THE DICTIONARY OF
CONTEMPORARY POLITICS
OF CENTRAL AMERICA
AND THE CARIBBEAN

THE DICTIONARY OF CONTEMPORARY POLITICS OF CENTRAL AMERICA AND THE CARIBBEAN

Phil Gunson and Greg Chamberlain
with additional material by
Andrew Thompson

SIMON & SCHUSTER
A Paramount Communications Company

New York   London   Toronto   Sydney   Tokyo   Singapore

First published 1991
by Routledge
11 New Fetter Lane, London EC4P 4EE

And in the USA by
Academic Reference Division
Simon & Schuster, 15 Columbus Circle
New York, NY 10023
A Paramount Communications Company

Set in Linotron Times and Helvetica by
Input Typesetting Ltd, London

Printed in England by T.J. Press (Padstow) Ltd, Cornwall

Library of Congress Cataloging-in-Publication Data
Gunson, Phil,
    The dictionary of contemporary politics of Central America and the
    Caribbean / Phil Gunson and Greg Chamberlain, with additional
    material by Andrew Thompson.
        p.   cm.
    Includes index.
    ISBN 0-13-213372-5
    1. Caribbean Area—Politics and government—1945– —Dictionaries.
    2. Central America—Politics and government—1951– —Dictionaries.
    I. Chamberlain, Greg. II. Thompson, Andrew, 1953– III. Title.
    F2183.G86   1991
    972.8'003—dc20   90–29902
                                                                  CIP

Contents

List of maps

Acknowledgements

The authors would like to acknowledge the generous assistance given by a number of specialists in the region. They include Tim Coone, Duncan Green, Richard Lapper, Lerna Llerena, James Painter, Trevor Petch and Ian Walker.

Abaco secession movement

After the announcement in 1971 of forthcoming independence for the Bahamas, the inhabitants of Abaco Island (40% of them white) demanded its secession, along with Grand Bahama Island, to become a British dependency. The Council for Free Abaco was led by Errington Watkins, a black policeman and opposition supporter. He was elected to parliament at the 1972 general election but the opposition Free National Movement expelled him and three other MPs from the party in 1973 for backing secession. Secret negotiations took place between the Abaconians and US and British businessmen, arms dealers and mercenaries. A month after independence in 1973, the Abaconian Independence Movement (AIM), led by Charles Hall, was set up to fight for secession by peaceful means. But support on the island faded by 1975. The AIM was renamed the Abaco Home Rule Movement and although its candidate won a seat at the 1977 general election, the secession movement then disappeared.
See also **Free National Movement; Bahamas.**

ABC islands

The three Dutch Caribbean islands of Aruba, Bonaire and Curaçao.
See also **Netherlands Antilles; Aruba.**

Abraham, Gen. Herard

b. 28 July 1940. President of Haiti 1990. Abraham rose through army ranks, after training in the US, to become assistant director of the military academy in 1981 and in 1982 deputy commander of the Leopards anti-subversion force. He was named director of the military academy in 1983. A few weeks after the collapse of the Duvalier dictatorship in 1986, he became information minister and a year later foreign minister. He became acting army commander when Gen. Prosper Avril seized power in 1988. Rebel officers tried to make him president during a revolt in 1989 but this was vetoed by the United States. He succeeded Avril as president for three days in 1990 before handing power to a woman supreme court judge, Ertha Pascal-Trouillot, signalling the Haitian army's first defeat in modern times at the hands of civilian politicians.
See also **Avril; Pascal-Trouillot.**

Action for the Defence of Democracy (ADED): see death squad.

Adams, (Sir) Grantley: see **Barbados Labour Party; Barbados Workers' Union; West Indies Federation; Barrow.**

Adams, John Quincy: see **Monroe doctrine.**

Adams, Peter: see **Anguilla secession.**

Adams, Tom
1931–85. Prime minister of Barbados 1976–85. A British-trained barrister and journalist, Adams returned to Barbados in 1962 and became assistant general secretary of his father Sir Grantley Adams's Barbados Labour Party (BLP) in 1965. He was elected to parliament in 1966; after the party's defeat in 1971, and his father's death a few months later, he became opposition leader in parliament and in 1973 leader of the BLP. He and the party won the 1976 elections and he became prime minister. He pursued a vigorous pro-US policy and campaigned against the left in the region, particularly the revolutionary regime in neighbouring Grenada from 1979. He offered Barbados as a staging post for the US invasion of Grenada in 1983 and sent police and troops to help rule it afterwards. He supported the US-sponsored Regional Security System aimed at curbing subversion in the eastern Caribbean. He died in office in 1985 in mysterious circumstances.
See also **Barbados Labour Party; Grenada, US invasion (1983); Regional Security System.**

Adolphe, Rosalie 'Madame Max': see **Tontons Macoutes.**

AFL-CIO: see **ORIT.**

African involvement (Cuba)
The involvement of Cuba with left-wing movements and governments in Africa dates from the early years of the revolution. The most notable military involvement prior to the mid-1970s was that of Ernesto Che Guevara and a small Cuban force which fought in the Congolese civil war in 1965. By the mid-1980s the Havana government had civilian or military advisers in some 17 African nations, with substantial numbers of troops in Angola (35–40,000), Ethiopia (11,000), Congo (3,000) and Mozambique (800), as well as in Algeria and Libya (around 3,500 in total). It has also provided support for the Polisario guerrillas in their campaign to win independence for the Western Sahara. Teachers, doctors and agronomists from Cuba are also present in large numbers in Africa. At its height, the Cuban presence on the continent, both military and civilian, was estimated to be around 65,000, and to account for approximately 10% of the Cuban budget.
   Although Cuban troops were often thought of as 'Soviet surrogates', the evidence suggests that their presence was primarily a Cuban initiative. The involvement in Angola dates from early 1975, when advisers were first sent to aid the MPLA independence movement, which subsequently won the civil war and became the government. Combat soldiers arrived in September 1975 and soon became involved in heavy fighting with South African troops who had invaded Angola. After the South Africans

retreated the Cubans' role became the defence of the capital, Luanda,
while MPLA units did most of the fighting. The scaling-down of the
Cuban presence, however, was reversed in 1977 after an abortive coup
against the Angolan government. The Cubans became more active in the
south of the country and their air superiority over the South Africans
eventually became an important factor. A previous policy of staying at
least 130 miles from the southern border was said to be untenable in
view of South African attacks, while Cuban expertise was necessary to
handle increasingly sophisticated Soviet-bloc weaponry. In 1987 Havana
admitted to the loss of 1,000 troops in Angola since 1975. In December
1989 it said 2,289 Cuban soldiers and civilians had died on foreign mis-
sions since the Castro regime came to power. Only 787 of these deaths
had occurred in combat, but over 2,000 Cubans had died in Angola.
Some foreign observers said the true figure was much higher.

In December 1988, South Africa, Angola and Cuba signed an agreement linking independence for Namibia with the withdrawal of the
approximately 50,000 Cuban troops then in Angola. Two-thirds of these
were to leave by April 1990, with the departure of the remainder taking
place by July 1991. The Ethiopian involvement dates from mid-1977
when Somalia invaded that country. At its height, the Cuban presence
amounted to over 24,000 troops, but it was later scaled down. Cuba
declined to be directly involved in the war against Eritrean and Tigrayan
separatists, many of whom it had trained prior to the Ethiopian revolution. In Mozambique the Cubans helped defend the country against
the South African-sponsored Renamo guerrillas.
See also **Guevara de la Serna.**

Afro-Caribbean Liberation Movement (ACLM): see **Antigua Caribbean Liberation Movement.**

Agrarian Labour Party (PLA): see **Labour Party** (Panama).

Aguero, Fernando: see **Somoza Debayle, Gen. Anastasio; Chamorro
Cardenal.**

Aguilar Bulgarelli, Oscar: see **Social Christian Unity Party.**

Aguiñada Carranza, Mario: see **Nationalist Democratic Union.**

AIFLD: see **American Institute for Free Labor Development.**

Albizu Campos, Pedro: see **Puerto Rico, nationalist violence.**

Alemán Valdés, Miguel
b. 1900. President of Mexico 1946–52, a period associated with rapid
economic growth along a capitalist development path; Alemán is sometimes referred to as the 'architect of modern Mexico'. After a term as
governor of Veracruz he went on to become interior minister under the
presidency of Manuel Avila Camacho, a post which put him in charge of
the secret police and gave him responsibility for eliminating subversive
activity and espionage by the Axis powers. German, Japanese and Italian

businesses were seized and a number of agents were arrested, charged with transmitting messages to German submarines in the Atlantic. In 1946 the ruling party, re-named the Institutional Revolutionary Party (PRI), nominated Alemán as the official candidate – the first civilian to be chosen for the presidency since Carranza.

In office he helped close the era of the revolutionary generals by cutting military expenditure to below 10% of the national budget. More generally, his administration has been seen as one in which a new generation of university-educated *técnicos* (technocrats) came to the fore, replacing the older revolutionary veterans. Inheriting an economy where industrialisation had already commenced, Alemán invested heavily in public works, particularly hydroelectric and irrigation projects and road building. The economy grew rapidly, to the benefit of the emerging middle classes; there was also a sharp concentration of wealth.

Relations with the United States, already good because of the Mexican participation in the war effort with the Allies, improved further. US investment and loans increased, and Alemán became the first Mexican president to pay an official visit to Washington. Tourism began to develop as an important industry. Alemán himself acquired land in seaside resorts like Acapulco, which later benefited from the construction of an airport, an oceanfront boulevard, and a highway linking it to Mexico City. Although still using revolutionary rhetoric, the Alemán government was conservative; wages were kept behind inflation and employers were encouraged to keep them down in pursuit of a competitive edge. Troops were sent to break up a strike by oil workers. The administration also became notorious for large-scale corruption, particularly in the awarding of public sector contracts.

See also **Avila Camacho; Institutional Revolutionary Party.**

Alexis, Francis

b. 3 October 1947. Grenadian politician. Alexis, a law professor, took over the right-wing Grenada Democratic Movement in 1983. After the US military invasion that year he failed to capture the leadership of the US-sponsored New National Party (NNP) coalition, which won general elections in 1984. The US-favoured Alexis became labour and local government minister under prime minister Herbert Blaize, whose leadership he criticised. In 1985 he defeated his rival, agriculture minister George Brizan, for the NNP deputy leadership. In 1987, after further power struggles, in which Alexis did not stand for re-election as NNP deputy leader, Blaize demoted him to attorney-general. He and Brizan resigned the same year to form the National Democratic Congress (NDC), with Alexis as deputy leader. He became attorney-general and local government minister when the NDC won the 1990 general election.

See also **National Democratic Congress; Brizan; New National Party; Blaize.**

ALIPO: see **Liberal Party** (Honduras).

Allen, Oscar: see **United People's Movement** (St Vincent).

Allfrey, Phyllis

1908–86. Co-founder of the Dominica Labour Party (DLP). Allfrey, a white Dominican and British Fabian socialist, daughter of the island's former crown attorney, founded the DLP in 1955 with trade union leader E. C. Loblack. She was elected to the West Indies federal parliament in 1958 and became federal minister of labour and social affairs and the only woman minister. She edited the DLP's *Dominica Herald*, but was expelled from the party in 1961 for alleged disloyalty, after which, in 1965, she founded an opposition newspaper, *The Star*, which appeared until 1982. She was a founder member of the Dominica Freedom Party in 1968. Allfrey published one of the earliest modern West Indian novels, *The Orchid House*, in 1953.

See also **Dominica Labour Party; Dominica Freedom Party.**

Alliance for Progress

A US-sponsored economic and social development programme for Latin America launched by President John F. Kennedy. The *Alianza para el Progreso* was largely conceived as a response to the revolutionary threat posed by Fidel Castro's victory in Cuba. Pressure was to be exerted on the continent's conservative élites to grant reforms, so as to reduce the appeal of revolutionary movements. As proposed by Kennedy, the Alliance was a re-working and broadening of an idea launched by President Juscelino Kubitschek of Brazil in 1958 under the title of 'Operation Pan America'. In a speech to Latin American diplomats on 13 March 1961, Kennedy called on the people of America 'to join in a new alliance for progress . . . a vast co-operative effort, unparalleled in magnitude and nobility of purpose, to satisfy the basic needs of the American people for home, work, and land, health, and schools'. The programme's targets included achieving a minimum of six years' schooling for all children, a literacy campaign, the eradication of malaria, a boost to house-building, and provision of drinking water to half the population.

Members of the Interamerican Economic and Social Council (IA-ECOSOC) of the OAS, with the exception of Cuba, signed the Declaration of the Peoples of America and the Charter of Punta del Este on 17 August 1961, which brought the Alliance into being. The declaration bound the signatories to take 'immediate and concrete actions to secure a better life, under freedom and democracy, for the present and future generations'. Total external funds deemed necessary for the ten-year programme were US$20bn, of which half was to come from the US as low-interest, long-term loans. To qualify for Alliance for Progress aid, countries had to submit long-range development plans for the approval of a panel of experts. The Alliance stressed land and tax reforms as essential for a better distribution of income. Although there was progress in some of the areas identified by the Alliance – including annual economic growth above the targeted 2.5% per capita in some years, by the late 1960s much of the impetus had been lost. The more conservative governments were unwilling to pursue even the mild land reform measures sought by the programme, and the local economies remained dependent on developments in international commodity markets.

All-Trinidad Sugar Estates and Factory (General from 1978) **Workers' Trade Union:** see Panday.

Alpha 66: see Omega 7.

Alvarez Bogaert, Fernando: see Balaguer.

Alvarez Córdova, Enrique: see Democratic Revolutionary Front.

Alvarez Martínez, Gen. Gustavo Adolfo
1937–89. Commander-in-chief of the Honduran armed forces, 1982–4. Alvarez was trained at the Honduran military academy, in the US and from 1958 to 1962 in Argentina. As commander of the 4th Infantry Batallion (La Ceiba) he intervened in 1975 at the request of the Standard Fruit Co. (which paid him a retainer) to arrest union leaders at the Las Isletas banana co-operative on charges of 'communism' and fraud. In 1980–81 he was commander of the Public Security Force (FUSEP), the militarised police. This was a period in which human rights organisations reported widespread and systematic abuses of police power. Alvarez was appointed armed forces chief in January 1982, becoming the first professionally-trained soldier to lead the Honduran military. He worked closely with the US embassy and the CIA on the contra campaign to undermine the Sandinista regime in Nicaragua, and agreed, without the knowledge of the National Congress, to allow the US to establish a military training facility (the CREMS) in Honduras, at which Salvadorean (as well as Honduran) soldiers were instructed by US advisers. This decision, along with the concentration of authority in the hands of a small military clique, helped precipitate his overthrow by fellow-officers on 31 March 1984. Other factors included discontent over conditions of service, the armed forces' growing reputation for human rights abuses, and Alvarez' own political ambitions, whose main vehicle was the Association for the Progress of Honduras (APROH), of which he was president. He went into exile in the US and in 1985 was dishonourably discharged from the army on grounds of corruption and abuse of power, although he was acquitted in 1986 (*in absentia*) of human rights violations. After returning to Honduras, he was murdered on 25 January 1989, apparently by Cinchonero guerrillas.
See also Association for the Progress of Honduras; Suazo Córdova.

'Amber and the Amberdines': see Vieques; Grenada, US invasion (1983).

Amerada Hess: see St Croix; Odlum, George.

American Federation of Labor (AFL): see general strike (Honduras).

American Institute for Free Labor Development (AIFLD)
Founded in 1962 by the US government, right-wing trade union leaders

and private corporations, with the aim of fostering anti-communist unions in the Americas, largely in response to the Cuban revolution. The bulk of its finance (over 95%) comes from the US Agency for International Development (AID), though the initial idea came from George Meany, head of the US labour federation AFL-CIO; and companies such as Shell, United Brands and W. R. Grace provide donations. The institute is a non-profit corporation, with a board originally comprising union officials and corporate executives, but now only the former. (The business/union link persists, however, in the related Citizens' Committee for the Pro-Democratic Forces in Central America, PRODEMCA, founded in 1984.) AIFLD's stated aim is 'the development of the democratic trade union movement in Latin America and the Caribbean', but it is frequently accused of efforts to divide and destroy union movements regarded as hostile to US interests. It trains union members and others, many at its training centres in Virginia and Maryland, and carries out other social projects, including housing schemes. According to former Central Intelligence Agency employees, AIFLD works closely with the CIA, as well as with ORIT, the western hemisphere affiliate of the International Confederation of Free Trade Unions (ICFTU). It is said to have assisted in the formation or re-establishment of well over 1,000 unions since 1976. AIFLD's largest programme in the region began in 1979 in El Salvador, where it played a major role in that country's controversial land reform. Its officials were expelled from Nicaragua in 1982 but it continued to channel funds to the anti-Sandinista opposition in that country. See also **ORIT.**

Anach: see Social Democratic Innovation and Unity Party.

Anaya, Herbert: see Democratic Revolutionary Front.

Anaya Montes, Mélida (Cmdte Ana María): see Popular Liberation Forces.

ANDES–21 de Junio: see Popular Revolutionary Bloc; Popular Liberation Forces.

Andonie Fernández, Miguel: see Social Democratic Innovation and Unity Party.

ANEP: see Romero Mena.

Angola (Cuban involvement in): see African involvement (Cuba).

ANGUILLA
   Capital: The Valley
   Area: 96 sq km
   Population (1987): 7,200
   Pop. growth rate: 5.9%
   Pop. density: 75/sq km
   Infant mortality: 27 per thousand
   Life expectancy at birth: 70

Literacy: 95%
GDP per capita (1987): US$3,562
Foreign debt per capita (1987): US$333
Main exports: tourism, salt, lobsters, livestock

Political system

The 1982 constitution formally restored the island to British rule with internal self-government, except for defence and external affairs. Anguilla was part of the state of St Kitts-Nevis-Anguilla until secession in 1967. An appointed British governor represents the titular head of state, Queen Elizabeth of Britain, and governs with a seven-member Executive Council. An 11-member (7 elected, 2 nominated, 2 ex-officio) parliament, the House of Assembly, is elected for a maximum of five years.
Governor: Brian Canty (1989)
Chief minister: Emile Gumbs (1984)
Last elections: 1989

Political organisations

Parties in parliament (leader) (elective seats): Anguilla National Alliance/ANA (Emile Gumbs) (3), f. 1980; Anguilla United Party/AUP (Ronald Webster) (2), f. 1980; Anguilla Democratic Party/ADP (Victor Banks) (1), f. 1984.
Parties outside parliament: Party for Anguilla's Culturation and Economy/PACE (Cuthwin Lake), f. 1988.
See also **St Kitts-Nevis**.

Anguilla Democratic Party (ADP)
Founded by Victor Banks (b. 1947) in 1984 after the defeat of chief minister Ronald Webster by changing the name of the Anguilla People's Party (APP). The APP had been founded by Webster in 1981 in succession to the Anguilla United Party, which he had formed in 1980 after a split in his People's Progressive Party. The party got two seats in the 1984 election, but only one in the 1989 poll.
See also **Webster**.

Anguilla National Alliance (ANA)
Political party in Anguilla. Founded in 1980 by chief minister Emile Gumbs after a split with former chief minister Ronald Webster and the People's Progressive Party. The party was defeated in elections in 1980 (6–1) and 1981 (2–5), but won in 1984 (4–3) and Gumbs became chief minister. It won only three seats in 1989, but Gumbs continued in power with the backing of an independent MP.
See also **Gumbs**.

Anguilla People's Party (APP): see Webster.

Anguilla secession (1967, 1969)
A revolt against rule by St Kitts which led to restoration of British colonial status. Anguilla had come under the authority of St Kitts since settlement in 1650. Without a plantation economy and with a different

mentality, Anguillans always resented Kittitian rule. This came to a head in 1967 when Britain granted St Kitts-Nevis-Anguilla associated statehood (internal self-government). Unwilling to tolerate the threats and authoritarian ways of the state premier, Kittitian Robert Bradshaw, 250 armed Anguillans on 30 May threw the Kittitian police force off the island and seized control. Anguillans voted in a referendum a month later to become independent. The island's only member in the St Kitts parliament, Peter Adams, and other Anguillan leaders then signed a quasi-agreement in Barbados in July to restore Kittitian rule but with a local Anguillan council.

The islanders rejected the accord and replaced Adams with Ronald Webster, who called for independence. Negotiations between Britain and Anguilla foundered and on 6 February 1969, after another referendum and egged on by American businessmen, Webster declared independence and a republic. On 19 March, 300 British troops and 50 police invaded Anguilla in Operation Sheepskin at Bradshaw's request. Webster accepted the British presence but ties with St Kitts were not restored.

In 1970, an enquiry chaired by Trinidadian judge Sir Hugh Wooding recommended Anguillan autonomy but under St Kitts. Anguilla rejected the report and refused to take part in state elections in 1971. Britain then reluctantly resumed formal control of the island, as requested by Webster, but faced hostility from Caribbean leaders who feared it would encourage fragmentation elsewhere in the region. The last British forces left in early 1972. Britain granted a constitution in 1976 and the title of chief minister to Webster. Anguilla was formally separated from St Kitts in 1980 with autonomy under a British governor. As a result of the secession, the island now has most of the public utilities it previously lacked.
See also **Webster; Bradshaw; Gumbs**.

Anguilla United Party (AUP): see Webster.

ANSESAL: see death squad.

Anticommunist Unification Party (PUA): see National Liberation Movement (Guatemala).

ANTIGUA-BARBUDA
Capital: St John's
Independence (from Britain): 1981
Area: 442 sq km
Population (1987): 81,100
Pop. growth rate: 1%
Pop. density: 183/sq km
Infant mortality: 21 per thousand
Life expectancy at birth: 72
Literacy: 90%
GDP per capita (1987): US$3,399
Foreign debt per capita (1989): US$3,205
Main exports: tourism, machinery, other manufactured goods, lobster, cotton, melons

Political system

Constitution: 1981. Titular head of state: Queen Elizabeth of Britain, represented locally by a figurehead governor-general. A 17-member House of Representatives is elected for a maximum five years. A 17-member Senate is nominated. Barbuda has its own island council with limited powers and elects one member of parliament.

Governor-general: Sir Wilfred Jacobs (1981)
Prime minister: Vere C. Bird (1976)
Last elections: 1989

Political organisations

Parties in parliament (leader) (seats in House of Representatives): Antigua Labour Party/ALP (Vere C. Bird) (15), f. 1951; United National Democratic Party/UNDP (Ivor Heath) (1), f. 1986; Barbuda People's Movement/BPM (Hilbourne Frank) (1).

Parties outside parliament: Antigua Caribbean Liberation Movement/ ACLM (Tim Hector), f. 1968; Barbuda Independence Movement (Arthur Nibbs), f. 1988.

Main trade unions: Antigua Trades and Labour Union/ATLU (Noel Thomas-Young), f. 1939; Antigua Workers' Union/AWU (Keithlyn Smith), f. 1967; Antigua Teachers' Union/ATU (Austin Josiah).

Employers' organisations: Antigua Manufacturers' Association/AMA (Peter Harker); Antigua Employers' Federation/AEF (H. Bass); Antigua and Barbuda Hotel Association/ABHA (John Hawley).

See also **Barbuda**.

Antigua Caribbean Liberation Movement (ACLM)

Left-wing party in Antigua. Founded in 1968 by schoolteacher Tim Hector as the Afro-Caribbean Liberation Movement, it gradually changed from a 'black power' group to a 'new left' party – in 1973 replacing 'Afro' by 'Antigua' in its name – and by 1980 dropped its refusal to take part in elections. The ACLM sought an alliance with the Progressive Labour Movement (PLM), which Hector had helped found, but eventually contested the 1980 poll alone and won only 1.1% of the vote. The subsequent disintegration of the PLM left the ACLM as the main opposition to the ruling Bird family's Antigua Labour Party. But when the opposition again failed to unite for the 1984 elections, the ACLM did not take part in the poll. It contested the 1989 general election but scored only 1.9% of the vote. However the ACLM's weekly organ, *Outlet*, became the island's most widely read newspaper because of its consistent exposure of official corruption and because of government harassment of the party and Hector. The government forced the paper to close in 1975–6.

See also **Hector; Bird, Vere C.; Walter; Progressive Labour Movement; Antigua Labour Party**.

Antigua Labour Party (ALP)

Growing out of the political committee (f. 1946) of the Antigua Trades and Labour Union (ATLU), the ALP was founded in 1951 by ATLU leader Vere C. Bird. It won unopposed all eight elective seats in the Legislative Council election in that year and in 1956. It won all 10 seats in both 1961 and 1965. After the ATLU split in 1967, the ALP was defeated 4–13 in the 1971 election by the new Progressive Labour Movement (PLM) of George Walter. But it returned to power with 11 seats to 6 in 1976, largely by promising to abolish personal income tax. The ALP increased its majority to 14–3 over the PLM in the 1980 elections and in 1984 swept the board by winning 16 seats to 1 for an independent from Barbuda.

The absence of official opposition then encouraged a split in the party. It centred around the fiercely pro-US prime minister Bird and his deputy, his son Lester, who criticised the old man's policies and vainly tried to get his elder brother Vere Jr dismissed from the government. Vere Jr was favoured by his father as his successor over Lester, party chairman since 1971.ʼ The infighting did not prevent the ALP winning the 1989 general election 15–2.

See also **Bird, Vere C.; Bird, Lester; Bird, Vere Jr; Progressive Labour Movement**.

Antigua Trades and Labour Union (ATLU): see **Bird, Vere C.; Antigua Labour Party; Walter**.

Antigua Workers' Union (AWU): see **Walter; Hector; Progressive Labour Movement; United National Democratic Party**.

Antilles of the Five
Name sometimes given to the Netherlands Antilles since the breakaway of Aruba in 1986, leaving only five islands in the state. All major Curaçao parties in the 1990 general election advocated Curaçao's withdrawal from the federation also. Holland proposed a two-part federation of Curaçao-Bonaire and of Sint Maarten, Saba and Statia.
See also **Netherlands Antilles**.

April revolt (Nicaragua): see **Chamorro Cardenal, Pedro Joaquín**.

APROH: see **Association for the Progress of Honduras**.

Aragón Quiñónez, Dr Héctor: see **National Liberation Movement** (Guatemala).

Arana, Francisco Javier: see **Sandoval Alarcón**.

Arana Osorio, Gen. Carlos
b. 17 July 1918. President of Guatemala, 1970–74. Born in Barbarena (Santa Rosa department), Arana graduated from the military academy in 1939. From 1964 to 1966 he served as military attaché in Washington and in 1966–8 as military commander of the Zacapa-Izabal zone. He earned the nickname 'Jackal of Zacapa' for his brutal counter-insurgency campaign, which is estimated to have cost 8,000 lives in six months. He was removed from the post amid the scandal surrounding the 1968 kidnap

of the Archbishop of Guatemala City (in which the army high command is said to have been involved), and appointed ambassador to Nicaragua. Arana became president after a fraudulent 1970 poll as the candidate of the far right MLN and the army party, the PID. Under a state of siege (1970–1) the armed forces and their allied 'death squads' engaged in massive repression. During Arana's presidency the army began to establish its own economic base and the Bank of the Army was founded. The general later formed his own party, the Organised Aranista Central (CAO, subsequently renamed CAN), which became part of the official coalition backing President Lucas García (1978–82), and in 1982 put up its own candidate for the presidency. Arana became wealthy through his tenure of the presidency, acquiring substantial interests in industry and large landholdings. In early 1990 he was said to be among the backers of a right wing military-civilian front seeking to present a military candidate in that year's elections.
See also **Authentic Nationalist Central; Institutional Democratic Party**.

Aranda, Theodore: see **United Democratic Party**; **People's United Party**.

Araujo, Arturo: see **Martínez, Gen. Maximiliano Hernández; Salvadorean Communist Party**.

Araujo, Manuel Enrique: see **National Guard** (El Salvador).

Arawaks: see **Caribs**.

Arbenz Guzmán, Lt.-Col. Jacobo
1913–1970. President of Guatemala 1951–4. Born in Quezaltenango, the son of a Swiss pharmacist, Jacobo Arbenz was the organiser of the coup which overthrew dictator Jorge Ubico's short-lived successor Gen. Federico Ponce on 20 October 1944. He participated in the three-man revolutionary junta which replaced him and which governed for five months while elections were organised. Minister of war in the government of Juan José Arévalo from December 1944, Arbenz was elected in 1950 to succeed Arévalo. When his term began, in March 1951, he embarked on a more ambitious series of reforms than those of his predecessor, including agrarian reform, for which legislation was introduced in 1952. The law was aimed at large estates and unused lands. Redistribution began in 1953: in all about 100,000 peasants (1965 OAS estimate) received land, and just over 1,000 plantations were affected, including those of the US transnational United Fruit Co., which owned over 500,000 acres (some sources say 800,000 or more) but cultivated less than 10%. Compensation was in government bonds based on 1952 tax returns. About 1.5m acres were distributed (including 1,700 owned by the president himself) and over $8m was paid in compensation. The government expropriated 387,000 acres from United Fruit and offered more than $1m in compensation. UFCO – backed by the US State Department – demanded 16 times as much for its Pacific coast holdings alone. The US (according to a later statement by President Eisenhower) regarded Arbenz as 'merely

a puppet manipulated by the communists'. Arbenz' own description of his aims was: 'first, to convert (Guatemala) from a dependent nation with a semi-feudal economy to an economically independent country; second, to transform our nation from a backward nation . . . to a modern capitalist country; and third, to accomplish this transformation in a manner that brings the greatest possible elevation of the living standards of the great masses of the people.' Trade union organisation grew rapidly under Arbenz: by 1954, 50% of the 600,000 workers and peasants were organised. United Fruit conspired with the US Central Intelligence Agency (CIA) and State Department and with internal opponents of Arbenz to overthrow him. This was achieved in June 1954 by a US-backed rebel army, led by Col. Carlos Castillo Armas, which invaded the country from neighbouring Honduras, although the main military action was bombing raids by US planes. Arbenz capitulated when his resignation was demanded by army representatives. He spent his later years in exile in Cuba, actively seeking the restoration of democracy in Guatemala.
See also **Arévalo Bermejo; Castillo Armas**.

Arce, Bayardo: see **Sandinista National Liberation Front**.

ARDE (*Alianza Revolucionaria Democrática*/Democratic Revolutionary Alliance)
An anti-Sandinista (contra) coalition founded in 1982 by the Nicaraguan Democratic Movement (MDN), the Sandino Revolutionary Front (FRS), Misurasata and the Nicaraguan Democratic Union/Nicaraguan Revolutionary Armed Forces (UDN/FARN) to engage in guerrilla war in Nicaragua. At its foundation Alfonso Robelo of the MDN became its political leader and Edén Pastora of the FRS its military commander. UDN/FARN left in early 1983, but returned in early 1984. The FRS and Misurasata had split with the Robelo wing in 1984 over the issue of alliance with the Nicaraguan Democratic Force (FDN), but both wings continued to use the ARDE name. In September 1984 the two wings agreed on co-ordination of actions wherever possible. The Robelo wing joined the FDN and the Nicaraguan Democratic Co-ordinator in the Nicaraguan Opposition Unity (UNO, later the Nicaraguan Resistance/RN) in 1985, and UDN/FARN became UNO/FARN. ARDE set up base camps in Costa Rica and the far south-east of Nicaragua, but the latter were destroyed in a 1985 Sandinista offensive and in mid-1986 Pastora gave up the struggle. Fernando 'El Negro' Chamorro took over as military commander but could not revive the 'southern front'. The relationship of ARDE leaders with the UNO/RN was fraught with problems: they often threatened withdrawal from the alliance and occasionally carried out their threats.
See also **Southern Opposition Bloc; Robelo Callejas; Pastora Gómez; Nicaraguan Resistance; Nicaraguan Democratic Co-ordinator; Nicaraguan Democratic Force**.

Ardito Barletta, Nicolás
b. 1938. President of Panama 1984–5. A former vice-president of the

World Bank, trained as an economist at North Carolina State University and the University of Chicago, Ardito Barletta formed strong ties with the US, numbering George Shultz and Henry Kissinger among his friends. He was chosen as the candidate of the official Democratic Revolutionary Party (PRD)-led Unade coalition for the 1984 elections, despite his lack of a firm political base, and became the first elected president of Panama in 16 years. His campaign was partly funded by US government sources, and his victory over Arnulfo Arias was widely believed to have been rigged by the military. His inability to introduce the austerity measures demanded by the IMF and World Bank without sparking popular and parliamentary opposition was partly responsible for his overthrow by the military in September 1985, but another factor was the announcement of an investigation into the murder of a political figure, Hugo Spadafora, allegedly killed by the defence forces. He was replaced by his vice-president Eric Arturo Delvalle.
See also **Noriega Morena; Delvalle**.

ARENA (*Alianza Republicana Nacionalista*/Nationalist Republican Alliance)
An extreme right-wing Salvadorean party, founded in 1981 (replacing the Broad National Front/FAN) to contest the March 1982 constituent assembly elections. Backed financially by the landed oligarchy and led by former intelligence officer Maj. (ret.) Roberto D'Aubuisson, ARENA is committed to nationalism, individualism, free enterprise and national security. It has frequently been accused of links with the death squads. It considers the Christian Democrats (PDC) to be 'crypto-communists'. ARENA gained considerable support from the lower middle class and some sectors of the peasantry in 1982 and won 19 (of 60) assembly seats. D'Aubuisson was elected president of the assembly, but lost to the PDC's José Napoleón Duarte in the run-off election for the presidency of the republic in March 1984, considered by many a US-engineered fraud. In the legislative elections of March 1985, the party lost control of the assembly, blaming its tactical alliance with the National Conciliation Party (PCN) for the loss of 6 seats. A splinter led by former vice-presidential candidate Hugo Barrera left to form the Free Nation Party (PPL). D'Aubuisson was replaced as president in September 1985, but retained the post of honorary president-for-life. His successor was businessman Alfredo Cristiani, a less controversial leader under whom the party took on a more modern form and broadened its appeal.

In July 1986, ARENA unveiled its 'National Peace Proposal' in which it declared its continued opposition to dialogue with the FMLN rebels, who, it said, should merely be allowed to join the existing political system; a formula which was well received on the right but dismissed by the FMLN. In January 1987, with other right-wing parties, ARENA boycotted National Assembly votes until the government withdrew a package of taxes aimed at making the very rich contribute to the war effort. It also backed a one-day strike to press home the point, while D'Aubuisson called for Duarte's resignation. In June 1987 the charismatic and rebel-

lious army officer Col. Sigifredo Ochoa resigned to join the party, providing it with a channel of communication to the far right in the army. In the 1988 assembly elections ARENA won half the 60 seats, securing an overall majority when a PCN deputy defected to ARENA. It also captured the bulk of municipalities and mayoralties, including that of San Salvador. In March 1989, Alfredo Cristiani won the presidency on the first ballot. His more moderate wing of the party currently competes for control with two other elements, one led by D'Aubuisson and the other controlling the death squads, with which D'Aubuisson is no longer thought to be directly involved.
See also **Cristiani; D'Aubuisson Arrieta; death squad**.

Arévalo Bermejo, Juan José
b. 1904. President of Guatemala 1945–51. Arévalo worked for the ministry of education prior to the Ubico dictatorship, during which he was exiled to Argentina. In 1934 he obtained a PhD in education from the University of La Plata, Argentina. He taught at several Argentine universities and founded and directed the Pedagogical Institute in San Luis. Supported by a new political group, the Revolutionary Action Party (PAR), Arévalo was elected president in December 1944, after the overthrow of Ubico, with 85% of the vote. He took office on 15 March 1945.

Arévalo described his politics as 'spiritual socialism', although he was a confirmed anti-communist (the party was banned under his presidency). Reforms carried out under the new constitution included a labour code giving the right to strike to both urban and rural workers and providing remedies for unfair dismissal; the introduction of a social security system; health and education advances including a large school- and hospital-building programme; and attempts to integrate the indigenous population. But although the constitution provided for the expropriation of idle land, Arévalo did nothing to reform the unbalanced system of land tenure – a source of growing tension – believing there was 'no agrarian problem'. He also failed to lift press censorship. None the less, his rhetoric in favour of the poor caused him to be labelled a communist by landowners. He handed over power to his elected successor, Jacobo Arbenz, in 1951. Following the overthrow of Arbenz in 1954, he was exiled to Mexico, returning in March 1963 after announcing his candidacy in the presidential elections of that year. Defence Minister Col. Enrique Peralta Azurdia pre-empted this staging a coup against President Miguel Ydígoras Fuentes (who had said he would allow Arévalo's candidacy) and cancelling the elections. Arévalo was appointed ambassador to France in 1970 but replaced in 1972. He is the author of several books on politics, including *The Shark & the Sardines* (1961) and *Anti-Kommunism in Latin America* (1963).
See also **Arbenz Guzmán; Guatemalan Labour Party; Ubico y Castañeda**.

Arguello, Leonardo: see Somoza García.

Arguello, Miriam: see Democratic Conservative Party of Nicaragua.

Arias, Harmodio: see Arias Madrid.

Arias Calderón, Ricardo

b. 4 May 1933. First vice-president, justice and interior minister of Panama 1989– . The leader of the Panamanian Christian Democrat Party (PDC), Ricardo Arias is also vice-president of the Christian Democrat International and was president of the Christian Democrat Organisation of America from 1981–5. An academic with a degree in philosophy and letters, he stood for the second vice-presidency of Panama on the Arnulfo Arias Madrid ticket in the 1984 elections. When the veteran politician was defeated, allegedly by government fraud, the younger man effectively took over the role of *de facto* leader of the opposition to the PRD-military alliance which ran the country. He strongly opposed the involvement of the defence forces in politics and became a leading figure in the National Civic Crusade (CCN), created to press for the 'demilitarisation' of the government. Arias sought the opposition presidential candidacy in the 1989 elections, but the fraction of Arias Madrid's old party, the PPA, represented in the ADOC coalition succeeded in imposing its own candidate and he stood instead for the first vice-presidency. Deprived of victory by fraud, the ADOC leadership was eventually installed as the government after the December 1989 US invasion of Panama. As minister of the interior (*gobernación*), Arias' main task was the reorganisation of the Panama Defence Forces into the new Public Force.

See also **Christian Democrat Party** (Panama); **National Civic Crusade; Democratic Alliance of Civic Opposition; Panama, US invasion (1989)**.

Arias Madrid, Arnulfo

1901–1988. President of Panama 1940–41; 1949–51; 1968. Born into a family which owned a medium-sized cattle ranch in Penonome, in the interior, Arnulfo Arias graduated in medicine from Harvard University. He first came to prominence when he led a successful coup against President Florencio Arosemena in 1931. Elections were called for 1932 and Arias' brother Harmodio became president, while Arnulfo was appointed minister of agriculture and public works. In 1934 he founded the National Revolutionary Coalition (CNR), forerunner of the Revolutionary National Party (PNR). In the late 1930s, as minister plenipotentiary, he spent several years in Europe, watching the growth of fascism at first hand. He was first elected president in 1940, and shortly afterwards a new constitution was approved which no longer legitimised foreign intervention in the country. Despite the enactment of many social reforms, including women's suffrage, Arias' government was marred by overtly racist and anti-semitic policies. His sympathy for the Axis powers in World War II and his attempt to maintain a stance of formal neutrality by refusing to grant territory for US bases or allow the arming of US-owned, Panamanian-registered ships led to his overthrow in a bloodless coup in 1941 and four years in exile. On his return he was jailed for seven months.

He was reinstated as president under the pressure of mass protest in 1949 after the death of President Domingo Díaz was followed by a succession of brief incumbencies. Arias was then ratified by the electoral

tribunal as the retroactive winner of the 1948 elections (which he had in fact won overwhelmingly). In 1950 he outlawed left-wing parties, and in the following year his announcement of the imminent suspension of the 1946 constitution provoked his overthrow for a second time, following which he was impeached and jailed for a year. In 1960 he founded the Panameñista Party. Defeated in the 1964 elections, whose result his supporters disputed, in 1968 he was declared the winner of a hotly-contested election but was deposed for the third time, after only 11 days in office, by the National Guard, whose two senior officers he had sought to replace. He was exiled in the US from 1968 to 1978 during the rule of Gen. Omar Torrijos, and later refused to take part in the 1980 elections. In 1984 he was narrowly defeated by the official candidate in elections which were widely alleged to have been fraudulent. His party changed its name to Authentic Panameñista Party (PPA), the name and symbols of the original PP having been appropriated by a pro-government group of former followers. Arias' career was marked by personal enrichment, allegedly derived in part from corruption. He was popularly known simply as 'el hombre' (the man).
See also **Authentic Panameñista Party**.

Arias Plan (Esquipulas II)

A Central American peace proposal unveiled on 15 February 1987 by Costa Rican president Oscar Arias, and for which he won the 1987 Nobel Peace Prize. At Washington's request the plan had been discussed with a high-level US delegation in Miami in January that year. In its original (leaked) form, the plan appeared to seek the isolation of Nicaragua and the neutralisation of the multi-nation Contadora process. Nicaragua was not invited to the February meeting in San José at which the presidents of Costa Rica, Honduras, El Salvador and Guatemala discussed the 'Procedure for the Establishment of a Firm and Lasting Peace in Central America'. But after seeing this modified version Nicaragua agreed to attend the summit meeting, set (after a number of postponements) for 6–7 August 1987 in Guatemala, to discuss the plan. Mexico, a leading Contadora nation, had expressed disagreement with the plan's 'democratisation' proposals, arguing that internal political arrangements were a matter for each nation, but in April Contadora endorsed the plan. The US was much more hostile to the amended version, which included no requirement for dialogue between the Nicaraguan government and the contra rebels, whose US aid would have to be cut off before 'democratisation' proposals came into effect. The US Senate, however, voted almost unanimously to take the plan seriously.

On the eve of the August summit the Reagan administration unveiled its own 'peace plan', backed by the Speaker of the House, Jim Wright, in what was seen as an administration bid to derail the Arias plan. Surprisingly, the latter was then signed by all five presidents, partly (it was said) because of resentment at the US move. Speaker Wright then switched to endorsement of the Arias plan. In its final form the plan called for parallel moves in every Central American country. There were to be talks between governments and their civilian political opponents (not with armed groups – but see below); amnesties and the formation of National Reconciliation Commissions; ceasefires in all armed conflicts; suspension of external aid to insurgent forces and an end to the use of signatory states' territories for aggression against their neighbours; restoration of civil liberties, including press freedom and political pluralism; free elections under existing constitutions, in the presence of international observers; and negotiations on arms reduction. The provisions of the treaty were to be treated as an indivisible whole and implemented simultaneously by signatories according to the timetable laid down. The central provisions were to come into force within 90 days.

Progress in implementation was patchy, and although talks were held with rebels in all three regional insurgencies, no firm agreements were reached. The greatest advances were made in Nicaragua, where press freedom was conditionally restored, an amnesty declared and a provisional ceasefire agreed with the contras. Definitive agreement with the contras was hindered by splits in their ranks. In February 1989 a Central American summit in San Salvador agreed to devise a plan for the disbandment of the contras in exchange for further measures by Nicaragua. The US refused to back this plan, but Congress declined to give further military aid to the rebels before the holding of the Nicaraguan elections, brought forward to February 1990. At the Tela summit in August 1989, the Central American presidents agreed a joint demobilisation plan for the contras to be completed by 5 December. This was not effective, and a new date of 25 April was set at Montelimar, Nicaragua, the following year, to coincide with the transfer of government to Violeta Chamorro. At Montelimar the presidents reiterated their commitment to all previous Esquipulas pledges.

See also **Arias Sánchez; Contadora Group; Central American Parliament**.

Arias Sánchez, Oscar

b. 13 September 1941. President of Costa Rica 1986–90. Born into a rich, coffee-growing family in Heredia, Oscar Arias trained as a lawyer, economist and political scientist in Costa Rica, and at the London School of Economics and the University of Essex (UK) where he obtained a PhD in political science. He was professor of political science at the University of Costa Rica, 1969–72, and served as a director of the National University, the Central Bank and the Technological Institute at different times between 1974 and 1977. In 1976 he became a member of the board of the Geneva-based International University Exchange Fund, and in 1977 a member of the North-South Round Table based in Rome.

Arias was counsellor on economic affairs to the presidency (1970–72) and Minister of Planning and Economic Policy (1972–7). From 1978 to 1982 he served as National Liberation Party (PLN) member for Heredia in the legislative assembly, having held the post of PLN secretary for international affairs since 1975. He became secretary general of the PLN (1978–81), but resigned the post to organise the successful campaign of his predecessor in the presidency, Luis Alberto Monge. He was re-elected secretary general in 1983, resigning again the following year to seek the presidential candidacy, which he obtained in January 1985. He won 54% of the vote in the 1986 election, becoming the youngest-ever Costa Rican president and the first since the civil war of 1948 not to belong to the 'Generation of '48'.

He had campaigned principally on foreign policy, as a champion of 'peace and neutrality' in the regional conflict. In early 1987 he unveiled what became known as the 'Arias plan' for peace in the region, subsequently ratified by all the Central American presidents in August that year as the 11-point 'Esquipulas II' agreement, which won him the 1987 Nobel Peace Prize. His opposition to the US-backed contra rebels and attempts to prevent them operating from Costa Rica earned him the enmity of the United States, which reduced its aid to the country and used its control over international financial bodies to exert further pressure. However, his government was not consistent in its stance on this issue.

Domestically, the president faced the problem of one of the highest per capita debts in the world, on which interest payments had not been kept up. He introduced austerity measures based on the demands of the IMF and Washington, cutting the public payroll despite a promise to create 25,000 new jobs, and restricting food subsidies. Pressure from farmers in his first year, however, led to concessions on price support and credit schemes which led the World Bank to suspend US$26m in aid disbursements. At the same time he sought a 'social contract' with labour and business based on wage rises of less than the inflation rate. He said his aims included the regeneration of industry, annual growth of 5% (achieved in practice) and rapid growth in non-traditional exports and domestic savings. His administration also explored alternative debt reduction methods, such as debt-for-bonds exchanges, and in late 1989 became the second Latin American government to announce a reduction of its debt under the US-sponsored Brady Plan; it also challenged the state-led development model of previous PLN governments by channelling IMF and World Bank funds directly to the private sector, bypassing the Central Bank.

Another top priority was a popular housing plan, aimed at curbing a housing deficit estimated at 214,000 units. Arias sought to strengthen local government by guaranteeing local authorities 10% of the national budget. Within months of taking power he was forced to set up a special commission on administrative corruption, due to the huge number of scandals which had surfaced. Costa Rica also emerged during his term as a major drug money laundering centre. Ironically, it benefitted from investors fleeing the instability in neighbouring Panama. Peace and stable government also helped encourage a tourist boom during the Arias years.

On stepping down, Arias said he would return to academic life as a writer and lecturer on Latin America at Harvard University.

See also **Arias Plan; National Liberation Party; Generation of '48**.

Aristide, Father Jean-Bertrand

b. 15 July 1953. Radical Haitian Roman Catholic priest. After studying in the Middle East and Europe, he began working in 1975 at the Salesian St Jean Bosco church on the edge of the Port-au-Prince slum of La Saline. In 1985 he started to preach against the Duvalier dictatorship and helped spark the revolt which brought it down. He became the best-known leader of the church's 'liberationist' wing and denounced the new regime's failure to uproot Duvalierism. The fiery Aristide attacked US 'imperialism' towards Haiti and called for revolution before overflowing congregations.

In 1987 he escaped death in a Duvalierist ambush. The church hierarchy ordered his transfer from the capital, but his followers occupied the national cathedral and forced the order to be dropped. In 1988 a Duvalierist gang attacked his church while he was preaching, killed 13 people and burned it down. The incident led to the overthrow of President Henri Namphy a few days later by disgusted junior officers. When Aristide's superiors once more ordered him to leave, this time for Canada, demonstrations again forced them to give in. The Salesians, encouraged by the conservative papal nuncio, Paolo Romeo, expelled him from the Order in late 1988 for his supposed 'incitement to hatred, violence and class struggle' and thus largely silenced him. He withdrew to run an orphanage in Port-au-Prince. A far left faction proposed him in 1990 as provisional president. See also **Haiti, Roman Catholic Church; Namphy; Duvalierism; Duvalier, Jean-Claude**.

Armed Forces of Liberation (FAL): see **Salvadorean Communist Party**.

Armed Forces of National Resistance (FARN): see **People's Revolutionary Army** (El Salvador).

Armed Liberation Group (*Groupe Liberation Armé*/GLA): see **Guadeloupe, independence movements; Reinette**.

Army in Defence of the National Sovereignty of Nicaragua (EDSN): see **Sandino**.

'arnulfismo': see **Authentic Panameñista Party; Endara Galimany**.

Arocena, Eduardo: see **Omega 7**.

Artola, Adán: see **Yatama**.

ARUBA

Capital: Oranjestad
Area: 193 sq km
Population (1990): 62,000
Pop. growth rate: 1%
Pop. density: 321/sq km
Infant mortality: 15.6 per thousand
Life expectancy at birth: 76
Literacy: 95%

GDP per capita (1989): US$13,145
Main exports: tourism, petroleum products

Political system

Formerly one of the six islands of the Netherlands Antilles, Aruba, which was constantly at odds with Curaçao, became self-governing ('status aparte') in 1986, with a Dutch-appointed figurehead Aruban governor, named for a six-year term, responsible for foreign affairs and defence while the island prepares for full independence. This was planned by 1996, but was postponed indefinitely in 1990 due to lack of post-independence guarantees by Holland. A 21-member parliament is elected for a maximum four years.

Governor: Felipe Tromp (1986)
Premier: Nelson Oduber (1989)
Last elections: 1989

Political organisations

Parties in parliament (leader) (seats): Aruban People's Party/AVP (Henny Eman) (8), f. 1942; People's Electoral Movement/MEP (Nelson Oduber) (10), f. 1971; Aruba Patriotic Party/PPA (Benny Nisbet) (1), f. 1949; New Patriotic Party/PPN (Eddy Werleman) (1), f. 1988; National Democratic Action/NDA (John Booi) (1), f. 1985.
Parties outside parliament: Democratic Action 86/AD86 (Arturo Oduber), f. 1986; Democratic Party of Aruba/PDA (Leonard Berlinski), f. 1983.
Main trade unions: Aruban Workers' Federation/FTA (Anselmo Pontilius); Public Workers' Union/SEPA (G. Wolf); Aruba Teachers' Union/SIMAR (B. Every); Aruban Government Worker's Union/GARBA (B. Gomez).
See also **Netherlands Antilles**.

Aruban People's Party (*Arubaanse Volkspartij*/AVP): see **Eman; Croes**.

Arzú Irigoyen, Alvaro: see **National Advance Party.**

Association for the Progress of Honduras (*Asociación para el Progreso de Honduras*/APROH)
A corporatist-type organisation, founded in 1981 by a group of businessmen led by Miguel Facussé and associated with the political ambitions of armed forces commander Gen. Gustavo Alvarez, who became its president. APROH was granted legal status in January 1983. Cutting across traditional political divisions and uniting the right within the armed forces, the private sector, trade unions and the academic world, it achieved a high degree of influence over the Suazo Córdova government. It was also linked with CAUSA, an affiliate of the Unification Church ('Moonies') of the Revd Sun Myung Moon. APROH's philosophy was based on anti-communism, the national security doctrine, free enterprise and stronger links with the US. Leaked proposals included a system of militarised

peasant co-operatives and a 'military solution' to the conflict with Nicaragua. Its leaders designed and executed a 'democratic front' tactic, whereby trade unions and other organisations were taken over by right-wing factions, backed ultimately by the Supreme Court (dominated by the ruling Liberal Party). In December 1983 they announced the formation of the US-based APROH Foundation, a right-wing pressure group backed by anti-Castro Cubans. APROH's influence declined after the March 1984 overthrow of Alvarez and in 1985 its legal status was annulled because of allegations of involvement in a plot to kill Suazo.
See also **Alvarez Martínez; Suazo Córdova; Callejas.**

Asturias, Rodrigo: see **Organisation of the People in Arms.**

Atlantic Coast (Nicaragua)
A remote, sparsely populated and ethnically distinct region, also known as the Mosquitia. In 1847 the British government set up the so-called 'Mosquito Kingdom' protectorate, extending from Belize in the north to Costa Rica in the south, whose 'kings' were locally appointed but subject to the authority of a British superintendent based in the port of Bluefields. US assertion of hegemony in the hemisphere and rising Liberal nationalism resulted in the departure of the British in 1894, after an abortive Royal Marine landing at Bluefields and Rio San Juan (though they had acknowledged Nicaraguan sovereignty in an 1843 treaty). Both the Honduran and Nicaraguan Mosquitia remained largely ignored until the present day. The border between Nicaragua and Honduras in this area was submitted to the arbitration of the Spanish crown under an 1894 treaty, but the 1906 ruling was rejected by Nicaragua until the World Court confirmed it in 1960.

The border has traditionally been regarded as a mere formality by the migratory Indian inhabitants of the Rio Coco frontier zone. An International Court of Justice ruling in 1960 redefining the border led to the requirement that they choose either Honduran or Nicaraguan citizenship, and those in Nicaragua were then prevented from carrying out their traditional seasonal cultivation on the Honduran side. Many were resettled by Nicaragua, but with inadequate resources. The precise size of the Indian populations is matter of controversy, but on the Nicaraguan side they are independently estimated at 70,000 Miskitos, 7,000 Sumos and 700 Ramas. Interspersed with the Indians, mainly on the coast, are some 26,000 English-speaking creoles (descendants of black slaves), 1,500 Garífuna ('black caribs') and 180,000 whites and mestizos.

The economy consists largely of fishing, lumber, gold-mining, sugar and African palm cultivation and subsistence agriculture. The withdrawal of foreign investors after the 1930s, due to banana plague, overfishing, depletion of lumber and run-down of mines, brought decline to the Mosquitia, and in 1988 the region was devastated by Hurricane Joan. The road to the Atlantic coast was begun only under the post-1979 Sandinista government. Heavy-handed treatment of the local population by the Sandinistas caused widespread resentment and was partly responsible for the growth of armed ethnic opposition. This in turn led to the

forced relocation of the Rio Coco border population in 1982. More sensitive handling in later years, including the granting of regional autonomy (enshrined in the 1987 constitution), helped ease tension and led to the return of refugees, although some armed activity continued prior to the change of government in 1990 and thousands of Miskito refugees remained on the Honduran side of the border. A locally-elected, 45-member regional council now governs each of the two provinces (Atlántico Norte and Atlántico Sur) which make up the region, under the terms of the autonomy statute approved by the National Assembly on 2 September 1987.
See also **Yatama; Sandinista National Liberation Front; Monroe doctrine.**

Austin, Gen. Hudson: see Revolutionary Military Council.

Authentic Institutional Party (PAISA): see National Conciliation Party.

Authentic Liberal Party: see Democratic Alliance of Civic Opposition.

Authentic Nationalist Central (*Central Auténtica Nacionalista*/CAN) A Guatemalan political party founded in 1979 as successor to the Organised Aranista Central (CAO, f. 1970), which was the political vehicle for the presidency of Carlos Arana Osorio (1970–74). The CAO had been formed by an alliance primarily composed of financiers, industrialists and military officers. It joined the official coalition behind candidates Gens Laugerud and Lucas in the 1974 and 1978 elections respectively. The party lost its ties with the Arana family in 1977, and although on the far right has sought to dissociate itself from the former president and his allies. It ran its own presidential candidate in 1982 but came last. In coalition with the National Liberation Movement (MLN) and the Institutional Democratic Party (PID), the CAN won 23 seats in the 1984 constituent assembly. It withdrew from the coalition in January 1985 when it was refused the vice-presidential candidacy and instead put up Chicago school economist and TV journalist Mario David García for the presidency. García obtained 6% of the vote and CAN won only one seat in the legislature. The party's weakness was partly attributed to the withdrawal of Arana supporters. It suffered further defections under the Cerezo presidency, apparently as a result of negotiating with the Christian Democrats (DCG). Secretary general (1989): Héctor Mayora Dawe.
See also **Arana Osorio; National Liberation Movement** (Guatemala).

Authentic Panameñista Party (*Partido Panameñista Auténtico*/PPA) The successor to the Panameñista Party (PP) of Arnulfo Arias Madrid, who in 1939 had declared his political platform to be 'our panameñismo [Panamanianism]', the 'only creed, the only doctrine' which should exist in the country. Like many other 'personalist' movements in the region, panameñismo (or arnulfismo) consists of a vague, essentially anti-communist, populist doctrine organised into a movement only at election time in support of its caudillo. Arias stood for the presidency for the third time in 1964, backed by the PP alone, and lost by only 11,000 votes to the candidate of the UNO coalition, Marco Robles. Accusations of fraud abounded. In 1968 the PP was just one of many parties in the National Union coalition which backed Arias in a victorious election campaign which led to a presidency of only 11 days, cut short by a coup d'état.

When party activity resumed, ten years later, Arias refused to register his party or take part in the 1980 legislative elections (which his followers termed a 'farce'), but two erstwhile allies (Alonso Pinzón and Luis Suárez) pre-empted him by registering the PP – with all its traditional symbols – in their own names. After the overthrow of President Royo, however, the regime persuaded Arias to overcome his reservations and register the 'Authentic' PP. In 1984 the PPA joined Molirena and the Christian Democrats (PDC) in the Democratic Opposition Alliance (ADO) which backed the candidacy of Arias against Nicolás Ardito Barletta, whose victory they later claimed was fraudulent. The PPA later lost the leadership of ADO and the opposition in general to the PDC, and after the death of Arias in August 1988 it split in two. One faction, favouring co-operation with the military-backed regime, put up its own leader, Hildebrando Nicosia, for the presidency; while the other succeeded in having its leader, Guillermo Endara, nominated by the opposition coalition for the ultimately abortive 1989 poll.

When Endara was installed as president after the December 1989 US invasion, his supporters registered themselves as the Arnulfista Party.
See also **Arias Madrid; Democratic Alliance of Civic Opposition.**

Authentic Party of the Mexican Revolution (*Partido Auténtico de la Revolución Mexicana*/PARM)

Emerged from a split in the ruling Institutional Revolutionary Party (PRI) in 1954, and thereafter followed a generally centrist, if somewhat erratic, course. During the 1960s and 1970s it was tolerated by the PRI as a token opposition, and served as a home for retired generals with political ambitions as well as for losers in successive internal PRI disputes. Its share of the congressional vote oscillated from 0.49% in 1961 to a high of 2.67% in 1976, taking its representation in congress to just over ten deputies. In 1976 and 1982 the PARM did not present a presidential candidate of its own, choosing instead to support the successful PRI candidates, José López Portillo and Miguel De la Madrid. In late 1987, however, it was the first party to offer the presidential nomination to the opposition candidate, Cuauhtémoc Cárdenas, who gained over 30% of the total vote in the July 1988 polls at the head of the National Democratic Front (FDN) coalition.
See also **Cárdenas, Cuauhtémoc; Institutional Revolutionary Party; National Democratic Front.**

Avila, César: see Communist Party (Cuba).

Avila Camacho, Gen. Manuel

1897–1955. A Mexican army officer and president (1940–46), who toned down the political radicalism and anti-clericalism of the revolution. Avila Camacho joined the revolutionary forces in 1914, working his way up the ranks to the cabinet as secretary of war under Lázaro Cárdenas. His reputation as a conservative made him a surprising choice for the succession by the radical Cárdenas, although the outgoing president appeared to be acknowledging the need to re-build bridges with the private sector. Because of his low profile before nomination, Avila Camacho was dubbed the 'unknown soldier'. His two-word answer to a question about the church during the electoral campaign, *'soy creyente'* (I am a believer), signalled the end of the anti-clerical campaign. He also proclaimed the revolution over, talking instead of the need to consolidate its social conquests and develop economic prosperity.

There was much less redistribution of land during his *sexenio*; profound economic changes were triggered instead by World War II, which led to strong US demand for Mexican minerals, metals, oil and food, and a process of import substituting industrialisation. Internal migration to urban areas began to gather pace. Relations with Washington improved; in 1942 the two countries signed the Bracero Agreement which allowed Mexican migrant workers to take up jobs on the northern side of the border. In April 1942, Mexico joined the war on the Allies' side after a German U-boat had sunk a Mexican tanker near Florida. Many Mexicans fought in the US army and in 1945 the country sent an air force squadron to the Philippines. In 1943, Avila Camacho met President Franklin Roosevelt on the border, the first meeting between the presidents of the two countries since 1909.

Left-wingers within the labour movement – including Vicente Lombardo Toledano, its leader during the Lázaro Cárdenas presidency – were removed and, in another reflection of the president's strong position, the military sector within the Mexican Revolutionary Party (PRM – later renamed the Institutional Revolutionary Party, PRI) was abolished.
See also **Cárdenas, Lázaro; Institutional Revolutionary Party; Lombardo Toledano.**

Avril, Gen. Prosper

b. 12 March 1937. President of Haiti 1988–90. Avril graduated first in his class at the Haitian military academy in 1961 and joined the presidential guard. He also studied law and underwent naval training in the US. In the late 1960s, he became chief bodyguard to dictator François Duvalier's son and heir Jean-Claude. After the younger Duvalier took power in 1971, Avril took charge of arms purchases and became manager of the family's estimated $500m fortune. In 1983 he was forcibly retired by interior and defence minister Roger Lafontant, the country's strongman. After Lafontant's fall, Duvalier brought him back as deputy commander of the presidential guard as the regime was crumbling in early 1986. Avril was one of the main negotiators of the Duvaliers' secret night flight into exile in February 1986, after which he joined the seven-man junta headed by Gen. Henri Namphy.

Six weeks later street demonstrations against Duvalierist holdovers forced him out of the junta, but he remained a top adviser to Namphy. He was a key figure in the overthrow of civilian President Leslie Manigat by junior officers in 1988 and Namphy, restored to power, was obliged to make him a general. When the sergeants ousted Namphy in September 1988 they named Avril president. He immediately began consultations with all political groups, said he wanted to establish democracy and promised elections within three years. He was almost deposed in a week-long army revolt in 1989. He declared a state of siege in January 1990 'to defend democracy' and deported seven opposition figures, but was forced by US, French and other pressure to cancel it after nine days. Opposition pressure and demonstrations, backed by the US, obliged him to resign in March and he was flown out of the country in a US military plane.

See also **Namphy; Manigat; Duvalier, Jean-Claude; Duvalier, François.**

Azcona Hoyo, José Simón

b. 26 January 1927. President of Honduras 1986–90. Born in Honduras of Spanish parents, Azcona lived with his grandparents in Santander, Spain, from 1935 to 1949. He returned to Honduras in 1949 after illegally crossing the frontier into Portugal to avoid military service. He studied at the National University of Honduras (UNAH) and qualified as a civil engineer; later he was to take up real estate investment. A long-standing Liberal Party (PL) member, he co-ordinated the PL's 1981 election victory and became minister of transport, public works and communications in the Suazo Córdova government. He was also chairman of the PL's executive (CCE), but he resigned in 1983 over internal party elections he considered fraudulent and began to construct his own *azconista* movement within the PL. When it became obvious that he stood no chance of being the official PL candidate in the 1985 elections, he backed a move by congressional president Efraín Bu Girón to challenge the government's control of the electoral process by dismissing five supreme court judges. The result was a constitutional crisis, which ended with agreement among the parties that the presidency would go to whichever candidate gained most votes within the majority party.

Azcona's popularity with Liberal voters gave him victory over the official candidate, Oscar Mejía Arellano, and though he won fewer votes than the PN's Rafael Leonardo Callejas the latter kept to the agreement. Before his inauguration, Azcona forged a 'National Unity Pact' with the PN, giving the latter control of the supreme court and certain other public appointments. He also named two PN members to his cabinet. At his inauguration, Azcona proposed a 'social pact' to overcome the country's problems. He also promised an end to corruption and an emphasis on rural development. Despite a nominal commitment to self-determination, non-intervention and support for the Contadora group, Azcona protected the Nicaraguan contras based in Honduras, and in office proved as strong a US ally as his predecessor. This was particularly evident in his reluctance to sign, and then to implement, the Arias peace plan. Honduras neither expelled the contras nor allowed the international verification commission to examine their bases, though it did urge the US to accept responsibility for their eventual resettlement. In July 1986, Azcona became the first

Honduran president since the 'football war' of 1969 to visit El Salvador, an act interpreted by some as primarily a response to US policy requirements.

Internally, both the alliance with the PN and the divisions within his own party caused him serious difficulties. One bipartisan agreement which was reached – the decision not to hold municipal elections in 1987 – was widely criticised as unconstitutional. The continued autonomy of the armed forces was demonstrated only days after Azcona's inauguration by the overthrow of their commander, Gen. Wálter López, carried out without reference to congress, which appointed him.

In the first half of Azcona's term inflation and the fiscal deficit were reduced and the national debt renegotiated, but despite government attempts to massage the figures, economic indicators later worsened markedly and labour unrest intensified. Both the IMF and the World Bank declared Honduras ineligible for further loans because of payment arrears, and by the end of his term the fiscal deficit still stood at around 12% of GDP. The PL lost the 1989 election to the PN.

See also **Liberal Party** (Honduras); **Suazo Córdova; Arias Plan.**

B

'Baby Doc': see **Duvalier, Jean-Claude.**

Baechli, Otto: see **Christian Democrat Party** (Guatemala).

BAHAMAS, Commonwealth of the

Capital: Nassau
Independence (from Britain): 1973
Area: 13,935 sq km
Population (1988): 234,000 (62% urban)
Pop. growth rate: 1%
Pop. density: 16.8/sq km
Infant mortality: 30 per thousand
Life expectancy at birth: 71
Literacy: 89%
GDP per capita (1988e): US$11,317
Foreign debt per capita (1988e): US$866
Main exports: tourism, offshore banking, petroleum products, chemicals, rum, pharmaceuticals, cement, salt, steel pipes, fish

Political system

Constitution: 1973. Titular head of state: Queen Elizabeth of Britain, represented locally by a figurehead governor-general. A 49-member House of Assembly is elected for a maximum five years. A 16-member Senate is appointed.
Governor-general: Sir Henry Taylor (1988)
Prime minister: Sir Lynden Pindling (1967)
Last elections: 1987

Political organisations

Parties in parliament (leader) (seats in House of Assembly): Progressive Liberal Party/PLP (Sir Lynden Pindling) (31), f. 1953; Free National Movement/FNM (Hubert Ingraham) (16), f. 1971.
Parties outside parliament: Vanguard Nationalist and Socialist Party (Lionel Carey), f. 1971.
Main trade unions: Bahamas Trade Union Congress/BTUC (Leonard Archer); Bahamas Hotel, Catering and Allied Workers' Union (Thomas Bastian), f. 1958; Bahamas Public Services Union, f. 1959; Bahamas Union of Teachers, f. 1945.

Employers' organisation: Bahamas Employers' Association.

Bahamas Democratic Party (BDP): see Free National Movement.

Bajeux, Jean-Claude: see KONAKOM.

Balaguer, Joaquín
b. 1 September 1906. President of the Dominican Republic 1960–61,
1966–78, 1986– . A poet and historian, Balaguer served as a diplomat in
Spain and Colombia before becoming dictator Rafael Trujillo's education
minister in 1950. In 1953 he became foreign minister and in 1957 vice-
president of the republic. He was appointed titular president in 1960,
holding the post when Trujillo was assassinated in 1961 and managing to
hang on until the army ousted him in 1962 after which he fled to the US.
He founded the conservative Reformist Party (PR) in 1964 and returned
from exile after the 1965 US invasion and occupation.
  He was elected president in 1966, defeating ex-president Juan Bosch,
and was re-elected in 1970 and 1974. During this time, especially 1966–70,
thousands of leftists were murdered by what he said were 'uncontrollable
elements' in the armed forces. Land reform measures gave him a strong
rural base. He was defeated in the 1978 presidential elections by the
Dominican Revolutionary Party's Antonio Guzmán, but not before US
President Jimmy Carter had intervened to prevent a coup after the military stopped vote-counting when they saw Balaguer was losing. When he
was narrowly elected president for the fourth time in 1986, thanks to a
split opposition, he was virtually blind from glaucoma. In 1985 he merged
his party with Fernando Alvarez Bogaert's Social Christian Revolutionary
Party (PRSC) to form the Social Christian Reformist Party (PRSC). He
launched an extensive public works programme, including construction of
the Faro Colón to mark the 500th anniversary of Columbus's arrival in
the Americas. He was re-elected president in 1990 with 35% of the vote.
See also **Trujillo; Bosch, Juan; Dominican Republic, US invasion (1965);
Guzmán; Jorge Blanco.**

'Bananagate': see López Arellano.

banana strike (Costa Rica, 1934)
The first successful strike in Costa Rica against a foreign monopoly,
staged by 10,000 United Fruit Co. employees in protest at working conditions in the Atlantic banana zone. The principal leaders were Carlos
Luis Fallas and Jaime Cerdas of the Communist Party. The port of
Puntarenas was paralysed and the government sent in troops, but after
several weeks of clashes United Fruit was forced to concede the workers'
demands, including limited recognition of union rights. Communist Party
influence over the banana workers was strengthened by the strike, but a
full labour code was not promulgated until the 1940s, under President
Rafael Angel Calderón Guardia.
See also **Communist Party** (Costa Rica).

Bangou, Henri
b. 11 November 1922. One of Guadeloupe's two senators in the French

parliament. A heart specialist, he was elected communist mayor of Pointe-à-Pitre in 1965, was a member of the island's General Council from 1967 to 1989, and was elected to the Senate in 1986.

Banks, Victor: see Anguilla Democratic Party.

Baquiaux Gómez, Rolando: see Democratic Party of National Cooperation.

BARBADOS
Capital: Bridgetown
Independence (from Britain): 1966
Area: 430 sq km
Population (1988): 254,000
Pop. growth rate: 0.3%
Pop. density: 591/sq km
Infant mortality: 11 per thousand
Life expectancy at birth: 73
Literacy: 99%
GDP per capita (1988e): US$4,233
Foreign debt per capita (1989): US$1,608
Main exports: tourism, electronic goods, sugar, cement

Political system

Constitution: 1966. Titular head of state: Queen Elizabeth of Britain, represented locally by a figurehead governor-general. A 27-member House of Assembly (dating from 1639) is elected for a maximum five years. A 21-member Senate is appointed.
Governor-general: Dame Nita Barrow (1990)
Prime minister: Erskine Sandiford (1987)
Last elections: 1986

Political organisations

Parties in parliament (leader) (seats in House of Assembly): Democratic Labour Party/DLP (Erskine Sandiford) (24), f. 1955; National Democratic Party/NDP (Richie Haynes) (4), f. 1989; Barbados Labour Party/BLP (Henry Forde) (3), f. 1938.
Parties outside parliament: Workers' Party of Barbados/WPB (George Belle), f. 1985; People's Pressure Movement/PPM (Eric Sealy), f. 1979.
Main trade unions: Barbados Workers' Union/BWU (Frank Walcott), f. 1941; National Union of Public Workers/NUPW (Nigel Harper), f. 1944; Barbados Union of Teachers/BUT (Ronald Jones), f. 1974; Barbados Secondary Teachers' Union/BSTU; Barbados Industrial and General Workers' Union/BIGWU (Bobby Clarke), f. 1981.
Employers' organisations: Barbados Hotel Association/BHA (Ralph Taylor); Barbados Manufacturers' Association/BMA (Lewis Kirton); Barbados Employers' Confederation/BEC.

Barbados Labour Party (BLP)

Conservative party in Barbados. Founded by moderate socialists in 1938 and the first modern political party to be formed in the Anglo-Caribbean, it changed its name a few months later to the Barbados Progessive League. It elected Grantley Adams (1898–1971) leader in 1939. By 1944 it had changed its name back to the Barbados Labour Party and in that year won eight seats in the house of assembly. It became the largest party in parliament after the 1946 elections and formed a ruling coalition with the Congress Party. It won an absolute majority in 1948 and in 1951 (16–8). Adams became the country's first premier in 1954.

The party split in 1955 when Errol Barrow broke away to form the Democratic Labour Party, but Adams easily won the 1956 elections (15–9). In 1958, Adams resigned to become West Indies federal prime minister and handed over the party and the premiership to Hugh Cummins. The BLP was heavily defeated 5–19 in the 1961 poll and Barrow became premier. The party lost again in 1966 (8–16), and in 1970 the ailing Adams resigned as leader in favour of Bernard St John. But the party was defeated 6–18 in the 1971 poll and in 1973 Adams's son Tom took over the party. The BLP regained power in 1976 (17–7) and Adams became prime minister. The party won 17–10 in 1981. Adams died in 1985 and was succeeded by St John. A year later, the BLP was badly defeated 3–24, with St John losing his seat as in 1971. He was replaced as party leader by Henry Forde. The party is a member of the Socialist International, although its policies are no longer left-wing. In 1989, the BLP was displaced as the official parliamentary opposition by the new National Democratic Party, which mustered four MPs.

See also **Forde; Adams, Tom; Barbados Workers' Union; Barrow; Democratic Labour Party** (Barbados); **West Indies Federation.**

Barbados Progressive League: see Barbados Labour Party.

Barbados Workers' Union (BWU)

Main trade union in Barbados. Founded in 1941, it became the backbone of the Barbados Progressive League/Barbados Labour Party. Its first general secretary was Hugh Springer, who was succeeded in 1948 by his deputy, Frank Walcott, while Grantley Adams became president-general. In 1949, Adams and the union led the revolt in the Caribbean against the communist-dominated World Confederation of Trade Unions and helped set up the rival International Confederation of Free Trade Unions. In 1954, Adams resigned as president-general to become premier and was soon estranged from Walcott, who in 1958, with much of the union, decided to back the opposition Democratic Labour Party of Errol Barrow. Walcott became a member of the house of assembly and later the senate.

See also **Walcott; Barbados Labour Party; Democratic Labour Party** (Barbados); **ORIT; National Workers' Union of Jamaica.**

Barbuda

Part of the twin-island state of Antigua-Barbuda.

Chief town: Codrington
Area: 160 sq km
Population: 1,100
Main exports: lobsters, sand, tourism

Political system

A nine-seat island council, half of whose members are elected every two years, has partial autonomy from the state government in Antigua. The island elects one member to the state parliament.
Island council chairman: Hilbourne Frank (1987)
Last elections: 1989

Political organisations

Parties in island council (leader) (seats): Barbuda People's Movement (Hilbourne Frank) (9).
Parties outside the council: Barbuda Independence Movement (Arthur Nibbs), f. 1988.
Once owned by the British Codrington family, Barbuda became a dependency of Antigua, 40 km away, in 1860. All land was held in common until 1981. The island was allotted its own parliamentary seat in 1961. Soon after Antigua-Barbuda won associated statehood (internal self-government) in 1967, talk of secession began. Barbuda was granted partial self-rule in 1976 with its own island council, but a successful campaign for further autonomy and more development money helped delay Antigua's independence until 1981. The islanders, who at one point wanted to return to direct British rule, now control all internal affairs except land and security matters. In 1988 former council chairman Arthur Nibbs founded the Barbuda Independence Movement to campaign for more self-government.
See also **Antigua-Barbuda; Frank; Burton.**

Barbuda People's Movement (BPM): see **Frank; Barbuda; Burton.**

barbudos: see **Cuban Revolutionary War.**

Barcenas-Meneses-Esguerra Treaty: see **San Andrés dispute.**

Barrera, Hugo: see **ARENA.**

Barrios, Justo Rufino: see **Ubico y Castañeda.**

Barrios de Chamorro, Violeta
b. 18 October 1929. President of Nicaragua 1990– . Violeta Chamorro (as she is usually known) was born Violeta Barrios in Rivas, southern Nicaragua. Her parents were wealthy landowners. In 1950 she married Pedro Joaquín Chamorro, who two years later became editor of the newapaper *La Prensa,* which his family owned. A leading opponent of the Somoza dictatorship, Chamorro was murdered in 1978, his death helping to spark off the national insurrection which led to the 1979 revolution. His wife succeeded him as publisher of *La Prensa,* and became

a member of the first post-revolutionary government. She resigned after
nine months, ostensibly on health grounds but in reality because of
political differences with the dominant Sandinistas (FSLN). *La Prensa*
became a vehicle for strident opposition to the government and was both
censored and closed down at different times. Her family is itself divided
politically: one son, Carlos Fernando, edits the FSLN newspaper *Barricada*, while another, Pedro Joaquín, was for a time a leader of the US-
backed contra rebels. He returned to Nicaragua in October 1989. Her
daughter Cristiana now edits *La Prensa*, but Claudia Chamorro, Cristiana's sister, is a pro-Sandinista diplomat. Although without a political
party of her own, Doña Violeta was chosen in September 1989 by the
National Opposition Union (UNO) as its presidential candidate for the
1990 elections, apparently under strong pressure from the United States.
She won an unexpected victory, taking 54% of the vote and becoming
the first elected woman president in Latin American history.

Her immediate problems were to negotiate the handover of power
from the FSLN and the disbandment of the contras, while not alienating
members of the ideologically diverse UNO coalition. Her decision to
retain Gen. Humberto Ortega as army chief of staff, while taking the
defence portfolio herself, aroused opposition in UNO, with some
appointees declining even cabinet posts in protest, while the contras
threatened to retain their weapons. Chamorro did, however, obtain an
agreement that the rebels would lay down their arms by 27 June 1990.
Difficulties within the coalition were harder to resolve, and UNO effectively split into two at the outset, with many members angry at the
way power was concentrated among Chamorro's advisers (seen as 'the
technocrats' and headed by her son-in-law, industrialist Antonio Lacayo)
rather than the professional politicians. On the economic front, Chamorro
announced a plan to 'wipe out inflation in 12 weeks' and introduce a new
currency at par with the US dollar. Politically, one of her first moves was
a sweeping amnesty law, pardoning all political crimes.

See also **National Opposition Union** (Nicaragua); **Chamorro Cardenal,
Pedro Joaquín; *La Prensa*.**

Barrow, Errol

1920–87. Premier, prime minister of Barbados 1961–76, 1986–7. A barrister, economist and British Royal Air Force bomber pilot during World
War II, Barrow returned to Barbados in 1950, joined Grantley Adams's
Barbados Labour Party (BLP) and was elected to the house of assembly
in 1951. He and others broke away in 1955 to form the Democratic
Labour Party (DLP), which was defeated in the 1956 general election,
with Barrow losing his seat. In 1958, after failing to get elected to the
West Indies federal parliament, he regained a seat in the Barbadian
parliament and was elected vice-president of the General Workers'
Union.

Barrow led the DLP to a 14–10 victory at the 1961 elections and
became premier. For the next 15 years, he intensively developed the
tourist industry and led the island to independence from Britain in 1966.

After the DLP lost the 1976 election, Barrow resigned as opposition leader and handed over to Frederick Smith, but resumed the job in 1978 when Smith resigned. He warned against excessive US influence in the region, including the 1983 invasion of Grenada. The DLP regained power in 1986 and Barrow became prime minister. He denounced militarisation of the region, criticised other Caribbean leaders for being too close to Washington and dismissed President Reagan as a 'cowboy' and a 'zombie'. He died in office in 1987. Barrow's sister, Dame Nita Barrow (b. 1917), a former Barbadian ambassador to the United Nations, was appointed the country's first woman governor-general in 1990.

See also **Democratic Labour Party** (Barbados); **Barbados Labour Party; Grenada, US invasion (1983); Regional Security System.**

Batista y Zaldívar, Gen. Fulgencio

1901–73. President of Cuba 1940–44, 1952–9. Fulgencio Batista was born in Banes and educated at Quaker missionary schools and state schools. After trying various jobs, he entered the army as a recruit in 1921. He later joined the ABC party which vehemently opposed the dictatorship of General Machado, and after Machado was ousted in a coup in August 1933, Batista (by then a sergeant-stenographer) led other NCOs in an uprising (motivated by discontent over pay and conditions) against the short-lived de Céspedes presidency on 4 September 1933. The rebels obtained the unexpected backing of Prof. Ramón Grau San Martín, leader of the Student Directorate (*Directorio Estudiantil*). Grau was given the task of forming a government, while Batista, now a colonel, became the power behind the throne, promoting his fellow-conspirators to senior positions. He forced Grau's resignation on 15 January 1934, replacing him with Col. Carlos Mendieta, whose government was only another in a succession of short-lived regimes.

From 1934 to 1940, Batista was armed forces chief of staff. He put together a 'Socialist Democratic Coalition' with the Communist Party (which had overcome its aversion to him as the 'fascist' who had smashed the soviets they set up during the Grau government and brutally put down the 1935 general strike). The coalition won 45 out of 81 seats in the constituent assembly of 1939, and Batista went on to stand successfully for president in 1940, though not under universal suffrage. Two years later he became the first Latin American president to include communist ministers in his cabinet. After his candidate for the succession (also backed by the Communists) was defeated in 1944, Batista left for Florida, where he stayed until 1948. On his return he formed the Unitary Action Party (PAU). He declared his candidacy on the PAU ticket in 1952, but staged a bloodless coup on 10 March 1952 against the government of President Prío Socarrás when it became obvious that he would not win.

Batista's second presidency was characterised by officially condoned vice and corruption: under it, Havana became the gambling and prostitution centre of the Caribbean. The torture and murder of dissidents also became commonplace, especially after the July 1953 Moncada incident, while the economy became even more heavily dependent on the US than

previously. In 1954 he staged an election in a bid for legitimacy, having formed a coalition with Liberals and National Democrats around the PAU's successor, the Progressive Action Party (PAP). During 1956–8, Batista was faced with a guerrilla insurgency led by Fidel Castro. On New Year's Day 1959 he fled to exile in the Dominican Republic and thence to the United States and later Europe, just before the victorious Castroite rebels marched into Havana. His chosen successor, Andrés Rivero Aguero, had won the elections in 1958 but was not permitted to take office. Batista died in Spain in 1973.
See also **Cuban Revolutionary War; Moncada assault.**

Bayo, Alberto: see **Caribbean Legion.**

Bay of Pigs invasion
An abortive attempt by the United States to overthrow the government of Fidel Castro in Cuba, using a US-trained invasion force of 1,400 Cuban exiles ('Brigade 2506'). Launched on 14 April 1961 from Puerto Cabezas in Nicaragua, the seaborne invasion landed on two beaches on the south coast of Cuba three days later. These were Playa Girón and Playa Larga in the Bahía de Cochinos (Bay of Pigs), 175 km south-east of Havana. An attempt had already been made to destroy Cuba's fledgling air force on the ground, but the bombing raid had largely failed, as had attempts to portray it as the work of Cuban defectors. This led President Kennedy to call off the planned air support for the invasion. The supply ships were driven back by air attack, and within 24 hours the brigade was surrounded by 20,000 troops of the Cuban regular army and the Matanzas militia, including tank and artillery forces. Within two days of the landing the invasion force had been crushed. A total of 1,180 prisoners were taken, three of whom were later executed for assassinations carried out under the Batista regime.
     Planning for the invasion had begun in January 1960 under President Eisenhower, who approved a $13m budget for it in August that year. The plan was drawn up and supervised by the Central Intelligence Agency, which organised the Cuban exiles into a 'Democratic Revolutionary Front' and trained the invasion force in the US and in Guatemala. A parallel effort to assassinate Castro was initiated at the same time, and Mafia boss Sam Giancano of Chicago and Santos Trafficante, former underworld boss in Havana, were recruited for the venture. Attempts were also made to organise an internal uprising to coincide with the invasion, but these never got off the ground. No Cuban was involved in the strategic planning, and when the invasion began, the 'Cuban Revolutionary Council' – which was supposed to form a provisional government – was kept under armed guard in a Florida air force base. The Bay of Pigs fiasco substantially strengthened the Castro regime and helped set the scene for the Cuban missile crisis of 1962.
See also **Castro Ruz, Fidel Alejandro; Cuban missile crisis; Batista y Zaldívar.**

Bay Street Boys: see **United Bahamian Party.**

Bazán, J. D.: see **Republican Party** (Panama).

Bazin, Marc
b. 6 March 1932. Conservative Haitian politician. A lawyer, Bazin was
a financial adviser to the Moroccan government and a World Bank official
in West Africa. He returned to Haiti to become finance minister in 1982
at the insistence of Haiti's international creditors. Five months later he
was dismissed after denouncing official corruption and returned abroad
to resume work for the World Bank. In 1986, after the fall of the Duvalier
regime, he came back to Haiti and founded the Movement for the Establishment of Democracy in Haiti (MIDH) and declared himself a candidate
for the presidency. He was regarded as the favourite of the US. After
the military and Duvalierists destroyed the 1987 elections, he and others
boycotted a new, regime-organised poll. He advocated dialogue with the
military government, however. He joined social democrat Serge Gilles
in 1989 to form a National Alliance for Democracy and Progress to
contest elections.
See also **Movement for the Establishment of Democracy in Haiti;
PANPRA; Gilles; Duvalier, Jean-Claude.**

Bazzaglia, Rogelio ('Marcelo'): see **Popular Liberation Forces.**

Beache, Vincent
b. 13 August 1931. St Vincent politician. Beache entered parliament in
1974 as a member of the St Vincent Labour Party (SVLP) and was named
trade and agriculture minister in 1978 under prime minister Milton Cato.
He became parliamentary opposition leader in 1985 after Cato's 1984
electoral defeat. He was elected SVLP leader in 1986 after the death of
the party leader Hudson Tannis, but lost his seat along with the party's
two other MPs at the 1989 general election.
See also **St Vincent Labour Party; Cato.**

'beans and bullets': see *fusiles y frijoles.*

Beckford, George: see **'black power'.**

BELIZE
   Capital: Belmopan
   Largest city: Belize City
   Independence: 1981 (from Britain)
   Area: 22,963 sq km
   Population (1989): 185,000 (50% urban)
   Pop. density: 8/sq km
   Pop. growth rate (1986e): 2.8%
   Infant mortality: 21 per thousand
   Life expectancy at birth: 69
   Literacy: 93%
   GDP per capita (1986): US$1149
   Foreign debt per capita (1987): US$611
   Main exports (1986): sugar (42.2%); garments (21.8%); orange juice
   (14.9%); fish products (9.9%); bananas (6.2%)

Political system

Constitution 1981. Titular head of state: Queen Elizabeth of Britain, represented by a figurehead governor-general. A 28-member House of Representatives is elected for a maximum five years. An eight-member Senate is nominated.

Governor-general: Dame Minita Gordon (1981)
Prime minister: George Price (1989)
Last elections: 1989

Political organisations

Political parties (leader) (seats in House of Representatives): People's United Party/PUP (George Price) (15), f. 1950; United Democratic Party/UDP (Manuel Esquivel) (13), f. 1973.
Main labour organisations (affiliation): National Federation of Workers/NFW (CLAT); Trades Union Congress/TUC (ORIT).
Employers' organisation: Belize Chamber of Commerce and Industry (Hugh Fuller/Billy Musa).
See also **Belize dispute.**

Belize Action Movement (BAM): see **United Democratic Party.**

Belize dispute

The independence of Belize, granted by the UK in 1981, was rejected by Guatemala, which has historically claimed Belize as a Guatemalan province. The basis of the claim is that the short-lived Federal Republic of Central America (1823–39) inherited the entirety of the Spanish colonial territories in the area, including Belize, and that when the Pact of Federation broke down in 1839, Guatemala was established on the territorial basis of the former Captaincy General of Guatemala. This too included sovereignty over the territory of Belize, which was subject to a usufruct concession in favour of Britain. Although it was not until 1862 that Belize was made a British Crown Colony (as British Honduras), the gradual establishment of colonial rule had been in progress since at least 1784. Britain never recognised the Federal Republic because of its refusal to yield on the issue of sovereignty, which remained in dispute even after the Anglo-Guatemalan Treaty of 1859 produced agreement on the boundaries of Belize. Guatemala subsequently argued that the treaty was a cession of territory in exchange for the building of a road by Britain from Guatemala City to the Belize coast. Since the road was never built, they said, the cession was void. The British view was that the treaty merely settled the boundaries of an established territory and that the building of the road was not a condition. A subsequent convention setting out responsibilities for the road project was not properly ratified.

The Belize issue was raised periodically by Guatemala over the next century, coming to a head in 1964 when Britain granted the colony self-government and Guatemala broke off diplomatic relations. Attempts at US mediation during 1965–8 failed, and in 1972 an invasion scare resulted in the reinforcement of the British garrison. In 1976 the British government attempted secretly to negotiate the cession of a corridor of land south of the Moho river (about 225 sq miles). This met with hostility from the Belizeans, who insisted on being party to future talks. Subsequent rounds included variants of this offer, which Guatemala seemed increasingly ready to accept. In March 1981 heads of agreement were signed, amounting to 15 points which included Guatemalan access to a sea corridor off the Belize coast; the use of two offshore cays; and free port facilities in Belize for Guatemalan exports. But negotiations broke down because of rioting in Belize, and independence was granted in September 1981 without Guatemalan recognition. It was subsequently revealed that Guatemala had sought the right to place a military installation on one of the cays.

In 1983, Guatemala modified its territorial claim and in its 1985 constitution dropped the formal claim altogether. For the first time since 1945 free negotiations on the issue would be allowed so long as any agreement was put to a referendum. The government of Manuel Esquivel (1984–9) in Belize declared its intention to be flexible (without ceding territory), while the civilian government of President Vinicio Cerezo in Guatemala (1986–90) restored consular and then full diplomatic relations with Britain in 1986. Cerezo announced his willingness to negotiate with Belize and not to insist on territorial concessions. However, the sovereignty claim was later reiterated, and at a meeting in April 1987 between the Guatemalan and Belizean foreign ministers territorial demands appeared to have been renewed. In May 1988 a Belize/Guatemala Joint Commission was set up to resolve the issue; the first time Guatemala had agreed to talk directly to Belize. Britain maintains a 1,600-strong military garrison in Belize, plus RAF Harrier jet fighters, helicopters and a small naval detachment. The Belize Defence Force is trained by the UK and US armies.

(NB. Mexico has a latent claim to part of northern Belize, but has said this would only be activated in event of the land's absorption into Guatemala. Honduras, too, has a latent claim to cays in the Bay of Amatique and would have to be taken into account in any agreement.)
See also **Price; People's United Party; Esquivel.**

Belize Popular Party (BPP): see People's United Party.

Bennett, Michèle: see Duvalier, Jean-Claude; Tontons Macoutes.

Benoit, François: see Movement for the Establishment of Democracy in Haiti.

Benoit, Victor: see KONAKOM.

Bentoera, Raymond: see Democratic Party (Netherlands Antilles).

Bequia
The main island of the St Vincent-administered part of the Grenadines chain.
Chief town: Port Elizabeth

Area: 15 sq km
Population: 2,600
Home of Vincentian prime minister James Mitchell. It is the last place
in the Caribbean where whaling is occasionally practised.
See also **Mitchell, James; Grenadines; St Vincent.**

BERMUDA
Capital: Hamilton
Area: 54 sq km
Population (1989): 58,800
Pop. growth rate: 1.2%
Pop. density: 1089/sq km
Infant mortality: 7 per thousand
Life expectancy at birth: 73
Literacy: 98%
GDP per capita (1987): US$24,210
Foreign debt per capita (1987): US$10,866
Main exports: tourism, offshore finance, petroleum products, pharma-
   ceutical products, rum, flowers

Political system
A British colony with internal self-government since 1968. An appointed
British governor responsible for defence and internal security represents
the titular head of state, Queen Elizabeth of Britain. Parliament com-
prises a 40-member House of Assembly elected for a maximum five years
and an appointed 11-member Senate.
   Governor: Sir Desmond Langley (1988)
   Premier: Sir John Swan (1982)
   Last elections: 1989

Political organisations
   Parties in parliament (leader) (seats in House of Assembly): United
   Bermuda Party/UBP (Sir John Swan) (22), f. 1964; Progressive Labour
   Party/PLP (Frederick Wade) (15), f. 1963; National Liberal Party/NLP
   (Gilbert Darrell) (1), f. 1985.
   Main trade union: Bermuda Industrial Union/BIU (Ottiwell Simmons).
   Employers' organisation: Bermuda Hotel Association/BHA.

Bermúdez, Col. Enrique: see Nicaraguan Democratic Force.

Berrios Martínez, Rubén
b. 21 June 1939. Social democratic leader of the Puerto Rican Independence Party (PIP). A British and US-educated lawyer, he took over the
party in 1969 after the death of its founder, Gilberto Concepción de
Gracia, in 1967. He was elected to the island's senate in 1972 and 1984
for four-year terms and won 5.4% of the vote when he ran for governor
in 1988.
See also **Puerto Rican Independence Party; Puerto Rico, nationalist violence.**

Best, Lloyd
b. 27 February 1934. Radical Trinidad politician and 'father' of the Caribbean 'new left'. An economist and academic, Best was a UN economic adviser to the Jagan government in Guyana (1962–3) and elsewhere in the Caribbean. He founded the New World Group of radical Caribbean intellectuals in 1963. The group split in 1968 and Best, then a lecturer at the University of the West Indies in Trinidad, founded the Tapia House Group the same year. He was an opposition senator from 1974 until 1976, when Tapia made a poor showing at general elections. He became opposition leader in the senate in 1981 after a three-party opposition alliance won 10 seats at a general election that year. In 1983 he resigned and went to work for the UN in French-speaking Africa. In 1986 he did not support the National Alliance for Reconstruction coalition which won power later that year with the backing of some Tapia figures.
See also **Tapia House Group; Williams; 'new left'; 'black power'.**

Bird, Ivor: see Bird, Vere C.

Bird, Lester
b. 21 February 1938. Deputy premier, deputy prime minister of Antigua–Barbuda 1976–   . When his father Vere's Antigua Labour Party (ALP) lost power at elections in 1971, Lester, a barrister, was nominated to the senate and became ALP chairman. When the ALP returned to office in 1976 and he was elected to parliament, he was appointed deputy premier and has largely run the government for his father since about 1980. After the landslide ALP victory in 1984, the cabinet split into factions supporting him or his father. Lester strove to ensure his succession while his father indicated he now favoured his eldest son Vere Jr, also a minister, whom he defended against corruption charges. Lester's faction managed to force Vere Jr's resignation in an arms smuggling scandal in 1990. Lester has questioned his father's fiercely pro-American position, which has resulted in generous military, communications and diplomatic facilities for the US in Antigua.
See also **Bird, Vere C.; Bird, Vere, Jr; Antigua Labour Party.**

Bird, Vere C.
b. 9 December 1909. Chief minister, premier, prime minister of Antigua-Barbuda 1960–71, 1976-   . A former Salvation Army captain, Vere Bird helped form the Antigua Trades and Labour Union (ATLU) in 1939 and became its president in 1943. He was elected to the legislative council in 1945 and in 1946 was named to the executive council. In 1951 he formed the Antigua Labour Party (ALP) which won all eight elective seats on the legislative council that year. In 1956, the ALP again won all eight seats and Bird became minister of trade and production and in 1960 chief minister. After winning elections in 1961, he began to turn the island away from sugar towards large-scale foreign-backed tourism development. He became premier in 1967 but the ATLU split the same year and Bird resigned as union president. He lost the 1971 general election to George

Walter, the leader of the split and head of a new party, the Progressive Labour Movement.

He regained his parliamentary seat and the premiership after an ALP victory in 1976 and in 1981 led the country to independence to become prime minister. From about 1980, everyday business was conducted through his son and deputy Lester. Although he was re-elected in 1984, corruption and scandal had begun to undermine his rule. In 1978 the government was found to have granted rights to a Canadian company, Space Research Corporation, laundering arms and ammunition to South Africa. After 1984, the cabinet split into factions around the fiercely pro-US Bird and his son Lester. The prime minister refused in 1987 to dismiss for corruption his eldest son (and public works minister) Vere Jr, Lester's chief rival to succeed their father. After a new scandal in 1990, he agreed to Vere Jr's resignation but claimed he was innocent. Another of Bird's sons, Ivor, runs the family radio station, ZDK.

See also **Antigua Labour Party; Bird, Lester; Bird, Vere, Jr; Progressive Labour Movement; Walter.**

Bird, Vere, Jr

b. 2 October 1936. Antiguan politician. A barrister and eldest son of Antiguan prime minister Vere C. Bird, he was elected to parliament in 1976. He was minister of public utilities, aviation and communications from 1984–7, and then public works and communications minister. In 1986 he was accused of involvement in a corrupt $11.5m deal with a French company to modernise the island's airport. The charges, implicitly confirmed in 1987 by an independent enquiry, aggravated a government split in which the prime minister refused to dismiss him and indicated he now favoured him as his successor over deputy prime minister Lester Bird. In 1990, he was accused by Israeli and Colombian authorities of secretly shipping arms through Antigua to Colombian drug barons and resigned from the government.

See also **Bird, Vere C.; Bird, Lester.**

Bishop, Maurice

1944–83. Prime minister of Grenada 1979–83. After training as a barrister in Britain, Bishop (who was born in Aruba of Grenadian parents) returned to Grenada in 1970 to found the radical Forum group and in 1972 the Movement for the Advancement of Community Effort (MACE). A few months later he co-founded the Movement for Assemblies of the People (MAP), which in 1973 merged with the Jewel Movement to form the New Jewel Movement (NJM). Premier Eric Gairy cracked down on the NJM, jailing Bishop briefly on independence in 1974. Bishop's father Rupert was shot dead by Gairy thugs during a general strike and demonstration two weeks earlier. Bishop was elected to parliament as a member of a three-party opposition group, the People's Alliance, in general elections in 1976 and was named opposition leader.

He became prime minister when the NJM seized power in 1979 while Gairy was out of the country and proclaimed a 'people's revolutionary government'. During his four years in office he was feared by fellow

Caribbean leaders for his potentially subversive example among their own people, but also admired for his probity and support for Caribbean cultural identity and regional economic and political interests. At a Caricom summit at Ocho Rios, Jamaica, in 1982, he extracted a regional pledge to respect ideological pluralism.

Serious conflict arose inside the NJM in 1982 when Bishop was blamed for inefficiency and later suspected of wanting to appease a hostile US government. In 1983 supporters of his radical deputy, Bernard Coard, persuaded him to agree to a plan for formally sharing national leadership with Coard. But he changed his mind and was arrested by the Coard faction soon after returning from a tour of eastern Europe in October 1983. Some 10,000 supporters freed him from house arrest on 19 October and he went to Fort Rupert, apparently to organise resistance to his rivals. But troops stormed the fort, killing nearly 100 people, and executed Bishop and three of his ministers. His body was burned. The assassination was one of the pretexts for the US military invasion of the island six days later. Bishop remains popular with Grenadians despite public dislike of his government in its last months. Coard and 13 others were sentenced to death in 1986 for his murder.

See also **New Jewel Movement; People's Revolutionary Government; Gairy; Coard; Grenada, US invasion (1983); Maurice Bishop Patriotic Movement; Radix; 'new left'.**

Black, Eli: see López Arellano.

Blackman, Don
b. 22 May 1935. Centre-left Barbadian politician. After his return from Canada and New York, where he taught African studies, Don Blackman was appointed ambassador to the UN in 1976 by the newly-elected Barbados Labour Party (BLP) government under Tom Adams. In 1978 he was appointed a senator and minister of labour. After his election to parliament in 1981 he became the transport and works minister and, later, minister of health. He was sacked, however, in 1983, and he resigned from the BLP just before the 1986 elections, accusing the party of promoting white control of the country. He joined the Democratic Labour Party and was re-elected to parliament, becoming transport and works minister once more in 1987.

See also **Adams, Tom; Democratic Labour Party** (Barbados); **Barbados Labour Party.**

'black power'
The goal of successive movements in the 20th-century English-speaking Caribbean aimed at ending domination by foreigners and local whites and 'Afro-Saxons'. The campaigns of the charismatic Jamaican Marcus Garvey in the 1920s and 1930s led to serious labour unrest in many countries and to the granting of self-government in the 1950s and 1960s. Influenced by Rastafarianism and spurred by the US 'black power' movement in the 1960s, black nationalism erupted again in the Anglo-Carib-

bean in the late 1960s fuelled by the ideas of regional intellectuals such as Walter Rodney, James Millette, Lloyd Best and George Beckford.

Pressure groups were founded in virtually every island and European-style dress and speech were often discarded by young people. The movement became violent in Jamaica and Bermuda in 1968, Curaçao in 1969 and in Trinidad in 1970, where black militants came close to overthrowing the government. By the mid-1970s, the movement had faded through the pressure of economic crisis and through recuperation by the 'new left' parties. But it had brought about a major advance in black consciousness and regional identity.

See also **Garvey;** *noirisme;* **Césaire; Rodney riots (1968); Social Independent Party-Workers' Liberation Front; Trinidad, 'black power' uprising (1970); Douglas, Rosie; Butler; Williams; National Joint Action Committee; Best; 'new left'; rastafarians; dreads; Duvalierism; Moyne Commission.**

Blaize, Herbert

1918–89. Chief minister, premier, prime minister of Grenada 1960–61, 1962–7, 1984–9. After working as a civil servant and then in Aruba for eight years as a clerk, Blaize returned to Grenada in 1952. He was elected to parliament in 1957 from his native Carriacou as a member of the Grenada National Party (GNP) (f. 1955) when the party won its first elections (6–2) as part of a coalition. Blaize was named minister of trade and production and became leader of the GNP. He was chief minister 1960–61. In 1962, after the dismissal of chief minister Eric Gairy, he narrowly won a general election on a platform of creating a unitary state with newly-independent Trinidad-Tobago and became chief minister again. In 1967, Blaize became premier with the granting of internal self-government (associated statehood) but lost elections later that year. He was opposition leader until 1976, after which he retired to practise law.

After a US military invasion removed the left-wing New Jewel government in 1983, Blaize was imposed by the US and others as compromise leader of a three-party conservative coalition, the New National Party (NNP), which won elections in December 1984, when he became prime minister. His autocratic style soon offended his colleagues and in 1987 three of his ministers resigned to form an opposition party. In early 1989, by then crippled with arthritis and dying of prostate cancer, he was deposed as NNP leader at a party convention by one of his ministers, Keith Mitchell, but remained prime minister. He lost his parliamentary majority a few months later after his sacking of Mitchell led to the resignation of two other ministers. He then announced the formation of The National Party (TNP) but died two days after being officially named its leader. He was succeeded as prime minister and TNP leader by his longtime lieutenant, Ben Jones.

See also **New National Party; Gairy; Mitchell, Keith; Grenada, US invasion (1983); Carriacou; Netherlands Antilles, oil refineries.**

'boat people'

Name given to the tens of thousands of economic and political refugees who since the early 1970s have fled desperate conditions in Haiti to seek a better life in the US. They travel in ancient, overloaded boats after paying exorbitant fees to Haitian captains. Many reach the Bahamas, from where they are ferried clandestinely to Florida. Their arrival aroused US public opinion, including Congress, against the Duvalier dictatorship in the mid-1970s and the bad publicity contributed to the regime's fall. They were systematically refused political asylum and hundreds were sent to detention camps all over the US to await deportation. In 1982 the US forced Haiti to allow the US Coast Guard to patrol Haitian waters to pick up and repatriate 'boat people'. Thousands have been returned, along with others who reached Cuba and the Bahamas, but the flow of refugees has continued despite the fall of the Duvaliers. Haitians use 'a boat people' as the singular form of the word.

Other 'boat people' in recent Caribbean history have included the 'Marielitos' – thousands who fled Cuba for the US in the late 1970s with US government approval – and the thousands who since the 1970s have crossed the shark-infested 120-km-wide Mona Passage from the Dominican Republic to Puerto Rico and often thence to the mainland US.
See also **Duvalier, Jean-Claude; Mariel exodus.**

Bodden, Jim
1930–88. Leader of the Cayman Islands 1976–84. A seaman and then salesman in the US, he returned to the islands in 1963 and became a real estate operator. He was elected to the legislative assembly in 1972, and was opposition leader until 1976, when he was elected to the executive council. His Unity and Teamwork group won seven of the 12 assembly seats in the 1980 election, but only three in 1984 and he handed over the assembly leadership to Benson Ebanks.
See also **Ebanks.**

Bodden, Norman
b. 2 October 1935. Leader of the Cayman Islands 1988- . An airline executive, he was elected to the legislative assembly in 1980 as a member of the Progress With Dignity group. He succeeded Benson Ebanks as island leader when he was elected to the executive council after the 1988 general election, at which Progress With Dignity increased its strength to 7 out of 12 elected assembly members. He took charge of tourism, aviation and trade.
See also **Ebanks.**

Boff, Leonardo: see liberation theology.

Bofill, Ricardo: see Cuban Human Rights Party.

bolsones: see border dispute (El Salvador/Honduras).

Bonilla, Policarpo: see Liberal Party (Honduras).

border dispute (El Salvador/Honduras)
The disputed territory consists of seven *bolsones* or areas of 'no-man's land' established by the Organisation of American States (OAS) after

the 1969 war between the two countries and amounting to some 1,300 sq km along 65 km of border, plus three insular territories in the Gulf of Fonseca. The frontier has never been fully agreed since colonial times. Prior to the war some border areas of Honduras lacked road connections with the capital and were economically a *de facto* part of El Salvador. The normal currency was the Salvadorean colón. Border incidents contributed to pre-war tension. After the war, roads were built and the areas were integrated into Honduras. The OAS patrolled a demilitarised border zone (DMZ) to avoid incidents.

In Mexico in 1973, Honduras presented a plan for the demarcation of the Gulf which would have ensured its control over the strategic island of Meanguera and hence access to the Pacific, but this was not accepted. In July 1976, after border clashes, the two sides met in Managua and agreed (in the 'Act of Managua') to resolve the dispute. In 1978, former Peruvian president José Luis Bustamante agreed to arbitrate, and on 30 October 1980 a peace treaty was signed under strong pressure from Washington, which was anxious to see joint action against the Salvadorean guerrillas, for whom the *bolsones* had become strongholds. Under the treaty the DMZ was abolished, and a bilateral frontier commission was to resolve the issue by 10 June 1986, failing which it would be referred to the International Court of Justice in The Hague. The commission met at intervals but made no progress.

El Salvador's 1983 constitution included a claim over Meanguera and the islet of Meanguerita, as well as stipulating the 'irreducibility' of Salvadorean territory. Expiry of the treaty deadline coincided with a change of government in Honduras: the incoming Azcona administration agreed to continue bilateral talks, but in May 1986 both countries opted for arbitration in The Hague. A ruling is expected some time between 1991 and 1993.

See also **'Football (Soccer) War'**.

Borge Martínez, Tomás

b. 13 August 1930. Founder-member of the Sandinista National Liberation Front (FSLN) of Nicaragua; interior minister of Nicaragua 1979–90. The son of a Matagalpa drugstore owner, Tomás Borge was a schoolfriend of FSLN ideologue Carlos Fonseca, whom he met when he was 13. He was active in the student movement in the 1950s while studying law at the National University, León. Sentenced to eight years' imprisonment after the assassination of President Anastasio Somoza García in 1956, he was freed under student pressure in 1958.

His earliest involvement with guerrilla activities was in the Olama y los Mollejones movement in 1958–9. He went secretly into exile in Costa Rica in the latter year, later becoming secretary of the Nicaraguan Revolutionary Youth (JRN, f. 1960) and the New Nicaragua Movement (MNN, f. 1961), considered forerunners of the FSLN. In 1960 he travelled to Cuba to ask Fidel Castro for support. In 1961, with Fonseca and Silvio Mayorga, he founded the FSLN at a meeting in Tegucigalpa, Honduras. He participated as a column leader in the attempts to establish guerrillas in 1963 (Río Coco) and 1967 (Pancasán). After travelling to Costa Rica to buy arms, he was arrested and sent to Colombia, and was subsequently exiled in Peru and Cuba for several years, returning to take charge of training and of the northern front. In 1972 he joined the Managua underground and he was responsible for training the commando which in 1974 won the release of Daniel Ortega and other political prisoners.

As the leading member of the 'Prolonged Popular War' (GPP) faction of the FSLN, Borge was instrumental in the 1975 expulsion of the Proletarian Tendency (TP). He was arrested in Managua in February 1976 and jailed for 9 months in Tipitapa prison, where he was severely tortured and at one stage given up for dead, before being sentenced to 180 years imprisonment by a military court. (His wife Yelba was killed by the National Guard in June 1979.) Borge was among 58 prisoners freed by Somoza in exchange for hundreds of hostages taken by the FSLN commando which seized the National Palace on 22 August 1978. Thereafter, he was the main spokesman for the GPP faction. He has been a member of the FSLN National Directorate since its formation on 7 March 1979.

After the FSLN victory he was appointed interior minister, responsible for police and state security, a post he held until the 1990 change of government. Although he has travelled widely on state visits, the US has consistently refused him a visa. A populist, Borge has often been described as a 'hard-liner' opposed to the more 'moderate' Ortegas, although this over-simplifies the differences between them.

See also **Sandinista National Liberation Front; Fonseca Amador.**

Borgonovo, Mauricio: see **Popular Liberation Forces.**

Bosch, Juan

b. 30 June 1909. President of the Dominican Republic 1963. A novelist and political theorist, Bosch lived mainly in Cuba from 1938–61 during the Trujillo dictatorship. He founded the leftist Dominican Revolutionary Party (PRD) in Havana in 1939. He became the country's first freely-elected president in February 1963, but after charges of communism and an abortive plan to invade Haiti, the military overthrew him seven months later with US encouragement and he was exiled to the US.

A leftist army revolt in 1965 aimed to restore him to power, but the US prevented him from returning from Puerto Rico and instead invaded and occupied the country. He later returned from exile but was defeated by Joaquín Balaguer in presidential elections in 1966, in which he was largely prevented from campaigning. He then went into exile in Europe until 1970, when he and his party boycotted the elections that year. He left the PRD in 1973 to form the marxist Dominican Liberation Party (PLD) after the PRD leadership, backing party secretary-general José Francisco Peña Gómez, voted to take part in the 1974 elections. Bosch and the PLD, which eventually became social democratic, took part in general elections from 1978 and won increasing support (1% in 1978, 10% in 1982, 18% in 1986, 34% in 1990). In the 1990 elections, Bosch was narrowly defeated for the presidency by Balaguer.

See also **Dominican Revolutionary Party; Dominican Republic, US invasion (1965); Balaguer; Trujillo.**

Bosch, Orlando: see Omega 7.

Bostwick, Henry: see Free National Movement.

braceros

The Mexican name for the migrant workers who cross the 2,000-mile-long northern border into the United States in search of employment. In the US they are often called 'wetbacks', from the time when most came over by swimming across the Rio Grande. The first accord governing the movement of these workers was the Bracero Agreement of 1942, which provided for the temporary employment of Mexicans in the US as part of the war effort. Given rapid Mexican population growth, the scarcity of good quality land, unemployment (all termed 'push' factors), together with the much higher levels of per capita income in the US and strong demand for cheap labour north of the border ('pull' factors), northwards migration has been a constant factor since World War II. By far the greater part of this migration has been illegal as far as the receiving country is concerned, and a source of tension between the two governments.

Between 1910 and 1930 some 500,000 to 800,000 Mexicans are estimated to have migrated to the United States, although an estimated 400,000 returned in 1930–33, the years of the Great Depression. During and after World War II the pace of migration intensified. In 1954 the US conducted the first of what were to become regular crack-downs on the illegal immigrants or *indocumentados*, deporting almost one million people during 'Operation Wetback'. When the Bracero Programme ended in 1964, a total of 4.6m temporary permits had been issued, but the real number of entries was estimated to have been many times that amount. In 1981 a US Select Commission estimated the number of illegal immigrants in the country as somewhere between 3 and 6 million, though not all were Mexicans. Estimates of Mexican *indocumentados* have been put around the 4 million mark, but the margin of error is considered very large. US border patrols estimate they capture and turn back as many as a million people a year. Responsibility for detecting and deporting illegal aliens falls to the Immigration and Naturalization Service (INS), known and hated by Mexicans as *la migra*. Mexican studies indicate that a large proportion of the *braceros* cross the border for seasonal employment on US farms, returning to Mexico for periods of time every year.

In the 1970s and 1980s many other nationals followed the route into the US through Mexico, particularly Central Americans fleeing both the political turmoil and the economic hardship of that area. The number of *indocumentados* from El Salvador living in the US in the late 1980s was estimated at almost 1 million, roughly 20% of El Salvador's total population. Most migrants pay professional smugglers known as *coyotes* to get them across the border and evade *la migra*. In October 1986, after years of discussion, the US Congress approved the Simpson-Mazzoli bill, designed to grant an amnesty to *indocumentados* with more than five years' residence in the country, but to repatriate newer arrivals and generally tighten up controls on the flow of *braceros*. The bill included provisions to make US employers liable for fines if they employed illegal immigrants. Despite protests from Mexico, Central America, and US civil rights groups, as well as by US farmers who rely on migrant labour, the Immigration Reform and Control Act became law in May 1987.

See also **Avila Camacho; Dominican Republic, Haitian canecutters.**

Bradshaw, Robert

1916–78. Chief minister, premier of St Kitts-Nevis-Anguilla 1966–78. After working at the island sugar factory, Bradshaw became vice-president of the Workers' League in 1943 and founded the St Kitts Trades and Labour Union in 1944. He formed the St Kitts Labour Party in 1946 and was elected to the legislative council that year. Bradshaw was appointed minister of trade and production in 1956. A year later, he handed over the post to his right-hand man, Paul Southwell, was elected to the West Indies federal parliament and became federal finance minister in 1958. After the Federation collapsed in 1962, he returned to St Kitts, was re-elected to the legislative council, became minister without portfolio and took over from Southwell as chief minister in 1966. When he became premier with the granting of associated statehood in 1967, Anguilla voted to secede, accusing Bradshaw of authoritarian rule. At his request, British police and troops invaded Anguilla in 1969 in a bid to restore his authority. But secession was irreversible by 1971, though Bradshaw, long one of the keenest advocates of Caribbean unity, angrily refused to recognise it for some years. He died in office in 1978.

See also **St Kitts-Nevis Labour Party; Anguilla secession.**

Bramble, Austin

b. 24 January 1931. Chief minister of Montserrat 1970–78. The businessman son of William H. Bramble (1901–88) – the island's first modern political leader (from 1952) and first chief minister (1961–70) – he was elected to parliament in 1966 as a member of the ruling Montserrat Labour Party. He became minister of communications and works, and then of social services. In 1970 he broke with his father to form the Progressive Democratic Party, which won the general election that year 7–0. A social democrat, he encouraged foreign investment while stressing economic self-reliance. He lost power in 1978 when former party colleague John Osborne and the People's Liberation Movement won every seat in a general election. He regained his seat in the 1983 elections, but lost it again in 1987 and announced his retirement from politics. He was named head of the island's stamp bureau in 1987.

See also **Osborne, John.**

Brandt, David: see Osborne, Bertrand.

Brathwaite, Nicholas

b. 8 July 1925. Grenadian prime minister 1990– . A schoolteacher, Brathwaite was Grenada's chief education officer 1969–74, after which he worked in Guyana as head of the Commonwealth Youth Centre. After the US military invasion in 1983 he was named chairman of the Advisory Council which governed the island and led it to general elections in 1984. He was elected leader of the opposition National Democratic Congress in 1989 in place of George Brizan and became prime minister and external affairs minister when the NDC won a general election the following year.

See also **Grenada, US invasion (1983); National Democratic Congress; Brizan; Carriacou.**

Brigade 2506: see **Omega 7.**

British Empire Workers' and Citizens' Home Rule Party (BEW & CHRP): see **Butler.**

British Honduras: see **Belize.**

BRITISH VIRGIN ISLANDS
Capital: Road Town
Area: 153 sq km
Population (1990e): 14,500
Pop. growth rate: 6.3%
Pop. density: 95/sq km
Infant mortality: 29 per thousand
Life expectancy at birth: 70
Literacy: 98%
GDP per capita (1990): US$10,345
Foreign debt per capita (1990): US$2,690
Main exports: tourism, offshore banking, fish, gravel, sand, livestock, fruit, vegetables

Political system

A British colony, with an appointed British governor in charge of defence, security and external affairs, representing the titular head of state, Queen Elizabeth of Britain. He chairs a six-member Executive Council. A 12-member (9 elected, 1 nominated, 2 ex-officio) parliament, the Legislative Council, is elected for a maximum four years.
Governor: Mark Herdman (1987)
Chief minister: Lavity Stoutt (1986)
Last elections: 1986

Political organisations

Parties in parliament (leader) (elective seats): Virgin Islands Party/VIP (Lavity Stoutt) (5), f. 1970; United Party/UP (Conrad Maduro) (1); Independent People's Movement/IPM (Omar Hodge) (1), f. 1989.

Brizan, George
b. 31 October 1943. Grenadian politician. A schoolteacher and economist, Brizan was an early member of the radical New Jewel Movement (NJM) but soon left it. He drafted much of the 1976 election manifesto

of the narrowly-defeated People's Alliance. In 1978 he founded a paper, the *People's Tribune*, which attacked the NJM. He nevertheless became a senior education ministry official under the NJM government and was briefly the island's chief education officer in 1983–4.

After the US military invasion in 1983 the centre-left Brizan founded the National Democratic Party in 1984 and brought it into the US-sponsored New National Party (NNP) alliance led by Herbert Blaize which won power in elections in 1984. He became agriculture and tourism minister. In 1985 he lost a contest for the NNP deputy leadership to his rival Francis Alexis. In 1986, when Alexis did not stand again, he lost a new contest to foreign minister Ben Jones. He was demoted in 1987 to education and fisheries minister. He and Alexis resigned the same year to form the National Democratic Congress (NDC), with Brizan as leader, but he stepped down as leader in 1989 in favour of Nicholas Brathwaite, who had headed the post-invasion interim government. He became finance, trade and industry minister when Brathwaite and the NDC won the 1990 general election.

See also **National Democratic Congress; New National Party; New Jewel Movement; Alexis; Blaize; Brathwaite.**

Broad National Front (FAN): see **D'Aubuisson Arrieta; ARENA.**

Broad Opposition Front (FAO): see **Chamorro Cardenal, Pedro Joaquín; Democratic Conservative Party of Nicaragua; Independent Liberal Party.**

Broad Popular Front (Frampo): see **National Liberation Coalition.**

Brown, Stanley: see **Social Independent Party-Workers' Liberation Front.**

Browne-Evans, Lois
b. 1927. Opposition leader in Bermuda 1968–72, 1976–85. The country's first woman lawyer, she joined the left-wing, black-dominated Progressive Labour Party (PLP) and was elected to parliament in 1963. As PLP deputy leader, she succeeded party leader Walter Robinson when he lost his seat at the 1968 election. She was replaced by Robinson when he won a seat at the 1972 election, but resumed the leadership just before the 1976 poll, which the PLP again lost. She expelled four right-wing PLP MPs who disputed her authority in 1984, but resigned as PLP leader after the party won only seven seats in the 1985 general election. She was succeeded by Frederick Wade.

See also **Progressive Labour Party** (Bermuda); **National Liberal Party.**

Brunei, Sultan of: see **Iran/contra affair.**

Bryan, Adelbert M.
b. 1943. US Virgin Islands politician. Bryan, a fiery former policeman and Vietnam war veteran from St Croix, lost the 1986 election for governor as candidate of the Independent Citizens' Movement. He campaigned against the 'invasion' of the islands by rich white Americans and poor

immigrants and won 36% of the vote. Bryan was a USVI senator until 1988. He was arrested for looting after Hurricane Hugo devastated St Croix in 1989.
See also **Independent Citizens' Movement; Hurricane Hugo.**

Bu Girón, Efraín: see **Liberal Party** (Honduras); **Azcona Hoyo.**

Bucareli agreements: see **Oil nationalisation** (Mexico).

Bueso Rosa, Gen. José: see **Suazo Córdova.**

Burton, Eric
b. 1932. Barbudan politician. A farmer, fisherman and shopowner, Burton, head of the Barbuda Committee party, was the island's representative in the Antigua-Barbuda parliament 1978–89, when he was beaten by Hilbourne Frank. Reaction to Burton's pro-government position (though he was titular leader of the Antigua-Barbuda opposition 1984–9) also helped Frank's Barbuda People's Movement win island council elections in 1987 and 1989.
See also **Barbuda; Frank.**

Bush, George: see **Iran/contra affair.**

Bustamante, Sir Alexander: see **Jamaica Labour Party; Shearer; Bustamante Industrial Trade Union; West Indies Federation.**

Bustamante, José Luis: see **border dispute** (El Salvador/Honduras).

Bustamante Industrial Trade Union (BITU)
Jamaica's main trade union. Founded in 1938 by Alexander Bustamante, who used it as a means to political power through its political arm, the Jamaica Labour Party, it controls some 60% of the workforce. By the early 1950s Hugh Shearer was Bustamante's heir-apparent in the union and he effectively took charge of it when the old man's health failed after 1964. From 1952 it was rivalled by the People's National Party union, the National Worker's Union.
See also **Jamaica Labour Party; Shearer; National Workers' Union of Jamaica.**

Butler, Tubal Uriah 'Buzz'
1897–1977. Caribbean trade union pioneer. Born in Grenada, Butler served in the British army in World War I and then migrated to Trinidad in 1921 to become a labourer in the oilfields. He worked with socialist activist Capt. A. A. Cipriani, became a powerful orator and saw himself as the saviour of all colonised West Indians, naming himself 'The Chief Servant'. In 1936 he formed the British Empire Workers' and Citizens' Home Rule Party on the grounds that the masses could not rely on Cipriani. His agitation in the oil belt made him a popular hero and an attempt to arrest him led to riots in June 1937, clashes with British troops and disturbances in other islands. He was jailed for sedition, 1937–9, and then detained without trial until 1945.
After his release he continued his campaign, which had already led to

the formation of the Oilfield Workers' Trade Union in 1937. He founded the British Empire Workers', Peasants' and Ratepayers' Union in 1946 and organised new strikes. He and his supporters got the most seats in the 1950 legislative elections but the governor did not allow him to take power. He spent 1951–6 in England and he and his party won only two seats at the 1956 elections. By 1961 he had been politically eclipsed by the ruling People's National Movement. Disorganised and eccentric, Butler, who had little formal education, had nevertheless set Trinidad and the rest of the Anglo-Caribbean on the road to independence. He was celebrated by the 1979–83 revolutionary government in Grenada.

See also **Moyne Commission; People's National Movement** (Trinidad-Tobago); **'black power'; People's Revolutionary Government.**

C

Caamaño Deñó, Col. Francisco

1932–73. Leader of the left-wing forces in the 1965 Dominican Republic civil war. Caamaño, the son of a notorious Trujillist general, was elected by a reconstituted congress as president of the short-lived 'constitutionalist' government set up by the left during the civil war. After the withdrawal of the US invasion forces he was exiled to London in early 1966 as military attaché. In October 1967, he left secretly for Cuba, where he began preparations for a guerrilla invasion of the Dominican Republic. However, the Cubans soon cut off any effective assistance to him, and when his 'invasion' force eventually landed, at Caracoles on the south coast on 3 February 1973, it consisted of only 10 men. Within two weeks Caamaño and the entire group had been killed by government troops. See also **Dominican Republic, US invasion (1965).**

Cabañas Barrientos, Lucio: see **Party of the Poor.**

Cabrera Hidalgo, Alfonso: see **Christian Democratic Party** (Guatemala).

CACIF: see **Cerezo Arévalo; Christian Democrat Party** (Guatemala).

cacique

A term widespread in hispanophone Latin America, said to be of Haitian or Cuban Indian origin, and originally meaning an indian chief. It is used throughout the region to refer to a political boss (hence *caciquismo* – a political system based on the boss figure). See also **caudillo, caudillismo.**

caciquismo: see *cacique*.

Calderón Fournier, Rafael Angel

b. 1949. President of Costa Rica 1990– . A conservative lawyer and son of former president Rafael Angel Calderón Guardia (1940–44), Calderón Fournier was born in Nicaragua, where his father was in exile as a result of the Costa Rican civil war. He went to school in Mexico. His godfather was Nicaraguan dictator Anastasio Somoza García. Widely known as 'Junior', he won a parliamentary seat at the age of 25 and founded the Social Christian Unity Party in 1983. He was foreign minister in the late 1970s and stood for the presidency twice (in 1982 and 1986) before defeating the PLN's Carlos Manuel Castillo by four percentage points in

1990. His party also won a majority in the Assembly, with 29 of the 57 seats. The campaign was marred by accusations on both sides of involvement with drug trafficking. Calderón himself denied a charge of having received half a million dollars for his 1985 campaign from Gen. Noriega of Panama.

In a populist campaign, Calderón promised to concentrate on domestic issues, in contrast to his predecessor, Oscar Arias, but to make no major changes in Arias' foreign policy stance. He had not, however, been an enthusiastic supporter of the Arias Central American peace plan, which he regarded as too favourable to Nicaragua's Sandinistas. With the International Monetary Fund (IMF) heavily involved in overseeing the country's economic reform programme and US aid due to be sharply cut, room for manoeuvre on the economy was limited, but the new president promised to reduce the massive budget deficit as well as enhancing welfare programmes. He also stressed the need to combat drug trafficking.

See also **Calderón Guardia; Arias Sánchez; Arias Plan; Noriega Morena.**

Calderón Guardia, Dr Rafael Angel

1900–1970. President of Costa Rica 1940–44. A physician, Dr Calderón was educated at the Colegio Seminario de Costa Rica and in France and Belgium, where he obtained an MD from the University of Louvain. He became chief surgeon at San Juan de Dios Hospital before going into politics. From 1934 to 1940 he served as a deputy, and was elected vice-president (1935–7) and president (1938–40) of the national congress.

Calderón was elected president of Costa Rica for the National Republican Party (PNR), which he led, in 1940. During his presidency he promulgated the country's first labour code; instituted the first social security legislation and public housing systems in Central America and began the development of the country's neglected Atlantic coast. Plans to reform the tax system into one based on the capacity to pay were abandoned, however. His government reached agreement with Panama on their disputed border, but it was seriously weakened by the defection from the PNR in 1941 of Calderón's predecessor as president, León Cortés, who could not accept his radical reforming programme and took much support with him in founding the Democratic Party (PD). US demands during World War II also weakened the government, which had to suppress local Germans and engage in costly road-building, leading to a serious fiscal and monetary crisis. But the Soviet alliance with the western allies led to Communist support for Calderón, which offset the loss of the Cortés faction. Calderón's social reforms and alliance with the Communist Party angered the right, however, and contributed to an atmosphere of tension during the 1944–8 government of his successor Teodoro Picado (also of the PNR).

In the 1948 elections, in which he sought re-election on the Liberal Party ticket, violence and tension reached a peak. The annulment of the elections, allegedly won by the opposition, sparked a civil war, in which the opposition under Pepe Figueres was victorious. Calderón went into exile in Mexico. In December 1948 his supporters, with the aid of the

Somoza government in Nicaragua, staged an invasion of Costa Rica in an attempt to restore his presidency, but this was abortive and an OAS intervention brought a cessation of hostilities. Another failed attempt took place in January 1955. Calderón finally returned in 1958, after being elected deputy once more, and staged an unsuccessful presidential bid (again for the PNR) in 1962. Later he was a prime mover behind the creation of the National Unification Party (PUN).
See also **Civil War** (Costa Rica); **Calderón Fournier.**

Calderonista Republican Party: see Social Christian Unity Party.

Calero Portocarrero, Adolfo
b. 1931. President of the Nicaraguan Democratic Force (FDN) guerrilla movement, 1983–89. A business administration graduate of Notre Dame University, USA, Adolfo Calero did postgraduate work at the University of Syracuse, New York. He also has a law degree from the University of Central America (UCA), Managua. In Nicaragua he was involved in the hotel and food industries (notably as shareholder and manager of the Coca Cola Company of Nicaragua), and became director of the Chamber of Commerce. He was also a founder member (and later co-ordinator) of the Authentic Conservative Party (PAC) from 1970 and dean of the economics and business studies faculty of the UCA in the early 1970s. As PAC representative on the Broad Opposition Front (FAO), Calero was briefly imprisoned by the Somoza dictatorship in May 1979.
He became the political co-ordinator of the Democratic Conservative Party (PCD) after the Sandinista victory of 19 July 1979, but left the country in 1982 to become head of the anti-Sandinista Nicaraguan Democratic Force (FDN). He was based in Miami and in Tegucigalpa, Honduras, until the Honduran government refused him entry in 1985. In mid-1985, with Alfonso Robelo and Arturo Cruz, he became joint leader of the United Nicaraguan Opposition (UNO), reportedly at the insistence of the CIA; but he was forced out in February 1987 for his opposition to reforms demanded by Cruz and Robelo. He retained the leadership of the FDN, and in May 1987 joined the directorate of the newly-formed umbrella group, the Nicaraguan Resistance (RN), taking on responsibility for international affairs. In November 1989 the directorate was replaced by a four-man commission, in a move Calero described as a 'military coup'.
See also **Nicaraguan Democratic Force; Nicaraguan Resistance.**

Callejas, Rafael Leonardo
b. 14 November 1943. President of Honduras 1990– . Born into a wealthy Tegucigalpa family, Rafael Leonardo Callejas was educated as an agronomist in the US. He was appointed to his first public office, as minister of natural resources, in 1975 by the then head of the military government, Gen. Juan Alberto Melgar Castro. In 1981 he stood for the vice-presidency of the National Party (PN) ticket with Ricardo Zúñiga. A successful banker and businessman, linked with the quasi-fascist Association for the Progress of Honduras (APROH), he led a group of

like-minded individuals who in the mid-1980s displaced the old guard in the leadership of the National Party (PN). This faction, known as MONARCA (*Movimiento Nacionalista Rafael Callejas*), emerged as the majority group from internal party struggles, and in 1985 Callejas obtained the PN presidential nomination. Despite winning more votes than any other candidate (41%), he was prevented from taking power because the total number of votes cast for Liberal Party (PL) presidential candidates exceeded those cast for PN candidates.

In 1989 he stood again, winning a clear victory over the PL's Carlos Roberto Flores Facussé and becoming the first elected opposition candidate to take power peacefully in 57 years. After the election he became vice-president and representative for Latin America of the International Democratic Union, the world federation of conservative parties. On his inauguration he immediately introduced a substantial package of economic measures, including the legalisation of a parallel exchange market and fiscal adjustments to curb a deficit running at about 12% of GDP. He also announced the opening up of the economy to international competition, with a phased reduction in tariff barriers. A boost to the privatisation programme half-heartedly initiated by the outgoing government was also anticipated. A major objective was the restoration of the creditworthiness of Honduras, which had been declared ineligible for further loans by both the World Bank and the IMF because of repayment arrears.

See also **National Party** (Honduras).

Calles, Gen. Plutarco Elías

1877–1945. Mexican revolutionary leader who was president in 1924–8 and *Jefe Máximo* (the effective leader of the country) 1928–34. Calles had worked as a teacher, store-keeper and flour mill manager before joining Madero's rebel forces in 1911 and later fighting in the ranks of the Constitutionalist Army under Gen. Alvaro Obregón. In 1915 he became governor of Sonora, concentrating resources on education and a school-building programme. In 1919 he became secretary of the interior in the Obregón administration. Obregón nominated him for the presidential succession but was forced to quell a rebellion by anti-Calles forces, including conservatives alarmed by his reputation as a radical.

On taking office in 1924, Calles established an authoritarian style of leadership. He stepped up the pace of land reform (distributing 8 million hectares in 1924–8, against only 3 million by Obregón), built up relations with the CROM labour confederation and invested in education, sanitation and health. Relations with the United States remained difficult, particularly over the issue of oil concessions. Relations with the church broke down completely following the implementation of the anti-clerical provisions of the 1917 constitution. Calles fought ruthlessly against the Cristero rebellion.

At the end of his term, in 1928, Calles supported his old mentor Gen. Obregón for the succession, perhaps in the hope of himself coming back in 1934. But Obregón was assassinated by a Cristero on 17 July 1928 as he celebrated his electoral victory. Calles therefore stepped back into the political centre stage, ruling the country as the real power behind a series of interim presidents up to 1934. This period is known as the *Maximato* in reference to Calles, the *Jefe Máximo*. The presidency was held first by Emilio Portes Gil, then, after new elections in 1929, by Pascual Ortiz Rubio. When Ortiz Rubio showed signs of independence, he too was replaced, this time by Gen. Abelardo Rodríguez.

One of Calles' main achievements was the creation of the National Revolutionary Party (PNR) in 1929, the forerunner of the Institutional Revolutionary Party (PRI). Politically, Calles veered to the right after 1928. Land distribution slowed down and the social programmes fell victim to growing corruption by officials. Repression of the labour movement began. Calles and other state officials built luxury homes in Cuernavaca, in an area which became known unofficially as the 'street of 40 thieves'. Calles chose Lázaro Cárdenas for the succession in 1934, hoping to control him like the others during the *Maximato*; but the new president established his independence dramatically in 1936 by ordering Calles' arrest and deportation, effectively ending his political career.

See also **Cárdenas, Lázaro; Cristeros; Institutional Revolutionary Party; Mexican Revolution.**

Camarena, Enrique: see De la Madrid Hurtado.

Campa, Valentín: see Communist Party (Mexico).

Canada and the Anglo-Caribbean
Canada's quiet influence in the Caribbean, through its banks, its former British ties and since 1986 a preferential trade package (Caribcan), has led some small island politicians to call for political union or association with Canada. Appeals from elements in Montserrat in 1975 and the Turks and Caicos Islands in 1970, 1974 and 1987 drew support from a few Canadian MPs, but the Ottawa government dismissed the idea. In 1990, Canada waived all outstanding development aid debts owed to it by Anglo-Caribbean countries – some US$152m.

See also **Turks and Caicos Islands; Montserrat; National Joint Action Committee; Trinidad, 'black power' uprising (1970).**

Cancún Declaration: see Contadora Group.

Candil group: see Popular Alliance.

Caraballeda Declaration: see Contadora Group.

Caracoles invasion: see Caamaño Deñó.

Carazo Odio, Rodrigo
b. 27 December 1926. President of Costa Rica 1978–82. Born in Cartago, Rodrigo Carazo graduated in economics from the University of Costa Rica in 1954. He occupied posts in the Figueres (1954–8) and Echandi (1958–62) governments and was the director of the National Housing Institute, 1954–9. From 1959 to 1963 he served as adviser on housing and

finance to the Banco Obrero of Venezuela, and in 1963–5 as director of the Central Bank of Costa Rica. He was elected to the legislative assembly in 1966 and held the post of assembly president 1966–7. Other jobs included president/director of Recope, the state firm responsible for the distribution of oil derivatives; professor of economics, administration, economic development and history; and visiting lecturer in the US and South America.

A businessman with interests in a large number of industrial and agricultural companies, Carazo belonged to the National Liberation Party (PLN) until he resigned in 1969 after failing to win the party's presidential nomination. He founded the Democratic Renovation Party in 1971 and came fourth in the presidential elections of 1974 as its candidate. In 1978 he was instrumental in creating the Opposition Unity (later, simply 'Unity') coalition, comprising the PRD and three other parties, and was elected president on the Unity ticket in that year.

The Carazo administration coincided with a period of acute economic difficulties, stemming partly from the second OPEC price shock of 1979, which it signally failed to tackle. Foreign debt tripled during his four-year term, to around US$3.5bn; the country developed a severe trade deficit; inflation rose to 60% and official unemployment to over 8%. At the same time, the government's gold and foreign currency holdings dwindled to almost nothing. The IMF reached two agreements with Costa Rica, but the government could not meet the terms, and by 1981 it had become the first in Latin America to decree a unilateral suspension of all debt repayments.

Carazo also had to deal with the situation arising from revolution in neighbouring Nicaragua, including border incursions. He chose to do this mainly through the Organisation of American States, proposing the expulsion of Somoza-led Nicaragua and at one point threatening to withdraw from the OAS if Nicaragua was not censured. He made powerful diplomatic use of Costa Rica's unarmed neutrality, and he persuaded the United Nations to back plans for a University of Peace and an Inter-American Court of Human Rights to be established in the country.
See also **Social Christian Unity Party.**

Cardenal, José Francisco: see Nicaraguan Democratic Force.

Cárdenas, Cuauhtémoc

b. 1 May 1934. A nationalist, left-wing, Mexican politician who in 1987 helped set up a dissident 'Democratic Current' within the ruling Institutional Revolutionary Party (PRI), going on to contest the 1988 presidential elections as an opposition candidate. The son of President Lázaro Cárdenas, Cuauhtémoc (named in honour of the last Aztec prince to resist the Spanish conquest) qualified as a civil engineer at the Universidad Nacional Autónoma de Mexico (UNAM). In the 1960s he joined the small leftist National Liberation Movement (MLN) along with the novelist Carlos Fuentes and other intellectuals. He then rose through the PRI to become deputy agriculture minister, a federal senator (1976) and governor of his home state of Michoacán (1980–86).

In 1987, however, he expressed opposition to the anti-democratic nature of the PRI-controlled presidential succession, helping to form the Democratic Current with other dissidents such as Porfirio Muñoz Ledo and Ifigenia Martínez. This dissident tendency demanded free internal party elections to choose the party's presidential candidate. When these demands were shunned by the ruling party the Democratic Current announced it would back Cárdenas as an opposition presidential candidate. He was also supported by nationalist left parties such as the Authentic Party of the Mexican Revolution (PARM) grouped together in the National Democratic Front (FDN), and the more orthodox left represented by the Mexican Socialist Party (PMS). The PMS had nominated its own candidate, Heberto Castillo, but he agreed to stand down in favour of Cárdenas.

Despite widespread allegations of pro-PRI fraud in the 6 July 1988 elections, Cárdenas did better than any opposition candidate in the previous half-century, gaining 31.06% of the vote according to the final official count. After the elections, he announced the creation of a new grouping, the Party of the Democratic Revolution (PRD), designed to form a single organisation to unify his supporters.

See also **Institutional Revolutionary Party; Cárdenas, Lázaro.**

Cárdenas, Lázaro

1895–1970. President of Mexico 1934–40. Possibly the most popular Mexican president in the twentieth century, whose term in office was marked by land reform and the nationalisation of the oil industry. Cárdenas worked his way up in the revolutionary forces, serving in armies loyal to Gens Alvaro Obregón and Plutarco Elías Calles. He reached the rank of brigadier general in the early 1920s, building up a power base in his native state of Michoacán, where he became governor in 1928–32. His administration there invested in education, established good relations with labour and peasant organisations and was able to carry out some modest land distribution. Cárdenas also established a reputation for going out to meet the people and for living modestly at a time of growing concern over corruption.

In 1933 he was nominated as the official candidate to succeed President Calles, who expected to remain the real power in the land. But as president Cárdenas began building up independent sources of power, appealing to the masses and wooing the army by introducing higher wages and special training programmes. In 1935 he began removing Calles appointees from his ministerial team and in 1936 he established his independence decisively by arresting and deporting his former mentor in what was subsequently hailed as a major historical turning-point. In the 23 years since the outbreak of the revolution a total of 26 million acres had been distributed. In the six subsequent years of the Cárdenas administration over twice that amount, 49 million acres, were shared out, mainly to *ejidos* (co-operatives).

Relations with the church remained strained. The president supported the efforts of Vicente Lombardo Toledano to forge a new labour group-

ing, the Confederation of Mexican Workers (CTM) to replace the corrupt CROM. But the Cárdenas government is perhaps best remembered for the nationalisation of the 17 oil companies operating in the country, on 18 March 1938. The decision was popular in Mexico and in the rest of Latin America, where it was seen as a symbolically important affirmation of national sovereignty. Cárdenas was also responsible for reorganising the National Revolutionary Party (PNR) and setting up the more widely based Mexican Revolutionary party (PRM). The last two years of his *sexenio* saw increasing economic difficulties, with inflation rising and the new state oil company, Pemex, struggling to overcome staff and equipment shortages and the closure of export markets. In opposition to the president's policies the private sector had cut back its investment programme. Acknowledging the changing climate, Cárdenas named a conservative, Manuel Avila Camacho, to succeed him.
See also **Oil nationalisation** (Mexico); **Mexican Revolution; Calles; Avila Camacho; Cárdenas, Cuauhtémoc.**

Cardenista National Reconstruction Front Party (PFCRN): see **Mexican Workers' Party; National Democratic Front.**

Carey, Lionel: see **Vanguard Nationalist and Socialist Party.**

Carías Andino, Tiburcio
1876–1960. President of Honduras 1933–48 (the longest term in Honduran history). Born into a mixed Indian/black family in Tegucigalpa, Carías was not only a politician and military leader but also a maths teacher and a farmer. He took part in the revolutions of 1893, 1894 and 1903 and participated in the 1907 war on the side of the Liberals, eventually commanding a detachment. When the Liberals won, he was rewarded with a law degree and the title of 'general'. In 1923, having changed sides, he became the Nationalist (Conservative) candidate for the presidency, obtaining the largest number of votes but no overall majority. A civil war ensued, in which his planes bombed Tegucigalpa. Carías emerged as a strong man, backed by the United Fruit Co., but he lost the elections of 1924 and 1928, winning at last in 1932.

He was originally elected for a four-year term and constitutionally barred from seeking re-election, but in 1936 congress extended his first term by two years and gave him another which ended in 1943. Then in 1939 they further extended this to 1949. Martial law was imposed for most of his presidency, which was a period of austerity and balanced budgets, as well as of suppression of the opposition both in the legislature and the press. The 1948 election was won by Carías' chosen successor, Juan Manuel Gálvez. None of the dictator's later efforts to return to power was successful.
See also **National Party Liberal Party** (Honduras).

Caribbean
The region comprises 15 independent states (Belize, Cuba, Jamaica, Haiti, Dominican Republic, the Bahamas, Antigua-Barbuda, St Kitts-

Nevis, Dominica, St Lucia, St Vincent, Barbados, Grenada, Trinidad-Tobago, Guyana).

Six other states are dependencies of Britain (Cayman Islands, Turks and Caicos, British Virgin Islands, Anguilla, Montserrat, Bermuda), two of the United States (Puerto Rico and the US Virgin Islands), two of France (Guadeloupe and Martinique) and two of the Netherlands (Netherlands Antilles and Aruba), all with different degrees of self-government.

Parts of many of the states have autonomy. These include Barbuda, Nevis, Tobago, and the Dutch Antilles islands of Curaçao, Bonaire, Sint Maarten, Saba and Statia.

Others have no statutory autonomy but regard themselves as separate, such as Saint Martin and Saint Barthélémy (both part of Guadeloupe) and St Croix (US Virgin Islands).

Guyana, the Bahamas and Bermuda are strictly speaking outside the region but are usually counted as part of it for reasons of shared history and similar economies. To a lesser extent, so are Suriname and French Guiana.

Spanish is the language of Cuba, the Dominican Republic, Puerto Rico and part of Belize; French Creole of Haiti, Guadeloupe, Martinique and parts of Dominica and St Lucia; Dutch is spoken in much of Suriname and parts of the Netherlands Antilles. English is the language of the other states.

The population of the Greater and Lesser Antilles (all the island states) is some 32 million – 0.6% of the total world population. The islands comprise 0.2% of the world's total land surface.

See also **Caribbean Community; Greater Antilles; Lesser Antilles.**

Caribbean Basin Initiative (CBI)

A US trade, tax and regional assistance package approved by Congress (as the Caribbean Economic Recovery Act) in July 1983, which came into effect on 4 January 1984 and has two main components: free trade status over 12 years for some 6,000 agricultural and industrial products (of which around 2,000 were already covered under the Generalised System of Preferences/GSP), on condition that 35% of the valued added was generated locally (25% if the product contained US parts); and a US$350m annual credit line for private industry to import US raw materials and semi-finished products. Fiscal incentives for US companies investing in the region, training and technical assistance for local personnel and co-ordination of development programmes with other countries were also included.

The stated aim was to enable beneficiaries to diversify exports, and thus to promote peace and prosperity in the region, mainly by strengthening private capital through increased US investment. Eligible countries (designated by the US president) included the nations of Central America, Panama, Guyana, Suriname, the Bahamas and all Caribbean nations except the overseas French departments; however, 'communist' nations were excluded. Other conditions included: acceptance of US criteria

when expropriating US property; co-operation with US narcotics authorities; acceptance of arbitration favourable to US citizens or companies;
maintenance of an extradition treaty with the US; avoidance of trade
treaties with other developed nations adversely affecting US trade; prohibition of unauthorised use of goods or services with US patents or
copyrights; equitable and reasonable US access to markets and natural
resources; US access to financial, tax, criminal and legal information;
presentation to the US of agricultural production plans; and co-operation
over the administration of exports to the US.

Excluded from the CBI were textiles covered by the Multi-Fibre Agreement; footwear, handbags and leatherwear designed before the
implementation of the law; tuna (prepared or preserved); and petroleum
and its derivatives (except plastics). Sugar eligibility was also strictly
limited, and cuts in US sugar quotas made serious inroads into CBI
benefits.

By 1986, amid growing US protectionism, the CBI was widely perceived as having failed in most parts of the region. A 1986 US congressional report concluded that of 285 businesses stated by the US
Commerce Department to have been set up in response to the CBI, only
37 had been greatly influenced by it in taking their decision, while more
than one-third were operational before it came into effect. Many island
nations complained that Central America was the real beneficiary, and
that finance to improve their infrastructure was an essential precondition
for investment. Potential investors complained that many nations had an
inadequate investment climate. In 1989 a CBI Enhancement Bill
('CBI-2') was introduced into the US congress, under which the initiative
would be extended indefinitely and broadened to reduce tariffs on some
products originally excluded altogether. Other provisions included a floor
for sugar imports and special consideration for the Eastern Caribbean
and Belize.

See also **Kissinger Report; San José Agreement; Caricom.**

Caribbean Community and Common Market (Caricom)

An economic and political grouping of 13 independent and non-indepen-
dent English-speaking Caribbean states with a total population of nearly
six million. It was launched in 1973 through the Treaty of Chaguaramas
as the expanded successor to the Caribbean Free Trade Association
(Carifta) (f. 1968) and has its headquarters in Georgetown, Guyana. It
and its associated institutions aim to promote regional political, economic
and cultural unity but have been continually obstructed by the economic
and political power of the external forces which have long dominated the
region. Attempts to abolish tariffs have been partly successful but divisions remain between the four biggest members (Trinidad-Tobago,
Jamaica, Barbados and Guyana) and the nine smaller members over the
share-out of production and investment.

Political unity efforts after the failure of the West Indies Federation
(1958–62) have made little headway despite constant declarations of
intent by small island leaders, especially concerning free movement of

citizens. Three years of talks between the 'Little Seven' (Barbados and six eastern Caribbean states) were abandoned in 1965, as were plans in 1971 (the Grenada Declaration) for a wider regional anglophone union. Plans in 1973 (the Petit St Vincent Initiative) for free movement of labour and capital between Grenada, St Vincent and St Lucia and in 1979 (the Declaration of St George's) for freedom of movement between Grenada, St Lucia and Dominica were also dropped. Further efforts at eastern Caribbean political union in 1987–8 also failed.

The six-member West Indies Associated States council of ministers (1966) and the Eastern Caribbean Common Market (1968) were replaced in 1981 by the Organisation of Eastern Caribbean States. In 1986 right-wing Anglo-Caribbean leaders formed the Caribbean Democratic Union. But both initiatives were linked with attempts by the United States to divide the region and oppose left-wing influence. Caricom's successes include maintenance of the University of the West Indies and of the regional airline, LIAT (Leeward Islands Air Transport).

The Turks and Caicos Islands and British Virgin Islands became associate members of Caricom in 1990.

Secretary-general: Roderick Rainford (Jamaica) (1983)

See also **West Indies Federation; West Indies Associated States; Organisation of Eastern Caribbean States; Declaration of St George's (1979); Caribbean Democratic Union; Regional Security System; University of the West Indies; Demas; McIntyre; Caribbean Basin Initiative.**

Caribbean Conference of Churches (CCC)
An ecumenical association of churches in 25 Caribbean states founded in 1973. The CCC sponsors and conducts research and educational and economic development and has been in the vanguard of the movement to forge a Caribbean identity. It balked however at condemning the 1983 US invasion of Grenada and allowed the US and Barbados to pressure its conservative wing into forcing out Rickey Singh, the high-profile editor of its popular monthly paper, *Caribbean Contact*, who had strongly condemned the invasion. The paper eventually continued with a similarly nationalist-minded editor, however.

See also **Singh; Grenada, US invasion (1983); Adams, Tom.**

Caribbean Contact: see **Singh; Caribbean Conference of Churches.**

Caribbean Democratic Union (CDU)
A US-sponsored alliance of eight conservative ruling Anglo-Caribbean political parties formed in 1986 and linked with the right-wing International Democratic Union. It is funded by the US Republican Party through the scandal-plagued National Endowment for Democracy and the far-right Heritage Foundation. It was originally led by Jamaican prime minister Edward Seaga, then the firmest US regional ally, and included Dominica (Eugenia Charles), Grenada (Herbert Blaize), St Lucia (John Compton), St Vincent (James Mitchell), Belize (Manuel Esquivel), St Kitts (Kennedy Simmonds), Nevis (Simeon Daniel) and Anguilla (Emile Gumbs).

See also **Caribbean Community; Seaga; Charles, Eugenia; Blaize; Compton; Mitchell, James; Simmonds; Daniel; Gumbs; Esquivel, Manuel.**

Caribbean Economic Recovery Act: see Caribbean Basin Initiative.

Caribbean Free Trade Area (Carifta): see Caribbean Community; Demas.

Caribbean Labour Congress (CLC): see Hart; Marryshow, T. A.

Caribbean Legion
A small, loosely grouped armed force comprising liberals and radicals of various Latin American nationalities committed to the 'overthrow of dictators' in the Caribbean and Central America, founded by José 'Pepe' Figueres, future president of Costa Rica, immediately after World War II through contacts made while in exile in Mexico. The Legion participated (as the 'Sandino Brigade') in the Cayo Confites expedition of 1947, with which Fidel Castro and Alberto Bayo were associated. (Bayo was a Spanish Republican adviser to the Legion who also gave military training to Ernesto 'Che' Guevara.) During the 1948 Costa Rican civil war it played a major role in the capture of Puerto Limón and was probably decisive in the victory achieved by Figueres' forces. It was formally disbanded in November 1948 after allegations by Nicaraguan dictator Anastasio Somoza García that it was training on Costa Rican soil to attack his regime, but it continued to meet informally. It was involved in the 1955 hostilities between Costa Rica and Nicaragua and in aggression against Honduras. Rumours in 1974 that it might be revived seem to have been unfounded.
See also **Figueres Ferrer; Civil War** (Costa Rica).

Caribbean Revolutionary Alliance (*Alliance Révolutionnaire Caraibe*/ARC): see **Guadeloupe, independence movements; Reinette.**

Caribs
The Amerindian inhabitants of the Caribbean when whites settled it in the 16th century. The Caribs, who had arrived in the region 500 years earlier and driven out the Arawak natives, were largely exterminated by the newcomers. Today, only about 500 full- or near full-blooded Caribs remain, plus some 1,500 part-Caribs, living in a 3,700-acre official reserve set up on the east coast of Dominica in 1903 around the village of Salibia, with an elected chief (Irvince Auguiste) and council. Violence erupted in 1987 over the government's refusal to permit the Carib Council to expel several non-Caribs from the reserve.
See also **Dominica.**

Caricom: see **Caribbean Community and Common Market.**

Carney, Fr James Francis ('Guadalupe'): see guerrilla movements (Honduras).

Carpio Nicolle, Jorge: see Union of the National Centre.

Carranza, Gen. Venustiano: see Mexican Revolution.

Carriacou
The main island of the Grenadian-administered part of the Grenadines chain.
Chief town: Hillsborough
Area: 34 sq km
Population: 8,000
Main exports: lobster, fish, tourism, limes, cotton
Home of Grenadian prime minister Nicholas Brathwaite and one of his predecessors (1984–9), Herbert Blaize, who represented it in parliament from 1957, until his death in 1989. Its inhabitants call themselves Kyacks.
See also **Blaize; Brathwaite; Grenadines; Grenada.**

Carrión, Luis: see Sandinista National Liberation Front.

Cartago, Battle of: see Civil War (Costa Rica).

Carter-Torrijos Treaties: see Panama Canal Treaties.

Casey, William: see Iran/contra affair.

Castillo, Carlos Manuel: see National Liberation Party; Oduber Quirós.

Castillo, Heberto: see Cárdenas, Cuauhtémoc; Mexican Workers' Party.

Castillo, Rolando: see Unitary Representation of the Guatemalan Opposition.

Castillo Armas, Col. Carlos
1914–57. President of Guatemala 1954–7. Born near Escuintla and educated at the military school, Castillo Armas studied military tactics and strategy in the US in 1945–6. As a conservative colonel, he was selected by the US embassy and the United Fruit Co. to carry out the 1954 overthrow of the elected government of Jacobo Arbenz. He had already been involved in an abortive revolt against the Arévalo government in 1949 and, after being imprisoned and sentenced to death, escaped to Honduras, where he gathered support from conservative Guatemalans.
Castillo Armas invaded Guatemala from Honduras on 18 June 1954 with a few hundred men. They captured some towns close to the border but failed to march on the capital, although US planes piloted by US mercenaries hired by the CIA carried out a series of virtually unopposed bombing raids on Guatemala City. On 27 June the Guatemalan officer corps demanded the president's resignation and Arbenz surrendered, resisting pressure from the left to organise civilian militias (the army would in any case not allow him to distribute arms to civilians). He was replaced by the head of the armed forces, Col. Enrique Díaz, by arrangement with US ambassador John Peurifoy, but Díaz said he would fight on against the invaders. His resignation in turn was secured by

Peurifoy, and after complex negotiations between the rebels and the high command, in which the ambassador acted as intermediary, Castillo was made president.

He suspended the 1945 constitution and ruled by decree, restoring many officials of the Ubico dictatorship to their former positions. He reversed most if not all of the reforms of the 1944–54 period, handing back virtually all the land redistributed under the 1952 agrarian reform law and supervising the killing of several hundred peasant and trade union leaders. An estimated 9,000 government opponents were jailed (and many of them tortured), while 8–10,000 fled the country. He founded an extreme right-wing political party, the National Liberation Movement (MLN), which was to have a major influence on Guatemalan politics. On 26 July 1957, while still in office, he was assassinated by a palace guard, in circumstances which were never fully clarified.

See also **National Liberation Movement** (Guatemala); **Arbenz Guzmán; Arévalo Bermejo.**

Castro Ruz, Fidel Alejandro

b. 13 August 1927.* Premier of Cuba 1959–76. President of Cuba, 1976– . First secretary of the Communist Party (PCC) and commander-in-chief of the armed forces. Born in Mayarí, Oriente, the son of a Spanish-born sugar plantation owner and his cook, Fidel Castro was educated at the Colegio Dolores, Santiago, the La Salle School and the Colegio Belén, Havana. As a boy he worked on his father's plantation before attending the University of Havana, where he became president of the Student Federation and obtained a doctorate in law in 1950.

As a student, Castro was involved in an unsuccessful attempt to overthrow the Trujillo dictatorship in the Dominican Republic in 1947. His politics gradually evolved from an early association with student political 'gangs', and he had strong disagreements with the Communist Party. On graduation he opened a law practice in Havana, working mainly with poorer clients. In 1952 he was a candidate for parliament on the 'Ortodoxo' (People's Party of Cuba) ticket, but Fulgencio Batista's coup intervened.

Castro unsuccessfully attempted to have the coup declared unconstitutional by the Court of Constitutional Guarantees, following which he took part in the formation of an opposition group which staged an armed attack on the Moncada barracks in Santiago on 26 July 1953. Castro and his brother Raúl were jailed for their part in the attack. At his trial, Castro gave a historic speech which concluded with the words: 'History will absolve me.'

Although sentenced to 15 years, he was released (along with Raúl and others) under an amnesty in May 1955 and left for Mexico City, where he formed a rebel force. With 81 others, he landed in Cuba on 2 December 1956 and, despite the immediate near-annihilation of the group, after two years of guerrilla war Batista's forces surrendered on New Year's Day 1959. Following the victory, Castro became commander-in-chief, taking over as prime minister in February 1959, but he resigned from the latter post in July 1959, taking it up once more after the appointment of Osvaldo Dorticós to the presidency in the same month.

Washington recognised the new government within a week, but relations were strained by expropriations of US property in response to President Eisenhower's suspension of Cuba's sugar quota in the US market, and were broken off on 3 January 1961 after Castro had declared that almost all US diplomats must leave Cuba. US congressional reports later (1975) showed that the CIA had made many attempts to kill Castro, beginning in March 1960. On 17 April 1961 the Agency staged an abortive invasion by Cuban exiles at the Bay of Pigs, whose net effect was to strengthen the Cuban regime. The increasing Cuban alignment with Moscow led to a decision to base Soviet nuclear missiles on the island, bringing about the October 1962 missile crisis.

On May Day 1961 Castro had publicly announced that Cuba was a socialist country, and in December that year he said he was a marxist-leninist. In February 1962 the Organization of American States (OAS) voted (at the instigation of the US) to exclude Cuba, and by late 1964 Mexico was the only Latin American country to maintain relations with Havana. Cuba was also excluded from the Latin American Group at the UN, except for the Law of the Sea caucus. Its isolation has now largely ended, and in the second half of the 1980s relations were re-established with six countries in the region. For a decade from 1964 the OAS imposed diplomatic and economic sanctions on Cuba, ostensibly because of its support for guerrilla insurgencies. US sanctions remain in force, although they were eased temporarily by President Carter in 1977, when interests sections were opened by both countries in each other's capital.

Despite increasing reliance on the USSR, Castro has usually sought to emphasise his independence in both foreign and domestic policy. Unlike the Soviet leadership, in the 1960s Castro favoured support for armed struggle as the only option for the left in Latin America and elsewhere. During 1966–8 there were serious disputes with Moscow over this and other issues, but Castro's willingness to back the Soviet invasion of Czechoslovakia in 1968 marked a return to the fold, apparently under heavy economic pressure. Revolutionary movements continued to receive backing, but the policy was increasingly subordinated to relations with governments and communist parties.

Cuban involvement in Africa (where Soviet and Cuban objectives often overlapped) became highly significant from the mid-1970s, and had the side-effect of bringing the suspension of talks on normalisation of Cuban-US relations. Cuba's role in Angola also enhanced Castro's stature in the Non-Aligned Movement, which in 1973 had debated Cuba's expulsion for alleged subservience to Moscow, although the sending of troops to Ethiopia threatened to reverse these gains. In 1979 Cuba hosted the Non-Aligned summit and Castro became the Movement's chairman for the next three years. A seat on the UN Security Council, which should have followed, was denied to Cuba after it declined to condemn the Soviet invasion of Afghanistan. Cuban support for guerrilla movements in Central America, including the victorious Sandinistas in Nicaragua, has also been a source of controversy, while in Grenada in 1983, US forces clashed directly with Cuban personnel when the former invaded the island.

Domestically, Castro has faced few serious threats to his leadership, but those opponents who have emerged have often received long prison terms. Perhaps his greatest shock was the 1980 Mariel exodus, in which around 125,000 Cubans opted for exile, a scale of discontent which apparently took the Cuban leadership by surprise.

The origins of this malaise were primarily economic, for despite enormous progress in social welfare and a sweeping agrarian reform in the early days of the revolution, the Cuban economy as a whole has failed to progress as Castro hoped, due in part to the US blockade. Consumer goods remain in short supply and rationing is still in force, although basic needs are assured and the economy fared better than most in Latin America in the 1980s.The country is highly dependent on Soviet aid, which since the mid-1970s (excluding military assistance) has equalled roughly 10% of the Cuban gross product. By the mid-1980s Cuban hard-currency revenues from the re-export of Soviet oil were three times higher than those from sugar, but the oil price slump removed this prop. Moscow has in recent years sought to use its leverage to force Havana to improve its management of the economy.

Immediately after the revolution, under Che Guevara's direction, the aim was rapid industrialisation to end dependency on sugar, but the failure of this effort led to renewed concentration on boosting sugar exports while aiming for more gradual diversification. The failure to reach the 10-million-tonne target in the 1970 sugar harvest, however, marked another change of direction after it was acknowledged that the whole economy had been disrupted by the diversion of labour into the cane fields. In the 1970s the Castro government turned to orthodox, Soviet-style central planning, but this too proved ultimately unsuccessful, resulting in inefficiency and an emphasis on output rather than quality.

In the early 1980s, partly in response to Mariel, there was a move towards decentralisation and the introduction of market forces, which was largely reversed in 1986, when a 'Campaign of Rectification of Errors' began, involving action against corruption and inefficiency, a return to the 1960s appeal to 'moral incentives', and unprecedentedly sweeping changes in the government and politburo. 'Rectification' is almost the polar opposite of the Soviet policy of perestroika, which involves increased acceptance of market forces, something Castro has said is not appropriate under Cuban conditions, and whose application to Cuban-Soviet trading relations he has reason to fear. On the international stage, Castro has repeatedly called for the repudiation by poorer nations of their massive debts, but Cuba has not taken unilateral action on this issue, pointing out that its own debt problems have not been brought about by corruption and capital flight.

Castro's domination of the political scene has been the primary feature of the past three decades of Cuban politics, but from 1970 the regime adopted a more formal structure. The first congress of the Communist

Party was held in 1975 and a new, Soviet-style constitution was adopted shortly afterwards which combined the roles of president and prime minister in the person of Fidel. In the age of glasnost Castro demonstrated a reluctance to liberalise Cuban politics, which remained tightly controlled, although policies towards, for example, religion and homosexuality, became more flexible. Reforms announced in February 1990 were explicitly stated to be aimed at 'perfecting a single, leninist party'.

* *Castro's parents added a year to his age when he was around eight, in order to make him eligible for enrolment in the La Salle school. Thus many sources give 1926 as the year of his birth. He even celebrated his 60th birthday (officially) in 1986.*

See also **Cuban Revolutionary War; Moncada assault; Batista y Zaldívar; Bay of Pigs; Communist Party** (Cuba); **'microfaction'; Cuban missile crisis; 26 July Movement; Havana, Declarations of;** *zafra de los diez millones*; **African involvement** (Cuba); **Guevara de la Serna; Mariel exodus; Ochoa case; Integrated Revolutionary Organisations; Matos; Castro Ruz, Raúl; Valladares.**

Castro Ruz, Raúl

b. 3 June 1931. Cuban revolutionary and minister of defence. Fidel's younger brother Raúl became second in power and influence only to the president himself and the only visible successor should the latter die or be incapacitated. Shortly after the rebels seized power, Fidel named Raúl as second-in-command of the 26 July Movement, to succeed him if he died. From his days as a law student at the University of Havana, Raúl was closer to the communists than Fidel and for a time belonged to the communist youth movement. He took part in the abortive Moncada barracks assault in 1953 and was jailed with the other surviving participants. In 1955 he went into exile in Mexico after being accused of an anti-government bomb plot, and later joined the 1956 invasion force led by Fidel. A noted military commander in the revolutionary war, he led a separate front during its later stages and was appointed commander-in-chief of the armed forces after the victory. Raúl entered the cabinet as armed forces minister in October 1959, and was appointed vice-premier in 1962. He is a member both of the secretariat and the political bureau of the Communist Party of Cuba.

See also **Castro Ruz, Fidel Alejandro; Cuban Revolutionary War.**

CATH (*Centrale Autonome des Travailleurs Haitiens*/Autonomous Federation of Haitian Workers)

Haitian trade union federation. It was founded underground in 1980 by Yves Richard (b. 28 May 1952), who later that year was arrested with other dissidents and expelled to Venezuela. Richard and CATH president Georges Fortuné, both of them in Caracas, soon quarrelled, however, and on their return to Haiti after the fall of the Duvalier dictatorship in 1986, both claimed the union leadership. The same year, Fortuné formed the rival CATH-CLAT, which was renamed in 1989 the Haitian Workers' Confederation (CTH). The banning of CATH and the arrest of its leaders after a general strike call in 1987 provoked demonstrations to which the government was forced to yield.

One of its leaders, Jean-Auguste Mésyeux, was jailed and severely beaten in 1989 for allegedly plotting to assassinate President Prosper Avril. CATH split in 1990, with Richard falling under the influence of the wealthy New York-based Stalinist Ben Dupuy and expelling Mésyeux and the confederation's other main leader, Gabriel Miracle.
See also **Duvalier, Jean-Claude; Avril.**

Cato, Milton

b. 3 June 1915. Chief minister, premier and prime minister of St Vincent 1967–72, 1974–84. A barrister, Cato founded the conservative St Vincent Labour Party (SVLP) in 1955. He was mayor of Kingstown and from 1958 to 1962 a member of the West Indies federal parliament. He entered the island parliament in 1961, led the SVLP to victory in elections in 1967 and became chief minister, then premier on associated statehood (internal self-government) in 1969. Cato was in opposition from 1972 until 1974, when the SVLP won a general election and he became premier of a coalition government with the People's Political Party. He led the country to independence in 1979 and became prime minister. Unpopular economic policies, political repression and scandals led to his defeat at elections in 1984, after which he retired from politics.
See also **St Vincent Labour Party; Union Island revolt (1979).**

caudillo, caudillismo

'*Caudillo*' means 'leader' in various senses, including 'chieftain' or military leader, but in Latin America its most common usage is as a rough equivalent of 'political boss'. The *caudillo* is the man to whom (typically) a rural dweller owes his allegiance, and for whose choice of candidate he will be required to vote at election time. In return, the boss is expected to dispense political favours, including jobs. '*Caudillismo*' is a pejorative term for the political structure based on this system, which, though less influential than before, remains an important factor in many parts of the region. It is often held to be at the root of the failure of constitutional régimes. Its origins lie in the system of 'debt peonage' and the company store, which appeared in the 17th century as a replacement for slavery. In the past, the worker would have been required to fight on behalf of his boss. The post-independence era has been referred to as the 'age of the *caudillos*'.

CAUSA: see **Association for the Progress of Honduras.**

CAYMAN ISLANDS

Capital: George Town
Area: 259 sq km
Population (1989): 25,800
Pop. growth rate: 5%
Pop. density: 96/sq km
Infant mortality (1989): 9 per thousand
Life expectancy at birth: 75

Literacy: 98%
GDP per capita (1988): US$20,160
Foreign debt per capita (1989): US$227
Main exports: offshore banking, tourism, chemicals, expatriates' cars

Political system

A British colony (the world's biggest offshore banking centre), with an appointed British governor in charge of defence and external affairs, representing the titular head of state, Queen Elizabeth of Britain. The governor chairs a seven-member Executive Council. Four members of the council are elected from the 12 elected members of a 15-member parliament, the Legislative Assembly, which is elected for a maximum four years.
Governor: Alan Scott (1987)
Island leader: Norman Bodden (1988)
Last elections: 1988

Political organisations

None. Only election-time alliances of independents. There are two shifting groups in parliament: Progress With Dignity (leader: Norman Bodden) (majority); Unity and Teamwork (Truman Bodden) (minority).

Cayo Confites expedition: see **Caribbean Legion.**

CELAM: see **Latin American Bishops' Council.**

Céleste, Christian: see **Guadeloupe, independence movements.**

Cenac, Neville: see **St Lucia Labour Party.**

Cenac, Winston: see **St Lucia Labour Party; Odlum, George; Josie.**

Central American Common Market (*Mercado Común Centroamericano*/MERCOMUN)
A regional body founded in 1960 by El Salvador, Guatemala, Honduras and Nicaragua, aimed at fostering economic integration along the lines of the European Economic Community (EEC). Costa Rica joined in 1962. In 1950 the five Central American nations had asked the UN Economic Commission for Latin America (ECLA/CEPAL) to examine the region's development possibilities. In 1951 the Charter of San Salvador was signed, setting up the Organisation of Central American States (ODECA), and in 1952 the Central American Economic Co-operation Committee (CCCE) was formed. ECLA favoured economic integration of the region as a means of expanding the domestic market of each of its nations. Internal income redistribution, which would also have increased demand for local goods, was unpopular with most governments.

   The earliest free trade agreements came into effect in 1959, and by 1963 most products had been freed from tariff restrictions. Member nations agreed on a common external tariff schedule, and partially freed both capital and labour markets. The original ECLA project, with planning provisions designed to protect the less developed economies, had undergone a transformation under the influence of the US, which had offered $100m in aid in return for a free market model more beneficial to its own investors. Foreign (especially US) investment grew considerably after the CACM was set up, but by the end of the decade it was apparent that local markets were saturated, and that the benefits of the CACM were unequally spread, with El Salvador and Guatemala gaining at the expense of their less developed neighbours (particularly Honduras and Nicaragua).

This disparity helped bring about the 1969 'soccer war' between El Salvador and Honduras, after which the latter withdrew from the CACM, although it retained observer status. Nicaragua, under Somoza, introduced measures to protect Somoza-owned industries (such as textiles). The Central American Economic Council (CEC), supposedly the highest CACM decision-making body, only met twice in the period 1969–85. The CACM was thus in serious difficulties even before the regional crisis which began in 1978 hit intra-regional trade (which fell 14% in 1978–9). The CACM Secretariat (SIECA) accepted in 1982 that bilateral treaties were inevitable.

In 1985 the Central American Tariff and Customs Council (CAAC) was set up and a new tariff regime approved, but breakdown once more loomed in 1986 when the Cerezo government in Guatemala introduced a multiple exchange rate for regional imports, and El Salvador, Costa Rica and Honduras retaliated with measures against Guatemalan goods. The disputes were patched up, but by this stage intra-regional trade was barely a third of its 1980 level. Export promotion had replaced import substitution as the focus of policy, and Costa Rica, for example, was sending 70% of its manufactured exports outside the region. In 1987–8, however, regional trade began to pick up and a UN Special Programme for Economic Co-operation held out hope of a CACM revival.

See also: **'Football (Soccer) War'; Organisation of Central American States.**

Central American Defence Council: see CONDECA.

Central American Democratic Community (*Comunidad Democrática Centroamericana*/CADC)

A short-lived, US-backed attempt to achieve the diplomatic isolation of the Sandinista regime in Nicaragua, the CADC was formed in January 1982 by Costa Rica, El Salvador and Honduras (joined later by Guatemala). In October 1982 it expanded into the Forum for Peace and Democracy, in which the original three were joined by Belize, Colombia, Jamaica and the US. Panama and the Dominican Republic attended as observers. Nicaragua and Guatemala were not invited. The Declaration of San José (4 October 1982), which Panama refused to sign, called for 'an end to the support, supply, training or command of terrorist or subversive elements operating against other states in the region; an end to arms trafficking' and limits to the arms race. The initiative collapsed and was superseded by the Contadora process.

See also **Contadora Group.**

Central American Development Corporation: see Kissinger
Report.

Central American Economic Co-operation Committee: see
Central American Common Market.

Central American Economic Council (CEC): see Central American Common Market.

Central American Parliament
The creation of a Central American parliament was originally proposed
by Guatemalan President Vinicio Cerezo, and the proposal was embodied
in the 'Declaration of Esquipulas' of 25 May 1986. The Declaration was
signed by the presidents of El Salvador, Honduras, Nicaragua and Costa
Rica, as well as Guatemala. The stated aim was to produce 'strategies,
analysis and recommendations' on the region's political and economic
problems. Twenty parliamentarians were to be elected per country and
sessions were scheduled to be held in Esquipulas, Guatemala, from 1990
onwards. According to the Arias plan of August 1987, direct elections
were to have taken place simultaneously in all signatory nations in the first
half of 1988 under Organisation of American States (OAS) supervision.
However, the elections were later postponed because of delays in ratification of the agreement by national legislatures in El Salvador, Honduras
and Costa Rica. The latter failed to approve the following bill by the
September 1989 deadline, leading to proposals that the parliament should
be constituted without it.
See also **Arias Plan.**

Central American Socialist Party (PSC): see Martí, Augustín Farabundo.

Central American Tariff and Customs Council (CAAC): see
Central American Common Market.

Central American Workers' Confederation (CCT): see CLAT.

Central Organisation of Latin American Workers: see CLAT.

Centre for the Study of National Problems (Costa Rica): see
Generation of '48 (Costa Rica); Second Republic (Costa Rica).

Cerdas, Jaime: see banana strike (Costa Rica).

Cerezo Arévalo, Marco Vinicio
b. 26 December 1942. President of Guatemala, 1986–90. A lawyer, teacher and notary, educated at the University of San Carlos, Guatemala
City, Vinicio Cerezo started his political career as a student leader. He
became president of the law students' association and led the Social
Christian Student Front (FESC) 1964–6. Between 1968 and 1974 he was
organisation secretary of the Christian Democrat Party (DCG) and in
the latter year he won a seat in the National Congress. In 1976 he became

secretary general of the party. A member of the 'progressive' wing of the DCG, Cerezo was a candidate for mayor of Guatemala City in 1978. During the government of Gen. Lucas García (1978–82) he was the target of at least three assassination attempts, although he is on record since 1977 as favouring a military-DCG alliance.

He won the presidency in the second round of the 1985 elections against Jorge Carpio Nicolle of the Union of the National Centre (UCN), becoming the first civilian president since 1970. Before taking office, however, he acknowledged that he would start out with only 30% of the power and was unlikely to achieve more than 70%. The armed forces retained most of their power under Cerezo, especially in matters of internal security and control of rural areas. His failure to support repeal of the military regime's amnesty, covering tens of thousands of political killings, was heavily criticised by human rights groups; while his refusal to contemplate agrarian reform alienated the landless. Unemployment, at around 45%, inflation of over 30%, a US$2.6bn national debt and a massive fiscal deficit were among the problems facing his presidency. An economic package (the PRES) introduced in March 1985 failed to resolve these problems, although the decline in economic growth was halted. Cerezo summed up his approach as the 'harmonisation' of conflicting sectors, in particular employers and unions. Both remained suspicious of government and each other, although Cerezo's links with the former were quite strong. The employers' organisation CACIF sought to block attempts at a mild reform of the country's uniquely regressive and inefficient tax structure (finally passed in late 1987), while the unions organised strikes against low pay and rising prices. In November 1989, partly as a result of low coffee prices, Cerezo was forced to float the Guatemalan currency, the quetzal.

Cerezo played a major role in the Central American peace process, basing his approach on 'active neutrality', a higher-profile version of the army's own policy, and was the prime mover behind the creation of the Central American Parliament. In practice, however, Guatemala has tended to line up on the side of the US. Moreover, despite holding one meeting with the Guatemalan National Revolutionary Unity (URNG) in Madrid in October 1987, Cerezo failed to fulfil the ceasefire and dialogue requirements of the Arias plan. An agreement to resume a dialogue was, however, signed in Oslo by the URNG and the National Reconciliation Commission set up under the plan, in March 1990. An amnesty for guerrillas, offered on Cerezo's inauguration, failed to reduce the military strength of the URNG. On a different front, diplomatic relations with Britain at ambassadorial level were restored in mid-1987 and direct negotiations with Belize over the territorial dispute began in 1988.

Cerezo faced coup attempts in both 1988 and 1989 which, although put down bloodlessly, succeeded in further curbing his freedom to act. The 1988 coup brought an end to talks with the URNG, forced changes in the government and in economic policy and increased the power of the army. Those involved were granted amnesty. One effect was a marked worsening of the human rights situation, which led the UN Human Rights

Commission in 1990 to appoint a special rapporteur for Guatemala. The government was also widely criticised for what the Bishops' Conference called 'unrestrained and blatant corruption'.

See also **Christian Democrat Party** (Guatemala): **Central American Parliament; Arias plan; Mutual Support Group; National Campesino Pro-Land Association; Guatemalan National Revolutionary Unity; Belize dispute.**

Cerro Maravilla: see **Puerto Rico, nationalist violence.**

Césaire, Aimé
b. 26 June 1913. Martinican poet, dramatist, cultural theorist and politician. A teacher, Césaire founded a magazine, *L'Etudiant Noir*, in 1934 with his friends Léopold Sédar Senghor and Léon-Gontran Damas. They preached a new theory of black pride and identity, which they called *négritude* and which inspired post-war African anti-colonial leaders and radical blacks in the US and the Caribbean.

Césaire was a member of the post-Liberation French Constituent Assembly in 1945 before being elected as a communist to the National Assembly in 1946, when Martinique became a *département* of France with its own representatives in parliament and with Césaire backing the move. He broke with the French Communist Party in 1956 over Hungary and the party's neglect of the French Caribbean possessions. He founded the Martinican Progressive Party (PPM) in 1958 and declared support for President Mitterrand's Socialist Party in 1981. He was elected mayor of Fort-de-France (1945) and in 1983–8 he was president of the island's regional council. In 1988 he refused an invitation to be French minister of state for human rights. In 1990, he was the longest serving member of the French National Assembly (since 1946).
See also **Martinican Progressive Party;** *noirisme;* **'black power'; rastafarians.**

César, Alfredo: see **Nicaraguan Resistance.**

Chaguaramas, Treaty of (1973): see **Caribbean Community.**

Chambers, George: see **People's National Movement.**

Chamorro, Carlos Fernando: see *La Prensa* (Nicaragua).

Chamorro, Jaime: see *La Prensa* (Nicaragua).

Chamorro, Violeta Barrios de: see **Barrios de Chamorro;** *La Prensa* (Nicaragua).

Chamorro Barrios, Pedro Joaquín, Jr: see **United Nicaraguan Opposition; Barrios de Chamorro.**

Chamorro-Bryan Treaty: see **Sandino.**

Chamorro Cardenal, Pedro Joaquín
1924–78. Editor of the Nicaraguan newspaper *La Prensa* (1952–78) and opponent of the Somoza dictatorship. Born into a conservative, news-

paper-publishing family, Pedro Joaquín Chamorro was educated at the Jesuit college, Granada. A member of the 'generation of '44', he was a student leader at university and was forced to complete his law degree in exile in Mexico. He was co-founder in 1948 (with Arturo Cruz) of the National Union of Popular Action (UNAP), a Christian Democrat movement of young conservatives which lasted until 1956 and was the forerunner of the Social Christian Party (PSC). Chamorro took part in the 1954 'April revolt' against the first Somoza and was jailed for two years. Arrested again after the assassination of Somoza García, he escaped to Costa Rica and later travelled to Cuba in an unsuccessful bid to win Havana's backing for the conservative-led 'Olama y Los Mollejones' invasion of mid-1959, after whose failure he was again imprisoned.

As a leading conservative, he sought without success to convert the party to revolutionary Christian Democracy, and eventually broke with party leader Fernando Aguero over his pact with Somoza's liberals. In January 1967, Chamorro was jailed yet again for his part in organising a demonstration which ended in the massacre of several hundred people by the National Guard. In 1974 he founded the Democratic Liberation Union (UDEL) coalition, which included dissident conservatives and liberals; the Socialist (communist) Party (PSN); the Social Christians (PSC) and the Independent Liberal Party (PLI). UDEL had informal links with the Sandinista National Liberation Front (FSLN) guerrillas and, even though the primarily middle-class base of the coalition found them excessively radical, Chamorro himself proclaimed their 'political legitimacy'. In December 1977, Chamorro handed over the leadership of UDEL to a conservative lawyer, Rafael Córdova Rivas.

On 10 January 1978 he was assassinated. Although no proof of the Somoza family's complicity was ever produced, the killing was widely attributed to them and brought about a small-scale uprising in Managua in January 1978 which in turn led to the FSLN's February 1978 offensive. UDEL as such soon ceased to exist, its membership being absorbed into the newly-formed Broad Opposition Front (FAO). Of the eight people arrested for the killing, three escaped in July 1979. All were eventually sentenced to between 18 and 30 years imprisonment, the fugitives *in absentia*.

Chamorro's son, Pedro Joaquín Chamorro Barrios, became editor of *La Prensa* but later joined the anti-Sandinista contra movement in exile. For a time he was on the directorate of the Nicaraguan Resistance (RN), but he was ousted in the July 1988 RN internal elections. Chamorro's widow, Violeta Barrios, was elected president of Nicaragua in 1990. See also *La Prensa* (Nicaragua); **Barrios de Chamorro.**

Chamorro Cardenal, Xavier: see *La Prensa* (Nicaragua).

Chapúltepec, Act of: see **Rio Treaty.**

Charles, Eugenia
b. 15 May 1919. Prime minister of Dominica 1980– . The barrister daughter of planter and politician J. B. Charles, she became president

of the Dominica Employers' Federation and then helped found the conservative Dominica Freedom Party (DFP) in 1968. She was appointed to the house of assembly in 1970 and elected to it in 1975. She led the DFP to a 17–4 electoral victory over the divided Labour Party in 1980 and became the Caribbean's first woman prime minister. In 1981, after violent incidents, she declared a state of emergency and announced she had foiled a plot to overthrow her. She disbanded the country's 100-member defence force and arrested its commander (who was executed in 1986) and former prime minister Patrick John. But there was a further coup plot that year.

Charles strongly backed the 1983 US invasion of Grenada as chairman of the Organisation of Eastern Caribbean States and was flown to Washington where she stood at President Reagan's side as he announced the invasion to the world. She later denied charges in the US that her government was paid $100,000 by the CIA for the gesture. She and Jamaican prime minister Edward Seaga launched the Caribbean Democratic Union of right-wing regional parties in 1986. Charles led the DFP to a 15–6 victory in general elections in 1985, but only narrowly won the 1990 poll (11–10).

See also **Dominica Freedom Party; John, Patrick; Grenada, US invasion (1983); Organisation of Eastern Caribbean States; Caribbean Democratic Union.**

Charles, George: see St Lucia Labour Party; Compton; Netherlands Antilles, oil refineries.

Charles, Lennox 'Bumber': see Union Island revolt (1979); rastafarians.

Chávez y González, Archbishop: see Romero, Archbishop Oscar Arnulfo.

Chiari, Roberto: see Liberal Party (Panama).

Christian base community (*comunidad eclesial de base*/CEB)
A group consisting of Christian laypeople who come together regularly to discuss community and social issues in the light of the Bible. The CEBs, which take various forms, grew up in the years following the Second Vatican Council (Vatican II) and are strongest today in Brazil, where there are tens of thousands of groups, though they are present almost everywhere in Latin America. The overwhelming majority of CEB members are poor. The emergence of the groups was due to a number of factors, including the decline in priestly vocations; the need for the church to relate to the laity in a more flexible way; the new emphasis on the 'option for the poor' and the need for groups to be smaller because of the opposition of many governments to this 'subversive' doctrine; and the legitimacy given to a more open, less hierarchical structure by Vatican II and the Medellín (1968) and Puebla (1979) Latin American bishops' conferences.

The latter aspect in particular implies a major change for the church:

the process of decentralisation involves an inversion of the traditional hierarchy and allows laypeople to take their own initiatives. This and the experience of coming together as peers to discuss concrete social problems and interpreting the Bible without the intervention of a priest has in many cases led to a profound process of political radicalisation, not least in Central America, where conservative church hierarchies have not always looked favourably on the so-called 'popular church'.
See also **liberation theology.**

Christian Democrat Party (El Salvador) (*Partido Demócrata Cristiano*/PDC)

Founded in 1960 by a group of professionals, the most prominent of whom was José Napoleón Duarte who in 1964 became mayor of San Salvador. That same year the party won control of 37 municipalities and 14 seats in the legislature. It explicitly sought a 'third way' between capitalism and socialism, and was backed by CD parties in Europe, especially West Germany and Italy. With the Catholic church it organised peasant unions (illegal under Salvadorean law), including in the late 1960s the Christian Federation of Salvadorean Peasants (FECCAS) which later joined the left. In 1972 and 1977 the PDC headed the reformist UNO alliance which backed Duarte for the presidency but 'lost the count'.

In 1979 the party joined the government formed after the overthrow of Gen. Romero, and stayed on even after the departure of its erstwhile UNO partners, the MDN and the UDN, forming part of the second and third juntas. It split over the issue of continued involvement, and a substantial left-wing faction led by Rubén Zamora joined the opposition FDR alliance as the Popular Social Christian Movement (MPSC). On 5 January 1980 the PDC effectively forged a coalition with the military (on condition that the latter agreed to the nationalisation of banks and foreign trade, to agrarian reform and to non-involvement of the private sector in the junta) which governed until the elections of March 1982, won by the far right. It was returned to power with the election of Duarte as president in March 1984, and in 1985 it consolidated its hold on the government by winning an overall majority in the legislative assembly elections. PDC candidates also took 200 of the 262 mayoral posts.

By mid-1987, however, the party was facing serious internal problems, principally over the presidential nomination for 1989. The two main contenders were Julio Adolfo Rey Prendes, minister of communications, and planning minister Fidel Chávez Mena. Supporters of the latter, considered the favourite of the private sector and the US embassy, began boycotting votes in the legislature in protest at the alleged undemocratic behaviour of Rey Prendes, who controlled much of the party machine. The split was seen as partly responsible for the PDC's loss of control of the assembly in 1988, when it won 23 of the 60 seats. An attempt by Duarte to impose a compromise candidate failed, and Rey Prendes led a breakaway from the party when Chávez Mena's nomination was eventually confirmed. The Authentic Christian Movement (MAC), an alliance between the *reyprendistas* and the Stable Centrist Republican Movement

(MERECEN), a small party of the right, was later granted legal status. Chávez Mena's platform, which stressed the 're-privatisation' of the economy, moved the PDC noticeably to the right but failed to prevent a first-round victory by Alfredo Cristiani of the extreme right ARENA party in the March 1989 election.

See also **Duarte, José Napoleón.**

Christian Democrat Party (Guatemala) (*Democracia Cristiana Guatemalteca*/DCG)

Founded in 1955 under the aegis of the Catholic church, out of the National Christian Affirmation Movement, as an 'alternative within the anti-communist tradition'. The DCG's leaders argued that the 1944–54 'revolution' had been leftist-led because of the absence of Christians from politics. They included René de León Schlotter, later president of the Christian Democrat World Organisation and development minister under the Cerezo government (*see below*). In the (annulled) elections of 1957 the DCG presidential candidate proposed combating communism with social justice. In the following year the party backed the candidate of the extreme right National Liberation Movement (MLN). Differences within the party over support for the military government of Enrique Peralta Azurdia led to the removal from the leadership of the right wing in 1964; an event which hastened the DCG's adoption of more reformist, 'developmentalist' positions.

The party began to win support among students, peasants and trade unionists, and with support from USAID backed the creation of co-operatives and unions. Two years later it was denied electoral participation on a technicality, though in 1968 it was granted legal status. For many years the Christian Democrats were the only legal party attempting serious opposition to the military regime. In the elections of 1970 they formed an alliance with the social democratic Revolutionary Democratic Union (URD, later known as the FUR) and several labour and women's groups. The alliance also won some support from Revolutionary Party (PR) dissidents and members of the unregistered Guatemalan Social Party (PSG) of its presidential candidate, Maj. Jorge Lucas Caballeros. It came third, but made a strong showing especially in the rural highlands. In 1974 it obtained substantial popular support, principally from the working class and the peasantry, and (as the main force in the National Opposition Front/FNO) was only cheated of victory by government fraud. Its candidate was Gen. (ret.) Efraín Ríos Montt. In 1978 (as part of the National Unity Front/Frenu) and 1982 (in the National Opposition Union/UNO alliance with the National Renewal Party/PNR) it was placed third in the presidential elections. The assassination of many of its leaders and threats against others did not affect its belief in electoral politics.

In recent years it has adopted a stance well to the right of most Christian Democrat parties in the region and refused to join opposition groupings to its left, provoking the defection of many members of its own left wing. In 1978 the bulk of the Christian Democrat trade union movement in Guatemala broke with the CLAT over this issue. For the

1982 poll it joined forces with the National Renewal Party (PNR) behind the latter's leader Alejandro Maldonado Aguirre. When the poll was annulled through a military coup the DCG backed the new regime's leader, former FNO candidate Ríos Montt. In 1984 it won the highest number of votes in the constituent assembly elections, taking 20 seats. In 1985 its candidate Vinicio Cerezo won the presidency and the party took 51 out of 100 seats in congress. Its government programme was highly conservative, ruling out land reform and emphasising overseas economic aid and debt renegotiation as the means of reactivating the economy. The business association CACIF contributed campaign funds and many senior army officers backed the DCG in 1985.

In 1987 the party sought to create an alliance around support for the democratic process, and this was partially achieved with the signing of the 'democratic commitment' by seven parties in mid-year, although the pact was rejected by three right-wing groups. In mid-1988 the party was shaken by accusations of corruption from a group of DCG dissidents (the DC National Front for Change/FCDC) led by deputy Otto Baechli. Despite being a target of corruption allegations, former foreign minister Alfonso Cabrera was chosen as DCG presidential candidate for 1990. De León Schlotter and a group of followers split with the party and allied themselves with the Social Democrats (PSD) in protest.
See also **Cerezo Arévalo; Ríos Montt; CLAT.**

Christian Democrat Party (Haiti): see **Haitian Christian Democratic Party.**

Christian Democrat Party of Honduras (*Partido Demócrata Cristiano de Honduras*/PDCH)
Founded in 1968 on the basis of a movement of students and peasants formed in the early 1960s and linked to two major labour organisations, the General Confederation of Workers (CGT) and the National Peasant Union (UNC). The least conservative of the Christian Democrat parties in Central America, the PDCH favours the withdrawal of US troops and the expulsion from Honduras of the Nicaraguan contras, believing the dispute with Nicaragua to have been artificially created. It has stated that in government it would initiate a comprehensive agrarian reform.

The party only achieved registration in July 1980, having been hindered by the majority Liberal (PL) and National (PN) parties. It succeeded in winning one congressional seat in 1981 and two in 1985. Several local PDCH organisers were kidnapped and tortured by security forces for alleged contacts with guerrilla organisations during Gen. Alvarez' tenure as head of armed forces (1982–4). In 1982 the party accused the government of seeking the extermination of its opponents. Congressional deputy Efraín Díaz Arrivillaga, often described as a 'one-man opposition' to the 1982–6 regime, was the only deputy to vote against the appointment of Alvarez. In 1984 he wrested the party presidency from right-wing leader Alfredo Landaverde, and the leadership remained in the hands of the 'progressive' faction under his successor, Rubén Palma. Attempts by the West German Christian Democrats, apparently with US backing, to force the PDCH into an alliance with the National Party by cutting off support funds were unsuccessful.

Christian Democrat Party (Panama) (*Partido Democracia Cristiana/* PDC)

Founded in 1960, the PDC emerged out of a movement at the National University inspired by European Christian Democracy and known from 1957 to 1960 as the National Civic Union (UCN). The PDC's leading figures were middle-class professionals, intellectuals and students, but support also came from the Federation of Christian Workers (FTC). It put up José A. Molino for president in 1964 and Antonio González Revilla in 1968, but neither made much impact. In both years it won one parliamentary seat. In 1968 the radical wing of the leadership was expelled *en masse*, as the increasingly right-wing party opted to support the government of populist Arnulfo Arias. It was backed by a tiny electorate consisting of urban professionals, a business group led by the Romero family, and the affiliates of the CIT (*Central Istmeña de Trabajadores*), the small DC labour federation. Arias chose a Christian Democrat as minister of education, but his government lasted only 11 days.

After reorganising itself in 1978, however, and with Arias' Panameñista Party not registered to participate, it came second in 1980 with 20% of the vote and won two seats in congress. A typical anti-communist Christian Democrat party, favouring the 'social market economy', it now plays a leading role in the Democratic Alliance of Civic Opposition (ADOC, formerly ADO), which was installed as the government after the 1989 US invasion. PDC president Ricardo Arias Calderón became first vice-president and interior and justice minister, and his party was allocated 27 Assembly seats.

See also **Arias Calderón; Democratic Alliance of Civic Opposition; National Civic Crusade; Panama, US invasion (1989).**

Christian Federation of Salvadorean Peasants (FECCAS): see **Christian Democrat Party** (El Salvador); **Popular Revolutionary Bloc.**

Cienfuegos, Fermán: see **Farabundo Martí National Liberation Front.**

Cipriani, A. A.: see **Butler.**

civil patrols (Guatemala) (*patrullas civiles*)

A counter-insurgency system set up under the government of Gen. Ríos Montt (1982–3) involving the recruitment of peasants into poorly-armed anti-guerrilla units which effectively monitor all movement in the countryside. It is said to be the most extensive of its kind in the world, involving at its height an estimated one million people (nearly 90% of adult male Indians in rural areas). Participation is supposedly voluntary, but human rights groups say objectors are subject to intimidation. The civilian government of President Vinicio Cerezo (1986–90) expressed a wish to phase them out, but by 1988 there remained an estimated 700,000 members. In mid-1989 the army announced that it would supply firearms to

some patrol members. A similar system, though on a much smaller scale, was attempted in El Salvador.
See also *fusiles y frijoles;* **Ríos Montt.**

Civil War (Costa Rica/1948)

An armed conflict lasting a little over a month which forestalled the return to power of Rafael Angel Calderón Guardia and established the so-called 'Second Republic' under José Figueres. The origins of the conflict lay in tensions which had grown up during the 1940–44 presidency of Calderón Guardia, principally over his programme of social reforms, which was backed by the Communist Party (Popular Vanguard/VP) and the Catholic church, and which the right sought to block. Calderón Guardia made a second bid for the presidency in 1948, hoping to succeed his ally, President Teodoro Picado. The opposition nominated Otilio Ulate Blanco of the National Union Party (PUN), a conservative newspaper publisher. Turnout on 8 February 1948 was extremely low, perhaps because of intimidation by the opposition, but Ulate was widely held to have won by around 10,000 votes. The electoral tribunal's confirmation of this, however, was only provisional, and Calderón alleged fraud.

On 1 March the legislative assembly, dominated by his supporters, declared the result null and void, apparently with the intention of nominating him as president at a later date. Two hours previously, armed police had fatally wounded the prominent oppositionist Dr Carlos Luis Valverde while seeking to arrest Ulate. The candidate was arrested the following day, but later released. Negotiations, mediated by Archbishop Víctor Sanabria, did take place, but on 13 March, Social Democrat leader Figueres started an uprising against the government, which declared a state of emergency. Aided by arms supplies from Figueres' foreign contacts (known as the Caribbean Legion), the rebels won some early victories. The government army of only 300 was aided by VP militias, a fact which helped boost US and opposition claims that the government was in the hands of the communists. On 11 and 12 April, Figueres' rebels took Limón and Cartago and prepared to advance on San José, the capital. The biggest battle of the war took place near Cartago on 13 April, when more than 200 government troops were killed, against fewer than 20 rebels. The government had received some help from the Somoza dictatorship in Nicaragua, but communist leader Manuel Mora said he would join Figueres if Nicaraguan forces entered the country.

On 19 April, President Picado signed a pact with Figueres' representative under which he offered his resignation in favour of the third designate to the presidency, Santos León Herrera. Both he and Calderón fled to Nicaragua, while the VP, which had agreed to lay down its arms, was outlawed. The 'National Liberation Army' entered San José on 24 April. An 11-man junta took power on 8 May and ruled for 18 months before Ulate was allowed to take power under a new constitution. Total casualties during the uprising were never finally determined: estimates range from a few hundred to as many as 5,000.

See also **Figueres Ferrer; Second Republic; Calderón Guardia; Caribbean Legion.**

Clark Memorandum: see good neighbour policy; Monroe doctrine.

CLAT (*Central Latinoamericana de Trabajadores*/Central Organisation of Latin American Workers)
The western hemisphere regional body of the World Confederation of Labour (WCL, formerly the International Federation of Christian Trade Unions/IFCTU). Founded in 1954 as the Latin American Confederation of Christian Trade Unionists (CLASC), it took its present name in 1971. CLAT has a history of anti-communism, but is generally perceived as being more critical of right-wing dictatorships than its pro-US counterpart, ORIT. Although formally autonomous it has very strong links with the Christian Democrat parties of Latin America, and in particular the Venezuelan party COPEI. In 1968 it signed an agreement with the pro-Moscow regional body, CPUSTAL, to promote unity in the Latin American labour movement, and it has several times issued strong criticisms of US-style capitalism and business unions. It is heavily involved with rural labour and the promotion of moderate agrarian reform, and to this end created the Latin American Peasant Federation (FCL).
   The CLAT Congress meets every four years (most recently in Mar del Plata, Argentina, in 1987). The Council meets annually, and a 23-member executive committee meets every six months. Subregional bodies include the Central American Workers' Confederation (CCT). Thirty-four national and 18 regional organisations in the Americas are members of CLAT, which has its headquarters in Caracas. It claims to represent 10.5m workers in 35 countries and territories.
See also **ORIT; CPUSTAL.**

Claude, Sylvio
b. 1 January 1934. Leader of the Haitian Christian Democratic Party (PDCH). A teacher and Protestant pastor of humble origins, he entered politics in 1978 after years as a small import-export merchant when he clandestinely founded the PDCH. He was arrested and exiled briefly to Colombia when he tried to stand in parliamentary elections in 1979. The PDCH went public a few months later and for the next seven years Claude was harassed, beaten, forced into hiding or imprisoned (for a total of nearly three years) by the Duvalier regime. He ran for president in aborted elections in November 1987, when he was tipped to win, and joined an opposition boycott of a new poll.
See also **Christian Democrat Party** (Haiti); **Duvalier, Jean-Claude.**

Clayton-Bulwer Treaty: see Monroe doctrine.

Clouthier, Manuel: see National Action Party.

Coalition of the Democratic Centre: see Robelo Callejas.

Coard, Bernard
b. 10 August 1944. Deputy prime minister of Grenada 1979–83. An

economist, the marxist Coard taught at universities in Jamaica and Trinidad before returning to Grenada in 1976 to help lead the opposition New Jewel Movement (NJM). He entered parliament in general elections that same year as part of the People's Alliance coalition. He became the dominant figure in a radical 'revolutionary socialist' group which had joined the NJM, the Organisation for Research, Education and Liberation (OREL) (f. 1975). After Coard was threatened with expulsion from the NJM for operating OREL inside the party, OREL was dissolved in 1978. But Coard maintained his radical influence as head of the NJM's organising committee, created the same year.

When the NJM seized power in 1979 he became deputy prime minister to Maurice Bishop as well as minister of finance, trade, industry and planning. Behind his moderate public front he privately tried to push sweeping radical policies, such as a proposal to seize all large landholdings on the island, and to repress dissent. He criticised his colleagues as 'petty bourgeois' and resigned from the NJM central committee in 1982. After Bishop went back on a party plan for him and Coard to share national leadership, Coard and his allies, with army backing, arrested Bishop on his return from eastern Europe in October 1983. After Bishop was freed by his supporters a few days later Coard sent troops after him, and Bishop and three cabinet ministers were executed. Coard covertly directed a Revolutionary Military Council which tried to govern for a week before it was swept away by a US military invasion.

Coard was arrested by US troops and he and 19 others were charged with murdering Bishop. After two years of legal disputes and delays and a trial plagued with irregularities, he and 13 others, including his influential Jamaican wife Phyllis, were sentenced to death in December 1986. See also **New Jewel Movement; Grenada, US invasion (1983); Revolutionary Military Council; Bishop.**

Colom Argueta, Manuel: see **Lucas García.**

Comandante Ana María: see **Popular Liberation Forces.**

Comandante Cero: see **Pastora Gómez.**

Committees for the Defence of the Revolution (*Comités por la Defensa de la Revolución*/CDR)

A national network of neighbourhood committees, created in Cuba on 28 September 1960. Originally intended both as an expression of 'direct democracy' and of vigilance against the ever-present counter-revolutionary threat, the CDRs were set up on every block and within a few years had over two million members. They play an important role in political education, popular mobilisation (for work brigades, etc.) and the dissemination of government policies, as well as in ensuring the equitable distribution of health and welfare entitlements. Critics, however, have increasingly seen them primarily as repressive organs linked to the police and state security. The eyes and ears of the CDRs have helped keep common crime to a minimum, but are also dedicated to rooting out all forms of opposition to the regime. The appointment, in February 1990, of Gen.

Sixto Batista to head the CDRs was seen by human rights activists as a
pointer to increased surveillance.

Commonwealth Caribbean

An association of all 16 former and present colonies of Britain in the
Caribbean, plus Guyana and Bermuda. All except Guyana, Trinidad-
Tobago and Dominica recognise the British monarch as titular head of
state who appoints a local notable as figurehead governor-general, in
practice someone chosen by the local government of the day.
See also **Caribbean Community.**

Communist Party (Costa Rica)

Organised in 1929 as the Workers' and Peasants' Bloc, the Costa Rican
Communist Party was formally founded in 1931. Its leader was law student Manuel Mora Valverde, who served as general secretary and later
president of the party until his expulsion in 1984. In 1934 the communists
took two seats in the congressional elections and led an important strike
of banana workers around the port of Limón which won a rise in minimum
wages. The party backed the losing candidate in the 1940 elections, but
subsequently switched its support to the winner, Rafael Angel Calderón,
as a consequence of the wartime alliance between the US and the USSR.
It played a major role in the social reforms of the Calderón government.
In 1943 it changed its name to Popular Vanguard (*Vanguardia Popular*)
to woo Catholic voters.

The alliance with the PNR continued under Calderón's successor Teodoro Picado, but with the beginning of the cold war attempts were made
to have the VP banned. The party declared its allegiance to the Comintern
and hostility to the US in 1948. The alliance with the PNR was not
renewed for the 1948 election, whose disputed result led to a civil war in
which the opposition and the US blamed the communists for the chaos.
After 1948 many members were imprisoned or exiled, and on 22 June
1948 the VP was proscribed. It fought elections under different names,
and in 1975 the constitutional ban was removed. In 1978 and 1982 the
communists joined the United People Party (PPU) coalition.

Now known as the Popular Vanguard party (VP), the old guard has
remained orthodox and pro-Moscow, with the bulk of its support still
coming from the banana zone of Puntarenas province and the working-
class areas of San José, Limón and Puntarenas city. Mora's breakaway
Costa Rican People's Party (PPC) formed the United People alliance, a
more pragmatic, reformist grouping. The two campaigned separately in
the 1986 elections, with the VP heading the Popular Alliance Coalition.
Each coalition won one seat. In 1990 they joined forces again under the
United People banner, winning one seat.
See also **Mora Valverde.**

Communist Party (Cuba)

The first communist party in Cuba was founded in Havana in 1925. It
adhered very strictly to Moscow (Comintern) policies, rejecting all
advances from other parties in its early years, although secretary general

César Avila later sought agreement with the dictator Machado in an attempt to avert direct US intervention. It rejected the 'revolutionary' administration of Grau San Martín in 1933 and firmly opposed the future dictator Fulgencio Batista in the early 1930s, but responded to the Comintern's 'popular front' phase by entering a coalition with him in 1937. In return he legalised the communist front party, the PUR, and allowed the communists to take control of the fledgling labour movement (the Confederation of Workers of Cuba/CTC). In 1939 the PUR and the clandestine communist movement merged into the legal Communist Revolutionary Union Party (PURC), which in coalition with Batista won the 1940 elections. Two PURC leaders (Carlos Rafael Rodríguez and Juan Marinello) held ministerial posts in the Batista government: both would subsequently play a major role in the Castro government.

In 1944 the PURC changed its name to Popular Socialist Party (PSP) in a bid to broaden its appeal. For most of its existence the PSP was headed by general secretary Blas Roca. In 1944 the PSP joined Batista in supporting Carlos Saladrigas for the presidency, but it later switched its allegiance to the victorious Ramón Grau San Martín. In 1948, standing alone, the party won 7% of the vote. Its influence waned after it lost control of the CTC under the anti-communist President Prío, and it was banned by Batista after his 1952 coup (though it continued to function). Operating semi-clandestinely, it supported Grau again in 1954. The PSP opposed Fidel Castro's revolutionary movement until just before its victory, calling the Moncada barracks attack 'adventurist'. However, in mid-1958, Carlos Rafael Rodríguez was sent to the Sierra Maestra to settle differences with Castro, and the PSP became the only non-Castroite party not banned by the revolution.

The modern Cuban Communist Party (*Partido Comunista Cubano/* PCC) was founded in October 1965 by the merger of Castro's July 26 Movement (M–26–7), the PSP and the Revolutionary Student Directorate (DER); a process which had begun with the creation of the Integrated Revolutionary Organisations (ORI) out of the same groups in late 1961 and its rapid transformation into the United Party of the Socialist Revolution (PURS). It did not hold its first congress, however, until December 1975, and was effectively controlled by an inner circle of Castro' and his associates (the politburo and secretariat met rarely in the early years). The 1976 constitution defines the party's role as 'the leading force in society and the state'. Internally, the ruling body is the party congress, which elects the 146 central committee members. The central committee in turn appoints the 16-member politburo and the five-member secretariat.

A PCC plenum in February 1990 ruled out a move to a multi-party system but announced a series of reforms aimed at streamlining and revitalising political institutions. In particular, the National Assembly of People's Power was to be strengthened and given a more parliamentary role. The party's fourth Congress was due to be held in 1991.

See also **26 July Movement; United Party of the Socialist Revolution; Integrated Revolutionary Organisations.**

Communist Party (El Salvador): see Salvadorean Communist Party.

Communist Party (Mexico) (*Partido Comunista Mexicano*/PCM)
Founded in November 1919 and recognised by the Comintern in Moscow,
the PCM grew steadily in the 1920s and 1930s, establishing considerable
influence in the trade unions and peasant co-operatives which grew out
of Mexico's revolutionary process. But PCM militants were persecuted
and the party itself was banned by President Calles after it had taken
part in an abortive revolt against his rule in 1929. This, however, did not
undermine its hold over important sectors of the intelligentsia – members
included the muralists Diego Rivera and David Alfaro Siqueiros. The
party recovered its legal status in 1935.

In this period it was decidedly Stalinist, supporting the Moscow trials
and participating in the assassination of Trotsky in Mexico City in August
1940. It also defended the Hitler-Stalin pact. But in the 1940s the party
fell victim to its own internal purges – both Hernán Laborde, the general
secretary, and Valentín Campa, the railway union leader, were expelled
for having opposed Trotsky's assassination. Dionisio Encinas, the new
general secretary, established a tight grip on the party for the following
two decades, a period in which the Stalinist and pro-Moscow line was
applied unremittingly. Membership during this period is estimated to
have fallen drastically from 30,000 to an estimated 3,000.

The PCM tried to recruit new members during the student unrest of
1968, but for the most part the new generation of political radicals ignored
the party. By the 1970s the PCM began to adopt a more 'Eurocommunist'
position. Although legal, the PCM was not on the electoral register until
1978. In the 1976 elections it was therefore not regarded as a contestant,
but supporters were nevertheless asked to write the name of Valentín
Campa (who had earlier been rehabilitated) on the presidential ballot
paper. Reports that Campa received up to 1 million of these unofficial
'write in' votes circulated for some time, but were never confirmed by
the electoral authorities.

Following electoral reforms under the López Portillo administration,
the PCM merged with the Popular Action Movement (MAP), the Socialist Action and Unity Movement (MAUS), the Mexican Peoples' Party
(PPM), and the Revolutionary Socialist Party (PSR) to form a single
leftist grouping, the Unified Socialist Party of Mexico (*Partido Socialista
Unificado de México*/PSUM). In 1982 the PSUM presidential candidate,
Arnaldo Martínez Verdugo, received 3.7% of the vote, and the party,
together with two other allied leftist groups, obtained 17 seats in the
chamber of deputies. In early 1987 the PSUM merged with the Mexican
Workers Party (PMT) to form the Mexican Socialist Party (*Partido Mexicano Socialista*/PMS), which ended up supporting the candidacy of
Cuauhtémoc Cárdenas in the July 1988 presidential elections. In this
process of realignments and alliances the PCM accepted a dilution of its
original ideological positions – the PMS, for example, explicitly rejected
the marxist-leninist doctrine of the dictatorship of the proletariat.
See also **Mexican Socialist Party.**

Communist Party of Guatemala (PCG): see Guatemalan Labour Party.

Communist Party of Honduras (*Partido Comunista de Honduras/* PCH)
An orthodox, Moscow-line party, founded in 1954, which played a key role (as the Honduran Democratic Revolutionary Party/PRDH) in the 1954 general strike. The PCH was influential in the formation of the first Honduran peasant union, FENACH, in the late 1950s, but with the destruction of FENACH by the military government in 1963 it turned to organising urban workers. It suffered splits in the 1960s and 1970s over its policy of working through existing unions, but resolved these in 1981 by forming a new union federation, the FUTH, affiliated to CPUSTAL. In 1960 and 1965–7 anti-Soviet factions broke away, resulting in 1967 in the formation of the pro-Chinese PCH-Marxist-Leninist. At its 1972 congress, the PCH adopted a new constitution reiterating its commitment to Marxism-Leninism. The Revolutionary Union of the People (URP), led by Tomás Natoví and Fidel Martínez and said to have links with the Cinchonero guerrillas, broke away in 1980 in an attempt to become a mass organisation. Natoví and Martínez were 'disappeared' (allegedly by the armed forces) in 1981. In the same year the PCH was granted legal status for the first time and joined the PCH-ML and the Socialist Party (PASOH) in the Patriotic Front (FPH) electoral alliance, following whose failure the PCH-ML opted for armed struggle and the PCH split into various factions. Rigoberto Padilla Rush became PCH secretary general. See also **guerrilla movements** (Honduras); **Honduran Patriotic Front; general strike** (Honduras 1954).

Communist Party of Honduras-Marxist Leninist: see Communist Party of Honduras; guerrilla movements (Honduras).

Communist Party (Panama): see People's Party of Panama.

Compton, John
b. 1 May 1926. Chief minister, premier, prime minister of St Lucia 1964–79, 1982– . Compton worked at the oil refinery in Curaçao before qualifying as a barrister and studying at the London School of Economics, later becoming a wealthy planter. He was elected to parliament as an independent in 1954. He joined the St Lucia Labour Party (SLP) in 1956 and was minister of trade and industry under chief minister George Charles, 1958–61, resigning to form the National Labour Movement. He merged this party with the People's Progressive Party in 1964 to form the United Workers' Party (UWP), led by himself.

When the UWP won the general election that year, the conservative Compton became chief minister and, on associated statehood in 1967, premier. He diversified the economy, stressing tourism and foreign industrial investment. But he lost the 1979 election, five months after leading the country to independence. He returned to power after winning elections in 1982 and was a leading advocate of the US invasion of Grenada the following year. After an unexpectedly narrow victory in 1987, he

called another election three weeks later, arguing the need for a stable majority, but only achieved the same one-seat margin. He then obtained the defection of SLP MP Neville Cenac by appointing him foreign minister.
See also **United Workers' Party; St Lucia Labour Party; Grenada, US invasion (1983); Caribbean Democratic Union.**

Concerned Citizens' Movement (CCM): see Nevis Reformation Party.

CONDECA (*Consejo de Defensa Centroamericano*/Central American Defence Council)
Formally established in 1964 as an adjunct to the Organisation of Central American States (ODECA) by the defence ministers of Guatemala, Honduras, El Salvador and Nicaragua. The US, which obtained full membership through its Panama Canal Zone-based Southern Command, was instrumental in its creation. Costa Rica and Panama were given observer status, with an option to join. CONDECA's objectives were: to coordinate action against internal subversion, under the guidance of US military representatives in the region and the US Central Intelligence Agency; to standardise training and equipment; and to minimise regional military rivalries. Two basic types of activity were contemplated: counter-insurgency and civic military action. The members conducted periodic joint counter-insurgency exercises, roughly a dozen in all between 1964 and 1976. After the 1972 Nicaragua earthquake, US, Salvadorean and Guatemalan troops were brought in to help maintain order; allegedly that same year the Nicaraguan and Guatemalan air forces helped crush a coup d'état in El Salvador.
CONDECA never fully achieved its objectives, however. Honduras effectively pulled out after the 1969 war with El Salvador (which CONDECA had done nothing to prevent), though it was reincorporated in the late 1970s, and the withdrawal of Nicaragua after the fall of Somoza in 1979 was a critical blow. During the 1978 Sandinista insurrection, Salvadorean and (allegedly) Guatemalan troops were in Nicaragua, but Somoza's last-minute call for aid in mid-1979 was rejected. Guatemala declined to go to the aid of Salvadorean dictator Gen. Romero during the October 1979 coup. By this stage the US had also ended its formal advisory role. However, CONDECA's permanent council continued to exist, with offices in Guatemala, and in the mid-1980s attempts were made to revive it as a regional front against the Nicaraguan government. These too foundered, partly on the unwillingness of the Guatemalan military government to become involved.
See also **'Football (Soccer) War'; Organisation of Central American States.**

Confederation of Central American Workers: see ORIT.

Confederation of Mexican Workers (*Confederación de Trabajadores Mexicanos*/CTM)
The country's largest labour confederation, founded in 1936 and closely

aligned with the ruling Institutional Revolutionary Party (PRI). It forms one of the three main sectors of the PRI (the other two are CNC, representing the peasants, and CNOP, representing public employees, professionals and military). The CTM was formed with backing of President Lázaro Cárdenas, who wanted a new organisation to overcome labour movement divisions and the corruption of the older Regional Confederation of Mexican Workers (CROM).

Under its first general secretary, Vicente Lombardo Toledano, the CTM adopted a strong anti-imperialist and anti-capitalist stance. The ruling group within the CTM, however, known as the 'five little wolves', included Fidel Velázquez, a staunch anti-communist, who emerged as the dominant leader after 1941. Under Velázquez' control the CTM managed government-labour relations, frequently damping down wage demands and heading off political challenges to the PRI's rule in return for government favours and patronage. Each successive president has dealt directly with the CTM in preference to various rival groupings. There was nevertheless a series of shifting alliances on the labour front: in the late 1950s, for example, the CTM joined the Workers' Unit Bloc (BUO) with other confederations in an effort to preserve its upper hand over rival unions grouped in the National Confederation of Mexican Workers (CNMT, often referred to as CNT). Although statistics on the relative strengths of the different labour organisations are contested, the CTM claims some 11,000 affiliated unions with a membership of over 6–7 million.

See also **Velázquez, Fidel; Lombardo Toledano; Institutional Revolutionary Party.**

Congo, Cuban involvement in: see African involvement (Cuba).

Conservative National Alliance Party: see Democratic Conservative Party of Nicaragua.

Conservative Popular Alliance Party: see Democratic Conservative Party of Nicaragua.

Constitutionalist Liberal Movement: see Nicaraguan Democratic Co-ordinator.

Constitutionalist Liberal Party: see Nicaraguan Democratic Co-ordinator.

Contadora Group *(Grupo Contadora)*
The name adopted by the governments of Mexico, Panama, Colombia and Venezuela when they came together in 1983 with the aim of 'promot(ing) detente and put(ting) an end to situations of conflict' in Central America. The group first met (8–9 January 1983) on Contadora Island, off the Coast of Panama. In July 1983 their presidents met at Cancún, Mexico, and on 17 July they issued the Cancún Declaration, calling on Central American governments and those of the US and Cuba to strive for peace. On 9 September the foreign ministers of Contadora, along with those of Guatemala, El Salvador, Honduras, Nicaragua and

Costa Rica, signed a 21-point 'Document of Objectives', which included proposals for a ban on 'foreign military bases or any other type of foreign military interference'; eventual removal of all foreign military advisers; an end to arms trafficking in the region and a variety of social and economic goals.

The efforts of three joint 'working commissions', on the political, security and socio-economic aspects of the crisis, set up on 8 January 1984, culminated in the 'Contadora Act for Peace and Co-operation in Central America', a draft treaty delivered to the Central Amercian governments on 8–9 June. The Nicaraguan government announced its willingness to sign the draft, while the other Central American nations called for modifications. These changes, backed by the US government and outlined in the Tegucigalpa Draft Agreement of 20 October 1984, sought to strengthen 'verification and control' mechanisms, while relaxing the rules against foreign military exercises and bases. They would also have reduced the value to Nicaragua of the built-in disputes procedure, by requiring 'consensus' as opposed to 'unanimity' and providing for appeal to the foreign ministers of 'the nine' (not those of Contadora alone). El Salvador, Honduras and Costa Rica – all closely identified with the US position – became known as the 'Tegucigalpa Group'.

The process remained bogged down until July 1985, when Latin American leaders meeting at the inauguration of Peruvian president Alan García agreed to form the Contadora Support Group (or 'Lima Group'), comprising Peru, Brazil, Argentina and Uruguay. The foreign ministers of the four met Contadora foreign ministers at Cartagena de Indias, Colombia, on 24–25 August 1985 and agreed on a role as consultative, supervisory and pressure group in favour of the Contadora objectives. Together, the two bodies became known as the Group of Eight. A modified 'Act for Peace' (*Acta de Paz*) was put to Central American nations for signing by 20 November 1985, but rejected by Nicaragua, which said it could not disarm while under attack by the US-backed contra rebels. A five-month moratorium was agreed in December 1985, but the process was revived in January 1986 by the Caraballeda Declaration of the Contadora and Lima Groups meeting in Venezuela, which called for a halt to foreign support for 'irregular forces' in the region; the suspension of foreign military manoeuvres; the withdrawal of foreign bases and advisers; and the reopening of US-Nicaraguan talks. The declaration was taken up by Central American heads of state meeting at the inauguration of Guatemalan president Vinicio Cerezo (14 January 1986) and endorsed by the Organisation of American States (OAS). Cerezo proposed the establishment of a Central American parliament.

The first concrete achievement of Contadora was an international civilian force to monitor the Nicaragua-Costa Rica border, agreed at a Punta del Este, Uruguay, meeting on 27–28 Feburary 1986, but this agreement later broke down. The June 1986 'Panama Message' contained a new version of the *Acta de Paz*, but Nicaragua refused to discuss limitations on its defence capabilities after the US Congress approved $100m in aid to anti-Sandinista forces in August. Guatemala proposed reopening discussions, but there was little response. In autumn 1986, after Nicaragua took Costa Rica and Honduras to the World Court for harbouring anti-Sandinista forces, the latter two countries withdrew from the Contadora process.

On 15 February 1987, Costa Rican president Oscar Arias proposed a peace settlement involving a ceasefire in the region, the suspension of aid to the contras and dialogue between governments and their internal opposition. At first seen as a challenge to Contadora, the 'Arias Plan' soon achieved widespread support, despite the opposition of the US government. After the plan was approved in August 1987, Nicaragua announced that it would suspend its case against Honduras and drop that against Costa Rica. Contadora assumed a supervisory and verification role under the plan. It also began to devote more of its time to other issues of common interest, notably the debt question. The presidents of the Group of Eight met in Acapulco on November 1987, with debt high on the agenda. Among other things, they agreed on an economic emergency plan to back up the Arias Plan. The summit was seen as a snub to Washington, which would usually convene such meetings. It became an annual event, with the 1988 meeting held in Uruguay. Panama's membership, however, was suspended after President Delvalle was dismissed by the head of the Defence Forces, Gen. Noriega. Mexico, Venezuela and Colombia announced the disbanding of Contadora on 29 March 1990, saying its objectives had been fulfilled.

See also **Arias Plan; Central American Parliament; Rio Group; Organisation of American States.**

continuismo

The practice whereby an incumbent president remains in office despite legal or constitutional provisions to the contrary. Notable exponents of *continuismo* in Central America and the Caribbean have been the Somoza family of Nicaragua (1936–79); dictators Ubico (Guatemala), Carías (Honduras) and Martínez (El Salvador) in the 1930s and 1940s; and the Duvalier family in Haiti (1957–86). Most constitutions in the region forbid consecutive terms of presidential office (an exception is Nicaragua). Techniques for overcoming this problem include the amendment of the constitution; plebiscites (usually fraudulent); the use of puppet presidents or juntas to provide a buffer period; and the replacement of the constitution by means of constituent assembly or referendum. An alternative is the total suspension of the constitution and rule by decree.

contra

An abbreviation of the Spanish *contrarrevolucionario* (counter-revolutionary), used to refer to members of the armed groups formed after the 1979 Nicaraguan revolution to overthrow the government of the Sandinista National Liberation Front (FSLN).

See also **Nicaraguan Resistance; Nicaraguan Democratic Force; United Nicaraguan Opposition; Southern Opposition Bloc; ARDE; Yatama.**

Córdova Rivas, Rafael: see Democratic Conservative Party of Nicaragua.

Coronado, Eduardo: see Independent Liberal Party.

Corrada del Río, Baltasar
b. 10 April 1935. Former leader of Puerto Rico's New Progressive Party (PNP). A lawyer, he was chairman of the island's civil rights commission, 1970–72. He was resident commissioner in Washington from 1977 until 1985, when he was elected mayor of the capital, San Juan. He became PNP leader on the resignation in 1985 of ex-governor Carlos Romero Barceló. But he was beaten for the governorship in the 1988 election by incumbent Rafael Hernández Colón and lost the party leadership to Romero Barceló in 1989.
See also New Progressive Party; Romero Barceló.

Cortés, León: see Calderón Guardia.

COSEP (*Consejo Superior de la Empresa Privada*/Higher Council of Private Enterprise)
The main Nicaraguan employers' federation, formerly known as COSIP. Originally embracing over a dozen private sector groups, now reduced to six, COSEP was founded in the early 1970s by business organisations not linked to the Somoza dictatorship. Almost all industrial and commercial sectors were represented. The organisation held its first large convention in 1974, at which it complained of 'unfair competition' by the Somoza regime. Members of COSEP contributed to the fall of Somoza through a series of business strikes in 1978 and 1979, but were reluctant to recognise the leadership of the Sandinista National Liberation Front (FSLN) in the revolutionary movement until just before the 1979 victory, after which COSEP became the focus of right-wing opposition to the Sandinista government. Many of its members were accused by the government of 'decapitalisation' and refusal to invest, and some were refused permission to travel abroad. Four COSEP leaders were jailed in October 1981 for breaking the Social and Economic Emergency Law.

The organisation was granted representation on the co-legislative Council of State (1979–84), but after initially taking up its six seats it attended only irregularly. In July 1981 it joined four opposition parties and two trade unions in the anti-Sandinista Nicaraguan Democratic Co-ordinator (CDN). In December 1983 it played a major part in drafting the nine conditions for CDN participation in the 1984 elections, which the latter eventually boycotted. In 1987, COSEP argued against participation in the dialogue between government and opposition established under the Central American peace plan (Arias Plan) but was overruled by the majority in the CDN. It later called for the formation of a 'government of national salvation' incorporating opposition figures.

COSEP supported the winning UNO coalition in 1990, and former COSEP president Enrique Dreyfus became foreign minister in Violeta Chamorro's government.
See also Nicaraguan Democratic Co-ordinator; National Opposition Union.

COSTA RICA, Republic of
Capital: San José
Independence: (from Spain) 1821; (from Central American Federation) 1838
Area: 50,900 sq km
Population (1988): 2.87m (50.3% urban)
Pop. growth rate (1980–88): 2.9%
Pop. density: 56/sq km
Infant mortality (1984): 18.8 per thousand
Life expectancy at birth (1980–85): 73.0
Literacy (1988): 92%
GDP per capita (1988e): US$2,235
Foreign debt per capita (1989e): US$1,558
Main exports (1988): coffee (24%); bananas (19%); meat (4%)

Political system

Constitution: 1949. Head of state/government: President Rafael Angel Calderón Fournier (PUSC) (1990–   ); succeeded Oscar Arias Sánchez (PLN) (1986–90). Legislature: single-chamber, 57-seat Legislative Assembly elected by universal compulsory adult (18+) suffrage and proportional representation in seven multi-member constituencies. Voters choose from rival party lists; the party deciding the rank order. The government subsidises electoral expenses (pro-rata, according to votes received in the last election) of any party obtaining over 5% of the vote. General elections are held every four years, most recently in February 1990. A 1969 constitutional amendment prohibits presidential re-election, and Assembly members cannot stand for consecutive terms. The president and vice-presidents must be over 30 and cannot be members of the clergy. During the year preceding the election a presidential candidate is not allowed to have held senior governmental posts nor to have been a supreme court judge. Governors of the seven provinces are appointed by the president.

(*Note*: the 1949 constitution abolished the army, and since 17 November 1983, Costa Rica has been formally committed to an international policy of permanent, unarmed, active neutrality.)

Political organisations

Parties in the Legislative Assembly (leader) (seats): National Liberation Party/PLN (Walter Coto Molina) (25); Social Christian Unity Party/PUSC (Rafael Angel Calderón) (29); United People coalition/PU (Alberto Salom Echeverría) (1); Generaleña Union (1); Cartagena Agricultural Union (1).
Other national parties: National Christian Alliance Party/PANC (Víctor Hugo González Montero); Revolutionary Workers' Party/PRT; National Progress Party; Independent Party/PI (Eugenio Jiménez Sancho); National Movement/MN (Mario Echandi Jiménez); Democratic Radical Party/PRD (Juan José Echeverría); Social Democratic Movement/MSD; Popular Democratic Party/PPD; National Republi-

can Party/PRN (Rolando Rodríguez Varela); Democratic National Party/PND (Rodolfo Cerdas Cruz); Costa Rican Ecological Party/PEC; People's Action/AP (Angel Ruiz Zúñiga); Costa Rican Concord Party (Emilio Piedra Jiménez); National Union Party (Olga Marta Ulate Rojas); New Alajuelita Party (Carlos Retana).

Main labour organisations (leader) (affiliation) belong to the Permanent Council of Workers/CPT, an umbrella organisation comprising: Democratic Workers' Authentic Confederation/CATD (Carlos Vargas) (independent); Costa Rican Confederation of Democratic Workers/CCTD (Luis Armando Gutiérrez) (ORIT); Unitary Confederation of Workers/CUT (Orlando Solano Mejías) (linked to the PU coalition); Costa Rican Workers Union/CTCR (Alsimiro Herrera Torres); National Confederation of Workers/CNT (linked to the PLN); Teachers' Front/Frente Magisterial.

Main employers' organisations: Chamber of Industries (Gustavo Gutiérrez Castro) and the Chamber of Commerce (Julio Ugarte).

Costa Rican People's Party: see Mora Valverde.

Courtenay, Harry: see People's United Party.

CPUSTAL (*Congreso Permanente de Unidad Sindical de los Trabajadores de América Latina*/Permanent Congress for Trade Union Unity of the Workers of Latin America)

Founded in 1964 in Brasilia, as the Trade Union Co-ordination Committee of Latin American Workers, CPUSTAL replaced the Confederation of Workers of Latin America (*Confederación de Trabajadores de América Latina*/CTAL). The original move for its creation came from a conference in Santiago de Chile in 1962, called by the Chilean CUT (*Central Unica de Trabajadores*) and the Cuban CTC (*Central de Trabajadores de Cuba*). Its first secretariat was based in Santiago, but after the Chilean military coup of September 1973 it moved to Lima, Peru, and thence to Panama City. It is now based in Mexico City. In the late 1960s, CPUSTAL signed an accord with the communist World Federation of Trade Unions (WFTU), based in Prague, to work for the unity of the Latin American trade union movement. Headed by a general council and a secretariat, it describes its aims as 'unitarian and anti-imperialist'. It does not publish membership/affiliates figures.

CREMS: see Alvarez Martínez.

Cristeros

Conservative Catholic guerrillas who fought the central government of Mexico in 1926–9. President Plutarco Elías Calles began to enforce the anti-clerical articles of the 1917 constitution, taking over churches, banning religious processions and preventing the clergy from voting, discussing politics, owning property or being involved in the education system. In 1926 he established an additional requirement, that all priests be licensed by the state. Catholic prelates responded by boycotting the state-regulated churches and refusing to officiate at mass, conduct baptisms

and marriages, or impart extreme unction. In Jalisco, Michoacán, Guana-
juato, Colima and Zacatecas, conservative peasants led by priests formed
guerrilla bands which attacked federal officials and institutions with the
battle cry *Viva Cristo Rey!* – hence the name 'cristeros'. The government
responded with fierce repression and there were atrocities on both sides.
Although a formal truce was achieved in 1929 with the re-opening of the
churches, anti-clericalism remained a strong force in the ruling party for
many years.
See also **Calles; Mexican revolution.**

Cristiani Burkard, Alfredo

b. 1947. President of El Salvador 1989– . Born in San Salvador, the son
of a coffee grower, 'Freddy' Cristiani was educated at the American
School in that city and later obtained a BA in business administration
from Georgetown University, Washington DC. Returning to El Salvador,
he devoted much of his time to sports and became national motocross
champion. He married into the oligarchy and became president of the
Coffee Exporters Association (1977) and vice-president of the National
Private Enterprise Association (1977–9). He took over a failing insurance
and investment business owned by his wife's family and built it into a
thriving concern. In 1984, Cristiani was elected director of the national
executive of the right-wing ARENA party, and in the following year he
succeeded Roberto D'Aubuisson as party president in a move aimed at
presenting a more 'moderate' image, particularly towards the US. In 1988
he became a member of the National Assembly, but he soon left to
campaign for the presidency. Critics said the party was still controlled by
its fundamentalist wing, a view which did not prevent Cristiani being
elected president with an absolute majority on the first ballot in March
1989. His election promises included dialogue with the guerrillas,
increased welfare spending and improvements in the administration of
justice. He also pledged to roll back state control of foreign trade and
banking and end the land reform programme introduced by the Christian
Democrats.

His attempts at negotiation with the FMLN, criticised at first for a lack
of seriousness, were further sabotaged by a bomb attack which killed ten
people at a trade union HQ on 31 October 1989. The guerrillas, who
blamed the army, suspended the dialogue and launched a huge offensive
on 11 November, in which they seized and held large areas of the capital.
During the offensive government troops murdered six Jesuit priests and
two women at the Central American University. This crime – part of a
general rise in human rights violations – once more called into question
US aid to El Salvador, especially as the government seemed incapable
of bringing its true authors to justice. Cristiani was weakened by the
offensive, and the extreme right in the Assembly immediately pushed
through a draconian reform of the penal code, outlawing many forms of
dissent. He gained some comfort, however, from a call by Central American presidents in December for an end to armed actions by the FMLN
and a resumption of dialogue. The February 1990 elections in Nicaragua,

which saw the defeat of the FMLN's allies, the Sandinistas, was even better news for Cristiani. On 5 April the government and the FMLN formally agreed to talks under UN auspices.
See also **ARENA.**

Croes, Betico

1938–86. Leader of Aruba 1975–85. A former schoolteacher, Croes joined the Aruban People's Party in 1967 with left-wing ideas, was elected to the island council and became education commissioner. He left the party in 1971 to found the People's Electoral Movement (MEP), which called for separation and eventual independence from the rest of the Netherlands Antilles.

Croes became island leader ('counsellor') after the MEP won the general election in 1975, and organised a referendum in 1977 in which Arubans voted for independence. In 1983 he persuaded the Netherlands to grant autonomy in 1986 (with independence in 1996), but his political following collapsed after the 1985 closure of the island's main employer, the Exxon-owned Lago oil refinery. He and the MEP were defeated in general elections in November 1985. A few weeks later, Croes (who had already been seriously wounded in an election rally shooting in 1983) was critically injured in a car crash on his way to the inauguration of the autonomy he had won for the island. He died in hospital in the Netherlands in 1986, after a year in a coma.
See also **People's Electoral Movement; Netherlands Antilles, oil refineries.**

Crusol, Jean

b. 20 September 1943. Martinican socialist, former member of the European parliament. A professor of economics at the University of Antilles-Guyane and a member of the French Economic and Social Council in Paris, he became a member of the parliament when he replaced French Socialist Party leader Lionel Jospin there in 1988 until new elections the following year.

Cruz, Ramón Ernesto: see **Liberal Party** (Honduras); **López Arellano.**

Cruz Porras, Arturo José

b. 1923. Nicaraguan banker and politician. A graduate of Georgetown University, Washington, Cruz co-founded a Christian Democrat movement of young conservatives in 1948. He worked for the Inter-American Development Bank in the 1970s and again after 1981. A member of the Conservative Party and of the 'Group of 12' opposition figures, he was jailed twice by the Somoza regime. After the 1979 revolution he was president of the Central Bank (1979–80) and a leading member of the Democratic Conservative Party (PCD). He served briefly as a member of the Junta of National Reconstruction and later as ambassador to Washington. After resigning in 1981 he became associated with the armed opposition.

Cruz was the presidential nominee of the Nicaraguan Democratic Co-ordinator (CDN) in the 1984 elections but declined to participate, alleging that the contest was unfair. When the CDN jointly set up the United

Nicaraguan Opposition (UNO) in 1985, Cruz was given responsibility for human rights. He several times threatened to resign from UNO, alleging that his views were being ignored. In February 1987 an ultimatum from Cruz brought the resignation from the UNO directorate of Adolfo Calero, but Cruz said he would still resign unless reforms (including the unification of contra forces) were carried out. Cruz's position was weakened by the admission that he had been receiving $6,000 a month out of a slush fund set up by Col. Oliver North. On 10 March 1987 he resigned, and when UNO was relaunched as the Nicaraguan Resistance in May he refused to join its leadership.

See also **Nicaraguan Democratic Co-ordinator; Nicaraguan Resistance; Democratic Conservative Party of Nicaragua; Calero Portocarrero; Iran/contra affair.**

Cuadra, Pablo Antonio: see *La Prensa* (Nicaragua).

cuartelazo

A military uprising; literally, 'a blow from the barracks (*cuartel*)'. The word '*cuartelada*' is also found.

CUBA, Republic of

Capital: Havana
Independence: (from Spain) 10 December 1898 under Treaty of Paris; became a republic on 20 May 1902, on withdrawal of US forces
Area: 114,524 sq km
Population (1987): 10.36m (70% urban)
Pop. growth rate (1986–7): 1.08%
Pop. density: 90/sq km
Infant mortality (1987): 18 per thousand
Life expectancy at birth: 74.7
Literacy: 96%
Per capita income (1983): US$1,590
Foreign debt per capita (1988): US$623
Main exports (1983): sugar and sugar products (75%); re-exported Soviet oil (9%); seafood (4%); nickel (3%)

Political system

Constitution: 1976. President: Dr Fidel Castro Ruz (1976–   ); formerly premier, succeeded Osvaldo Dorticós. Executive power is in the hands of the Council of Ministers. Legislative functions are carried out by the National Assembly of People's Power (president: Dr Juan Escalona Reguera), elected for a five-year period by the Municipal Assemblies on the basis of universal adult (16+) suffrage. Deputies are subject to recall at any time by their electors. A Council of State elected from among the Assembly members replaces the Assembly when the latter is not in session. The current National Assembly dates from 1986. Both the Council of Ministers and the Council of State are headed by the President, whose functions are assumed by the First Vice-President (currently Gen. Raúl Castro Ruz) in the event of his absence or death.

Political organisations

The Cuban Communist party (PCC) is the only legal political party. In 1990 it turned down requests for recognition from the Social Democratic Party/Pascu and the Cuban Human Rights Party. The constitution assigns it the role of 'highest leading force in society and the state'. President Fidel Castro is First Secretary of the PCC.

Main labour organisation: Cuban Workers' Federation/CTC (secretary general: Pedro Ross Leal).

Cuban Human Rights Party (*Partido Pro-Derechos Humanos en Cuba*)

A small, illegal organisation formed in mid-1988 by former members of the Cuban Human Rights Committee founded by dissident sociologist Ricardo Bofill (b. 1943). Bofill himself is now in exile, along with many of the other leaders of the committee. Members of both organisations are accused by the Cuban government of being counter-revolutionaries under the control of the United States. Bofill was jailed three times, the first of these from 1968 to 1972 as a result of the so-called 'microfaction' trial. His other two periods of imprisonment took place in 1980–82 and 1983–86. In 1985 he was adopted as a prisoner of conscience by Amnesty International. In July 1987, Bofill had announced that the Committee would form a Pro-Human Rights Party, an illegal act under the Cuban constitution. Described in its own communiqués as 'a vehicle for spontaneous social mobilisation', the 'party' sought to incorporate the Universal Declaration of Human Rights into the preamble to the Cuban constitution. Its acting head, Hiram Abi Cobas, was arrested with other dissidents in August 1989 and charged with spreading false stories to the foreign media concerning the Ochoa corruption case. He was sentenced to 18 months in prison. Nine more party members, including secretary general Tania Díaz Castro, were arrested in April 1990.

See also **'microfaction'; Ochoa case.**

Cuban missile crisis

A fortnight of confrontation between the US and the USSR (16–29 October 1962) over the presence of Soviet nuclear ground-to-ground missiles on Cuban soil. On 22 October, President John F. Kennedy announced that he was mounting a full-scale naval blockade of Cuba to prevent further deliveries of offensive weapons, pending a decision by Moscow to remove existing missiles. His move was backed by the North Atlantic Treaty Organisation (NATO) and the Organisation of American States (OAS). Moscow at first refused to confirm or deny the presence of the missiles and gave Soviet ships orders to repel any attempted boarding. However, the ships eventually turned back to avoid confrontation, and on 26 October, in a personal letter to Kennedy, Soviet premier Nikita Krushchev confirmed the presence of nuclear weapons, saying they were under his country's control.

On 27 October a U2 spyplane belonging to the US was shot down over Cuba, but Kennedy resisted calls for reprisals. Doubts persist over

whether the plane was brought down by Cuban or Soviet personnel, but at the time Washington assumed it was a provocation carried out on Krushchev's orders. On the same day Krushchev proposed the removal of the missiles in exchange for the removal of US bases in Turkey, but this was modified on the following day to a call for a US commitment not to invade Cuba. Agreement was reached on this basis (without Cuban participation) and the missiles were removed on 29 October. Castro refused to agree to a US demand for territorial inspection, on which its 'no invasion' promise was contingent, despite a request from the UN secretary general. The US maintained its quarantine of Cuba and added a demand that Soviet IL–28 light bombers also be removed from the island. The USSR subsequently claimed that the missiles had been sent at the request of the Cubans, who feared a US attack. However, this version was later refuted by Cuba's leader, Fidel Castro, who said they had been sent at the insistence of Krushchev 'to strengthen international socialism'. The crisis severely strained Soviet-Cuban relations and permanently damaged the trust formerly displayed by Havana towards Moscow (though Castro conceded in 1975 that he had been wrong to criticise Krushchev's accommodation with the US). It also substantially reduced the role of the old guard communists in the Cuban government.
See also **Castro Ruz, Fidel Alejandro; Bay of Pigs invasion.**

Cuban Revolutionary Council: see **Bay of Pigs invasion.**

Cuban Revolutionary Party: see **Martí, José.**

Cuban Revolutionary War

Rebel forces led by Fidel Castro took two years to oust the dictator Fulgencio Batista, from 2 December 1956 when the original group of 82 landed on the southern coast, to 1 January 1959 when Batista fled the country. Immediately located by the government army, the rebels had initially been reduced by casualties, capture and desertion to under 20. When it became clear that Castro had survived, however, Batista suspended civil rights in January 1957. Gradually, the rebels' numbers swelled and they established support among the local population of the Sierra Maestra mountains in the south-east of the island, where they were based. Occasional betrayals were a problem, particularly that of peasant leader Eutimio Guerra, whose instructions enabled the government to bomb the rebel camp. Guerra also agreed to rejoin the group and assassinate Castro, but failed to do so. He was later executed by his former comrades.

In February 1957, Castro was interviewed by Herbert Matthews, a senior editor with the *New York Times*, whose article (which eventually reached the Cuban public) did much to increase the credibility of the rebel leader, both at home and abroad. Fuelled by Batista's growing brutality, even moderate politicians began to plot his downfall and Castro began to receive increased financial support from business leaders. A student group, the Revolutionary Directorate (DR) staged an abortive attack on the presidential palace in March 1957, spurring Batista to new excesses of repression, including for a time the forced relocation of the population of the Sierra Maestra. Tensions emerged between the force in the mountains and their civilian allies of the 26 July Movement (M–26–7) in the cities, who sought to establish the primacy of the urban struggle and convince Castro of the need for a detailed programme. Eventually, Castro did put his name to a moderate document, the Sierra Maestra manifesto, but he seems to have done so for purely tactical reasons.

In September 1957, NCOs sympathetic to Castro staged a poorly-planned uprising which was also bloodily repressed. By early 1958 the rebel force had assumed the structure of a formal army on three separate fronts and was moving to a war of positions. An attempt at a general strike to precipitate Batista's removal in April 1958 was wholly unsuccessful and its failure allowed Castro to take complete control of the M–26–7. Batista then mounted a massive army operation in Oriente province which included bombing the civilian population. By August he was forced to pull his troops out. Copying the successful plan of the independence fighters of 1895, Castro mounted a nationwide offensive with the aim of isolating the cities. Che Guevara's role was to split the country in two and, after he succeeded in establishing a united front with the guerrillas of the DR in the central province of Las Villas, the rebels (by now known as the *'barbudos'*, or bearded ones) consolidated their grip. Batista fled to the Dominican Republic and the advance units of the Las Villas forces arrived in Havana on 2 January 1959.

See also **Castro Ruz, Fidel Alejandro; Batista y Zaldívar; 26 July Movement; Guevara de la Serna;** *Granma.*

Culebra

A small island 30km east of Puerto Rico, of which it is part. The island was used as a US navy gunnery range until 1974, when local protests forced the US to abandon the range. The island was devastated by Hurricane Hugo in 1989.

See also **Vieques; Puerto Rico; military bases (foreign) in the Caribbean; Dog Island.**

Cummins, Hugh: see **Barbados Labour Party.**

D

Daaga, Makandal: see National Joint Action Committee.

Dada, Héctor: see Democratic Convergence.

Dalton, Roque: see People's Revolutionary Army.

Daniel, Simeon
b. 22 August 1934. Premier of Nevis 1983– . Daniel was a teacher before going to London to work as a clerk for nearly ten years. He qualified as a barrister in 1966 and returned to Nevis to found the Nevis Reformation Party (NRP) in 1970 in order to fight for autonomy from St Kitts. He became chairman of the Nevis island council when the NRP won the 1971 local elections. Elected to parliament in 1975, he became leader of the opposition. After the 1980 election Daniel's NRP joined the People's Action Movement (PAM) in a coalition which ended 28 years of Labour Party rule, and Daniel himself became vice-premier and finance minister. His successful demands for Nevisian self-rule delayed the state's independence until 1983, after which he also became premier of Nevis. After PAM increased its majority at the 1984 elections Daniel was demoted to minister of natural resources and the environment.
See also **Nevis; Nevis Reformation Party; People's Action Movement.**

Darrell, Gilbert: see National Liberal Party.

Darsières, Camille
b. 19 May 1932. President of Martinique's regional council 1988– , member of the general council and secretary-general of the Martinican Progressive Party (PPM) 1970– . He was vice-president of the regional council from 1983 until 1988, when he succeeded PPM leader Aimé Césaire as president, though he had fulfilled the function on Césaire's behalf since 1983.
See also **Martinican Progressive Party; Césaire.**

D'Aubuisson Arrieta, Roberto
b. 23 August 1943. Director of the Salvadorean intelligence service under the presidency of Gen. Romero; later, leader of the ARENA party. Trained at the International Police Academy, Washington DC (1965), and in the Panama Canal Zone (1971), D'Aubuisson reached the rank of major but was forced to resign from the army in October 1979 by the new reformist junta. In late 1979/early 1980 he formed a series of extreme

right-wing groups, based on the supposedly outlawed paramilitary force ORDEN, in alliance with landowners and sectors of the armed forces and business community. These included the Salvadorean Nationalist Movement and the National Democratic Front. On 22 December 1979 he founded the Broad National Front (FAN), with the aim of replacing the junta with a coalition of right-wing businessmen and officers.

Often accused of heading death squads (particularly the White Warriors' Union/UGB), D'Aubuisson was described by US ambassador Robert White in 1980 as a 'pathological killer'. He is blamed by the Christian Democrats (PDC) for the murder of party member Attorney General Mario Zamora on 23 February 1980 (the PDC threatened to resign from the government if D'Aubuisson was not brought to justice, though the threat was never carried out). He was also accused of plotting to overthrow the military/PDC junta. After the plot was foiled on 2 May 1980, he was arrested on 8 May along with 23 alleged co-conspirators, in whose possession were found incriminating documents, including one linking D'Aubuisson with the murder of Archbishop Oscar Romero (whom he had publicly threatened). In 1985 a former Salvadorean intelligence officer also accused the ex-major of involvement in this crime. The 24 were released after five days. Eight out of 14 garrisons supported him against the reformist junta member Col. Majano, and Majano was stripped of his command of the army.

In September 1981, D'Aubuisson became president of the newly-formed ARENA party, which won 19 constituent assembly seats, and was elected assembly president. He lost the 1984 presidential elections to the PDC's José Napoleón Duarte, and after a poor showing in the 1985 legislative elections he resigned from the party presidency, though remaining honorary life president. His bad image in the US, where he was accused of drug smuggling as well as death squad murders, encouraged the party to lower his profile.

See also **ARENA; death squad; Romero, Archbishop Oscar Arnulfo; ORDEN.**

death squad (*escuadrón de la muerte*)

A phrase coined in the 1960s in Brazil by unofficial units within the police which specialised in the torture and murder of alleged criminals and later (1969) turned their attention to 'subversives', with the assistance of the army. The technique has also been used by Central American armies and security forces, as well as in Haiti. 'Counter terror' was an integral part of the counter-insurgency doctrine taught by the US military to Latin Americans. More direct financial and organisational involvement by the Pentagon and the Central Intelligence Agency (CIA) has often been alleged.

The first recorded Guatemalan group, known as Action for the Defence of Democracy (ADED), was formed in 1963, but not until 1966, after the election of civilian president Méndez Montenegro, did death squads begin to proliferate. One source lists 31 separate groups formed between 1966 and 1980. The Regional Centre for Telecommunications, an intelligence agency based inside the presidential palace, drew up lists for political killings after top-level discussions. The army and the police both carried out the murders. In 1981, Amnesty International reported that nearly 5,000 people had been killed in this way since 1978.

In El Salvador security forces and the paramilitary organisation ORDEN provided personnel for death squads prior to 1979–80, when army units became involved on a large scale. Killings were co-ordinated by the intelligence agency ANSESAL, and by senior army officers. In the worst year, 1981, at least 13,500 non-combatants were murdered by army and security forces. Death squad killings declined, but did not stop, after the 1984 election of José Napoleón Duarte as president. They increased again with the ARENA government (1989–), including the murder of six Jesuits at the Central American University (UCA) in November 1989.

In Honduras such killings have been much less common, but reached a peak under armed forces commander Gen. Gustavo Alvarez (1981–4). Among the names used by death squads (apart from *Escuadrón de la Muerte*) have been:

An Eye for an Eye (*Ojo por Ojo*) (Guatemala): operated in 1970, its main target being the University of San Carlos, Guatemala City.

Anti-communist Action Alliance (*Alianza de Acción Anticomunista/* AAA): active in the Alvarez years in Honduras. Re-emerged with death lists in 1988.

Central American Anti-communist Hand (*Mano Anticomunista Centroamericana/*MACA): said to have originated in Guatemala; appeared in El Salvador in December 1988.

Eastern Solidarity Committee (*Comité de Solidaridad Oriental/*COSOR): emerged in late 1988, focusing on El Salvador's San Miguel province.

FALANGE (*Fuerzas Armadas de Liberación-Guerra de Eliminación/* Armed Forces of Liberation-War of Elimination): El Salvador, 1975.

Honduran Anticommunist Movement (*Movimiento Anticomunista Hondureño/*MACHO): emerged in 1980–81 with threats against students expressing solidarity with the Salvadorean left.

Jaguar of Justice (*Jaguar de Justicia/*JJ): Guatemala, 1989.

Maximiliano Hernández Martínez Brigade: El Salvador, from 1980.

Organisation for Liberation from Communism (*Organización por la Liberación del Communismo/*OLC): El Salvador, 1977.

Revolutionary Anticommunist Extermination Action (*Acción Revolucionaria Anticomunista de Exterminación/*ARDE): emerged in El Salvador in late 1988.

Secret Anti-Communist Army (*Ejército Secreto Anticomunista/*ESA): emerged in Guatemala during a general strike in 1978. ESA letterheads were said by a defector to have been stored at the Interior Ministry. This name was also used in El Salvador in recent years by the self-styled armed wing of the 'National Liberation Party', which staged kidnaps and issued death lists aimed at the National University (UES). The (or an) ESA was again active in Guatemala in the late 1980s.

White Hand (*Mano Blanca*, aka MANO): emerged in Guatemala in 1966 and was reorganised around 1977. (An organisation with the same name was formed at this time in Nicaragua, and another operated in Honduras in the early 1980s.) MANO was said to have been founded by Col. Enrique Trinidad Oliva (assassinated 1967) and led (until his death in 1968) by Raúl Lorenzana. In 1968, *Mano Blanca* was involved in the kidnap of Archbishop Mario Casariego, apparently with the aim of provoking a coup by rightist groups within the armed forces. A *Mano Blanca* was again claiming responsibility for killings in 1988.

White Warriors' Union (*Union Guerrera Blanca*/UGB): emerged in El Salvador in the mid-70s at a time of agrarian reform proposals by the Molina government. In June 1977 it accused the church of backing communism and threatened to kill all Jesuits in El Salvador. It published a leaflet with the slogan 'Be a patriot – kill a priest'. Maj. Roberto D'Aubuisson, a former National Guard intelligence chief and latterly a leading right-wing politician, is said to have been linked with the UGB.

See also **ORDEN; Tonton Macoutes; National Guard** (El Salvador); **Mutual Support Group**.

'Death to Somoza' operation: see **Pastora Gómez**.

Debray, Régis: see *foquismo*.

de Céspedes, President: see **Batista y Zaldívar**.

déchoukage ('uprooting')
A creole term used in Haiti after the fall of the Duvalier dictatorship in 1986 to describe the movement to purge the country of all Duvalierists or anyone else who offended, either by chasing them out of their jobs or more commonly looting or destroying their homes. In July 1987 a radical Catholic bishop, Willy Romélus (b. 17 January 1931) of Jérémie, popularised what he said should be a further stage of *déchoukage* – 'raché manyok, ba nou tè a blanch!' (Pull up your manioc and leave us clean ground!)

See also **Duvalierism; Duvalier, Jean-Claude; Haiti, Roman Catholic Church**.

Declaration of St George's (1979)

Statement of intent by the then left-wing leaders of Grenada, Dominica and St Lucia to allow freedom of movement between their countries. It was never put into practice.

See also **Caribbean Community; Organisation of Eastern Caribbean States**.

dedazo: see *destape*.

de Haenen, Rémy

b. 12 February 1916. Former political leader of the French Caribbean island of Saint Barthélémy. De Haenen, a British-born former naval officer and commercial pilot, settled in the island in 1952 and began to develop it as a tourist resort. A strong right-winger, he was mayor of the island 1962–77. Violence erupted in 1975 over a new tax he proposed

and against his authoritarian rule, and French riot police were sent to the island. One of the rebel leaders, Charles Querrard, was elected mayor in his place in 1976. De Haenen is leader of the Guadeloupe branch of the extreme right-wing National Front.
See also **Saint Barthélémy**.

Déjoie II, Louis

b. 28 May 1928. Conservative Haitian politician. The son of Louis Dejoie, a wealthy mulatto senator who officially lost the 1957 presidential election to François Duvalier, Dejoie junior, an agronomist, built up a prosperous construction business during a 25-year exile in Puerto Rico. After briefly joining the exiled Leslie Manigat's RDNP party in 1981, he revived his father's National Agricultural and Industrial Party (PAIN) (f. 1956) the following year to reclaim the family's political legacy. He returned to Haiti after the fall of the dictatorship in 1986 and was a candidate in aborted presidential elections of 1987.
See also **Duvalier, François; Manigat**.

de la Espriella, Ricardo: see Noriega Morena.

de la Guardia, Antonio (Tony): see Ochoa case.

De la Madrid Hurtado, Miguel

b. 1934. President of Mexico 1982–8. Studied law at the Universidad Nacional Autónoma de México (UNAM). His rise within the Institutional Revolutionary Party (PRI) was regarded as indicative of the strengthening of the more 'technocratic' wing of the party, at the expense of the political old guard. Apart from law, De la Madrid also studied economics, taking a postgraduate degree at Harvard University from where he returned to embark upon an essentially administrative career. He worked at the Banco de México, was assistant director of finance at Pemex, the state oil company (1970–72), director of public sector credit and under-secretary of finance. Under the presidency of José López Portillo he was secretary for planning and the budget, one of the key ministerial posts in the admistration, in 1979–80.

Nominated by López Portillo as the official PRI candidate, De la Madrid won the July 1982 presidential elections with 71.6% of the votes cast. He took office in December 1982, only months after the country defaulted on its foreign debt payments. A financial conservative, the new president pursued austerity policies for the length of his six-year term, signing stand-by agreements with the IMF and rescheduling Mexico's commercial bank debt. The administration's cautious economic policy, coupled with the disastrous Mexico City earthquake of September 1985 and the collapse of international oil prices in early 1986, meant that throughout the *sexenio* living standards fell sharply and, in view of most analysts, underlying social tensions increased.

Allegations of blatant electoral fraud in municipal and state elections in 1984, 1985, 1986 and 1987 led to violent protests by supporters of the right-wing opposition National Action Party (PAN). Although De la Madrid sought improved relations with the United States and was generally seen as less openly critical than his predecessors of US Central American policies, there remained points of tension with Washington. One of the most sensitive was the drugs issue, particularly after the kidnapping and murder of a US Drug Enforcement Agency (DEA) employee, Enrique Camarena, in Guadalajara in February 1985.

In domestic politics, relations between the president and Fidel Velázquez, the leader of the CTM labour grouping, came under strain. Velázquez ensured that the union movement accepted wage restraint, but felt insufficiently recompensed by the president. He was particularly annoyed at the choice of Carlos Salinas de Gortari in October 1987 as the candidate to succeed De la Madrid.

See also **Institutional Revolutionary Party; National Action Party; Salinas de Gortari; Echeverría Alvarez**.

de Lugo, Ron

b. 2 August 1930. Delegate of the US Virgin Islands in the US Congress 1973–79, 1981–   . A real estate dealer, former radio journalist and member of the Democratic Party, de Lugo was elected to the USVI senate in 1956 and served until 1966. He was administrator of St. Croix from 1961–2. He was the USVI representative in Washington from 1969 until 1972, when he was elected as the first Virgin Islands delegate to the US Congress. He became chairman of the House of Representatives insular affairs committee. In 1974 and 1978 he ran unsuccessfully for governor.

See also **Luis.**

Delvalle, Eric Arturo

b. 2 February 1937. President of Panama, 1985–8. The leader of the right-wing Republican Party (PR), Delvalle served as first vice-president to Nicolás Ardito Barletta from 1984 until the latter's overthrow by the Defence Forces in September 1985, whereupon he replaced him as president. He is president of one of the country's largest sugar companies as well as of nine other businesses, most of them in the service sector.

Delvalle's government was seriously threatened by strikes and demonstrations which began in mid-1987 aimed at ousting the country's military strong man, Gen. Noriega. It responded by censoring the opposition press, banning demonstrations against the government and ordering the arrest of around 40 opposition leaders. The country's economy deteriorated sharply and in October the government was forced to introduce an emergency economic programme, including budget cuts. The National Banking Commission stated that capital flight due to the crisis had reached a billion dollars in a few months. Relations with the US, which backed the opposition National Civic Crusade, became very strained as military and economic aid was cut off and the US Senate called for Noriega's resignation. Delvalle's vice-president, Roderick Esquivel, was excluded from the government after calling for an independent commission to investigate the charges against Noriega, a political amnesty and an end to censorship. His party, the Liberals (PL), withdrew from the ruling Unade coalition.

In February 1988, after Noriega was indicted on drugs charges in the US, Delvalle, with the backing of Washington, tried to dismiss him as head of the Defence Forces. Instead, he was himself removed from the presidency and replaced by Manuel Solís Palma, the education minister. Delvalle went into hiding and then into exile, while the US stepped up its economic sanctions in an attempt to remove the general. Recognised by the US as the legitimate president, Delvalle was seen as a possible mediator between Washington and Panama. The Christian Democrats (PDC) and the Nationalist Republican Liberal Movement (Molirena) initially backed the US call for the ex-president to head a government of reconstruction, but Delvalle's importance declined after the abortive May 1989 elections as his claim to the presidency faded. The post-invasion government issued a warrant for his arrest on suspicion of having misused government funds.
See also **National Liberation Coalition; Noriega Morena**.

Delvalle, Max: see **Republican Party** (Panama).

Demas, William
b. 14 November 1929. Caribbean economist. After training in Britain, Demas was an economic adviser to the government of his native Trinidad, 1959–69. He became a pioneer in regional economic unity efforts as the first secretary-general of the regional body Carifta in 1970 and of its successor, Caricom, in 1973. He succeeded Sir Arthur Lewis as president of the Caribbean Development Bank in 1974. He resigned in 1988 to become governor of the Trinidad-Tobago central bank.
See also **Caribbean Community; Lewis, Sir Arthur**.

Democratic Accord Committee (*Comité d'Entente Démocratique*/CED): see **Gilles**.

Democratic Action Congress (DAC): see **Robinson; Tobago; National Alliance for Reconstruction**.

Democratic Alliance of Civic Opposition (*Alianza Democrática de Oposición Cívica*/ADOC)
A coalition of right-wing parties founded (as the Opposition Democratic Alliance/ADO) to fight the 1984 Panamanian elections, in which it won 27 seats out of 67. The founding members of ADO were the Christian Democrats (PDC), the Authentic Panameñista Party (PPA) and the Liberals (Molirena). Two other groups, the People's Action Party and the Authentic Liberal Party, subsequently joined the alliance. ADO's presidential candidate in 1984 was Arnulfo Arias, three times president of Panama and leader of the PPA. The Alliance claimed the elections, in which Arias was officially beaten by less than 2,000 votes out of 600,000 cast, were fraudulent, an allegation widely accepted both within Panama and internationally. The PPA was still calling in 1987 for the results to be reassessed and Arias awarded victory, while other sectors of ADO favoured the election of a constituent assembly to prevent further electoral frauds.

In July 1987, following accusations of fraud, assassination and drug trafficking against defence forces chief Gen. Noriega by an ousted subordinate, ADO demanded the speedy replacement of the 'current militarist regime' with a new government and the 'immediate removal' of Noriega. It also backed the formation of the National Civic Crusade (CCN), a broad coalition of opposition groups committed to 'demilitarising' the government. ADO leaders, notably Ricardo Arias of the PDC, were individually prominent in the CCN, although the parties themselves did not become members.

Prior to the 1989 elections ADO suffered a serious internal dispute over the presidential candidacy, which eventually went to Guillermo Endara, leader of the PPA faction still in the alliance (along with the PDC, Molirena and the PLA). Renamed ADOC, the coalition was universally held – except by the government – to have won by a substantial majority. The election results were annulled, but ADOC was installed as the government of Panama after the December 1989 US invasion.
See also **Endara Galimany; Panama, US invasion (1989); National Civic Crusade; Christian Democrat Party** (Panama); **Authentic Panameñista Party; Arias Calderón; Arias Madrid**.

Democratic Conservative Party of Nicaragua (*Partido Conservador Demócrata*/PCDN)

Founded in 1979 by three factions of Nicaragua's traditional Conservative Party which had participated in the anti-Somoza Broad Opposition Front (FAO), the PCDN represents the political tradition of the anti-Somoza Conservative Pedro Joaquín Chamorro. One of its leaders, Rafael Córdova Rivas, joined the Junta of National Reconstruction (JGRN) (1980–84), though not as a PCDN representative. In 1984 the PCDN split in two over the issue of electoral participation, with those opposed (dubbed 'legitimists') forming the Nicaraguan Conservative Party (PCN). Led by Miriam Arguello and Mario Rappaccioli, the PCN joined the abstentionist Nicaraguan Democratic Co-ordinator (CDN). The PCD (*Agueristas*) took part in the 1984 elections, nominating Clemente Guido for the presidency. He won 14% of the vote, and the PCD became the largest opposition party in the national assembly, with 14 seats. It then suffered a further split, with four deputies under Enrique Sotelo Borgen (all of whom had been expelled for allegedly taking bribes from the US embassy) forging a pact with the Independent Liberals (PLI). This faction became known as the 'non-officialist' PCDN.

Guido declined to sign the 1987 constitution, but his alternate (stand-in) deputy did sign. In mid-1987, Córdova Rivas staged a hunger strike in an attempt to restore party unity, which suffered from the need to seek broad support while retaining the backing of the landowners who provide the PCDN's financial base. The party remained split, however, with one faction led by Eduardo Molina and the other (now called the Conservative National Alliance Party/PANC) by Hernaldo Zúñiga. The PDCN stood alone in the 1990 elections, with Molina as its presidential candidate. The PANC, though not legally recognised, joined the victorious UNO coalition. The PCN, now called the National Conservative Party/PNC, itself later split, with Miriam Arguello forming the Conservative Popular Alliance Party/PAPC. Both halves joined UNO, and Arguello was elected leader of the National Assembly after the 1990 elections. See also **Nicaraguan Democratic Co-ordinator; Chamorro Cardenal, Pedro Joaquín; National Opposition Union**.

Democratic Convergence (*Convergencia Democrática*)

An alliance formed in El Salvador in November 1987 between two member parties of the Democratic Revolutionary Front (FDR) and the Social Democrat Party (PSD, f. 1986). The two FDR parties are the National Revolutionary Movement (MNR), a member of the Socialist International, which began as group around lawyer and university teacher Dr Guillermo Ungo in 1964 and commenced public activities in 1965; and the Popular Social Christian Movement (MPSC), a 1980 breakaway from the Christian Democrat Party (PDC) led by Dr Rubén Zamora. The MNR was granted legal status in 1967 and won two seats in the 1968 legislative elections, but lost them in 1970 after an internal split. Its leaders were unwilling at this stage to join forces with the groups on the left such as the Communist Party (PCS). In the 1972 and 1977 elections, however, they opted to participate with the communist front party, the UDN, and the PDC in the National Opposition Union (UNO) alliance, which is widely believed to have been defrauded of victory on both occasions. The MNR joined a similar but broader coalition, the Popular Forum, in 1979, and with the UDN and the PDC took part in the military/civilian government which followed the reformist coup of 15 October 1979, leaving – along with the UDN – in January 1980, and eventually (April 1980) becoming a founder member of the FDR. The FDR in turn formed an alliance with the guerrillas of the Farabundo Martí National Liberation Front (FMLN).

Dr Ungo, who had been a member of the post-coup junta, succeeded the murdered FDR president Enrique Alvarez in late 1980. The MPSC leader, Rubén Zamora, was minister of the presidency in the post-October 1979 government, while co-founder Héctor Dada had belonged to the ruling junta. Zamora became a member of the FDR's 7-strong political-diplomatic commission. Following the signing of the Arias peace plan in August 1987, Zamora took the lead in testing the possibility of a return to civilian politics, and on 26 November 1986, with Ungo and PSD leader Mario Reni Roldán, confirmed the formation (announced three weeks earlier) of the Democratic Convergence at a meeting in San Salvador. The PSD stated that the agreement (which allowed for the autonomy of each party) did not imply its allegiance to the principles of the FDR, while the political and military (FMLN) wings of the rebel organisation said there was no question of a split between them over the tactic. The aims of the CD include an end to US interference in El Salvador, a ceasefire and free elections, agreement on a programme to combat economic injustice, non-alignment and respect for human rights. Ungo and Roldán stood for the presidency and vice-presidency in El Salvador in

1989 but won only about 3% of the votes, a result which Ungo blamed partly on disruption by the FMLN.
See also **Democratic Revolutionary Front** (El Salvador); **Ungo**.

Democratic Current: see **National Democratic Front; Institutional Revolutionary Party;** *destape*.

Democratic Front Against Repression (FDCR): see **Peasant Unity Committee**.

Democratic Front of El Salvador (FDES): see **Democratic Revolutionary Front**.

Democratic Labour Party (DLP) (Barbados)
A social democratic party founded in 1955 by Errol Barrow as a break-away from Grantley Adams's Barbados Labour Party, the DLP lost the general election in 1956 (4–20) and failed to win any seats in the West Indies federal elections in 1958. The party won the 1961 elections 14–10 and Barrow became premier. The DLP won again in 1966 (14–10) and 1971 (18–6) but was beaten 7–17 in 1976 partly as a result of hardship caused by the rise in world oil prices. Barrow resigned and handed over the party to Frederick Smith, but he became leader again in 1978 when Smith resigned. The DLP lost the 1981 elections 10–17 but, helped by a promise of tax reforms and by the death of prime minister Tom Adams, beat the BLP 24–3 in 1986 and Barrow returned to power. Erskine Sandiford became party leader and prime minister after Barrow died in 1987.
See also **Sandiford; Barrow; Barbados Labour Party; Adams, Tom**.

Democratic Labour Party (DLP) (Trinidad-Tobago): see **Robinson**.

Democratic Left: see **Liberal Party** (Honduras).

Democratic Liberation Union (UDEL): see **Chamorro Cardenal, Pedro Joaquín**.

Democratic National Union (Unade): see **National Liberation Coalition**.

Democratic Party (Costa Rica): see **Calderón Guardia**.

Democratic Party (DP) (Netherlands Antilles)
A conservative Curaçao-based party, founded in 1944 by Efrain Jonckheer, which formed the first coalition government when the state was granted autonomy in 1954. Jonckheer was premier until 1968, when he handed over to Ciro Kroon. After an uprising of petroleum industry workers in Curaçao in 1969, Kroon resigned and Ernesto Petronia became party leader and the country's first black premier. The party's mainly-white leadership was challenged by younger figures led by Sylvius 'Boy' Rozendal. But Ronchi Isa, a lawyer of Lebanese origin, became party leader and premier in 1971. He was replaced a few months later by O.

Beaujon but then returned as premier until 1973, when the DP won only four seats at a general election and yielded power to the National People's Party after 19 years.

The DP recovered to win six seats at the 1977 poll and Rozendal became premier. In the 1979 elections it won only three seats and was eclipsed by the new social democratic New Antilles Movement of Don Martina, who succeeded Rozendal as premier. Businessman Agustín Díaz then became party leader. The DP retained its three seats in the 1982 and 1985 general elections, but acquired only one in the 1990 poll.

See also **New Antilles Movement; National People's Party; Martina; 'black power'**.

Democratic Party of National Co-operation (*Partido Democrático de Cooperación Nacional*/PDCN)

Founded in Guatemala in 1983 by individuals with close ties to the co-operative movement and some left-wing support, the PDCN failed to win any seats in the 1984 constituent assembly elections and was taken over by engineering professor, businessman and 'born again' Protestant Jorge Serrano Elías, a veteran anti-communist. Serrano, who belonged to the fundamentalist 'Church of the Word' sect and was head of the unelected council of state under Gen. Riós Montt, reoriented the party towards the business community, from which it then received financial support. Backing also came from some cotton and coffee producers, many of them former supporters of the National Liberation Movement (MLN). It entered a coalition with the Revolutionary Party (PR) in July 1985, with Serrano as presidential candidate, which won 11 seats. It stressed co-operativism and Protestant fundamentalism as strong elements in its conservative programme. After the election, in which Serrano won 14% of the vote, he withdrew from the party to organise the Solidarity Action Movement (MAS), while the PDCN itself formed a tacit alliance with the Christian Democrat (DCG) government. With the PR and the Nationalist Revolution Party/PAR, it put forward the presidential candidacy of former foreign minister Fernando Andrade in 1990, but Andrade withdrew at an early stage of the campaign. Rolando Baquiaux Gómez was elected PDCN secretary general in 1986.

See also **National Liberation Movement; Ríos Montt**.

Democratic Party of the (US) Virgin Islands (DPVI): see Farrelly; Independent Citizens' Movement; de Lugo; Evans.

Democratic Renovation Party (PRD): see Carazo Odio; Social Christian Unity Party.

Democratic Revolutionary Alliance: see ARDE.

Democratic Revolutionary Front (Cuba): see Bay of Pigs invasion.

Democratic Revolutionary Front (El Salvador) (*Frente Democrático Revolucionario*/FDR)

A political coalition founded on 18 April 1980 in El Salvador to oppose the military-Christian Democrat junta installed in March 1980. The FDR

was the successor to the short-lived Democratic Front of El Salvador
(FDES), founded on 4 April by the Popular Liberation Movement (MLP,
a civilian organisation linked to the PRTC guerrillas), the Popular Christian Democrat Tendency (TPDC, later MPSC), the National Revolutionary Movement (MNR) and several trade union, student and professional
organisations. The crucial addition was the Revolutionary Co-ordinating
Committee of the Masses (CRM), comprising the so-called 'popular
organisations' – broad-based worker-student-peasant coalitions, each
linked to a guerrilla group. These were: the Popular Revolutionary Bloc
(BPR), the 28 February Popular Leagues (LP–28) and the Unified Popular Action Front (FAPU). The MLP was also a member of the CRM, as
was the illegal Communist Party's (PCS) front organisation, the nationalist Democratic Union (UDN), though neither could match the size of
the other three.

The FDR proclaimed its 'decisive task' to be the installation of a
'democratic revolutionary government' which, among other things, would
replace the 'security forces' with a police force; nationalise the banking
and financial system, along with foreign trade, oil refining and electricity
distribution; and carry out a thorough agrarian reform. On 27 November
six FDR leaders, including its president, former agriculture minister
Enrique Alvarez Córdova, were abducted by troops in San Salvador and
murdered. The FDR was effectively driven underground by late 1980: its
political-diplomatic commission (including president Guillermo Ungo of
the MNR and MPSC leader Rubén Zamora) became the external diplomatic wing of the insurgency.

In 1983 the FDR/FMLN, fortified by military successes, sought to gain
international recognition for the 'state of belligerency' in El Salvador.
US special envoy Richard Stone held talks with FDR leaders in Costa
Rica in August, and two rounds of talks were held with the Salvadorean
government 'peace commission'; but no progress was made. In January
1984 the FDR/FMLN abandoned the installation of a 'democratic revolutionary government' as an immediate aim, substituting a 'broad-based
provisional government' (GAP). This would include representatives of
manual workers, peasants, teachers, white-collar workers, professionals,
universities, political parties, business interests, an army purged of
'repressive elements', and the FDR/FMLN itself. It would end the state
of siege; free political prisoners; abolish the security forces (but not the
army), the death squads and the ARENA party (accused of death squad
links); purge the army and incorporate FMLN combatants; investigate
human rights abuses; implement an emergency reconstruction plan and
literacy campaign; and prepare for elections.

On 15 October 1984, President Duarte met FDR/FMLN leaders for
peace talks in La Palma, El Salvador, but little progress was made beyond
an agreement to 'humanise' the war. At a subsequent meeting in Ayagu-
alo (1985) the FDR/FMLN proposed a 'phased settlement' involving a
government of conciliation representing both sides and the integration of
their armies, but this was not accepted and the talks stalled. Tactical
differences between the FDR and FMLN led to increasingly strained

relations. In 1985 it was agreed that the FMLN would have autonomy in military matters and the FDR on the diplomatic front. (A new alliance between the two fronts, including a more detailed redefinition of the relationship, was signed on 30 November 1986.)

On 10 July 1986 the FDR/FMLN made a further concession as part of a 'programmatic proposal for national dialogue': the resolution of the problem posed by the two armies would be left to a transitional government representing both sides. But a meeting planned for September 1986 inside El Salvador was not attended by the FDR/FMLN because the army had refused to demilitarise the site of the talks. In May 1987 an 18-point proposal by the FDR/FMLN for the humanisation of the war, including an end to the laying of mines and the bombing of the civilian population, was turned down by Duarte. The two sides met in San Salvador on 4–5 October 1987 within the framework of the Central American peace plan (the Arias Plan), but agreed only on the establishment of two joint commissions. The work of these commissions was disrupted by the assassination, on 26 October, of Herbert Anaya, president of the Salvadorean (non-governmental) Human Rights Commission, which led the FMLN to pull out of a scheduled meeting. Further offers of talks by the FDR/FMLN were turned down.

However, on 6 November 1987 the MNR and the MPSC, together with the internal Social Democrat Party (PSD – not an FDR member), announced that Ungo and Zamora would return to El Salvador to examine the possibility of working politically inside the country. Their visit was marked by a unilateral FMLN ceasefire. Fresh FDR/FMLN overtures met with silence from the government, but the MNR-MPSC-PSD initiative (named the 'Democratic Convergence') took root, opening up new electoral possibilities. However, despite the FMLN's insistence that there was no split, a tour of Latin America by FMLN leaders alone in late 1988 seemed to confirm that the FDR as such had effectively ceased to exist.

See also **Democratic Convergence; Farabundo Martí National Liberation Front; Ungo; Franco-Mexican declaration; Duarte; Christian Democrat Party** (El Salvador).

Democratic Revolutionary Party (*Partido Revolucionario Democrático*/PRD)

Founded in Panama in 1978 at the instigation of Gen. Omar Torrijos, the PRD is sometimes referred to as the Torrijista Party. Its original function was to maintain and promote the general's political philosophy, despite his formal transfer of power to Aristides Royo (who became a PRD member), and the PRD was closely associated with the political role of the Defence Forces (formerly the National Guard). It was composed of various factions, including former Communist Party (PPP) youth members and student leaders, as well as Christian Democrats and Liberals, reflecting support among the wealthy who benefited from a corrupt military regime as well as among the poor who remained loyal to the populist tradition. Blacks tended to support it, in part because of the racist policies when in office of its erstwhile major opponent Arnulfo Arias.

Despite the death of Torrijos (its *de facto* leader) in 1981, the PRD continued to play a major role in Panamanian politics. Although a consultative member of the Socialist International (from which it was expelled after the 1989 elections), it moved to the right under the influence of Defence Forces commander Manuel Noriega. In 1984 its candidate for president, Nicolás Ardito Barletta, won a disputed election against ex-president Arias, and the PRD-led coalition Unade took the majority of seats in the national assembly. However, Ardito Barletta was ousted by the National Guard in September 1985 and replaced by his vice-president, Eric Arturo Delvalle, leader of the Republican Party (PR). In late 1986, PRD influence over the government was made evident when it imposed cabinet changes on a reluctant President Delvalle. The move was also seen, however, as an attempt to resolve deep internal divisions in the PRD, principally between the former communists of the so-called 'tendency' and the 'business sector' of the party.

In the (subsequently annulled) May 1989 elections, PRD leader Carlos Duque stood as presidential candidate of the official COLINA alliance. In the aftermath of the December 1989 US invasion the PRD was invited to join the commission allocating seats in the legislature. It withdrew, however, on finding that it was to be given only six.

See also **Torrijos Herrera; Noriega Morena; Delvalle; Ardito Barletta; Panama, US invasion (1989).**

Democratic Socialist Party (PSD) (Guatemala): see Socialist (Second) International.

Denoon, Lennox: see Tobago.

député-maire
In France and its overseas possessions, someone simultaneously holding the posts of deputy (member) of the French National Assembly and of mayor of a town. It is frequently translated in error as deputy (assistant) mayor.

de Ronceray, Hubert
b. 20 August 1932. Haitian politician. A sociologist, de Ronceray set up a research institute, CHISS, in Haiti in 1966 and taught at the state university. He was deputy education minister, 1972–4, and labour and social affairs minister, 1978–80, after which he was named Haitian ambassador to Unesco in Paris, becoming chairman of its human rights committee in 1984. He spoke out against the Duvalier regime from 1983 and was briefly jailed in 1984 and 1985. After the fall of the dictatorship he formed the Mobilisation for National Development (MDN) party. In the re-run presidential election in 1988 he officially came second, but some reliable reports say he unofficially won. He was deported to the US in early 1990 after a state of siege was declared.

See also **Duvalier, Jean-Claude.**

desaparecidos

The 'disappeared ones' – the name given to the victims of political persecution who, after being kidnapped, are never traced. The kidnapping of political opponents has a long history in Latin America's conflicts; but it was only after the 1950s that the practice of 'disappearances' was refined and used systematically for purposes of repression by the state.

The massive use of secret police and military units to kidnap and execute political dissidents, while the central government denied all involvement, made its appearance in Guatemala after the 1954 coup d'état, although examples of this form of repression can be found under earlier Central American military regimes. Estimates of the total number of 'disappeared' in Guatemala in the three decades after 1954 range as high as 30,000. Disappearances were widespread under the Somoza dynasty in Nicaragua. The technique later moved to the Southern Cone of Latin America, appearing in Brazil (after the 1964 coup), Chile (after 1973), Uruguay (after 1973) and Argentina (from the early 1970s, but particularly after the 1976 coup). In Argentina's 'dirty war' of the 1970s a minimum of 9,000 people disappeared, although the actual figure is believed to be higher. In virtually all these cases they were kidnapped by police and army personnel, wearing civilian clothes and driving unmarked cars. Military units maintained secret lists of names detailing those targeted for abduction, torture and murder; the 'disappeared' were held in clandestine places of detention known as *'pozos'* ('holes').

In the late 1970s large-scale disappearances took place in El Salvador, in a process linked to extreme state repression and the emergence of guerrilla insurgencies. They were also used in the 'dirty war' between the Peruvian military and the *Sendero Luminoso* (Shining Path) guerrillas in the 1980s, in which over a thousand people disappeared after being arrested by the military. Even in more stable societies such as Mexico, politically motivated 'disappearances' have played a role in attempts to quell protest movements.

A separate phenomenon in both Peru and Colombia in the late 1980s (though going back many years in the Colombia case) was the spread of 'commercial' kidnapping rings. Most countries in which 'disappearances' have taken place have also developed human rights organisations struggling either to trace the *desaparecidos* or at least to determine the circumstances of their deaths and the identity of those repsonsible. Among the better-known groups of relatives of the disappeared are the Mothers of the Plaza de Mayo in Argentina and the Mutual Support Group (GAM) of Guatemala.

destape

The traditional process by which the Mexican president reveals the identity of his successor, who will be adopted as the official candidate of the ruling Institutional Revolutionary Party (PRI). Although the *destape* ritual remained unchanged for decades, it was affected by growing pressure for reform in the late 1980s. Under the terms of the ritual, the various potential candidates are known as the *tapados* ('covered ones'), of whom only one will be *destapado* ('uncovered' or unveiled). The art of politics for many members of the PRI has been to correctly anticipate who will be chosen (who will be *el bueno* – the good one) and to express support for him before his elevation, thereby increasing the chances of being rewarded with the offer of a ministry or other post. The *destape* normally occurs some nine months before the elections. While theoretically it is the result of internal consultations within the party, in practice most analysts agree that it is the incumbent president who directly nominates his successor after hearing the opinions of the main pressure groups. This process is also popularly referred to as *el dedazo* (the pointing finger), to emphasise the authoritarian nature of the succession.

In 1987–8 a sector of the PRI led by Porfirio Muñoz Ledo and Cuauhtémoc Cárdenas criticised the succession procedure, calling for a more open and democratic system with party members voting for the candidate of their choice. The dissidents formed the 'Democratic Current' but were shunned by the party leadership. As a concession to the demands for change, however, President Miguel De la Madrid for the first time formally announced a list of six pre-candidates for the succession, from among whom Carlos Salinas de Gortari was chosen in the traditionally secretive manner, going on to win the July 1988 elections by a small margin and amid allegations of fraud. Cárdenas, who stood as an opposition candidate, claimed to be the true victor of the electoral contest. See also **Institutional Revolutionary Party; Salinas de Gortari; Cárdenas, Cuauhtémoc**.

Díaz, Adolfo: see Somoza García.

Díaz, Agustín: see Democratic Party (Netherlands Antilles).

Díaz, Domingo: see Arias Madrid.

Díaz, Col. Enrique: see Castillo Armas.

Díaz, Mauricio: see Popular Social Christian Party.

Díaz, Gen. Porfirio: see Mexican Revolution.

Díaz, Col. Roberto: see Noriega Morena.

Díaz Arrivillaga, Efraín: see Christian Democrat Party of Honduras.

Díaz Ordaz, Gustavo

1911–79. President of Mexico, 1964–70. Considered one of the most conservative presidents of Mexico in recent times, Díaz Ordaz succeeded in maintaining a good rate of economic growth (on average 6% per annum), but is remembered most of all for the bloody repression of student protest in 1968. Born in the strongly Catholic state of Puebla, he held a variety of judicial and administrative posts there, rising to be president of the state supreme court and later sitting in both houses of the federal congress in the period 1946–52. Appointed secretary of the interior (*secretario de gobernación*) under the presidency of Adolfo López Mateos, he was quickly identified with hard-line policies. Under his orders police were sent in to break the 1959 railway strike. Following the failed US-supported attempt to invade Cuba through the Bay of Pigs in 1961, Díaz Ordaz was involved in a crack-down on domestic leftists. He applied the laws on 'social dissolution' to arrest David Alfaro Siqueiros and other PCM members.

Standing as the Institutional Revolutionary Party (PRI) candidate in 1964, he obtained 88.8% of the total vote. In power, he at first appeared ready to support a major reform of the ruling party, signalled by his appointment of Carlos Madrazo as the PRI president. But when Madrazo tried to clean up nomination procedures within the PRI, the party old guard rebelled and forced Díaz Ordaz to sack him. The president increased spending on education and urban renewal and was a driving force behind the signing of the Tlatelolco Treaty on nuclear non-proliferation. But it was the Tlatelolco massacre – the killing of up to 300 student demonstrators in the Plaza de Tlatelolco in October 1968, just before the start of the Olympic Games in Mexico City – which earned the government international notoriety and condemnation. In the last two years of his presidency, Díaz Ordaz retreated into isolation.

See also **Tlatelolco massacre; López Mateos; Echeverría**.

Díaz Serrano, Jorge: see **López Portillo**.

Diego, Wycliffe: see **Yatama**.

Dignity Battalions (*Batallones de Dignidad*)
A civilian militia force, thought to comprise as many as 10,000 individuals loyal to Gen. Manuel Noriega, the *de facto* ruler of Panama prior to the 1989 US invasion. Established in 1988 in response to the internal and external threats to Noriega, the Dignity Battalions achieved international notoriety after the abortive elections of 7 May 1989, when their brutal attacks on civilian demonstrators, including top opposition leaders, were widely publicised by the foreign media. After the December 1989 US invasion some militia members went into hiding, along with former members of the security forces. Two armed opposition groups later appeared: the 20 December movement (M–20) and the movement for the liberation of Panama (MLP), both of them thought to comprise former Battalions members, among others.

See also **Noriega Morena**.

Dog Island
A small uninhabited island 25 km north-west of Anguilla sought by the US in 1975 as a replacement gunnery range for Culebra (Puerto Rico), which had been abandoned after local protests. The Pentagon offered rent and infrastructural aid to Anguilla and the island's part-owner, Emile Gumbs. Gumbs became chief minister of Anguilla in 1980 but the deal did not go through because of local and regional objections.

See also **Gumbs; Anguilla; Culebra; military bases (foreign) in the Caribbean**.

dollar diplomacy

A phrase coined during the presidency of William Howard Taft in the US (1909–13) to describe a financial technique whereby Washington would grant loans to Central American and Caribbean nations with which they might repay onerous European debts, in exchange for US customs receivership. This method, which brought several nations (including Honduras, Nicaragua, Haiti and the Dominican Republic at different dates) under US control, was excused by Taft as a means of avoiding the recovery of the debts by military force. It was eventually repudiated by President Franklin D. Roosevelt in the 1930s. The phrase itself came to have a wider connotation, namely the use of US foreign policy to protect the interests of US transnational corporations in Latin America.
See also **Monroe doctrine; good neighbour policy.**

DOMINICA

Capital: Roseau
Independence (from Britain): 1978
Area: 751 sq km
Population (1988e): 81,200
Pop. growth rate: 1.3%
Pop. density: 108/sq km
Infant mortality: 16 per thousand
Life expectancy at birth: 66
Literacy: 95%
GDP per capita (1987): US$1,550
Foreign debt per capita (1987): US$813
Main exports: bananas, light manufactures, soap, coconut oil, grapefruit, tourism, limes

Political system

Constitution: 1978, setting up a republic within the British Commonwealth. A figurehead president is nominated by parliament for a five-year term. A 31-member (21 elected members, 9 nominated senators, 1 ex-officio member) House of Assembly is elected for a maximum of five years.
President: Sir Clarence Seignoret (1983)
Prime minister: Eugenia Charles (1980)
Last elections: 1990

Political organisations

Parties in parliament (leader) (elective seats): Dominica Freedom Party/DFP (Eugenia Charles) (11), f. 1968; United Workers' Party/UWP (Edison James) (6), f. 1988; Dominica Labour Party/DLP (Michael Douglas) (4), f. 1955.
Main trade unions: Waterfront and Allied Workers Union/WAWU (Louis Benoit), f.1964; Civil Service Association/CSA (Alvin Thomas), f.1968; Dominica Amalgamated Workers Union/DAWU (Darryl Gage), f.1961; Dominica Trade Union/DTU (Leo Jules), f.1945;

National Workers Union/NWU (Rawlings Jemmott), f.1977; Dominica
Farmers' Union/DFU (Frank Walters), f.1978; Dominica Hucksters
Association (Cecil Joseph), f.1983.
Employers' organisations: Dominica Association of Industry and
Commerce/DAIC (Edward Lambert), f.1973; Dominica Employers
Federation/DEF (Francis Emmanuel), f.1966; Dominica Banana
Growers Association/DBGA (Conrad Cyrus), f.1985.
See also **Caribs**.

Dominica Freedom Party (DFP)

Founded in 1968 by wealthy barrister Eugenia Charles and others, the
party, which initially attracted such disillusioned Labour Party veterans
as Phyllis Allfrey and E. C. Loblack, won two seats at the 1970 election
and three at the 1975 poll. In 1980 it defeated a split Dominica Labour
Party (DLP) 17–4 and Charles became prime minister. The DFP's
majority fell to 15–6 in the 1985 general election, but increased subsequently to 17–4 after a by-election and a DLP defection. The party was
narrowly returned (11–10) at the 1990 election.
See also **Charles, Eugenia; Dominica Labour Party; Allfrey**.

Dominica Labour Party (DLP)

Formed in 1955 as a moderate socialist party by E. C. Loblack, founder
of the island's first trade union, the Dominica Trade Union, and Phyllis
Allfrey, a radical member of the white planter class. The DLP won three
out of eight legislative council seats in the 1956 election. It won 7–4 in
1961 and party leader Edward Leblanc became chief minister. Allfrey
was expelled from the party a few months later. At the 1966 election the
party increased its majority to 10–1. It then split, with Leblanc forming
the Leblanc Labour Party which won the 1970 elections (7–4).

Leblanc retired in 1974 and Patrick John became premier and leader
of a reunited party. The DLP won the 1975 election (16–5), but scandals
and John's eccentric and repressive rule split the party in 1979. John was
replaced by Oliver Seraphin (b. 2 August 1943), who formed the Dominica Democratic Labour Party (DDLP) and ruled until the defeat (17–4)
of both Labour factions at the 1980 general election by the Dominica
Freedom Party (DFP) of Eugenia Charles.

Seraphin's ex-deputy, Michael Douglas, formed another faction, the
United Dominica Labour Party (UDLP), in 1981. The DDLP rejoined
John's DLP in 1983 with Seraphin as leader and John as deputy. In 1985,
Douglas and his UDLP returned to the DLP and elected Douglas as
leader, seconded by Seraphin. At the general election later that year the
DLP won 5 seats to the DFP's 15, but it later lost two of them, one in
a by-election and another through defection. John, who had been arrested
in 1981 for plotting to overthrow the government, lost the seat he had
won after he was jailed for 12 years following the 1985 election. The
party won four seats in the 1990 election but was eclipsed as the main
opposition by the new United Workers' Party.
See also **John, Patrick; Douglas, Michael; Allfrey; Charles, Eugenia**.

Dominican Liberation Party (Partido de Liberacion Domini-
cana/PLD): see Bosch, Juan.

DOMINICAN REPUBLIC

Capital: Santo Domingo
Independence (from Haiti): 1844
Area: 48,422 sq km
Population (1989e): 7m (59% urban)
Pop. growth rate: 1.4%
Pop. density: 145 sq km
Infant mortality: 70 per thousand
Life expectancy at birth: 66
Literacy: 69%
GDP per capita (1989): US$957
Foreign debt per capita (1990): US$690
Main exports: tourism, sugar, light manufactures, coffee, nickel, gold,
cocoa, tobacco, rum

Political system

Constitution: 1966. A president and vice-president are elected every four
years, along with a 120-member Chamber of Deputies and a 30-member
Senate elected by proportional representation.
President: Joaquín Balaguer (1986)
Vice-president: Carlos Morales Troncoso (1986)
Last election: 1990

Political organisations

Parties in parliament (leader) (seats in Chamber of Deputies/Senate):
Social Christian Reformist Party/PRSC (Joaquín Balaguer) (42/16), f.
1985; Dominican Liberation Party/PLD (Juan Bosch) (44/12), f. 1973;
Dominican Revolutionary Party/PRD (José Francisco Pĕna Gómez)
(30/2), f.1939; Independent Revolutionary Party/PRI (Jacobo Majluta)
(2/0), f.1989; Socialist Bloc (Rafael 'Fafa' Taveras) (1/0), f.1984; Dominican Workers' Party/PTD (José González Espinosa) (1/0), f.1979.
Other parties and groups: Quisqueyan Democratic Party/PQD (Elias
Wessin Chavez), f.1968; National Progressive Force/FNP (Marino Vinicio Castillo) f.1980; The Structure Party/PLE (Andres Vanderhorst),
f.1985; Dominican Communist Party/PCD (Narciso Isa Conde), f.1944;
Communist Labour Party/PCT (Rafael Chaljub Mejía), f.1980; Council
of Popular Unity/CUP (Virtudes Alvarez), f.1989.
Main trade unions: General Workers' Union/CGT (Francisco Antonio
Santos, Antonio Froilan), f. 1972; Sectoral Workers' Union/CTC (Rad-
hames Castro), f. 1985; United Workers' Union/CUT (Efraín Sanchez
Soriano), f. 1978; National Confederation of Dominican Workers/
CNTD (Mariano Negrón Tejado), f. 1972; Majority Workers'
Union/CTM (Nelsida Marmolejos), f. 1983; Autonomous Confeder-
ation of Sectoral Trade Unions/CASC (Gabriel del Río), f. 1962; Domi-
nican General Workers Union/UGTD (Juan Pablo Gómez), f. 1978;

Dominican Teachers' Association/ADP (Rafael Santos), f. 1970; Dominican Medical Association/AMD (Eusebio Garrido), f. 1891; Independent Peasants' Union/UCA (Manuel Félix Santana), f. 1979.
Employers' organisations: National Council of Businessmen/CNHE (Luis Augusto Ginebra Hernández), f. 1963; Dominican Retailers' Federation/FDCD (Abigail Soto), f. 1976; Association of Industrial Firms of Herrera (Antonio Isa Conde), f. 1979; National Association of Importers/ANI (Fernando Rodríguez); Dominican Employers' Confederation/CPRD (Heriberto de Castro); Dominican Sugar Cane Planters' Federation (César Contreras).

Dominican Republic, Haitian border massacre (1937)
Some 20,000 Haitian migrants, who had come to cut sugar cane, the Dominican Republic's main crop, were massacred during three days in October 1937 on the orders of Dominican dictator Gen. Rafael Trujillo, most of them along the border between the two countries. Sugar mills in Cuba had closed and Haitian workers were expelled, swelling the number who normally migrated to the Dominican Republic, where the mills had also closed. The killings were fuelled by the racism of Dominicans, who also disdained the manual labour which Haitians performed in conditions of near-slavery. Dominican troops carried out the killings, identifying Haitians by forcing them to say the word '*perejil*' (parsley). (Haitians pronounce an 'r' as a 'w'.) The killings began in the town of Dajabon, on the Massacre River. Trujillo, who later settled white immigrants in a buffer zone along the border, agreed in 1938 to pay $525,000 compensation to the victims and their families in response to Haitian President Stenio Vincent's feeble and apologetic protests. Only about half the money was paid.
See also **Trujillo; Dominican Republic, Haitian canecutters**.

Dominican Republic, Haitian canecutters
Many of the 400,000 Haitians living in the more prosperous neighbouring Dominican Republic, most of them illegally, work in semi-slave conditions in the sugar industry, until recently the country's main source of foreign earnings, cutting cane or working in grinderies. Dominicans are reluctant to take such poorly-paid work. The army rounds up hundreds of Haitians and sells them to the industry at the start of the harvest. Each year up to 20,000 workers are also recruited in Haiti and bought and sold by the sugar industry and for a few dollars each by army intermediaries. From 1966 a clandestine agreement earned the Haitian government some US$2m a year for supplying the canecutters. After the operation's miserable conditions were denounced at home and abroad, the Haitian government ended the accord in 1986 after the fall of the Duvalier dictatorship. Recruitment and migration continues clandestinely.
See also **Dominican Republic, Haitian border massacre (1937); braceros.**

Dominican Republic, US invasion (1965)
After the CIA-backed assassination of dictator Rafael Trujillo in 1961 and the US-encouraged army overthrow of elected President Juan Bosch

in 1963, US interests in the Dominican Republic were looked after by a civilian junta until left-wing army officers rebelled on 24 April 1965 and demanded the restoration to office of the exiled Bosch. Right-wing generals Elías Wessin y Wessin and Antonio Imbert Barrera agreed to a US request to invade the country on 28 April to crush the revolt and prevent what President Lyndon Johnson claimed would be 'another Cuba'.

The rebels, who set up a 'constitutionalist' government, managed to hold the centre of the capital, Santo Domingo, for five months against some 23,000 US troops and the rightist forces, headed by Gen. Imbert's 'Government of National Reconstruction'. The invaders were soon dressed up as an Organisation of American States 'inter-American peace force' nominally headed by a Brazilian general. US envoys, led first by McGeorge Bundy and then by diplomat Ellsworth Bunker, negotiated a political settlement and oversaw the installation of Héctor García Godoy, once Bosch's foreign minister, as provisional president after the rightists had refused his one-time agriculture minister, Antonio Guzmán. García Godoy ruled until elections in 1966, when the pro-US Joaquín Balaguer, once nominal president under Trujillo, defeated Bosch, who was largely prevented from campaigning. The occupation troops finally withdrew in September 1966. About 3,000 people are thought to have died during the civil war and invasion.

See also **Bosch, Juan; Wessin y Wessin; Imbert Barrera; Caamaño Deñó; Reid Cabral; Dominican Revolutionary Party; Peña Gómez; Guzmán; Balaguer; Trujillo; invasions and occupations by the United States; military bases (foreign) in the Caribbean; Grenada, US invasion (1983).**

Dominican Revolutionary Party (*Partido Revolucionario Dominicano*/PRD)

A social democratic party in the Dominican Republic, founded in Havana in 1939 as a moderate leftist party by Juan Bosch. On dictator Rafael Trujillo's assassination in 1961, its leaders were the first political exiles to return and Bosch became the country's first freely-elected president in February 1963. But, encouraged by a suspicious United States, the army overthrew him seven months later. The 1965 civil war was fought over an attempt by leftist army officers to restore Bosch and the PRD to power, but Bosch was defeated in carefully-controlled elections in 1966.

The party boycotted the 1970 elections in protest against President Joaquín Balaguer's seeking re-election. In 1973 it split when Bosch's proposal to boycott the 1974 elections was rejected and he walked out to form the marxist Dominican Liberation Party (PLD). The PRD was left in the hands of the more moderate José Francisco Peña Gómez, its general secretary since 1963. It formed a five-party coalition (the Santiago Accord) for the 1974 elections, with the PRD's Antonio Guzmán and rightist Gen. Elías Wessin y Wessin as candidates for president and vice-president. But the coalition boycotted the poll at the last minute in protest at government-inspired repression.

The PRD returned to power in 1978, when Antonio Guzmán was

elected president after US President Jimmy Carter had intervened to block a coup. The military had stopped the vote count when they saw incumbent President Joaquín Balaguer was losing. Guzmán killed himself in 1982 after discovering close aides were corrupt. Salvador Jorge Blanco was elected to succeed him in 1982, but by 1985 a serious left-right split had arisen between supporters of Peña Gómez and businessman Jacobo Majluta, who as vice-president had briefly succeeded Guzmán. Majluta won the PRD nomination for the presidency in the 1986 elections after a bitter fight which included a shoot-out during the party convention. Peña Gómez took little part in the election campaign and Majluta was defeated. Majluta, who had formed his own group, *Partido La Estructura* (The Structure Party), inside the PRD in 1985, claimed control of the party, but Peña Gómez retained the loyalty of most members and expelled Majluta from the PRD in 1987. The national electoral council later annulled the expulsion.

The PRD's prestige was further damaged by the indictment in 1987 of Jorge Blanco for corruption while in office, and his flight into exile to avoid imprisonment. In 1989, because of the party split, Peña Gómez and Majluta set up their own groups to run in the 1990 elections, but Peña Gomez was later named the party's candidate and came third with 23% of the vote.

See also **Peña Gómez; Majluta; Bosch, Juan; Jorge Blanco; Guzmán; Balaguer; Dominican Republic, US invasion (1965); Trujillo**.

Dorsilien, Jacques: see **Théodore; Unified Haitian Communist Party**.

Dorticós Torrado, Osvaldo
b. 1919. President of Cuba 1959–75. Born in Cienfuegos into an upper-middle-class family, Osvaldo Dorticós was educated at Catholic primary schools, the Colegio Champagnat and the Instituto de Segunda Enseñanza, Cienfuegos; then at the University of Havana (philosophy and law). He obtained a doctorate in civil law in 1941. Dorticós had been a student leader and a successful lawyer, as well as commodore of the Cienfuegos Yacht Club, before he joined Fidel Castro's struggle against the Batista dictatorship. He had also briefly belonged to the Communist Party, serving as secretary to its president. In 1957–8 he led the underground resistance movement in Cienfuegos. Arrested and jailed in the latter year, he escaped to Mexico, returning shortly after the overthrow of Batista. Castro appointed him to the cabinet, as minister of revolutionary laws, and he became president in July 1959 on the resignation of Manuel Urrutia. He served until 1975 when a new constitution combined the roles of president and prime minister, a job assumed by Castro himself.

See also **Castro Ruz, Fidel Alejandro; Cuban Revolutionary War**.

Douglas, Denzil: see **St Kitts–Nevis Labour Party**.

Douglas, Michael
b. 26 April 1940. Leader of the opposition in Dominica 1985–90. After joining the Dominica Labour Party (DLP), he entered parliament in 1975 and under prime minister Patrick John was minister of agriculture

(1975–6) and communications and works (1976–8), after which he was
sacked for what John called 'communism'. He then formed the National
Alliance Party, which became the Dominica Democratic Alliance, and
took it into the four-party left-wing Dominica Liberation Movement
Alliance which contested the 1980 election. When John was forced to
resign in 1979, Douglas became finance minister and deputy to prime
minister Oliver Seraphin until the DLP's electoral defeat in 1980. In 1981
he formed the United Dominica Labour Party, but in 1985 rejoined the
DLP, which elected him leader and Seraphin as his deputy. He later
made an alliance with the leftist Dominica Liberation Movement of Bill
Riviere.
See **Dominica Labour Party; John, Patrick; Douglas, Rosie.**

Douglas, Rosie
b. 15 October 1942. Marxist politician in Dominica and brother of ex-
opposition leader Michael Douglas. As a student he was involved in the
destruction of a computer centre at Sir George Williams University in
Montreal in 1969 by 'black power' activists. He was eventually jailed for
18 months in 1973–4 and finally deported to Dominica in 1976, where he
founded the Popular Independence Committee. He was appointed a
senator in 1979, but was sacked soon afterwards for supposedly inviting
Cuban troops to Dominica after Hurricane David had devastated the
island. Prime minister Oliver Seraphin obliquely admitted that the US
had demanded the sacking in exchange for relief aid. Douglas was elected
to parliament as an independent at the 1985 general election, but lost his
seat at the 1990 poll.
See also **Douglas, Michael; 'black power'.**

dreads
A group of rastafarian youths whose anarchistic activities, including violence, in Dominica in the early 1970s led to passage of a law in 1974 (the
Dread Act) authorising anyone to shoot them on sight and providing for
mandatory jail sentences for anyone dressing like them. One of their
number, Desmond Trotter, who was also a left-wing activist, was arrested
in 1974 and accused of murdering a white American tourist. He was
sentenced to death the same year on evidence later admitted to be false.
The case provoked an international outcry. His conviction was overturned
and his sentence commuted to life imprisonment. He escaped from prison
in the political confusion of 1979 and was later pardoned. The Dread Act
was repealed in 1981.
See also **Dominica; John, Patrick; rastafarians; 'black power'.**

Duarte, José Napoleón
1926–90. President of El Salvador 1980–2, 1984–9. Educated at the University of Notre Dame in Indiana. A practising civil engineer until 1964,
Duarte was a founder member of the Christian Democrat Party (PDC)
and its first general secretary (1960–64). He was elected mayor of San
Salvador in 1964 by a large majority, and during three consecutive terms
he introduced street lighting, improved the efficiency of the taxation

system and built up community development programmes (and an important political power base) in the slum areas. He was elected president of the PDC in 1972 and stood as presidential candidate for the National Opposition Union (UNO) alliance formed by the PDC, the National Revolutionary Movement (MNR) and the Nationalist Democratic Union (UDN).

Deprived of victory by blatant fraud, he lent belated support to the subsequent coup d'état in his favour, which was crushed with the loss of some 200 lives. He sought asylum in the Venezuelan embassy, but government soldiers entered to arrest him. After torture, during which his cheekbones were broken with rifle butts and the tips of three fingers cut off, he was allowed to flee abroad. In exile in Venezuela (1972–9) he forged strong links with leading Christian Democrats of the COPEI party. He returned in 1980 to join the 'third junta' formed after the 1979 coup, amid a growing civil war.

Appointed president in November 1980 with the backing of the US and the Salvadorean military, he was removed from office in April 1982 by the newly-elected constituent assembly, dominated by the far right, but was elected president (in a poll boycotted by the left) in March 1984. He consolidated his power by winning an outright legislative majority in 1985, although he lost this again in 1988. As president, Duarte sought a negotiated settlement of the civil war with the left-wing FDR/FMLN, but his room for manoeuvre was limited by the armed forces and the right-wing business community. His peace terms were in any case rejected as a surrender demand by the rebels, who in September 1985 severely embarrassed Duarte by kidnapping his daughter and releasing her only in exchange for FMLN prisoners. An attempt to resume the dialogue in 1987, under the terms of the Central American peace accord (the Arias Plan) also broke down.

Duarte's problems worsened after an earthquake destroyed much of central San Salvador in October 1986. The inadequacy of relief and reconstruction efforts, handed over by Duarte to the private sector, contributed to a decline in his popularity. This was followed by labour unrest, a dispute with the right over electoral and taxation policy (leading to a parliamentary boycott by the right in early 1988) and the worst drought for 30 years. The slump in the PDC's support among organised labour was dramatically underlined when the pro-Duarte UPD confederation split. By the end of his term, the president could barely even control his own party, which was riven by disputes over the succession, and his administration seemed reduced to impotence. Corruption scandals, which even touched his own son, and a resurgence of the death squads, added to his problems. The crisis deepened when Duarte was diagnosed in 1988 as suffering from the cancer which was to lead to his death in 1990.
See also **Christian Democrat Party** (El Salvador); **Arias Plan.**

Duncan, D. K.: see **People's National Party** (Jamaica).

Dupuy, Ben: see CATH.

Duque, Carlos: see National Liberation Coalition.

Durazo Moreno, Arturo

The chief of police in Mexico City in 1976–82, who became notorious for his part in corruption. A childhood friend of President José López Portillo, Durazo, known as 'El Negro', had worked in the Federal Judicial Police. At the time of his appointment to head the capital's police in 1976 he already faced indictment in the US on drug trafficking charges. During his time in office he was alleged to have been heavily involved in abuses of power and corruption; a special force of plain clothes detectives, the Department for the Prevention of Delinquency, ran an extortion racket. At the end of the López Portillo presidency he went into exile in the United States. According to a former aide he had been responsible for accepting bribes, dealing in cocaine and ordering the killing of a rival Colombian drug gang (the 'Tula River' murders).

In 1984, Durazo was charged *in absentia* for tax evasion and his assets in Mexico were seized. Charges were also filed against him for extortion, smuggling and possession of illegal weapons. Among his confiscated assets were property at the Pacific resort of Zihuatanejo and a $2.5m mansion in Mexico City, complete with casino and racetrack, which was later opened to the public as a 'Museum of Corruption'. He was arrested in the United States in June 1984, and eventually extradited to Mexico. See also **López Portillo.**

Durham, Alden: see Progressive National Party.

Duvalier, Dr François

1907–71. President of Haiti 1957–71. The son of a teacher, Duvalier trained as a doctor, worked in the countryside and joined a group of nationalist intellectuals (The Griots) at the end of the US occupation of Haiti in the 1930s to praise *noirisme*, or the primacy of blacks over mulattos in Haiti's colour-conscious society. He was secretary-general of Daniel Fignolé's *noiriste* Worker-Peasant Party (MOP) in 1946. President Dumarsais Estimé, considered a noiriste by some, made him minister of health and labour in 1949. In 1950 on Estimé's overthrow, Duvalier went underground.

He emerged as president from months of political turmoil in 1957 after officially defeating Louis Déjoie, a rich mulatto businessman, in an army-rigged election. Opposition violence and invasions led him to create a private militia, the National Security Volunteers (VSN), or Tontons Macoutes, in 1958. With their help he emasculated the army and clamped down on all opposition. In 1959, in constant bad health and pain, he began a seven-year reign of terror in which many thousands of people, including prominent mulattos and black opponents, were murdered. The US cut off aid in 1963 after failing to oust him. He declared himself 'president-for-life' in 1964, expelled foreign priests and seized control of the Catholic Church, appointing the first black and Haitian archbishop. Nicknamed 'Papa Doc' by all, he died of a diabetes-induced heart attack

in 1971 after appointing his 19-year-old son Jean-Claude as his succcessor
to rule a ruined and internationally shunned country.
See also **Duvalierism;** *noirisme*; **Duvalier, Jean-Claude; Tontons Macoutes; Fignolé; Haiti, Roman Catholic Church.**

Duvalier, Jean-Claude

b. 3 July 1951. President of Haiti 1971–86. After doing poorly at school
and escaping assassination in 1963, Duvalier was named in 1971 by his
dying father, François Duvalier, to succeed him as ruler and the country's
ninth 'president-for-life'. A referendum 'approved' the choice by
2,391,916 votes to 1. For most of his reign he was the puppet, first of his
mother and sisters and then of his father's top aides, who kept the
dictatorship going for their own profit. He was nicknamed 'Baby Doc'
by the foreign press and Haitians adopted the name. At first his youth
made him popular and US aid was restored. Political tension eased,
especially between 1977 and 1980. But in May 1980 he married Michèle
Bennett, the domineering daughter of a rich mulatto businessman, defy-
ing his mother and leading Duvalierists, who were shocked at the sym-
bolic reconciliation with the old ruling class his father had fought.
   A crackdown on journalists and dissident politicians, most of whom
were deported, ended the liberal period six months later. Growing corruption, palace intrigues, foreign pressure, Church activism and continued economic decline finally provoked a nationwide rebellion after
regime thugs shot dead four schoolchildren in Gonaïves in November
1985. US aid was suspended and after a week-long state of siege in which
hundreds were murdered, the US government secretly flew Duvalier and
his relatives into exile in France in February 1986 aboard a military plane.
Washington's promise to France to receive the Duvaliers a few days
later was then withdrawn. Attempts to recover some of the Duvaliers'
estimated $500m fortune were dropped in 1989 by the government of
Gen. Prosper Avril, who was once the Duvaliers' financial manager.
Supporters of the dictatorship are still powerful in Haiti.
See also **Duvalier, François; Duvalierism; Tontons Macoutes; Namphy;
Avril.**

Duvalierism

The practices and policies of the Duvalier family dictatorship in Haiti
from 1957 to 1986, loosely tied to *noirisme*, or the primacy of black over
mulatto. After a decade of brutality and repression by François Duvalier,
his son and successor Jean-Claude said in 1971 that his father had made
the 'political revolution' (ostensibly, though not in reality, breaking the
traditional mulatto ruling class) and that he would now embark on the
'economic revolution'. However, nothing of the sort happened and the
ruined economy continued to decline. In 1977, Duvalier's advisers proclaimed the doctrine of 'Jean-Claudism', which they said was Duvalierism
'refined, reconsidered and corrected', and set up a National Council of
Jean-Claudist Action (CONAJEC). This half-hearted ideological effort
began to fade after Duvalier angered his supporters, especially the *noir-
istes*, by marrying the daughter of a rich mulatto merchant in 1980.

Old guard Duvalierists were sometimes called 'the dinosaurs'. The 1987 constitution barred 'notorious' Duvalierists from general elections later that year. They and their supporters in the army then waged a campaign of violence, culminating in election day killings which led to cancellation of the poll in mid-vote on 29 November.

See also **Duvalier, François; Duvalier, Jean-Claude; Tontons Macoutes;** *noirisme.*

E

Eastern Caribbean Common Market (ECCM): see **Caribbean Community**

Ebanks, Benson
b. 18 February 1935. Leader of the Cayman Islands 1984–8. A banker and businessman, he was elected to the legislative assembly in 1965 and became a member of the executive council in 1969. His Progress With Dignity group won 5 of the 12 elected seats in the 1980 elections. In the 1984 poll, with five again, it became the largest group and Ebanks succeeded Jim Bodden as leader of the assembly and senior member of the executive council, with responsibility for health, education and social services. He was replaced as leader by Norman Bodden after the 1988 general election and took charge of education.
See also **Bodden, Norman; Bodden, Jim.**

ECAM Foundation: see **Christian Democrat Party** (Panama).

Echeverría Alvarez, Luis
b. 17 January 1922. President of Mexico 1970–76. From a middle-class Mexico City family, Echeverría studied law at the Universidad Nacional Autónoma de México (UNAM). He was appointed deputy interior minister in 1958 under the Adolfo López Mateos administration, a job which carried responsibility for the intelligence services. As interior minister (*secretario de gobernación*) under President Gustavo Díaz Ordaz he was involved in the repression of student unrest, culminating in the 1968 Tlatelolco massacre; he was therefore considered a political hard-liner. Yet on becoming president in 1970 (he won the elections as the official PRI candidate with 85.8% of the vote) he promised a democratic opening and released imprisoned student activists. When right-wing paramilitary *'halcones'* carried out a new attack on student demonstrators in 1971, killing at least 30 people, the president sacked the police chief and the mayor of Mexico City, consolidating his power. He then offered many leftist intellectuals government jobs. While clashing with the private sector at home, Echeverría's pursuit of closer relations with Cuba and the Popular Unity government in Chile antagonised the United States. He adopted a vocal nationalist and 'Third Worldist' position.

Towards the end of his administration the president encountered a growing political and economic crisis. Widening budget deficits encouraged inflation and capital flight and on 31 August 1976 the peso was devalued for the first time in 22 years. Then, only 11 days before leaving office, Echeverría expropriated large tracts of private farmland in Sonora state, triggering rumours of a coup d'état. Although in the end he handed power to his chosen successor, José López Portillo, without mishap, the period is remembered as one of the tensest transitions between *sexenios*. See also **Díaz Ordaz; López Portillo; Tlatelolco Massacre.**

Economic Commission for Latin America and the Caribbean (ECLAC) (*Comisión Económica para América Latina y el Caribe/* CEPAL)

A United Nations organisation set up in 1948 to co-ordinate policies for the promotion of regional economic development. The commission meets every two years. Its main work involves collaboration between governments to analyse economic development issues and formulate development plans. ECLAC headquarters are based in Santiago de Chile; the executive secretary is Gert Rosenthal of Guatemala (his immediate predecessors were Enrique Iglesias of Uruguay and Norberto González of Argentina). The executive secretariat comprises divisions on development, statistics, documentation and other specialist tasks. ECLAC's share of the United Nations budget for the two years 1988–9 was $43m; it also received other voluntary contributions.

The commission's member countries are: Antigua-Barbuda, Argentina, Bahamas, Barbados, Belize, Bolivia, Brazil, Canada, Chile, Colombia, Costa Rica, Cuba, Dominica, Dominican Republic, Ecuador, El Salvador, France, Grenada, Guatemala, Guyana, Haiti, Honduras, Jamaica, Mexico, Netherlands, Nicaragua, Panama, Paraguay, Peru, Portugal, St Kitts-Nevis, St Lucia, St Vincent and the Grenadines, Spain, Suriname, Trinidad-Tobago, United Kingdom, USA, Uruguay, and Venezuela. ECLAC economists established a reputation for a structuralist analysis of local economies (as distinct from a monetarist analysis), stressing the need for the removal of production bottlenecks in resolving problems such as inflation and persistent balance of payments deficits. See also **Latin American Economic System.**

Edgar Ibarra Guerrilla Group/Front (GEI): see **Rebel Armed Forces; Guerrilla Army of the Poor.**

Edgar Macías faction: see **Popular Social Christian Party; Social Christian Party.**

Eighth Army of Liberation: see **Joshua, Ebenezer.**

Eisenhower, Dwight D: see **Arbenz Guzmán; Bay of Pigs invasion; Monroe doctrine; Omega 7.**

Eleta, Carlos: see **Labour Party.**

EL SALVADOR, Republic of
Capital: San Salvador

Independence: (from Spain) 1821; (from Mexico) 1823; (from Central American Federation) 1839; republic formally established 1841
Area: 20,935 sq km
Population (1988): 5.03m (48.2% urban)
Pop. growth rate (1980–88): 1.3%
Pop. density: 239/sq km
Infant mortality (1985–90): 57.4 per thousand
Life expectancy at birth (1985–90): 62.2.
Literacy (1988): 49%
GDP per capita (1988e): US$955
Foreign debt per capita (1988e): US$356
Main exports (1987): coffee (60%); sugar (3%); seafood (2%)

Political system

Constitution: 1983. President: Alfredo Cristiani (ARENA) (1989–   ), succeeded José Napoleón Duarte (PDC) (1984–9). Elections are held every five years for president, with a run-off round if there is no clear winner; consecutive presidential terms are not permitted. Every three years there are elections for a 60-member unicameral Legislative Assembly. The last legislative elections were held in March 1988. Seats are divided among the 14 departments (provinces), based on population, with the results determined by a quotient system. The quotient is derived by dividing the number of valid votes per department by its number of assembly seats; parties are entitled to one seat for each full quotient obtained, with the remaining available seat(s) going to the party with the most residual votes. There is universal compulsory adult (18+) suffrage.

Political organisations

Parties in the Assembly (leader) (seats obtained at the last election): Nationalist Republican Alliance/ARENA (Roberto D'Aubuisson; Mario Repdaelli) (32); Authentic Christian Democrat Movement/MADC (Guillermo Guevara Lacayo) (13); Christian Democrat Party/PDC (Fidel Chávez Mena) (4); National Conciliation Party/PCN (Ciro Cruz Zepeda) (6).
Parties outside the Assembly: Democratic Convergence/CD alliance, comprising the National Revolutionary Movement/MNR (Guillermo Ungo), Popular Social Christian Movement/MPSC (Rubén Zamora) and Social Democrat Party/PSD (Mario Reni Roldán); Democratic Action/AD; Stable Centrist Republican Movement/MERECEN (Juan Ramón Rosales); and Central American Unionist Party/PUCA (Gabriel Pilopa Araujo).
Parties with no legal status (1989) include: Businessmen, Peasants and Workers Party/ECO (Luis Rolando López); Independent Democratic Party/PID (Eduardo García Tobar); Salvadorean Centrist Party/PACES (Tomás Chafoya Martínez). The Nationalist Democratic

Union/UDN (Mario Aguiñada), a member of the FDR (see below), declined to take part in the 1989 presidential elections, despite having an open political presence. The National Action Movement/MAN has not sought party status.

The following parties were deprived of their legal status by the electoral council in October 1989 for having failed to obtain the minimum 0.5% of the vote in the March elections: Liberation Party/PL, Salvadorean Institutional Party/Paisa (Roberto Escobar García); Salvadorean Popular Party/PPS (Francisco Quiñónez Avila) (these three formerly allied in the Popular Union/UP coalition, f. 1988); Popular Orientation Party/POP; and Party of Restorative Action/PAR (Ernesto Oyarbide). Democratic Action/AD (Ricardo González Camacho) was threatened with a similar fate but might avoid it on the grounds that it was in coalition with the PDC.

Main labour organisations (leader) (affiliation): National Unity of Salvadorean Workers/UNTS (Marco Tulio Lima and others (independent) [an umbrella organisation of worker and peasant groups including the National Union Federation of Salvadorean Workers/ FENASTRAS, the Federation of Independent Associations and Unions of El Salvador/FEASIES, the food and clothing workers' federation FESTIAVCES, the Salvadorean Unitary Trade Union Federation/FUSS and the National Indigenous Association/ANIS]; National Union of Workers and Peasants/UNOC (Amanda Villatoro and others) (independent) [an umbrella organisation of worker and peasant groups including the Confederation of Democratic Workers/CTD (ORIT) and the construction and transport workers' federation FESINCONTRANS (ICFTU)]; Salvadorean Workers' Central/CTS (Félix Blanco) (CLAT); Democratic Peasant Alliance (Félix Blanco, Simón Parada and others) [links peasant organisations belonging to different confederations].

Main employers' organisations: National Private Enterprise Association/ANEP (Juan Maldonado); Salvadorean Industrialists Association/ASI (Roberto Ortiz Avalos); Coffee Association of El Salvador/ ACES (Francisco García Rossi); Association of Coffee Processors and Exporters/Abecafe (Miguel Angel Salavarría); Society of Salvadorean Traders and Industrialists/SCIS; Chamber of Commerce and Industry of El Salvador/CCI (Ricardo Flores Cena); Salvadorean Construction Industry Chamber/CASALCO. In March 1986 the SCIS, the CCI, the ASI, CASALCO and ANEP formed the Salvadorean Productive Unity/UPS to oppose the economic policy of the PDC government.

An armed insurgency began in the mid-1970s and has been co-ordinated since 1980 by the Farabundo Martí National Liberation Front/FMLN. Civilian organisations backing the FMLN belong to the Democratic Revolutionary Front/FDR, which has declined in importance since its two leading members, the MNR and the MPSC, formed the Democratic Convergence.

Eman, Henny

b. 20 March 1948. Premier of Aruba 1985–9. Eman took over the leadership in 1981 of the conservative Aruban People's Party (AVP) founded in 1942 by his grandfather. Because of discontent caused by the 1985 closure of the Exxon-owned Lago oil refinery, Aruba's biggest employer, Eman, a Christian Democrat, and the AVP in coalition with three other parties defeated Betico Croes and the People's Electoral Movement (MEP) at that year's general election. Eman, as premier, led the island to autonomy a few weeks later on New Year's Day 1986. The AVP was defeated in the 1989 general election and he was succeeded by MEP leader Nelson Oduber.

See also **Netherlands Antilles, oil refineries; Croes; People's Electoral Movement; Oduber, Nelson.**

Encinas, Dionisio: see Communist Party (Mexico).

Endara Galimany, Guillermo

b. 12 May 1936. President of Panama 1989– . A labour lawyer who studied at New York University, Guillermo Endara was secretary to the veteran populist and three times president Arnulfo Arias. He was selected by the ADOC coalition as its presidential candidate for 1989 as a compromise after the parties had been unable to agree. The divisions in Arias' Authentic Panameñista Party (PPA) left him effectively without a party of his own. Deprived of his election victory by a massive fraud on behalf of the country's de facto ruler, Gen. Manuel Noriega, Endara was among opposition leaders beaten by Noriega's paramilitary forces after the elections, and was hospitalised for several days. After the October 1989 coup attempt he fled the country, but he was installed as president when the US invaded on 20 December; the swearing-in took place on a US military base in Panama. Many Latin American nations were reluctant to recognise his government as a result of these circumstances, despite the subsequent ratification of his victory by the electoral tribunal.

In the aftermath of the invasion his supporters moved to revive the tradition of Arias by forming the Arnulfista Party. Seen by many observers as rather ineffectual, Endara concentrated his initial efforts on attempting to persuade Washington to expedite economic aid to mend the country's shattered economy. He even went on hunger strike 'in solidarity with the people of Panama', while insisting he was not seeking to pressure the US. His government soon encountered serious criticism, especially over its alleged failure to create an effective security force to replace the defunct Panama Defence Forces (FDP).

See also **Democratic Alliance of Civic Opposition; Panama, US invasion (1989); Authentic Panameñista Party; Arias Madrid.**

Escalante, Aníbal: see 'microfaction'; Integrated Revolutionary Organisations.

Escuela de Golpes: see School of the Americas.

Esquipulas, Declaration of: see Central American Parliament.

Esquipulas II: see Arias Plan.

Esquivel, Manuel
b. 2 May 1940. Prime minister of Belize 1984–9. A physics teacher, he joined the opposition Liberal Party in the early 1970s before it became part of the United Democratic Party (UDP). He was elected UDP chairman in 1976, appointed a senator in 1979 and became party leader in 1983. He led the UDP to victory at the 1984 elections, ending the 24-year rule of George Price.

Esquivel, more pro-US than Price, joined the right-wing Caribbean Democratic Union of regional leaders in 1986 and US presence in Belize increased, with a larger embassy, and more aid and Peace Corps volunteers. The opposition accused him of permitting arms shipments through Belize to the US-financed Nicaraguan Contra rebels. He was also criticised for setting up a secret police in 1987. Esquivel narrowly lost power at the 1989 general election to Price and the People's United Party.
See also **United Democratic Party; Price; Belize dispute; Caribbean Democratic Union.**

Esquivel, Roderick: see **Liberal Party** (Panama); **Delvalle; National Liberation Coalition.**

Estrada Palma, Tomás: see **Platt Amendment.**

Ethiopia (Cuban involvement in): see **African involvement** (Cuba).

Eugène, Grégoire
b. 12 March 1925. Conservative Haitian politician. A lawyer, he was a junior minister in two governments in 1957. He taught law at the University of Haiti from 1964 until he founded the Haitian Social Christian Party (PSCH) in 1979 and opposed the Duvalier dictatorship through the party organ, *Fraternité*. He was deported to the US with other opposition figures in 1980 but was allowed to return in 1984. He stood in the heavily boycotted, army-organised presidential elections in 1988 and officially came fourth.
See also **Duvalier, Jean-Claude.**

Evans, Melvin
1917–84. Governor of the US Virgin Islands 1969–75. A surgeon, he was the last appointed (1969) and the first popularly-elected governor (1970) of the USVI. A Republican (and former Democrat), he was defeated for re-election in 1974 by Cyril King. He was US ambassador to Trinidad-Tobago 1981–4.
See also **Farrelly.**

Evertsz, Juancho: see National People's Party.

Eye for an Eye (*Ojo por Ojo*): see death squad.

F

Facussé, Miguel: see Association for the Progress of Honduras.

Fagoth, Steadman: see Yatama.

Falange: see death squad.

Fallas, Luis: see banana strike (Costa Rica).

Family Islands

All the score or so of inhabited islands of the Bahamas chain except for the main island, New Providence, seat of the capital, Nassau. The term was brought into use in 1972 by Bahamian prime minister Lynden Pindling. They were formerly known as the Out Islands.
See also **Bahamas; Pindling.**

FAPU (*Frente de Acción Popular Unificada*/United Popular Action Front)

Originally formed in 1974 by an alliance of peasants, students, labour unions, church groups and teachers opposed to the eviction of 15,000 people by the government of Col. Armando Molina for the building of the Cerrón Grande dam, FAPU was the first of the so-called 'popular organisations' of the Salvadorean left. It argued that the Molina regime was fascist, that the electoral path was exhausted, and that a broad front of all 'democratic and revolutionary' groups should be created. It broke up after only six months amid fierce disputes over control, but was reorganised in 1976 as a mass front for the National Resistance (RN) guerrillas. It gained considerable support among urban trade unionists (most importantly the power workers), winning some unions away from government control and others from the Communist Party (PCS). It did not join the Popular Forum, which participated in the post-coup government of 1979, though its largest affiliate, the union federation FENASTRAS, did; withdrawing shortly after the coup. In 1980, with other popular organisations, FAPU formed the Revolutionary Mass Co-ordinating Body (CRM), and through it became part of the Democratic Revolutionary Front.
See also **Democratic Revolutionary Front** (El Salvador).

Farabundo Martí National Liberation Front (*Frente Farabundo Martí para la Liberación Nacional*/FMLN)

A guerrilla front, founded in El Salvador in October 1980 by the Popular

Liberation Forces (FPL), the People's Revolutionary Army (ERP) and the Salvadorean Communist Party (PCS), which jointly made up the Unified Revolutionary Directorate (DRU). The FMLN was named after a Communist Party leader executed in 1932. By December 1980 the remaining two Salvadorean guerrilla groups – the National Resistance (RN) and the Revolutionary Party of Centralamericanist Workers (PRTC) – had also joined. The 15-strong DRU became the co-ordinating body for the five groups, while its executive commission, made up of the five general secretaries, became the general command structure. The FMLN was 'directly linked' to the Democratic Revolutionary Front (FDR) via a body known as the political-diplomatic commission (CPD) on which both were represented.

The combined guerrilla army was said to number 11–12,000 by 1984, with the ERP and the FPL accounting for over three-quarters of them and the FARN (Armed Forces of the RN) for most of the remainder. In addition to the 5–6,000 members of the 'mobile force', twelve 500-strong 'strategic batallions' were formed, but these had to be split into smaller units in 1984 as a result of the improved artillery and air power of armed forces and their use of US military intelligence data. Regular guerrilla forces declined to under 6,000 (according to foreign observers) under sustained, US-backed counter-insurgency efforts by the government, but by 1988 the FMLN appeared to be back to its previous strength. The FPL has always been strongest in the northern department of Chalatenango, while the ERP has its stronghold in the north-eastern department of Morazán. The main base of the FARN was on the Guazapa volcano north of San Salvador. Four 'war fronts' were designated by the FMLN upon its foundation: the 'Modesto Ramírez' Central Front' the 'Feliciano Ama' Western Front; the Paracentral 'Anastasio Aquino' Front; and the 'Francisco Sánchez' Eastern Front.

The FMLN responded to army counter-insurgency tactics by spreading the war to previously untouched areas; fighting a war of attrition; returning to urban operations and stepping up political work. In 1985 it announced that it would integrate all combatants into a single army and that the tactics of laying mines and halting road traffic would be intensified. By 1986 a unified command structure had been established, although the ultimate objective of a single political organisation remains a distant one. Current (1990) members of the general command are: Jorge Schafick Handal (PCS), Salvador Sánchez Cerén ('Leonel González') (FPL), Eduardo Sancho ('Fermán Cienfuegos') (RN), Joaquín Villalobos (ERP) and Francisco Jovel ('Roberto Roca') (PRTC).

In October/November 1988, Villalobos and González headed an FMLN diplomatic offensive in Latin America, seeking support for a political solution to the war. The tour seemed to emphasise the guerrillas' autonomy from their erstwhile civilian allies of the FDR, despite the insistence that there was no split. In January 1989 the FMLN offered to recognise that year's presidential elections, in which FDR candidates were standing, in exchange for a postponement of the poll and guarantees of impartiality. After the proposal was rejected they disrupted the poll, seriously affecting the vote for FDR/Democratic Convergence (CD) leader Guillermo Ungo, although they supported the CD's decision not to pull out. This marked the beginning of the 'strategic counter-offensive', in which the FMLN combined insurrectionary tactics with a push for a negotiated settlement. In talks with the new Cristiani government the Front offered a ceasefire and moves towards becoming a political party, in exchange for judicial and political reforms, a purge of the armed forces and an end to repression, plus the establishment of an interim government in which it would not demand a role. The talks were halted after a bomb attack on a trade union HQ, and on 11 November 1990 the FMLN mounted a massive, nationwide offensive lasting two weeks. Its forces held off government troops in the capital for a week and forced a major overhaul of counter-insurgency policy. Talks with the government resumed, this time under UN auspices, in May 1990.

See also **People's Revolutionary Army** (El Salvador); **Popular Liberation Forces; Democratic Revolutionary Front** (El Salvador); **Villalobos; Democratic Convergence; Martí, Agustín Farabundo; Cristiani.**

FARO: see **Romero Mena.**

Farrelly, Alexander A.
b. 29 December 1923. Governor of the US Virgin Islands 1987– . A corporate lawyer from St Croix, former assistant US attorney and ex-senator (1967–71), he ran as a Democrat in the first popular elections for governor in 1970 but was defeated by Republican Melvin Evans. He lost to Independent Citizens' Movement candidate Cyril King in 1974, but in 1986 became the first Democrat to be elected governor.
See also **Evans.**

Fawkes, Randol: see **Progressive Liberal Party.**

FECCAS-UTC: see **Popular Revolutionary Bloc; Popular Liberation Forces.**

Federation of Christian Workers (FTC) (Panama): see **Christian Democrat Party** (Panama).

FENACH: see **Communist Party of Honduras.**

FENASTRAS: see **FAPU.**

Fergus, Howard
b. 25 July 1937. Historian and speaker of the Montserrat parliament. After university in Britain, Fergus returned to Montserrat to teach and become chief education officer and then a senior lecturer at the University of the West Indies. He was elected the first speaker of the island's legislative council (parliament) in 1975. He was the first Montserratian to act as governor, in the absence of the British official appointed by London. He has written most of the current books on the history of Montserrat. In 1987 he declined an invitation by the two main opposition parties to head an opposition electoral alliance.
See also **Montserrat.**

Ferrey, Azucena: see Social Christian Party.

FERRG: see Guerrilla Army of the Poor.

15 September Legion: see Nicaraguan Democratic Force.

Fignolé, Daniel

1915–86. President of Haiti 1957. A spell-binding orator and pioneer in the political use of the non-élite Creole language, Fignolé, who trained as a teacher, was named education minister in the Estimé government in 1946 but resigned after a few months. He emerged as provisional president in the turmoil of 1957, but was overthrown by the army after only 19 days. Hundreds of his supporters in the capital's slums were massacred. He returned from 29 years' exile in New York to a hero's welcome in 1986, but died of cancer a few months later. His party, the *noirist* Movement of Organisation of the Country (MOP) (formerly the Worker-Peasant Movement/MOP), survived under the leadership of Gérard Philippe-Auguste, who came third in heavily-boycotted presidential elections in 1988 and was agriculture minister in the government of Leslie Manigat. The MOP split the same year.

See also **Duvalier, François;** *noirisme*.

Figueres Ferrer, José María Hipólito ('Pepe')

1906–90. Provisional president of Costa Rica 1948–9; president 1953–8; 1970–74. Born in San Ramón, the son of Catalan immigrants, and educated at the University of Costa Rica, the University of Mexico and MIT, Pepe Figueres was the founder of the National Liberation Party (PLN). His academic and diplomatic posts included: visiting professor of Latin American affairs at Harvard University (1963–5); delegate to the UN Conference on Development and World Trade (1964); visiting professor at the University of New York (1967); and consultant to the UN human rights division (1967) and the Food and Agriculture Organisation.

As a young man, Figueres spent four years in the US (mainly in New York). On his return to Costa Rica he became a successful farmer. He first came to public attention with a verbal attack on President Calderón Guardia on 8 July 1942. His accusation that the government was under communist control led to his immediate arrest and exile to Mexico, on charges of collaboration with Germans and leaking military secrets. In exile he made contact with other Latin American dissidents and signed the Pact of the Caribbean, pledging to oust dictators from Central America and the Caribbean.

The opposition alleged fraud in the elections held in March 1944, in which Teodoro Picado Michalski had won the presidency for the National Republican Party. The newly-formed Democratic Action (AD) party launched a newspaper supporting Figueres which prepared the ground for his return on 23 May 1944, when he called for military action to oust the government and establish a 'Second Republic'. In March 1945, AD joined the Centro group in forming the Social Democratic Party (PSD), which in turn joined forces with the Democrat Party and the National Unionists to form a united opposition for the 1946 mid-term elections.

They accused Picado of over-reliance on the four communists in congress. In February 1947, unable to secure the opposition presidential nomination, Figueres became campaign manager for the candidate, Otilio Ulate.

Four months after the mid-term elections the Social Democrats attempted an armed uprising, in which Figueres, who thought it mistaken, took no part. Some 200 prisoners, with arms and ammunition, were captured by the government. But Figueres' group, while continuing political participation, made plans for a terror campaign and strengthened its links with supporters in the region. Ulate claimed victory in the 1948 elections, but the government had them annulled. Within weeks Figueres launched an insurrection in southern San José province, aided by foreign supporters from his days in exile, who became known as the Caribbean Legion.

After winning the 1948 civil war Figueres became provisional president of the Founding Junta of the Second Republic, which nationalised the banks and made changes in the structure of government, abolished the army and banned the Communist Party. A constituent assembly ratified Ulate's victory, and Figueres handed over the presidency to him in 1949. In 1951 he founded the National Liberation Party (PLN), his vehicle for the 1953 election, which he won by a wide margin. In office he expanded the social reforms begun by Calderón, extended state control of the economy and ran up a substantial public sector deficit. The period was marred by deep hostility between Figueres and the Nicaraguan dictator Somoza García, who sponsored an abortive invasion attempt by *calderonista* exiles in 1955.

Figueres declined the PLN nomination in 1966, but won easily when he stood again in 1970. During 1970–74 he consolidated earlier reforms and sought economic diversification. His image was tarnished, however, by allegations of impropriety in his relationship with the fugitive US financier Robert Vesco, who settled in Costa Rica in 1972. In 1976, during the Oduber presidency, Figueres caused a split in the PLN over his proposed constitutional amendment allowing two successive presidential terms. He withdrew from party activities and declined to campaign in 1978 for Luis Alberto Monge, who lost to the opposition candidate, Rodrigo Carazo. During Monge's presidency (1982–6), Figueres was appointed roving ambassador, but he was forced to resign in 1985 after staging a 'peace crusade' to the Nicaraguan border, followed by a visit to the People's Republic of China. In 1983 he was re-elected as PLN president and used his influence to back the presidential aspirations of Oscar Arias (1986–90).

See also **Civil War** (Costa Rica); **National Liberation Party; Caribbean Legion; Calderón Guardia; Somoza García; Arias Sánchez.**

flag riots

Disturbances in Panama in 1964 arising out of the refusal of US students and their parents to allow a Panamanian flag to fly alongside the Stars and Stripes over a Canal Zone high school. Demonstrations involving

some 30,000 people led to at least 22 deaths, 300–450 injuries, 500 arrests and damage valued at $2m. US troops were ordered to fire warning shots at demonstrators, then shoot to kill. The government of Panama broke diplomatic relations, but restored them after the US agreed to allow the flag to be flown and to negotiate a new canal treaty.
See also **Panama Canal Treaties.**

Fleming, Albert
b. 22 July 1936. Political leader of the French Caribbean possession of Saint Martin. A wealthy owner of construction and property firms, Fleming was elected independent conservative mayor of the main town, Marigot, in 1977. He was re-elected in 1983, but the election was annulled in 1984. He won in a new vote the same year. There were calls in 1988 for his removal because of his authoritarian rule and his residence in the Dutch part of the island so as to avoid French taxes.
See also **Saint Martin.**

Fletcher, Raphael: see Grenada United Labour Party.

Flores Facussé, Carlos: see Liberal Party (Honduras).

foco: see *foquismo*.

Fonseca Amador, Carlos
1935–76. Founder of the Sandinista National Liberation Front (FSLN), Nicaragua. Carlos Fonseca was born in Matagalpa. As a schoolboy he played an active role in the formation of a student committee. At the age of 19 he joined the law school at the National Autonomous University (UNA). In 1955 he founded a university revolutionary cell whose members were loyal to the memory of revolutionary heroes Augusto César Sandino and Benjamín Zeledón. He joined the Socialist (communist) Party (PSN) in 1956, and was arrested and tortured in the same year after the assassination of President Anastasio Somoza García, in which he was not involved. In 1957 he went to Moscow as a delegate to the Sixth Congress of the World Federation of Democratic Youth, and was subsequently imprisoned and tortured by the Somoza regime. On his release he organised 'popular committees' in the city of León and wrote on politics for *Nueva Nicaragua* magazine, as well as arguing for revolution at public meetings.

Fonseca's earliest involvement in guerrilla activity was in 1958, as a member of a small group under the command of Gen. Ramón Raudales, a veteran of Sandino's army. In 1959 he formed the Rigoberto López Pérez column, which was ambushed by the National Guard. He was seriously wounded, arrested again and jailed in Honduras, before being deported to Guatemala (1960) and held there for a time. In 1961–3 he was exiled in Cuba, Costa Rica and Honduras. He organised (with former followers of Sandino) the New Nicaragua Movement (MNN) and, later, the FSLN. Fonseca insisted on the relevance of the tradition of Sandino to contemporary Nicaragua (hence 'Sandinismo'), and as the Frente's most important theorist, argued for a revolutionary coalition of marxists, radical Christians and liberals. He entered Nicaragua secretly in 1963, but was captured in June 1964 in Managua and imprisoned. Deported to Mexico six months later, he returned in 1966. In 1969 he was again arrested (this time in Costa Rica) while on an FSLN mission, but FSLN pressure secured his release and deportation to Cuba.

Fonseca was secretary general of the FSLN from 1966 to his death in 1976, a period spent mostly in Cuba writing on Nicaraguan history, as well as travelling to a number of countries. He returned to Nicaragua in 1976 in an attempt to heal the split between the three internal tendencies of the FSLN, and was killed in a National Guard ambush on 7 November 1976 near Zinica. Fonseca, who is second only to Sandino in the FSLN pantheon, is buried in the Plaza de la Revolución, Managua, where an eternal flame commemorates his death.

See also **Sandinista National Liberation Front; Somoza García; Sandino.**

'Football (Soccer) War'

The popular name for the five-day war of July 1969 between El Salvador and Honduras, so-called because of the erroneous notion that it was fought over the result of a World Cup qualifying round match. The origins of the conflict lay partly in the resentment felt by the Hondurans over the flooding of their country's markets by Salvadorean products, imported under the terms of the Central American Common Market, of which both were members. El Salvador, being the more highly industrial-ised nation, was able to take greater advantage of the lack of tariff barriers. Honduras had also been flooded in recent years with Salvadorean immigrants, most of whom had been landless in their own country. Between 1961 and 1971 the number of landless peasants in El Salvador increased from 30,000 (11% of the rural population) to 112,000 (29%), due in large measure to an expansion of the area under cotton. Salvadorean migrants in Honduras at the time of the war were estimated at 300,000.

Tension between the two countries had waxed and waned for decades, and numerous clashes had taken place along their disputed common border. In 1966 it had risen sharply after an attempt by the Salvadorean military to install a government in Honduras which would be more favour-able to the Common Market. The government of Gen. Oswaldo López Arellano in Honduras, seeking to distract its people from internal diffi-culties, blamed Salvadorean immigrants for taking land belonging to Hondurans. Instead of embarking upon serious land reform, which would have involved confrontation with major landowners, it expropriated land belonging to Salvadoreans (April 1969) and expelled them from Hondu-ras. An ultra-right group calling itself *Mancha Brava* began forcibly evicting Salvadoreans, who in June 1969 started crossing the border in hundreds (ultimately totalling 20–50,000). The Honduran government had invoked a section of the 1962 agrarian reform law which required that owners of land be 'Honduran by birth', and given those who were not 30 days to leave.

On 14 July 1969, the Salvadorean air force bombed Toncontín airport,

Tegucigalpa. During the 100-hour war, the Salvadorean army penetrated deeply into Honduras in some areas before a ceasefire was arranged via the Organisation of American States (OAS). Economic and political ties between the countries were cut and Honduras pulled out of CACM altogether. A peace treaty was finally signed in October 1980, under pressure from the United States, which was concerned about lack of co-ordination between the two armies in border areas where the Salvadorean FMLN guerrillas had strongholds. The treaty did not resolve the border dispute, however.

See also **border dispute** (El Salvador/Honduras); **López Arellano; Central American Common Market.**

foquismo

A theory of guerrilla war which emerged from the Cuban revolution, was refined by Ernesto 'Che' Guevara and popularised by the French marxist philosopher Régis Debray (though Debray later acknowledged its limitations). Its essence, as expressed by Guevara, was that 'it is not necessary to wait until all conditions for making a revolution exist; the insurrection can create them'. In practice, this meant starting a guerrilla *'foco'* (centre, or nucleus) in a remote, preferably mountainous region, which could provide the model for the rural population and eventually a catalyst for mass revolt. Both Guevara and Debray stressed that this should not be considered in isolation from work among the urban proletariat, through they tended to minimise this requirement, and this was a prime factor in the downfall of most *foquista* experiments.

The theory began to lose credibility after the failure of Guevara's 1967 Bolivian *foco*, which led to his death. In Central America it was put into practice by the Guatemalan FAR (1960–68) and the Nicaraguan FSLN (1963–7), but the virtual military annihilation of both movements led to a profound reassessment, culminating in a change of strategy, with much greater emphasis laid on slow, painstaking political work. The Revolutionary Party of Centralamericanist Workers (PRTC) failed in attempts to establish a Honduran *foco* in 1983 and 1984, while denying that its tactics were *foquista*.

See also **Guevara de la Serna; Rebel Armed Forces; Sandinista National Liberation Front.**

Forde, Henry

b. 20 March 1933. Barbadian politician. A barrister, he joined the Barbados Labour Party (BLP) in 1971 and was elected to parliament the same year. After the BLP returned to power in 1976, he was named attorney-general and external affairs minister, posts he held until 1981. After the party's defeat at the 1986 general election, he succeeded Bernard St John as party leader in 1987. He was official leader of the opposition until the BLP was displaced in 1989 by the more numerous MPs of Richie Haynes's new National Democratic Party.

See also **Barbados Labour Party; Haynes.**

Fort Dimanche

Haiti's most notorious political prison. A military post built on the marshes on the edge of Port-au-Prince, it became the main centre of torture and murder under the 28-year Duvalier family dictatorship (1957–86). Many thousands died there of disease, torture or execution. Under foreign human rights pressure the regime announced its closure, but it remained in operation. In 1986, after the Duvaliers fled, six people died when police opened fire on demonstrators who went to the prison to mark the anniversary of a 1963 massacre. A new massacre of 46 regime opponents was reported there in November 1987. The Avril government announced in 1988 that it would be closed, but ignored calls to make it a memorial to the dead.

See also **Duvalier, François; Duvalier, Jean-Claude; Tontons Macoutes; Duvalierism.**

Fortuné, Georges: see CATH.

Forty Thieves: see United Bermuda Party.

Forum for Peace and Democracy: see Central American Democratic Community.

'Forum' groups: see 'new left'.

Forum of Democratic Guatemalans (*Foro de Guatemaltecos Democráticos*/FGD)

A group of prominent Guatemalan exiles in Mexico, including academics, journalists and trade union leaders. Since 1986 the FGD has made the return to Guatemala of its members conditional on a series of reforms, including repeal of the 1986 amnesty for members of the armed forces guilty of human rights violations; trials for those guilty of such crimes; the demilitarisation of the countryside; and the dismantling of civil patrols and the 'apparatus of clandestine repression'. After a 5-day visit to the country in November 1987, members of the group concluded that the conditions for their open participation in politics did not exist.

See also **Cerezo Arévalo; civil patrols; Unitary Representation of the Guatemalan Opposition.**

Foster, Kenneth: see St Lucia Labour Party.

Fountain Valley massacre (1972): see St Croix.

Four H's, The: see People's National Party; National Workers' Union of Jamaica.

fourteen families

The ruling clique of El Salvador was traditionally said to comprise fourteen families. One version is that they were the Dueño, Regalado, Hill, Mes Ayau, De Sola, Sol Millet, Guirola, Alvarez, Meléndez, Menéndez Castro, Deininger, Quiñónez, García Preto and Vilanova families, although others are mentioned. Most of their wealth came originally from coffee. The Meléndez and Quiñónez clans founded a political dynasty which held the presidency from 1913 to 1931, but after the 1932 uprising 'the 14' did not rule directly. Instead, they left formal government largely in the hands of the army, up to the coup of October 1979, which curtailed their power.

See also **Matanza (1932 massacre)**.

Frampo: see **National Liberation Coalition**.

Francis, Nathaniel 'Bops': see **Progressive National Party**.

Franco-Mexican declaration

A joint statement by the French and Mexican governments, sent to the chairman of the UN security council on 28 August 1981, in which they recognised the Democratic Revolutionary Front-Farabundo Martí National Liberation Front (FDR-FMLN) of El Salvador as a 'representative political force' whose participation in negotiations to resolve the country's crisis was 'legitimate'. Their stance won little international support, and was rejected not only by the Salvadorean government but by many other Latin American governments as interference in the country's internal affairs.

See also **López Portillo; Farabundo Martí National Liberation Front; Democratic Revolutionary Front** (El Salvador).

Frank, Hilbourne

b. 1932. Barbudan politician. A former schoolteacher and electrical engineer, he campaigned against Barbuda's becoming independent in 1981 as part of Antigua and favoured either separate independence or continued colonial status. His Barbuda People's Movement controlled the Barbuda council 1979–85 (with Frank as chairman) and again from 1987. It held all nine seats after elections in 1989 and Frank became chairman again. Frank was elected the island's representative in the state parliament the same year, defeating the incumbent Eric Burton.

See also **Barbuda; Burton.**

Free National Movement (FNM)

Conservative party in the Bahamas, founded in 1971 by Cecil Wallace-Whitfield as successor to the white-dominated United Bahamian Party (UBP). Education minister Wallace-Whitfield led three other ministers and four MPs out of the ruling Progressive Liberal Party (PLP) in 1970 and with the four remaining UBP MPs founded the Free National Movement in 1971, led by Henry Bostwick and then Wallace-Whitfield. A secessionist movement in Abaco island, opposing Bahamian independence, attached itself to the FNM in 1971. The party was beaten 28–9 by the PLP at the 1972 elections and the PLP defectors, including Wallace-Whitfield, lost their seats. Four FNM MPs were expelled from the party in 1973 for sympathising with the Abaco secessionists.

Kendal Isaacs became party leader until 1975, when Wallace-Whitfield returned. Quarrels led to resignations and formation of the Bahamas Democratic Party (BDP) by Bostwick, which contributed to another election defeat in 1977, when the FNM won 5 seats and the BDP 3 to the PLP's 30. The FNM then reabsorbed the BDP and Isaacs became leader once more in 1981. But the FNM lost again in 1982 (11–32) and in 1987 (16–33), with the party unable to counter the public belief that it was still the instrument of the old white ruling class and, in 1987, also secretly backed by the US government. Isaacs was replaced as leader again by Wallace-Whitfield in 1987. When Wallace-Whitfield died in 1990, former PLP housing minister Hubert Ingraham was elected party leader.

See also **Wallace-Whitfield; Isaacs; United Bahamian Party; Progressive Liberal Party; Abaco secession movement.**

Free Nation Party (PPL): see ARENA.

Fuentes, Carlos: see Cardenas, Cuauhtémoc.

Fuentes Mohr, Dr Alberto: see Lucas García.

Fuentes Pieruccini, Mario: see Revolutionary Party (Guatemala).

fusiles y frijoles

A counter-insurgency campaign initiated by the government of Gen. Efraín Ríos Montt in Guatemala in 1982 and known in English as 'rifles and beans' or 'beans and bullets'. In secret army documents the campaign was identified as part of the 'Victory 82' plan. It consisted of the depopulation of guerrilla areas by a scorched earth policy and the killing of civilians; the establishment of 'model villages' (after Vietnam-style strategic hamlets), and the rapid expansion of obligatory civil defence patrols.

See also **Ríos Montt; 'civil patrols.'**

FUTH: see Communist Party of Honduras.

G

Gairy, Sir Eric

b. 18 February 1922. Chief minister, premier, prime minister of Grenada 1961–2, 1967–79. An ex-teacher, Gairy returned to Grenada in 1949 from Aruba, where he had worked as a clerk and was a trade union organiser. In 1950 he founded the Grenada Manual and Mental Workers' Union (from 1972 the Grenada Maritime and Intellectual Workers' Union) as well as the Grenada People's Party (from 1951 the Grenada United Labour Party/GULP). He led strikes and demonstrations in 1951 and was elected to the legislative council.

Gairy served as minister of trade and production 1956–7, before the GULP lost the 1957 elections, after which he was disenfranchised for five years for disrupting a political meeting. He became chief minister after the GULP's 1961 election victory, but the British-appointed governor dismissed him the following year for alleged corruption. In 1967, when the GULP returned to power, he became premier. After a series of strikes in 1970, Gairy became increasingly repressive and eccentric, claiming that he was appointed by God and intimidating opponents with a band of thugs known as the Mongoose Gang. However, in 1974 he led the country to independence from Britain amid a general strike against his rule, and became prime minister.

Gairy's government was overthrown by the left-wing opposition New Jewel Movement (NJM) in 1979 while he was in New York to lecture the UN General Assembly about flying saucers. The US government blocked his extradition to face charges of conspiracy to murder. After the US invasion of Grenada in 1983 he was allowed to return the following year, but he was not a candidate in the 1984 general elections in which the GULP won a third of the votes. He called for US troops to return to Grenada to provide jobs, defend against future invasion and counter 'communism'. He stood for parliament in the 1990 elections, though virtually blind, and was narrowly beaten, but the GULP won four seats. See also **Grenada United Labour Party; New Jewel Movement; Grenada, US invasion (1983); Netherlands Antilles, oil refineries.**

Gallisá, Carlos: see **Mari Bras.**

Gálvez, Juan Manuel: see **Carías Andino.**

García, Mario David: see **Authentic Nationalist Central.**

149 general strike (Honduras/1954)

García Godoy, Héctor: see Dominican Republic, US invasion (1965).

García Pérez, Alan: see Lima Group.

Gardner Dunn, Archibald: see Popular Liberation Forces.

Garífuna: see Atlantic Coast (Nicaragua).

Garvey, Marcus
1887–1940. A Jamaican-born pioneer in the fight for the dignity and freedom of Afro-Caribbeans and Afro-Americans, Garvey was the major inspiration for generations of blacks in the Caribbean, North America and Europe and those who were to lead independent Africa.

Travels in Central America, the Caribbean and England between 1909 and 1914 convinced him of the wretched plight of blacks. On his return to Jamaica in 1914, he founded the Universal Negro Improvement Association (UNIA) with the aim of creating a country for blacks. In 1916 he went to the United States where the UNIA drew huge support. He proclaimed himself 'provisional president of Africa', founded an international black newspaper (*The Negro World*), a black shipping company (the Black Star Line, 1919) and a chain of small businesses. He organised an international black convention in New York in 1920 and advocated that blacks return to Africa to regain control of it from its white masters. Garvey's popularity and eccentricity provoked hostility from rival black leaders in the US and from the white authorities and led to his trial and conviction for mail fraud in 1923. He was jailed from 1925 to 1927, after which he was deported to Jamaica, where he was greeted as a messiah by the poor. After further travels, he founded the radical People's Political Party in Jamaica in 1929 and while in prison was elected to Kingston city council in 1930.

He became disillusioned and left for England in 1935, where he died penniless in 1940. His body was returned to Jamaica in 1964 and he was officially proclaimed a 'national hero'. His talk of Ethiopia as the promised land for blacks and of a black king in Africa led to the rastafarian movement in Jamaica. The UNIA's red, black and green flag was adopted by the rastas.
See also **rastafarians; 'black power';** *noirisme*; **Césaire.**

Gayot, Archbishop François: see Haiti, Roman Catholic Church.

General Confederation of Workers (Honduras): see Christian Democrat Party of Honduras.

general strike (Honduras/1954)
A stoppage which began among United Fruit port workers in Puerto Cortés in April 1954 and became a general strike involving 50,000 workers and lasting until July. It was the most significant industrial action in the country this century. The original grievance concerned overtime payments for Easter Sunday, but soon all United Fruit workers were involved. On 1 May, Standard Fruit employees came out in support. The principal demands were union recognition and a 50% pay rise. All north-

ern ports were crippled, the fruit industry halted and communications with the capital cut. At the end of May the strike leaders were arrested and ORIT-trained, anti-communist leaders took control. The American Federation of Labor (AFL), led by George Meany, played a major role in persuading managements to grant recognition to unions. The strikers eventually won 10–15% pay rises, improved conditions, and – for the first time in Honduras – the right to organise legal unions, the most important of which was SITRATERCO, the United Fruit workers' union. The Communist Party (PCH), which had helped organise the strike, retained some influence with the labour movement, but ORIT and the AIFLD came to dominate it.

See also **American Institute for Free Labor Development; Communist Party of Honduras: ORIT.**

General Union of Guadeloupean Workers (*Union Générale des Travailleurs Guadeloupéens*/UGTG): see **Guadeloupe, independence movements.**

General Workers' Union (Belize): see **People's United Party; Price.**

General Generation of '48 (Costa Rica)

The political generation whose predominance lasted from their victory in the civil war of 1948 until the mid-1980s. Most were associated in the pre-war years with the Centre for the Study of National Problems and (from 1945) the Social Democrat Party. They formed the nucleus of the National Liberation Party (PLN) from its foundation in 1951, and most remained members.

See also **Civil War** (Costa Rica); **National Liberation Party; Figueres Ferrer.**

Generation of '44 (Nicaragua): see **Chamorro Cardenal, Pedro Joaquín; Independent Liberal Party.**

Giancano, Sam: see **Bay of Pigs invasion.**

Gibbons, (Sir) David: see **United Bermuda Party.**

Gilles, Serge

b. 5 January 1936. Haitian social democratic leader. In exile from 1962, mostly in Paris, Canada and the Dominican Republic, he founded the leftist Charlemagne Peralte Patriotic Action Committee in 1972 to oppose the Duvalier dictatorship. In 1980 he formed another left group, IFOPADA. After returning to Haiti on the fall of the Duvaliers in 1986, he rejected efforts to turn the party further left and broke away to found the more moderate PANPRA. In 1986–7 he was unofficial co-ordinator of the mainstream opposition as executive secretary of the Democratic Accord Committee (CED). In 1989, he joined conservative Marc Bazin's Movement for the Establishment of Democracy in Haiti (MIDH) to form a National Alliance for Democracy and Progress to contest elections.

See also **PANPRA; Bazin; Movement for the Establishment of Democracy in Haiti; Duvalier, Jean-Claude.**

Girón, Fr Andrés: see National Campesino Pro-Land Association.

Glasspole, Sir Florizel: see Jamaica; National Workers' Union of Jamaica.

Godett, Wilson 'Papa': see Social Independent Party-Workers' Liberation Front.

Godoy, Dr Virgilio: see Independent Liberal Party; National Opposition Union.

Gómez, Juan Gualberto: see Platt Amendment.

Gomez, M. F. da Costa: see National People's Party.

Gómez Morín, Manuel: see National Action Party.

Gonsalves, Ralph
b. 8 August 1946. Left-wing politician, St Vincent. A lawyer and former politics lecturer at the University of the West Indies in Barbados, the marxist Gonsalves became leader of the Youlou Liberation Movement (Yulimo) (f. 1974) in the late 1970s. In 1979 he led the three-party, left-wing United People's Movement (UPM) alliance to win 14.4% of the vote at a general election. The Barbados government had by then banned him from returning and he was forced out of his university job. In 1982 he broke away from the UPM to form the Movement for National Unity, which won 2% of the vote at the 1984 and 1989 general elections. In 1988 he criticised a narrow leninist approach as 'the path to political self-destruction in the Caribbean'.
See also **Movement for National Unity; United People's Movement; 'new left'.**

González, Leonel: see Popular Liberation Forces; Farabundo Martí National Liberation Front.

González Luna, Efraín: see National Action Party.

González Revilla, Antonio: see Christian Democrat Party (Panama).

good neighbour policy
A 'non-interventionist' stance adopted by US Presidents Herbert Hoover and Franklin D. Roosevelt towards Latin America in particular (though as originally formulated it referred to international relations in general). Espoused by Hoover with his acceptance of the 1928 Clark Memorandum on the Monroe Doctrine, the stance was reiterated by FDR in his inaugural address in 1933 and formally stated to be official policy by Secretary of State Cordell Hull at the 7th Pan American Congress in Montevideo that same year. Hull declared that 'no government need fear any intervention on the part of the United States'. In Montevideo he signed the Convention on the Rights and Duties of States, article 8 of which affirmed that 'No state has the right to intervene in the internal affairs of another.' The policy led to the abrogation of the Platt Amendment relating to Cuba, the withdrawal of US troops from Haiti and the 1936 signing of a non-intervention pact by the US and Panama.
See also **Monroe doctrine; Platt Amendment.**

Gourgue, Gérard

b. 1 December 1925. Haitian politician and human rights leader. A lawyer and school principal, Gourgue co-founded the Haitian Human Rights League in 1978 and took over the leadership later that year. He cautiously criticised the repression of the Duvalier family and was beaten by government thugs who broke up a human rights meeting he was addressing in 1979. After the dictatorship fell in 1986 he was named a member of the ruling junta and justice minister. He resigned after only a few weeks, complaining that reform was being obstructed. Though a conservative, he was chosen as presidential candidate by the leftist National Co-operation Front (FNC) in aborted elections in 1987 in a bid to reassure the US. The army and the Duvalierists forced cancellation of the vote, claiming it was being rigged in Gourgue's favour. He resigned as head of the Human Rights League in 1988. His successor, Joseph Maxi (b. 1926), was named interior minister in 1990 by provisional president Ertha Pascal-Trouillot. See also **Duvalier, Jean-Claude; Namphy; KONAKOM; Pascal-Trouillot.**

Grace, W. R.: see **American Institute for Free Labor Development.**

Grande, Fr Rutilio: see **Romero, Archbishop Oscar Arnulfo.**

Granger, Geddes: see **National Joint Action Committee; Trinidad, 'black power' uprising (1970).**

Granma

(1) a 58-ft cabin cruiser, bought for US$15,000 with money provided by Carlos Prío Socarrás, in which Fidel Castro and 81 others sailed from Mexico to Cuba in 1956 to begin the revolution. The trip lasted from 25 November to 2 December. Less than half of the 82 were to survive the initial clash with the dictator Batista's troops, and the nucleus of the revolutionary army was reduced to a score of men.
(2) a Cuban daily paper, the official organ of the Central Committee of the Communist Party of Cuba.
See also **Cuban Revolutionary War; Castro Ruz, Fidel Alejandro; Guevara de la Serna.**

Grau San Martín, Prof. Ramón: see **Batista y Zaldívar; Communist Party** (Cuba).

Greater Antilles

The larger islands of the Caribbean – Cuba, Jamaica, Hispaniola (Haiti and the Dominican Republic) and Puerto Rico.
See also **Lesser Antilles.**

Greaves, Philip

b. 19 January 1931. Deputy prime minister of Barbados 1987– . A barrister and former teacher, Greaves joined the Democratic Labour Party (DLP) in 1966. He was appointed a senator and home affairs minister and then elected to the house of assembly in 1971. He was then minister of housing and labour until the DLP's defeat in 1976. When the party regained power 10 years later, he was named minister of transport, works and communications. After the death of Errol Barrow in 1987, the new prime minister Erskine Sandiford appointed him his deputy. See also **Sandiford; Democratic Labour Party** (Barbados); **Barrow.**

GRENADA
Capital: St George's
Independence (from Britain): 1974
Area: 344 sq km
Population (1987): 103,400
Pop. growth rate: 1.3%
Pop. density: 301/sq km
Infant mortality: 17 per thousand
Life expectancy at birth: 67
Literacy: 85%
GDP per capita (1987): US$1,346
Foreign debt per capita (1990): US$546
Main exports: tourism, nutmeg and mace, bananas, cocoa

Political system

Constitution: 1974. Titular head of state: Queen Elizabeth of Britain, represented by a figurehead governor-general. A 15-member House of Representatives is elected for a maximum five years. A 13-member Senate is appointed.
Governor-general: Sir Paul Scoon (1978)
Prime minister: Nicholas Brathwaite (1990)
Last elections: 1990

Political organisations

Parties in parliament (leader) (seats in House of Representatives): National Democratic Congress/NDC (Nicholas Brathwaite) (8), f. 1987; Grenada United Labour Party/GULP (Sir Eric Gairy) (2), f. 1951; The National Party/TNP (Ben Jones) (2), f. 1984; New National Party/NNP (Keith Mitchell) (2), f. 1984.
Parties outside parliament: Maurice Bishop Patriotic Movement/MBPM (Terry Marryshow), f. 1984.
Main trade unions: Technical and Allied Workers' Union/TAWU (Chester Humphrey), f. 1958; Seamen and Waterfront Workers' Union/SWWU (Eric Pierre), f. 1952; Commercial and Industrial Workers' Union/CIWU (Anselm DeBourg), f. 1956; Public Workers' Union/PWU (Lauret Clarkson), f. 1959; Grenada Union of Teachers/GUT (Hudson McPhail), f. 1960; Bank and General Workers' Union/BGWU (Derek Allard), f. 1978; Agricultural and Allied Workers' Union/AAWU (Patsy Frame), f. 1984; Grenada Taxi Owners' and Drivers' Association/GTODA (Vivian Charles), f. 1968.
Employers' organisations: Grenada Employers' Federation/GEF (Angela Smith), f. 1962; Grenada Co-operative Nutmeg Association/GCNA (Norris James) f. 1947; Grenada Cocoa Association/GCA (Raymond Rush), f. 1964; Grenada Banana Co-operative Society/-

GBCS (R. M. Bhola), f. 1954; Grenada Hotel Association/GHA (Gus Cruikshank); Grenada Manufacturers' Association/GMA (George Williamson).
See also **Carriacou; Grenadines.**

Grenada Declaration (1971): see **Caribbean Community.**

Grenada Democratic Movement (GDM): see **Alexis; Mitchell, Keith.**

Grenada Manual and Mental (Maritime and Intellectual from 1972) **Workers' Union (GMMWU/GMIWU):** see **Gairy.**

Grenada National Party (GNP): see **Blaize.**

Grenada United Labour Party (GULP)
Founded in 1951 by trade union leader Eric Gairy by renaming the Grenada People's Party he launched the previous year, it won general elections for the legislative council in 1951 (6–2) and 1954 (6–2), losing in 1957 (2–6), winning again in 1961 (8–2), losing in 1962 (4–6) and winning in 1967 (7–3), 1972 (13–2) and 1976 (9–6). Gairy was overthrown in a coup by the New Jewel Movement while abroad in 1979. In elections in 1984 after the US military invasion the GULP, backed by the rural poor and centred on the charismatic personality of Gairy (who did not campaign), won 36% of the vote but only one seat. Gairy decided to boycott parliament and expelled his lone MP, Marcel Peters, from the party when Peters took his seat in 1985 and was named parliamentary opposition leader. Peters and others then formed a new party. In 1987, Gairy named academic Raphael Fletcher as deputy GULP leader and his eventual successor but soon dismissed him for supposed Libyan connections. The party won four seats and 28% of the vote at the 1990 general election. Gairy narrowly failed to be elected and one GULP MP defected to the government to give it an absolute majority, but the GULP was still the largest opposition party. A retired teacher, Winifred Strachan (b. 8 September 1930), was appointed parliamentary opposition leader. A few weeks later, another GULP MP left the party.
See also **Gairy; New Jewel Movement.**

Grenada, US invasion (1983)
After four years of economic and political harassment of Grenada's left-wing government by Washington, 7,000 US troops, followed by a token 150 soldiers from Jamaica and 250 from five other Anglo-Caribbean countries, invaded Grenada on 25 October 1983. The official aim was to 'rescue' several hundred US medical students at the 'offshore' University of St George's, to restore order and 'democracy' after the arrest and execution a week earlier of prime minister Maurice Bishop and to eradicate a supposed Cuban-Soviet threat to US security. The invasion had been rehearsed several times by the US, notably in 1981 on the Puerto Rican island of Vieques when 120,000 troops in the 'Ocean Venture' exercise 'invaded' the island, which they named 'Amber and the Amberdines'.

Caricom member-governments were planning a blockade of the extremist post-Bishop regime, the Revolutionary Military Council (RMC), led by Gen. Hudson Austin and Bernard Coard, when the invasion took place. A smaller group, the Organisation of Eastern Caribbean States (OECS), led by Dominica, St Lucia and St Vincent, claims it requested the intervention at the insistence of the sidelined figurehead Grenadian governor, Sir Paul Scoon. Sir Paul signed a formal letter of request only after the invasion, however, and at Washington's suggestion. Two weeks earlier the US had proposed to conservative Barbados an operation to 'rescue' the arrested Bishop. OECS chairwoman Eugenia Charles of Dominica was flown to Washington to stand at President Ronald Reagan's side as he announced the invasion, which was supported by all Caricom states except Trinidad-Tobago, Guyana, the Bahamas and Belize, and by most Grenadians. Cuba's rejection of the RMC's plea for help reportedly clinched the US decision to invade.

The military operation, codenamed Urgent Fury and involving all four US services, was a débâcle because of faulty intelligence and inter-service rivalry and the island was not under control until three days later. The only fighting took place between US troops and about 650 partly-armed Cuban construction workers building the island's new airport. There was also some Grenadian resistance. A third of the 20 Americans officially killed died in unrelated accidents. At least 10 other Americans were killed during a secret commando operation on the island just before the invasion. Forty-five Grenadians – including 18 inmates of a mental hospital bombed in error – and 24 Cubans were killed.

The US authorities arrested a score of the leaders of the Austin-Coard group, who were eventually tried and 14 of them sentenced to death in 1986 for murdering Bishop. A nine-member Advisory Council of government, headed by schoolteacher Nicholas Brathwaite, was formed and Barbadian officials brought in to head the police and army. Twenty tons of government and party documents were seized by the US, which published a faintly damning selection to back up its official psychological warfare effort on the island. The Bishop government's educational and community organisations were dismantled and US officials arrived to 'reorganise' the island's trade unions. Secretary of State George Shultz, visiting the island in 1984, described it as 'a lovely piece of real estate'.

Most US troops left after two months. The remaining 250 were gradually withdrawn, the last leaving in June 1985 along with the Caribbean troops. Elections organised in December 1984 during the occupation were won by the conservative New National Party, a coalition put together under US auspices and led by Herbert Blaize. The US launched a $15m military aid programme to the eastern Caribbean after the invasion and set up small, locally-manned para-military Special Service Units within each island's defence force. President Reagan visited Grenada in February 1986.

See also **Revolutionary Military Council; Coard; Bishop; Organisation of Eastern Caribbean States; Charles, Eugenia; Caribbean Community; Brathwaite; People's Revolutionary Government; invasions and occu-**

(…)

pations by the United States; Vieques; military bases (foreign) in the Caribbean; Special Service Units; Caribbean Conference of Churches; Singh; McIntyre; Blaize.

Grenadines

A string of 20 or so islands, nine of them permanently inhabited, stretching the 104 km between St Vincent and Grenada.

Area: 79 sq km
Population: 18,000
Main exports: lobster, fish, tourism, limes, cotton

Most are part of St Vincent, including Bequia, Union, Canouan, Mustique, Palm Island, Petit St Vincent and Mayreau (total 45 sq km). Grenada has Carriacou and Petit Martinique (total 34 sq km). The islands are dry but popular with foreign yachting enthusiasts. The islands elect one member to the Grenadian and two to the Vincentian parliament.

See also **Bequia; Carriacou; Mustique; Union Island revolt (1979); St Vincent; Grenada.**

Group of Eight: see Rio Group; Contadora Group.

Group of 57: see KONAKOM.

Group of 14: see National Opposition Union (Nicaragua).

Groves, Wallace: see Hawksbill Creek Agreement.

Guadeloupe

Capital: Basse-Terre
Area: 1,705 sq km
Population (1990): 386,600
Pop. growth rate: 2.1%
Pop. density: 227/sq km
Infant mortality: 19 per thousand
Life expectancy at birth: 73
Literacy: 90%
GDP per capita (1985): US$3,600
Foreign debt per capita (1987): US$157
Main exports: tourism, bananas, wheat flour, rum, sugar

Political system

A commissioner (prefect) appointed by and sent from Paris for (generally) a two-year term governs in consultation with a 42-member General Council (elected for six years, with half the council renewed every three years) and a 41-member Regional Council elected every five years. Guadeloupe, with its five smaller island dependencies, is officially a *département* (province) of France and is represented in the French parliament by four National Assembly deputies and two senators. It was granted more self-government in 1982 and the Regional Council (which controls longer-term policy) was created in 1983.

Commissioner (prefect): Jean-Paul Proust (1989)
President of General Council: Dominique Larifla (FSG) (1985)

President of Regional Council: Felix Proto (FSG) (1986)
Deputies: Frédéric Jalton (FSG) (1981), Ernest Moutoussamy (PCG) (1981), Lucette Michaux-Chevry (RPR) (1988), Dominique Larifla (FSG) (1988).
Senators: Henri Bangou (PCG) (1986), François Louisy (FSG) (1986).
Last elections: June 1988 (National Assembly), October 1988 (General Council), March 1986 (Regional Council).

Political organisations

Parties (leader) (seats in General/Regional Councils): Guadeloupean Socialist Federation/FSG (Felix Proto) (14/12), f. 1971; Guadeloupean Communist Party/PCG (Christian Céleste) (8/10), f. 1944; Rally for the Republic/RPR (Daniel Beaubrun) (9/15), f. 1976; Union for French Democracy/UDF (Simon Barlagne) (3/4), f. 1978.
Other parties: Popular Union for the Liberation of Guadeloupe/UPLG (Claude Makouke), f. 1978; Popular Movement for an Independent Guadeloupe/MPGI (Luc Reinette), f. 1982; Caribbean Revolutionary Alliance/ARC (Luc Reinette), f. 1983; Revolutionary Socialist Group/GRS (Alex Lollia).
Main trade unions: General Union of Guadeloupean Workers/UGTG (Rosan Mounien), f. 1973; General Confederation of Guadeloupean Workers/CGTG (Claude Morvan), f. 1973; Union Confederation of Guadeloupean Workers/CSTG (Alain Mephon), f. 1987.
Employers' organisations: Employers' Union of Guadeloupe/UPG (Amedée Huyghues-Despointes); Association of Medium-sized and Small Industries/MPI (Bernard Aubéry), f. 1974; Sugar and Rum Producers' Association/APSR (Amedée Huyghues-Despointes); Hotel and Tourism Association/CSMTG (Jean-François Rozan).
See also **Saint Martin; Saint Barthélémy.**

Guadeloupe, independence movements
France's policy of assimilation of Guadeloupe to France since 1946 has spawned a series of determined, though marginally-backed independence movements, which also oppose the presence of French troops and immigration of whites from France.

In 1967, 49 people were killed when police attacked a pro-autonomy demonstration in Pointe-à-Pitre staged by the Guadeloupean National Organisation Group (GONG) (f. 1963). The Armed Liberation Group (GLA), founded in 1979 by Luc Reinette, claimed responsibility for bombings in 1980 but was broken up the following year. In 1983 the Caribbean Revolutionary Alliance (ARC) emerged in another spate of bombings, some of them in Martinique, Paris and French Guiana. The French government outlawed the ARC in 1984. The same year, four people were blown up by their own bombs. In February 1985, ARC leader Luc Reinette and nine others were jailed for their part in the 1983 bombings. In June, Reinette escaped and in 1986 the ARC claimed credit for a score of explosions. Reinette was recaptured in St Vincent in 1987 but freed under an amnesty with eight other militants in 1989. The

National Council of the Guadeloupean Resistance (CNRG) brought together the underground movements.

The Popular Movement for an Independent Guadeloupe (MPGI) (f. 1982) has been considered a front for the ARC since 1984. The more moderate Popular Union for the Liberation of Guadeloupe (UPLG), founded in 1978 and led by Claude Makouke (b. 17 September 1937), opposes violence. It has won only 6% of the vote in local polls but a romantic image of independence, despite the relative affluence of life under French rule, provides it with wider public sympathy for its campaigns. In 1990, the UPLG watered down its stand to advocate 'associated statehood' as a transition to independence. France has meanwhile relaxed its grip, however. In 1974, French overseas possessions minister Olivier Stirn called for the 'reinvention of genuine West Indian culture' and one of his successors, Paul Dijoud, admitted in 1979 that strict imposition of French culture on the islands was wrong.

Several trade unions are pro-independence – notably the General Union of Guadeloupean Workers (UGTG), the Trade Union Confederation of Martinican Workers (CSTM) and the General Union of Martinican Workers (UGTM) – and publish numerous magazines. In 1988 the influential Guadeloupean Communist Party (PCG) (f. 1958) – which controls the island's two main towns, Pointe-à-Pitre and Basse Terre, and five others – elected Christian Céleste as its new leader and declared it favoured full independence for the island.

See also **Reinette; Bangou; military bases (foreign) in the Caribbean.**

Guadeloupean Communist Party (*Parti Communiste Guadeloupéen*/PCG): see Guadeloupe, independence movements.

Guadeloupean National Organisation Group (*Groupe d'Organisation Nationale de la Guadeloupe*/GONG): see Guadeloupe, independence movements.

Guadeloupe Party (*Le Parti de Guadeloupe*/LPG): see Michaux-Chevry.

Guantánamo base

A US naval base on the southern shore of Cuba, close to the island's eastern point, acquired under a 1903 treaty pursuant to the Platt Amendment to the Cuban constitution. Land at Honda Bay was also originally included but was exchanged in 1912 for an expansion at Guantánamo. The government of Fidel Castro does not accept the US right to the base but has been unable to secure its closure, despite the mutual abrogation of the Platt Amendment in 1934.

See also **Platt Amendment.**

GUATEMALA, Republic of

Capital: Guatemala City
Independence: (from Spain) 1821; (from Mexico) 1823; (from Central American Federation) 1838; independent republic established 1839
Area: 108,889 sq km

Population (1988): 8.7m (34.3% urban; approx. 60% indigenous)
Pop. growth rate (1980–88): 2.9%
Pop. density: 79/sq km
Infant mortality (1988): 53.6 per thousand
Life expectancy at birth (1988): 62.6
Literacy (1988): 48%
GDP per capita (1988e): US$1,502
Foreign debt per capita (1988e): US$318
Main exports (1988): coffee (35%); bananas (9%); sugar (6%); cardamom (5%)

Political system

Constitution: 1985 (took effect in January 1986). Head of state/government: President Marco Vinicio Cerezo Arévalo (DCG) (1986–90); replaced the *de facto* military regime of Gen. Oscar Humberto Mejía Víctores. Elections are held every five years for national and municipal authorities. The most recent general elections were in November/December 1985 (two rounds). There is a 100-seat legislature, of which 25 members are elected on a national list and 75 for districts or departments. voting is by universal adult (18+) suffrage, except for police and active-duty military personnel, and is compulsory for all but the illiterate, invalids and those over 70. The Communist Party (PGT) is banned from participation. Parties not obtaining 4% of the vote in the 1984 constituent assembly elections had their registration withdrawn.

Political organisations

Parties in parliament (leader) (seats): Guatemalan Christian Democrat Party/DCG (Alfonso Cabrera) (51); Union of the National Centre/UCN (Jorge Carpio Nicolle) (22); National Liberation Movement/-MLN (Mario Sandoval Alarcón) and Institutional Democratic Party/PID (Oscar Humberto Rivas García) (12 in coalition); Democratic Party of National Co-operation/PDCN (Rolando Baquiaux Gómez) and Revolutionary Party/PR (Carlos Enrique Chavarría Pérez) (11 in coalition); Democratic Socialist Party/PSD (Mario Solórzano) (2); National Renewal Party/PNR (Alejandro Maldonado Aguirre) (1); Nationalist Authentic Central/CAN (Héctor Mayora Dawe) (1).
Parties outside parliament: National Unity Front/FUN (Gabriel Girón Ortiz/Enrique Peralta Azurdia); Emergent Movement for Harmony/MEC (Dario Chávez/Arturo Ramírez/Col. Francisco Gordillo); Guatemalan Democrat Party/PDG (Jorge Antonio Reyna Castillo); Movement of Solidarity Action/MAS (Jorge Serrano); Front for National Advance/FAN (Col. Abundio Maldonado); Organised National Union/UNO; United Revolutionary Front/FUR (comprising New Force [Carlos Rafael Soto], Humanist Movement for Democratic Integration [Victoriano Alvarez], 20th October Movement [Marco Antonio Villamar Contreras] and Democratic Socialist Party/PSD [Mario Solórzano] [see above]); Democratic Action/AD (Leopoldo Urrutia); National Integration Party/PIN; Popular Alliance–5/AP–5; Socialist

Christian Party/PCS; Popular Democratic Force/FDP (Francisco Reyes
Ixcamey); National Advance Party/PAN (Alvaro Arzú Irigoyen); Gua-
temalan Nationalist Party/PANAC (Mario Castejón García Prendes);
National Unification Movement/MUN (Gen. Héctor Mario López
Fuentes); Guatemalan Unity (Luis Zurita Tablada) (a May 1988 splin-
ter from the PSD); Military Front (Gen. Aníbal Guevara); Feminine
Party of Guatemala/PFG (Tysbee Payeras de Muñoz).

In April 1988, seven parties fought the municipal elections as an
alliance: they were the MLN, MAS, PID, CAN, FUN, PNR and MEC.
The alliance won only 34 out of 272 districts, while the DCG won 140
and the UCN 56.

Labour confederations (affiliation): Unity of Trade Union and Popular
Action/UASP; Confederation of Guatemalan Trade Union
Unity/CUSG (led by Francisco Alfaro Mijangos) (ORIT) (a member
of the UASP); Trade Union of Workers of Guatemala/UNSITRAGUA
(independent, no legal status) (a member of UASP); General Co-
ordinating Body of Guatemalan Workers/CGTG (CLAT) (the main
force in the pro-government Unitary Union Co-ordinator/COSU).
Other important unions (all members of UASP) include the Peasant
Unity Committee/CUC; electricity workers/STINDE; bank employees/
FESEBS; university students/AEU; state employees/FENASTEG and
education workers/STEG.

Main employers' organisation: Co-ordinating Committee for Agricultural, Commercial, Industrial and Financial Associations/CACIF
(Arturo Pellecer Arellano).

An armed insurgency whose origins go back to 1960 is now co-
ordinated by the Guatemalan Nationalist Revolutionary Unity/URNG.

Guatemalan Labour Party (*Partido Guatemalteco del Trabajo*/PGT)
An orthodox communist party, founded in 1949 as the Communist Party
of Guatemala (PCG), the PGT took its present name in 1951. It was
active in organising the workers' movement during the 'revolution' of the
late 1940s and early 1950s, although banned under the Arévalo government (1945–51). It held some government posts, especially in agrarian
reform, under Jacobo Arbenz (1951–4), whose presidential candidacy it
had backed, and had four seats in congress. After Arbenz' overthrow it
was again banned and has remained illegal ever since, although it has
retained an influential role in the Guatemala City labour movement and
among south coast agricultural workers in particular. In 1961 it defined
its support for armed struggle, which it put into practice at first alone
and later alongside the 13 November Revolutionary Movement (MR–13),
the two coalescing in 1962 to form the Rebel Armed Forces (FAR).
The PGT was assigned the political leadership, but gradually abandoned
practical support for armed struggle, so that in 1968–71 the FAR broke
with the communists. In 1966 and again in 1972 the bulk of the PGT
leadership was captured and murdered by the armed forces.

By the mid-1970s its formal abandonment of guerrilla warfare had led
to a serious split in the ranks. In 1981 the so-called 'National Leadership

Nucleus' (*PGT-Núcleo de Dirección Nacional*) broke away over the issue
of armed struggle and in 1982 helped found the URNG guerrilla front,
though it failed to develop a serious military structure and later left the
URNG by mutual agreement. In 1985 the faction known as the 'PGT–6
January' broke away from the Central Committee. By this stage there
were at least five different PGT factions, although the Leadership Nucleus
and the Central Committee came to operate as one and aligned with the
URNG.

See also **Guatemalan National Revolutionary Unity; Arbenz Guzmán;
Rebel Armed Forces.**

Guatemalan National Revolutionary Unity (*Unidad Revolucionaria Nacional Guatemalteca*/URNG)

A guerrilla front founded in January 1982 by all four Guatemalan armed
revolutionary groups (EGP, FAR, ORPA and PGT-Leadership Nucleus)
around a five-point programme. Its demands were: an end to repression;
an end to domination by the rich; equality for the indigenous population;
representation in government for all 'patriotic, popular and democratic
sectors'; and self-determination and non-alignment. Military fusion did
not take place until early 1985, when the General Command (*Comandan-
cia General*) was set up. By then the PGT was split into five factions,
and though still formally a member of the URNG, had no military
presence. The command had overall control of political and military
strategy. It emphasised a flexible response to the national and international context and the avoidance of 'stale' debates on the relative
merits of insurrection and prolonged war. It declined to disrupt the 1985
elections but insisted the poll was solely a 'manoeuvre' by the army.

The URNG stated that it would not seek to hinder government reform
efforts, and in May and October 1986 the guerrillas proposed preliminary
negotiations with Cerezo, who had also expressed a willingness to engage
in 'talks'. They called, among other things, for the security forces to be
purged of those responsible for human rights violations, something which
Cerezo had always rejected. The president eventually declared that the
rebels must lay down their arms before any dialogue could take place.
In February 1987 the URNG repeated its call for talks, suggesting that
they should be aimed at creating 'the broadest alliance in Guatemalan
history', but this was again rejected, first by the army and then by the
government. Following the signing in August 1987 of the Central American peace plan (the Arias Plan), the offer was renewed, and this time
Cerezo proposed preliminary talks between the URNG and the National
Reconciliation Commission (CNR) set up under the plan. In October
1987 'low level' talks were held in Madrid between the government and
the guerrillas, with army officers present as observers, but these were
accompanied by an intensification of military activities on both sides. The
URNG had proposed the dismantling of 'the military power structure',
the humanisation of the war and a broad national dialogue. Inconclusive
CNR-URNG meetings were held in Costa Rica in late 1988/early 1989,

but at a meeting in Oslo in March 1990 the two sides agreed to resume a dialogue.

The URNG currently claims 3,000 combatants and is seeking to double this figure, although some observers put its strength at only 1,500. In 1989 it stepped up military activity, opening new fronts including one in the capital. The General Command (1990) comprises: Rolando Morán (EGP), Pablo Monsanto (FAR), Rodrigo Asturias ('Gaspar Ilom') (ORPA) and Carlos González (PGT).

See also **Guerrilla Army of the Poor; Organisation of the People in Arms; Rebel Armed Forces; Guatemalan Labour Party**.

Guatemalan Social Party: see **Christian Democrat Party** (Guatemala).

Guerra, Eutimio: See **Cuban Revolutionary War**.

Guerra-Meneses Treaty: see **San Andrés dispute**.

Guerrilla Army of the Poor (*Ejército Guerrillero de los Pobres*/EGP) A Guatemalan guerrilla group founded in 1972 by former leaders of the Rebel Armed Forces (FAR), forced into exile in the 1960s by military defeat, who had sought to retain control from Cuba. Their efforts were rejected and they were replaced as leaders. Fifteen EGP founders entered Guatemala from Mexico in January 1972 to begin organising both in the northern provinces of Quiché and Huehuetenango and on the south coast plantations. The group was originally known simply as New Organisation of Combatants (NORC). Its strategy was based on that of the Edgar Ibarra Guerrilla Group (GEI), one of the constituent parts of the FAR, but this was rejected by the new FAR in a pamphlet entitled 'Our Conception of the War'.

Based initially in northern Quiché province, by 1982 the EGP was operating on seven fronts and was the only guerrilla group with a truly national structure. It worked closely with the Peasant Unity Committee (CUC) and was the first group to incorporate large numbers of Indians into its ranks, in the belief that the 'ethnic-national contradiction' was a key factor in mobilising for revolution. (In the mid-1980s the distinction between the EGP and the CUC virtually disappeared, the latter having been 'paramilitarised'.) Linked urban organisations included the student front FERRG and the shanty-town-dwellers' union UPT. Arguing that political and military work went hand in hand, the group did not form separate structures to handle each. Its first public act was the killing of a notorious landlord known as the 'Tiger of Ixcán' in 1975, which set off a huge army counter-insurgency campaign. In 1982 the EGP joined forces with other guerrilla groups to form the Guatemalan National Revolutionary Unity (URNG).

The counter-insurgency campaigns of the 1980s took a heavy toll of its civilian supporters, many thousands of whom were murdered, forcibly relocated or compelled to flee the country. By late 1985 it had concentrated its forces in northern Quiché (the 'Ho Chi Minh Front') and

northern Huehuetenango (the 'Ernesto Che Guevara Front') provinces once again. Leader (1990): Rolando Morán.
See also **Guatemalan National Revolutionary Unity; Peasant Unity Committee; Rebel Armed Forces.**

guerrilla movements (Honduras)

There are half a dozen left-wing guerrilla groups in Honduras, totalling probably less than 1,000 combatants. The Popular Action Front (FAP) emerged in the 1960s in the department of Yoro, headed by peasant leader Lorenzo Zelaya (killed in action in 1965). His name was later taken by the Lorenzo Zelaya Popular Revolutionary Forces (FPL-LZ), set up in 1979 by students at the National University and dedicated to 'prolonged, popular, revolutionary war'. FPL actions have included attacks on embassies and the seizure of radio stations. An attempt to infiltrate guerrillas from Nicaragua in 1984 led to the exposure of part of the FPL network.

Founded in March 1980, the Cinchonero Popular Liberation Movement (MPL-Cinchoneros) is also of student origin. Named after Serapio Romero ('Cinchonero'), a peasant leader who organised an uprising in 1865, its strategy is similar to that of the FPL, although there are ideological differences and its operations have been more spectacular. In September 1982 it seized 105 hostages at the Chamber of Commerce in San Pedro Sula, including the ministers of finance and the economy. Demands included the release of 160 political prisoners and the expulsion of foreign military advisers and the Nicaraguan contras, but the guerrillas eventually flew to Cuba apparently without achieving their aims. In January 1989 the Cinchoneros claimed responsibility for the murder of former armed forces chief Gen. Alvarez Martínez.

The Morazanista Front for the Liberation of Honduras (FMLH), linked with the Marxist-Leninist Communist Party (PCH-ML), dates from 1979 and specialises in attacks on US troops. In May 1990 it said it was abandoning the armed struggle. The Revolutionary Party of Central Americanist Workers of Honduras (PRTC-H), founded in 1977, appeared publicly in May 1983, arguing that a single vanguard movement had to be formed at regional level. The PRTC-H announced the formation of the National Unitary Directorate (DNU), which supposedly also comprised the FPL, the Cinchoneros and the Communist Party (PCH). No joint actions were subsequently undertaken, however. The PRTC-H's biggest action to date was the infiltration of almost 100 guerrillas from Nicaragua in July 1983 under the command of Dr José María Reyes Matta. The group's chaplain was the US-born priest James Francis ('Guadalupe') Carney, expelled from Honduras in 1979 for 'subversion'. The operation ended in defeat after two months. Reyes Matta and Carney were said to have died, although the bodies were never produced. Government opponents and the Carney family alleged that they were tortured to death. The PRTC-H attempted a similar operation, with the same results, a year later. Smaller groups include the Revolutionary Union of the People (URP), the Honduran Popular Forces (FPH) and the Patriotic Resistance Army–1927 (ERP–27). The Honduran Revolutionary Movement (MRH) now claims to co-ordinate guerrilla actions. See also **Communist Party of Honduras.**

Guevara, Gen. Aníbal: see Institutional Democratic Party.

Guevara de la Serna, Ernesto Che

1928–67. Argentine-born revolutionary and guerrilla leader. Born in Rosario into a well-to-do family, Guevara's early schooling was sporadic, due to the asthma which persisted throughout his life, but he graduated from the Buenos Aires School of Medicine in 1953. His parents were both involved in left-wing politics. As a student he travelled through several Latin American countries and spent a month in Miami. On his return he took part in a failed anti-Peronist plot. He had intended to go after graduation to Caracas, Venezuela, to work in a leper colony, but instead found himself eventually in Guatemala during the period of the US-backed overthrow of the Arbenz government. After taking a small part in the resistance, but failing in his attempt to be sent to the front, he was forced to flee via the Argentine embassy to Mexico, where he met Fidel Castro in 1955.

He agreed to join Castro in an attempt to overthrow the Batista government in Cuba, and set out on the *Granma* expedition in November 1956. Nicknamed 'Che' after the familiar Argentine form of address, he initially acted as a doctor but soon took up arms, gaining the highest rank (*comandante*, or major) and command of the 2nd (later renamed the 4th) column in the Sierra Maestra campaign. Two books based on these experiences (*Guerrilla Warfare* and *Reminiscences of the Cuban Revolutionary War*) became classics in their field. After the victory of the guerrilla forces in 1958 he toured widely (especially in the communist nations) explaining the nature of the revolution. Naturalised as a Cuban (under the name Ernesto Che Guevara) in January 1959, he held the posts of industrial director of the agrarian reform agency INRA; president of the National Bank; head of the Department of Instruction in the armed forces ministry (responsible for the development of the militias); director of the National Planning Board; and Minister of Industries. He may also have helped set up the G2 secret police unit. In 1961 he headed the Cuban delegation to the Punta del Este conference at which the Alliance for Progress was enacted.

From April to December 1965, under the code name 'Tatú', he fought with 200 Cuban troops in the Congolese civil war, in which the US Central Intelligence Agency and Cuban exile mercenaries were involved on the other side. There followed two years of planning for guerrilla campaigns on the mainland of South America, the aim being (as he put it) to create 'two, three, many Vietnams'. Having decided on Argentina as the ideal location for a guerrilla '*foco*' he later changed his mind and opted for Bolivia, setting up the National Liberation Army (ELN) training base at Ñancahuazú. The campaign, however, was a failure. Neither the local population nor the Bolivian Communist Party provided the necessary support and, with CIA help, Bolivian army rangers tracked down and annihilated the guerrillas. Che was captured on 8 October 1967 and after being identified by Cuban CIA agents was executed the next day by Sgt Mario Terán. His body was buried secretly, but his severed hands and his campaign diary were later sent clandestinely to Cuba. See also **Cuban Revolutionary War;** *foquismo;* **Castro Ruz, Fidel Alejandro.**

Guido, Clemente: see **Democratic Conservative Party of Nicaragua.**

Gumbs, Emile

b. 18 March 1928. Chief minister of Anguilla 1977–80, 1984– . Gumbs, a seaman, was one of the Anguillan delegation to a conference in Barbados with Britain and St Kitts in 1967 which tried in vain to persuade the Anguillans to return to Kittitian rule. He rebelled against Ronald Webster's leadership of the People's Progressive Party and was elected to the island council in 1972 as the lone opposition member. He later became minister of works, communications and trade but led a rebellion against Webster in 1977 and was named chief minister in his place. As leader of the Anguilla National Alliance (ANA), he lost power to Webster at elections in 1980, but returned to office after the 1984 elections which the ANA won. The ANA fell back to three seats in the 1989 election, but Gumbs formed a new government with the backing of an independent MP.
See also **Anguilla secession; Webster; Anguilla National Alliance; Dog Island.**

gusano

A pejorative term for an anti-Castro Cuban, supposedly derived from the name given in Cuba to the large bags in which emigrants took away their possessions. The more usual translation of 'gusano' is 'worm'. By 1979–80 the Cuban press had adopted the term *'mariposa'* (butterfly) instead, to signal President Castro's efforts at dialogue with the exiles, but the Mariel exodus of 1980 brought a renewal of mutual hostility.
See also **Mariel exodus; Omega 7.**

Gutiérrez, Gustavo: see **liberation theology.**

Guyana, Republic of

Although situated on the north-east coast of South America, Guyana is generally counted as part of the Caribbean because of its shared colonial history and economic similarity to the Anglo-Caribbean states. Guyana is a member of the Caribbean Community and Common Market (Caricom), which has its headquarters in the Guyanese capital, Georgetown.
See also **Caribbean Community.**

Guzmán, Antonio

1911–82. President of the Dominican Republic 1978–82. A wealthy rancher, Guzmán was nevertheless agriculture minister in the brief left-wing government of President Juan Bosch in 1963 and joined the leftist side during the 1965 civil war. The rightists refused a US proposal to make him provisional president after the US invasion. Bosch chose him as his running mate in the 1966 presidential election, which he lost. Guzmán was chosen as the PRD's presidential candidate in 1974 but at the last minute the party boycotted the election in protest at government-inspired repression.

In 1978, he was elected president, defeating President Joaquín Balaguer, after US President Jimmy Carter had intervened to block a coup by troops who stopped the vote count when they saw Balaguer was losing. Guzmán notably tamed the powerful armed forces, but shot himself dead in July 1982 after learning that his daughter and brother-in-law, who were close aides, were involved in corruption.

See also **Dominican Revolutionary Party; Bosch, Juan; Balaguer; Dominican Republic, US invasion (1965).**

Habib, Philip: see **Popular Social Christian Party.**

HAITI, Republic of
Capital: Port-au-Prince
Independence (from France): 1804
Area: 27,749 sq km
Population (1988): 6.3m (26% urban)
Pop. growth rate: 1.8%
Pop. density: 226/sq km
Infant mortality: 108 per thousand
Life expectancy at birth: 55
Literacy: 25%
GDP per capita (1988): US$319
Foreign debt per capita (1988): US$121
Main exports: light manufactures, coffee, mangoes, sugar, cocoa, essential oils

Political system

Constitution: 1987, creating a prime minister and reducing the power of the president, to be elected for a five-year term. An 83-member Chamber of Deputies is to be elected every four years. Members of a 27-seat Senate are to be elected for a six-year term, with one third of the seats renewed every two years. The constitution was suspended and parliament dissolved after a military coup in June 1988. The army was forced out of power by the opposition and the US government in 1990. A Supreme Court judge, sharing power with a 19-member Council of State, was named provisional president to organize elections.
President: Ertha Pascal-Trouillot (1990)
Last elections: 1988

Political organisations

Parties and groupings (leader): Haitian Nationalist Progressive Revolutionary Party/PANPRA (Serge Gilles), f. 1986; Movement for the Establishment of Democracy in Haiti/MIDH (Marc Bazin), f. 1986; National Committee of the Congress of Democratic Movements/ KONAKOM (Victor Benoit), f. 1987; National Agricultural and Industrial Party/PAIN (Louis Déjoie II), f. 1956; Haitian Christian Democratic Party/PDCH (Sylvio Claude), f. 1978; Unified Haitian Communist Party/PUCH (René Théodore), f. 1969; Rally of National Progressive Democrats/RDNP (Leslie Manigat), f. 1979; Mobilisation for National Development/MDN (Hubert de Ronceray), f. 1986; Democratic Unity Confederation/KID (Evans Paul), f. 1987; Worker-Peasant Movement/MOP (Gérard Philippe-Auguste/Emmanuel Beauvois), f. 1946; National Popular Assembly/APN (Ben Dupuy, François Pierre-Louis), f. 1986; Haitian Social Christian Party/PSCH (Grégoire Eugène), f. 1979; Papaye Peasant Movement/MPP (Chavannes Jean-Baptiste), f. 1986.

Main trade unions: Haitian Workers' Confederation/CTH (Jean-Claude Lebrun), f. 1989; Federation of Unionised Workers/FOS (Joseph Senat), f. 1984; Autonomous Federation of Haitian Workers/CATH (Yves Richard), f. 1980; Union of Metropolitan Area Public Transport Drivers/CSTPM (Lexius Cajuste), f. 1986; Union Federation of Haitian Drivers/CSTH (Nally Beauharnais), f. 1987; Independent General Haitian Workers' Organisation/OGITH (Schiller Marcelin), f. 1988; National Confederation of Haitian Teachers/CNEH (Carl Henri Guiteau), f. 1986; Haitian Journalists' Association/AJH (Raymond Exumé), f. 1986.

Employers' organisations: Haitian Industries Association/ADIH (Jurgen Anderson), f. 1980; Haitian Chamber of Commerce and Industry/CCIH (Ludovic Louisdhon), f. 1895; Haitian American Chamber of Commerce/HAMCHAM (André Apaid), f. 1979.

Haiti, Roman Catholic Church

Haiti's official church was dominated by white foreign priests (mainly Bretons) who occasionally crusaded against voodoo, the religion of most Haitians, until President François Duvalier's reign of terror began in 1959. He expelled its French archbishop, François Poirier, in 1960 and was excommunicated. In 1966 the Vatican yielded the right to name Haitian bishops and Duvalier appointed François Wolf Ligondé (b. 17 February 1928) as the first black and Haitian archbishop and head of the Church. In 1969 more priests were expelled, for leftist sympathies.

In 1978 the church opened a radio station, Radio Soleil, run by reform-minded foreign priests, which began criticising the dictatorship. The radio became the backbone and informal co-ordinator of the rising rebellion against the Duvaliers and the voice of the developing grassroots *Ti Legliz* (Little Church) movement. The Duvaliers expelled the station's managers and briefly closed it down, to no avail. The Pope had given a boost to the rebellion when he visited Haiti in 1983 in exchange for regaining control of naming bishops and declared that 'something must change here'.

The hierarchy is dominated by conservatives, led by Archbishop François Gayot (b. 12 July 1927) of Cap Haitien, who has eclipsed the widely-disliked Ligondé. The radicals, led by Father Jean-Bertrand Aristide, grew in influence after the Duvaliers fell. The hierarchy warned against 'communism' and denounced the 'liberationist' priests in 1987 despite

public support for them and forbade use of the term 'people's church'. In 1988 the church effectively abandoned its ambitious literacy plan, Misyon Alfa, launched in 1986, in a bid to curb the liberationists it said were 'politicising' it. Attempts to kill Aristide culminated in a government-inspired massacre during one of his services in 1988. A few days later disgusted junior army officers overthrew President Henri Namphy. Church efforts to transfer Aristide abroad from his Port-au-Prince slum parish failed in the face of strong public protests but he was expelled from the Salesian Order in 1988 and thus largely silenced. In 1989 the hierarchy, encouraged by the powerful papal nuncio (1984–90), Paolo Romeo, purged Radio Soleil of its pro-liberationist staff.
See also **Aristide; Duvalier, François; Duvalier, Jean-Claude; Namphy; Papaye Peasant Movement.**

Haitian Christian Democrat Party (*Parti Democrate Chrétien Haitien*/PDCH)
Founded in 1978 by Protestant pastor Sylvio Claude as the first non-government party for more than 20 years, the PDCH did not operate openly until 1979. The party's offices were soon ransacked by Duvalier regime agents, Claude imprisoned and the party's magazine, *Conviction*, seized. But all three continued to operate spasmodically over the next seven years, sometimes as the only internal opposition to the regime, until the Duvaliers fell. Claude was a candidate in aborted presidential elections in 1987 which he was tipped to win.
See also **Claude; Duvalier, Jean-Claude.**

Haitian Human Rights League (*Ligue Haitien des Droits Humains*/LHDH): see **Gourgue.**

Haitian Social Christian Party (*Parti Social Christien d'Haiti*/PSCH): see **Eugène.**

Haitian Workers' Confederation (*Confédération des Travailleurs Haitiens*/CTH): see **CATH.**

halcones: see **Echeverría Alvarez.**

Hall, Robert: see **Progressive Labour Movement; Walter.**

Hall, Robert: see **Progressive National Party** (Turks and Caicos Islands).

Handal, Schafick Jorge: see **Salvadorean Communist Party; Farabundo Martí National Liberation Front.**

Hanna, Arthur: see **Pindling.**

Havana, First Declaration of
The name given by Fidel Castro to a speech he delivered on 2 September 1960 before an estimated half-million Cubans in response to the Organisation of American States' (OAS) 'Declaration of San José' of the previous month. The OAS had implicitly condemned Cuban 'totalitarianism' and Soviet 'extra-continental' intervention, in a resolution which only Cuba

itself opposed. Castro's reply was to declare that Havana would establish diplomatic relations with the People's Republic of China and would accept Soviet missiles for defence against the United States. He also called on Latin American nations to emulate Cuba's rejection of US ties. See also **Castro Ruz, Fidel Alejandro; Havana, Second Declaration of.**

Havana, Second Declaration of

A document issued by Fidel Castro in response to the January 1962 expulsion of Cuba from the Organisation of American States (OAS). Like the first Declaration (see above), it urged Latin Americans to emulate Cuba by rising up against 'US imperialism'. The document was poorly received in Moscow, where the leadership was pursuing a policy of 'peaceful coexistence', and it highlighted the differences between Castro and the Cuban Communist Party.
See also **Castro Ruz, Fidel Alejandro; Havana, First Declaration of; Communist Party** (Cuba).

Hawksbill Creek Agreement

A 99-year agreement signed in 1955 between the white Bahamian authorities and a US businessman with underworld links, Wallace Groves (1901–88), to develop 600 sq km (about half) of Grand Bahama Island, only 130 km off the coast of Florida, into a freeport and tourist centre with sweeping tax concessions. Groves' Grand Bahama Port Authority, which had British and Canadian backing, from 1960 built a deep-water harbour at Freeport, a residential estate, an oil refinery and cement and pharmaceutical plants. Most land and business concessions went to white foreigners, as did most jobs. Charges of huge payoffs by the developers to Bahamian politicians contributed to the electoral downfall of the country's white rulers and the advent of the first black government under Lynden Pindling in 1967, though Pindling received similar financial backing. The government began to regain control over the island from 1969, notably over immigration in 1970, but foreign capital then fled. Grand Bahama did not recover for 10 years, and then only partially.
See also **Progressive Liberal Party; Pindling.**

Haya de la Torre, Víctor Raúl: see *indigenismo*.

Hay-Bunau Varilla Treaty: see Panama Canal Treaties.

Hay-Herrán Treaty: see Panama Canal Treaties.

Haynes, Richie

b. 10 June 1936. Leader of the opposition in Barbados 1989– . Trained in Britain as a doctor, Haynes was elected to parliament in 1978 as a member of the opposition Democratic Labour Party (DLP). He became finance minister when the DLP returned to power in 1986 and was seen as a possible successor to prime minister Errol Barrow. Soon after Erskine Sandiford took over on Barrow's death in 1987, Haynes resigned over policy differences and denounced Sandiford for failing to consult him. He formed the National Democratic Party in 1989 and, backed by three

other defecting DLP MPs, became official opposition leader, displacing BLP leader Henry Forde, whose party had only three MPs.
See also **Sandiford; Democratic Labour Party** (Barbados); **Barrow; Forde.**

Heath, Ivor: see **United National Democratic Party.**

Hector, Tim
b. 24 November 1942. Left-wing Antiguan politician. A schoolteacher, Hector was a leader of the new Antigua Workers' Union in 1967 and co-founder with George Walter in 1968 of the Progressive Labour Movement, becoming its first chairman. The same year, he founded the Afro-Caribbean (later Antigua Caribbean) Liberation Movement (ACLM) and became one of the pioneers of the regional 'new left'. In 1970 he broke away from the PLM. Spurning electoral politics until 1980, he campaigned vigorously against government corruption and became the main opposition to the ruling Bird family, although few Antiguans chose to step beyond the traditional parties to vote for him. He has been constantly harassed by the government and in 1985 was sentenced to six months in jail for libelling a cabinet minister. However, the sentence was declared unconstitutional.
See also **Antigua Caribbean Liberation Movement; Walter; Progressive Labour Movement.**

Helms, Jesse: see **Panama Canal Treaties.**

Herbert, Billie: see **People's Action Movement.**

Hernández Colón, Rafael
b. 24 October 1936. Governor of Puerto Rico 1973–7, 1985- . A former law professor, he was secretary (minister) of justice 1965–7 under Governor Roberto Sánchez Vilella. He became a Popular Democratic Party (PPD) senator in 1968 and was senate president 1969–72. He was elected governor in 1972 but was defeated both in 1976 and narrowly in 1980 by Carlos Romero Barceló. He regained the post in 1985 and was re-elected in 1988, after which he announced he would organise the first referendum since 1967 on the country's status – to choose between independence, US statehood or the present autonomy.
See also **Popular Democratic Party; Romero Barceló.**

Hernández Galicia, Joaquín: see **La Quina.**

Hodge, Omar: see **United Party; Virgin Islands Party.**

el hombre: see **Arias Madrid.**

Honduran Anticommunist Movement (MACHO): see **death squad.**

Honduran Patriotic Front (*Frente Patriótico Hondureño*/FPH)
An electoral alliance formed in 1981 by the Communist Party of Honduras (PCH), the Marxist-Leninist Communist Party (PCH-ML) and the Socialist Party (PASOH) which presented candidates in three out of the 18

departments (provinces) but failed to win any seats. In 1986 some members of the FPH joined with sectors of the Christian Democrat Party (PDCH), the Innovation and Unity Party (PINU) and the M-Lider faction of the Liberal Party (PL) in setting up a new Honduran Patriotic Front, described as 'moderate left'. The remnants of this form the nucleus of the San Pedro Sula-based Popular Unity group.
See also **Communist Party of Honduras.**

Honduran Popular Forces: see guerrilla movements (Honduras).

Honduran Revolutionary Movement (MRH): see guerrilla movements (Honduras).

HONDURAS, Republic of
Capital: Tegucigalpa
Independence: (from Spain) 1821; (from Mexico) 1824; (from Central American Federation) 1838
Area: 112,088 sq km
Population (1988): 4.83m (42.2% urban)
Pop. growth rate (1980–88): 3.5%
Pop. density: 43/sq km
Infant mortality (1983): 78.6 per thousand
Life expectancy at birth (1980–85): 59.9
Literacy (1988): 60%.
GDP per capita (1988e): US$851
Foreign debt per capita (1988e): US$694
Main exports (1987): bananas (40%); coffee (25%); wood (5%); beef (3%)

Political system
Constitution: 1965 (revised 1981 and 1982). Head of state/government: President Rafael Leonardo Callejas (PN) (1990–), succeeded José Simón Azcona Hoyo (PL) (1986–90). There is a single-chamber National Congress, comprising 134 deputies elected by universal compulsory adult (18+) suffrage under a proportional system on departmental (provincial) lists. (In 1987 Congress voted to reduce the number of deputies to a basic 128, but also to give seats to unsuccessful presidential candidates.) General elections are held every four years; the most recent were in November 1989. A president may not serve two successive terms.

Political organisations
Parties in Congress (leader) (number of seats): National Party/PN (Rafael Leonardo Callejas) (71) Liberal Party/PL (Carlos Flores Facussé) (55); Social Democratic Innovation and Unity Party/PINU-SD (Miguel Andonie Fernández) (2).
Parties outside Congress: Christian Democrat Party of Honduras/PDCH; Honduran Revolutionary Party/PRH (Francisco Rodolfo Jiménez Caballero) (no legal status); Social Democrat Party of Hon-

duras/PSDH; Honduran Patriotic Front/FPH; Communist Party of Honduras/PCH (Rigoberto Padilla Rush); Socialist Party/PASOH (Mario Virgilio Caras/Rogelio Martínez Reina).

There are also several illegal left-wing armed organisations, including: the Marxist-Leninist Communist Party/PCH-ML (with its armed wing, the Morazanista National Liberation Front/FMLNH); the Revolutionary Party of Central Americanist Workers-Honduras/PRTCH (linked to PASOH); the Popular Liberation Movement/MPL (or 'Cinchoneros'); the 'Lorenzo Zelaya' Popular Revolutionary Forces/FPL-LZ; the People's Revolutionary Forces/FRP; the Popular Action Force (FAP); the Revolutionary Action Movement/MAC.

Main labour organisations (leader) (affiliation): General Workers Central/CGT (Julio Chávez) (CLAT, but now allied to PN); Confederation of Honduran Workers/CTH (Francisco Guerrero/Luis Yáñez) (ORIT); Unitary Federation of Honduran Workers/FUTH (Héctor Hernández) (CPUSTAL); Honduran Northern Workers Trade Union Federation/FESITRANH (Francisco Guerrero) (part of CTH); Independent Federation of Honduran Workers/FITH; Federation of Agrarian Reform Co-operatives/FECORAH; National Rural Workers' Central/CNTC (Oscar Mejía); (two factions: [i] led by Lucas Aguiler and affil. to CGT/CLAT; [ii] led by Marcial Caballero and linked to PN); Organisation of Honduran Peasants/OCH (two factions: [i] led by Marcial Euceda and linked to PDCH; [ii] led by René Muñoz and affil. to APU); Honduran Federation of Peasant Women/FEHMUC (linked to UNC-Caballero); Council for the Integral Development of the Peasant Woman/CODIMCA (Rosa Dilia Rivera) (linked to OCH-Euceda); National Association of Honduran Peasants/ANACH (Luis Lagos) (part of CTH). The Co-ordinating Body of Honduran Peasant Confederations/COCOCH is an umbrella body representing all peasant organisations except the UNC-Caballero and the OCH-Euceda.

Main employers' organisation: Honduran Private Enterprise Confederation/COHEP (Richard Zablah).

Hoover, Herbert: see good neighbour policy.

Hudson-Phillips, Karl

b. 20 April 1933. Conservative Trinidadian politician. A barrister, Hudson-Phillips was elected to parliament for the ruling People's National Movement in 1966. He became minister without portfolio in 1969 and a few months later attorney-general. He was widely criticised for drafting a repressive Public Order Bill after the failure of the 1970 'black power' uprising and the bill was withdrawn. He was forced to resign in 1972 after indicating he wanted to succeed prime minister Eric Williams, who had said he would retire.

He founded the conservative Organisation for National Reconstruction (ONR) in 1981 and the party won 22% of the vote at the general election that year but no seats. Hudson-Phillips took the ONR into a four-party opposition National Alliance for Reconstruction in 1985, becoming one of its two deputy leaders. The coalition won the 1986 general election,

but Hudson-Phillips did not stand for parliament or take a cabinet post. A leading regional lawyer, he secured the jailing in 1979 for corruption of Antiguan ex-premier George Walter. In 1985–6, he led the prosecution team in the Bishop murder trial in Grenada.
See also **National Alliance for Reconstruction; Williams; People's National Movement** (Trinidad-Tobago); **Walter; Grenada, US invasion (1983); Coard; Bishop.**

Hueck, George: see Social Independent Party-Workers' Liberation Front.

Huerta, Gen. Victoriano: see Mexican Revolution.

Hull, Cordell: see good neighbour policy.

Hull-Alfaro Treaty: see Panama Canal Treaties.

Hunte, Julian
b. 14 March 1940. Leader of the opposition, St Lucia, 1984- . An insurance and property agent, Hunte joined the United Workers' Party (UWP) (he is UWP leader John Compton's brother-in-law) and was mayor of Castries 1971–2, resigning to become a member of the left-wing St Lucia Action Movement. He later left to join the St Lucia Labour Party, becoming deputy chairman after the party's 1982 election defeat and party leader in 1984 in a contest with left-winger Peter Josie. His refusal to make an electoral alliance with the Progressive Labour Party of George Odlum narrowly cost him victory in the two general elections in 1987, when he was elected to parliament for the first time.
See also **St Lucia Labour Party; Progressive Labour Party; Josie; Compton.**

Hurricane Hugo (1989)
The strongest hurricane to hit the eastern Caribbean for a quarter of a century, Hugo devastated the islands of Désirade, northern Guadeloupe, Montserrat, Nevis, St Croix, Vieques, Culebra and eastern Puerto Rico between 16 and 18 September 1989. Although only about 40 people were killed, total damage was estimated at up to $4bn, including $1bn in Puerto Rico, $600m in Guadeloupe and $500m in the US Virgin Islands. Some 1,000 US troops were flown to St Croix after widespread looting broke out in which local police and officials took part. Former USVI state senator and ex-gubernatorial candidate Adelbert Bryan was among those arrested.
See also **St Croix; Bryan.**

ICFTU: see American Institute for Free Labor Development.

IFOPADA: see Gilles.

Illescas, Jorge: see Social Democratic Innovation and Unity Party.

Ilom, Gaspar: see Guatemalan National Revolutionary Unity.

Imbert Barrera, Gen. Antonio

b. 3 December 1920. Right-wing leader in the 1965 Dominican Republic civil war. Imbert Barrera was a small businessman when he was drawn into a CIA-backed plot to murder dictator Rafael Trujillo in 1961. He is the last survivor of the team that carried out the assassination, for which he was given the official title of national hero and made an honorary general. He was a member of the provisional government from 1962 until elected President Juan Bosch took office in 1963. When civil war broke out in 1965, he was named head of the right-wing pro-US junta, the Government of National Reconstruction. He was named armed forces minister by President Joaquín Balaguer in 1986 but was dismissed in 1988.

See also **Dominican Republic, US invasion (1965): Trujillo; Balaguer; Bosch, Juan.**

Independent Citizens' Movement (ICM)

Political party in the US Virgin Islands. Founded in 1968 by Democratic Party dissidents led by Cyril King, it took a strong nationalist position. King was defeated in the 1970 election for governor, but won in 1974. He was succeeded on his death in 1978 by another ICM figure, Juan Luis. But the party did not support him when he was elected governor later that year and in 1982. The ICM candidate, Adelbert Bryan, lost the governorship race in 1986 to the Democrats but won 36% of the vote, campaigning against white minority control of the country and immigration problems. Party leader: Senator Virdin Brown.

See also **Luis; Bryan.**

Independent Liberal Party (*Partido Liberal Independiente*/PLI)

A 1944 offshoot of the official Liberal Party of Nicaraguan dictator Anastasio Somoza García, the PLI was formed by anti-Somoza intellectuals and members of the urban middle classes, the so-called 'generation of '44', who objected to Somoza's extension of his rule. The party's traditional base was the city of León and the cotton growers. Its ideology has historically been anti-marxist liberalism, and today it belongs to the Liberal International. The PLI joined the opposition UDEL coalition in 1974 and the Broad Opposition Front (FAO) in 1978, but left the FAO in December 1978 with other groups opposed to compromise with the regime. After the 1979 revolution it was allied to the Sandinista National Liberation Front (FSLN) until the Patriotic Front of the Revolution (FPR) was dissolved in April 1984. Its leader, Virgilio Godoy, was labour minister until March 1984.

The Godoy faction called for a boycott of the 1984 elections, but too late to achieve anything except a reduced vote. It occupied its nine seats in the legislature, insisting that this did not confer legitimacy on the government, and forged a temporary pact with a faction of the Democratic Conservatives (PCD). The PLI aligned itself with the abstentionist parties of the Nicaraguan Democratic Co-ordinator (CDN) in mid-1986 in calling for a general amnesty and new elections. It also advocated the depoliticisation of the army and the mass organisations and the conversion of agrarian reform titles to private property titles. The Godoy faction did not take part in the constitutional debate and refused to sign the 1987 constitution. However, a centre-left faction led by Eduardo Coronado, representing about 40% of members, did take part. This faction broke away in 1988 to form the PLI of National Unity (PLIUN).

The PLI formed part of the victorious UNO coalition in 1990, and Godoy became vice president of Nicaragua. However, differences between his group and that around President Violeta Chamorro were immediately apparent.

See also **Generation of '44; United Nicaraguan Opposition; Somoza García.**

Independent People's Movement (IPM): see **United Party.**

indigenismo: A 20th-century intellectual and political movement concerned with the revival of indigenous culture in the Americas. Its greatest contribution to politics was in post-revolutionary Mexico, especially under President Lázaro Cárdenas (1934–40) and in the APRA movement created by the Peruvian Víctor Raúl Haya de la Torre, who proposed that Latin America should be renamed 'Indo-America'. Although the indigenistas challenged the theory of white racial supremacy, hardly any were themselves Indians, and the movement was in many respects paternalistic. One of its tenets was that the mixing of the races in the Americas would result in a superior '*raza cósmica*' (cosmic race).
See also **Cárdenas, Lázaro.**

Indigenous Border Defence Militias: see **Yatama**.

indocumentados: see *braceros*.

Institutional Democratic Party (*Partido Institucional Democrático/* PID)
Founded in 1965 by members of the Guatemalan army, technocrats linked

to the oligarchy and conservative businessmen, led by the then president of Guatemala, Col. Enrique Peralta Azurdia. Despite being the official party, the PID lost the 1966 elections, but in coalition with the National Liberation Movement (MLN) it was successful in 1970 (Gen. Carlos Arana) and 1974 (Gen. Kjell Laugerud). In 1978 it joined forces with the Revolutionary Party (PR) to back the successful candidacy of Gen. Romeo Lucas. An attempt to repeat this formula in 1982, in alliance with the PR and the National Unity Front (FUN), failed when a coup unseated the president-elect, Gen. Aníbal Guevara. It won five constituent assembly seats in 1984 and subsequently renewed its coalition with the MLN, gaining one seat in the congress elected in 1985. The PID believes in unfettered private enterprise. It has no significant social base, having depended in the past largely on the official bureaucracy and the armed forces. Its current secretary general is Oscar Humberto Rivas García (re-elected in 1986). In 1989 it expressed support for the presidential candidacy of Gen. Efraín Ríos Montt.
See also: **Ríos Montt.**

Institutional Revolutionary Party (*Partido Revolucionario Institucional*/PRI)
The PRI grew out of the Mexican revolution and dominated the country's political system for more than half a century after 1929. It has been credited both with Mexico's long period of political stability and with creating the country's authoritarian power structure. Founded in 1929 by President Plutarco Elías Calles, one of a generation of revolutionary generals, the PRI was first named the National Revolutionary Party (PNR). It absorbed the various socialist and liberal factions, the approximately 400 different parties which had come into being during the revolutionary process, and also the emerging state bureaucracy and the armed forces. From the start the party was made virtually synonymous with the state, adopting the colours of the Mexican flag. In the period 1929–88 it won every single presidential and state election, maintained an overwhelming majority in both houses of congress and controlled most other elected offices down to municipal level.

In 1938, President Lázaro Cárdenas reorganised and renamed the PNR, calling it the Mexican Revolutionary Party (PRM) and dividing it into four sections: military, labour, agrarian and popular. In 1946 the incoming president, Miguel Alemán, carried out a new reorganisation, dropping the military sector and giving the party its present name. The three sectors became the Confederation of Mexican Workers (CTM) for labour; the National Peasant Confederation (CNC) for the peasantry; and the National Confederation of Popular Organisations (CNOP) for government employees and professionals, including the army. Successive presidents helped shape the PRI into a massive network for social control and the distribution of patronage within which numerous interest groups operated. Although not formally recognised as on a par with the labour, peasant or popular sectors, the business lobby played a very influential role in the party through organisations such as the Management Co-ordinating Council (CCE).

Analysts noted that while the top positions within the party were controlled by members of what they called the 'revolutionary family', it also developed powerful mechanisms of co-option, to absorb or deflect challenges to its rule. One technique was the proliferation of smaller opposition parties effectively controlled by the PRI itself. Nevertheless, as the economic crisis grew in the 1970s and 1980s it became difficult for the PRI to maintain its control. The party's traditional electoral boast, *de todas, todas* – to sweep the board in all key elections – began to be confronted increasingly by allegations of fraud. Within the party the euphemistic phrase used was *alquimia electoral* – electoral alchemy – which encompassed a wide variety of corrupt practices, ranging from buying votes to stuffing ballot boxes. An internal conflict began to emerge between the old guard *políticos*, identified with the operation of the party machine, and the younger conservative *técnicos*, seeking to overhaul and modernise the economic system.

Following the 1976 election, in which the PRI candidate José López Portillo stood unopposed and won a claimed 98.7% of the vote, official figures showed dwindling support, with 71.6% for Miguel De la Madrid in 1982 and 50.7% for Carlos Salinas de Gortari in 1988. The PRI's share of the three-yearly congressional polls also dwindled: 1976 – 84.9%; 1979 – 68.3%; 1982 – 65.0%; 1985 – 65.0%; 1988 – 51.9%. In the 1988 elections the combined vote for the opposition candidates came very close to exceeding that for the PRI's Salinas de Gortari (49.26% against 50.74%). Opposition leaders in any case claimed that the figures had been manipulated to give the official candidate a credible majority. Salinas de Gortari himself recognised that Mexico could no longer be considered a one-party state. One of the opposition candidates, Cuauhtémoc Cárdenas, had earlier led a dissident PRI faction, the Democratic Current, criticising the authoritarian nature of the party's selection of the candidate. The PRI's crisis was underlined in July 1989 when for the first time the authorities recognised an opposition victory in a gubernatorial race (a win by the National Action Party in Baja California). At the same time, however, the government refused to accept claims of a similar gubernatorial victory by the pro-Cárdenas Party of the Democratic Revolution (PRD) in Michoacán.

See also *destape*; **Cárdenas, Cuauhtémoc; Confederation of Mexican Workers; Salinas de Gortari.**

Insurrectional Tendency: see Sandinista National Liberation Front.

Integrated Revolutionary Organisations (*Organizaciones Revolucionarias Integradas*/ORI)

A transitional political organisation founded in Cuba in late 1961 to bring together pro-revolutionary groups prior to the formation of a full-scale party. It comprised the 26 July Movement (M–26–7), the Revolutionary Student Directorate (DER) and the Popular Socialist Party (PSP). M–26–7 was numerically dominant, with 13 members on the ruling body compared with ten for the PSP and two for the DER, but the PSP leaders held key positions. In March 1962, however, Fidel Castro denounced ORI's secretary, Aníbal Escalante of the PSP, as a sectarian. He was forced into exile in Moscow and the balance swung away from the stalinist old guard. Largely a forum for discussion, ORI never became a mass movement and was replaced in 1963 by the United Party of the Socialist Revolution (PURS).

See also **Communist Party** (Cuba); **United Party of the Socialist Revolution; 'microfaction'.**

Inter-American Defence Board

An advisory committee of the Organisation of American States (OAS) dealing with military co-operation issues. Originally created after the Rio de Janeiro foreign ministers' meeting of January 1942 to co-ordinate the Allied war effort in the Americas during World War II. Headquartered in Washington, it liaises with member governments to plan the joint defence of the western hemisphere. It also runs the Inter-American Defence College.

See also **Organisation of American States; Rio Treaty.**

Inter-American Development Bank (IDB)

Created in 1959 within the framework of the Inter American system, the IDB provides project finance to public and private sectors within the region. Its aims are defined as the promotion of development in the region by the funding of economic and social enterprises, and the provision of technical assistance. The membership includes 44 countries: Argentina, Austria, Bahamas, Barbados, Belgium, Bolivia, Brazil, Canada, Chile, Colombia, Costa Rica, Denmark, Dominican Republic, Ecuador, El Salvador, Finland, France, Guatemala, Guyana, Haiti, Honduras, Israel, Italy, Jamaica, Japan, Mexico, Netherlands, Nicaragua, Panama, Paraguay, Peru, Portugal, Spain, Suriname, Sweden, Switzerland, Trinidad-Tobago, United Kingdom, USA, Uruguay, Venezuela, West Germany, Yugoslavia. The board of governors is the main decision-making body; it meets annually and is composed of one governor and one alternate for each member country. The US holds 35% of the votes on the IDB board. In 1988, Enrique Iglesias (Uruguay) was elected president to replace the long-serving Antonio Ortiz Mena (Mexico). The cumulative total of IDB lending to end–1987 was over US$36bn, of which most was destined for projects in the energy sector ($10.9bn), followed by agriculture and fisheries ($8.5bn), industry and mining ($6.2bn), transport and communications ($5.1bn) and others. IDB capital is replenished every four years. In 1988 ordinary capital resources stood at $34.5bn, with an additional $8.3bn for the Fund for Special Operations.

See also **Economic Commission for Latin America; Latin American Economic System.**

Interamerican Labour Confederation (CIT): see Monge Alvarez.

Interamerican Regional Organisation of Workers: see ORIT.

International Confederation of Free Trade Unions (ICFTU):
see **American Institute for Free Labor Development; ORIT; Barbados Workers' Union.**

International Federation of Christian Trade Unions (IFCTU):
see **CLAT.**

International Red Aid: see Martí, Agustín Farabundo.

invasions and occupations by the United States
In what it said was defence of the Monroe doctrine of US political hegemony over Latin America and especially the Caribbean, the US has invaded and occupied six Caribbean Basin countries in the 20th century: Cuba (1898–1902, 1906–09), Nicaragua (1912–24, 1925–33), Haiti (1915–34), the Dominican Republic (1916–24, 1965–6), Grenada (1983–5) and Panama (1989). The US also seized Puerto Rico from Spain in 1898 and Panama from Colombia in 1902.

See also **Monroe doctrine; Panama, US invasion (1989); Grenada, US invasion (1983); Dominican Republic, US invasion (1965); Puerto Rico, nationalist violence.**

Iran/contra affair
A political scandal in the United States involving, among other things, the diversion to the Nicaraguan contra rebels of funds derived from secret arms sales to Iran. The scandal became public on 25 November 1986, when Attorney General Edwin Meese stated that Lt.-Col. Oliver North, a National Security Council (NSC) aide, had been dismissed for his role in organising the deal. Vice-Admiral John Poindexter, the National Security Adviser, who had approved it, resigned. Apart from the illegality of the transfer of funds, a congressional ban on US government assistance for contra military operations had been in force from October 1984 to October 1986. Attempts to circumvent this had already been partially revealed. Aides to Vice-President George Bush were shown to have had close contact with the covert supply operation, and the involvement of US diplomats and military advisers in Central America was also revealed. Col. North had devised a so-called 'private network' to replace official US government funds and was involved in secret deals, approved by President Reagan, to sell arms to Iran – initially via Israel – in an attempt to have US hostages freed by Iran or its allies. No firm proof that the president knew of the diversion of Iran arms profits to the contras was produced.

The 'private network' grew out of a scheme called 'Project Democracy', whose covert aspects were headed by Col. North from 1984 onwards with the aim of pursuing secret foreign policy initiatives. The sum transferred from the arms sales to the contras was first put at between $8m and $30m, but was finally reduced to $3.5m. Leaders of the main contra forces denied receiving the money, which North apparently spent trying to create a 'southern front' against Nicaragua. The main groups (in particular the Nicaraguan Democratic Force/FDN) survived on funds mostly provided by Saudi Arabia ($32m from July 1984 to March 1985).

Assistance was also obtained from the Sultan of Brunei (US$10m, which ended up in the wrong account) and Taiwan ($2m in 1986). South Korea, Singapore and Israel were also approached.

North's chief assistant, both in the Iranian and contra elements of the operation, was retired air force major general Richard Secord. Another key associate was retired major general John Singlaub, head of the World Anti-Communist League. The head of the CIA, William Casey, was also involved, although his death from cancer shortly after the scandal broke prevented the details emerging. All four of Nicaragua's Central American neighbours were implicated, including Costa Rica under President Monge. Press reports also stated that the presidential campaign of Rafael Angel Calderón, who lost in 1986 to Oscar Arias (but became president in 1990), was partly funded by the 'private network'.

Investigations in the US were carried out by a joint congressional panel, by the three-man Tower Commission, headed by former senator John Tower, and by special prosecutor Lawrence Walsh, the latter two appointed by President Reagan. By mid-1988, five people, including North and Poindexter, had been indicted on conspiracy and other charges arising from the affair. North went on trial in January 1989, accused of twelve separate criminal offences including deceiving congress and participating in tax fraud. Charges of conspiracy and theft had to be dropped when US intelligence agencies refused access to secret documents. Acquitted on most charges, he did not go to jail and on appeal most of his convictions were ruled to have been improperly obtained. Poindexter was convicted on five charges in April 1990.

See also **Nicaraguan Resistance; United Nicaraguan Opposition; Nicaraguan Democratic Force.**

Irish, J. A. George

b. 17 May 1942. Montserrat politician. In 1973, Irish, a lecturer in Spanish at the University of the West Indies in Jamaica and one-time teacher in the Dominican Republic, formed the Montserrat Allied Workers' Union as a centre-left challenge to chief minister Austin Bramble. In 1983 he formed the United National Front, which contested the general election that year and won 6% of the votes but no seats. He is a notable promoter of Montserratian cultural activities.

See also **Bramble.**

Isaacs, Kendal

b. 23 July 1925. Opposition leader in the Bahamas 1972–6, 1981–7. A barrister, Isaacs was solicitor-general, 1955–63, then attorney-general 1963–5. He became a senator in 1965. He was elected to parliament in 1972 and succeeded Cecil Wallace-Whitfield as leader of the Free National Movement (FNM) until 1976, when Wallace-Whitfield resumed the post. Isaacs took over again in 1981 until the FNM's general election defeat in 1987, when Wallace-Whitfield replaced him once more as party leader.

See also **Free National Movement; Wallace-Whitfield.**

Las Isletas Co-operative: see Alvarez Martínez, Gen. Gustavo Adolfo.

Isthmian Workers' Central (CIT): see Christian Democrat Party (Panama).

Ixcán, Tiger of: see Guerrilla Army of the Poor.

J

Jaipail Mission (1975)

A three-man mission sent to Montserrat by the United Nations Decolonisation Committee at Britain's invitation in 1975. Headed by Trinidadian Rikhi Jaipail, it concluded that the islanders were content with their self-governing colonial status but made minor recommendations about further self-rule.

See also **Montserrat**.

Jalton, Frédéric

b. 21 February 1924. One of Guadeloupe's four deputies in the French National Assembly. A doctor, Jalton became a National Assembly deputy for the Guadeloupean Socialist Federation in 1973, lost his seat in 1978 and regained it in 1981. He was a member of the European parliament 1978–81 and was elected mayor of his home town of Abymes in 1977.

JAMAICA

Capital: Kingston
Independence (from Britain): 1962
Area: 10,991 sq km
Population (1988): 2.4m (51% urban)
Pop. growth rate: 1.4%
Pop. density: 221/sq km
Infant mortality: 18 per thousand
Life expectancy at birth: 70
Literacy: 89%
GDP per capita (1988e): US$1,843
Foreign debt per capita (1988): US$1,875
Main exports: tourism, alumina/bauxite, petroleum products, clothing, machinery, sugar, bananas, coffee, rum

Political system

Constitution: 1962. Titular head of state: Queen Elizabeth of Britain, represented locally by a figurehead governor-general. A 60-member House of Representatives is elected for a maximum five years. A 21-member Senate is nominated.

Governor-general: Sir Florizel Glasspole (1973)
Prime minister: Michael Manley (1989)
Last elections: 1989

Political organisations

Parties in parliament (leader)(seats in House of Representatives): People's National Party/PNP (Michael Manley)(45), f. 1938; Jamaica Labour Party/JLP (Edward Seaga)(15), f. 1943.
Parties outside parliament: Workers' Party of Jamaica/WPJ (Trevor Munroe), f. 1978; Jamaica American Party/JAP (James Chisholm), f. 1986.
Main trade unions: Bustamante Industrial Trade Union/BITU (Hugh Shearer), f. 1938; National Workers' Union of Jamaica/NWU (Michael Manley), f. 1952; Trades Union Congress of Jamaica/TUC (Hopeton Caven); Dockers and Marine Workers' Union/DMWU (Milton Scott); Jamaica Teachers' Association/JTA (Pat Robinson); Jamaica Union of Public Officers and Public Employees/JUPOPE (Claude O'Reagan); University and Allied Workers' Union/UAWU (Trevor Munroe).
Employers' organisations: Private Sector Organisation of Jamaica/PSOJ (Delroy Lindsay), f. 1976; Jamaica Manufacturers' Association/-JMA (Anthony Barnes); Jamaica Hotel and Tourist Association/JHTA (Peter Rousseau); Cane Farmers' Association/CFA (Trevor Mignott); Jamaica Banana Growers' Association/JBGA (Bobby Pottinger).

Jamaica Labour Party (JLP)
A conservative party, founded in 1943 by Alexander Bustamante (1884–1977) as the political arm of his Bustamante Industrial Trade Union (BITU) because of his dislike of the leftists in the People's National Party (PNP) with which he was allied. The party won legislative council elections in 1944 (22–10) and Bustamante became communications minister and leader of the government and, from 1953, chief minister. The JLP had won again in 1949 (17–15), but lost 14–18 to Norman Manley's PNP in 1955 and was defeated again in 1959 (29–16). Bustamante then campaigned successfully against Jamaica's remaining in the West Indies Federation and beat the PNP (26–19) at elections on the eve of independence in 1962, thereby becoming the country's first prime minister a few months later.
In 1964, ailing and elderly, he made finance minister Donald Sangster acting prime minister. When the JLP won the 1967 election (35–20), Bustamante resigned in favour of Sangster, but Sangster (b. 1911) died a month later. Hugh Shearer, the *de facto* leader of BITU, then became prime minister. After the JLP was defeated 16–36 in 1972, Shearer was replaced in 1974 by Edward Seaga. After another defeat (47–13) in 1976 the party, with strong US support and covert US attempts at destabilisation, won the 1980 elections (51–9) and Seaga became prime minister. The JLP won all 60 seats in the 1983 election because the PNP boycotted the poll. In 1986 it was heavily defeated by the PNP in local elections and lost power nationally at the 1989 elections, going down to a 15–45 defeat at the hands of the PNP.
See also **Seaga; Shearer; Bustamante Industrial Trade Union; People's National Party; Manley, Michael; West Indies Federation.**

James, C. L. R. (Cyril Lionel Robert)

1901–89. A Trinidad-born marxist historian and author, James left the island in 1932 to teach and write in Britain and the US. He returned to Trinidad in 1958 to edit the ruling People's National Movement (PNM) organ, *The Nation*, and become secretary of the West Indies Federal Labour Party. After quarrelling with PNM leader Eric Williams, he was expelled from the PNM in 1961 on the trumped-up charge of embezzling party funds. Other PNM left-wingers joined him in 1965 to form the Workers' and Farmers' Party, which advocated radical land reform, nationalisation of the sugar and oil industries and ties with Cuba. James was briefly put under house arrest as a subversive. After the party won only 3.5% of the vote and no seats at the 1966 general election, James returned abroad, to live in the US and Britain. His best-known works are *The Black Jacobins* (1938), a history of the Haitian war of independence, and *Beyond a Boundary* (1963), about cricket and Caribbean society.

See also **People's National Movement** (Trinidad-Tobago)**; Williams; 'black power'; West Indies Federation.**

Jarquín, Agustín: see Social Christian Party.

Jean-Baptiste, Chavannes: see Papaye Peasant Movement.

Jefferson, Thomas

b. 13 April 1941. Financial secretary, Cayman Islands, 1982- . A former seaman and military policeman, Jefferson joined the civil service and rose to become financial secretary, succeeding Vassel Johnson.

See also **Johnson.**

JM/WAVE programme

A massive programme of activities mounted in the 1960s by the US Central Intelligence Agency against the Cuban government of Fidel Castro, including assassination plots. Based at the University of Miami, the JM/WAVE headquarters was for a time the largest CIA base in the world other than that at Langley, Virginia. It made extensive use of the Cuban exile community, although in retrospect part of its aim seems to have been to keep the armed exiles busy; thoughts of an invasion having been abandoned after the Bay of Pigs and the Cuban missile crisis.

See also **Bay of Pigs invasion; Cuban missile crisis; Omega 7.**

John, Kenneth: see United People's Movement (St Vincent).

John, Patrick

b. 8 January 1937. Prime minister of Dominica 1974–9. A teacher and shipping clerk, John formed the Seamen and Waterfront Workers' Union (later the Waterfront and Allied Workers' Union) in 1964. He was mayor of Roseau 1965–8 and was elected to parliament for the ruling Dominica Labour Party (DLP) in 1970, when he became minister of communications and works. In 1973 he was named home affairs minister and later that year deputy premier and finance minister. He succeeded Edward

Leblanc as premier in 1974 with the aim of crushing subversion, 'agents of international communism', and 'pseudo-intellectuals'.

John appointed himself a colonel in 1975 and his rule became increasingly eccentric and repressive. A 1974 law allowed people to shoot rastafarians (dreads) on sight and he cracked down on trade unions, the press and demonstrations. He led Dominica to independence from Britain in 1978, but then became involved in a mercenary plan to invade Barbados. He also secretly planned to lease part of the island to a US corporation to build a freeport and tourist and gambling centre, negotiated to launder oil and arms exports to South Africa through Dominica, and proposed that the US build a submarine base on the island. Demonstrations and a general strike forced him to resign in 1979 in favour of Oliver Seraphin. He lost his seat at the 1980 general election.

John was arrested after involvement in a 1981 attempt to overthrow prime minister Eugenia Charles with the help of the army and foreign mercenaries. He was acquitted in 1982 but after a retrial in 1985 was jailed for 12 years. When the divided DLP reunited in 1983, he lost the leadership to Seraphin, to whom he became deputy. He became DLP secretary-general in 1985 and regained a seat in parliament at the general election that year before being jailed and losing it. He resigned from the DLP in 1988, accusing it of exploiting him. He was freed from jail after the 1990 general election.

See also **Dominica Labour Party; dreads; Charles, Eugenia.**

Johnson, Vassel
b. 18 January 1922. Architect of the Cayman Islands as a tax haven. A Jamaican-born accountant, he rose through the ranks of the civil service and became the colony's financial secretary in 1965, when he began promoting the country as a place where companies could officially register without paying taxes. The islands are now the world's largest offshore banking centre. Johnson retired in 1982 and was succeeded by Thomas Jefferson. He remained a member of the legislative assembly and in 1984 took responsibility for development and natural resources. He retired from politics in 1988.
See also **Jefferson.**

Jonckheer, Efrain: see **Democratic Party** (Netherlands Antilles).

Jones, Ben: see **New National Party; Blaize; Brizan.**

Jorge Blanco, Salvador
b. 5 July 1926. President of the Dominican Republic 1982–6. A lawyer, Jorge Blanco was attorney-general in the leftist provisional government during the 1965 civil war and helped to negotiate the withdrawal of the US invasion force later that year. He became president of the Dominican Revolutionary Party (PRD) in 1977 and a senator, but failed to win the party's nomination for president in 1978. He was elected president of the republic in 1982. He did not stand for re-election in 1986 and mediated in vain to prevent rival candidates splitting the party and so losing the election for the PRD. In 1987, President Joaquín Balaguer encouraged

his indictment for the embezzlement of $35m in a scandal over bogus or poor quality arms purchases while in power. He fled to the Venezuelan embassy to escape imprisonment and, pleading heart trouble, was allowed to leave for the United States. He was sentenced *in absentia* in 1988 to 20 years in jail, after which, proclaiming his innocence and aware of a legal obligation to retry him, he returned to the Dominican Republic and surrendered to the authorities.

See also **Dominican Revolutionary Party; Balaguer; Dominican Republic, US invasion (1965).**

Joshua, Ebenezer

b. 23 May 1908. Chief minister of St Vincent 1961–7. A teacher and trade union leader, Joshua was elected to the legislative council in 1951 as a member of the short-lived Eighth Army of Liberation party. He formed the People's Political Party (PPP) later that year. He was twice expelled from the island's executive council for supposed sedition and communist sympathies. The PPP won elections in 1957 (5–3) and Joshua became minister of trade and production in 1958. He was named chief minister after the PPP won the 1961 elections (6–3). The PPP narrowly won (5–4) in 1966, but one member defected. After disturbances, the British authorities dismissed Joshua and at new elections in 1967, he was defeated 3–6 and became opposition leader.

When the PPP and the St Vincent Labour Party (SVLP) won six seats each in the 1972 poll he allied himself with independent MP James Mitchell, who became premier with Joshua as his deputy. He quarrelled with Mitchell in 1974 and the government fell. Joshua then teamed up with SVLP leader Milton Cato and when the SVLP won the election the same year (10 seats to the PPP's 2), he became trade and agriculture minister. Joshua's wife Ivy, a former minister, was then named token opposition leader to prevent Mitchell getting the job. Joshua was sacked in 1978. The PPP failed to win any seats in the 1979 election and in 1980, Joshua retired from politics. In 1987 the party changed its name to the People's National Movement, but it later disappeared.

See also **Mitchell, James; Cato; St Vincent Labour Party.**

Joshua, Ivy: see Joshua, Ebenezer.

Josie, Peter

b. 26 September 1941. Left-wing St Lucian politician, leader of the Seamen, Waterfront and General Workers Union. An agronomist, Josie joined George Odlum in the radical St Lucia Action Movement in the early 1970s. He joined the St Lucia Labour Party in 1973 and entered parliament at the 1974 elections. When the party came to power in 1979 he was named agriculture and labour minister. After the Louisy government collapsed in 1981 and Odlum resigned, Josie broke with him and became foreign and trade and industry minister under prime minister Winston Cenac. He became party leader, but the SLP lost the the 1982 elections and having lost his own seat he was replaced by Neville Cenac. In 1984, businessman Julian Hunte was elected leader with Josie as his deputy. Josie failed to persuade Hunte to link up with Odlum and the Progressive Labour Party for the 1987 elections and the SLP was narrowly defeated.

See also **St Lucia Labour Party; Odlum, George; Hunte.**

junta

Literally, 'board, council or executive committee', the word has characteristically been used to denote the body exercising *de facto* control of state power, often in military regimes. Some of the first ruling juntas came into being during the 19th-century independence struggle against Spain. In the region covered by this book the junta has been a less frequent phenomenon than in South America, with even military regimes such as those of El Salvador or Guatemala usually preferring the presidency of a succession of individual officers. These have typically been selected by the leadership of the armed forces and their rule 'legitimised' by the holding of regular, if fraudulent, elections. The appearance of a junta is usually a sign that the system is in crisis, as in the case of the post-1979 civilian-military juntas in El Salvador or the 1982 Ríos Montt military junta in Guatemala. Dictator Anastasio Somoza Debayle of Nicaragua ruled through a 'puppet' civilian junta (known as the triumvirate), 1972–4, while retaining *de facto* control. An 11-man civilian junta held power for 18 months in Costa Rica after the 1948 civil war in that country.

See also **Second Republic** (Costa Rica); **Somoza Debayle, Gen. Anastasio; Ríos Montt.**

K

Kennedy, John F.: see **Bay of Pigs invasion; Cuban missile crisis; Monroe doctrine; Omega 7.**

King, Cyril: see **Independent Citizens' Movement; Luis; Evans; Farrelly.**

Kisan: see **Yatama.**

Kissinger, Henry: see **Kissinger Report; Ardito Barletta.**

Kissinger Report
The report of the 12-member US National Bipartisan Commission on Central America, chaired by former Secretary of State Dr Henry Kissinger, delivered on 10 January 1984. The Commission was set up in mid-1984 to advise on 'a long-term US policy that (would) best respond to the challenges of social, economic and democratic developments in the region, and to internal and external threats to its security and stability'. Among its recommendations were: an emergency economic stabilisation programme involving an additional $400m in bilateral assistance in fiscal 1984; new trade credit guarantees and a new debt initiative; $8bn in bilateral assistance between 1985 and 1990 (roughly doubling the 1983 level); a review of non-tariff trade barriers; the promotion of democratic institutions and processes, strong and diversified economies and improved income distribution; the establishment of a Central American Development Corporation to promote private investment; an expansion of the Peace Corps and the creation of a 'Literacy Corps'; 10,000 US scholarships for Central Americans; and significantly increased military aid to El Salvador, contingent on human rights improvements.

There was no specific recommendation on aid to the US-backed Nicaraguan rebels (contras), but two members added individual calls for it to be suspended. Many of the recommendations were taken up, including the introduction in December 1984 of a five-year, $300m p.a. federal guarantee programme to insure against Central American countries defaulting on loans.

See also **Caribbean Basin Initiative.**

KONAKOM (*Comité National du Congrès des Mouvements Démocratiques*/National Committee of the Congress of Democratic Movements)
Centre-left Haitian political party which grew out of a congress in Port-au-Prince in January 1987 of more than 300 grassroots organisations from

all over the country. The congress called for broad political and economic reforms, including recognition of Creole and voodoo as part of national culture. It also set up KONAKOM, headed by schoolteacher Victor Benoit (b. 26 September 1941), which was the core of the Group of 57 coalition that led anti-government protests in mid-1987. Benoit lost a contest for the presidential nomination of the subsequently formed National Co-operation Front (FNC) to human rights lawyer Gérard Gourgue later that year. KONAKOM officially became a political party in 1989, with Benoit as leader and a former priest, Jean-Claude Bajeux, as his deputy.

See also **Gourgue**.

Kroon, Ciro: see **Democratic Party** (Netherlands Antilles).

Krushchev, Nikita: see **Cuban missile crisis**.

L

Laborde, Hernán: see **Communist Party** (Mexico).

Labour Party (Panama) (*Partido Laborista*/PALA)
Formed in Panama in 1982, PALA has its origins in the Agrarian Labour Party (PLA), founded in 1960 and re-registered in 1979. Azael Vargas, who claimed that the PLA had been hijacked, split with it to found the Authentic PLA (PLAA). He then joined with Carlos Eleta, scion of one of the '20 families', to found the National Renovation Movement (MNR), which in 1982 changed its name to the Conservative Party. An attempt to join forces with the Republican Party (PR) to form the Conservative Republican Party was frustrated by the electoral tribunal, and Vargas and Eleta then went on to form PALA. The party mounted an expensive publicity drive and was accused of fraudulently boosting its membership figures.

Despite its name, and its use of the spade (*pala*) as its symbol, it is extremely conservative and hostile to organised labour. With backers among Panama's wealthy élite, PALA initially supported the presidential aspirations of National Guard chief Gen. Rubén Darío Paredes in 1984. When Paredes withdrew it opted for official candidate Nicolás Ardito Barletta, joining the Unade coalition and obtaining three seats in Ardito's cabinet. PALA became the second most important force within Unade, but was weakened in 1987 by a power struggle in which Eleta was ousted as party president, apparently as part of a move by the defence forces to take greater control over the party. A member of Unade's successor, the National Liberation Coalition (COLINA), PALA was expected to be allocated one seat in the post-US invasion legislature in 1990.
See also **National Liberation Coalition**; *rabiblancos*; **Panama, US invasion (1989).**

Lacayo, Gonzalo: see **Ortega Saavedra**

ladino
Originally a pejorative term for a 'latinised' (i.e. hispanicised) Indian in Spanish America. Later, any individual not identifiably Indian in dress or behaviour, including those of Spanish descent. It is also used to mean a sly or cunning person in some countries. The opposite of '*indio*' (a usually pejorative term) or '*indígena*'. Nowadays most widely used in Guatemala, where pure-blooded Indians are a larger proportion of the

population than elsewhere in the region. '*Ladinización*' refers to the adoption of 'western', or hispanic, dress and customs.

Lafontant, Roger: see Tontons Macoutes; Avril.

Lago refinery: see Netherlands Antilles, oil refineries.

Lagos, Luis: see Social Democratic Innovation and Unity Party.

Lakas, Demetrios: see Torrijos Herrera.

Landaverde, Alfredo: see Christian Democrat Party of Honduras.

land reform (Guatemala): see National Campesino Pro-Land Association; Arbenz Guzmán; Arévalo Bermejo.

Larifla, Dominique
b. 6 July 1936. One of Guadeloupe's four deputies in the French National Assembly. A heart specialist, Larifla was secretary of the Guadeloupean Socialist Federation, 1983–7, and was elected to the General Council in 1985 when the left won control of the council. He became its president at the same time, replacing conservative Lucette Michaux-Chevry as president. He was elected to the National Assembly in 1988 and as mayor of his home town of Petit-Bourg in 1977.

Larue, Frank: see Unitary Representation of the Guatemalan Opposition.

latifundio
A large, private agricultural estate, sometimes only partially worked, which may take the form of a plantation, ranch or hacienda, and which typically depends for seasonal labor on landless, or semi-landless peasants. Hence, '*latifundismo*': a land tenure system based on large estates. The *latifundio* is usually associated with the '*minifundio*', which is defined as a plot too small to support a family and whose owner or tenant must therefore seek employment from the large landowner. This is sometimes known as the '*latifundio-minifundio* complex'. In many countries and regions of Latin America the bulk of land is taken up by *latifundia*, while the vast majority of farms are *minifundia*, the latter often forming part of the large estate. Forms of labour are frequently (but not always) semi-feudal, in that a cash wage may not be paid, or may be only part of the remuneration. The *latifundio* has been the target of many land reform programmes, but even when broken up it sometimes reappears when rich landowners find ways of circumventing the law; a process defined as '*neo-latifundismo*'. The large landowner, known as a *latifundista*, naturally has better access to credit, irrigation and modern technology than the smallholder, as well as to centres of political power.

Latin American Bishops' Council (*Consejo Episcopal Latinoamericano*/CELAM)
Founded in 1955 with four stated objectives: to study matters of interest to the Catholic church in Latin America; to co-ordinate activities; to

promote and assist Catholic initiatives; and to prepare conferences of Latin American bishops, to be convoked by the Holy See. Its members are the bishops' conferences of South and Central America and of the Caribbean. In addition to the general secretariat (based in Bogotá, Colombia) there are five under-secretariats, dealing with the preservation and propagation of the faith; the supervision of diocesan clergy and religious institutions; the dissemination of religious education for youth; the apostolate of the laity; and social action/social assistance. In 1968, Pope Paul VI became the first pontiff to visit Latin America when he attended the second conference of Latin American bishops in Medellín, Colombia. Pope John Paul II followed him when he addressed the third, in Puebla, Mexico, in 1979. In recent years, CELAM has suffered from deep divisions between left and right. The most prominent conservative is Cardinal Alfonso López Trujillo of Colombia, while Cardinal Aloisio Lorscheider, archbishop of Fortaleza, Brazil, is usually considered the leading progressive.

See also **liberation theology.**

Latin American Confederation of Christian Trade Unionists (CLASC): see CLAT.

Latin American Economic System (*Sistema Económico Latino Americano*/SELA)

Set up in October 1975 largely on the initiatives of Presidents Luis Echeverría of Mexico and Carlos Andrés Pérez of Venezuela. The group includes 25 Latin American countries, and is conceived as a co-ordination and consultation body. SELA places great emphasis on the need for joint Latin American action on a number of issues, independently of the different forms of economic or political organisation of member states. Unlike other regional organisations, SELA excludes the United States but includes Cuba in its active membership. It sees itself very much as representing the South in terms of the North-South dialogue. SELA has sought to promote joint marketing of Latin American commodities so as to defend international price levels; it has also campaigned against protectionism in the industrialised countries and has tried to promote the formation of bi-national or multinational companies through which local producers might compete more effectively on world markets. In the early 1980s SELA also took an active interest in the foreign debt problem.

The top decision-making body within SELA is the Latin American Council, which meets annually and is composed of ministers from each member state. The permanent secretariat is based in Caracas. The membership is composed as follows: Argentina, Barbados, Bolivia, Brazil, Chile, Colombia, Costa Rica, Cuba, Dominican Republic, Ecuador, El Salvador, Grenada, Guatemala, Guyana, Haiti, Honduras, Jamaica, Mexico, Nicaragua, Panama, Peru, Suriname, Trinidad-Tobago, Uruguay, Venezuela. Executive secretary: Dr Sebastián Alegrett.

See also **Latin American Integration Association; Organisation of American States.**

Latin American Energy Organisation (*Organización Latinoamericana de Energía*/OLADE)
Founded in November 1973 at the Third Latin American Consultative Meeting of Ministers of Energy and Petroleum, held in Lima, Peru. The Lima Convention, setting up the organisation, came into effect on 18 December 1974 and was signed by the following countries: Argentina, Brazil, Colombia, Cuba, Costa Rica, Chile, Dominican Republic, Ecuador, El Salvador, Guatemala, Guyana, Honduras, Jamaica, Mexico, Nicaragua, Panama, Paraguay, Peru, Trinidad-Tobago, Uruguay, Venezuela. Since then, Barbados, Bolivia, Dominica, Grenada, Haiti and Suriname have joined, while Argentina now has only observer status. OLADE's objectives are to promote joint action in the utilisation and defence of the natural resources of each country and the region as a whole, including the identification and resolution of specific energy problems which constitute a barrier to development; promote the rational exploitation and conservation of energy resources; develop a Latin American energy market and a common regional approach to energy issues; and develop a financial arm to channel funds into energy projects. It collaborates with the UN Development Programme on the Latin American Energy Co-operation Programme. OLADE's executive secretary is headquartered in Quito, Ecuador. The annual meeting of ministers is the body's highest authority. It elects a committee of six ministers on a geographical basis.

Latin American Integration Association (LAIA) (*Asociación Latinoamericana de Integración*/ALADI)
Created in August 1980 to replace the Latin American Free Trade Association (LAFTA), which had been in existence since February 1960. The objectives of LAFTA had been: to increase trade between members; to promote regional integration and development; and to lay the basis for what would eventually become a Latin American Common Market. But progress towards these aims was slow – the tariff reduction programme in particular proved problematic, with LAFTA agreements accounting for only 14% of trade among members by 1980. The change to LAIA on expiry of the original LAFTA protocols was designed to create a less ambitious, more flexible association. The LAIA framework stresses a regional tariff preference for goods coming from other member countries, economic preference areas, and partial scope agreements (involving specific goods and groups of member countries). Despite these efforts, the proportion of members' total exports covered by LAIA agreements fell from 13% in 1981 to 8.1% in 1985, recovering to 10.3% in 1987.

LAIA comprises the 11 original LAFTA members, grouped into three categories: most developed – Argentina, Brazil, Colombia and Mexico; intermediate – Chile, Peru, Uruguay and Venezuela; and least developed – Bolivia, Ecuador and Paraguay. Tariff treatment varies by category, with the least developed countries getting the best terms. The main decision-making body is the council of ministers – made up of foreign ministers of member countries. The secretariat, LAIA's technical body, is based in Montevideo, Uruguay. General secretary: Norberto Bertaina (Argentina).

Latin American Peasant Federation (FCL): see CLAT.

Laugerud García, Gen. Kjell: see Institutional Democratic Party; National Liberation Movement (Guatemala); Authentic Nationalist Central; Riós Montt.

Leblanc, Edward: see Dominica Labour Party.

Leeward Islands
In the Anglo-Caribbean, the north-easterly islands of Anguilla, Antigua, Barbuda, St Kitts, Nevis and Montserrat. In the Netherlands Antilles, the three southerly islands of Curaçao, Aruba and Bonaire.

León Herrera, Santos: see Civil War (Costa Rica).

Lesser Antilles
The smaller eastern islands of the Caribbean, stretching from the Virgin Islands to Trinidad and the Netherlands Antilles.
See also **Greater Antilles**.

Lewis, Sir Allen: see St Lucia Labour Party.

Lewis, Sir Arthur
b. 23 January 1915. Caribbean economist. After lecturing in British universities and advising the British government variously between 1935 and 1948, Lewis worked in Africa in the early 1950s. He was principal of the University College of the West Indies 1959–62 and then vice-chancellor when it became the University of the West Indies in 1962, until 1963. He taught at Princeton University, 1963–70, and was first president of the Caribbean Development Bank, 1970–74. St Lucian-born Lewis won the Nobel prize for economics in 1979. He is credited with the concept of 'industrialisation by invitation' which inspired Puerto Rico's Operation Bootstrap crash development plan.
See also **Operation Bootstrap; University of the West Indies; Demas**.

Liberación: see National Liberation Party.

Liberal Party (Belize): see United Democratic Party; Esquivel, Manuel.

Liberal Party (Costa Rica): see Calderón Guardia.

Liberal Party (Honduras) (*Partido Liberal*/PL)
Founded in 1891 in the classic liberal mould under the leadership of Policarpo Bonilla, the PL comprises two basic currents, one of which is conservative and largely rural, the other more reformist and based around the urban centres of Tegucigalpa and San Pedro Sula. Its most recent presidents have been Mejía Colindres (1929–33), Villeda Morales (1957–63), Suazo Córdova (1982–6) and Azcona Hoyo (1986–90). Villeda sought to organise the PL and give it a formal programme, but failed. In

1963 he was overthrown in a military coup. The PL boycotted the 1965 constituent assembly, but took seats when the assembly became a legislature. For the 1971 elections it agreed to a 'pact of national unity' with the National Party (PN), involving a 50–50 division of congress under an elected president (Ramón Ernesto Cruz of the PN, who was overthrown by the army in 1972).

From 1970 the PL was increasingly factionalised, initially between the conservative followers of Modesto Rodas Alvarado (*rodistas*) and the more progressive Popular Liberal Alliance (ALIPO, founded in 1978 as a merger of the Villeda Morales Movement and the Democratic Left), which under Carlos Roberto Reina and Jorge Arturo Reina developed social democrat leanings. Rodas died in 1979, shortly before the armed forces handed back power to elected civilians, and *rodista* Dr Roberto Suazo Córdova led the PL to power in 1981. The *rodistas* successfully split ALIPO in 1983 and the Reina brothers were ousted from its leadership, going on in 1984 to form the Revolutionary Democratic Liberal Movement (M-Líder), also within the PL. ALIPO retained control of the newspaper *Tiempo*, and remained centred on the banking and commercial interests of the group associated with leading San Pedro Sula businessman Jaime Rosenthal. In 1985 the *rodistas* also split, with the ruling *suazocordovista* faction backing Oscar Mejía Arellano for the presidency, while other groups formed around congressional president Efraín Bu Girón and former public works minister José Azcona Hoyo, who subsequently won the 1985 elections in alliance with ALIPO.

A second 'National Unity Pact' (or Patriotic Accord) with the PN gave the latter control of the supreme court and other key political and administrative positions, and Azcona appointed two PN ministers. The struggle within the party for the presidential nomination in 1989 began almost immediately, and by 1987 there were seven clear contenders. In September 1987, Carlos Roberto Flores Facussé, former minister of the presidency to Suazo Córdova and majority shareholder in the newspaper *La Tribuna*, emerged as front-runner when he took control of the party executive, and in July 1988 he forged an unexpected alliance with the M-Líder group. In December that year he won the nomination. Flores had been forced to step down as presidential candidate in 1985 in favour of Mejía Arellano. His short history as a PL member (he joined in 1980) and his Arab ancestry had counted against him in the past. He lost the 1989 election by a margin of about 7% to Rafael Callejas of the PN, and the Liberals went into opposition.

See also **Azcona Hoyo; Suazo Córdova; Villeda Morales; National party.**

Liberal Party (Panama) (*Partido Liberal*/PL)

Originally the Panamanian branch of the Colombian Liberal Party, from which it split in 1932, the PL led the National Opposition Union (UNO) coalition which won the presidency in 1960 (Roberto Chiari) and 1964 (Marcos A. Robles). It failed to win in 1968, when David Samudio was candidate, partly because of the defection of ex-president Chiari to the victorious Panameñista Party (PP). A right-wing member of the Liberal

International, the PL places great emphasis on private enterprise. It agreed to take part in the controversial 1980 elections, despite the abstention of two other Liberal factions and an internal dispute over the presidency of the party, and won 5 of the 19 available seats, even though it obtained only two-thirds as many votes as the Christian Democrats (PDC) who won two. It was given seats in the PRD-led cabinet in 1982, and joined the PRD-led Unade coalition which won the controversial 1984 election. When President Ardito Barletta was replaced by his vice-president, Eric Arturo Delvalle, PL president Roderick Esquivel in turn became vice-president. But in July 1987 Esquivel proposed an independent inquiry into charges of murder and corruption against Defence Forces (FDP) chief Gen. Noriega. From then on he was marginalised from the government, and in October that year his goverment offices were seized by the FDP. Although he still refused to resign, the PL said it would withdraw from Unade. In January 1989, however it joined the new official coalition, COLINA.

See also **National Liberation Coalition; Molirena.**

Liberal-Progressive Party: see Ubico y Castañeda.

liberation theology

The popular name for an approach to the expression of Catholic beliefs developed by Latin American theologians, both priests and laypeople. Their inspiration came from the teachings of Pope John XXIII, the documents of the Second Vatican Council (1962–5) and the Second General Conference of Latin American Bishops at Medellín (Colombia) in 1968. (The term was popularised by Peru's best-known theologian, Gustavo Gutiérrez, in the title of a 1971 book.) Among its key concepts are the 'preferential option for the poor', and their liberation from all forms of oppression, including 'institutionalised violence', to which the violence of the poor is a sometimes justifiable response. Archbishop Oscar Romero's espousal of this doctrine helped bring about his murder in San Salvador in 1980.

Liberation theologians adopted as an analytical tool some of the methodology of Marxism. Their ideas were derived in large measure from the everyday experience of the 'ecclesial base communities' (*comunidades eclesiales de base*, or CEBs) in which ordinary people came together to reflect on their lives in the light of the teachings of the Bible. The Vatican has looked askance at certain aspects of liberation theology as practised in Latin America, in particular its links with Marxism. Cardinal Joseph Ratzinger, head of the Vatican's Congregation for the Doctrine of the Faith, has been pursuing its exponents with particular hostility since the 1970s. In 1985, in a lengthy criticism deplored by Brazilian bishops, the Congregation described a book by Brazilian theologian Leonardo Boff as 'unsustainable' and as 'placing at risk the sound doctrine of the faith'. Boff had in September 1984 become the first theologian ever to be summoned to Rome to be personally confronted. A year's silence was imposed on him (1985–6), during which he was not to give lectures to those outside his religious community; however, this was cut short after 11 months.

Nicaragua has been a particular focus of the clash between established and 'popular' churches, because of the involvement of the latter in supporting – and even occupying senior positions in – the Sandinista government (1979–90). The Vatican and the local hierarchy sought, unsuccessfully, to have priests withdrawn from the government. Church spokesmen even expressed support for the contra rebels, and in 1986 a bishop and a priest were expelled from the country.

See also **Christian base community; Haiti, Roman Catholic Church; Romero, Archbishop Oscar Arnulfo; Latin American Bishops' Conference.**

Liberia-Peters, Maria

b. 20 May 1941. Premier of the Netherlands Antilles 1984–5, 1988– . A former nursery schoolteacher, Liberia-Peters was elected to the Curaçao island council in 1974 and was island health commissioner 1977–8. In 1982 she was appointed acting lieutenant-governor of Curaçao and became leader of the National People's Party (PNP). In 1983 she was named economic affairs minister under premier Don Martina. But she resigned as minister in 1984 and later that year was appointed the country's first woman premier after Martina lost his majority. Following new elections in 1985, Martina again became premier. When he lost his majority once more in 1988 Liberia-Peters formed her second government. She led the PNP to victory in the 1990 elections and continued in office.

See also **National People's Party; Martina.**

Ligondé, Archbishop François Wolf: see Haiti, Roman Catholic Church.

Lima Group: see Rio Group.

Lindo, Dean: see United Democratic Party.

Lise, Claude

b. 31 January 1941. One of Martinique's four deputies in the French National Assembly. A doctor, Lise joined the Martinican Progressive Party (PPM) in 1978 after the dissolution of the Martinican Socialist Party he had founded two years earlier. He was named to the General Council to fill out a term in 1980 and was elected to it in 1985 and to the French National Assembly in 1988. He is also an assistant mayor of Fort-de-France.

See also **Martinican Progressive Party.**

Literacy Corps: see Kissinger Report.

'Little Seven': see Caribbean Community.

Loblack, E. C.: see Dominica Labour Party; Allfrey; Dominica Freedom Party.

Lodge, Henry Cabot: see Monroe doctrine.

Lombardo Toledano, Vicente

A left-wing Mexican labour leader who rose to prominence in the 1930s and 1940s. As leader of the socialist General Worker and Peasant Confederation of Mexico (CGOCM), Lombardo was supported by President Lázaro Cárdenas, who wanted to undermine the position of corrupt union leaders associated with the *Maximato* period. Lombardo went on to become the first general secretary of the Confederation of Mexican Workers (CTM) in 1936, but by the early 1940s he had been displaced by more conservative leaders such as Fidel Velázquez. In 1948, Lombardo Toledano set up the Popular Party (later to become the Popular Socialist Party /PPS) and he ran as an opposition presidential candidate in 1952. See also **Confederation of Mexican Workers; National Democratic Front.**

López Arellano, Gen. Oswaldo

b. 30 June 1921. President of Honduras 1963–71, 1972–5. López Arellano joined the armed forces in 1939. He studied at the US School of Military Aviation and Flight Training. As army commander, he staged a right-wing coup in 1963 against the Liberal (PL) administration of Ramón Villeda Morales (1957–63). He was elected president for the National Party (PN) in rigged elections in 1965, and in his first term ended the reforms initiated by Villeda and repressed trade unions and PL members. Later he adopted a more reformist stance, reviving the agrarian reform and promoting peasant co-operatives. In 1969 he began expelling Salvadoreans from their land in Honduras in response to an escalation of tension in the countryside, a move which helped bring about the 'soccer war' of that year. The war revealed the incompetence and corruption of the army and strengthened the hand of younger, reform-minded officers.

López allowed elections in 1971 which were won by Ramón Ernesto Cruz (PN). But in December 1972 he staged another coup, supported this time by progressive business groups and reformist unions, against the increasingly unpopular Cruz. In the second presidency he initiated state-backed industrialisation and more sweeping land redistribution; although again he was met by opposition, particularly from landowners, 1972–6 saw the allocation of roughly 70% of all land redistributed between 1962 and 1981. But corruption eventually brought down the government. In February 1975, Eli Black, chairman of the fruit company United Brands, committed suicide. A subsequent investigation showed the company had paid a $1.25m bribe to a Honduran official in exchange for banana tax concessions. López and his economy minister, Abraham Bennatón (the alleged recipient of the bribe) were forced to resign as a consequence of what became known as the 'bananagate' scandal. Col. Juan Melgar Castro (president 1975–8) was López' replacement.

López retired from politics to concentrate on his business interests, which included vast landholdings (much of them acquired during his time as president), and the national airline, TAN-SAHSA. He also became president of the bankers' association, AHIBA. From 1984 to January 1986 his nephew, Gen. Wálter López Reyes, was head of the armed forces. In June 1985, López Arellano made public statements critical of

the Suazo Córdova government's hostility towards Nicaragua. The true enemy of Honduras, he said, was El Salvador.
See also **National Party; 'Football (Soccer) War'**.

López Fuentes, Gen. Héctor Mario: see National Liberation Movement (Guatemala).

López Mateos, Adolfo

1911–70. President of Mexico 1958–64. López Mateos brought a more populist style to the rule of the Institutional Revolutionary Party (PRI), contrasting with the conservatism of the preceding two administrations. The son of a small-town dentist, he served as labour minister under Adolfo Ruiz Cortines and built up a reputation for being on the centre-left. But although supported by radicals such as former president Lázaro Cárdenas, he took a hard line against what he considered the anti-democratic left, including the Communist Party. During his term some communist leaders were jailed and troops were used to break up a communist-led rail strike in 1959.

He accelerated the pace of land reform, which had ground to a virtual halt under the previous two administrations. During his *sexenio* a total of 30m acres was distributed, second only to the amount handed out under Cárdenas in the 1930s, although the quality of the land was inferior. The public sector expanded, the state purchasing majority shareholdings in a number of foreign firms, including US- and Canadian-owned electricity companies. Social welfare spending also increased and important advances were made in the fight against diseases such as tuberculosis, polio and malaria. López Mateos also initiated large-scale housing programmes for low-income groups. He took steps to implement clauses in the 1917 constitution calling for profit-sharing for workers in industry.

In foreign policy he refused to follow the US lead in condemning the revolutionary government in Cuba. With President J. F. Kennedy, he agreed to resolve the Chamizal territorial dispute, caused by changes in the course of the Rio Grande near Ciudad Juárez/El Paso. Conscious of the need to liberalise the political system, he introduced partial proportional representation in an effort to guarantee a greater voice in congress for the smaller parties without threatening the PRI's dominant position. Shortly after leaving office, López Mateos suffered a stroke and he remained in a coma until his death in 1970.
See also **Institutional Revolutionary Party; Organisation of American States.**

López Nuila, Col. Reynaldo: see Romero, Archbishop Oscar Arnulfo.

López Pérez, Rigoberto: see Somoza García.

López Portillo y Pacheco, José

b. 16 June 1920. President of Mexico 1976–82. López Portillo presided over the country's oil boom of the late 1970s, a period of rapid but unbalanced economic growth and heavy foreign borrowing which came to an abrupt end during the 1982 foreign payments crisis. Trained as a lawyer, he taught political theory and public administration at the Universidad Nacional Autónoma de México (UNAM). He first held government posts during the Gustavo Díaz Ordaz presidency, rising to become under-secretary of the presidency. A childhood friend of the next president, Luis Echeverría, López Portillo benefited from a series of appointments, becoming first under-secretary for national patrimony, then head of the Federal Electricity Commission and, in May 1973, finance minister. He was an unexpected choice for the presidential succession: Echeverría was expected to acknowledge the need for better relations with the private sector by appointing someone with a reputation as a financial conservative.

After standing unopposed in the July 1976 elections and winning with 92% of the vote cast, López Portillo restored business confidence by agreeing to an IMF austerity programme; he also introduced political reforms to give opposition parties more representation. In foreign policy, his administration opposed the US line on Central America, supporting the Nicaraguan revolution and calling for the Salvadorean guerrillas to be recognised as a representative political force. The discovery of massive oil reserves led after 1978 to an economic boom, with output, government spending, foreign borrowing and inflation all accelerating. The economy eventually overheated, and following a drop in oil prices in mid-1981 a process of capital flight began. In February 1982, after promising to defend the value of the peso 'like a dog', López Portillo was forced to devalue it by 40%. Following new devaluations, the government announced the suspension of payments on the foreign debt in August.

In September, with only a few months left before the end of his term in office, the president nationalised the privately owned banks and imposed sweeping exchange controls. During this period his popularity plummetted – there was growing anger and generalised suspicion of wholesale corruption, nepotism and personal enrichment. After the end of his term the new government considered, but dismissed, the idea of prosecuting López Portillo on corruption charges, concentrating instead on his associates. They included Jorge Díaz Serrano, the former head of the state oil company Pemex, and General Arturo 'El Negro' Durazo, the former head of police in Mexico City, both of whom were charged with fraudulent use of public funds and other crimes. The US columnist Jack Anderson, quoting CIA sources, claimed that López Portillo had personally misappropiated over $1bn during his term in office.
See also **Durazo Moreno; Franco-Mexican declaration; De la Madrid Hurtado; Echeverría Alvarez.**

López Reyes, Gen. Wálter: see Azcona Hoyo; López Arellano.

López Rivera, Oscar: see National Liberation Armed Forces.

López Trujillo, Cardinal Alfonso: see Latin American Bishops' Council.

Lordinot, Guy
b. 30 January 1944. One of Martinique's four deputies in the French

National Assembly. A pharmacist, Lordinot founded the Renewal of Sainte-Marie party in 1982 (renamed Union for Renewal in 1988) and became the town's mayor the following year. He was elected to the National Assembly in 1988 as a left-wing independent, but usually aligns himself with the Socialist Party.

Lorenzo Zelaya Popular Revolutionary Forces (FPR-LZ): see guerrilla movements (Honduras).

Lorscheider, Cardinal Aloisio: see Latin American Bishops' Council.

***Los Doce*:** see Sandinista National Liberation Front.

Louis-Joseph-Dogué, Maurice
b. 15 January 1927. One of Martinique's four deputies in the French National Assembly, a socialist member of the island's General Council and mayor of his home town of Ducos. He was elected to the National Assembly in 1986.

Louison, George
b. 29 November 1951. Grenadian politician. Louison, a teacher, small farmer and youth organiser, became education minister when the radical New Jewel Movement seized power in 1979. He was appointed agriculture minister in 1981. The main backer of prime minister Maurice Bishop during the 1983 leadership crisis, he resigned after Bishop's arrest and was jailed. He was freed after the US invasion and with fellow ex-minister Kendrick Radix founded the Maurice Bishop Patriotic Movement.
See also **Maurice Bishop Patriotic Movement; New Jewel Movement; Grenada, US invasion (1983); Bishop; Radix.**

Louisy, Allan: see St Lucia Labour Party; Odlum, George.

Lozano Díaz, Julio: see Villeda Morales.

Lucas Caballeros, Maj. Jorge: see Christian Democrat Party (Guatemala).

Lucas García, Gen. Fernando Romeo
b. 5 July 1924. President of Guatemala 1978–82. Lucas served as chief of staff in the Zacapa region under Col. Arana Osorio (with whom he was closely associated) in 1966–8. During the government of Gen. Kjell Laugerud he was defence minister in 1975–6 and in July 1978 he was selected to succeed Laugerud. As the candidate for the Institutional Democratic Party (PID), the Organised Aranista Central (CAO – Arana's party) and the Revolutionary Party (PR), he gained some middle-class support but was primarily backed by the cotton and coffee oligarchies. In government he acquired a reputation for political murders and other human rights violations. Among those killed were the prominent social democratic opposition leaders Manuel Colom Argueta and Alberto Fuentes Mohr. On 31 January 1980 a group of peasants occupied the Spanish embassy in a protest over army killings. The government sent

in its Comando 6 ('SWAT') counter-insurgency unit, despite pleas for negotiations by the ambassador. The building caught fire and 38 people died (including one who was kidnapped from hospital and shot). As a result, the Spanish government broke off diplomatic relations. Lucas' brother, Gen. Benedicto Lucas, a prominent counter-insurgency strategist, was army chief of staff during his presidency.

The Lucas regime was overthrown in a coup d'état just before the planned inauguration as president of Gen. Aníbal Guevara, the chosen successor. Gen. Efraín Ríos Montt took over the government and the Lucas brothers retired to their large estates in the north of the country, from where they continued to exert political influence. Benedicto Lucas was chosen in 1990 to be the presidential candidate of the Emergent Movement for Harmony (MEC).

See also **Arana Osorio; Peasant Unity Committee; Ríos Montt.**

Lucas García, Gen. Manuel Benedicto: see Lucas García, Gen. Fernando Romeo.

Luis, Juan
b. 1941. Governor of the US Virgin Islands 1978–87. A member of the Independent Citizens' Movement (ICM), which broke away from the Democratic Party, he was elected lieutenant-governor under governor Cyril King in 1974. He became governor when King died in 1978 and won election to the post without the backing of the ICM later that year, defeating Democratic Party leader Ron de Lugo. He was re-elected in 1982, beating his lieutenant-governor, Henry Millin.

See also **Independent Citizens' Movement; de Lugo.**

Luna, Alfonso: see *Matanza* (1932 massacre).

M

M–26–7: see 26 July Movement.

McCartney, J. A. G. S.: see People's Democratic Movement.

McCartney, John: see Vanguard Nationalist and Socialist Party.

McIntyre, Alister
b. 29 March 1931. Caribbean economist. McIntyre was director of the Institute of Social and Economic Research at the University of the West Indies in Jamaica before becoming secretary-general of Caricom, 1974–9. He then became director of the commodities division of the UN Conference on Trade and Development (UNCTAD). In 1984, he refused an invitation to head the post-US invasion interim government in his native Grenada, and the same year became a deputy secretary-general of UNCTAD. He was named UN assistant secretary general for development and international economic co-operation in 1987 until the following year when he was appointed vice-chancellor of the University of the West Indies. In 1989 he was also named UN mediator in the Guyana-Venezuela territorial dispute.
See also **Caribbean Community; Grenada, US invasion (1983); University of the West Indies.**

Machado, Gen. Gerardo: see Batista y Zaldívar.

Los Macheteros (Puerto Rican Popular Army/*Ejército Popular Boricua*/EPB)
A guerrilla organisation fighting for Puerto Rico's independence and led by Filiberto Ojeda Rios (b. 1933). Founded in 1978, it claimed responsibility for attacking a US navy bus in 1979, and in 1981 for destroying nine US planes at a military base on the island and the bombing of a power station. It was accused of staging a $7m armed robbery in Connecticut in 1983. Fifteen people, including Ojeda, were arrested for the robbery in 1985 and their trial began in the US in 1988. Three were given 15-year jail sentences in 1989.
See also **Puerto Rico, nationalist violence; National Liberation Armed Forces; Puerto Rican Independence Party.**

Madero, Francisco: see Mexican Revolution.

Madero, Pablo Emilio: see National Action Party.

Madrazo, Carlos: see Díaz Ordaz.

Maduro, Conrad: see United Party.

Majano, Col. Adolfo: see D'Aubuisson Arrieta.

Majluta, Jacobo
b. 9 October 1934. President of the Dominican Republic 1982. A lawyer, Majluta was finance minister in the short-lived government of President Juan Bosch in 1963. He was secretary-general of the Dominican Revolutionary Party (PRD) 1962–3. He was elected vice-president of the republic in 1978 under the PRD's Antonio Guzmán. When Guzmán killed himself in July 1982, just before the end of his term, Majluta became president for 42 days. He was president of the senate 1982–6.

In 1985 he founded the conservative Structure Party (PLE) group within the PRD as part of a bitter but successful campaign to wrest the PRD nomination for the 1986 presidential elections from the party's left-wing leader, José Francisco Peña Gómez. He was narrowly defeated in the election by Joaquín Balaguer, thanks to the PRD's divisions. He broke with the PLE after Balaguer's re-election. He was expelled from the PRD in 1987 but the country's Central Electoral Council annulled the move a year later. In 1989 he set up a new group, the Independent Revolutionary Party, to run in the 1990 elections, but won only 7% of the vote.
See also **Dominican Revolutionary Party; Guzmán; Peña Gómez; Balaguer; Bosch, Juan.**

Makouke, Claude: see Guadeloupe, independence movements.

Maldonado Aguirre, Alejandro: see Christian Democrat Party (Guatemala).

Mallet, George: see United Workers' Party.

Management Co-ordinating Council (CCE): see Institutional Revolutionary Party.

Managua, Act of: see border dispute (El Salvador/Honduras).

Mancha Brava: see 'Football (Soccer) War'.

Manigat, Leslie
b. 16 August 1930. President of Haiti 1988. Manigat became a foreign ministry official in 1953 and in 1958 founded a school of international studies under the aegis of President François Duvalier. He fell out with Duvalier, who briefly jailed him in 1961, and went into exile in 1963. For the next 23 years he taught at universities in the US, France, Trinidad and Venezuela. In 1968, Duvalier had him sentenced to death *in absentia* for subversion. In 1979 he founded the centre-left Rally of National Progressive Democrats (RDNP).

He returned to Haiti in 1986 and was a candidate for the presidency in aborted elections in 1987. He declined to join an opposition boycott of a new poll in 1988 and the ruling armed forces, encouraged by the United States, allowed him to win the heavily-shunned vote against 10 minor candidates. In power, February-June 1988, he failed to gain opposition support or resumption of suspended foreign aid. As a result, when he attacked corruption and army-controlled smuggling and violence and tried to reshuffle the army command he was overthrown, despite his alliance with a key army commander, Col. Jean-Claude Paul. He went into exile once more and resumed university teaching.

See also **Namphy; Avril; Duvalier, François; Déjoie.**

Manley, Michael

b. 10 December 1924. Prime minister of Jamaica 1972–80, 1989– . The son of one of the 'fathers' of Jamaican independence, Norman Manley (1893–1969), he returned from England in 1951 with an economics degree and journalistic experience. In 1953 he was given the task of organising the country's sugar workers into the new National Workers' Union launched by his father's People's National Party (PNP), becoming union vice-president in 1955 and president from 1984. He was president of the Caribbean Bauxite, Mine and Metal Workers' Federation 1964–74. Appointed a PNP senator in 1962, he was elected to parliament in 1967 and in 1969 became party leader on the retirement of his father.

Manley led the PNP to victory in the 1972 election after a campaign in which he appealed to national cultural pride and talked of 'liberation'. In 1974 he declared himself a democratic socialist and began enacting left-wing nationalist measures, curbing foreign companies and taking vigorous Third Worldist positions, as well as opening friendly relations with neighbouring Cuba and encouraging others in the regional left. He was re-elected in 1976, but by the 1980 election was under heavy economic and political pressure, open and covert, from the United States and the International Monetary Fund, which helped ensure the failure of his socially-oriented domestic policies.

He was defeated in that election by the strongly pro-US Edward Seaga and the Jamaica Labour Party. Although Manley condemned the 1983 US invasion of Grenada, he admitted errors during his time in power, broke with the PNP's most left-wing elements and made peace with Washington. He and the party returned to power in an electoral landslide in 1989, advocating limited privatisation, conservative economic policies and co-operation with the US, although he also promised higher social spending and cautious resumption of ties with Cuba. He became a vice-president of the Socialist International in 1979.

See also **People's National Party; National Workers' Union of Jamaica; Seaga; Grenada, US invasion (1983).**

Manley, Norman: see **People's National Party; West Indies Federation; Manley, Michael; National Workers' Union of Jamaica; Hart.**

Manning, Patrick

b. 17 August 1946. Leader of the opposition, Trinidad-Tobago, 1987– . Manning, a geologist, was elected to parliament as a member of the

ruling People's National Movement (PNM) in 1971 and was a parliamentary secretary to various economic ministries 1971–8. In 1978 he became junior finance minister and then chief of information in the prime minister's office. In 1981 he was named industry and commerce minister and later the same year energy minister. He was elected PNM leader in 1987, as one of the party's three MPs who survived its crushing 1986 general election defeat.
See also **People's National Movement** (Trinidad-Tobago); **Williams.**

Mari Bras, Juan

b. 2 December 1927. A lawyer, he founded in 1959 the Movement for Independence (MPI), which became marxist-leninist and changed its name to the Puerto Rican Socialist Party (PSP) in 1971. It took part in elections from 1976 but gained no more than 1% of the vote. Mari Bras resigned as party leader in 1982 and was succeeded by Carlos Gallisá.
See also **Puerto Rican Independence Party; Puerto Rico, nationalist violence.**

Mariel exodus

The departure of an estimated 125,000 disaffected Cuban citizens in 1980 via the port of Mariel, near Havana. The sequence of events began in April with the occupation by a group of several hundred dissidents of the Peruvian embassy. Police protection had been removed from the embassy following earlier incidents at the Peruvian and other embassies, in one of which a guard had been killed. As the news spread the number of occupiers grew, eventually reaching around 10,000, and there were more ugly incidents between defectors and loyalists. Other western embassies, notably those of Ecuador, Venezuela and the Vatican, were also occupied as US President Carter declared that all those with relatives in the US would be accepted as immigrants. The Andean Pact nations also agreed to take some refugees. A flotilla of up to 3,000 boats arrived off Mariel to ferry the Cubans to Miami. An estimated 300,000 applied to leave, and the Cuban government took advantage of the opportunity to rid itself not only of dissidents and political prisoners but of homosexuals, mental patients, drug addicts and common criminals. Many of the latter were subsequently involved in violent crime in the US.

The bulk of the exodus was halted in late June, when the US authorities ended their 'open arms' policy, though '*marielitos*' (as the Cubans called them) continued to arrive for several more months at a lesser rate. In December 1984, Cuba agreed to take back 2,749 criminals and mental patients in exchange for the normalisation of immigration policy by Washington, which said it would accept up to 20,000 Cubans a year. The agreement broke down, however, after the US government-funded anti-Castro propaganda station Radio José Martí went on the air in May 1985, and was not revived until November 1987, when it sparked off serious rioting among *marielitos* in US jails. Although the Mariel exodus was something of an embarrassment for Cuba, and brought its relations with some Latin American countries to a new low, the eventual effect was probably to strengthen the revolution by ridding the country of 'undesirables'.

See also **boat people**; *gusano;* **Radio Martí.**

marielitos: see **Mariel exodus.**

Marinello, Juan: see **Communist Party** (Cuba).

Marryshow, T. Albert

1887–1958. Grenadian politician and anti-colonial pioneer. Marryshow founded *The West Indian* newspaper in 1915 to campaign for self-rule and a West Indian federation. When partial representation was granted in 1925 he was elected to the legislative council, on which he sat until his death. He praised Africa, socialism and black pride and co-founded the Grenada Workingmen's Association in 1931 to demand votes for all. He campaigned constantly in the region and on visits to England to meet British officials.

In 1945, Marryshow was elected first president of the Caribbean Labour Congress, the first attempt to bring together the region's trade unions and pro-independence movements. He was eclipsed by Eric Gairy in the early 1950s and died the year the West Indies Federation he had worked for was launched, soon after being nominated to the federal senate. He is often called the 'Father of Federation'. Marryshow was celebrated as a national hero by the 1979–83 left-wing government in Grenada.

See also **West Indies Federation; Garvey; Gairy; People's Revolutionary Government; Marryshow, Terry.**

Marryshow, Terry

b. 9 November 1952. Grenadian left-wing politician. A grandson of T. A. Marryshow, the island's pioneer anti-colonial leader of the 1920s and 1930s, Terry Marryshow taught in Grenada until the leftist New Jewel Movement seized power in 1979, when he joined the People's Revolutionary Army and was appointed commander of Camp Butler. From 1979 to 1986 he studied medicine in Cuba, after which he was in effect barred from practising in Grenada. He was elected leader of the Maurice Bishop Patriotic Movement in May 1988 in place of Kendrick Radix.

See also **Maurice Bishop Patriotic Movement; New Jewel Movement; Radix; Marryshow, T. A.**

Martí, Agustín Farabundo

1893–1932. Salvadorean Communist Party leader. The natural son of a wealthy landowner in a remote part of El Salvador, Martí first entered politics as a student to oppose the government of Jorge Meléndez. This resulted in his deportation in 1920 to Guatemala, where he worked as teacher, construction worker and agricultural labourer. He lived for a time among the Indians of Quiché province, and is also reputed to have visited Mexico and gained the rank of sergeant in the Red Workers' Battalions of the Mexican Revolution. In 1925 he took part in founding the Central American Socialist Party (PSC) and was expelled from Guatemala. Returning to El Salvador, he played an active role in the Regional

Federation of Salvadorean Workers (FRTES, founded 1924), becoming its principal organiser.

By the late 1920s he was the representative in El Salvador of the Caribbean Bureau of International Red Aid, which provided legal and financial help to persecuted communists, and he was thus the main link between communists in El Salvador and the Comintern. Jailed by President Pío Romero Bosque in 1927, he went on hunger strike to demand release. The demand was met, partly due to supporting action by trade unionists, and Martí travelled to New York, Mexico, Cuba and Jamaica. In 1928 he returned to Central America and found his way to the guerrilla camp of General Sandino in Nicaragua. He worked for a time as Sandino's private secretary, assisting with international relations, and was given the rank of colonel, but they eventually fell out (due largely to Sandino's anti-communism), and Martí was forced to leave Nicaragua in 1929.

After travelling to Mexico, he returned to El Salvador in mid-1930, following the foundation of the Salvadorean Communist Party (PCS). Further periods of arrest and exile followed, but Martí was back in El Salvador for the preparation of the abortive January 1932 uprising. Captured on 19 January 1932 with two communist student leaders prior to the uprising, he was executed with them by firing squad on 1 February. See also **Salvadorean Communist Party;** *Matanza* (1932 massacre); **Sandino.**

Martí, José

1853–95. Cuban patriot, poet and journalist. Born in Havana, the son of Spanish parents loyal to the crown (his father was a sergeant in the Spanish army), Martí nevertheless became the most powerful advocate of Cuban independence, for which he argued in his journal *Patria Libre* in 1869. He was jailed in 1870 for alleged 'apostasy' but pardoned in the following year and eventually exiled to Spain, where he studied at the universities of Madrid and Zaragoza, obtaining degrees in philosophy and letters and law. In the year of his arrival in Spain (1871), he published a tract called 'Political Imprisonment in Cuba' and this was followed by 'The Spanish Republic and the Cuban Revolution' with which he tried to convince the prime minister of the newly-declared First Spanish Republic that Cuba merited independence. In 1875–6 he lived in Mexico, and after 1881 in New York, where he set about organising a revolution in Cuba, while officially working as a journalist.

In 1892 he founded the Cuban Revolutionary Party (PRC) among exiles in the US, and inspired the 1895 revolt. With half a dozen others, he landed at Playitas (Oriente) in April 1895 and led the rebel troops until his death a few weeks later in a skirmish with Spanish soldiers. The revolutionary regime founded in 1959 hails Martí as its ideological forerunner, but his name is also invoked by anti-Castro Cubans, and was given to a counter-revolutionary radio station set up in Florida by the administration of President Reagan, which began broadcasting in 1985. See also **Radio Martí.**

Martina, Don

b. 1 May 1935. Premier of the Netherlands Antilles 1979–84, 1985–8. A civil engineer, Martina was elected to the Curaçao island council in 1971 and was island justice commissioner 1972–6. He had founded the social democratic New Antilles Movement (MAN) in 1971. When MAN became the largest party in parliament at general elections in 1979, he was appointed premier. His ruling coalition broke up in 1984 and he was succeeded by National People's Party leader Maria Liberia-Peters. Although the MAN did poorly in the 1985 election, Martina put together another coalition and became premier again. His government fell in 1988 after it once more lost its parliamentary majority, and he was succeeded again by Liberia-Peters.

See also **New Antilles Movement; Liberia-Peters.**

Martínez, Boris: see Torrijos Herrera.

Martínez, Fidel: see Communist Party of Honduras.

Martínez, Ifigenia: see Cárdenas, Cuauhtémoc.

Martínez, Gen. Maximiliano Hernández

1882–1966. President of El Salvador 1931–4, 1935–44. Martínez, who was of Indian origin, spent much of his childhood as a water-carrier. He used his maternal surname because he had no legal title to his father's name, Hernández. After attending the military academy (Escuela Militar Politécnica) in Guatemala, he entered the Salvadorean army and was commissioned in 1903. Promoted to major in 1906 for service in the war against Guatemala, he attained the rank of brigadier general in 1919. For a year he sat in on a law course at the National University. He studied theosophy and became a vegetarian, saying his guiding principle was that 'It is a greater crime to kill an ant than a man – for a man on dying is reincarnated, while an ant remains dead.' After attaining the post of chief of staff, Martínez stood for the presidency in the 1930 elections, but at the last moment he threw in his lot with the candidate of the Salvadorean Labour Party (PLS), Arturo Araujo. When Araujo won, Martínez became vice-president and minister of war.

On 2 December 1931 he assumed the presidency after a group of young officers overthrew Araujo, although his personal complicity in the coup remains unclear. His presidency was confirmed by congress in February 1932, but the US embassy withheld diplomatic recognition from the regime for two years (though it refused to support Araujo, who fled to Guatemala). When a peasant revolt, semi-led by the Communist Party (PCS), broke out in January 1932, Martínez crushed it with great loss of life. Subsequently all party and trade union activity was banned, with the exception of his own Pro-Patria Party. His rule was noted for its ruthless efficiency and occult overtones. In 1934, Martínez resigned the presidency to meet the requirements for standing in the 1935 election, which he won. He amended the constitution in 1939 to remain in power, but an attempt at further constitutional manipulation in 1944 led to a general strike supported by workers, doctors, bank employees and students which toppled him in May 1944, aided by the withdrawal of US support following the killing by a policeman of a 17-year-old US national, Joe Wright. Martínez spent the remainder of his life in exile in Honduras. See also *Matanza* (1932 massacre).

Martínez Verdugo, Arnaldo: see **Communist Party** (Mexico).

Martinican Progressive Party (*Parti Progressiste Martiniquais*/PPM) Main left-wing party in Martinique. Founded in 1958 by Fort-de-France mayor Aimé Césaire after he broke with the French Communist Party over Hungary and in protest against the party's inattention to the problems of the French Caribbean islands. The PPM opposed *département* status and sought a 'Martinican region in a French federal structure'. In 1967 it called for autonomy. It also accused France of 'genocide by substitution' in the Caribbean through encouraging emigration to France from the islands. After the Socialist Party victory in France in 1981, the party dropped its autonomy stance to back the socialists' decentralisation policy. The party's secretary-general, Camille Darsières, became president of Martinique's regional council in 1988, succeeding Césaire.
See also **Césaire; Darsières; Guadeloupe, independence movements.**

MARTINIQUE

Capital: Fort-de-France
Area: 1,100 sq km
Population (1990): 359,800
Pop. growth rate: 1.1%
Pop. density: 327/sq km
Infant mortality: 15 per thousand
Life expectancy at birth: 74
Literacy: 94%
GDP per capita (1985): US$4,761
Foreign debt per capita: US$83
Main exports: tourism, bananas, petroleum products, rum, pineapples, fertilisers

Political system

A commissioner (prefect) appointed by and sent from Paris for (generally) a two-year term governs in consultation with a 45-member General Council (elected for six years, with half the council renewed every three years) and a 41-member Regional Council elected every five years. Martinique, a *département* (province) of France, is represented in the French parliament by four National Assembly deputies and two senators. It was granted more self-government in 1982 and the Regional Council (which controls longer-term policy) was created in 1983.
Commissioner (prefect): Jean-Claude Roure (1989)
President of General Council: Emile Maurice (RPR) (1970)
President of Regional Council: Camille Darsières (PPM) (1988)
Deputies: Aimé Césaire (PPM) (1946), Maurice Louis-Joseph-Dogué

(PS) (1986), Claude Lise (PPM) (1988), Guy Lordinot (indep. left) (1988).
Senators: Rodolphe Désiré (PPM) (1986), Roger Lise (UDF) (1977).
Last elections: June 1988 (National Assembly), October 1988 (General Council), March 1986 (Regional Council).

Political organisations

Parties (leader) (seats in General/Regional Councils): Martinican Progressive Party/PPM (Aimé Césaire) (12/11), f. 1958; Rally for the Republic/RPR (Stephen Bagoë) (11/11), f. 1976; Union for French Democracy/UDF (Jean Maran) (5/9), f. 1979; Martinican Socialist Federation/FSM (Michel Yoyo) (5/5), f. 1971; Martinican Communist Party/PCM (Armand Nicolas) (3/2), f. 1957; Martinican Independence Movement/MIM (Alfred Marie-Jeanne) (1/0), f. 1974.

Other parties: National Council of Popular Committees/CNCP (Robert Saé), f. 1983; Revolutionary Socialist Group/GRS (Gilbert Pago), f. 1972; Combat Ouvrier (Gérard Beaujour), f. 1971; Communist Party for Independence with Socialism/PKLS (Jean-Pierre Etilé), f. 1984; Union for Renewal (Guy Lordinot), f. 1988.

Main trade unions: Workers' Force/FO (René Fabien); General Federation of Martinican Workers/CGTM (Luc Bernabé, Ghislaine, Joachim-Arnaud), f. 1967; Trade Union Confederation of Martinican Workers/CSTM (Daniel Marie-Sainte, Marc Pulvar), f. 1976; General Union of Martinican Workers/UGTM (Léon, Bertide), f. 1981; Martinican Democratic Workers' Union/CDMT (Denis Lange), f. 1979.

Employers' organisations: Martinique Chamber of Commerce and Industry/CCIM (Marcel Osénat); Employers' Association/CP (Baudoin Lafosse-Marin); Association of Medium and Small-sized Industries/MPI (Bernard Petitjean-Roget).

Matanza (1932 massacre)

The killing of between 10,000 and 50,000 people in El Salvador by the government of Gen. Maximiliano Hernández Martínez after an abortive uprising in January 1932. The Salvadorean Communist Party (PCS) had planned to lead the insurrection, but the plot was discovered and party leaders were arrested on 18 January. (Agustín Farabundo Martí, Mario Zapata and Alfonso Luna were executed on 1 February.) Fighting, which broke out on 22–23 January and continued for several days, was centred on the western coffee regions, where the peasants' main grievance was the seizure of their lands. Not more than 30 civilians are estimated to have died at the hands of the rebels, but the military government proceeded, after putting down the revolt, to slaughter systematically those deemed to have supported it. The most widely accepted death toll is 15–20,000. To have 'Indian features' or wear Indian costume was often regarded as proof of guilt, and this episode marked the virtual end of a distinctive indigenous culture in El Salvador. It also ushered in half a century of uninterrupted military rule – the longest in any Latin American country to date. So effective was the 'pacification' that even today the

western provinces (*departamentos*) of Sonsonate and Ahuachapán are the least affected by the current guerrilla insurgency.
See also **Martínez, Gen. Maximiliano Hernández; Salvadorean Communist Party; Martí, Agustín Farabundo.**

Matos, Huber
b. 26 November 1918. A veteran of the Cuban revolutionary war and military commander of Camagüey province under the Castro government, Matos became the most prominent political prisoner in Castro's Cuba. A rice grower from Manzanillo, he had been appointed commander of the Antonio Guiteras Column (Column IX) during the war. He resigned his Camagüey post in October 1959 in protest at growing communist control of the revolution. A score of other officers resigned with him, and all were arrested as counter-revolutionaries. Matos was put on trial in December 1959, charged with 'anti-patriotic and anti-revolutionary conduct'. He was alleged to have obstructed the agrarian reform programme in Camagüey and to have conspired with others elsewhere in the country who shared his views. Matos was sentenced to 20 years' hard labour and on completion of his sentence went into exile in Venezuela, where in 1980 he chaired a conference of counter-revolutionary groups plotting to overthrow Castro. His son, also called Huber, also became a prominent counter-revolutionary figure.
See also **Cuban Revolutionary War.**

Matthews, Herbert: see **Cuban Revolutionary War.**

Maurice, Emile
b. 8 July 1910. President of Martinique's General Council 1970– . A supporter of the Gaullist Rally for the Republic (RPR), he became a member of the General Council in 1957 and mayor of St Joseph in 1959. After the 1988 elections he remained president of the council despite the left's narrowly winning control.

Maurice Bishop Patriotic Movement (MBPM)
Left-wing party in Grenada. Formed in 1984 by supporters of the murdered Grenadian prime minister Maurice Bishop and led by two of his ex-cabinet ministers, Kendrick Radix and George Louison. After initial hesitation the MBPM stood in the 1984 elections, but won only 5% of the vote and no seats. However its newspaper, *Indies Times*, was widely read. The party denounced the leaders of the government faction jailed for killing Bishop and others in 1983. Radix stepped down as leader in 1988 and was succeeded by Terry Marryshow. The party's share of the vote dropped to 2.4% at the 1990 general election.
See also **Marryshow, Terry; Radix; Louison; New Jewel Movement; Grenada, US invasion (1983); Bishop.**

Maxi, Joseph: see **Gourgue.**

Maximato: see **Calles, Gen. Plutarco Elías.**

Maximiliano Hernández Martínez Brigade: see death squad; Romero, Archbishop Oscar Arnulfo.

Maynard, Clement
b. 11 September 1928. Deputy prime minister of the Bahamas 1985- . A medical technician, Maynard became leader of the senate and minister without portfolio when the Progressive Liberal Party came to power in 1967. He was elected to parliament in 1968 and served successively as minister of works (1968–9), tourism (1969–79) and labour and home affairs (1979–84). In 1984 he was appointed minister of foreign affairs and tourism, retaining both posts when he became deputy prime minister in 1985. He was replaced as foreign minister in 1989.
See also Pindling; Progressive Liberal Party.

Mayora Dawe, Héctor: see Authentic Nationalist Central.

Mayorga, Silvio: see Sandinista National Liberation Front.

Meany, George: see American Institute for Free Labor Development; general strike (Honduras 1954).

Medrano, Gen. José Alberto ('Chele'): see ORDEN.

Meese, Edwin: see Iran/contra affair.

Mejía Arellano, Oscar: see Azcona Hoyo.

Mejía Colindres, President: see Liberal Party (Honduras).

Mejía Victores, Gen. Oscar Humberto
b. 1931. Head of state/minister of defence of Guatemala 1983–6. Mejía joined the army in 1948 and by 1980 had reached the rank of brigade general. His posts included commander of the Quezaltenango military brigade; director of the Instituto Adolfo V. Hall del Norte in Alta Verapaz; commander of the Gen. Justo Rufino Barrios barracks in Guatemala City; inspector general of the army; and deputy defence minister. He was actively involved with the élite paratroop and *Kaibiles* units. Mejía was appointed minister of defence under the presidency of Gen. Efraín Ríos Montt and served as interim president for 48 hours in December 1982 when Ríos Montt visited the US. On 8 August 1983 he led a coup against the Ríos Montt regime, one of whose aims was to restore the political authority of the high command. An extreme anti-communist, Mejía (who never took the title of president) pursued with vigour the extermination of those deemed to be guerrilla supporters. Internationally, he brought Guatemala closer to the US (which supported his coup), but was restrained from fully implementing the active anti-Nicaraguan role in the region which he clearly favoured. He maintained close ties with the far right in the region, including Maj. Roberto D'Aubuisson in El Salvador and Gen. Gustavo Alvarez in Honduras. He promised 'free elections' from the beginning of his rule, and eventually handed over to an elected civilian successor, Vinicio Cerezo, in January 1986.
See also Ríos Montt; Cerezo Arévalo.

Meléndez, Jorge: see Martí, Agustín Farabundo.

Melgar Castro, Col. Juan: see López Arellano.

Menchú, Rigoberta: see Unitary Representation of the Guatemalan Opposition.

Méndez, Julín: see Social Democratic Innovation and Unity Party.

Méndez Montenegro, Julio César: see Revolutionary Party.

Méndez Montenegro, Mario: see Revolutionary Party; death squad.

Mendieta, Col. Carlos: see Batista y Zaldívar.

MERCOMUN: see Central American Common Market.

MERS: see Popular Revolutionary Bloc; Popular Liberation Forces.

Mésyeux, Jean-Auguste: see CATH.

Mexican Oil Workers' Union (STPRM): see Oil nationalisation (Mexico); La Quina.

Mexican Revolution

The uprisings of 1910–11 against the regime of Gen. Porfirio Díaz (the Porfiriato) set off one of the major social and political revolutions of the 20th century, antedating the Russian revolution. The term 'Mexican revolution' is used to refer to the immediate uprising and the subsequent internecine warfare, but also to the wider process of social change. The main achievements of the Mexican upheaval were significant land reform, the liberal 1917 Constitution (which embodied such novel features as the defence of labour rights and a declaration of state ownership of land and minerals), the eventual suppression of warlordism, and the emergence of political stability through the establishment of the single ruling party, the Institutional Revolutionary Party (PRI).

The post-revolutionary political system has not been free from criticism, particularly over the loss of the momentum of reform, the emergence of corruption and the domination of the country by an élite sometimes referred to as the 'revolutionary family'. For some academics the political system is essentially authoritarian, while others stress what they see as a kind of interest-group democracy working within the PRI.

The revolution itself can be divided up into various periods. The first uprising, of 20 November 1910, was led by Francisco Madero, a liberal reformer incensed by his imprisonment and exclusion from presidential elections earlier that year. Madero had earlier stated his claim to the presidency in his *Plan de San Luis Potosí*, in which he condemned Díaz' perpetuation in power and proclaimed the slogan 'effective suffrage, no re-election'. Although the rising itself failed, Madero was able to join up with the new rebel forces which had sprung up in Chihuahua under the leadership of Pancho Villa and Pascual Orozco. This rebel army forced Díaz to flee the country in May 1911, and in October that year Madero was elected president.

In office, however, he stopped well short of implementing the land reform measures demanded by Villa and other revolutionary commanders such as Emiliano Zapata in Morelos. In September 1911, Madero sent a force under Gen. Victoriano Huerta to crush Zapata's army. Zapata was forced into hiding, from where he issued his *Plan de Ayala*, which condemned Madero as a traitor and called for a new revolution, economic as well as political. A second period began in February 1913, when Gen. Huerta led a counter-revolution, taking power after his men had murdered Madero. He initiated a phase of intense repression with the backing of landowners, the church and the United States (a fact which explains in part the animosity felt by the revolutionaries towards all three). But there were new rebellions against him, led by Venustiano Carranza in the north. Villa's forces won the battle of Zacatecas in June 1914, but it was Carranza's close ally, Gen. Alvaro Obregón, who entered Mexico City first in July 1914 and forced Huerta to flee. US marines had meanwhile seized the port of Veracruz in April 1914 in a dispute with Huerta; they did not leave until November that year.

Once in power Carranza, like Madero, was unwilling to decree sweeping land reform. When a political convention ignored his position and voted to support key aspects of the Plan de Ayala, he ordered his supporters to withdraw. Villa and Zapata's peasant armies, then numbering about 50,000, marched on the capital while Carranza and Obregón withdrew to Veracruz. Zapata stayed only briefly in the capital; Villa set up a chaotic administration which collapsed in January 1915, providing the opportunity for Obregón to retake Mexico City and reinstate Carranza as president. Villa, his forces dwindling, withdrew to the north and ceased to be a challenge to central government. But Carranza found Zapata's forces more difficult to quell. A long and bloody civil war was fought, lasting even after Zapata himself was murdered by government troops on 9 April 1919.

Meanwhile, a constituent assembly meeting at Querétaro approved the 1917 constitution, which provided for considerable autonomy for the states but counterbalanced this with the creation of a powerful federal presidency. Although Carranza was finally forced to adopt many tenets of the Plan de Ayala, with the economy ravaged by war and a new government bureaucracy emerging there was little real land reform. Carranza and Obregón quarrelled in 1920, in part because Carranza had failed to pick his long-time lieutenant for the presidential succession due in 1921. Obregón's forces under Gen. Plutarco Calles marched down from Sonora to Mexico City and as Carranza withdrew he was murdered by his own soldiers on 21 May 1920.

Obregón's presidency initiated a new period of revolutionary consolidation. Land reform at last began to gather speed and the first moves were made towards establishing a strong central state. Obregón's successor, Calles, undertook economic modernisation, enforced the anti-clerical clauses of the 1917 Constitution (sparking off the Cristero wars) and forged most of the roughly 400 parties and movements which emerged

from the revolution into a single organisation, the National Revolutionary Party (PNR), later to become the PRI.
See also **Cristeros; Institutional Revolutionary Party.**

Mexican Revolutionary Party (PRM): see **Institutional Revolutionary Party.**

Mexican Socialist Party (*Partido Mexicano Socialista*/PMS)
A new grouping on the Mexican left, formed in 1987 by the merger of the Unified Socialist Party of Mexico (PSUM) and the Mexican Workers' Party (PMT). The PSUM was itself the product of a 1981 coalition of various groups, including the Communist Party (PCM). At that time the PMT had been involved in unity talks but these had foundered over the choice of presidential candidate for the July 1982 polls. The PMS explicitly rejected the marxist-leninist doctrine of the dictatorship of the proletariat, and maintained that religion was not necessarily the opiate of the masses. As such it represented another stage in the attempt to fuse nationalist and leftist traditions. In 1987 the PMS decided to choose Heberto Castillo, the former PMT leader, as its presidential candidate for the July 1988 polls. In June 1988, Castillo decided to stand down, however, announcing that the PMS would join the National Democratic Front (FDN) in supporting Cuauhtémoc Cárdenas for the presidency. After the elections, in which Cárdenas came second with over 31% of the votes, the PMS agreed to join the new *cardenista* Party of the Democratic Revolution (PRD).
See also: **Mexican Workers' Party; Communist Party** (Mexico).

Mexican Workers' Party (*Partido Mexicano de los Trabajadores*/PMT)
This party emerged from Mexico's student protests of 1968. In September 1971, Heberto Castillo, a university professor who had been jailed for his part in the events of 1968, brought together a group of independent leftists to discuss the formation of a new party. In fact, two parties emerged from these meetings. One strand of thinking led to the formation of the Socialist Workers' Party (PST), later re-named (in 1987) the Cardenista National Reconstruction Front Party (PFCRN). In its early days the PST sought to support 'nationalist' elements in the government and therefore moved close to the administration of Luis Echeverría. The other strand of thinking took a tougher opposition line and led to the creation of the PMT under Castillo. The PMT campaigned on a number of issues, but particularly on the question of the misuse of Mexico's oil resources. The party was refused electoral registration in 1982 (partly because it dismissed President López Portillo's electoral reforms as 'meaningless'); it achieved registration in July 1984. In the 1985 congressional elections it joined a coalition with other leftist parties; and in 1987 it merged with the Unified Socialist Party of Mexico (PSUM) to form the Mexican Socialist Party (PMS).
See also: **Mexican Socialist Party.**

MEXICO (United Mexican States)

Independence: (from Spain) 1821
Capital: Mexico City
Area: 1,967,183 sq km
Population (1988): 84.89m (70.3% urban)
Pop. growth rate (1980–88): 2.4%
Pop. density: 43/sq km
Infant mortality (1980–85): 49.9 per thousand
Life expectancy at birth (1980–85): 65.7
Literacy (1988): 84%
GDP per capita (1988e): $2,588
Foreign debt per capita: $1,198
Main exports (1988): manufactures (46%); hydrocarbons (32%); food products (15%)

Political system

Constitution: 1917. Head of state/government: President Carlos Salinas de Gortari (PRI) (1988–   ); elected to succeed Miguel De la Madrid (PRI) (1982–8). The president is elected by universal adult suffrage (18+) for a six-year term known as a *sexenio*; the office has wide-ranging powers, including the power to intervene in the states. Both houses of Congress are also elected by direct suffrage. There are 64 senators (two from each state and two from the Federal District) who also serve six-year terms. There are 500 deputies who are elected for three-year terms. In each election 300 of the seats in the lower chamber are awarded on a first-past-the-post basis; one for each of the 300 electoral districts into which the country is divided. The remaining 200 seats are distributed on a proportional representation basis to parties obtaining a national vote of at least 1.5%. General elections were held in July 1988.

Political organisations

Parties: (seats in Senate/Chamber of Deputies): Institutional Revolutionary Party/PRI (60/260); National Democratic Front/FDN (4/139); National Action Party/PAN (-/101). The FDN stood as a coalition comprising the Cardenista Front for National Reconstruction/PFCRN, the Popular Socialist Party/PPS, the Authentic Party of the Mexican Revolution/PARM and the Mexican Socialist Party/PMS.
The following parties have no congressional representation: Mexican Democratic Party/PDM, Workers Revolutionary Party/PRT.
Main labour organisation: Confederation of Mexican Workers/CTM.
Main employers' organisations: National Chamber of Processing Industries/CANACINTRA; Confederation of Industrial Chambers/CONCAMIN.

Michaux-Chevry, Lucette

b. 5 March 1929. One of Guadeloupe's four deputies in the French National Assembly and mayor of Gourbeyre. A lawyer, Michaux-Chevry achieved prominence by organising relief for refugees from the eruption of the island's Soufrière volcano in 1976. She was elected to the general council in 1976 as a socialist but left the party in 1981 to campaign for the re-election of conservative French President Valéry Giscard d'Estaing. As president of the general council (1982–5) she led a right-wing coalition to victory in elections for the regional council in 1983. She founded the Guadeloupe Party in 1984 but joined the Gaullist Rally for the Republic in 1985. In 1986 she was elected a National Assembly deputy, giving up her seat the same year when she was named a junior minister in charge of promoting the French language, a post she held until 1988. She was re-elected as a deputy in 1988.

'microfaction'
The term applied by the Cuban authorities to a group of Moscow-line dissidents, led by Aníbal Escalante, who in the late 1960s criticised Fidel Castro's policies, particularly his support for armed struggle. Escalante and 36 followers were arrested in January 1968 and put on trial, some of them ending up with 12-year jail sentences. Despite this clear signal of his refusal to toe the Moscow line, Castro was soon compelled, primarily by economic pressure, to abandon his independent foreign policy.
See also **Cuban Human Rights Party.**

Mien, John: see **Rebel Armed Forces.**

military bases (foreign) in the Caribbean
The United States has the most military bases in the region. The largest are at Roosevelt Roads (Puerto Rico) and Guantánamo (Cuba). Others are in Puerto Rico, the Bahamas and Antigua. In 1979, soon after the left-wing seizure of power in Grenada, the US established a military Caribbean Joint Task Force based in Key West, Florida. Shortly before its 1983 invasion of Grenada, the US began training and equipping small island forces employing Antigua as a base for its military surveillance of the eastern Caribbean. The invasion itself was rehearsed several times, notably on the Puerto Rican island of Vieques in 1981.

The Soviet Union has maintained some 8,000 troops in Cuba since the mid-1960s. France has about 5,000 troops stationed in Guadeloupe and Martinique, but no base as such. Britain and the Netherlands no longer have military bases in the region. All four Western countries co-operate militarily and stage US-led war games in the area most years.
See also **Regional Security System; Special Service Units; Grenada, US invasion (1983); Dominican Republic, US invasion (1965); Guantánamo base; Puerto Rico, nationalist violence; invasions and occupations by the United States; Vieques; Culebra.**

Millette, James: see **'black power'.**

minifundio: see *latifundio.*

Miracle, Gabriel: see **CATH.**

Misick, Ariel: see **Turks and Caicos Islands; Progressive National Party.**

Miskito Indians: see **Atlantic Coast** (Nicaragua).

Misurasata: see ARDE; Yatama.

Misyon Alfa: see Haiti, Roman Catholic Church.

Mitchell, James 'Son'

b. 15 March 1931. Premier, prime minister of St Vincent 1972–4, 1984– .
An agronomist, Mitchell joined the St Vincent Labour Party (SVLP) and
was elected MP for his native Grenadines in 1966, becoming minister of
trade, agriculture and tourism in 1967. He resigned from the SVLP in
1972 and was returned as the sole independent in a general election that
year which his resignation had provoked. The SVLP and the People's
Political Party (PPP) tied with six seats each. Mitchell allied himself with
the PPP and was named premier, with PPP leader Ebenezer Joshua as
his deputy. In 1972 he launched the concept of indigenous tourism in the
Caribbean, as opposed to large-scale foreign-owned package tourism, in
a speech which he called 'To Hell With Paradise'. In 1974, Joshua
resigned and Mitchell called new elections which were won by former
premier Milton Cato, who then teamed up with Joshua. The new government prevented Mitchell from becoming opposition leader by naming
Joshua's wife Ivy to the post.

In 1975 he founded the centrist New Democratic Party (NDP), which
won two seats at the 1979 election. But Mitchell, who had switched to a
mainland seat, failed to be elected. He regained his Grenadines seat at
a by-election in 1980 and became official opposition leader in 1983. The
NDP won the 1984 general election and he became prime minister.
Though he strongly favoured the 1983 US invasion of Grenada, he
rejected as wasteful, subversive and potentially repressive the concept of a
regional army which the US subsequently proposed to eastern Caribbean
states. He led the NDP to win all the seats in parliament at the 1989
election.

See also **New Democratic Party; St Vincent Labour Party; Joshua, Ebenezer; Grenadines; Bequia; Special Service Units; Regional Security System;
Caribbean Democratic Union; Grenada, US invasion (1983).**

Mitchell, Keith

b. 12 November 1946. Grenadian politician. A university mathematics
lecturer in the US and once a member of Herbert Blaize's Grenada
National Party, Mitchell joined the right-wing Grenada Democratic
Movement and after the 1983 US invasion of the island was elected to
parliament as a member of the victorious New National Party (NNP)
coalition in the 1984 elections. He was named communications, works
and utilities minister by Blaize, the new prime minister. In 1986 he
became general secretary of the NNP and in 1989 was elected NNP leader
by a party convention, deposing Blaize. A few months later, Blaize
sacked him from the government.

See also **New National Party; Blaize; Alexis.**

M-Líder: see Liberal Party (Honduras).

Mobilisation for National Development (*Mobilisation pour le Développement National*/MDN): see **de Ronceray.**

Molina, Col. Arturo: see **FAPU; ORDEN; Romero Mena.**

Molino, José A.: see **Christian Democrat Party** (Panama).

Molirena (*Movimiento Liberal Republicano Nacionalista*/Nationalist *Republican Liberal Movement*)
A Panamanian political party of the right, founded in 1981. Sometimes described as a 'patchwork' party, Molirena was formed out of fractions of the Liberal and Republican parties and of the defunct Third Nationalist Party (*Tercer Partido Nacionalista*). It joined the Opposition Democratic Alliance (ADO) coalition for the 1984 elections and maintained a position of hostility towards the regime of Defence Forces commander Gen. Noriega, supporting the National Civic Crusade campaign to remove the military from politics. In 1989 Molirena leader Guillermo (Billy) Ford was a vice-presidential candidate of the Alliance (renamed ADOC). He achieved worldwide prominence when members of Noriega's paramilitary Dignity Battalions were photographed beating him up during an opposition march to protest at the government fraud. After the US invasion of Panama in December 1989, ADOC was installed in government and Ford became second vice-president and minister of planning. Molirena was allocated 15 Assembly seats by the electoral tribunal.
See also **Democratic Alliance of Civic Opposition; Noriega Morena.**

MONARCA: see **National Party** (Honduras).

Moncada, José María: see **Somoza García.**

Moncada assault
An attack on the Moncada barracks in Santiago de Cuba on 26 July 1953, led by Fidel Castro, which was intended to spark off a general revolt against the Batista dictatorship. The 'Moncada Manifesto' was an 11-point programme of nationalist reforms, combined with an explanation of the uprising and an exhortation to join it. A simultaneous attack on the barracks at Bayamo was designed to prevent reinforcements being sent from there. Both attacks failed, and the Moncada attackers, who numbered over 100, were easily defeated. Eighty of those captured, along with some who had not participated, were later murdered, many after being tortured. Thirty-two were put on trial, with twice as many other innocent defendants (eventually acquitted). Castro acted as his own lawyer, to such effect that he was soon excluded from the trial. After his followers had been sentenced, Castro's own trial began again, less publicly. He delivered a two-hour speech, which later became known by its final words, 'History will absolve me', and was reproduced in a pamphlet in 1954. Sentenced to 13 years imprisonment, he was taken, with the other male prisoners, to the Presidio Modelo jail on the Isle of Pines. On 7 May 1954 Batista granted an amnesty and the Moncada prisoners were set free. Castro subsequently organised a new political movement called the '26 July Movement' in commemoration of the Moncada assault,

and since the revolution the date has been the most important annual celebration in Cuba.

See also **Castro Ruz, Fidel Alejandro; 26 July Movement; Batista y Zaldívar.**

Monge Alvarez, Luis Alberto

b. 29 December 1925. President of Costa Rica 1982–6. Born in Palmares into a middle-class peasant family and educated at the University of Costa Rica and University of Geneva, Luis Alberto Monge was a member of the Rerum Novarum labour federation from 1947 and later its president. A leading member of the Costa Rican Confederation of Democratic Workers (CCTD), he became vice-president of the Interamerican Labour Confederation (CIT). He was a member of Pepe Figueres' National Liberation Army in 1948 and in 1949 was elected as the youngest representative in the national constituent assembly.

Monge was a co-founder of the National Liberation Party (PLN) in 1951 and served as the party's secretary general for 12 years. He worked for the International Labour Organisation (ILO) in Geneva for three years and was secretary general of the Interamerican Regional Organisations of Workers (ORIT) for six years, as well as being a visiting lecturer at several universities in the US, Panama, Mexico and Peru. Monge served in the ministry of the presidency under Figueres in 1955 and was subsequently the first Costa Rican ambassador to Israel. After resigning from his ORIT post he was elected to the legislative assembly in 1958 and 1970 and served as president of the assembly 1970–74.

After an unsuccessful presidential campaign in 1978 he was elected president in 1982 as successor to Rodrigo Carazo. The Monge administration abruptly departed from the 'import substitution' model of economic development of the post-war years, opening up the ecomony to market forces. He succeeded in reducing inflation and the budget deficit, stablising the exchange rate and renegotiating the heavy foreign debt. But the price was adherence to IMF guidelines and a declining GDP. The government ultimately proved unable to meet its commitments to these organisations and aid disbursements were suspended for the last months of the Monge presidency. Internationally, Monge may be best remembered for his proclamation of neutrality in 1983 (although his attempt to have this incorporated into the constitution was defeated in the assembly). Despite this, the president was subsequently revealed to have been collaborating with the secret US support network for the Nicaraguan contra rebels, and his foreign policy was markedly anti-Nicaraguan.

Washington blatantly used the country's economic weakness as a lever to ensure support for its regional policies. Under the cover of a 'Northern Security and Colonisation Plan' financed by the US and Israel, US military engineers went to work along the Nicaraguan border, from where contra forces were operating, while US Special Forces personnel came to Costa Rica to train a 'Rapid Response' battalion. Costa Rica also became the first country to set up its diplomatic mission in Jerusalem in defiance of the United Nations. Monge's term of office also coincided with an increase in the militarisation of Costa Rica's police and security forces and the growth of civilian paramilitary groups. Allegations of corruption undermined his government's popularity and in September 1987, Monge himself was put on trial for alleged embezzlement of state funds during his term of office. He was, however, cleared of the charges. See also **National Liberation Party.**

Mongoose Gang: see **Gairy.**

Monroe doctrine

A unilateral foreign policy statement by US President James Monroe in his 2 December 1823 State of the Union address (drafted by Secretary of State John Quincy Adams) whereby the US rejected the colonisation of the Americas by European powers, in exchange for non-interference by the US in the colonial affairs of the latter. Monroe stated that any attempt 'to extend their system to any portion of this hemisphere' would be considered 'dangerous to our peace and safety'. The enunciation of the doctrine was prompted by European threats to intervene in order to suppress independence movements in the Spanish colonies. It has remained a major (though largely tacit) element in US foreign policy, despite modifications (such as F. D. Roosevelt's 'good neighbour policy' of the 1930s) to its interventionist overtones and the support ultimately given to the UK against Argentina in the 1982 Falklands/Malvinas war. It was restated and strengthened by President James K. Polk in 1845 over the attempt by Yucatán to secede from Mexico to Britain and Spain.

The curb on British plans in Central America imposed by the Clayton-Bulwer Treaty of 1850 was one of the doctrine's most important practical applications. In 1895, Secretary of State Richard Olney coined the Olney corollary to the doctrine, over a border dispute between Venezuela and British Guiana. He described the US as 'practically sovereign on this continent'. The Roosevelt corollary, set out by President Theodore Roosevelt in 1904, extended the doctrine to cover US intervention in Latin America in response to 'chronic wrongdoing, or an impotence which results in a general loosening of the ties of civilised society'. This justification ostensibly lay behind subsequent US 'police actions' in Haiti, the Dominican Republic and Nicaragua. On 12 August 1912, Congress approved the Lodge corollary, drafted by Senator Henry Cabot Lodge, which further extended the doctrine to cover an Asian country (Japan) and a private company in that country (which had sought to acquire Magdalena Bay in Baja California, Mexico). The Roosevelt corollary was repudiated in the 1928 Clark Memorandum. President Eisenhower affirmed the relevance of the doctrine over Soviet involvement with the Castro regime in Cuba, but his successor John F. Kennedy never invoked it. However, in the late 1980s senior US figures, including Secretary of State George Shultz have confirmed (à propos of Soviet support for Nicaragua, for instance) that the doctrine is still held to be valid.
See also **invasions and occupations by the United States; dollar diplomacy; good neighbour policy.**

Monsanto, Pablo: see Rebel Armed Forces; Guatemalan National Revolutionary Unity.

Montenegro de García, Nineth: see Mutual Support Group.

MONTSERRAT

Capital: Plymouth
Area: 102 sq km
Population (1987): 11,900
Pop. growth rate: 0%
Pop. density: 117/sq km
Infant mortality: 40 per thousand
Life expectancy at birth: 68
Literacy: 76%
GDP per capita (1988): US $4,000
Foreign debt per capita (1987): US$176
Main exports: electrical components and polythene bags, clothing, peppers, tomatoes, cotton, tourism

Political system

A British colony, with an appointed British governor in charge of defence, internal security, external affairs and (since a corruption scandal in 1989) offshore finance, representing the titular head of state, Queen Elizabeth of Britain. He chairs a 7-member Executive Council. An 11-member (7 elected, 2 nominated, 2 ex-officio) parliament, the Legislative Council, is elected for a maximum five years.
Governor: David Taylor (1990)
Chief minister: John Osborne (1978)
Last elections: 1987

Political organisations

Parties in parliament (leader) (elective seats): People's Liberation Movement/PLM (John Osborne) (4), f. 1976; National Development Party/NDP (Bertrand Osborne) (1), f. 1984; Progressive Democratic Party/PDP (Eustace Dyer) (1), f. 1970.
Main trade unions: Montserrat Trade Union Congress/MONTUC (Joseph Meade), f. 1990; Montserrat Allied Workers Union/MAWU (Vereen Thomas), f. 1973; Montserrat Union of Teachers/MUT (Joseph Meade), f. 1957; Civil Service Association/CSA; Seamen and Waterfront Workers' Union/MSWWU (G. Edward Dyer), f. 1961.

Montserrat Allied Workers' Union (MAWU): see Irish.

Montserrat Labour Party (MLP): see Bramble.

Moon, Revd Sun Myung: see Association for the Progress of Honduras.

Moore, Lee
b. 15 February 1939. Premier of St Kitts-Nevis 1979–80. A British-trained

lawyer, Moore returned to the island to become a top aide to premier Robert Bradshaw and his public relations officer in 1967. He was elected a vice-president of the St Kitts-Nevis Trades and Labour Union. Attorney general from 1971, he became premier on the death of Paul Southwell in 1979 and until the Labour Party was defeated at the 1980 general election. He then became official opposition leader. He lost his seat at the 1984 general election but remained party leader and head of the union. After again failing to win a seat at the 1989 election, he resigned as party leader and was replaced by Denzil Douglas.
See also **St Kitts-Nevis Labour Party; Bradshaw.**

Morales Troncoso, Carlos
b. 29 September 1940. Vice-president of the Dominican Republic 1986– . Morales Troncoso was general manager of the Gulf and Western-owned sugar, tourism and cattle interests in the Dominican Republic 1974–85, and in 1986 was elected vice-president of the republic at the same time Joaquín Balaguer regained the presidency. Balaguer appointed him head of the State Sugar Council (CEA) in 1986 but dismissed him in 1989 and named him ambassador to Washington. He retained the vice-presidency.
See also **Balaguer.**

Morán, Rolando: see **Guerrilla Army of the Poor; Guatemalan National Revolutionary Unity.**

Morán Castañeda, Rafael: see **National Conciliation Party.**

Mora Salas, Manuel: see **Mora Valverde.**

Mora Valverde, Manuel
b. 1908. A leading figure in the Costa Rican Communist Party for more than half a century, Manuel Mora was born in San José and trained as a lawyer and notary. He served as general secretary and then president of the Communist Party (later known as the Popular Vanguard Party/PVP) from 1934 to 1984, when he was expelled by the pro-Soviet leadership for alleged 'opportunism'. He and his followers then formed a breakaway group which became the Costa Rican People's Party (*Partido del Pueblo Costarricense*/PPC). Mora was a deputy in the legislative assembly 1934–48 and 1970–74. He stood for the presidency in 1940 and 1974. The author of many political works, he became the president of the United People (PU) coalition of the Communist and Socialist parties on its foundation in 1978. Mora's son, Manuel Mora Salas, is also a PU politician.
See also **Communist Party** (Costa Rica); **Civil War** (Costa Rica).

Morazanista Front for the Liberation of Honduras (FMLH): see **guerrilla movements** (Honduras).

Moscoso, Teodoro: see **Operation Bootstrap.**

Mosquitia: see **Atlantic Coast** (Nicaragua).

Mosquito Kingdom: see Atlantic Coast (Nicaragua).

Moutoussamy, Ernest
b. 7 November 1941. One of Guadeloupe's four deputies in the French National Assembly. A teacher, Moutoussamy was elected to the National Assembly for the Guadeloupean Communist Party in 1981 and in 1989 to both the island's General Council and the mayoralty of Saint-François.

Movement for National Unity (MNU)
Founded in 1982 by Ralph Gonsalves as a breakaway from the left-wing United People's Movement in St Vincent, it won 2% of the vote at the 1984 and 1989 elections.
See also **Gonsalves; United People's Movement.**

Movement for the Establishment of Democracy in Haiti (*Mouvement pour l'Instauration de la Démocratie en Haiti*/MIDH)
Conservative party founded in 1986 by ex-finance minister Marc Bazin after the fall of the Duvalier dictatorship. Bazin was the party's US-favoured presidential candidate in aborted elections in 1987. The MIDH boycotted a new army-sponsored election in 1988. The party's deputy leader, François Benoit, was ambassador to Washington 1988–90. In 1989, the party joined up with Serge Gilles' PANPRA to form a National Alliance for Democracy and Progress to contest elections.
See also **Bazin; PANPRA; Gilles.**

Movement of Organisation of the Country (*Mouvement d'Organisation du Pays*/MOP): see **Fignolé.**

Movement for the Liberation of Panama (MLP): see **Dignity Battalions.**

Moyne Commission
A British royal commission, chaired by Lord Moyne, sent to the British Caribbean in 1938 to investigate the social and economic causes of unrest and rioting there in the mid-1930s. Publication of the commission's report in 1939 was delayed until 1945 for fear its recommendations might cause colonial unrest in wartime. The report called for more money to be spent on the colonies, and for better wages, encouragement of trade unions and more self-government. The recommendations were followed.

Mozambique, Cuban involvement in: see **African involvement** (Cuba).

MR–13: see **Rebel Armed Forces.**

Muñoz Ledo, Porfirio: see **Cárdenas, Cuauhtémoc.**

Muñoz Marín, Luis
1898–1980. Governor of Puerto Rico 1949–65. The son of a prime minister under Spanish rule, Muñoz Marín was educated in the US and entered politics as a socialist and a nationalist. He returned to Puerto Rico to join the Liberal Party, was elected a senator in 1932 and campaigned for

autonomy and against the sugar barons. He was expelled from the party in 1937 and founded the Popular Democratic Party (PPD) in 1938, which won 38% of the vote at the elections in 1940. Muñoz, backed by a sympathetic US governor, Rexford Tugwell, became senate president and government leader. The PPD won the 1944 elections and Muñoz abandoned the idea of independence from the US. In the mid-1940s he launched what became known as Operation Bootstrap to lure foreign investors to industrialise the country and develop tourism.

In 1949 he became the island's first elected governor, and by 1952 he had won autonomy ('free associated statehood') for the island from the US. In 1965 he retired and his deputy, Roberto Sánchez Vilella, became governor. He is regarded as 'the father of modern Puerto Rico'. His daughter Victoria, a senator 1982–4 and 1988– , made a strong showing in the 1984 election for mayor of the capital, San Juan.
See also **Popular Democratic Party; Operation Bootstrap.**

Munroe, Trevor
b. 10 December 1944. Founder and general secretary of the marxist Worker's Party of Jamaica (WPJ). Munroe, a lecturer in politics at the University of the West Indies, founded the marxist Workers' Liberation League (WLL) in 1974 to give 'critical support' to Michael Manley's government. He renamed the WLL the WPJ in 1978 but his later offer to form an alliance with the increasingly radical ruling People's National Party was ignored. Munroe's strong ties with the radicals who took control of the Grenadian revolution in 1983 lost him support after Maurice Bishop's murder. When his deputy and other top figures resigned on the eve of the 1988 party congress, complaining of his rigidity and domination, Munroe admitted errors and promised a more democratic style. But he rejected demands to abandon marxism-leninism. Munroe is also founder and president of the University and Allied Workers' Union.
See also **Workers' Party of Jamaica; People's National Party.**

Murphy Act: see **Panama Canal Treaties.**

Musa, Said: see **People's United Party.**

Mustique
An island of the St Vincent Grenadines chain.
   Area: 5 sq km
   Population: 100
It has been owned since 1958 by a minor British aristocrat, Colin Tennant, who has made it into an exclusive private resort favoured by members of the British royal family. The French cruise liner *Antilles* ran aground off the island in 1971 and its rusting hulk has never been removed.
See also **Grenadines; St Vincent.**

Mutual Support Group (*Grupo de Apoyo Mútuo*/GAM)
A Guatemalan human rights organisation founded in June 1984 by relatives of disappeared prisoners. Several of its leading members, including its press officer, were killed during the Mejía Víctores government

(1983–6), allegedly by the security forces. The GAM represents more than 250 families of disappeared prisoners and was nominated for the 1986 Nobel Peace Prize by British parliamentarians. It expressed dissatisfaction with the response of the civilian government of Vinicio Cerezo (1986–90) to its demands, which included information on the whereabouts of up to 40,000 people 'disappeared' under military governments since 1954; the repeal of the 'unconstitutional' decree 8–86, which gave immunity to military officers responsible for human rights abuses; and the formation of an international commission to investigate the disappearances. In 1986, GAM presented habeas corpus petitions on behalf of around 2,000 individuals. The government, which had previously agreed to convene an investigatory commission, went back on its promise, arguing that the courts would have to deal with the matter. A fresh commitment in 1987 was reversed after the May 1988 coup attempt, which also led to intensified persecution of GAM. Leader (1989): founder-member Nineth Montenegro de García.

See also **Cerezo Arévalo; death squad; Mejía Víctores.**

N

Namphy, Gen. Henri

b. 2 October 1932. President of Haiti 1986–8. The illegitimate son of a member of parliament and a poor shopkeeper, Namphy joined the army in 1952 and rose through the ranks via the presidential guard and several provincial commands. He became deputy army commander in 1981 and head of the army, then a relatively powerless post, on the death of Gen. Roger St Albin in 1984.

When President Jean-Claude Duvalier fled in February 1986 before a popular revolt, Namphy assumed the presidency. Welcomed at first because of his genial disposition and apparent democratic intentions, he became disillusioned with the lack of civilian leadership and from mid–1987, soon after 99.8% of voters had approved a new liberal constitution, gave free rein to Duvalierists and fellow-soldiers seeking to destroy elections scheduled for November that year. After street protests forced him to reverse two repressive laws in July, he cut himself off from civilian politicians. He proclaimed himself armed forces commander for three years shortly before the poll. When the elections were called off amid officially-inspired violence he blamed foreigners, the Catholic church and leftists.

Namphy organised heavily-boycotted new elections in 1988 which the army allowed university professor Leslie Manigat to win. He stepped down as president, but when Manigat sacked him as army chief, junior officers rebelled and restored him to power in June 1988. Namphy ruled out further attempts at democracy and moved closer to leading Duvalierist politicians. After a church massacre and burnings by Duvalierists in the capital, he was overthrown in September 1988 by disgusted sergeants and exiled to the Dominican Republic.

See also **Manigat; Haiti, Roman Catholic Church; Duvalier, Jean-Claude; Duvalierism;** *déchoukage*.

National Action Party (*Partido de Acción Nacional*/PAN)

Mexico's main right-wing opposition party, founded in September 1939 as a conservative, Catholic response to the radicalism of the Cárdenas presidency. PAN's first leaders, Manuel Gómez Morín and Efraín González Luna, stressed the importance of individual over state or collective rights and emphasised the party's 'social-Christian' credentials. But the advent of the Alemán administration in the late 1940s, which opened the door to the private sector and was generally conservative in outlook, drew many businessmen away from PAN and back into co-operation with the state. The party nevertheless maintained its opposition image and gradually became a natural focus for protest votes against the ruling PRI. Between 1952 and 1970, PAN increased its share of the presidential vote from 7.8% to 13.8%. It began to build up considerable middle-class backing, winning a number of municipal elections and at times forcing the PRI to resort to fraud to retain a state governorship. In the 1970s, however, it was hit by internal dissent and it failed to field a candidate in the 1976 presidential elections because of a dispute over the nomination.

The party none the less staged a strong recovery in 1982. Its candidate, Pablo Emilio Madero, a businessman and nephew of the revolutionary leader Francisco Madero, took 16.4% of the vote and in the new chamber of deputies 55 out of 500 seats went to PAN. The party did particularly well in states near the US border. In municipal elections in 1983 it gained control of 5 out of 31 state capitals, but in state and municipal elections in 1985 and 1986, PAN accused the PRI of using wholesale fraud to stop further victories and regain control of a number of municipalities. The party organised a series of protests, including the occupation of town halls to stop PRI mayors taking office and the blocking of bridges across the US-Mexican border, many of which led to clashes with police.

In the July 1988 presidential elections the PAN candidate, Manuel Clouthier, came third with 16.81% of the vote. The party subsequently won a major victory when it took the governorship of Baja California in July 1989. The successful candidate, Ernesto Ruffo, was the first opposition figure to win a state election in more than half a century.

See also **Cárdenas, Lázaro; Alemán Valdés; Institutional Revolutionary Party.**

National Advance Party (*Partido de Avanzada Nacional/PAN*)
A Guatemalan party of the centre-right, founded in 1989 by the then mayor of Guatemala City, Alvaro Arzú Irigoyen, as a vehicle for his presidential ambitions. Arzú, who was director of the Guatemalan tourist board 1978–81, resigned as mayor in January 1990 to become the PAN candidate in that year's elections. Although little known outside the capital, he was seen as a competent administrator and potentially a strong contender. With Jorge Carpio Nicolle of the UCN, Arzú was one of those regarded favourably both by the US embassy and by the business community. A possible PAN/UCN alliance was mooted, but considered unlikely because of the personal ambition of both candidates.

See also **Union of the National Centre.**

National Agricultural and Industrial Party (*Parti Agricole et Industrial National/PAIN*): see **Déjoie.**

National Alliance for Democracy and Progress (*Alliance Nationale pour la Démocratie et le Progrès/ANDP*): see **Movement for the Establishment of Democracy in Haiti; PANPRA.**

National Alliance for Reconstruction (NAR)

A political party in Trinidad-Tobago, founded in 1985 as a four-party coalition of the East Indian-dominated United Labour Front (leader: Baseo Panday), the Tobago-based Democratic Action Congress (A. N. R. Robinson), the Organisation for National Reconstruction (Karl Hudson-Phillips) and the Tapia House Movement (Lloyd Best). The NAR, an expansion of the three-party alliance which won ten seats at the 1981 general election, was regarded as a rare success among attempts to unite the country's two main racial groups, the East Indians and the Afro-Trinidadians. However, Tapia leader Lloyd Best did not support it at the 1986 election, when the NAR, with Robinson as leader, ended the 30-year rule of the People's National Movement by winning 33 out of 36 seats.

The coalition split in late 1987, and by early 1988 four ministers, led by foreign minister Panday, who had accused Robinson of dictatorial government, had been dismissed. The rebels, charging discrimination against Indians, set up Club 88 and three of them were expelled from the NAR later that year. They founded the United National Congress party in 1989, with Panday as leader.

See also **Robinson; Panday; Hudson-Phillips; Best; Tapia House Group; People's National Movement** (Trinidad-Tobago).

National Campesino Pro-Land Association (*Associación Nacional Campesina Pro-Tierra*/ANC)

A peasant land rights movement formed in Guatemala in February 1986 by Father Andrés Girón, a Catholic priest. Land reform has been a forbidden subject in Guatemala since the 1954 'counter-revolution', although 67% of arable land is accounted for by only 2% of farms. Pressure has mounted in recent years owing to the decline in demand for labour, the failure of wages to keep pace with the cost of living, and the expectations aroused by the return to civilian government. Girón began by calling together 7,000 landless peasants to petition President Vinicio Cerezo for land. Cerezo promised to help, but nothing happened. He also ignored a subsequent petition signed by 35,000. In April-May 1986, Girón led a 100-mile march of 15,000 from Nueva Concepción to Guatemala City, modelled on the civil rights marches in the US in the 1960s in which he had taken part as a student. He stressed that the ANC was religious rather than political and avoided confrontation with landowners, preferring to seek government mediation.

Opponents have charged that his schemes will do nothing to alter the unjust structure of land tenure which gives rise to landlessness. From the outset, Cerezo promised the private sector that there would be no land reform. Instead, the government programme involves the purchase of farms for sale to groups of landless peasants. The aim was to aid 18,000 families in the first two years, although this is less than the rate of increase in the number of landless families. In the first year, six farms were handed over, of which two went to groups belonging to the ANC. By 1990, the figure had risen to 16. Girón claims that the ANC has 100,000 members,

but although his is the most prominent there are other land movements, some of which have adopted more confrontational tactics. In March 1990 Fr. Girón announced that he would leave the church and campaign for the Christian Democrats (DCG) in that year's elections. He said he hoped to be the DCG's vice-presidential candidate.
See also **Cerezo Arévalo; Arbenz Guzmán; Castillo Armas.**

National Christian Affirmation Movement: see **Christian Democrat Party** (Guatemala).

National Civic Crusade (*Cruzada Civilista Nacional*/CCN)
An opposition alliance formed in Panama in June 1987 and centred on the Panamanian Chamber of Commerce. The Crusade was set up to call for the resignation of Defence Forces commander Gen. Noriega and the immediate restoration of full civilian rule. Its nucleus consisted of around 35 business, professional and other organisations which joined forces after Noriega's former chief of staff publicly accused him of corruption, ballot-rigging and complicity in murder. Eventually it claimed the support of some 200 such groups. It was also backed by five right-wing opposition parties, but not by the two major trade union organisations, despite the latter's opposition to the government. Its tactics included strikes, street demonstrations, processions of cars and 'masses for peace'.

The government's first response was a three-week state of siege and the use of troops to quell the protests, which were subsequently banned. It censored the opposition media and ordered the arrest of CCN leaders, mainly right-wing businessmen. Government repression largely succeeded in preventing significant demonstrations after October 1987, although a strike virtually paralysed the country in the second half of March 1988. In January 1988 the CCN issued a 'Programme for a Transition to Democracy', which proposed the establishment of a provisional ruling junta to prepare for elections, restructure the legal system and work for economic reactivation. Two of its three members would be chosen by the CCN and the other by the opposition parties. During the rule of the junta, which would not be more than 18 months, a national commission would study possible constitutional reforms.

The Crusade's leaders continued to meet after the installation of the Endara government, and were highly critical of its performance, especially in relation to the new Public Force (successor to the Defence Forces). The CCN's co-ordinator (1990) is Dr Fernando Boyd.
See also **Democratic Alliance of Civic Opposition; Noriega Morena; Panama, US invasion (1989); Endara Galimany.**

National Civic Union (UCN): see **Christian Democrat Party** (Panama).

National Conciliation Party (*Partido de Conciliación Nacional*/PCN)
A Salvadorean party founded in September 1961 by Col. Julio Adalberto Rivera, leader of the right-wing counter-coup of that year against a reformist junta, and president 1962–7. The PCN inherited the tradition of 'official' parties and was the direct successor to the Revolutionary Party

of Democratic Unification (PRUD) of presidents Osorio and Lemus, to which many of its officials had belonged. It was the ruling party from 1961 under a succession of fraudulently elected military presidents until the overthrow of Gen. Carlos Humberto Romero on 15 October 1979. The president of the republic acted as 'general co-ordinator' of the party, which though dominated by the military was a source of patronage for civilian officials and supporters and reflected the interests of the business élite.

It re-emerged in 1982 as a conservative, anti-reformist, civilian party retaining strong links with the military, and won 14 seats in a 60-seat constituent assembly, obtaining four cabinet posts in the interim coalition government; but it quickly split in two, with the right wing setting up the Authentic Institutional Party (PAISA). In coalition with the Nationalist Republican Alliance (ARENA), the PCN won 12 seats in 1985; but the coalition broke down when the results were declared and an attempt by three PCN leaders, by agreement with ARENA, to have the elections declared void led to their expulsion from the party. In January 1987, with the two other right-wing parties in the assembly, the PCN boycotted parliamentary votes to force the government to repeal an electoral measure giving greater power to the ruling Christian Democrats (PDC) and an austerity package including a new war tax. In mid-1987 it announced that it would resume 'the social democratic line which guided it at its birth in 1961'; seemingly a reference to reformist elements in its original platform, 'betrayed' by Rivera. The move appeared largely cosmetic, aimed at improving its chances of participating in government. In the March 1988 assembly elections the PCN won seven seats, but one member subsequently defected to ARENA. Its presidential candidate, Rafael Morán Castañeda, polled only 4.2% in 1989. In July 1989 the party formed an alliance with the PDC and the Democratic Convergence 'to promote dialogue with the guerillas', but withdrew from this two months later.

See also **ARENA; Romero Mena.**

National Confederation of Mexican Workers (CNMT/CNT): see Confederation of Mexican Workers.

National Confederation of Popular Organisations (CNOP): see Institutional Revolutionary Party.

National Conservative Party: see Democratic Conservative Party of Nicaragua; Nicaraguan Democratic Co-ordinator.

National Co-operation Front (*Front National de Concertation*/FNC): see KONAKOM; Gourgue.

National Council of the Guadeloupean Resistance (*Conseil National de la Résistance Guadeloupéenne*/CNRG): see Guadeloupe, independence movements.

National Democratic Congress (NDC)

Grenadian political party founded in 1987 by three dissident members of

prime minister Herbert Blaize's government – George Brizan, Francis Alexis and Tillman Thomas – who accused Blaize of autocracy and inefficiency. The party, which is centrist, drew other MPs to hold 6 of the 15 seats in parliament. Brizan was elected party leader, but stepped down in 1989 in favour of Nicholas Brathwaite, former head of the post-invasion Advisory Council interim government. The NDC won seven seats in the 1990 general election and after one MP had defected to it, formed a government with an absolute majority.
See also **Alexis; Brizan; Brathwaite; Blaize.**

National Democratic Front (*Frente Democrático Nacional*/FDN)
A coalition of Mexican parties created in early 1988 to support the presidential candidature of Cuauhtémoc Cárdenas. They included the Democratic Current (a dissident sector of the ruling Institutional Revolutionary Party/PRI); the Authentic Party of the Mexican Revolution (PARM); the Popular Socialist Party (PSP); and the Cardenista National Reconstruction Front Party (PFCRN). In June 1988 the Mexican Socialist Party (PMS) also joined the FDN coalition. At the beginning of July a senior FDN official, Francisco Xavier Ovando Hernández, was shot dead in Mexico City together with an assistant. The party came second in the presidential race and also secured the second largest bloc of seats in congress.
See also **Cárdenas, Cuauhtémoc.**

National Democratic Party (NDP) (Barbados): see **Haynes.**

National Democratic Party (NDP) (Grenada): see **Brizan.**

National Development Party (NDP): see **Osborne, Bertrand.**

National Endowment for Democracy: see *La Prensa* (Nicaragua).

National Guard (El Salvador) (*Guardia Nacional*/GN)
A paramilitary force under the control of the defence ministry, created in 1912 by President Manuel Enrique Araujo as a rural constabulary modelled on the Spanish *Guardia Civil*. Training was initially given by Spanish officers. As worker and peasant militancy increased, the National Guard adopted a more explicitly political role in putting it down. The Agrarian Law of 1907, as reinforced in 1942 by President Martínez, included the requirement that 'The agents of the National Guard shall immediately upon the demand of any *hacendado* or farmer, arrest the person or persons whom he indicates to them as suspicious.' On larger estates it was common for members of the GN (usually those of lower status) to be assigned to protect the landowner and his property. (He would pay for their maintenance.)

Currently organised in 14 companies (one per department) and totalling 3,600 men, the GN has operated as a frontline counter-insurgency force during the civil war (1980–). It has frequently been accused of grave human rights violations. Five former members of the GN were given 30-year sentences for the rape and murder in 1980 of four US churchwomen – the first instance of army or security force personnel being sentenced

for crimes against civilians. Two others, given similar prison terms for the 1981 murder of two US advisers and the head of the Agrarian Reform Institute, were freed under amnesty in 1987.
See also: **D'Aubuisson Arrieta; death squad; ORDEN.**

National Guard (Nicaragua) (*Guardia Nacional*/GN)

A military organisation founded in 1925 by the US forces occupying Nicaragua as a 'professional, apolitical' force capable of replacing the traditional factional (Liberal or Conservative) armies. (A similar model was applied in Haiti, the Dominican Republic and the Philippines.) In 1933, US marines withdrew from Nicaragua, leaving the GN in the hands of its first Nicaraguan commander, Gen. Anastasio Somoza García, who in 1936 seized power and established a 43-year dynastic dictatorship whose principal power base was the GN. The Guard was responsible for both army and police functions, as well as communications, immigration, the health service and internal revenues. At election time the GN supervised the count. Officers made considerable sums from control of gambling, prostitution, smuggling and other illegal activities. On the death of Somoza García, command of the GN passed to his son, Anastasio Somoza Debayle. In 1978 an élite unit known as the Basic Infantry Training School (EEBI) was set up under the command of Anastasio Somoza Portocarrero, grandson of the first Somoza.

The GN was destroyed as an institution by the Sandinista revolution of 1979. Hundreds of its members were put on trial for acts of brutality, though many were subsequently given early release. Some of these, along with those who had fled abroad, later joined one of the US-backed counter-revolutionary ('contra') organisations (in particular the Nicaraguan Democratic Force/FDN). Their presence at senior levels was opposed by some contra groups and hindered the unification of the armed opposition.
See also **Somoza García; Somoza Debayle, Gen. Anastasio; Nicaraguan Democratic Force.**

National Independence Party (NIP): see People's United Party; United Democratic Party.

National Joint Action Committee (NJAC)

Trinidadian political party, founded in 1969 as a 'black power' coalition of radical trade unions and student and youth groups. It protested against the trial of West Indian students who smashed a computer centre at Sir George Williams University in Montreal in 1969 and then against 'Canadian imperialism' in the Caribbean. The protests grew into 'black power' demonstrations in Trinidad in early 1970, headed by the charismatic NJAC leader Geddes Granger (who later africanised his name to Makandal Daaga), and a mutiny by radical sympathisers in the army in April that year. NJAC contested its first election in 1981 and won 3.3% of the vote. In 1986 it scored only 1.5%.
See also **'black power'; Trinidad, 'black power' uprising (1970); Canada and the Anglo-Caribbean; Douglas, Rosie.**

National Liberal Party (NLP)

Political party in Bermuda, formed in 1985 by four right-wing dissident members (led by Gilbert Darrell, b. 30 June 1923) of the social democratic Progressive Labour Party (PLP) who were expelled from the PLP when they demanded party leader Lois Browne-Evans's resignation in 1984. At the 1985 general election, the NLP won two seats, but only one (held by Darrell) at the 1989 election.
See also **Progressive Labour Party** (Bermuda); **Browne-Evans**.

National Liberation Armed Forces (*Fuerzas Armadas de Liberación Nacional*/FALN)

A guerrilla organisation fighting in the US for Puerto Rico's independence. Founded in 1974 by members of three earlier guerrilla groups, it staged some 130 bomb attacks on political and military targets in the United States between 1974 and 1983. Many of its members were sentenced to long jail terms, including its leader, Oscar López Rivera, in the US in 1981 for conspiracy.
See also **Puerto Rico, nationalist violence; Macheteros; Puerto Rican Independence Party**.

National Liberation Army: see **Civil War** (Costa Rica).

National Liberation Coalition (*Coalición Nacional de Liberación*/COLINA)

An alliance of seven Panamanian pro-government parties, formed to succeed the ruling Unade (Democratic National Union) alliance which won the controversial 1984 elections. Unade's presidential candidate, Nicolás Ardito Barletta, beat opposition leader Arnulfo Arias by a narrow margin in a poll widely denounced as fraudulent. Unade took 40 of the 67 parliamentary seats. Its six original members were the Democratic Revolutionary Party (PRD), the Broad Popular Front (Frampo), the Labour Party (PALA), the Liberal Party (PL), the Panameñista Party (PP) and the Republican Party (PR). The strongest of these was the PRD, followed by PALA. Frampo and the PP were deprived of their legal status in November 1984, although by 1987 the PP had gained sufficient affiliations to reapply. In September 1985, Ardito Barletta was replaced as president by Eric Arturo Delvalle of the PR. Tensions arose within Unade (whose members had already complained that they were excluded from key decisions) over the repression of anti-government media and demonstrators in the second half of 1987. After statements critical of the government, vice-president Roderick Esquivel of the PLN was effectively marginalised, and the PL withdrew from Unade, although Esquivel at first refused to resign.

The PL did, however, join the new COLINA grouping, formed to fight the 1989 elections, which also included the PRD, PALA, the PR, the Revolutionary Panameñista Party (PPR), the People's Party of Panama and the Democratic Workers' Party. The official result gave COLINA's candidate Carlos Duque a 2:1 victory over Guillermo Endara of the ADOC alliance. However, most observers agreed that the latter won by

around 3:1. Under pressure at home and abroad, the government annulled the results, which were eventually partially reinstated after the December 1989 US invasion.
See also **Democratic Revolutionary Party; Labour Party; Republican Party (Panama); Ardito Barletta; Delvalle; Panama, US invasion (1989).**

National Liberation Movement (Guatemala) (*Movimiento de Liberación Nacional*/MLN)

An extreme right-wing political party and paramilitary organisation, founded in Guatemala in 1960, the MLN represents the political tradition of Col. Castillo Armas' invading army of 1954 and is the successor to the National Democratic Movement (MDN). It is dominated by its veteran leader, Mario Sandoval Alarcón (vice-president under Kjell Laugerud, 1974–8). Supporters have traditionally included landowners both large and small, middle-ranking traders and bureaucrats, with an emphasis on the agro-export sector. The MLN shared political dominance with the Revolutionary Party (PR) during the Peralta Azurdia government (1963–6). It lost the 1966 elections but participated in government from 1970 to 1978 in alliance with the Institutional Democratic Party (PID). In 1978 and 1982 it ran as an opposition party and lost. MLN members were suspected of a coup plot against the Ríos Montt government in August 1982. Leading member Leonel Sisniega split with the party and in 1983 formed the Anticommunist Unification Party (PUA).

In 1984 the MLN won 23 seats in the constituent assembly in coalition with the Authentic Nationalist Central (CAN). This agreement ended in January 1985, and the MLN-PID coalition was restored for the November 1985 elections, in which it won 12 seats and presidential candidate Sandoval obtained 12.6% of the vote. It has consistently criticised the Cerezo government's policy of 'active neutrality' in the Central American conflict, and in December 1986 said it was training 8,000 volunteers at a secret site in Central America to fight with the Nicaraguan contra rebels. It has also accused the government of leading the country towards communism and has called at various times for its resignation and the suspension of the constitution. It declined to sign the 'democratic commitment' with other parties in 1987. The party's decline is partly attributable to a loss of support within the armed forces, whose 'statist' tendencies the MLN opposed and who needed to hand over to a moderate civilian successor.

The party suffered a further split in early 1986 with the departure of a group led by secretary general Dr Héctor Aragón Quiñónez to set up the Organised National Unity (UNO) party.
See also **Sandoval Alarcón; Castillo Armas; Authentic Nationalist Central; Institutional Democratic Party.**

National Liberation Movement (MLN) (Mexico): see Cárdenas, Cuauhtémoc.

National Liberation Party (*Partido Liberación Nacional*/PLN)

The dominant political force in Costa Rica since its foundation in 1951 as the successor to the Social Democratic Party (PSD, f. 1945), the PLN has held a continuous majority in the legislative assembly except for the period 1978–82. The group of social democrats around José 'Pepe' Figueres who founded the party said their aim was to put an end to the 'intolerable level of misery' among the population. Moderate economic and social reform has been the keynote of PLN policy, along with the restructuring of government and the creation of autonomous agencies to administer the nationalised sector of the economy.

Often referred to simply as *Liberación*, the PLN claims to belong to the Latin American tradition of 'people's parties' in the mould of the Peruvian APRA and has been affiliated to the Socialist International since the early 1960s. From the beginning, however, it lacked a working-class base, being an élitist-led party dedicated to opposing the populism of the Calderón Guardia era. Figueres was chosen as the party's candidate for the 1953 elections, which he won comfortably. The party split in 1955, however, with the breakaway faction headed by finance minister Jorge Rossi fighting the 1957 election as the Independent Party and winning 3 seats, against 20 for the PLN itself. This gave it the balance of power in the legislative assembly. The PLN subsequently held the presidency for the periods 1962–6 and 1970–74 (Figueres); 1974–8 (Daniel Oduber); and 1982–6 (Luis Alberto Monge). It won a further consecutive term in 1986 with Oscar Arias Sánchez.

An internal power struggle over the 1986 candidacy resulted in the marginalisation of the 'generation of '48' – the original patriarchs of the PLN (although Figueres remained party president). Foreign policy under Monge had been pro-US, anti-Nicaragua, but Arias came to power on a 'peace ticket', seeking a regional peace settlement. This helped ease some of the tension between the Socialist International and the PLN, which has many times objected to Sandinista influence in the SI. In economic terms, too, the party had distanced itself from social democracy under the pressure created by Costa Rica's enormous foreign debt. The battle for the 1990 candidacy between the conservative and progressive wings of the party began as early as 1987 and was fuelled by issues such as privatisation of state enterprises and banking reform, as well as drugs scandals involving party figures. Conservative Carlos Manuel Castillo won the nomination but lost the election to Rafael Angel Calderón of the PUSC.

See also **Civil War** (Costa Rica); **Figueres Ferrer; Oduber Quirós; Monge Alvarez; Arias Sánchez; Calderón Guardia.**

National Opposition Front: see **Christian Democrat Party** (Guatemala).

National Opposition Union (UNO) (El Salvador): see **Democratic Convergence; Duarte; Salvadorean Communist Party.**

National Opposition Union (Nicaragua) (*Unión Nacional Opositora*/UNO)
Originally known as the Group of 14, UNO is a coalition of Nicaraguan

parties formed to challenge the ruling Sandinistas (FSLN) in the 1990 elections. Its membership fluctuated, but by the time of the elections it comprised 12 legal and two unrecognised parties (*see country entry for details*). UNO accused the other opposition parties of being government 'stooges', but in August 1989 it signed an agreement with them and the FSLN calling for the disbandment of the US-backed armed opposition (the contras), in exchange for government concessions relating to the 1989–90 election campaign. The FSLN, for its part, alleged that UNO and the contras were one and the same. UNO won an unexpected victory at the polls, taking about 55% of the vote, and its candidate, Violeta Barrios de Chamorro, was elected president. Its 51 Assembly seats were not enough, however, to amend the Sandinista-designed constitution. Moreover, splits in the coalition were evident even during the election campaign, and after the election UNO divided into two opposing wings, with eight of its member parties (including the Independent Liberals/PLI of vice-president Virgilio Godoy) hostile to the Chamorro group's hand-ling of the transition. They particularly objected to the retention of Sandinista defence minister Gen. Humberto Ortega to head the army. Miriam Arguello, of the Conservative Popular Alliance Party (PAPC) was elected to lead the Assembly against the wishes of Chamorro, who had proposed Alfredo César of the Social Democrats (PSD). Clashes were also foreseen over the handling of the economy, and especially over demands by the right within UNO for wholesale privatisations.

See also **Barrios de Chamorro; Nicaraguan Democratic Co-ordinator;** *La Prensa* (Nicaragua); **Independent Liberal Party.**

National Opposition Union (UNO) (Panama): see Liberal Party (Panama).

National Party, The (TNP) (Grenada): see Blaize; New National Party.

National Party (*Partido Nacional*/PN)

One of the two 'traditional' parties in Honduras, the PN became a coherent political force in 1923 under the influence of Tiburcio Carías, after attempts dating back to the 1890s to unite its factions. It had originated as a split from the Liberal Party (PL) but was traditionally more conservative, deriving the bulk of its support from rural areas dominated by large landowners. From 1912 until after World War II the PN was the party of the US transnational United Fruit Co., while the PL was dominated by the rival Cuyamel company (taken over by UFCo in 1929). It held power from 1933 to 1957 and (in alliance with the PL) in 1971–2.

After the foundation of the modern Honduran army in 1952 the National Party developed close links with the officer corps, often acting as the 'army party' (e.g. in the early years of the López Arellano govern-ment and from 1975 to 1981). This alliance was effectively broken by the PL victory in the 1981 elections. During 1981–5 the PL systematically undermined PN unity, backing a pro-government minority faction, the

Movement for Unity and Change (MUC) under Juan Pablo Urrutia, whose right to control the party was upheld by the supreme court and the electoral tribunal (TNE), both dominated by the PL. Under a so-called 'little pact' (*pactito*) between the armed forces and the PN in 1985, the legitimate leadership of the PN was restored, and the newly-formed MONARCA faction under Rafael Leonardo Callejas succeeded in winning all 63 PN seats in the 1985 election.

Although the PL received more votes than the PN, Callejas was more popular than the PL's Azcona, who was none the less declared president under a pre-election agreement that the majority candidate from the winning party would take office. Callejas was thus able to force on the Liberals a coalition agreement (the National Unity Pact/PUN), under which the PN was granted four out of nine places on the congressional directorate and effective control of the judiciary and the TNE, as well as a large share of more minor posts. Azcona named PN members to head the foreign and labour ministries. Ideological differences between *azconistas* and *callejistas* are small: both are politically conservative and believers in private enterprise. However, Callejas' most prominent rival within the PN, Oswaldo Ramos Soto, extreme right-wing rector of the National University, strongly opposed the PUN, which was officially dissolved in January 1987 but continued in practice until the end of that year. Callejas took his party's nomination for the 1989 elections unopposed and won the presidency with about 50% of the vote.

See also **Callejas; Carías Andino; López Arellano.**

National Peasant Confederation (CNC) (Mexico): see Institutional Revolutionary Party.

National Peasant Union (UNC): see Christian Democrat Party of Honduras.

National People's Party (*Partido Nashonal di Pueblo*/PNP; *Nationale Volkspartij-Unie*/NVP)
Political party in the Netherlands Antilles, founded in 1945 by M. F. da Costa Gomez as a social Christian party backed mainly by middle and lower-middle-class Afro-Antilleans. Gomez headed a coalition government from 1951 until elections in 1954, when the PNP lost power to the Democratic Party (DP).

Juancho Evertsz took over the party on Gomez' death in 1969 and became premier after the PNP emerged as the dominant party, with five seats, at the 1973 election ending 19 years of DP rule. Evertsz was premier until the 1977 poll, when the PNP won only three seats and handed power back to the DP. Gilbert de Paula then became party leader until 1982, when he was succeeded by Maria Liberia-Peters. The party sank to only two seats at the 1979 election but improved to three in the 1982 poll. Liberia-Peters became premier in 1984 for a year after premier Don Martina of the New Antilles Movement lost his majority. The PNP doubled its seats to six at the 1985 election, but could not form a government. However, Liberia-Peters became premier again in 1988 when the

Martina government broke up. The party won seven seats at the 1990 election on a platform of Curaçao's secession from the Netherlands Antilles federation after Aruba's example and Liberia–Peters continued in office.

See also **Liberia-Peters; Martina; New Antilles Movement; Democratic Party** (Netherlands Antilles); **Workers' Liberation Front-Social Independent Party.**

National Renewal Party (PNR): see Christian Democrat Party (Guatemala).

National Renovation Movement (MNR): see Labour Party (Panama).

National Republican Party (PNR): see Calderón Guardia.

National Rescue and Conciliation Movement (MRCN): see Southern Opposition Bloc.

National Revolutionary Coalition (CNR): see Arias Madrid.

National Revolutionary Movement (MNR): see Democratic Convergence.

National Revolutionary Party (PNR): see Calles; Institutional Revolutionary Party; Mexican Revolution.

National Security Volunteers (*Volontaires de la Sécurité Nationale*/VSN): see Tontons Macoutes.

National Trade Union Unity Committee (CNUS): see Peasant Unity Committee.

National Unification Coalition: see Social Christian Unity Party.

National Unification Party (PUN): see Calderón Guardia.

National Union coalition: see Authentic Panameñista Party.

National Union of Freedom Fighters (NUFF): see Trinidad, 'black power' uprising (1970).

National Union of Popular Action (UNAP): see Chamorro Cardenal, Pedro Joaquín.

National Union of Workers (UNT): see Salvadorean Communist Party.

National Union Party (PUN): see Civil War (Costa Rica/1948); Social Christian Unity Party.

National Unitary Directorate (DNU): see guerrilla movements (Honduras).

National Unity Front (Frenu): see Christian Democrat Party (Guatemala).

National Unity Pact: see Azcona Hoyo.

National Workers' Union of Jamaica (NWU)

Jamaica's second biggest trade union, controlling some 30% of the work-force. It was founded by the opposition People's National Party (PNP) in 1952 to fill the gap left after PNP leader Norman Manley purged the party of leftists who had done virtually all the work of building the party up from the grassroots. The leftists, centred on the Trade Union Congress (TUC) and led by 'The Four H's' (Ken Hill, Richard Hart, Frank Hill and Arthur Henry), had resisted Manley's request to break with the communist-dominated World Federation of Trade Unions. The new union, led initially by Florizel Glasspole (b. 25 September 1909) and others, managed to draw substantial support thanks to the past political work of the left, the split in the TUC and the efforts of Manley's energetic son Michael among the sugar workers. The new union was a key element in the PNP's first general election victory in 1955. Michael Manley became its president in 1984.

See also **People's National Party; Manley, Michael.**

National Democratic Front: see D'Aubuisson Arrieta.

Nationalist Democratic Union (*Unión Democrática Nacional-ista*/UDN)

A Salvadorean political party, founded in 1969, incorporating several leaders of the liberal/social democrat Party of Restorative Action (*Partido de Acción Renovadora*/PAR – 'Nueva Linea'), but essentially the legal front for the Salvadorean Communist Party (PCS, banned in 1932). The UDN participated in the UNO reformist coalition in the 1972 and 1977 elections, and later in the Popular Forum (*Foro Popular*, f. 1979), a similar broad front. It joined the government after the coup of October 1979, holding five cabinet posts (notably the labour ministry), but left in January 1980. It was a founder-member of Democratic Revolutionary Front (FDR) opposition coalition in 1980. The UDN re-entered civilian politics in 1988, saying it was seeking to contribute to the search for a negotiated settlement of the war, but that it would not participate in the 1989 elections. General secretary: Mario Aguiñada Carranza.

See also **Salvadorean Communist Party; Democratic Revolutionary Front (El Salvador); Democratic Convergence.**

Nationalist Revolutionary Civic Association (*Asociación Cívica Nacionalista Revolucionaria*)

A small guerrilla movement which was active in the early 1970s in the Mexican state of Guerrero. It was led by Genaro Vázquez Rojas, a schoolteacher, who was forced to flee persecution by hired gunmen; he and a small group of followers took to the hills from where they began their campaign. Vázquez Rojas worked closely with Lucio Cabañas Barri-entos, leader of another Guerrero rebel movement, the Party of the Poor. The movement petered out in the face of 'dirty war' counter-insurgency tactics and after Vázquez Rojas' death in a car crash in 1972.

See also **Party of the Poor.**

Nativí, Tomás: see **Communist Party of Honduras.**

NETHERLANDS ANTILLES

Capital: Willemstad
Area: 800 sq km
Population (1989): 194,700 (92% urban)
Pop. growth rate: 1%
Pop. density: 243/sq km.
Infant mortality: 15 per thousand
Life expectancy at birth: 77
Literacy: 95%
GDP per capita (1985): US$6,110 (incl. Aruba)
Foreign debt per capita (1987): US$5,338
Main exports: petroleum and petroleum products, tourism

Political system

The Netherlands' last overseas possession, the five-island federation (Curaçao, Bonaire, Sint Maarten, Sint Eustatius (Statia) and Saba) has internal self-government under its 1954 constitution. Aruba broke away from the federation in 1986 but remains under nominal Dutch rule. The state is sometimes referred to as the Antilles of the Five. In 1990, Holland proposed dividing the federation into two parts – Curaçao-Bonaire and the three smaller islands in the north.

An Antillean figurehead governor representing titular head of state Queen Beatrix of the Netherlands has responsibility for foreign affairs. A 22-member parliament (the Staten) is elected for a maximum four years. Fourteen seats are reserved for Curaçao, three each for Bonaire and Sint Maarten and one each for Saba and Statia. Each island also has its own lieutenant-governor and partly-elected local council.
Governor: Jaime Saleh (1990)
Premier (minister-president): Maria Liberia-Peters (1988)
Last elections: 1990

Political organisations

Parties in parliament (leader) (seats): National People's Party/ PNP/NVP (Maria Liberia-Peters) (7), f. 1945; New Antilles Movement/ MAN (Don Martina) (2), f. 1971; Democratic Party (Curaçao)/DP (Raymond Bentoera) (1), f. 1944; Sint Maarten Democratic Party/ PSM (Claude Wathey) (2), f. 1951; Sint Maarten Patriotic Alliance/SPA (Vance James) (1); Bonairean Patriotic Union/UPB (Rudi Ellis) (3); Social Independent Party-Workers' Liberation Front/SIFOL (George Hueck) (3), f. 1990; Nos Patria (Chin Behilia) (1), f. 1990; Windward Islands Progressive Movement/WIPM (Will Johnson) (1); Democratic Party (Statia)/DP-Statia (Kenneth van Putten) (1).
Main trade unions: Union of Curaçao Trade Unionists/KSC/KVC (Errol Cova); Curaçao Federation of Workers/CFW (H. J. van Sichem), f. 1964. Petroleum Workers' Federation of Curaçao/

PWFC/FTPK (L. Janzen), f. 1955; General Union of Curaçao Workers/CGTC (Erwin Koense); Bonairean Labour Federation/FEDEBON (William Cicilia); Windward Islands Federation of Labour/WIFOL (René Richardson).
See also **Aruba; Sint Maarten; Antilles of the Five.**

Netherlands Antilles, oil refineries

The refineries were a major magnet for emigration in the region between 1920 and 1955 and the source of political awakening of many future leaders of the Eastern Caribbean, including Eric Gairy and Herbert Blaize (Grenada) and George Charles (St Lucia). Most influential was Exxon's Lago refinery, which began operating at Sint Nicolaas, on Aruba, in 1929. At its peak in the 1950s, it employed some 9,000 people. The refinery gradually cut back its operations and finally closed in 1985, dealing a body blow to the Netherlands Antilles economy and helping to bring about the electoral defeat of Aruba's nationalistic leader Betico Croes and his People's Electoral Movement. The same year, Shell sold its refinery on Curaçao (built in 1916) at a nominal price to the government, which averted closure by leasing it to a Venezuelan company. Large oil trans-shipment terminals built during the oil boom in the mid-1970s were also superseded a decade later. In 1989 a Texas company, Coastal Corporation, announced plans to reopen the Aruba refinery in 1991.
See also **Croes; People's Electoral Movement; Aruba; Gairy; Blaize.**

Nevis

Part of the twin-island federal state of St Kitts-Nevis.
Capital: Charlestown
Area: 93 sq km
Population: 9,500
Main exports: tourism, light manufactures, offshore finance, cotton

Political system

A five-member Assembly is elected for a maximum five years. The assembly and a premier have limited powers. The island elects three members of the state National Assembly. A figurehead deputy governor-general represents the titular governor-general of the state.
Deputy governor-general: Weston Parris (1983)
Premier: Simeon Daniel (1983)
Last elections: 1987

Political organisations

Parties in island Assembly (leader) (seats): Nevis Reformation Party/NRP (Simeon Daniel) (4), f. 1970; Concerned Citizens' Movement/-CCM (Vance Amory) (1), f. 1987.
Parties outside Assembly: Nevis National Party/NNP (Andrea Procope), f. 1987.
The island came under rule by St Kitts in 1882. Economic neglect by a heavy-handed Kittitian central government and the 1967 revolt in Angu-

illa fuelled demands for secession after Anguilla's example. The pro-secession Nevis Reformation Party won control of the island council in 1971 and, by 1975, of both the Nevisian seats then allocated in the state parliament. The council voted for secession in 1974, and 99% of Nevisians voted likewise in a referendum in 1977. In 1979, Britain at first agreed to and then rejected the island's request to remain under British rule after the state's independence.

In 1980, island leader Simeon Daniel joined the St Kitts-based People's Action Movement in a coalition which ousted the anti-secession Labour Party from power after state general elections that year. St Kitts-Nevis independence was delayed until 1983 as Daniel, then the state's vice-premier and finance minister, fought for Nevisian self-rule. This was granted, with a guaranteed share of revenue and an option of full indepen-dence. Daniel was named premier of Nevis and the island was given its own Assembly. In 1989, Daniel announced that Nevis would soon secede from St Kitts.

See also **St Kitts-Nevis; Nevis Reformation Party; Daniel; Anguilla secession; People's Action Movement; St Kitts-Nevis Labour Party.**

Nevis Reformation Party (NRP)

Political party in Nevis. Founded in 1970 by lawyer Simeon Daniel to fight for autonomy from St Kitts, it won elections for the Nevis island council in 1971 and Daniel became council chairman. The party won one of the two Nevisian seats in the state parliament in the 1971 elections, and both of them in 1975. Britain rejected the party's demands that Nevis be made a British dependency like Anguilla as a way of escaping rule by St Kitts.

In 1980 the party joined with the Kittitian opposition People's Action Movement (PAM) to oust the Labour Party from power in the state parliament after elections that year. Daniel became vice-premier and finance minister. The NRP won all five seats in the Nevis assembly in 1983, but lost one of them in the 1987 poll to the Concerned Citizens' Movement (CCM). In the 1989 general election it also narrowly lost one of the (now) three Nevisian parliamentary seats to the CCM, which won 37% of the vote in Nevis.

See also **Nevis; Daniel; People's Action Movement; St Kitts-Nevis Labour Party.**

New Antilles Movement (*Movimentu Antiyas Nobo*/MAN)

Political party in the Netherlands Antilles. Founded as a social democratic party in 1971 by Don Martina, it merged immediately with the Workers' Liberation Front. It broke with the Front in 1977 and at the 1979 elections became the largest party in parliament, with 7 out of 22 seats. Martina became premier of a coalition government, succeeding Sylvius Rozendal. The withdrawal of the Aruban People's Electoral Movement from the coalition in 1981 caused new elections in 1982, at which MAN won only six seats. Martina put together a four-party coalition to continue in power, but lost his majority and the premiership in 1984. Though the party won only four seats at the 1985 election, he managed to construct a new coalition which lasted until 1988, when he again lost his majority and the premiership to Maria Liberia-Peters of the National People's Party. The MAN won only two seats at the 1990 election. The party advocates Curaçao's withdrawal from the Netherlands Antilles federation after the example of Aruba.

See also **Martina; People's Electoral Movement; Liberia-Peters; National People's Party; Aruba.**

New Democratic Party (NDP)

Political party in St Vincent. Founded in 1975 by former premier James Mitchell, the centre-right NDP won two seats at the 1979 general election. Mitchell and the party were not recognised as the official opposition until 1983. The NDP came to power with Mitchell as prime minister after winning the 1984 election (9–4). It won all 15 elective seats in parliament at the 1989 election.

See also **Mitchell, James.**

New Jewel Movement (NJM)

Left-wing Grenadian political party. The NJM came into being in 1973 as a result of the merger of the year-old Movement for Assemblies of the People (leaders: Maurice Bishop and Kendrick Radix) and the Joint Endeavour for Welfare, Education and Liberation (JEWEL) (Unison Whiteman). Both parties grew out of the 'black power' movement of the time. Bishop was chosen as leader of the NJM, which was seen as one of the region's burgeoning 'new left' parties led by young, foreign-educated, middle-class intellectuals. Prime minister Eric Gairy, denouncing 'communism', harassed the increasingly popular NJM, briefly jailing Bishop on independence in 1974 soon after his men had shot dead Bishop's father Rupert during an opposition demonstration. The NJM joined with two other parties – Herbert Blaize's Grenada National Party and Winston Whyte's United People's Party – in the People's Alliance to contest general elections in 1976. The NJM won three of the six seats captured by the Alliance and Bishop became opposition leader.

The party began secretly to develop along marxist-leninist lines in 1974 and by 1977 had become a leninist vanguard-type party with tightly restricted membership. Bishop's deputy, Bernard Coard, became its leading ideologist as head of a hard-line faction, the Organisation for Research, Education and Liberation (OREL), which had joined the NJM in 1976. This was dissolved in 1978 at the insistence of his rivals, but Coard's influence continued as head of the party's organising committee.

The party seized power in March 1979 while Gairy was abroad. During the four years of the People's Revolutionary Government the NJM continued as a 'vanguard' party, with never more than 200 full members who organised and led 'mass organisations' aimed at creating grassroots democracy. The membership of the party's central committee, along with Coard's 1982 resignation from the committee, was never publicised. The growing split between supporters of Bishop and Coard was accompanied by increasing isolation from the population and damaging ideological rigidity and naïveté. Bishop accepted a central committee vote in September 1983 that he should share national leadership with Coard, but then changed his mind. He was arrested a month later and Coard supporters executed him and three of his ministers on 19 October 1983.

After the subsequent US military invasion the NJM lost virtually all its support. Bishop's surviving colleagues founded the Maurice Bishop Patriotic Movement (MBPM) in 1984. Former central committee member Ian St Bernard announced the revival of the NJM and denounced the MBPM leaders as traitors. The new NJM comprised mainly hardline supporters abroad.

See also **People's Revolutionary Government; Maurice Bishop Patriotic Movement; Bishop; Radix; Coard; 'new left'; Gairy; Blaize; Grenada, US invasion (1983).**

'new left'

The various left-wing movements which emerged in the Anglo-Caribbean in the late-1960s, led mainly by foreign-educated, middle-class intellectuals who questioned the effectiveness of the 'Westminster system' of British-inherited democratic forms in solving the region's serious economic, social and political problems. The 'new left' was influenced by the 'black power' movement in the United States and by Marxism, but was uninterested in ties with Moscow. Its adherents also stressed economic dependency theories and called for the region to take control of its own natural resources and to rediscover and promote West Indian culture.

The first major group, which for many years inspired the others, was the Tapia House Group, founded in Trinidad in 1968 by Lloyd Best, which grew out of the New World Group of Caribbean intellectuals he had founded in 1963. Many of the 'new left' leaders met in mid-1970 at Rat Island, off St Lucia, to discuss the situation in the wake of the 'black power' disturbances in Trinidad. After the conference, attended by radicals from eight countries, 'Forum' groups were set up in several islands (St Lucia, St Vincent, Grenada and Dominica) to promote socialism.

The 'new left' declined to take part in elections at first but began to do so in the mid-1970s. High points in its influence were Grenada in 1976, where the New Jewel Movement, soon to become clandestinely a marxist-leninist party, won control of the parliamentary opposition at a general election; St Vincent, where a left-wing coalition won 14% of the vote at a general election in 1979; and St Lucia, where the 'new left' shared control of the government between 1979 and 1981 before being pushed out by the right. In other countries its followers won only a few hundred votes at elections.

After the collapse of the New Jewel government in Grenada and the US invasion, the left, 'new' or otherwise, was effectively discredited throughout the region.

See also **'black power'; Rodney riots (1968); Tapia House Group; Best; New Jewel Movement; St Lucia Labour Party; United People's Movement (St Vincent); Gonsalves.**

New National Party (NNP)

Conservative party in Grenada. The NNP was founded in 1984 under pressure from the US and neighbouring Barbados, St Vincent and St Lucia as a three-party coalition to prevent victory by former prime minister Sir Eric Gairy and his Grenada United Labour Party in elections in December that year. After difficult negotiations, the three parties – the Grenada National Party (GNP) (Herbert Blaize), National Democratic Party (George Brizan) and the Grenada Democratic Movement (Francis Alexis) – named Blaize as compromise NNP leader and the coalition, with heavy US financial help and Jamaican and Barbadian political advisers, won 14 out of 15 seats in the election.

Blaize's autocratic style soon provoked dissent and from 1985 there was undeclared war inside the party. Blaize's closest political ally, foreign minister Ben Jones, was elected deputy NNP leader in 1986, beating Brizan, and in 1987 three ministers, including Brizan and Alexis, resigned and formed the National Democratic Congress to oppose Blaize. Other officials followed. The NNP was left as a right-wing rump based narrowly on Blaize's GNP. In 1989, Blaize was voted out as party leader and replaced by the NNP secretary-general, Keith Mitchell. A few months later, Blaize sacked Mitchell and party chairman Larry Joseph from the government. Two more ministers then resigned and Blaize lost his parliamentary majority. He then announced the formation of a rival group, The National Party, which was led after his death in 1989 by his right-hand man, Jones. The NNP won only two seats at the 1990 elections. See also **Blaize; Alexis; Brizan; Mitchell, Keith; National Democratic Congress; Gairy; Grenada United Labour Party.**

New Nicaragua Movement (MNN): see Borge Martínez; Fonseca Amador.

New Organisation of Combatants (NORC): see Guerrilla Army of the Poor.

New Progressive Party (*Partido Nuevo Progresista*/PNP)

Political party in Puerto Rico, advocating that the island become the 51st state of the US. Founded in 1967 by Luis Ferré (b. 17 February 1904) and Carlos Romero Barceló. Thanks to a split in the ruling Popular Democratic Party (PPD), Ferré was elected governor the following year despite a 1967 plebiscite (61%) against statehood. He was defeated in the governorship election in 1972 by the PPD's Rafael Hernández Colón, but Romero Barceló regained the governorship for the PNP in 1976. The party lost control of the House of Representatives in the 1980 elections and almost lost the governorship.

Splits and scandals during 1981–3 saw senior party figures opposed to Romero Barceló, including the PNP vice-president and the mayor of the capital, forced out of the party. The San Juan mayor, Hernán Padilla (b. 5 May 1938), formed the Puerto Rican Renewal Party, whose 4% score at the 1984 elections caused Romero Barceló's defeat. Romero Barceló resigned as party leader in 1985. He was succeeded by Baltasar Corrada

de Río, who lost to Hernández Colón at the 1988 gubernatorial election. Romero Barceló regained the party leadership in 1989.
See also **Romero Barceló; Corrada del Río; Popular Democratic Party; Hernández Colón.**

New World Group: see Best; 'new left'; Tapia House Group.

Nibbs, Arthur: see Barbuda.

NICARAGUA, Republic of
Capital: Managua
Independence: (from Spain) 15 July 1821; (from Mexico) 1 July 1823; (from Central American Federation) 1838
Area: 139,000 sq km
Population (1988): 3.6m (59.4% urban)
Pop. density: 26/sq km
Pop. growth rate (1980–88): 3.4%
Infant mortality (1980–85): 61.7 per thousand
Life expectancy at birth (1980–85): 59.8
Literacy (1988): 88%
GDP per capita (1988e): US$819
Foreign debt per capita (1989e): US$2,600
Main exports (1987): coffee (44.7%); cotton (15.5%); meat (4%)

Political system

Constitution: 1987. President: Violeta Barrios de Chamorro (UNO) (1990–   ), succeeded Daniel Ortega Saavedra (FSLN) (1984–90). General elections are held every six years, most recently in 1990. The 1990 elections were brought forward to February under the terms of a 1989 agreement among the five Central American presidents concerning the disbanding of US-backed Nicaraguan rebels (contras). The Constitution was amended in October 1989 to allow the president and Assembly members to take office two months later, rather than in January 1991 as originally established. There is no ban on consecutive presidential terms. Ninety National Assembly members are elected by proportional representation under universal adult (16+) suffrage; the country being divided into nine regions, 17 departments (including the two autonomous Atlantic region departments, Atlántico Norte and Atlántico Sur) and 143 districts for national and local voting purposes. Losing presidential candidates are also entitled to a seat in the Assembly, provided they obtain a certain percentage of the vote. The 1990 Assembly comprised 92 seats. Fifty-five votes would be required for amendments to the constitution.

Political organisations

Parties in the National Assembly (leader) (seats): Sandinista National Liberation Front/FSLN (Daniel Ortega) (39); National Opposition Union/UNO coalition (Violeta Chamorro) (51 in total) (see below); Movement of Revolutionary Unity/MUR (Moisés Hassan & Francisco Samper) (1); Social Christian Party/PSC/Yatama (Erick Ramírez) (1).

[UNO comprises: Independent Liberal Party/PLI (Virgilio Godoy) (5); Democratic Party of National Confidence/PDCN (Agustín Jarquín & Adán Fletes) (5); National Conservative Party/PNC (Silviano Matamoros) (5); Conservative Popular Alliance Party/PAPC (Miriam Arguello) (5); Social Democrat Party/PSD (Guillermo Potoy & Alfredo César) (5); Constitutionalist Liberal Party/PLC (Jaime Cuadra & José Ernesto Somarriba) (3); Neo-Liberal Party/PALI (José Luis Tijerino) (3); Nicaraguan Socialist Party/PSN (Gustavo Tablada) (3); Communist Party of Nicaragua/PCdeN (Eli Altamirano) (3); National Action Party/PAN (Eduardo Rivas Gasteazoro) (3); Nicaraguan Democratic Movement/MDN (3); Central American Integrationist Party/PIAC (3); Popular Social Christian Party (UNO faction)/PPSC-UNO (2); Conservative National Alliance Party/PANC (2); UNO-Yatama (Brooklyn Rivera) (1).]

Parties outside the Assembly (leader): Democratic Conservative Party of Nicaragua/PCDN (Clemente Guido); Independent Liberal Party of National Unity/PLIUN (Eduardo Coronado); Popular Social Christian Party/PPSC-Díaz faction (Mauricio Díaz); Marxist Leninist Popular Action Movement/MAP-ML (Isidro Téllez); Workers' Revolutionary Party/PRT (Bonifacio Miranda); Central American Unionist Party/PUCA (Blanca Rojas & Giovani D'Ciofalo); Social Conservatism Party/PSOC (Fernando Aguero/José María Zavala).

Parties seeking registration include the Labour Conservative Party (José María Icabalceta), the Democratic Party of National Renovation-/PDRN (Leonidas Arévalo) and the Democratic Action Party.

A US-backed insurgency, dating from 1981 and led by the Nicaraguan Resistance (RN) alliance, informally known as the contras, was formally ended on 10 June 1990.

Main labour organisations (affiliation) (leader): Sandinista Workers' Central/CST (FSLN) (Lucio Jiménez); National Workers' Front/FNT (FSLN) (Lucío Jiménez); Association of Rural Workers/ATC (FSLN) (Edgardo García); Nicaraguan Workers' Central/CTN (CLAT) (Carlos Huembes); Trade Union Action and Unification Central/CAUS (PCdeN); General Confederation of Independent Workers/CGT-i (CPUSTAL) (Carlos Salgado); Confederation of Trade Union Unification/CUS (ORIT) (Alvin Guthrie). The Permanent Workers' Council/CPT is an umbrella group of pro-government unions.

Main employers' organisation: Higher Council of Private Enterprise/COSEP (Enrique Bolaños).

Nicaraguan Conservative Party (PCN): see **Nicaraguan Democratic Co-ordinator.**

Nicaraguan Democratic Co-ordinator (*Coordinadora Democrática Nicaragüense-Ramiro Sacasa Guerrero*/CDN)
An opposition coalition founded in 1981 by the Nicaraguan Democratic Movement (MDN), the Social Christian Party (PSC) and the Social Democratic Party (PSD). Six business groups and two trade unions also joined. The CDN took the name of the leader of the Constitutionalist

Liberal Movement (MLC, f. 1967) who had died in a car crash in September 1981. The MDN left in 1982 to join the armed opposition in exile, while the MLC (which became the Constitutionalist Liberal Party/PLC in March 1982) took its place. The CDN chose former junta member Arturo Cruz Porras as its presidential candidate for the 1984 elections but in mid-1984, under pressure from Washington, opted not to participate, on the grounds that they were not 'free and fair'. The newly-formed Nicaraguan Conservative Party (now the National Conservative Party/PNC) began to take a leading role in the CDN, but was not granted legal status. Member parties were proscribed in August 1984 under the electoral law for having called for abstention.

The CDN formally joined forces with the armed opposition in June 1985, establishing the United Nicaraguan Opposition (UNO) with the Nicaraguan Democratic Force (FDN) and the Democratic Revolutionary Alliance (ARDE), but also maintained a presence inside Nicaragua. Both the abstention decision and the establishment of links with the contras heightened tensions within the CDN, with the PSC in particular expressing dissent. The CDN responded to the 1986 state of emergency by calling for a general amnesty and fresh elections, but the government rejected its offer of talks. In February 1987 it again called for a national dialogue to include the armed opposition, and for elections at all levels. CDN member parties joined in the dialogue with the government under the terms of the August 1987 Arias peace plan. In early 1989 it called for international supervision of the 1990 elections and for constitutional reforms to give more freedom to opposition parties. With the formation of the National Opposition Union (UNO), which won the 1990 elections, the CDN's influence declined.

See also **Cruz Porras; Social Christian Party; Democratic Conservative Party of Nicaragua; Nicaraguan Resistance.**

Nicaraguan Democratic Force *(Fuerza Democrática Nicaragüense/*FDN)

The largest anti-Sandinista (contra) guerrilla group, founded in 1981 under the auspices of the Central Intelligence Agency and trained first by Argentine and then by US instructors. Its nucleus was an alliance of the 15 September Legion, formed by some 60 ex-National Guard officers and associates of dictator Anastasio Somoza shortly after his overthrow in July 1979, and the Nicaraguan Democratic Union (UDN), then headed by businessman José Francisco Cardenal. In December 1982 formal control was assumed by a civilian-dominated National Directorate of seven, hand-picked by the CIA. A four-strong Military-Civilian Command (*Comando Cívico-Militar*) was created within the directorate in October 1983, with Adolfo Calero as president of the directorate and commander-in-chief. By 1985, the FDN claimed 15–18,000 members (independent sources suggest 8–12,000), the majority based in camps on the Honduran side of the Nicaraguan border and consisting of disaffected or kidnapped Nicaraguan peasants. The military leadership, headed by Col. Enrique Bermúdez, was overwhelmingly ex-GN.

In 1984 the FDN claimed responsibility for the mining of Nicaraguan ports, later found to have been carried out by the CIA. The US Congress subsequently cut off military aid and prohibited CIA involvement, but the restrictions were lifted in late 1986. Somoza connections made an alliance with the Costa Rica-based ARDE contras difficult, but the FDN – at the instigation of Washington – joined with the Misura and ARDE groups in September 1984 to form UNIR (Nicaraguan Unity for Reconciliation). This was succeeded in June 1985 by the Nicaraguan Opposition Unity (UNO), to which the civilian opposition group CDN also affiliated, and in May 1987 the Nicaraguan Resistance, an alliance of UNO and the Costa Rica-based Southern Opposition Bloc (BOS), was formed.

See also **Nicaraguan Resistance; United Nicaraguan Opposition; Calero Portocarrero; National Guard** (Nicaragua); **Iran/contra affair; Nicaraguan Democratic Co-ordinator.**

Nicaraguan Democratic Movement (MDN): see Nicaraguan Democratic Co-ordinator; Robelo Callejas.

Nicaraguan Democratic Union (UDN): see Nicaraguan Democratic Force.

Nicaraguan Resistance (*Resistencia Nicaragüense*/RN)
The contra umbrella group, founded in May 1987 by the United Nicaraguan Opposition (UNO) under Pedro Joaquín Chamorro and the much smaller, Costa Rica-based Southern Opposition Bloc (BOS) under Alfredo César. Intended to heal a serious split within the UNO leadership and present a more appealing face to the US Congress, the new alliance was headed by a seven-strong directorate, chosen by a 54-member assembly representing nine economic, political and military groups. The original directorate included Chamorro, César, Adolfo Calero, controversial head of the biggest contra army, the FDN, and Alfonso Robelo, who had resigned from UNO the month before. Arturo Cruz, another former UNO leader, withheld his support from the new group, which claimed to have 14,000 combatants (the Nicaraguan government put the number at 8,000).

The 'Arias Plan' for peace in Central America, signed in August 1987, was a serious blow to the US-funded RN because it called for an end to external aid for insurgent forces. The US Congress declined administration requests for military funding from 1987, badly affecting contra morale. Although the Arias Plan did not require political negotiations with armed opposition groups, the Nicaraguan government agreed for the first time to indirect talks with the contras, which began in December 1987 in Santo Domingo, mediated by Archibishop Obando y Bravo. In January 1988 the government agreed to direct talks, this time in Costa Rica, and on 23 March a preliminary, two-month ceasefire agreement was reached at the border town of Sapoá. Later sessions were held in Managua and by May hopes had risen that a settlement might be possible, despite sweeping demands by the RN and a mutiny in its ranks. Hard-

liner Calero had been replaced at the head of the delegation by the more
moderate César, who, it emerged, had been engaged in secret diplomacy
with the government. But military commander Enrique Bermúdez repudiated the deal and in June the talks broke down after the RN presented
fresh demands at the last minute, including the election of a constituent
assembly before the end of 1988.

In July 1988 the election of a new RN directorate, including Bermúdez,
led to the withdrawal of the southern front (BOS) amid accusations of
vote-rigging. In August 1989 (in Tela, Honduras) the Central American
presidents set a deadline of early December that year for the disbandment
and voluntary repatriation of the contras, and a UN force was set up
to oversee the process. The RN, backed by the Bush government in
Washington, rejected the plan, insisting that it would not disarm until
after the February 1990 elections in Nicaragua. With its political leadership drifting back to Managua and Bermúdez marginalised by field commanders led by Israel Galeano (Commander Franklin), the military did
agree to UN-sponsored talks with the Sandinistas, but no agreement was
reached. Following the opposition victory in the February 1990 elections,
the RN signed the Toncontín Accord on 23 March, agreeing to demobil-
ise. The Central American Presidents made a more specific call, in the
Montelimar Declaration of 3 April, for demobilisation to be completed
no later than 25 April, the date of the inauguration of Violeta Chamorro.
The contras responded with demands that senior Sandinista officers be
removed from the army, but eventually agreed to a 27 June demobilisation debate.

See also **United Nicaraguan Opposition; Calero Portocarrero; Cruz
Porras; Robelo Callejas; Southern Opposition Bloc; Arias Plan.**

Nicaraguan Revolutionary Youth (JRN): see Borge Martínez.

Nicaraguan Unity for Reconciliation (UNIR): see Nicaraguan
Democratic Force; United Nicaraguan Opposition.

Nicosia, Hildebrando: see Authentic Panameñista Party.

noirisme

The belief, especially among intellectuals in Haiti, in the worth, African-
ness and superiority of a country's black majority in the face of the
attacks and privileges of the traditional ruling mulatto and white minorit-
ies. *Noirisme* is a more active form of Aimé Césaire's *négritude*. Coincid-
ing with the Garveyite black nationalist movement in Jamaica and the
US, it reached a peak in Haiti in the 1930s, largely in reaction to the
racist brutalities of the US occupation, during which the mulattos were
favoured. Its advocates, who also opposed the Catholic Church's attacks
on voodoo, helped bring down the mulatto president Elie Lescot in a
remarkable popular ferment in 1946 and install the black Dumarsais
Estimé in his place. The doctrine was brandished by François Duvalier
to justify extermination of his opponents during his harsh 14-year rule,
1957–71.

See also **Duvalierism; Duvalier, François; Garvey; 'black power'; Césaire; rastafarians; Tontons Macoutes.**

Non-Aligned Movement (NAM)

Founded in 1961 by emerging Third World nations with the aim of avoiding involvement in the East-West conflict, the NAM comprises 101 sovereign states and one movement (the PLO). It has four basic principals: (1) peaceful coexistence; (2) non-participation in military pacts; (3) no bases for the superpowers; (4) support for national liberation struggles. Today, it is most closely identified with the struggle for a New International Economic Order (NIEO), the principles of which were drawn up at the Algiers summit of 1973. They were based on the 'centre-periphery' analysis pioneered by leading Latin American economist Raúl Prebisch. The NAM also holds funds for agricultural development, the maintenance of buffer stocks of commodities and the enhancement of food production. The organisation is run by the 17-member Co-ordination (or 'Co-ordinating') Bureau of the Non-Aligned Countries (or 'Movement').

Cuba was a founding member, but remained alone among western hemisphere nations until 1970. Thereafter, a number of Latin American and Caribbean countries joined, reflecting a shift in the region away from unquestioning reliance on and support of the United States. Of the countries dealt with in this volume, the following also became members (date of accession in brackets): Jamaica (1970), Trinidad-Tobago (1970), Panama (1976), Grenada (1979), Nicaragua (1979), Bahamas (1983), Barbados (1983), Belize (1983), St Lucia (1983). Antigua, Costa Rica, El Salvador and Mexico have permanent observer status, although Costa Rica withdrew from 1989–91. In 1979 the Non-Aligned Conference was held in Havana, Cuba, and Fidel Castro became chairman of the movement, despite his controversial stance as a pro-Soviet 'non-aligned' leader.

At the September 1989 summit in Belgrade the issue of Panama proved to be one of the most divisive, with Nicaragua and Cuba calling for non-intervention while other members, notably Venezuela, favoured fresh elections.

Noriega Morena, Gen. Manuel Antonio

b. 11 February 1938. Head of the Panamanian Defence Forces (PDF), and *de facto* ruler of Panama 1983–9. Noriega joined the PDF (then known as the National Guard) in 1960 and won a scholarship to Chorrillos military academy in Peru, where in 1962 he graduated as a military engineer. He subsequently attended courses at the School of the Americas, and in the US and Peru, dealing with such subjects as counter-insurgency, psychological warfare and narcotics. He played an important role in putting down the 1969 coup attempt against Gen. Omar Torrijos and accompanied him at the signing of the Canal Treaties in 1977. Noriega served Torrijos as head of security and intelligence for 12 years, becoming head of the PDF in 1983, two years after the death of Torrijos, on the retirement of Torrijos' successor, Gen. Rubén Darío Paredes.

Despite the existence of a formal democracy in Panama, the PDF exercised *de facto* control over the government, and between 1982 and 1988 they stepped in four times to replace a civilian president. Noriega was responsible for the removal of Presidents Ricardo de la Espriella (February 1984), Nicolás Ardito Barletta (September 1985) and Eric Arturo Delvalle (February 1988). Ardito Barletta had sought to set up a commission to investigate the murder of former health minister Hugo Spadafora, a well-known opponent of Noriega whom the PDF were widely suspected of having killed. Noriega declined to investigate the crime. Delvalle had attempted to dismiss Noriega after the general was indicted on drugs charges in Florida. He was forced to go into hiding when an arrest warrant was issued for him. The majority of the Panamanian cabinet and members of parliament remained loyal to the general, who controlled a television channel and three newspapers as well as having influence with six radio stations.

US pressure on Panama in the mid-1980s over its involvement in the Contadora peace process in Central America included leaks to the press suggesting that Noriega was involved in illegal drugs and arms trading, as well as money laundering, pro-Cuban espionage and assistance to left-wing guerrillas in Colombia; accusations the general continued to deny even after his indictment by two US grand juries. Witnesses claimed Noriega had been earning up to $10m a month by collaborating with Colombian drug traffickers. Despite such allegations Noriega had a reputation not only as a pragmatic and skilled politician but as a mediator in regional quarrels. A long-time CIA 'asset', his relationship with former CIA director and presidential candidate George Bush became an issue in the 1988 US presidential election. In June 1987 the removal of the Defence Forces chief of staff, purportedly for 'health reasons', had led to street violence in protest at the role of the military in politics, after the dismissed officer, Col. Roberto Díaz (a cousin of Torrijos), accused Noriega of having rigged the 1984 elections, as well as of complicity in the deaths of Spadafora and Torrijos. A 'National Civic Crusade' was set up by centrist and right-wing groups to orchestrate demands for Noriega's resignation, which were echoed by the US Senate. Rejecting the demands, Noriega said the campaign was a US-sponsored attempt to prevent the re-establishment of Panamanian sovereignty over the Canal.

Washington stepped up the pressure, cutting all military and economic assistance in July 1987 and freezing Panamanian deposits in US banks in February 1988. It also sent an extra 2,000 troops to its bases in the Canal Zone. In March 1988 an attempted coup against Noriega failed, and the general dismissed at least 18 officers. US attempts to reach a negotiated settlement, under which Noriega would step down in return for immunity from prosecution, broke down in May 1988, with the general still in power, despite the severe economic crisis induced by the US boycott. In the May 1989 general election, Noriega's hand-picked candidate for president, Carlos Duque, was so heavily defeated that even a massive fraud could not conceal the fact, and the result was anulled.

Four months later a *de facto* administration under Francisco Rodríguez was installed, against a background of additional US sanctions, aimed specifically at Noriega's closest associates. Another coup attempt was defeated in October that year, but it was clear that the cohesion of the PDF had been seriously affected. The general himself seemed to be moving towards a formal assumption of political power when the unelected Assembly of Corregimiento Representatives named him its co-ordinator and 'leader of the national liberation process'. In December 1989 Noriega declared that a state of war existed between Panama and the US. On 16 December a US soldier was shot dead by PDF troops. Four days later the US invaded Panama and Gen. Noriega went into hiding, eventually seeking asylum in the Vatican embassy. On 3 January 1990, after ten days of intense negotiations, he surrendered and was flown to Miami to stand trial.

See also **Panama, US invasion (1989); Ardito Barletta; Delvalle; Iran/contra affair; National Civic Crusade; Torrijos Herrera.**

North, Col. Oliver: see **Iran/contra affair.**

November 13 Revolutionary Movement (MR–13): see Rebel Armed Forces.

Obando y Bravo, Cardinal Miguel

b. 2 February 1926. Archbishop of Managua 1970– . Born in La Libertad, Chontales province, the son of a coalminer, Miguel Obando y Bravo was educated in Granada and at a seminary in El Salvador, of which he later became principal. He was ordained in Guatemala in 1958 as a member of the Salesian order, becoming auxiliary bishop of Managua in March 1968. He taught in seminaries and served as auxiliary bishop of Matagalpa before being appointed the first native-born archbishop of Managua in 1970. An outspoken critic of the Somoza regime, Obando mediated between the government and the Sandinista guerrillas during the 1974 and 1978 hostage crises. In February 1978 he suggested that armed opposition was acceptable to the church under the 'just war' doctrine. He helped form moderate opposition groups which sought a negotiated end to the dictatorship in the late 1970s.

From 1980 onwards he was an equally outspoken opponent of the Sandinista government, despite his initial acceptance of its legitimacy and of the role of priests in government (later condemned by the Vatican). He accused the FSLN of responsibility for the regional crisis, while the government alleged that he was linked with the contra rebels, with whom he argued they should negotiate directly. He is firmly opposed to the 'theology of liberation' and the so-called 'popular church'. When appointed cardinal in April 1985 by Pope John Paul II his first public act after leaving Rome was to celebrate mass in Miami for Nicaraguan exiles, including leaders of the contra groups. He was also accused of receiving money from Oliver North's 'Iran/contra' secret network. In 1987 the Sandinista government appointed Obando to the Commission of National Reconciliation set up under the terms of the Arias peace plan. He also agreed to mediate in talks between the government and the contra leaders and became co-director of the ceasefire verification commission. Controversy arose in late 1988 over his acceptance (and misuse) of US AID funds for the commission, which he at first denied receiving.

See also **liberation theology; Arias Plan; Iran/contra affair.**

Obregón, Gen. Alvaro: see Mexican Revolution.

Ochoa case

On 12 June 1989 a group of officials of the Cuban interior and armed forces ministries were arrested on corruption charges. The most senior

was Gen. Arnaldo Ochoa Sánchez, a hero of the Angolan war. It subsequently came to light that the officials had been involved with Pablo
Escobar, head of the so-called Medellín cocaine cartel of Colombia, in
trafficking drugs through Cuba into the United States. Ochoa and a
subordinate, Capt. Jorge Martínez Valdés, together with Antonio (Tony)
de la Guardia and Amado Padrón of the interior ministry, were later
sentenced to death by a military tribunal and executed by firing squad
on 13 July. Ten other officials of the de la Guardia group, including his
brother Patricio, were jailed for between ten and 30 years. De la Guardia
had for seven years been head of the MC department of the ministry
(formerly Department Z), whose task was to find ways of circumventing
the US trade embargo. His group said they had moved about six tonnes
of cocaine through Cuba since 1987, making about $3.4m, which they at
first claimed they had passed to the state as part of their normal trading
income.

The case was a severe embarrassment to the Cuban government, even
though no evidence suggesting the involvement of more senior revolutionary leaders was uncovered. The United States had for years been insisting
that there was a 'Cuban connection' in Caribbean cocaine trafficking, a
charge which Havana had consistently portrayed as 'counter-revolutionary propaganda'. Some Cuban exiles and dissidents suggested that the
case had its origins in a coup plot by Ochoa. Three human rights activists
were jailed in late 1989 for 'spreading false news' after telling foreign
journalists that the Ochoa case defendants had been drugged and subjected to psychological torture.
See also **Cuban Human Rights Party.**

Odlum, George
b. 24 June 1934. Left-wing politician in St Lucia. An economist, Odlum
worked in the ministry of trade and industry and at the Commonwealth
Secretariat in London before becoming executive secretary to the West
Indies Associated States council of ministers in 1967. He co-founded the
leftist Forum and the St Lucia Action Movement (SLAM), which in 1973
led a lengthy strike in the banana industry. The same year, Odlum merged
SLAM with the opposition St Lucia Labour Party (SLP). He became
president of the St Lucia Farmers' and Farm Workers' Union. Hampered
by a 'black power' image, he was defeated for the SLP leadership in 1977
by Allan Louisy but became his deputy.

Odlum's popularity among banana workers and his attack on the US
firm Amerada Hess's strict terms for building a $150m oil terminal clin-
ched the SLP victory at the 1979 elections and he became foreign minister
and deputy prime minister. Encouraged by the US, Louisy reneged on
an agreement to hand over the premiership to him after a few months.
Odlum was sacked as deputy prime minister in 1980 and dismissed in
1981 as deputy leader of the SLP. When Louisy finally resigned in 1981,
after pro-Odlum MPs had helped vote down the budget, he handed the
premiership to Winston Cenac instead.

Odlum then founded the Progressive Labour Party (PLP) and was part

of a brief all-party coalition in 1982 headed by his deputy, Michael Pilgrim. Odlum lost his seat at the 1982 elections, at which the PLP won 27% of the vote but only one seat. New SLP leader Julian Hunte refused an alliance with the PLP for the 1987 elections. As a result, the PLP drew off 9% of the vote and the SLP narrowly lost.
See also **St Lucia Labour Party; Progressive Labour Party** (St Lucia); **Josie; West Indies Associated States; 'black power'; 'new left'.**

Odlum, Jon: see **Progressive Labour Party** (St Lucia); **St Lucia Labour Party; Odlum, George.**

Oduber, Nelson
b. 7 February 1947. Premier of Aruba 1989– . Oduber, who was elected to the central parliament in Curaçao in 1975, took over the leadership of the People's Electoral Movement (MEP) in 1986 after the death that year of the party's founder, Betico Croes, to whom he had long been chief aide and party secretary-general. He led the MEP to victory in the 1989 general election and became premier at the head of a three-party coalition, succeeding Henny Eman.
See also **Croes; People's Electoral Movement; Eman.**

Oduber Quirós, Daniel
b. 25 August 1921. President of Costa Rica 1974–8. Born in San José, Daniel Oduber was educated at the University of Costa Rica, McGill University, Canada, and the Sorbonne, where he obtained a doctorate in law and philosophy. He was a prominent member of the group which planned and carried out the successful 1948 rebellion and was secretary general of the founding junta of the Second Republic (1948–9). He later served as ambassador to the UN (1949) and ambassador at large in Europe (1949–50). In 1951–3 he was head of public relations for the National Liberation Party (PLN), which he co-founded, and he was its secretary general 1956–8. A deputy in the legislative assembly, 1958–62, he was foreign minister 1962–4 and an unsuccessful PLN presidential candidate in 1966. Between 1970 and 1974 he was president of the assembly, and he served as PLN party president 1970–77 and again in the 1980s.
Oduber succeeded PLN founder José Figueres as president of Costa Rica in 1974, and his term of office was notable for expansionary, state-interventionist economic policies. The foreign debt, which was to become such a heavy burden for later governments, expanded dramatically, with public sector debt alone rising threefold by 1978, when the second OPEC price shock badly hit oil-importing Costa Rica. Oduber rejected an IMF package in the final days of his presidency, saying it would mean transfer-ring economic sovereignty to Washington. His term also saw the begin-ning of the final phase of the revolution in neighbouring Nicaragua, into which Costa Rica threatened to be drawn. As president, he turned down military assistance offers from abroad on the grounds that they were inconsistent with the country's non-military tradition.
After 1978 he remained a powerful figure in the PLN, but with the

Oilfield Workers' Trade Union (OWTU)

260
nomination of Oscar Arias as candidate for the 1986 election the 'Generation of '48' was pushed into the background. Oduber had backed Carlos Manuel Castillo for the nomination. Although by no means pro-Sandinista, in the 1980s Oduber, by now a vice-president of the Socialist International, opposed US aid to the Nicaraguan contra rebels. He said the Central American conflict was a problem of social justice rather than East-West relations. In 1989 he was obliged to testify before the legislature after admitting receiving a million *colones* (around US$12,500) political contribution from an alleged drug trafficker. The resulting scandal cost him his post as head of the PLN political committee and led to his suspension from the party for a year.

See also **National Liberation Party; Civil War** (Costa Rica); **Generation of '48** (Costa Rica).

Oilfield Workers' Trade Union (OWTU): see Butler; Panday.

Oil nationalisation (Mexico)

The nationalisation of the oil industry by Mexican president Lázaro Cárdenas on 18 March 1938 was one of his most popular decisions, regarded subsequently as a major affirmation of national sovereignty and a model for the rest of Latin America. Oil had first been discovered in 1901 and production expanded rapidly as US and British companies stepped up their operations. Most of the oilfields were far from areas of conflict during the revolution, and production rose steadily throughout the period. But when the 1917 constitution asserted the state's ownership of the subsoil, the companies and their governments protested. The companies went so far as to finance the army of a local caudillo opposed to the central government of Venustiano Carranza.

The oil issue was to remain central to the US-Mexican quarrel for the following two decades. In 1920, Washington refused to recognise the new president, Alvaro Obregón, until the oil question was settled. A compromise solution was eventually reached, through the 1923 Bucareli agreements, which converted the companies' property rights into virtually indefinite concessions and provided for a new production tax. But a new law in 1925 limited concessions to 50 years and gave rise to renewed protests by the companies. Mexico was forced to give way in 1928, reinstating indefinite concessions. In 1931 a labour code was introduced which stipulated that 90% of oil company employees must be Mexican nationals.

On taking office in 1934, Cárdenas sponsored the formation of a new Mexican oil workers' union (the STPRM), under a radical leadership. In May 1937 the STPRM went on strike over the companies' refusal to let union officials inspect their books as part of wage negotiations. The government ordered arbitration, which led in December that year to a ruling that the companies had been earning excess profits and must pay a 27% increase, as well as providing other benefits. The companies appealed to the supreme court but lost; when they continued to avoid paying the rise, Cárdenas accused them of an 'arrogant and rebellious attitude' and ordered the immediate nationalisation of the assets of the 17 US and British companies.

The sudden nationalisation decision brought an economic slump, a damaging boycott of Mexican oil products by US companies, and a break in diplomatic relations with the UK. But in political terms it was a major success and was widely applauded in Latin America. Not until the outbreak of World War II was compensation agreed and relations normalised. The companies had asked for US$220m but eventually settled for $24m.

See also **Cárdenas, Lázaro.**

Ojeda Rios, Filiberto: see Macheteros.

Omega 7

One of many armed Cuban exile groups, mainly Florida-based, whose origins go back to the years following the overthrow of Batista. In August 1960, President Eisenhower approved funding for a Cuban 'paramilitary organisation', and thereafter the Central Intelligence Agency was closely involved in arming and training the Cubans. The groups retain links with the CIA, although they are not always responsive to Agency control. In 1978 the House Select Committee on Assassinations put at 20 the number of exile groups with the 'motivation, capability and resources' to have assassinated President J. F. Kennedy in 1963. Omega 7 first came to prominence in the mid-1970s, with minor bomb attacks on Cuba's UN mission and other targets considered 'pro-Castro'. The group's leader, Eduardo Arocena ('Omar') was later convicted of these and other attacks, including the 1980 murder of a Cuban attaché at the UN. Orlando Bosch of Omega 7 was accused of the bombing of a Cuban airliner in 1976 in which 73 people died. Bosch (b. 1926) spent over 11 years in custody in Venezuela, despite being acquitted three times, and was arrested for a 1974 parole violation on his return to the US in 1988. In 1968 he had been sentenced to ten years for firing a bazooka at a Polish cargo vessel. The Justice Department was in late 1989 seeking his 'deportation as a dangerous terrorist'.

Other groups include Brigade 2506 (Military Command), a splinter from the Bay of Pigs Association – Assault Brigade 2506; Alpha 66, which says it has undertaken dozens of acts of sabotage inside Cuba; and the United Revolutionary Organisations Co-ordinating Group.

See also **Bay of Pigs invasion**; *gusano*; **JM/WAVE.**

O'Neal, Ralph: see Virgin Islands Party; United Party.

Operation Bootstrap

A 'self-help' scheme launched by Puerto Rican leader Luis Muñoz Marín in the mid-1940s to industrialise the island rapidly by means of luring massive foreign investment with the promise of tax holidays and cheap labour. The operation was directed by Teodoro Moscoso, later to be the first administrator of the US Alliance for Progress. It was based on St Lucian economist Sir Arthur Lewis's advocacy of 'industrialisation by invitation' and, as the 'Puerto Rican model', was held up as an example to the rest of the Caribbean. For 25 years, the results were impressive and nearly 2,000 firms came to the island. But by 1970 the policy was under attack by both economists and radicals as leading to ruinous economic dependency, massive debt, unemployment, large-scale emigration to the US, social tensions and destruction of the environment.

In 1976 the economy was boosted by a new tax incentive scheme, known as Section 936, which exempted US firms from federal income tax on profits from their Puerto Rican operations provided that 10% of these profits were deposited in the local Government Development Bank. When the US Congress threatened in 1984 to abolish the scheme, Puerto Rico headed off the threat with a 'twin-plant' concept to invest the deposited funds in Caribbean Basin Initiative (CBI) beneficiary countries which would finish semi-manufactured goods from Puerto Rico.

See also **Muñoz Marín; Lewis, Sir Arthur; Caribbean Basin Initiative; Puerto Rican Independence Party.**

Operation Sheepskin (1969): see Anguilla secession.

ORDEN (*Organización Democrática Nacional*/National Democratic Organisation)

A mass-based paramilitary organisation linked to the Salvadorean security forces, founded secretly around 1964–5 by Col. (later Gen.) José Alberto 'Chele' Medrano, commander of the First Infantry Regiment and head of the 'Security Service' (later the Salvadorean Intelligence Service). The acronym means 'order' in Spanish. Its identity was not made public until 1967, when the post of Supreme Chief of ORDEN was assumed by the presidency. Medrano, then head of the National Guard, remained its executive director. It was revitalised by the government of Col. Arturo Molina in 1975 and had members in virtually every community – an estimated 100,000 – by 1979. These were recruited primarily from the ranks of army reservists, who became informants and agents provocateurs, in return for which they were favoured with jobs and other privileges and allowed to carry firearms. Medrano said the organisation's purpose was that of 'combating the infiltration of the peasantry by communism'.

The establishment of ORDEN was assisted by US agencies, working under the cover of the AID Public Safety Program. Among those who held the post of ORDEN chief was Col. (later Gen.) Carlos Humberto Romero, president of El Salvador 1977–9. By the 1970s ORDEN was also acting as a 'death squad'. After the October 1979 coup, the new regime formally ordered its disbandment, declaring all acts done in its name illegal. In practice, however, the structure remained intact, and later re-emerged in other forms, including civil defence groups. Medrano, who formed the Nationalist Democratic Front (FDN) on the 'dissolution' of ORDEN, had been forcibly retired from the army in 1970, and was assassinated in March 1985.

See also **death squad.**

OREL (Organisation for Research, Education and Liberation): see Coard; New Jewel Movement.

Organisation for National Reconstruction (ONR): see Hudson-Phillips; National Alliance for Reconstruction.

Organisation of American States

The main inter-American regional organisation, designed to strengthen political, economic and social ties and defend sovereignty, territorial integrity and independence. Its origins lie in: (1) the First Congress of American States, convened by Simón Bolívar in Panama City in 1826, attended by Colombia, United Provinces of Central America, Peru and Mexico; and (2) the International Union of American Republics, set up in 1890, later renamed the Pan American Union (PAU). The 9th International American Congress under the PAU framework in Bogotá set up the OAS in April 1948. The OAS charter was modified in 1970, establishing the General Assembly as the dominant body in the organisation and replacing the Inter-American Conferences.

The main OAS bodies are the following: the General Assembly, which meets annually and operates on the basis of one country, one vote; the consultative meeting of foreign ministers, which is convened to consider urgent problems; the Inter-American Judicial Committee; the Inter-American Commission on Human Rights; and the General Secretariat (based in Washington). In 1962 the OAS supported the US in its demands for the removal of Soviet nuclear missiles sited in Cuba; and the organisation voted to suspend Cuban membership. In 1964 member states voted to impose sanctions against Cuba. Interventions in other regional political conflicts included: mediation in the US-Panama dispute of 1964; backing for US intervention in the Dominican Republic in 1965; investigation of human rights violations and recommendation of a ceasefire in El Salvador-Honduras war of 1969; condemnation of the military coup in Bolivia in 1980; a call for a ceasefire in the Peru-Ecuador border clashes of 1981; and a request to Britain and Argentina in 1982 to cease hostilities over the Falklands/Malvinas islands and negotiate a settlement, taking account of Argentina's 'rights of sovereignty' and the interests of the islanders. In November 1984 the General Assembly recognised the need to 'revitalise' the organisation. In 1987 and 1988 the OAS was involved in Central American peace efforts, in support of the Arias peace plan (August 1987) and the Nicaraguan ceasefire (April 1988). In 1989 the OAS sent a mission to Panama in an attempt to mediate in the crisis caused by the annulment of the elections by Gen. Manuel Antonio Noriega.

General Secretary: João Baena Soares (Brazil – succeeded Alejandro Orfila of Argentina). Assistant General Secretary: Christopher Thomas (Trinidad-Tobago). Membership: Antigua-Barbuda, Argentina, Bahamas, Barbados, Bolivia, Brazil, Chile, Colombia, Costa Rica, Cuba (suspended), Dominica, Dominican Republic, Ecuador, El Salvador, Grenada, Guatemala, Haiti, Honduras, Jamaica, Mexico, Nicaragua, Panama, Paraguay, Peru, St Kitts-Nevis, St Lucia, St Vincent-

Grenadines, Suriname, Trinidad-Tobago, US, Uruguay, Venezuela. Canada joined in 1989.
See also: **Dominican Republic, US invasion (1965); 'Football (Soccer) War'.**

Organisation of Central American States (*Organización de Estados Centroamericanos*/ODECA)

Founded in 1951 under the Charter of San Salvador, with its secretariat (the Central American Bureau) in that city, ODECA was an unsuccessful move towards economic and social federation among the five republics. Its consolidation was hampered by the prevailing hostility towards the reformist government of Guatemala, which was overthrown three years later. Guatemala withdrew in 1953 and ODECA did not begin to function until 1955, when (with Guatemala once more a member) it became a peace-keeping organisation under the terms of the UN Charter. ODECA's own charter was revised in 1962 in Panama City, and Panama was invited to join. The organisation sought to introduce uniform legislation among its members, and established the Central American Court of Justice, comprising the presidents of its member nations' supreme courts. The Central American Defence Council (CONDECA) was set up as an arm of ODECA. By 1973 events (including the 1969 'football war' between Honduras and El Salvador) had revealed its impotence, and it was effectively reduced to nominal status.
See also **Central American Common Market; CONDECA; 'Football (Soccer) War'; Arbenz Guzmán.**

Organisation of Eastern Caribbean States (OECS)

A grouping of seven small English-speaking eastern Caribbean islands (Antigua-Barbuda, Dominica, Grenada, Montserrat, St Kitts-Nevis, St Lucia and St Vincent) founded in 1981. The aim was to work out a joint economic approach within the region and towards the outside world, along with joint diplomatic representation. After the 1983 US invasion of Grenada, for which the OECS (chaired by Dominican prime minister Eugenia Charles) provided a formal invitation with Washington's encouragement, the emphasis moved towards defence co-operation at the instigation of the US. In 1987, OECS heads of government decided to work towards creation of a unitary state, but little progress was made.
Director-general: Vaughan Lewis (St Lucia) (1982)
See also **Grenada, US invasion (1983); Charles, Eugenia; Caribbean Community; West Indies Associated States; West Indies Federation.**

Organisation of the People in Arms (*Organización del Pueblo en Armas*/ORPA)

A Guatemalan guerrilla group, founded in 1971 in Mexico but not publicly launched until 1979. Like the Guerrilla Army of the Poor (EGP), it was founded by ex-members of the Rebel Armed Forces (FAR) who believed FAR's position on the 'Indian question' to be racist. It incorporated large numbers of Indians into its ranks but unlike the EGP was organised as a purely military group with no mass fronts. Initial organisational work was done on or close to the Pacific coast, but in September 1971 ORPA moved into the coffee region of the Sierra Madre mountains. In 1981 it was badly hit by an army intelligence operation (aided by Argentine counter-insurgency specialists) which uncovered several safe houses and virtually destroyed the organisation in Guatemala City created between 1975 and 1977. By then ORPA rural fronts were active in many different areas, notably the populous districts of San Marcos and Sololá departments.

The group has been a member of the URNG guerrilla front since its January 1982 foundation. Like the other groups, its strength (though not necessarily its size) was severely depleted by army counter-insurgency operations in the early 1980s, but by the late 1980s it was growing again and may even have re-established a presence in the capital. Commander-in-chief (1990): Rodrigo Asturias, son of the Nobel Prize-winning novelist Miguel Angel Asturias, from whose novel *Men of Maize* he takes his nom de guerre, 'Gaspar Ilom'.
See also **Guatemalan National Revolutionary Unity; Rebel Armed Forces.**

ORIT (*Organización Regional Interamericana de Trabajadores*/Interamerican Regional Organisation of Workers)
A trade union international, founded in 1951 by the International Confederation of Free Trade Unions (ICFTU) as its western hemisphere branch, and with the specific aim of combating 'communist infiltration' in the labour movements of the region. From its headquarters in Mexico City it co-ordinates anti-communist unions throughout the Americas (including the US and Canada). Its sub-regional organisations include the Confederation of Central American Workers (CTCA) and the Caribbean Confederation of Labour (CCL).

Despite taking a stand in its early days against dictatorships of the right (e.g. that of Trujillo in the Dominican Republic), ORIT has been linked with US-backed coups against left-leaning governments, including those of Jacobo Arbenz (Guatemala, 1954), João Goulart (Brazil, 1964) and Cheddi Jagan (Guyana, 1964). There have been frequent accusations that it serves as a tool of US foreign policy and the CIA. The AFL-CIO of the US is by far the dominant organisation within ORIT (though it withdrew from the ICFTU in 1969), and other member organisations have expressed opposition to its close identification with US interests. Even the ICFTU has distanced itself in recent years from its affiliate.

ORIT's congress meets every four years, most recently in Caracas in 1990. The organisation is run by a 22-member executive council and a 12-member executive committee. It has 33 full members and claims to represent around 35 million workers in 24 countries and territories.
See also **American Institute for Free Labor Development.**

Orozco, Pascual: see Mexican Revolution.

Ortega Saavedra, Daniel
b. 11 November 1945. President of Nicaragua 1984–90. Born in La Libertad (Chontales department), son of a mine company accountant who

later ran an import-export company in Managua, Daniel Ortega was educated at the Instituto Pedagógico and the Instituto 'Maestro Gabriel' in Managua. As a young man he was active in the Catholic church. He attended the law faculty of the Central American University (UCA), Managua, but owing to his political work he only lasted a few months. A student activist in anti-dictatorship protests in the early 1960s, he joined the FSLN in 1962–3 and within three years was responsible for its student movement. He founded the *El Estudiante* newspaper. In 1965 he was appointed to head the FSLN's 'internal front' and elected to the leadership. He took part in the assassination of national guard sergeant Gonzalo Lacayo (October 1967) and was imprisoned and tortured that year by the Somoza regime but freed in 1974 in exchange for hostages seized in the 'Chema' Castillo operation.

In 1975 he headed the FSLN's northern front. When the movement split, he became a leader of the insurrectional tendency (Terceristas) with his brother Humberto (who became defence minister in 1979) and helped devise the successful strategy for the overthrow of Somoza. He led the southern front in 1977–9 and became a member of the nine-man national directorate of the FSLN. Given the highest Sandinista rank (Commander of the Revolution) after the victory, he was a member of the Junta of National Reconstruction (JGRN) from 1979 and co-ordinator of the JGRN and the Council of State, 1981–4. He was elected president on the FSLN ticket in November 1984. In 1985 he was appointed head of the FSLN; by that time the 'Ortega faction' was widely regarded as having consolidated its power and influence, and to have overcome possible rivals such as interior minister Tomás Borge. The replacement as head of economic planning of a Borge ally, Henry Ruiz, by an associate of Daniel Ortega was one of a number of signs that the Ortegas' control extended to the economy.

Ortega's presidency was dominated by the war against the US-backed contras and the severe economic problems stemming largely from the war and the US boycott of Nicaragua. In mid-1988 he took steps towards the introduction of a free market, ending most state subsidies and freeing wages and prices. Inflation in 1988 was officially put at almost 22,000% and per capita incomes had slumped to the levels of the 1940s. In January 1989, Ortega introduced a drastic austerity plan, cutting the national budget by 44% and sacking 35,000 state employees. The following month he moved to consolidate the regional peace process by announcing early elections (February 1990), a pardon for political prisoners and improved conditions for opposition parties. After losing the 1990 elections to Violeta Chamorro and the UNO coalition he officially took on the role of leader of the parliamentary opposition. In practice this task fell to his 'alternate,' former vice-president Sergio Ramírez, while Ortega devoted himself to other forms of party activity.
See also **Sandinista National Liberation Front; contra; Arias Plan.**

Ortiz Rubio, Pascual: see Calles.

Osborne, Bertrand

b. 18 April 1935. Opposition leader in Montserrat, 1987– . A wealthy building contractor, merchant and hotelier and the island's leading businessman, Osborne founded the National Development Party (NDP) in 1984, saying he feared premature independence from Britain. He later started the *Montserrat Reporter*, which became the island's only newspaper. He was elected to parliament in the 1987 general election, at which the NDP won two seats and 32% of the vote and became the main opposition party. The party's second MP, lawyer David Brandt, resigned from the NDP in 1989 after its veiled criticism of his role in the island's offshore banking sector.

Osborne, John

b. 27 May 1936. Chief minister of Montserrat 1978– . A wealthy boat-builder, property developer and farmer, he was elected to parliament in 1966 as a member of the Montserrat Workers' Progressive Party. In 1970 he was a founder-member of the Progressive Democratic Party (PDP), which won the general election that year. and was appointed minister of agriculture, trade, lands and housing. He broke with PDP leader Austin Bramble in 1973 and formed the People's Liberation Movement (PLM) in 1976. The party won all seven seats in parliament at the general election in 1978 and conservative Osborne became chief minister. He and the PLM won again in 1983 (5–2) and 1987 (4–3). He favours eventual independence from Britain.
See also **Bramble.**

Outlet: see **Antigua Caribbean Liberation Movement.**

Ovando Hernández, Francisco Xavier: see **National Democratic Front.**

P

Padilla, Hernán: see New Progressive Party; Romero Barceló.

Pact of Espino Negro: see Sandino.

Padilla Rush, Rigoberto: see Communist Party of Honduras.

PAIN: see Déjoie.

PAISA: see National Conciliation Party.

PALA: see Labour Party (Panama).

Palma, Rubén: see Christian Democrat Party of Honduras.

Panama, Republic of
Capital: Panama City
Independence: (from Colombia) 1903
Area: 77,082 sq km
Population (1988): 2.32m (50.6% urban)
Pop. growth rate (1980–88): 2.2%
Pop. density: 30/sq km
Infant mortality (1986): 22.7 per thousand
Life expectancy at birth (1980–85): 71
Literacy (1988): 85.8%
GDP per capita (1988e): US$2,229
Foreign debt per capita (1987): US$2,301
Main exports (1988): bananas (27%); shrimps (19%); sugar (2%).
[N.B. Less than one quarter of Panamanian GDP is traditionally derived from primary, manufacturing and construction sectors.]

Political system

Constitution: 1972 (amended 1978 and 1983). Head of state/government: President Guillermo Endara Galimany (ADOC) 1990– . Panama came under a *de facto* government following the annulment of the May 1989 elections amid widespread allegations of fraud and government complaints of 'foreign interference'. The United States invaded on 20 December 1989 and installed the election winners, the ADOC coalition, in government. Under normal circumstances the president, two vice-presidents and members of the 67-seat Legislative Assembly are elected for five-year terms by compulsory popular vote. In the event that no presidential candidate obtains a majority, the Assembly is empowered to appoint the president. In February 1990 the electoral tribunal allocated 57 Assembly seats on the basis of available returns. One seat is allocated to the party with the most votes among those winning no seat directly. This was expected to go to PALA. Fresh elections were due to be called in August 1990 for the remaining seats.

Political organisations

Parties in National Assembly (leader) (seats): Democratic Alliance of Civic Opposition/ADOC coalition (51 in total) (see below); Democratic Revolutionary Party/PRD (Carlos Duque) (6); Labour Party/PALA (Ramón Sieiro and Carlos Eleta) (1). [ADOC comprises: Christian Democrat Party/PDC (Ricardo Arias Calderón) (27); Nationalist Republican Liberal Movement/Molirena (Guillermo Ford and Alfredo Ramírez) (15); Authentic Liberal Party/PLA (Jaime Ortega) (9).]

Parties outside the Assembly (leader): Republican Party/PR; Panamanian People's Party/PPP (Rubén Darío Sousa); Revolutionary Panameñista Party/PPR (Luis Gaspar Suárez); National Action Party/PAN; Democratic Workers' Party/PDT; Authentic Panameñista Party/PPA (Hildebrando Nicosia).

Parties without legal status: Arnulfista Party/PA (Guillermo Endara) (in formation); National Liberal Party/PLN (Rodolfo Chiari); Panameñista Party/PP (Luis Suárez/Alonso Pinzón); Broad Popular Front/Frampo (Renato Pereira); Popular Nationalist Party/PNP (Olimpo Sáez); Popular Action Party/PAPO (Carlos Iván Zúñiga); United Popular Front/Frepu; Socialist Workers' Party/PST; Revolutionary Workers' Party/PRT; Independent Democratic Movement/MID; Democratic Socialist Party/PSD; Agrarian Labour Party/PLA; Panamanian Social Democrat Party/PSD (Carlos González de la Lastra); Non-Aligned Revolutionary Movement; Popular Nationalist Federalist Party/PFNP; Independent Working Class Party/PICO.

The government coalition for the annulled 1989 elections was the National Liberation Coalition/COLINA, comprising the PRD, PALA, the PLN, the PPP, the PPR and the PRT.

Main labour organisation (leader) (affiliation): National Council of Organized Workers/CONATO (Martín González/Eduardo Ríos), comprising the Confederation of Workers of the Republic of Panama/CTRP (Ricardo Monterrey Calderón) (ORIT), National Workers' Central/-CNTP (CPUSTAL), and Isthmian Workers' Central/CIT (Julio César Pinzón) (CLAT).

Main employers' organisation: National Private Enterprise Council/CONEP (Alberto A. Boyd Jr).

Panama Canal Area: see Panama Canal Zone

Panama Canal Treaties
(1) The 1902 Hay-Herrán Treaty between the US and Colombia, by which the former would have obtained rights to the Panama canal route, was refused ratification by the Colombian senate. This provided the main

motivation for the US-backed secession of Panama from Colombia in the following year, for which Washington eventually paid US$25m in reparations to Colombia under a 1921 agreement.
(2) The 1903 Hay-Bunau Varilla Treaty, signed immediately after Panama's secession from Colombia, gave the US the right to build a trans-isthmian canal and hold it – together with an 8 km strip of land either side – 'in perpetuity', in return for $10m, plus a $250,000 annuity in gold coin, beginning in 1912. (This was increased to $430,000 in 1933 and $1.93m in 1955.) The US agreed to guarantee Panamanian freedom (i.e. from reincorporation into Colombia) and assumed responsibility for the maintenance of law and order in the country. The US government purchased the canal rights for $40m from the French company which had failed in its bid to dig the canal. Construction was completed in 10 years at cost of about $380m. The US invoked its right to intervene in Panamanian internal affairs on several occasions between 1903 and 1930, usually at the request of one or other Panamanian political faction. Interventions included election supervision; the stationing of a US occupation force in Chiriquí province for two years; and US involvement in the quelling of rent riots in 1925. Washington's non-intervention in the 1931 coup marked a new phase in relations.
(3) The first successful revision of the 1903 agreement was the Hull-Alfaro Treaty of 1936 (ratified in 1939). This explicitly recognised Panamanian sovereignty and ended the country's 'protectorate' status by abrogating the US guarantee of Panamanian independence and the concomitant right to intervene. US rights in the Canal Zone (CZ) were stated to apply only for purposes of 'maintenance, operation, sanitation and protection' of the canal. But the US was granted the right to conduct military manoeuvres in the Republic of Panama.
(4) In 1955 an increase in annuity was agreed, along with a single basic wage scale for canal employees regardless of nationality (though this was not implemented in practice), and a cut-back on those commercial operations in the CZ not essential to the operation of the canal. Panama conceded rent-free occupation of 8,000 ha of its territory as US military bases for 15 years.
(5) The two Carter-Torrijos Treaties, signed on 7 September 1977 and effective from 1 October 1979, resulted from the Torrijos government's rejection of the so-called 'three-in-one' treaties, whose ratification had been prevented by the 1968 coup. Panamanian sovereignty over the CZ and the canal was restored when the treaties went into effect. Full operational control and defence of the canal is due to pass into Panamanian hands at noon on 31 December 1999, when US military personnel stationed in Panama (currently numbering around 11,000) must withdraw. [N.B. US law 96–70, also known as the Murphy Act, which was approved unilaterally in 1977, in effect nullifies some of the clauses relating to the handover, including the neutrality of the canal. The Noriega government had asked for its amendment.] In the meantime the Panamanian Canal Commission, a US government agency controlled by a board comprising US and Panamanian citizens, runs the waterway. In 1990 a Panamanian

became the Commission's senior officer. The treaties also gave Panama a greater share in shipping toll revenues, which by 1987 accounted for 8% of national income. During the US-Panamanian confrontation of 1988–89 these were withheld by the US government.

In 1986 Panama had demanded payment of $54m from the US under the terms of the treaties, alleging the deliberate falsification of operating costs in order to avoid payment of the agreed $10m per annum. Washington refused to pay.

Panama Canal Zone (CZ)
Administrative capital: Balboa Heights
A strip of territory five miles wide on either side of the Panama Canal, demarcated in 1903 as a zone to be held in perpetuity by the United States. The issue of Panamanian sovereignty was left vague, and only clarified by a succession of treaty revisions. The Zone was administered by the Panama Canal Co., a self-sustaining corporate body, founded in 1951 to replace the Panama Railroad Co. and responsible to the US Department of Defense. Only employees of the Canal Co. were permitted to live in the CZ: the majority of these were Panamanian citizens. The US Southern Command is based in the Zone (known as the Panama Canal Area since sovereignty reverted to Panama), and under the terms of the 1977 Carter-Torrijos treaties the US is entitled to retain its military bases there until the year 2000.
See also **flag riots; Panama Canal Treaties; School of the Americas.**

Panama, US invasion (1989)
After two years of confrontation between the US and Panama's *de facto* ruler, Gen. Manuel Noriega, Washington invaded the country in the early hours of 20 December 1989. Its stated objectives were: to protect the lives of US citizens; to arrest Noriega and take him to Miami to face trial on drug trafficking charges; to safeguard the operations of the Panama Canal; and to restore democracy to Panama. The operation had been planned for the beginning of January 1990, but was precipitated by a speech in which the general declared that a 'state of war' existed between the two countries and by incidents involving the death of one US officer and threats to another at the hands of the Panama Defence Forces (FDP). An attempted coup on 3 October 1989 had been bloodily put down by Noriega, and the George Bush administration in Washington had been criticised in Congress for failing to give the attempt adequate support.

'Operation Just Cause', as the invasion was designated, involved the largest US military airlift since the Vietnam war and the biggest combat paratroop drop (over 3,000) since World War II. A total of 26,000 troops were involved, of whom almost half were already on US bases in Panama before the invasion began. Although PDF resistance was quickly put down, sporadic fire-fights continued for some days and Noriega himself evaded capture. A million-dollar reward was offered for information on his whereabouts, but he eventually sought asylum in the papal nunciature on 24 December, where he remained until a negotiated settlement resulted in his surrender and transfer to Miami on 3 January. By 13 February all extra US troops had been withdrawn, although the US military retained a security function in Panama.

The destruction of the PDF and the failure of US troops to police the country resulted in an estimated $1bn in losses from looting in the immediate aftermath of the invasion. Total losses were put at around $2bn. The Panama Canal was closed for 24 hours for the first time in its history, and operations remained restricted for about a week. Twenty-three US soldiers died and 324 were wounded, but the number of casualties on the Panamanian side remained a matter of controversy. Washington said 202 civilians and 314 PDF members were killed, but later admitted that only 51 PDF bodies had been identified. A team of US doctors put civilian deaths at over 300, while Panamanian sources claimed up to 7,000 had died.

The invasion was widely condemned in Latin America, with many countries refusing to recognise the Endara government, sworn in on a US base as the operation began. The OAS voted 20:1 to deplore it. Several governments called for fresh elections to legitimise the new regime, a demand rejected by Panama.

See also **Noriega Morena; Endara Galimany; Panama Canal Treaties.**

Panameñismo: see **Arias Madrid; Authentic Panameñista Party.**

Pancasán: see **Sandinista National Liberation Front.**

Panday, Basdeo
b. 25 May 1932. Social democratic Trinidadian politician. A British-trained lawyer, economist and former actor, Panday returned to Trinidad in 1965 and ran unsuccessfully for parliament in 1966 as a member of the leftist Workers' and Farmers' Party. He became legal adviser to the Oilfields Workers' Trade Union and was appointed an opposition senator in 1972. In 1973 he became head of the All-Trinidad Sugar Estates and Factory Workers Trade Union. In 1975, he led a strike which won major improvements in working conditions and then with three other unions (oilfields, transport and industrial, cane farmers) helped put together the predominantly East Indian United Labour Front (ULF) in 1975. After the Front won 10 seats at the 1976 general election, he became opposition leader. He was ousted as ULF leader in 1977 by left-winger Raffique Shah but regained the post in 1978. He was part of the opposition Alliance group which won 10 seats at the 1981 general election.

In 1985, Panday became one of the two deputy leaders of the new four-party National Alliance for Reconstruction (NAR). When the NAR came to power in the 1986 elections, Panday was named foreign minister. He was sacked in 1988 and later the same year expelled from the party, along with two other dismissed ministers, after accusing the prime minister, A. N. R. Robinson, of autocratic rule. Panday and five other dissident MPs formed the United National Congress party in 1989, with Panday as leader.

See also **National Alliance for Reconstruction; Robinson.**

PANPRA *(Parti Nationaliste Progressiste Révolutionnaire Haitien/* Haitian Nationalist Progressive Revolutionary Party)
Haitian social democratic party. Founded after the fall of the Duvalier dictatorship in 1986 by Serge Gilles, after he broke away from IFOPADA, which he founded in 1980 and some of whose leaders wanted to move further left. In 1989, PANPRA, strongly backed by the French Socialist Party and after admission to the Socialist International, joined with Marc Bazin's Movement for the Establishment of Democracy in Haiti (MIDH) to form a National Alliance for Democracy and Progress (ANDP) to contest elections. Its deputy leaders are former filmmaker Arnold Antonin and Dully Brutus.
See also **Gilles; Movement for the Establishment of Democracy in Haiti; Bazin.**

'Papa Doc': see **Duvalier, François.**

Papaye Peasant Movement *(Mouvement Paysan de Papaye/*MPP)
Founded in 1986 by Haitian Catholic lay worker Chavannes Jean-Baptiste (b. 17 February 1947) in the area of the central Haitian town of Papaye, to defend peasant interests and provide cheap credit, the movement launched a nationwide boycott of payment of market taxes. The peasants said they received no services in exchange for paying the tax. The MPP organised a national peasants' congress at Papaye in March 1987, backed by Caritas, the Catholic Church's development body. The movement split in 1990.
See also **Haiti, Roman Catholic Church.**

Paredes, Gen. Rubén Darío: see **Labour Party** (Panama).

Party of Restorative Action (PAR): see **Nationalist Democratic Union.**

Party of the Poor *(Partido de los Pobres)*
A small guerrilla movement active in the Mexican state of Guerrero in the early 1970s and led by a former schoolteacher, Lucio Cabañas Barrientos. The movement came into being as a result of the harsh repression of local peasants by landowners and hired gunmen. It carried out a number of armed actions, including kidnappings in Acapulco. Cabañas, who became a folk hero, was killed in combat in 1974. The army used 'dirty war' tactics against the movement: many of Cabañas' relatives, for example, were held incommunicado in the First Military Camp in Mexico City for extended periods.
See also **Nationalist Revolutionary Civic Association.**

Party of the Salvadorean Revolution (PRS): see **People's Revolutionary Army** (El Salvador).

Pascal-Trouillot, Ertha
b. 13 August 1943. President of Haiti 1990–   . Pascal-Trouillot qualified as Haiti's first woman lawyer in 1971 and married legal historian Ernst Trouillot, president of the Port-au-Prince bar association. She became a

judge in 1980 and was named to the supreme court in 1986 after the fall of the Duvalier dictatorship. On the overthrow of President Prosper Avril in 1990, she accepted an opposition invitation to become provisional president, sharing power with a council of state, with the task of organising elections.

See also **Avril; Abraham.**

Pastora Gómez, Edén

b. 1937. Nicaraguan politician and guerrilla leader. Pastora was born into a Conservative farming family of Sicilian origin in Matagalpa. His father was killed by the National Guard in 1942. Edén was educated at a Jesuit boarding school in Granada and in the 1950s studied medicine in Mexico. In his twenties he was active in the social democratic Sandino Revolutionary Front (FRS), an armed organisation opposed to the Somoza dictatorship. In 1966–7 he took part in the Conservative election campaign. He became associated with the Sandinista National Liberation Front (FSLN) in 1967 but fled abroad after the Pancasán defeat. Amnestied, he turned to tobacco farming. He left the FSLN in 1972 and was briefly involved with a guerrilla group led by the Chamorro Rappaccioli brothers. In 1973 he set up a shark-fishing business in Costa Rica, and took Costa Rican nationality, rejoining the FSLN as a member of the 'Tercerista' faction in 1977.

He achieved international prominence as 'Comandante Cero' (Commander Zero), his code name in the FSLN's 'Death to Somoza' operation of August 1978, in which several hundred hostages were taken at the National Palace. In the September 1978 insurrection and the final offensive of May-July 1979 he commanded the Southern Front. After the July 1979 overthrow of Somoza he was given the rank of guerrilla commander and appointed deputy interior minister and later (December 1979) deputy defence minister in charge of militias. He left Nicaragua in 1981, supposedly to fight alongside other guerrilla movements, but formally broke with the Sandinistas in April 1982, accusing them of having betrayed the revolution. In exile in Costa Rica he set up the second Sandino Revolutionary Front (FRS), a founding member of the Democratic Revolutionary Alliance (ARDE). In April 1983 he launched a guerrilla war from bases in Costa Rica and southern Nicaragua, but with limited success.

Expelled from ARDE in early 1984 because of his objections to an alliance with the *somocista* Nicaraguan Democratic Force, he continued to use the ARDE name and later reached agreement with its leaders on mutual consultation. An assassination attempt on him (allegedly involving the CIA) failed in 1984. The Pastora wing of ARDE was a founder member of the Southern Opposition Bloc (BOS) in 1985. In March 1986, Pastora signed a unity agreement with the FDN, but this quickly broke down over the issue of the command structure. In May 1986 most FRS commanders abandoned Pastora to join the UNO coalition, of which the FDN was a part. A week later, Pastora applied for political asylum in Costa Rica. In December 1989 he returned to Nicaragua to campaign for the Social Christian Party (PSC), with whom he had signed a pact the previous year, but went back to Costa Rica before the 25 February 1990 elections.

See also **ARDE; Nicaraguan Resistance; Sandinista National Liberation Front; Social Christian Party.**

Patriotic Front of the Revolution (FPR): see Independent Liberal Party.

Patterson, P.J. (Percival)

b. 10 April 1935. Deputy prime minister of Jamaica 1976–80, 1989– . A barrister, Patterson became a member of the People's National Party (PNP) executive in 1964, a senator in 1967 and in 1969 PNP vice-chairman. He was elected to parliament in 1970 and was industry, tourism and trade minister from 1972 until 1976, when he was named foreign minister and deputy prime minister, posts he held until the PNP's electoral defeat in 1980 when he lost his own seat. As leader of the conservative wing of the party, he briefly left the PNP executive in 1981, rejoining after leftists had resigned and became party chairman. He became deputy prime minister and minister of production and planning when the PNP returned to power in 1989.

See also **People's National Party; Manley, Michael.**

Peasant Unity Committee (*Comité de Unidad Campesina*/CUC)

A semi-clandestine Guatemalan peasant organisation, formed between 1976 and 1978. The CUC first came to prominence when it took part in the 1978 May Day demonstration in Guatemala City organised by the National Trade Union Unity Committee (CNUS), which had played a part in its creation. It significance was that it was Indian-led and succeeded in organising for the first time the country's majority Indian population in the highland regions alongside poor *ladinos*. It was aided in this task by the Indians' pattern of migratory labour in the coastal plantations, where in March 1980 the CUC organised a successful, large-scale strike for higher wages. Members of the CUC took part in the January 1980 occupation of the Spanish embassy which ended in the deaths of 38 people when police stormed the building. A year later it formed the 31 January Popular Front (FP–31) with other labour, student and popular organisations sympathetic to the armed struggle. Since 1979 it had been a member of the Democratic Front Against Repression (FDCR), a broader-based organisation.

The CUC did not publicise details of its leadership, but in 1980–81 many leaders and activists were murdered and the organisation was forced to go underground and into exile. Despite this, CUC members took part in another embassy occupation in May 1982 to publicise army repression. In March 1987 it joined the newly-created Unity of Labour and Popular Action (UASP) and showed signs of returning to open political work within Guatemala. However, the authorities threatened to respond by arresting CUC members for subversion.

See also **National Campesino Pro-Land Association; Guerrilla Army of the Poor.**

Pemex: see Cárdenas, Lázaro.

Peña Gómez, José Francisco
b. 6 March 1937. Social democratic leader in the Dominican Republic. Peña Gómez was left behind by his Haitian-born parents when they fled dictator Rafael Trujillo's 1937 massacre of some 20,000 Haitians living in the border area. He became secretary-general of Juan Bosch's Dominican Revolutionary Party (PRD) in 1963, the year Bosch was elected president and then overthrown. In 1965, with dissident left-wing soldiers, he seized the country's main radio station, announced the fall of the Reid Cabral provisional government, called for an uprising to restore Bosch, and thereby sparked off civil war and the subsequent US invasion.

Peña Gómez became party leader when Bosch resigned in 1973 after his proposal to boycott the 1974 elections was rejected. He was mayor of Santo Domingo from 1982 until 1986, when after a bitter fight, including a convention gun-battle involving his supporters, he lost the party's nomination for the presidency to conservative Jacobo Majluta. He agreed to be Majluta's vice-presidential candidate but then withdrew and took little part in the election campaign. Majluta was narrowly defeated and continued his quarrel with Peña Gómez, who nevertheless retained the loyalty of most PRD supporters. Peña Gómez, who is also vice-president of the Socialist International for Latin America, became party president in 1986. Because of the party split he set up a new group in 1989, the Institutional Social Democratic Bloc (BIS), to run in the 1990 national elections but he was eventually named the PRD's presidential candidate and won 23% of the vote. Peña Gómez' black skin and Haitian origins have caused him to be ostracised by the country's white élite.

See also **Dominican Revolutionary Party; Majluta; Bosch, Juan; Dominican Republic, US invasion (1965); Reid Cabral; Dominican Republic, Haitian border massacre (1937); Trujillo.**

People's Action Movement (PAM)
Conservative party in St Kitts-Nevis. Founded in 1965 by lawyer Billie Herbert, its pro-Anguillan leaders were arrested in 1967 for subversion after Anguillan secessionists attacked St Kitts police headquarters. The charges were dismissed. The conservative PAM formed a trade union, the Working People's Union (later renamed the United Workers' Union), but the party, allied with opposition politicians in Nevis, lost general elections in 1966 (2–7), 1971 (1–8) and 1975 (0–9) despite receiving about a third of the vote. Herbert was replaced as leader in 1976 by Kennedy Simmonds. At the 1980 general election, with Simmonds promising abolition of personal income tax, PAM won three seats to Labour's four. Simmonds became premier with a one-seat majority in coalition with the Nevis Reformation Party, which had won two seats, and thereby ended 28 years of Labour Party rule. PAM won the 1984 elections with six

seats, to the NRP's three and Labour's two. The party again won six seats in the 1989 election.

See also **Simmonds; Powell; Nevis.**

People's Alliance: see **New Jewel Movement; Bishop; Brizan.**

People's Democratic Movement (PDM)

Political party in the Turks and Caicos Islands. Founded in 1975 by Oswald Skippings and nightclub owner J. A. G. S. McCartney, the originally pro-independence PDM won a general election 6–5 the following year and McCartney became chief minister. McCartney was killed in a plane crash in the US in 1980 and Skippings succeeded him for a few months until the general election that year which the party lost 3–8. Skippings was replaced as party leader by Clement Howell (1935–87) (whose deputy he became) just before the 1984 election, which the PDM again lost 3–8. Skippings, who was accused of arson by a 1986 commission of enquiry, replaced Howell in 1987. The party won the 1988 general election 11–2 after Britain restored constitutional rule, and Skippings became chief minister again.

See also **Skippings.**

People's Electoral Movement (*Movimentu Electoral di Pueblo*/MEP)

Social democratic political party in Aruba. Founded in 1971 by Betico Croes to fight for separation and eventual independence from the rest of the Netherlands Antilles, the party won the general election in 1975 and Croes became island leader. After Arubans voted 82% for independence in a 1977 referendum the MEP was excluded from the central government in Curaçao (of which it had been part since 1973) and boycotted the federal parliament. The party joined a central government coalition headed by Don Martina and the New Antilles Movement in 1979, but withdrew from it in 1981 when the government insisted that any oil discovered off Aruba would belong to the whole federation.

Closure of Aruba's Exxon-owned Lago oil refinery in 1985 caused the party's 13–8 defeat in elections that year. Croes was critically injured in a car crash a few weeks later and the party's secretary-general, Nelson Oduber, became MEP leader. He led the party to power at the 1989 general election, when the MEP became the largest party, with 10 of the 21 seats, and Oduber formed a coalition with two small parties.

See also **Croes; Oduber, Nelson; Netherlands Antilles; oil refineries; Martina; New Antilles Movement; Aruba.**

People's Liberation Movement (PLM): see **Osborne, John.**

People's National Movement (PNM) (St Vincent): see **Joshua, Ebenezer.**

People's National Movement (PNM) (Trinidad-Tobago)

Political party in Trinidad-Tobago. Founded in 1956 by Eric Williams, who attracted young nationalist intellectuals tired of traditional political parties and eager to break with British colonial rule. The party won general elections 13–11 in September 1956, only eight months after its foundation, and Williams became chief minister. The PNM won re-election in 1961 (20–10), 1966 (24–12), 1971 (36–0) (because of an opposition boycott) and 1976 (24–12). Williams died in 1981. His successor, George Chambers, won the general election of 1981 (26–10) but he and a wearied and corrupt PNM were defeated 3–33 in 1986 by an opposition alliance led by A. N. R. Robinson. Former energy minister Patrick Manning, one of the three PNM MPs to survive, was elected party leader in 1987.

See also **Williams; Manning; 'black power'; Butler; Trinidad, 'black power' uprising (1970); 'new left'; James, C.L.R.**

People's National Party (PNP)

Jamaican social democratic party. Founded in 1938 by Norman Manley as a socialist party, the PNP was beaten by Alexander Bustamante's Jamaica Labour Party (JLP) at general elections in 1944 (27–5) and 1949 (19–13). In 1952, Manley purged it of its powerful left wing, which had refused his request to disaffiliate from the communist-dominated World Federation of Trade Unions. The left's leaders (Ken Hill, Richard Hart, Frank Hill and Arthur Henry) were known as 'The Four H's'. Manley founded the National Workers' Union immediately afterwards to profit from their considerable grassroots work and the union was a key factor in the party's first general election victory (18–14) in 1955. Manley became chief minister and the PNP increased its majority to 29–16 in 1959, when he became premier. After voters in 1961 rejected Manley's proposal to stay in the West Indies Federation the party was defeated 26–19 at the 1962 general election by the JLP and Bustamante, who led the country to independence a few months later. The party was beaten again in 1967 (35–20).

The ailing Manley's son Michael was elected party leader in 1969 and defeated the JLP 36–16 in the 1972 elections and became prime minister. From 1974, Manley declared his aim was democratic socialism, and the party turned left domestically (nationalisation) and internationally (defence of Third World interests and ties with Cuba) under the guidance of party general secretary D. K. Duncan and others. It won again 47–13 in 1976 but by then had roused the strong hostility of the business class. US pressure and covert attempted destabilisation, poorly organised reforms and the resultant economic collapse led to the party's 51–9 defeat in a violence-plagued general election in 1980 by the JLP and its strongly pro-US leader, Edward Seaga.

Under pressure from party conservatives, such as former deputy prime minister P. J. Patterson who briefly resigned from the PNP, Manley dropped the left in 1981, broke ties with the marxist Workers' Party of Jamaica and generally moderated his policies. The PNP boycotted the 1983 election in protest against the absence of promised electoral reforms. It won control of nearly all the island's towns in local elections in 1986 and returned to power nationally at the 1989 elections, beating the JLP 45–15. Manley became prime minister once more.

See also **Manley, Michael; National Workers' Union of Jamaica; Workers' Party of Jamaica; Seaga; Patterson; Jamaica Labour Party; West Indies Federation; Munroe.**

People's Party of Panama (*Partido del Pueblo de Panamá*/PPP)

Founded in 1925 as the Labour Party (*Partido Laborista*), the PPP took its present name in 1943, having previously been known as the Communist Party. Its hostility to the US presence resulted in proscription after 1950, with a consequent loss of influence. It declared its adherence to Marxism-Leninism in 1951. Never a mass movement, it none the less developed some strength in the labour and student movements, as well as among peasants and intellectuals. It has held seats in the National Assembly. After 1970 it gave 'critical support' to the Torrijos regime, while its youth wing (which controlled the student federation, the FEP) broke away and gave unconditional support, eventually taking a leading role (as 'the tendency') in the Torrijista party, the PRD. In international outlook the PPP was pro-Soviet, while economically it approved of a role for the private sector. It won legal recognition in 1981 but performed poorly in the 1984 elections and temporarily lost legal status. In 1989 it joined the official COLINA alliance for the subsequently annulled 1989 elections, but was allocated no seats by the Electoral Tribunal when the results were re-examined under the Endara government in early 1990.
See also **Democratic Revolutionary Party; Torrijos Herrera.**

People's Political Party (PPP): see Joshua, Ebenezer.

People's Progressive Party (PPP): see Webster; Gumbs; Anguilla Democratic Party.

People's Revolutionary Army (El Salvador) (*Ejército Revolucionario del Pueblo*/ERP)

Formed in 1972 by former Christian Democrats of predominantly middle-class origin, the ERP was affected almost immediately by an internal dispute. This pitted the militaristic, *foquista* majority in the leadership against a faction headed by the noted poet Roque Dalton, who favoured the development of a mass movement dedicated to 'national resistance'. The majority faction turned towards Maoism, at first tolerating the existence of competing views but in 1975 deciding to crush the dissenters. On 10 May, Dalton and one of his supporters were shot as 'right-wing revisionists'. A bloodbath was only averted by the intervention of the Popular Liberation Forces (FPL), and the dissenting group took much of the membership with it to set up the Armed Forces of National Resistance (FARN). The ERP rump was reviled by much of the left as a result, with many accusing it of being in league with the CIA. Between 1975 and 1977 the hard-liners in the leadership were purged, but the ERP strategy remained insurrectionist, opposed to 'prolonged popular war'. The group set up the Party of the Salvadorean Revolution (PRS), which argued for a broad front, but the PRS was a largely artificial creation which failed to conceal the ERP's uncompromising stance.
The ERP leadership built a powerful military apparatus based primarily

in the eastern province of Morazán, and in 1977 it united with one of the smaller 'popular organisations', the 28 February Popular Leagues (LP–28), formed earlier that year after the 28 February 1977 massacre of demonstrators by the military regime. After the coup of October 1979 the ERP was the only guerrilla group to call for an immediate insurrection. However, its attempt to mount one was a costly failure. Despite continued antipathy between the ERP and FARN, the former joined the new guerrilla front in March 1980. Since the death of FPL leader Cayetano Carpio in 1983 the ERP has been regarded as the most powerful group within the FMLN front and its leader, Joaquín Villalobos, as the senior guerrilla commander.

See also **Farabundo Martí National Liberation Front; Villalobos; Popular Liberation Forces.**

People's Revolutionary Army (PRA) (Grenada): see People's Revolutionary Government; Marryshow, Terry.

People's Revolutionary Government (PRG)

The left-wing government in Grenada (1979–83) led by Maurice Bishop following the 1979 overthrow of prime minister Sir Eric Gairy. It began as a coalition between the New Jewel Movement (NJM) and sympathetic businessmen, played down its socialist nature and hid the marxism of its leaders. It faced the immediate hostility of the United States, which fought to destroy it diplomatically, economically and probably also by destabilising covert action (the leadership escaped a bomb assassination attempt in 1980). Washington pointed to Grenada's new ties with Cuba, the Soviet Union and other communist states. The PRG expanded the army, renamed the People's Revolutionary Army, from a few hundred to nearly 2,000 and also formed a volunteer militia. Other regional governments feared Grenada-inspired subversion but were also impressed by the PRG's sincere attempts to tackle the region's endemic problems of dependency, narrow-based economies, corruption and foreign domination. US attempts to recruit regional allies were therefore not always effective.

The PRG launched self-help campaigns to improve education, literacy, housing, roads and agricultural self-sufficiency and to create the beginnings of a welfare state, including health care and free education. For the first time, Grenadians were also officially encouraged to take a pride in their culture and language. Cuban help was obtained to build a new international airport financed from various sources, both East and West. The airport, which the US claimed was for military purposes, distorted the economy, which the PRG's economic supremo, Bernard Coard, had earlier restored to some degree of efficiency.

The PRG at first said it would hold general elections but then dropped the idea, saying the 'Westminster system' was unsuitable for Grenada. It set up local councils and, with the NJM, various 'mass organisations' aimed at establishing grassroots democracy. But after some success they foundered on inefficiency and increasingly tough ideological direction from the centre, which lost the government much support. Opposition media were not tolerated and free speech generally diminished.

Internal pressures, ideological rigidity and naïveté, aggravated by foreign harassment, caused the collapse of the PRG in October 1983 after a split which led to Bishop's arrest and murder. The US invaded and occupied the island a week later.

See also **New Jewel Movement; Bishop; Coard; Grenada, US invasion (1983); Revolutionary Military Council; Gairy.**

People's United Party (PUP)

A Belizean political party, founded in 1950 as the People's Committee, a radical nationalist movement closely linked to the General Workers' Union, favouring an economy based on consumer and producer co-operatives. The PUP's support has traditionally been stronger among Spanish-speakers, ladinos, Catholics and Indians than among blacks, who have tended to favour more West Indian-oriented politicians. In 1951–4 the PC was believed to have had close contacts with the reformist Arbenz government in Guatemala. In 1954, as the PUP, it won eight out of nine elective seats on the newly-established legislative assembly (six members were nominated by the UK government), after campaigning on a platform of self-government. Its leaders, predominantly Catholic radicals, at one time imprisoned as 'subversives', were accepted on to the colonial executive council. In 1956 it split in two, with the more pro-British elements forming the National Independence Party (NIP – later part of the opposition United Democratic Party/UDP).

In 1957 the PUP won all nine assembly seats. By 1961 the assembly had been reformed, and the PUP won all 18 elected seats (against four nominated). Party leader George Price became premier, a post he retained until 1984, when the PUP lost control of the (now independent) government for the first time. Following its massive electoral defeat, the party was at first weakened by factional fighting and could count on majority support only in the mestizo north of the country. In the municipal elections of March 1985 the PUP lost virtually the whole of its local power base. The party is often described today as 'social democratic', although it has traditionally been dominated by conservatives and George Price has called himself a Christian democrat. It favours a mixed economy and controlled foreign investment and is generally pro-US. The left wing of the PUP, led by Said Musa and (formerly) Assad Shoman, would like to see redistribution of land and wealth, but has never won control of the party.

In the aftermath of the 1984 defeat, leftist Harry Courtenay was nominated senator by the party and Said Musa, despite having lost his own seat, acquired a more prominent role in the party as chairman. This was seen by some as presaging a general move to the left, at the expense of the rightist faction led by party chairman Louis Sylvestre, who left the PUP in 1985 to found the Belize Popular Party (BPP). In 1988, however, the small Christian Democratic Party of former UDP leader Dr Theodore Aranda fused with the PUP, helping consolidate the position of the

centrist faction under Florencio Marin, the leader of the opposition, whose strength lies primarily among the northern sugar farmers. In 1989 the PUP was returned to power with 15 seats to the UDP's 13, and George Price once more became prime minister. Said Musa was given the foreign affairs, economic development and education portfolios; Aranda those of health and urban development; while Marin became deputy prime minister and minister of industry.
See also **Price.**

Peralta Azurdia, Col. Enrique: see Arévalo Bermejo; Christian Democrat Party (Guatemala); Institutional Democratic Party.

Permanent Congress for Trade Union Unity of the Workers of Latin America: see CPUSTAL.

Peters, Marcel: see Grenada United Labour Party.

Petit St Vincent Initiative (1973): see Caribbean Community.

Petronia, Ernesto: see Democratic Party (Netherlands Antilles).

Philippe-Auguste, Gérard: see Fignolé.

Picado, Teodoro: see Calderón Guardia; Civil War (Costa Rica).

Pilgrim, Michael: see St Lucia Labour Party; Odlum, George; Progressive Labour Party (St Lucia).

Pindling, Sir Lynden
b. 22 March 1930. Premier, prime minister of the Bahamas 1967– . A lawyer, Pindling joined the Progressive Liberal Party (PLP) soon after its foundation in 1953 and was elected to parliament in 1956, when he became party leader. He was appointed leader of the opposition in 1964 and premier after the 1967 general election, when independents backed him after the PLP had tied 18–18 with the white-dominated opposition United Bahamian Party. He launched a programme of 'Bahamianisation' of the colonial society and led the country to independence from Britain in 1973.

In 1983 the US media charged that he and other top officials were being paid by fugitive international financier Robert Vesco and Colombian drug king Carlos Lehder to allow smuggling of cocaine and marijuana to the US through the Bahamas. A government-appointed royal commission in 1984 confirmed the reports except that it could not prove the charges against Pindling, now a multi-millionaire. Pindling sacked two cabinet ministers named by the commission and two others who called for his resignation. Deputy prime minister Arthur Hanna resigned in protest against his behaviour. Pindling survived by stressing his links with poor black Bahamians and because of the weakness of the opposition. New allegations in 1987 linked him with Lehder, but he and the PLP won the 1987 general election 31–18 and the US government reportedly refused to authorise his indictment.

See also **Progressive Liberal Party; United Bahamian Party; Family Islands.**

Pinilla, Col. José María: see Torrijos Herrera.

PINU: see Social Democratic Innovation and Unity Party.

Pinzón, Alonso: see Authentic Panameñista Party.

Platt Amendment
Seven articles proposed by Sen. Orville H. Platt of Connecticut as an amendment to the US Army Appropriation Bill of 1901–2 and subsequently added (under US pressure) to the Cuban constitution of 1901. The amendment gave the US the 'right to intervene for the preservation of Cuban independence [and] the maintenance of a government adequate for the protection of life, property and individual liberty', as well as the right to buy or lease land for 'coaling or naval stations' and prevent other powers from establishing such base(s); and the right of surveillance over the Cuban customs and excise and public health systems. Conditions were placed on Cuba's ability to contract debts. The amendment was included as a condition for the withdrawal of US troops, which had been sent ostensibly to assist Cuba in gaining its independence from Spain but occupied the country from 1898 to 1902. It was also included (as an annexe) in the Cuban-US treaty of 1903. The opposition, led by black politician Juan Gualberto Gómez, succeeded in delaying but not preventing its approval by a small parliamentary majority.
  Over the next 30 years the US made continual use of the amendment, intervening to supervise elections or suppress 'disorder'. During 1906–9 a US-imposed 'provisional revolutionary government' was in power, after troops were sent at the request of President Tomás Estrada Palma. The amendment was abrogated by Cuba in 1934 with the consent of the US President F. D. Roosevelt, but the US continues to assert the right to occupy the Guantánamo naval base, acquired under the Platt Amendment.
See also **Guantánamo base; good neighbour policy.**

Playa Girón: see Bay of Pigs invasion.

Poindexter, Vice Admiral John: see Iran/contra affair.

Polk, James K.: see Monroe doctrine.

Ponce, Gen. Federico: see Ubico y Castañeda.

Ponce, Col. René Emilio: see *tanda*.

Pope John XXIII: see liberation theology.

Pope John Paul II: see Latin American Bishops' Council.

Pope Paul VI: see Latin American Bishops' Council.

Popular Action Front (FAP): see guerrilla movements (Honduras).

Popular Alliance: see **Communist Party** (Costa Rica).

Popular Christian Democrat Tendency (TPDC): see **Democratic Revolutionary Front** (El Salvador).

'popular Church': see **Christian base community.**

Popular Democratic Party (*Partido Popular Democrático*/PPD)
Political party in Puerto Rico, supporting the island's present autonomous status, which it fought for and obtained in 1952. Founded in 1938 by Luis Muñoz Marín, it won half the seats in the legislature in the 1940 general election with 38% of the vote (a one-vote majority in the senate, but no majority in the house of representatives) and Muñoz became government leader as senate president. It won again in 1944 (64%), 1948 (63%) and 1952 (65%) and became a social democratic party. In 1965, Muñoz retired after 16 years as governor and party leader and handed over to his deputy Roberto Sánchez Vilella.

After a split with Muñoz, Sánchez Vilella failed to win nomination in 1968 for a second term as governor and ran on a minor party ticket, splitting the vote and ensuring victory for the new pro-statehood New Progressive Party (PNP) despite a 1967 plebiscite (61%) against statehood. Rafael Hernández Colón won back the governorship for the PPD in 1972, but was beaten by the PNP in 1976 and 1980. But the PPD won control of both houses of the legislature in 1980 and, helped by splits and scandals during the rule of the PNP's Carlos Romero Barceló, it recaptured the governorship with Hernández Colón in 1984. He was re-elected in 1988.
See also **Muñoz Marín; Hernández Colón.**

Popular Forum: see **FAPU; Romero Mena.**

Popular Independence Committee: see **Douglas, Rosie.**

Popular Liberation Forces (*Fuerzas Populares de Liberación-Farabundo Martí*/FPL-FM)
A guerrilla organisation founded in March 1970 by breakaway members of the Salvadorean Communist Party (PCS) led by secretary general Salvador Cayetano Carpio, a former baker's union leader. Nameless for the first two years of its existence, it then adopted the name of El Salvador's communist leader of the 1930s. The split with the PCS was largely over the latter's refusal to contemplate armed struggle. During the 1970s the FPL carried out sabotage actions against local and foreign companies, executed government collaborators, and attacked army and national guard barracks, as well as other government installations; kidnapped several businessmen, government officials and diplomats, including foreign minister Mauricio Borgonovo in 1977 and South African ambassador Archibald Gardner Dunn in 1979. Both men were killed when the FPL's demands were not met, but ransom money acquired by the group during this period totalled millions of dollars. By the end of the decade it had established a stronghold in the northern department (province) of Chalatenango, and on joining forces in 1980 with other

guerrilla groups to form the FMLN was regarded as the largest and most important. By the late 1970s, in common with the other groups, it had formed a civilian front organisation (*organización popular*), the Popular Revolutionary Bloc (BPR), whose mass base was strongest among peasants (FECCAS-UTC), slumdwellers (UPT), teachers (ANDES–21 de Junio) and students (UR–19 and MERS).

Up to 1983 the FPL maintained a strategy of 'prolonged popular war', viewing the insurrectionary 'final offensive' of January 1981 as an error and looking askance at proposals by other groups for negotiations with 'progressive sectors' in the armed forces. But by early 1983 a powerful minority within its leadership, headed by second-in-command Mélida Anaya Montes (Comandante Ana María) was pushing for an accommodation over strategy with the leaders of the ERP in particular. On 6 April 1983, Ana María was assassinated in Managua by a group led by Rogelio Bazzaglia ('Marcelo'), an FPL leader close to Carpio. Six days later Carpio himself, who had been abroad at the time of the murder, took his own life, according to the official version. The outcome was a much weakened organisation which lost hegemony within the FMLN to the ERP and the Communist Party (whose strategy became dominant). Salvador Sánchez Cerén ('Leonel González') eventually emerged as Carpio's successor.

See also **Farabundo Martí National Liberation Front; Popular Revolutionary Bloc; Martí, Agustín Farabundo; Salvadorean Communist Party; People's Revolutionary Army** (El Salvador).

Popular Movement for an Independent Guadeloupe (*Mouvement Populaire pour une Guadeloupe Indépendante*/MPGI): see **Reinette; Guadeloupe, independence movements.**

Popular Party (PP): see **Lombardo Toledano.**

Popular Revolutionary Bloc (*Bloque Popular Revolucionario*/BPR)
A mass organisation founded in El Salvador in 1975 in response to an army attack on a student demonstration on 30 July 1975. The founding members of the BPR were the Christian Federation of Salvadorean Peasants (FECCAS), the Union of Rural Workers (UTC), the Union of Slumdwellers (UPT), the National Association of Salvadorean Teachers (ANDES–21 de Junio), the Revolutionary Students (UR–19) and the Movement of Secondary School Students (MERS). Although FECCAS had been founded by Catholic priests, the BPR was from the outset explicitly socialist, favouring a worker-peasant alliance and linked with the Popular Liberation Forces (FPL) guerrilla movement. Like the FPL it believed in a strategy of 'prolonged struggle', dismissing the electoral participation put forward by the UNO coalition and the 'anti-fascist broad alliance' proposed by the United Popular Action Front (FAPU). In January 1980 the BPR (which at the time claimed over 80,000 members) joined with other 'popular organisations' to form the Revolutionary Mass Co-ordinating Committee (CRM), which later became part of the Democratic Revolutionary Front (FDR).

See also **Popular Liberation Forces; Democratic Revolutionary Front** (El Salvador); **FAPU.**

Popular Social Christian Party (*Partido Popular Social Cristiano/* PPSC)
Founded in 1976 as a rurally-based left-wing splinter from the Social Christian Party (PSC) and originally known as the Nicaraguan Social Christian Party (PSCN) or 'Edgar Macías' faction. At one time the PPSC had greater influence over the CTN union confederation than did the PSC. It joined the Broad Opposition Front (FAO) in 1978 but left shortly afterwards in protest at US manipulation. It was a founder member, in February 1979, of the pro-Sandinista National Patriotic Front (FPN), and of its post-revolution successors, the BPP and the FPR. It presented a presidential candidate (general secretary Mauricio Díaz) in the 1984 elections and came fourth, with six seats, in the national assembly elections, 40% of its vote coming from urban areas. The PPSC favours the promotion of co-operatives to extend workers' control, and has a small trade union affiliate, the CTN(A). Díaz was strongly criticised in early 1987 by PPSC members and others both for signing a '9-point peace proposal' with extra-parliamentary groups and for holding talks with US envoy Philip Habib in Costa Rica. In 1989, however, he expressed reservations about a grand alliance of the opposition because of the links between some parties and the US-backed contra rebels. The PPSC left the ranks of the opposition UNO alliance in late 1989 for an electoral pact with the PSC in the February 1990 elections.
See also **Social Christian Party.**

Popular Socialist Party (PSP) (Cuba): see **Communist Party** (Cuba).

Popular Socialist Party (PSP) (Mexico): see **Lombardo Toledano; National Democratic Front.**

Popular Union for the Liberation of Guadeloupe (*Union Populaire pour la Libération de la Guadeloupe/*UPLG)**:** see **Guadeloupe, independence movements.**

Popular Unity: see **Honduran Patriotic Front.**

Popular Vanguard (VP): see **Communist Party** (Costa Rica).

Populism
A term used in the Latin American context to describe mass popular movements involving a multi-class alliance, based on an emotive call (e.g. nationalism, social justice), and often organised around a single charismatic leader. The exact definition of the concept remains the subject of academic debate. Although at times it is used to refer to the attempt by intellectuals to work with the rural poor (a 'back to the land' movement), its most frequent usage is in the context of urban politics. Perhaps the best-known contemporary Central American populist figure was Arnulfo Arias of Panama, whose campaigns sought to bring together a

multi-class coalition around strong nationalist rhetoric. In Latin America as a whole examples include the movements led by Gen. Juan Domingo Perón in Argentina (Peronism) and Getúlio Vargas in Brazil (*trabalhismo*), both of which, in different ways, sought to introduce the demands and aspirations of the urban working classes and sectors of the rural poor to the political system. There have been many other movements which can be described as wholly or partly populist – they include Víctor Raúl Haya de la Torre's APRA in Peru and Assad Bucaram's Concentration of Popular Forces (CFP) in Ecuador.
See also **Arias Madrid.**

Portes Gil, Emilio: see Calles.

Powell, Michael
b. 10 April 1939. Deputy prime minister and minister of agriculture of St Kitts-Nevis 1983– . After becoming general secretary of the opposition-controlled Working People's Union, Powell was elected vice-president of the opposition People's Action Movement (PAM) in 1976 when Kennedy Simmonds was elected party leader. He became deputy prime minister to Simmonds when PAM came to power after elections in 1980.
See also **People's Action Movement; Simmonds.**

premier (Anglo-Caribbean)
The leader of an internally self-governing country in the English-speaking or Commonwealth Caribbean. On full independence, the title changes to prime minister. Under the British colonial system, the first degree of self-government in the 1950s produced cabinets chaired by the white British governor but led by a local politician who took the post of minister of trade and production. The next stage produced a cabinet headed by a chief minister, followed by one led by a premier.

La Prensa (Nicaragua)
A Nicaraguan daily paper, founded in 1926 by the Chamorro family. *La Prensa* was edited until his assassination in 1978 by Pedro Joaquín Chamorro, a prominent Conservative opponent of the Somoza dynasty whose murder was attributed to gunmen linked to the Somozas. The newspaper had become the voice of opposition business and professional groups and was often censored under the dictatorship. On one occasion it was shut down for a year, and during the 1978–9 revolution its offices were bombed and shelled by the National Guard. After the Sandinista victory of 1979 it became an equally fervent opponent of the new government. In 1980, 160 of its staff, under Xavier Chamorro Cardenal (Pedro Joaquín's brother), left to form an independent, pro-Sandinista paper, *El Nuevo Diario*.

Pedro Joaquín Chamorro Barrios, son of his murdered namesake, edited *La Prensa* until 1984, when he went into exile to join forces with the armed opposition, leaving his uncle, Jaime Chamorro, and his mother, Violeta Barrios de Chamorro (a member of the revolutionary junta until April 1980), in charge, along with editor Pablo Antonio Cuadra. (The other Nicaraguan newspaper, the official Sandinista organ

Barricada, is also edited by a family member, Pedro Joaquín Jr's brother, Carlos Fernando.) Forty editions of *La Prensa* were recalled for violations of censorship regulations before it was closed down on 26 June 1986 for allegedly acting as a mouthpiece for the US administration and accepting money from the CIA. The ban was imposed one day after the US Congress approved $100m in aid to the contras. *La Prensa* has received several hundred thousand dollars from a semi-official US institution, the National Endowment for Democracy, which was set up in 1983.

The reopening of *La Prensa* on 21 September 1987 was in fulfilment of the government's commitments under the terms of the Arias peace plan. The newspaper immediately went on the offensive, blaming the government for the war and refusing to condemn US support for the contras. It was again closed, for two weeks, in July 1988. In 1990 Violeta Chamorro was elected president of Nicaragua at the head of the victorious UNO coalition.

See also **Chamorro Cardenal, Pedro Joaquín; Barrios de Chamorro.**

Price, George

b. 15 January 1919. Prime minister and foreign minister of Belize 1981–4; Prime minister, finance, defence and internal affairs minister 1989– .
Educated at St John's College, Belize City, George Price studied for the priesthood at St Augustin Seminary, Mississippi, but decided against taking holy orders. Before entering politics he worked as secretary to a wealthy trader. He became a city councillor (1947–62) and was mayor of Belize City in 1956. From 1947–1952 he was president of the General Workers' Union, and in 1950 he became a founder member of the People's United Party (PUP). He served as party secretary 1950–56, becoming leader of the PUP in 1956. From 1954–1960 he was a member of the legislative council, although in 1957 he was dismissed by the British government for having had contact with Guatemalan diplomats in London. He subsequently served as a member of the legislative assembly (1960–65); first minister (1961–3); member of the house of representatives (1965–84) and premier and minister of finance and economic development (1964–81). Price, who has described himself as a 'Christian democrat', led the country to independence in 1981 and became its first prime minister. He lost his own seat in the 1984 elections, but retained the post of party leader, to which he was re-elected again in 1986. In September 1989 he won a narrow election victory over Manuel Esquivel's UDP and once more became prime minister.

See also: **Belize dispute; People's United Party; United Democratic Party.**

Prío Socarrás, Carlos: see *Granma.*

PRODEMCA: see American Institute for Free Labor Development.

Progressive Action Party (PAP): see Batista y Zaldívar.

Progressive Democratic Party (PDP): see Bramble; Osborne, John.

Progressive Labour Movement (PLM)

Former Antiguan political party. Founded in 1968 by Antigua Workers' Union leader George Walter and radical schoolteacher Tim Hector, it came to power after beating the Antigua Labour Party 13–4 at the 1971 general election. Walter's mildly repressive rule led to the PLM's defeat 5–12 at the 1976 poll. When Walter was jailed in 1979 for corruption, Robert Hall, a white planter, took over as leader. The party lost the 1980 election 3–14. The Antigua Workers' Union broke with the party the same year and Walter left it as well. The PLM won only 9% of the vote at the 1984 elections and unofficially merged with the United National Democratic Party before the 1989 general election.
See also **Walter; Antigua Labour Party; Hector.**

Progressive Labour Party (PLP) (Bermuda)

Founded in 1963 as a socialist party to express the rising demands of Bermuda's poor and powerless black majority. Led by lawyer Walter Robinson, it won six seats in parliament at elections later that year. The party won 10 of the 40 seats in the 1968 election, but Robinson was defeated. He was succeeded by his deputy, Lois Browne-Evans, who took a centre-left, pro-Caribbean stance. The party again won 10 seats at the 1972 election. Robinson was elected and resumed the leadership but stepped down again in favour of Browne-Evans in 1976. The PLP lost the 1976 election 14–26 to the white-dominated United Bermuda Party (UBP). The party then dropped socialism and toned down its racial militancy. But Browne-Evans and the PLP campaigned against the execution of a black Bermudan for the 1973 murder of the British governor, Sir Richard Sharples, warning of a racial explosion. The hanging was carried out in 1977 and serious rioting erupted.

The party came within 150 votes of winning power at the 1980 election, losing 18–22 to the UBP. After it lost again (14–26) in the 1983 election, the party split over whether or not to move left. Browne-Evans expelled four right-wing PLP MPs, who in 1985 formed the National Liberal Party (NLP). At the general election later that year, the PLP won only seven seats, while the NLP rebels captured two. Browne-Evans was replaced as leader by her deputy, lawyer Frederick Wade (b. 1939). The party doubled its representation at the 1989 election, which it lost 15–25. The PLP officially advocates independence but has not made it a priority.
See also **Browne-Evans; National Liberal Party; 'black power'; United Bermuda Party.**

Progressive Labour Party (PLP) (St Lucia)

Left-wing party in St Lucia. Founded in 1981 by former deputy prime minister George Odlum, when he and other radicals broke away from the St Lucia Labour Party (SLP) after Odlum lost a fight for the leadership. Former SLP minister Michael Pilgrim became deputy PLP leader and then interim prime minister of a three-party coalition for four months until general elections in 1982. The party obtained 27% of the vote but only one seat, won by Odlum's brother Jon. The SLP leader, Julian Hunte, refused to ally himself with the PLP for the two 1987 elections and the SLP was narrowly defeated. The PLP won 9.2% of the vote but no seats.

See also **Odlum, George; St Lucia Labour Party; Josie; Hunte.**

Progressive Liberal Party (PLP)

Political party in the Bahamas. Founded in 1953 to fight against the corruption and racism of the white ruling class known as the 'Bay Street Boys', it won 6 of the 28 elective seats in parliament in the 1956 elections and lawyer Lynden Pindling became the party's leader. A long taxi-drivers' strike in 1958 organised by left-wing trade union leader Randol Fawkes (b. 20 March 1924) led to constitutional advances and the PLP won five more seats at by-elections in 1960. But the white-dominated United Bahamian Party (UBP) won a surprise 19–8 victory over the PLP at the 1962 general election.

Parliamentary violence by PLP MPs and a subsequent PLP split in 1965 failed to harm the party and, financed by foreign gambling interests, it tied 18–18 with the UBP at the 1967 general election. Fawkes and a white independent held the balance and agreed to allow Pindling to become premier, thereby inaugurating black majority rule. The party increased its majority to 29–9 at the 1968 elections. In 1970, education minister Cecil Wallace-Whitfield, three other ministers and four more PLP MPs broke away and formed the Free National Movement (1971). But the PLP was little affected and won elections in 1972 (28–10), 1977 (30–8), 1982 (32–11) and 1987 (31–18).

See also **Pindling; United Bahamian Party; Free National Movement; Wallace-Whitfield; 'black power'.**

Progressive National Party (PNP)

Political party in the Turks and Caicos Islands. Founded as the Progressive National Organisation by Norman Saunders and Nathaniel 'Bops' Francis (b. 6 May 1912) before the 1976 general election, which it lost 4–7. It changed its name to the PNP, opposed independence, won the 1980 elections and Saunders became chief minister. The PNP won the 1984 election 8–3, but in 1985 Saunders was arrested with two government members in Miami and jailed in the US on drug conspiracy charges. He was replaced as chief minister by his deputy, Francis. An official enquiry in 1986 into corruption and arson declared Francis unfit for public office. Commerce, development and tourism minister Ariel Misick (b. 11 August 1951) resigned and Francis and his government were forced to quit. The governor then imposed direct rule. Francis was replaced as party leader in 1987 by Dan Malcolm. The party lost the 1988 general election 2–11, and Robert Hall became its leader, with Alden Durham its parliamentary leader.

See also **Saunders, Norman.**

Progress With Dignity: see Ebanks; Bodden, Norman.

Project Democracy: see Iran/contra affair.

Pro-Patria Party: see Martínez, Gen. Maximiliano Hernández.

Public Order Law (El Salvador): see Romero Mena.

Puerto Ordaz Agreement: see San José Agreement.

Puerto Rican Independence Party (*Partido Independentista Puertorriqueno*/PIP)
Main pro-independence party in Puerto Rico. Founded in 1946 by Gilberto Concepción de Gracia as a breakaway from the Popular Democratic Party to campaign against the dangers to local cultural independence of the massive North American industrialisation of Operation Bootstrap. Concepción de Gracia died in 1967 and was succeeded in 1969 by Rubén Berrios. The party stands for democratic socialism and has toned down its calls for independence in recent years. The PIP won 19% of the vote at the 1952 elections, but its share has since fallen to around 5%. The PIP won two seats in the house of representatives and one in the senate at the 1988 elections. Pro-independence groups boycotted a 1967 plebiscite, which voted 60% to retain the island's 'commonwealth' status. A new plebiscite is planned for 1991.
See also **Berrios; Puerto Rico, nationalist violence; Mari Bras; Operation Bootstrap.**

Puerto Rican model: see Operation Bootstrap.

Puerto Rican Popular Army (*Ejercito Popular Boricua*/EPB): see Macheteros.

Puerto Rican Renewal Party: see New Progressive Party; Romero Barceló.

Puerto Rican Socialist Party (*Partido Socialista Puertorriqueño*/PSP): see Mari Bras.

PUERTO RICO, Commonwealth of
Capital: San Juan
Area: 8,959 sq km
Population (1988): 3.3m (75% urban)
Pop. growth rate: 0.5%
Pop. density: 368/sq km
Infant mortality: 37 per thousand
Life expectancy at birth: 75
Literacy: 89%
GDP per capita (1988): US$6,171
Foreign debt per capita (1988): US$3,637
Main exports: chemicals, pharmaceuticals, petroleum, textiles and clothing, tourism, rum, electronics

Political system
An internally self-governing possession (since 1898) of the United States, and (since 1952) officially a 'free associated state' or 'commonwealth'. A plebiscite will be held on 4 June 1991 to choose between this status, independence and statehood as the 51st state of the USA. Puerto Ricans

have US citizenship and serve in the US armed forces, but do not vote in US elections or pay US taxes. They elect a non-voting member (resident commissioner) of the US House of Representatives. Under the 1952 constitution, the islanders elect their own governor, a 53-member House of Representatives and a 27-member Senate every four years.

Governor: Rafael Hernández Colón (1985)
Resident commissioner in the US: Jaime Fuster (1985)
Last elections: 1988

Political organisations

Parties in the Legislative Assembly (leader) (seats in House/Senate): Popular Democratic Party/PPD (Rafael Hernández Colón) (36/18), f. 1938; New Progressive Party/PNP (Carlos Romero Barceló) (15/8), f. 1967; Puerto Rican Independence Party/PIP (Rubén Berrios Martínez) (2/1), f. 1946.

Parties and groups outside parliament: Puerto Rican Socialist Party/PSP (Carlos Gallisá), f. 1971; National Liberation Armed Forces/FALN (Oscar Lopez Rivera), f. 1974; Los Macheteros (Puerto Rican Popular Army/EPB) (Filiberto Ojeda Ríos), f. 1978; Industrial Mission/MI (Wilfredo López); National Ecumenical Movement of Puerto Rico-Prisa/MENPR-Prisa (Eunice Santana).

Main trade unions: International Ladies' Garment Workers' Union/ILGWU (Clifford Depin); General Workers' Council/CGT (Luis Amaury Suárez Zayas), f. 1940; Puerto Rican Hotel and Restaurant Employees' Union/La Gastronómica; Electrical and Irrigation Workers' Union/UTIER (Herminio Martínez Rodríguez); General Workers' Union/UGT (Osvaldo Romero Pizarro), f. 1948; Puerto Rican Workers' Federation/CPT (Federico Torres), f. 1982; General Union of Puerto Rican Workers/UGTPR (Adolfo Martínez), f. 1948; Puerto Rico Industrial Workers' Union/PRIWU (David Muñoz Vázquez); Unión de Tronquistas (Teamsters) (José Cadiz); Puerto Rico Teachers' Association/AMPR (José Eligio Vélez).

Employers' organisations: Puerto Rico Manufacturers' Association (Hector Jiménez Juarbe), f. 1928; Pharamaceutical Industry Association of Puerto Rico/AIFPR (Iris Santini); Puerto Rico Farmers' Association/AAPR (Antonio Alvarez).
See also **Vieques; Culebra.**

Puerto Rico, nationalist violence

The first major clash in modern times was an armed attack on the governor's mansion in San Juan in October 1950 led by nationalist Pedro Albizu Campos (1891–1964). Governor Luis Muñoz Marín was uninjured and Albizu was jailed. Two days later, gunmen attacked Blair House in Washington, President Harry Truman's temporary residence. Subsequent violence on the island left 32 dead. In 1954, three men and a woman opened fire in the US House of Representatives, wounding four congressmen. They served 25 years in prison.

In July 1978, police murdered two pro-independence militants on Cerro

Maravilla mountain, near Ponce, claiming the two youths had intended to attack a television transmitter. They had been lured there by a police spy. The government tried to cover the affair up, but between 1985 and 1987, a total of five ex-policemen were jailed for up to 30 years for the killings. In 1981, the Macheteros group claimed responsibility for blowing up nine planes at a US military base on the island.

Half a dozen small, pro-independence guerrilla groups have staged bombings and other attacks in the island and the US since the late 1960s. Prominent among them have been the Armed Liberation Commandos (CAL), the National Liberation Armed Forces (FALN), the Macheteros, also called the Puerto Rican Popular Army (EPB), and the Organisation of Volunteers for the Puerto Rican Revolution. The FALN and the Macheteros announced in 1979 that they were joining forces. In 1987 the existence of secret Puerto Rican police files on more than 100,000 suspected militants was disclosed.

See also **Macheteros; National Liberation Armed Forces; Puerto Rican Independence Party; Mari Bras; Romero Barceló; invasions and occupations by the United States.**

Q

Querrard, Charles: see **Saint Barthélémy; de Haenen.**

La Quina (*Hernández Galicia, Joaquín*)
b. 1922. A powerful and politically influential Mexican oil workers' leader who was arrested in early 1989 in a dramatic move by the new president, Carlos Salinas de Gortari. The son of an oil worker and a welder by trade, La Quina rose through the ranks of Local 1 of the STPRM (*Sindicato de Trabajadores Petroleros de la República Mexicana*). In 1962 he was elected general secretary of the STPRM. Although he later stepped down from this post, he continued to control the union from his base in Ciudad Madero, building up a network of union, political and business interests. His success was attributed to a combination of charisma, Mafia-style strong-arm tactics and the placing of friends and supporters in key union posts. Aligned with the Institutional Revolutionary Party (PRI) old guard, La Quina was opposed to the choice of Salinas de Gortari for the presidential succession, even suggesting that oil workers should vote for the opposition instead. He also made his opposition to Salinas' economic policies clear. In January 1989 the new president ordered police and army units to arrest La Quina on charges of gun-running and corruption. The union leader was seized after a gun battle, and attempts to organise a national oil workers' strike on his behalf failed. The pre-emptive strike against him by Salinas de Gortari was widely considered a successful and popular move.
See also **Confederation of Mexican Workers; Salinas de Gortari.**

Quisqueyan Democratic Party (*Partido Quisqueyano Democrata*/PQD): see **Wessin y Wessin.**

R

'rabiblancos'

Literally, 'white-tailed ones'. A slang term for the Panamanian oligarchy, comprising the so-called '20 families' who ran the country until the 1968 Torrijos coup and who remain dominant in the economy.

Radio Martí

A US government-funded, Spanish language, propaganda station, based at Marathon, Florida, and aimed at Cuba. Named after Cuba's national hero, Radio Martí went on the air on Cuban independence day, 20 May 1985, resulting in a sharp deterioration in relations between Washington and Havana. Cuba immediately suspended immigration agreements with the US, including one signed the previous December, and announced plans to jam US commercial radio stations and to abrogate its anti-hijack accord with the US. The emigration of Cubans to the US did not resume until September 1986, and it was November 1987 before the full scope of previous immigration agreements was restored. The Voice of America (VOA) network is responsible for Radio Martí programming. In September 1987 the station's Miami bureau chief resigned, alleging that reporters were being compelled to gather intelligence and that most professional journalists had already left the organisation. In March 1990 the VOA began TV Martí broadcasts to Cuba. Havana immediately retaliated by jamming the signal and disrupting radio stations in Florida.
See also **Martí, José**.

Radio Soleil: see **Haiti, Roman Catholic Church**.

Radix, Kendrick

b. 25 November 1941. Grenadian politician. Radix and fellow-barrister Maurice Bishop founded the leftist Movement for Assemblies of the People in 1972, which a year later merged with another group to form the New Jewel Movement (NJM). Radix, one of the four senior NJM leaders, became minister of legal affairs when the NJM seized power in 1979. He was forced out of the NJM central committee in 1982 by radicals around deputy prime minister Bernard Coard and resigned as minister of industrial development, legal affairs, agroindustries and fishing after Bishop's arrest during the 1983 leadership crisis. The anti-Bishop faction jailed him and he was freed after the US invasion. He then founded, with fellow ex-minister George Louison, the Maurice Bishop Patriotic

Movement. He yielded the party leadership to Terry Marryshow in 1988 and became party president.

See also **New Jewel Movement; Maurice Bishop Patriotic Movement; Marryshow, Terry; Grenada, US invasion (1983); Bishop; Coard; Louison.**

Rally of National Progressive Democrats (*Rassemblement des Démocrates Nationaux Progressistes*/RDNP): see **Manigat.**

Rama Indians: see **Atlantic Coast** (Nicaragua).

Ramírez, Erick: see **Social Christian Party.**

Ramos Soto, Oswaldo: see **National Party.**

Rappaccioli, Mario: see **Democratic Conservative Party.**

rastafarians

A loosely-organised religious sect which grew up in the slums of Kingston, Jamaica, in the 1930s around the belief that the Ethiopian Emperor Haile Selassie (Ras Tafari) was the god-king of all Africans and that blacks should aim to return to Africa, their true spiritual home. Haile Selassie visited Jamaica in 1966. The rastas were inspired by the black nationalism of Marcus Garvey, who idealised Ethiopia as the symbol of Africa and had said that the crowning of a black king in Africa would mean deliverance was near. Haile Selassie subsequently came to the throne and was crowned in 1930. Garvey later denounced Haile Selassie as a tyrant, however.

Rastas usually wear their hair in long matted braids (dreadlocks), africanise their names, spurn material possessions, are frequently vegetarians and often smoke *ganja* (marijuana), which they regard as holy. Rastafarianism helped fuel the 'black power' movement, but otherwise its political influence is limited by the refusal of most rastas to vote in elections, which they regard as part of the corruption of 'Babylon' (non-rastafarian society). Jamaican rastafarian musician and superstar Bob Marley (1945–81) introduced reggae music to the world in the 1970s, popularised rastafarianism and became a symbol of black pride and nationalism.

Rastafarians have frequently been persecuted in the Caribbean for their lifestyle. They were harassed, brutalised and jailed by police in Jamaica until the mid-1960s. In Dominica the government passed a law in 1974 known as the Dread Act, authorising citizens to shoot rastas dead on sight. The law was prompted by local violence blamed on rastas. In Grenada, the left-wing government which seized power in 1979 at first tried to embrace the rastas as part of its pioneering efforts to foster Caribbean culture. But the regime turned against them in 1981 when they proved intractable, and arrests were made.

Rastafarians were involved in a brief revolt on Union Island in 1979 against the St Vincent government. Its leader, a rasta called Lennox 'Bumber' Charles, was protesting against government neglect of the island.

See also **dreads; Garvey; 'black power'; People's Revolutionary Government; Union Island Revolt (1979);** *noirisme*; **Césaire.**

Rat Island meeting (1970): see **'new left'.**

Ratzinger, Cardinal Joseph: see liberation theology.

Raudales, Gen. Ramón: see Fonseca Amador.

raza cósmica: see indigenismo.

Rebel Armed Forces (*Fuerzas Armadas Rebeldes*/FAR)
A Guatemalan guerrilla group, founded in 1962, which originated in an abortive 13 November 1960 army revolt led by Col. Rafael Sessán Pereira against President Ydígoras Fuentes. The two lieutenants who were involved, Marco Antonio Yon Sosa and Luis Augusto Turcios Lima, returned clandestinely from a brief exile to organise the 'Alejandro de León' November 13 Revolutionary Movement (MR–13), named after a rebel officer killed in combat, which went into action in the Sierra de las Minas in February 1962, sparking a widespread popular revolt which was none the less crushed with relative ease within two months. In December 1962 the MR–13 joined the Communist Party (PGT) and radical student activists in forming FAR, whose role was to co-ordinate surviving guerrilla units. Political leadership was in the hands of the PGT-dominated United Resistance Front (FUR), on which MR–13 had no representation. The low priority given to the armed struggle by the communists led to tension, and for a time the FAR guerrillas were closer to the 4th International ('Posadas' section). Turcios Lima, however, was unhappy with the Trotskyist line, and in 1964 he led the FAR (Edgar Ibarra Front) in a split with Yon Sosa's MR–13. Yon Sosa too broke with the Trotskyists in 1966, though his differences were less ideological and his strategy did not change. Turcios Lima died that same year in a mysterious car accident.

   In 1967 the two wings were reunified under Yon Sosa, and in January 1968 a formal break took place between FAR and the PGT, with the former accusing the communists of supplying the ideas while they supplied the combatants. The PGT response was to form its own FAR, whose initials stood for 'Revolutionary' Armed Forces. In 1968, FAR took credit for the assassination of US ambassador John Mien. By the end of the decade the guerrillas were effectively defeated by a US-assisted counter-insurgency campaign. In the early 1970s the surviving FAR leaders re-established bases in the northern jungle (Petén department) and in the east around Lake Izabal, after acknowledging the inadequacy of their previous *foquista* strategy. They also resumed working with the PGT, and concentrated most of their efforts on union organising among urban and rural workers. In January 1982 they joined other guerrilla groups in the URNG coalition. In 1983 they kidnapped the sister of President Ríos Montt and later the sister of his successor, Gen. Mejía Víctores. Both were released after FAR propaganda was published in the press. Forced back into Petén by the early 1980s counter-insurgency drives, FAR continued low-intensity operations, claiming five fronts in mid-1985, including Alta Verapaz and Chimaltenango. Leader (1990): Pablo Monsanto. See also *foquismo*; **Guatemalan National Revolutionary Unity.**

Reformist Party (*Partido Reformista*/PR): see **Balaguer.**

Regalado, Antonio: see **Romero, Archbishop Oscar Arnulfo.**

Regional Centre for Telecommunications: see **death squad.**

Regional Confederation of Mexican Workers (CROM): see **Confederation of Mexican Workers.**

Regional Federation of Salvadorean Workers (FRTES): see **Martí, Agustín Farabundo.**

Regional Security System (RSS)

A military alliance between six small Eastern Caribbean states at the instigation of the US, Britain and Barbados and aimed at the prevention of coups d'etat and subversion. It was mainly inspired by the advent of the left-wing government in Grenada (1979) and revolts in Union Island (St Vincent) (1979) and Dominica (1981). It was launched in 1982 when Antigua-Barbuda, Dominica, St Lucia, St Vincent and Barbados signed a memorandum of understanding, but it received its chief impetus after the 1983 US invasion of Grenada. St Kitts-Nevis joined on independence in 1983 and Grenada in 1985.

The main features of the RSS are the presence of US-trained and equipped Special Security Units (SSUs) on four of the islands, the 300-member Barbados defence force and co-operation between national coastguard forces. Britain and Canada also help finance and train the RSS forces. Barbadian prime minister Tom Adams was a leading organiser of the RSS, which has its headquarters in Barbados. The use of the RSS was questioned by Adams's successor Errol Barrow and St Vincent's James Mitchell, who opposed upgrading the 1982 memorandum into a full treaty.
See also **Special Service Units; Grenada, US invasion (1983); Union Island revolt (1979); Adams, Tom; Barrow; Mitchell, James; military bases (foreign) in the Caribbean.**

Reid Cabral, Donald

b. 9 June 1923. President of the Dominican Republic 1963–5. A lawyer and car dealer, Reid Cabral served on the provisional council of state, 1962–3, before becoming in late 1963 president of a civilian junta which had taken over after the army's overthrow of President Juan Bosch that year. Reid's disastrous economic policies, increasing repression, his self-appointment as armed forces minister in 1965 and his plan to cut the military budget led to his overthrow in April 1965 by a leftist army revolt which sparked a US military invasion. He was foreign minister under President Joaquín Balaguer 1986–8.
See also **Bosch, Juan; Dominican Republic, US invasion (1965); Balaguer.**

Reina, Carlos Roberto and Jorge Arturo: see Liberal Party (Honduras).

Reinette, Luc
b. 9 August 1950. Pro-independence Guadeloupean politician. A former housing official, Reinette was briefly jailed in 1981 in connection with bomb attacks by the Armed Liberation Group (GLA), which he founded in 1979. He helped found the Popular Movement for an Independent Guadeloupe (MPGI) in 1982. He was also leader of the Caribbean Revolutionary Alliance (ARC), which emerged in 1983, and was sentenced to 23 years in jail in 1985 for a series of bombings in the island and elsewhere in 1983. However, he escaped from prison later that year. Reinette and other ARC leaders were recaptured in St Vincent in 1987 after they fled Martinique in a small plane to Guyana and then Suriname, both of which refused to admit them. He was released under amnesty in 1989.
See also Guadeloupe, independence movements.

Republican Front of Guatemala: see Ríos Montt.

Republican Party (Costa Rica): see Social Christian Unity Party.

Republican Party (Panama) (*Partido Republicano*/PR)
A Panamanian party whose distant origins lie in the Renovatory Liberal Party (PLR) founded in 1932. The PR was created in 1960 by J. D. Bazán and Max and Eric Arturo Delvalle, all of them Jewish and backed by the Jewish business community. Bazán was briefly vice-president to Arnulfo Arias in his 11-day government of 1968, despite Arias' well-known anti-semitism. The party was reborn in 1981 with a view to participating in the 1984 elections, though this time the 'Jewish vote' was more widely dispersed. Bazán and the Delvalles were again at its head, and the party was even more clearly allied to the country's wealthy élite, with policies of untramelled free enterprise and embryonic authoritarianism. It joined the Unade coalition behind official candidate Nicolás Ardito Barletta in 1984, winning two seats. Eric Arturo Delvalle became first vice-president, taking over the presidency when Ardito Barletta was overthrown by the military in 1985, but he in turn was ousted in February 1988 when he tried to dismiss Defence Forces chief Gen. Noriega. The PR joined the official COLINA coalition for the 1989 elections.
See also Delvalle; National Liberation Coalition.

Rerum Novarum labour federation: see Monge Alvarez.

Revolution (Cuba): see Cuban Revolutionary War.

Revolution (Mexico): see Mexican Revolution.

Revolution (Nicaragua): see Sandinista National Liberation Front.

Revolutionary Action Party (PAR): see Arévalo Bermejo.

Revolutionary Co-ordinating Committee of the Masses (CRM): see Democratic Revolutionary Front (El Salvador).

Revolutionary Democratic Liberal Movement (M-Líder): see Liberal Party (Honduras).

Revolutionary Democratic Union (URD): see Christian Democrat Party (Guatemala).

Revolutionary Military Council (RMC)
After the murder of Grenadian prime minister Maurice Bishop on 19 October 1983, his rivals in the New Jewel Movement regime announced a 15-man Revolutionary Military Council nominally headed by the army chief, Gen. Hudson Austin, but in fact directed by Bishop's one-time deputy Bernard Coard and several radical army officers. The council declared a round-the-clock curfew and tried unsuccessfully to soften regional hostility. Cuba's refusal of Austin's request for support apparently clinched a US decision to invade on 25 October. Austin, Coard and others were arrested, tried and in December 1986 sentenced to death for murdering Bishop.
See also Coard; Grenada, US invasion (1983); People's Revolutionary Government; Bishop.

Revolutionary National Party (PNR): see Arias Madrid.

Revolutionary Party (Partido Revolucionario/PR)
A Guatemalan party with support in the middle classes and the bureaucracy, founded in 1957 by former participants in the 1944 'revolution', including Mario Méndez Montenegro, who was defeated in the presidential poll of 1958. The more reformist elements in the PR were expelled at the 1959 convention. Méndez Montenegro died before he could contest the 1966 election and his brother Julio César was nominated in his place. Although the latter was elected to the presidency, his reformist plans were frustrated by the army, which had tied his hands through a secret agreement signed before the election. The party lost office in 1970 and after a period of internal struggle emerged as a clearly right-wing force, forming an alliance with the Institutional Democratic Party (PID) to elect Gen. Romeo Lucas in 1978.

In 1982 the PR once more backed the official candidate, Gen. Aníbal Guevara. It won ten constituent assembly seats in 1984, and later that year forged a 'centrist' alliance with the newly-formed Union of the National Centre (UCN) and the Party of National Renewal (PNR). In July 1985, having withdrawn from this alliance, it joined forces with the Democratic Party of National Co-operation (PDCN), signalling a slight leftward drift. The two parties presented a joint presidential candidate (the PDCN's Serrano Elías) in 1985 and he obtained 14% of the vote. The party's presidential candidate in 1990 was to have been former foreign minister Fernando Andrade Díaz Durán. However, Andrade dropped out and PR leaders later spoke of backing for a military candidate. Secretary General (1990): Carlos Enrique Chavarría Pérez.
See also Democratic Party of National Co-operation; Institutional Democratic Party; Union of the National Centre.

Revolutionary Party of Centralamericanist Workers (PRTC) (El Salvador): see Farabundo Martí National Liberation Front; *foquismo.*

Revolutionary Party of Centralamericanist Workers-Honduras (PRTC-H): see guerrilla movements (Honduras).

Revolutionary Party of Democratic Unification (PRUD): see National Conciliation Party.

Revolutionary Student Directorate (DER): see Communist Party (Cuba); Integrated Revolutionary Organisations.

Revolutionary Union of the People (URP): see guerrilla movements (Honduras); Communist Party of Honduras.

Reyes Matta, Dr José María: see guerrilla groups (Honduras).

Rey Prendes, Julio Adolfo: see Christian Democrat Party (El Salvador).

Richard, Yves: see CATH.

Richards, Sir Edward: see United Bermuda Party.

'rifles and beans': see *fusiles y frijoles.*

Rio Group (*Group of Eight*)
Officially known as the Permanent Mechanism of Consultation and Political Coordination, the Rio Group (f. 1986, in Brazil) comprises the four nations of the Contadora Group, plus the four South American nations known as the Contadora Support Group (or Lima Group) formed on 29 July 1985. The support group initiative came from President Alan García of Peru, at whose inauguration the agreement was sealed. The other three nations are Argentina, Brazil and Uruguay, all of them recently restored to civilian rule. On 24/25 August 1985 the Lima Group met the Contadora foreign ministers in Cartagena, Colombia, to discuss implementation of the Contadora Act. On 11/12 January 1986 the foreign ministers of the eight issued the Caraballeda Message, defining the conditions for lasting peace in Central America and calling for a fresh impetus to the peace talks. This message was subsequently supported by the Central American nations and welcomed by the European Community. The Lima Group took part in many subsequent meetings of the Contadora Group, and the first formal Group of Eight summit took place in Acapulco, Mexico, in 1987. The second was held in Punta Arenas, Uruguay, the following year.

The Group's focus of attention was gradually broadened, and when in October 1989 the foreign ministers met at Ica, Peru, they discussed drug trafficking, the foreign debt and terrorism. Panama's membership of Contadora was suspended in February 1988, and the original title of 'Rio Group' revived in place of 'Group of Eight'. After the US invasion of December 1989 the Group called for fresh elections in Panama. The

Group said it might consider membership applications from Panama, as well as from Bolivia, Chile, Ecuador and Paraguay at its November 1990 summit in Caracas. In March 1990 the Contadora Group was wound up as an independent entity.
See also **Contadora Group.**

Rio Treaty (Inter-American Treaty on Reciprocal Assistance)
A regional security pact signed in Rio de Janeiro, Brazil, in 1947 and also known by its Spanish acronym, TIAR. Signatories (the US and most Latin American nations) agree to assist one another in the event of armed aggression within the hemisphere, and to consult one another in the event of armed aggression outside the hemisphere or of other types of aggression within it. The central principle of the treaty is that 'an armed attack by any State against an American State shall be considered as an attack against all', a principle enunciated in the Rio declaration of 1942 and embodied in the Act of Chapúltepec, 1945. Signatories also pledge not to resort to war, and to submit disputes for peaceful settlement within the organisation before resorting to the United Nations. The decision-making body for treaty purposes is a consultative meeting of foreign ministers of the Organisation of American States (OAS), though provisional decisions can be taken by the OAS Permanent Council. A two-thirds vote by ministers is binding on members. Sanctions contemplated by the treaty include diplomatic, economic and military measures. A protocol to the treaty was agreed in 1975 against US objections, though it has yet to be ratified. This would recognise 'ideological pluralism' and make the lifting of sanctions more straightforward. The treaty has been invoked on a score of occasions since its introduction, most of them involving situations in the Caribbean basin.
See also **Organisation of American States.**

Ríos Montt, Gen. José Efraín
b. 1927. President of Guatemala and commander-in-chief of the armed forces 1982–3. Born in Huehuetenango, Ríos Montt joined the army in 1943 and rose through the ranks. He studied at Fort Gulick (Canal Zone), at Fort Bragg, N. Carolina (counter-guerrilla operations), and at the Army School of War, Italy. His posts included commander of the Honour Guard Brigade and of the Mariscal Zavala Brigade; chief of the army general staff under President Carlos Arana; director of the Polytechnic (Military) School; Guatemalan representative on the Inter-American Defense Board and military attaché in Washington DC.

Ríos Montt retired from the army to fight the 1974 election as presidential candidate for the National Opposition Front (FNO), formed around the Christian Democrat Party (DCG), but was deprived of victory by a fraud in favour of the official candidate, Gen. Kjell Laugerud. Under protest, he was restored to active army status and ordered to take up the post of military attaché in Madrid (1974–8).

In 1978 he became a convert to a fundamentalist Protestant sect from California, the Church of the Word, and retired from the army again, but re-entered political life as the beneficiary of the 23 March 1982 coup

against President Lucas and president-elect Gen. Guevara; first as head
of a 3-man military junta and minister of defence; then (in June 1982) as
self-proclaimed president and commander-in-chief.

He replaced elected town mayors with his own appointees, introduced
the death penalty for a wide range of offences and ruled by decree under
state of siege regulations. In the fight against left-wing guerrillas he
initiated a large-scale scorched earth policy in rural areas. Under the
official title of *'fusiles y frijoles'* (literally 'rifles and beans') the army
concentrated the rural Indian population into 'model villages' and
expanded the civil defence patrols. Ríos Montt was overthrown by the
army on 8 August 1983 and replaced by Gen. Oscar Humberto Mejía
Víctores, in a move which restored the authority of the army hierarchy.
In 1989 a group of right-wing parties declared their support for his
presidential candidacy, and although this was ruled as unconstitutional
because of his previous assumption of power by force the general said
he would stand in the 1990 elections. The Republican Front of Guatemala
was created to back his candidacy.

See also *fusiles y frijoles*.

Rivas García, Oscar Humberto: see Institutional Democratic Party.

Rivas Gasteazoro, Eduardo: see Social Christian Party.

Rivera, Brooklyn: see Yatama.

Rivera, Diego: see Communist Party (Mexico).

Rivera, Julio Adalberto: see National Conciliation Party.

Rivero Aguero, Andrés: see Batista y Zaldívar.

Riviere, Bill: see Douglas, Michael.

Robelo Callejas, Alfonso
Nicaraguan businessman and politician. Trained in the US as a chemical
engineer, Alfonso Robelo founded the GRASCA cooking oil company
and other businesses in Nicaragua which were confiscated when he joined
the armed opposition. He was director of the University of Central
America (UCA), Managua, 1970–72, president of the Chamber of Commerce until 1975 and director of the Nicaraguan Development Institute
(INDE) up to 1978. Robelo entered politics in 1977. He founded the
Nicaraguan Democratic Movement (MDN) in April 1978 and played a
prominent part in the non-Sandinista opposition to the dictator Somoza
(notably the Broad Opposition Front/FAO), for which he was briefly
jailed by Somoza in May 1979. The MDN, whose initial base was among
cotton growers in the north-west, represented middle-ranking anti-
Somoza businessmen seeking a degree of social reform. Robelo was a
member of the first post-revolution junta, from which he resigned in
April 1980. He chaired the opposition Nicaraguan Democratic Co-ordinator (CDN) before going into exile in Costa Rica in 1982 and founding
ARDE with Edén Pastora, a decision which split the MDN.

In 1985 he was a joint founder, with Arturo Cruz and Adolfo Calero, of the United Nicaraguan Opposition. Robelo resigned from the directorate of UNO in April 1987, citing differences with Calero, but said he would continue to work with the organisation. The following month, with new UNO director Pedro Joaquín Chamorro, he announced the formation of the Nicaraguan Resistance (RN), but in early 1988 he formally withdrew from the contra movement to avoid expulsion from Costa Rica. Robelo endorsed the formation of the Coalition of the Democratic Centre (CCD) within the RN in October 1988. In late 1989 he announced his return to Nicaragua to join the opposition coalition (also known as UNO) under Violeta Chamorro. After Chamorro's victory he was appointed ambassador to Costa Rica.

See also **ARDE; Nicaraguan Resistance.**

Robinson, A. N. R. (Arthur Napoleon Raymond) (Ray)

b. 16 December 1926. Prime minister of Trinidad-Tobago 1986– . After qualifying as a barrister in England, Robinson returned home in 1955 and helped found the People's National Movement (PNM), which won power the following year. A member of the West Indies federal parliament 1958–60, he was elected to the Trinidad-Tobago parliament in 1961 from his native Tobago, defeating the political leader of that island, A. P. T. James. He was minister of finance (1962–7), then of external affairs (1967–70), as well as deputy leader of the PNM and deputy to prime minister Eric Williams. He resigned from the government and the party in 1970 after reportedly trying to depose Williams during unrest led by 'black power' organisations.

He then formed the Action Committee for Dedicated Citizens and linked up with the East Indian-dominated Democratic Labour Party, but boycotted general elections in 1971. He renamed his party the Democratic Action Congress (DAC) and it won Tobago's two parliamentary seats in the 1976 and 1981 elections. He was elected to one of the seats. The DAC also won control of the new Tobago house of assembly in 1980 (8–4) and Robinson chaired the assembly until 1986. He helped form the state-wide, four-party National Alliance for Reconstruction (NAR) in 1985 and became its leader. The NAR won the 1986 general election and Robinson became prime minister. His leadership was severely challenged in late 1987 and early 1988 and he sacked four of his ministers, including foreign minister and deputy NAR leader Basdeo Panday.

See also **National Alliance for Reconstruction; Tobago; Williams; People's National Movement** (Trinidad-Tobago); **Trinidad, 'black power' uprising (1970); Panday.**

Roca, Blas: see **Communist Party** (Cuba).

Roca, Roberto: see **Farabundo Martí National Liberation Front.**

Rodas Alvarado, Modesto: see **Liberal Party** (Honduras).

Rodney riots (1968)

At the height of 'black power' feeling in the United States, the Jamaican government of Hugh Shearer in October 1968 refused entry after a trip abroad to the popular Guyanese 'black power' historian Walter Rodney (1942–80), a lecturer at the University of the West Indies campus in Jamaica. Riots followed which spread to the slum areas of Kingston. The episode was a protest against Jamaica's white-dominated ruling class. It was also a watershed in Anglo-Caribbean political consciousness and inspired the growth over the next decade of 'new left' movements in the region. Rodney went back to his old university job in Tanzania and in 1974 returned to Guyana. He was barred from the university there and founded the left-wing Working People's Alliance. He was murdered in June 1980 by a government agent who handed him a bomb hidden in a walkie-talkie. His main works were *The Groundings with My Brothers* (1969), *How Europe Underdeveloped Africa* (1972) and *A History of the Guyanese Working People* (1980).

See also **'black power'; 'new left'; Shearer.**

Rodríguez, Gen. Abelardo: see Calles.

Rodríguez Rodríguez, Carlos Rafael

b. 23 May 1913. Vice-president of the Cuban Council of State and Council of Ministers. Educated at the University of Havana, where he received an economics doctorate in 1939, Carlos Rafael Rodríguez was a senior member of the Cuban communist party (the Popular Socialist Party/PSP) at the time of Fidel Castro's revolutionary war. He had joined the party in 1932 and become a member of its Central Committee by the end of the decade. During the 1933 revolution he was mayor of Cienfuegos, and in 1942 he became a minister in the government of Fulgencio Batista – with Juan Marinello (appointed at the same time), one of the first two communists ever to join a Latin American cabinet.

Rodríguez travelled to the revolutionary army's Sierra Maestra head-quarters in 1957 to sign a pact with Castro which offered PSP support to the revolution, despite opposition from within the party. After the victory he became editor of the communist newspaper *Hoy* (1959–62), and in 1961 he assumed a leading economic policy role in the Integrated Revolutionary Organisations (ORI). In 1962–4 he headed the agrarian reform institute. When the Cuban Communist Party (PCC) was set up in 1965, Rodríguez became a member of its secretariat, and although he was out of favour for several years after this, he was appointed to the politburo in 1975 and to the council of state in the following year. As the number three in the Cuban hierarchy, he has had an enormous influence over both economic and foreign policy.

See also **Communist Party** (Cuba); **Cuban Revolutionary War; Integrated Revolutionary Organisations.**

Roldán, Mario Reni: see Democratic Convergence.

Romélus, Bishop Willy: see *déchoukage.*

Romeo, Paulo: see Haiti, Roman Catholic Church; Aristide.

Romero, Archbishop Oscar Arnulfo

1917–80. Archbishop of San Salvador 1977–80. Born in Ciudad Barrios, El Salvador, Oscar Romero studied theology at the Gregorian University, Rome, 1937–43, and was ordained a priest in Rome in 1942. From 1943 to 1967 he worked in El Salvador, successively as a parish priest; director of the Chaparrastique seminary; rector of the interdiocesan seminary, San Salvador; secretary general of the bishops' conference; and executive secretary of the Episcopal Council of Central America and Panama (CEDAC). He was appointed bishop of Tambee in 1967, auxiliary to Archbishop Chávez y González in 1970 and bishop of Santiago de María in 1974. He became archbishop in February 1977, two days after Gen. Carlos Humberto Romero took power following fraudulent elections, and he soon became an outspoken critic of the government's human rights record. When chosen, he had been regarded as a cautious conservative, but he developed the habit of giving publicity in his Sunday homilies (broadcast on national radio) to kidnappings and murders investigated by the *Socorro Jurídico* (legal aid) group, founded in 1975 by Catholic lawyers to give legal representation to the poor.

In June 1977, Romero gave official recognition to Socorro, which became the archdiocese's own human rights body. He also spoke out strongly on socio-economic issues. The murder of a left-wing priest, Fr Rutilio Grande, three weeks after Romero's ordination as archbishop, made a significant impression on him and may have helped radicalise him. He was awarded honorary doctorates by US and Belgian universities and nominated for the Nobel Peace Prize by UK parliamentarians in 1978. By early 1980 he openly supported the 'popular organisations' of the left. On 17 February 1980 he sent a letter to US President Carter, urging him not to send arms to the military-Christian Democrat junta. In his final sermon he called on soldiers and members of the security forces to disobey orders to kill.

Archbishop Romero was shot dead on 24 March 1980 while saying mass. The judge put in charge of the investigation was himself the victim of an assassination attempt and had to flee the country. From exile he accused ARENA party leader Roberto D'Aubuisson and former National Guard Col. José Medrano of being behind the murder. In late 1987 the Romero case was reopened, having been excluded from the 5 November 1987 amnesty law, and a Salvadorean officer, Capt. Alvaro Rafael Saravia, was detained in the US pending extradition on a murder charge. President Duarte reaffirmed that D'Aubuisson was behind the crime. D'Aubuisson responded by naming deputy public security minister Col. Reynaldo López Nuila as the murderer. López Nuila, accused by human rights groups of heading the Maximiliano Hernández Martínez Brigade death squad, was forced to resign from the army and the cabinet on 1 January 1988. Saravia's extradition from the US was barred by the Salvadorean supreme court in late 1988 and the attorney general who had been pressing for it sacked. In early 1989 the government named

Antonio Regalado, former head of security at the National Assembly, as the gunman. He was believed to be in Guatemala.
See also **D'Aubuisson Arrieta; death squad.**

Romero, Serapio: see guerrilla movements (Honduras).

Romero Barceló, Carlos

b. 4 September 1932. Governor of Puerto Rico 1977–85. A lawyer, Romero Barceló joined pro-statehood movements in the mid-1960s and then co-founded the pro-statehood New Progressive Party (PNP) in 1967. He was mayor of the capital, San Juan, 1969–77, was elected governor in 1976 and served two terms until 1985. But his tenure was marred by fierce party infighting and scandals. After his narrow re-election in 1980 he was obstructed by an opposition Popular Democratic Party (PPD) majority in the legislature. During 1981 eight ministers and other government officials resigned in protest at his leadership. In 1983 party vice-president and PNP leader in the house of representatives Angel Viera Martínez was expelled from the party for demanding he resign. Hernán Padilla, mayor of San Juan, left the PNP and formed the Puerto Rican Renewal Party. There were charges of corruption and of a police cover-up in the 1978 murder of two pro-independence militants on Cerro Maravilla mountain. Romero Barceló lost the 1984 election to Rafael Hernández Colón and resigned as PNP leader in 1985. He was succeeded by Baltasar Corrada del Río, but regained the party leadership in 1989.
See also **New Progressive Party; Puerto Rico, nationalist violence; Corrada del Río; Hernández Colón; Popular Democratic Party.**

Romero Bosque, Pío: see Martí, Agustín Farabundo.

Romero Mena, Gen. Carlos Humberto

b. c. 1926. President of El Salvador 1977–9. Born in the northern town of Chalatenango, Carlos Humberto Romero was educated at the Capitán General Gerardo Barrios military school and received later military training at the Escuela de Armas y Servicios and the Commando and General Staff School. His posts included regimental commander, cavalry; 2nd officer, 1st Infantry Regiment; deputy director of the Escuela de Armas y Servicios; head of personnel on the general staff; military attaché to Mexico and chief of staff to the presidency. He also headed the paramilitary organisation ORDEN. He was appointed minister of defence in the government of Col. Arturo Molina (1972–7) and served as president of the Central American Defence Council (CONDECA) 1973–7.

The candidate of the ruling National Conciliation Party (PCN) for the 1977 elections, Romero had taken effective power in 1976 after the employers' association ANEP and the newly-formed eastern region Farmers' Front FARO had forced Molina to abandon plans for mild agrarian reform. The election is generally held to have been won by the opposition UNO coalition, but an elaborate fraud brought Romero to power. In response, UNO organised the occupation of a square in central San Salvador by up to 100,000 people, which lasted several days. On 28 February 1977 security forces, backed up by the army, attacked the

demonstration, killing over 100 participants. In government, Romero sharply increased the repression of dissidents, introducing a draconian public order law. The US government cut economic and military aid to El Salvador on human rights grounds, although the Salvadorean government pre-empted the move by rejecting the aid in advance. US pressure forced Romero to repeal the public order law and issue an election timetable. As pressure from the 'popular organisations' and the guerrillas mounted, Romero was overthrown on 15 October 1979 by a group of officers close to the opposition 'Popular Forum', with the passive assent of the US embassy.
See also **CONDECA; ORDEN.**

Romney, Cyril
b. 1 March 1931. Chief minister, British Virgin Islands 1983–6. A US-educated economist and schoolteacher, Romney was elected to the legislative council and was a senior civil servant from 1960, including a period as financial secretary until 1973. After the 1983 general elections when the two main parties tied, Romney, as the sole independent, was made chief minister by the United Party, whose leader, Willard Wheatley, became his deputy. After allegations that he was involved in laundering drug money, Romney called a general election in 1986 in which he retained his seat but lost power to former chief minister Lavity Stoutt and his Virgin Islands Party.
See also **Wheatley; United Party; Stoutt; Virgin Islands Party.**

Roosevelt, Franklin D.: see **Avila Camacho; good neighbour policy.**

Roosevelt, Theodore: see **Monroe doctrine.**

Rose, Renwick: see **United People's Movement** (St Vincent).

Rossi, Jorge: see **National Liberation Party.**

Roumain, Jacques: see **Unified Haitian Communist Party.**

Royo, Dr Aristides: see **Torrijos Herrera.**

Rozendal, Silvius 'Boy': see **Democratic Party** (Netherlands Antilles).

Ruffo, Ernesto: see **National Action Party.**

Ruiz, Henry: see **Sandinista National Liberation Front; Ortega Saavedra.**

Ruiz Cortines, Adolfo
b. 1891. President of Mexico 1952–8. Ruiz Cortines maintained the pace of economic growth inherited from the Alemán administration before him but took steps to reduce corruption, forcing public officials to disclose their financial assets. Like Alemán, his path to the presidency had been via the governorship of Veracruz state and the interior ministry. Considered reliable and efficient, once in office he followed the path of capitalist economic development mapped out by his predecessor. Foreign

investment grew considerably, particularly after the 1953 devaluation of the peso.

Politically, Ruiz Cortines' main achievement was the extension of the franchise to women. Despite economic growth and the extension of the social security system, the government was unable to push up real wages at a time of average annual inflation of 7.3%. Towards the end of his term, Ruiz Cortines became increasingly aware of the growing problems posed by rapid population growth and urbanisation; the population of Mexico City rose from 3m to 4.5m during his presidency. In his last address to congress he recognised that economic development had taken place at the expense of social justice and that many of the promises of the revolution remained unfulfilled. His decision to choose his labour minister, Adolfo López Mateos, for the presidential succession was seen as an attempt to relieve the strain on the system by bringing in a dynamic populist.

See also **Institutional Revolutionary Party; Alemán Valdés; López Mateos.**

S

Sacasa, Juan Bautista: see Somoza García.

Sacasa Guerrero, Ramiro: see Nicaraguan Democratic Co-ordinator.

Saint Barthélémy (Saint Barth)
One of the five dependencies of the French Caribbean possession (département) of Guadeloupe.
Capital: Gustavia
Area: 25 sq km
Population: 4,000
Deputy Commissioner (prefect) (also for Saint Martin): Michel Magnier (1989)
Mayor: Daniel Blanchard (1983)
The island was a Swedish colony from 1784 until 1877, when it was sold to France. It retained its freeport privileges and became a centre of smuggling. Violent anti-government demonstrations against tax proposals and in support of a local doctor and politician, Charles Querrard, erupted in 1975 and French riot police were sent to the island. The French authorities ruled in 1985 that income tax could be collected and there were further protests. Most of the population are of white Norman origin. The island has become a favourite retreat for rich foreigners, including US banker David Rockefeller, who owns an estate there. Saint Barth and nearby Saint Martin have asked France to grant them joint autonomy. See also de Haenen; Guadeloupe; Saint Martin.

St Bernard, Ian: see New Jewel Movement.

St Christopher-Nevis. The official name for the state of St Kitts-Nevis.

St Croix
The biggest of the US Virgin Islands.
Capital: Christiansted
Area: 218 sq km
Population: 52,000
Main exports: petroleum products, ethanol, meat, rum
Political system: The island has some autonomy from the state government in St Thomas, which is represented by a lieutenant-governor who is from St Croix.

Lieutenant-governor: Derek M. Hodge (1987)
The island contains two major elements in the USVI economy – the Amerada Hess oil refinery (the world's biggest) and a bauxite smelter, owned by Marc Rich, part of which has been converted to ethanol production. Their presence, and that of wealthy American tourists and retirees, has caused racial tension. In 1972 eight people, including four white American tourists, were shot dead by masked black militants on a golf course at Fountain Valley owned by the Rockefeller family. The incident (though never established as racially motivated) and other subsequent killings of whites destroyed the island's tourist trade for several years. In 1989, 1,200 US troops were flown to St Croix for two months to restore order when widespread looting broke out after the island was devastated by Hurricane Hugo.
See also **'black power'; US Virgin Islands; Hurricane Hugo (1989).**

St John, Bernard: see Barbados Labour Party.

ST KITTS-NEVIS
Capital: Basseterre
Independence (from Britain): 1983
Area: 269 sq km
Population (1987): 46,500
Pop. growth rate: 1.5%
Pop. density: 173/sq km
Infant mortality: 35 per thousand
Life expectancy at birth: 65
Literacy: 90%
GDP per capita (1987): US$2,119
Foreign debt per capita (1987): US$473
Main exports: sugar, clothing and shoes, tourism, cotton

Political system

Constitution: 1983, creating a federation of St Kitts and Nevis. Titular head of state: Queen Elizabeth of Britain, represented locally by a figurehead governor-general. A 14-member National Assembly (11 elected members, 3 nominated senators) is elected for a maximum five years.
Governor-general: Sir Clement Arindell (1983)
Deputy governor-general (Nevis): Weston Parris (1983)
Prime minister: Kennedy Simmonds (1980)
Premier of Nevis: Simeon Daniel (1983)
Last elections: 1989

Political organisations

Parties in parliament (leader) (elective seats): People's Action Movement/PAM (Kennedy Simmonds) (6), f. 1965; St Kitts-Nevis Labour Party/SKNLP (Denzil Douglas) (2), f. 1946; Nevis Reformation Party/NRP (Simeon Daniel) (2), f. 1970; Concerned Citizens' Movement/-CCM (Vance Amory) (1), f. 1987.

Parties outside parliament: Progressive Liberal Party/PLP (James Sutton), f. 1987; Nevis National Party/NNP (Andrea Procope), f. 1987. *Main trade unions:* St Kitts Trades and Labour Union/SKTLU (Lee Moore), f. 1944.
See also **Nevis.**

St Kitts-Nevis Labour Party (Workers' League) (SKNLP)

Founded by Robert Bradshaw in 1946 and based on the Workers' League (f. 1932) and Bradshaw's St Kitts Trades and Labour Union, it won all elective seats on the legislative council in the first universal suffrage elections in 1952. In 1957 it won 5–3. It won all the general elections – 1966 (7–2), 1971 (7–2) and 1975 (7–2) – until Bradshaw's death in 1978. A power struggle then erupted between Paul Southwell, who succeeded Bradshaw, and attorney-general Lee Moore, who became premier on Southwell's death in 1979.

This infighting, earlier hints by Moore about a possible one-party state, the decline of the sugar industry and the party's hostility towards Nevis produced a poor showing at the 1980 general election. Although with four seats it was the largest single party, it was ousted from power after 28 years by a coalition of the People's Action Movement and the Nevis Reformation Party. It won only two seats at the 1984 election and Moore lost his own seat, though he remained party leader. Moore again failed to win a seat at the 1989 election, when the party again lost (2–9) and Denzil Douglas, a doctor, replaced him as leader. The party added Nevis to its name in 1983.
See also **Bradshaw; Moore; Nevis.**

St Kitts-Nevis Trades and Labour Union (SKTLU): see **Bradshaw; St Kitts-Nevis Labour Party.**

ST LUCIA

Capital: Castries
Independence (from Britain): 1979
Area: 616 sq km
Population (1987): 142,400
Pop. growth rate: 2.1%
Pop. density: 231/sq km
Infant mortality: 20 per thousand
Life expectancy at birth: 71
Literacy: 90%
GDP per capita (1987): US$1,400
Foreign debt per capita (1989): US$79
Main exports: tourism, bananas, paper and board, clothing, light manufactures

Political system

Constitution: 1979. Titular head of state: Queen Elizabeth of Britain, represented locally by a figurehead governor-general. A 17-member

House of Assembly is elected for a maximum five years. An 11-member
Senate is appointed.
Governor-general: Stanislaus James (1988)
Prime minister: John Compton (1982)
Last elections: 1987

Political organisations
  Parties in parliament (leader) (seats in House of Assembly): United
  Workers' Party/UWP (John Compton) (10), f. 1964; St Lucia Labour
  Party/SLP (Julian Hunte) (7), f. 1950.
  Parties outside parliament: Progressive Labour Party/PLP (George
  Odlum), f. 1981.
  Main trade unions: St Lucia Workers' Union/SLWU (Titus Francis),
  f. 1939; National Workers' Union/NWU (George Goddard); Seamen,
  Waterfront and General Workers' Union/SWGWU (Peter Josie); St
  Lucia Farmers' and Farm Workers' Union/SLFFWU; St Lucia Teach-
  ers' Union/SLTU (John Sealy); Civil Service Association.
  Employers' organisations: St Lucia Manufacturers' Association/-
  SLMA; St Lucia Hotels' Association/SLHA; St Lucia Banana Growers'
  Association/SLBGA (Charles Cadet); National Farmers' Association/-
  NFA (Darnley Lebourne).

St Lucia Action Movement (SLAM): see Odlum, George; Josie;
Hunte; St Lucia Labour Party.

St Lucia Labour Party (SLP)
Founded in 1950 by George Charles (b. 7 June 1916), leader of the St
Lucia Workers' Co-operative Union, and Allen Lewis (b. 26 October
1909), who became its first president. The party won the 1951 and 1954
general elections (5–3 each time). Charles was appointed to the executive
council in 1956 and became minister of social services. The SLP increased
its majority to 7–1 in the 1957 poll and Charles became its political leader.
In the 1961 election, after Charles had become chief minister (1960), it
won 9–1. It was defeated (8–2) in 1964 by the new United Workers'
Party, founded partly by SLP dissidents, including the new premier, John
Compton, whose defection had brought about the poll. Charles stepped
down as SLP leader in 1967 in favour of Kenneth Foster. The party lost
elections in 1969 (3–7) and 1974 (7–10).
   In 1977 retired judge Allan Louisy (b. 1916) was elected leader over
George Odlum, who became his deputy. Odlum and other 'new left'
figures from the St Lucia Action Movement – his brother Jon and Peter
Josie – had joined the party in 1973. The SLP won the 1979 elections
(12–5) largely through this group's efforts and despite charges of 'communism'. Louisy became prime minister and a few months later Odlum,
with a 7–5 majority among SLP MPs, pressed him to hand over the job to
himself. With US encouragement and saying he feared Cuban influence,
Louisy refused and when he resigned in 1981 gave it to attorney-general
Winston Cenac. But he too resigned a few months later, in 1982, as the
party split worsened. Josie was elected leader. After a four-month all-

party coalition government under an SLP defector, Michael Pilgrim (b. 3 January 1947), the party was defeated 15–2 at general elections in 1982 and the UWP returned to power.

Neville Cenac became party leader, but in 1984 businessman Julian Hunte was elected leader over leftist Peter Josie, who became his deputy. Hunte's refusal to ally himself with Odlum's Progressive Labour Party caused the SLP to be narrowly beaten 9–8 in elections in 1987. When new elections produced the same result, prime minister Compton obtained a 10–7 majority after Neville Cenac defected from the SLP in exchange for the job of foreign minister.

See also **Hunte; Odlum, George; Josie; 'new left'; United Workers' Party; Compton.**

Saint Martin

One of the five dependencies of the French Caribbean possession (départ-ement) of Guadeloupe. It is the larger part of an island of the same name divided between Holland and France.

Capital: Marigot
Area: 54 sq km
Population (1990): 28,000
Pop. growth rate: 9.8%
Pop. density: 519/sq km
Deputy Commissioner (prefect) (also for St Barthélémy): Michel Magnier (1989)
Mayor: Albert Fleming (1977)

Leaders of Saint Martin and neighbouring St Barthélémy have asked France to grant them joint autonomy.

See **Fleming; Guadeloupe; Sint Maarten; St Martin.**

St Martin

An 88 sq km island in the northeastern Caribbean divided between France and The Netherlands since 1648 but without frontier formalities. It developed into a major tourist resort in the 1970s but also a centre for crime, drugs and smuggling. It is a magnet for immigration from other Islands.

Population (1990): 52,000

See also **Saint Martin; Sint Maarten.**

ST VINCENT and the Grenadines

Capital: Kingstown
Independence (from Britain): 1979
Area: 389 sq km
Population (1989): 112,600
Pop. growth rate: 1.1%
Pop. density: 289/sq km
Infant mortality: 23 per thousand
Life expectancy at birth: 71
Literacy: 85%
GDP per capita (1988): US$1,148

Foreign debt per capita (1989): US$507
Main exports: bananas, tourism, vegetables, arrowroot, fruit, flour, animal feed, tennis rackets

Political system

Constitution: 1979. Titular head of state: Queen Elizabeth of Britain, represented locally by a figurehead governor-general. A 22-member House of Assembly (15 elected members, 6 nominated senators and a speaker) serves a maximum five years.
Governor-general: David Jack (1989)
Prime minister: James Mitchell (1984)
Last elections: 1989

Political organisations

Parties in parliament (leader) (elective seats): New Democratic Party/NDP (James Mitchell) (15), f. 1975.
Parties outside parliament: St Vincent Labour Party/SVLP (Vincent Beache), f. 1955; United People's Movement/UPM (Adrian Saunders), f. 1979; Movement for National Unity/MNU (Ralph Gonsalves), f. 1982; People's Popular Movement/PPM (Percival Stapleton), f. 1988; National Reform Party/NRP (Joel Miguel), f. 1989.
Main trade unions: Commercial, Technical and Allied Workers' Union/CTAWU, f. 1962; St Vincent Union of Teachers/SVUT; National Workers' Movement/NWM (Noel Jackson); National Farmers' Union/NFU; St Vincent Workers' Union/SWU; Workers' and Peasants' Union; Civil Service Association/CSA.
Employers' organisations: St Vincent Employers' Federation; St Vincent Banana Growers' Association, f. 1954.
See also **Grenadines; Bequia; Mustique; Union Island Revolt (1979).**

St Vincent Labour Party (SVLP)

Founded in 1955 by Conservative barrister Milton Cato with middle-class support, it lost the elections of 1957 (3–5), 1961 (3–6) and 1966 (4–5) to the People's Political Party of Ebenezer Joshua. After disturbances following the 1966 vote the British authorities dismissed chief minister Joshua and at new elections in 1967 the SVLP won 6–3 and Cato became chief minister. In the 1972 elections it tied 6–6 with the People's Political Party and went into opposition when the PPP took power in alliance with independent MP James Mitchell, whose resignation as an SVLP MP had caused the previous government to fall.

The party won elections 10–3 in 1974 and Cato returned to power in coalition with the PPP. The party won 11–2 in 1979 but was defeated 4–9 in 1984 elections by Mitchell's New Democratic Party. Cato retired from politics and former deputy prime minister Hudson Tannis took over the party. When Tannis was killed in a plane crash in 1986 Vincent Beache became SVLP leader. The party lost all its seats in parliament at the 1989 election.
See also **Cato; Beache; Mitchell, James; Joshua, Ebenezer.**

Saladrigas, Carlos: see **Communist Party** (Cuba).

Salinas de Gortari, Carlos

b. 3 April 1948. President of Mexico, 1988– . An economist, educated at the Universidad Nacional Autónoma de México (UNAM) and Harvard, Salinas joined the ruling Institutional Revolutionary Party (PRI) in 1966. More a technocrat than a politician in his early career, he worked as an analyst at the finance ministry, later becoming head of planning at the treasury before moving on to the ministry of planning (*secretaría de programación y presupuesto*). In 1982–7 he served as minister of planning under President Miguel De la Madrid and was regarded as the intellectual architect of the economic austerity programme pursued during those years. He was the youngest member of the cabinet; because of his small size and energetic style, his critics dubbed him the 'atomic ant'. In June 1986, together with interior minister Manuel Bartlett, Salinas helped oust finance minister Jesús Silva Hérzog, then regarded as a strong candidate for the presidential succession. He was selected by De la Madrid as the PRI's official candidate in the 1988 elections, despite the misgivings of trade union leaders and others within the ruling party, who wanted someone with more political experience.

As a candidate, Salinas signalled a change in emphasis, saying that domestic economic growth would take precedence over servicing Mexico's foreign debt. During the campaign he also promised modernisation of the economy, greater political pluralism and a new emphasis on the redistribution of wealth. He was declared the winner of the 6 July 1988 elections with 50.74% of the vote, the lowest achieved by the PRI in many years, and was hit by bitter allegations of fraud by opposition parties. Although a beneficiary, Salinas himself was believed to oppose the use of fraud by the old guard of the party, and immediately after the elections he claimed that one-party rule in Mexico was coming to an end. Only a month after taking office, Salinas de Gortari moved spectacularly against his opponents in the labour movement old guard by ordering the arrest of the oil workers' leader 'La Quina'. He followed this up by ordering the arrest of top stock exchange brokers also accused of corrupt practices. By common agreement, Salinas came to the presidency in the midst of the country's most severe political crisis, in which the viability of the whole political system was being questioned as never before.

See also **De la Madrid Hurtado; Institutional Revolutionary Party; La Quina.**

Salvadorean Communist Party (*Partido Comunista Salvadoreño/* PCS)

Founded in 1930 on the basis of urban artisan unions, the PCS gave cautious backing to the 1930 election winner, Arturo Araujo of the Salvadorean Labour Party (PLS). It turned against him, however, when the collapse of the international coffee market led him to abandon promised reforms. As social unrest grew, the party was able to organise some 80,000 coffee workers into highly militant unions. After the overthrow of Araujo by Gen. Martínez in December 1931, the PCS was allowed to participate in the January 1932 municipal elections, but these were suspended when it showed signs of winning seats. It was obliged by pressure from below to attempt an insurrection but this was abortive. Leader Farabundo Martí and others were executed, but although outlawed, leaderless and almost wiped out it remained the only organised source of left-wing opposition to the regime for the next four decades. After the overthrow of Martínez in 1944 it began to expand its union base, organising the National Union of Workers (UNT) into a 50,000-strong body.

Over the next 30 years the PCS concentrated on labour issues and eventually on electoral strategy via a legal front organisation, the Nationalist Democratic Union (UDN, f. 1969). In 1972 and 1977 the UDN participated in the National Opposition Union (UNO) coalition which backed Christian Democrat José Napoleón Duarte for the presidency but 'lost the count'. The refusal of the PCS to contemplate armed struggle led to internal splits, the most serious of which was the departure of secretary general Salvador Cayetano Carpio ('Marcial') in 1969 to found the Popular Liberation Forces (FPL). In April 1979, at its 7th party congress, the PCS voted for armed struggle, but when the 15 October 1979 coup took place the UDN joined the government, withdrawing along with the National Revolutionary Movement in January 1980 in favour of an alliance with the guerrilla organisations. It became part of the FDR/FMLN rebel coalition, with a small (*c.* 500 combatants) armed wing known as the Armed Forces of Liberation (FAL). It has consistently favoured a negotiated settlement of the war. Secretary general: Schafik Jorge Handal (1973–   ).

See also **Martí, Agustín Farabundo; Martínez, Gen. Maximiliano Hernández;** *Matanza* **(1932 massacre); Nationalist Democratic Union; Democratic Revolutionary Front; Farabundo Martí National Liberation Front; Popular Liberation Forces.**

Salvadorean Labour Party (PLS): see **Martínez, Gen. Maximiliano Hernández; Salvadorean Communist Party.**

Salvadorean Nationalist Movement: see **D'Aubuisson Arrieta.**

Samudio, David: see **Liberal Party** (Panama).

Sanabria, Archbishop Victor: see **Civil War** (Costa Rica).

San Andrés dispute

Sovereignty over the Caribbean islands of San Andrés and Providencia (with their associated cays of Roncador, Quitasueño and Serrana) is disputed by Colombia and Nicaragua. A 1928 treaty (known alternatively as the Esguerra-Barcenas, Barcenas Meneses-Esguerra or Guerra-Meneses Treaty) in which Nicaragua ceded the islands to Colombia was declared null and void by the Nicaraguan government on 4 February 1980 on the grounds that the islands were in its territorial waters (extended to 200 miles in December 1979) and that the treaty had been signed under US pressure by a 'traitorous' regime in Managua (US troops occupied

Nicaragua at the treaty date). Colombia, which bases its claim on an order of the Spanish crown of 1803, then recalled its ambassador. Panama (which also has a dormant claim to the islands) offered to mediate. Under the same treaty, Colombia had renounced its claim to the Miskito coast of Nicaragua and the offshore Mangle islands.

The San Andrés archipelago lies about 180 km from the Nicaraguan coast and 480 km from Colombia. It holds Colombia's most important tourist complex and the San Andrés freeport. The possible presence of oil in the surrounding waters complicates the issue. A 1972 treaty (Sánchez-Vásquez Carrizosa or Vázquez-Sakio) between Washington and Bogotá granted US recognition of Colombian sovereignty and returned a number of islets which had been under US occupation. Nicaragua requested in 1979 that it not be ratified by Washington, but despite this the US Senate ratified it on 31 July 1981. In March 1980, Colombia took the dispute to the UN Law of the Sea conference, but in May 1980 Nicaragua and Colombia agreed to indefinite bilateral talks on the issue. Further friction was evident in 1986, when Nicaragua again insisted on its claim and Colombia despatched warships to the islands. In August that year Honduras renounced its own claim to many of the smaller cays in a treaty with Colombia.

Sánchez-Vásquez Carrizosa Treaty: see San Andrés dispute.

Sánchez Vilella, Roberto: see Popular Democratic Party; Muñoz Marín; Hernández Colón.

Sandiford, Erskine
b. 24 March 1937. Prime minister of Barbados 1987– . A teacher, Sandiford became a personal aide to prime minister Errol Barrow in 1966, entered parliament as a Democratic Labour Party (DLP) senator in 1967 and was minister of education (1967–75) and health (1975–6). He was elected to the house of assembly in 1971. He was DLP general secretary 1967–71 and party president and deputy DLP parliamentary leader from 1976. He led the DLP in support of the 1983 US invasion of Grenada during the absence from the island of party leader Barrow, who opposed it. Nevertheless he became Barrow's deputy prime minister, as well as education minister, when the DLP returned to power in 1986, and succeeded him on his death in 1987.
See also **Democratic Labour Party** (Barbados); **Barrow; Grenada, US invasion (1983).**

Sandinista Defence Committees (CDS): see Sandinista National Liberation Front.

Sandinista National Liberation Front (*Frente Sandinista de Liberación Nacional*/FSLN)
Nicaraguan guerrilla movement (later a political party) founded in July 1961 in Tegucigalpa, Honduras, by Carlos Fonseca, Tomás Borge and Silvio Mayorga, to overthrow the Somoza dictatorship. Originally called the National Liberation Front, it took its present name in 1963 in memory

of Augusto César Sandino, a Nicaraguan general who fought against the US occupation of his country in the 1930s. Its first armed actions were launched from Honduras in 1963. After initial military setbacks it spent the period 1963–7 primarily on urban political work. In 1967 it resumed its military offensive, building up a guerrilla infrastructure around Pancasán mountain, about 50 km east of Matagalpa. But in August 1967 the National Guard (GN) located and decimated the Pancasán units, killing 13 senior members of the FSLN, including Silvio Mayorga.

A further period of urban consolidation followed, despite setbacks such as the 15 July 1969 National Guard attack on a Managua 'safe house', in which five militants (including a member of the national leadership) were killed. In 1970, partly as result of this blow, the FSLN became a wholly clandestine movement, forswearing combat except as a last resort. Immediately prior to this it had staged its last guerrilla operation of the period, in the mountains of Matagalpa, where the combatants were, for the first time, mostly peasants. Also for the first time, the guerrilla column succeeded in escaping a military cordon and inflicting serious losses on government forces. By 1974, despite significant gains on the urban front, the FSLN was losing ground to the Communist Party (PSN), and had suffered the loss of another safe house. Its leaders saw the need for a spectacular action, and on 27 December 1974, 13 guerrillas seized the house of Somoza confidant 'Chema' Castillo, taking prominent hostages in exchange for whom Somoza was forced to release several political prisoners and hand over a $2m ransom. During the ensuing three-year state of siege the FSLN was pinned down by the GN and carried out few military operations. By November 1976, when Fonseca was killed in a GN ambush, it had split into three tendencies.

The **Prolonged Popular War** (GPP) faction, led by Henry Ruiz and Tomás Borge, believed in a 'gradual accumulation of forces' in rural and urban areas. Its main strength was in the northern mountains.

The **Proletarian Tendency** (TP), led by Jaime Wheelock and Luis Carrión, split away in October 1975. It believed in the vanguard role of the proletariat and the need for a marxist-leninist party and its main strength was among students and workers in Managua.

The **Insurrectional Tendency**, or *Terceristas*, led by Daniel and Humberto Ortega and Víctor Tirado López, emerged as mediators and developed a plan for a popular insurrection in alliance with other opposition sectors.

The Terceristas, who had the best international contacts, launched a new series of military operations in October 1977 and February 1978, despite criticism from the other tendencies. A group of 12 prominent professionals (*'Los Doce'*) publicly announced in October 1977 that there could be no solution to the political crisis without the FSLN's participation; they were to play a key role in the ensuing months. By mid-1978 the possibility of an insurrection was evident, and all three backed the formation of the United People's Movement (MPU) as a mass front, together with the Civil Defence Committees (CDCs, later renamed Sandinista Defence Committees/CDS). The August 1978 Tercerista seizure of the National Palace, with hundreds of hostages, was supported by the whole of the FSLN. The operation won the release of 58 prisoners and a ransom of several million dollars.

On 9 September 1978 the Terceristas called for a national insurrection, soon supported militarily by the rest of the FSLN. León, Chinandega, Masaya and Estelí were seized, the latter holding out for two weeks. Reunification of the three tendencies followed in March 1979, with the creation of the National Directorate (DN), comprising three leaders from each.

In early 1979 there was a second, week-long occupation of Estelí and an attempt to open a south-eastern front which led to the deaths of 128 combatants. The final offensive began on 31 May. On 16 June a provisional government (Junta of National Reconstruction) was named in Costa Rica. On 17 July, Somoza fled to Miami. The FSLN took over on 19 July, after Somoza's designated successor, Francisco Urcuyo, had also fled.

As the dominant force on the junta and in the co-legislative council of state, the FSLN held *de facto* power until January 1985, when an elected FSLN government under President Daniel Ortega was inaugurated after winning 67% of the vote in the November 1984 general elections. The FSLN (now a political party) was still headed by the 9-man DN, which was in turn led by an executive committee drawn from its number whose membership was changed or ratified each year. The replacement by this committee (chaired by president Ortega, who has held the party leadership since 1985) of the political commission headed by Bayardo Arce, an ally of Borge, was widely seen as a consolidation of the Ortegas' control of the party.

The tendencies were formally disbanded after the victory but continued to have some significance; the pragmatic Terceristas wielded almost unchallenged power. Humberto Ortega, now a four-star general, had sole command of the army. The Sandinista Assembly, convened at irregular intervals, was the debating forum for an élite of about 100 party members, nominated by the DN. Membership of the whole party was about 37,500. However, after the 1990 elections, which the FSLN lost with about 41% of the vote, steps were taken to alter the party structure, introducing internal democracy and converting the Front into an essentially social democratic party. Humberto Ortega resigned from the DN in order to remain as head of the army. Daniel Ortega was expected to be elected general secretary.

See also **Sandino; Somoza Debayle, Gen. Anastasio; Fonseca Amador; Borge Martínez; Ortega Saavedra; National Guard** (Nicaragua); **Pastora Gómez.**

Sandino, Augusto César

1895–1934. Nicaraguan guerrilla leader, 1927–33. Born in Niquinohomo, Masaya department, Sandino became a Liberal general in 1926 on his return to Nicaragua after several years abroad, during which he had worked in a sugar mill in Honduras, on a banana plantation in Guatemala and in the Mexican oilfields. He fought Nicaraguan government and US troops in the mountains of northern Nicaragua after rejecting the Pact of Espino Negro (Stimson-Moncada pact) of 1927 between the Liberal and Conservative Forces, which ended a civil war at the cost of US domination. He withdrew to El Chipote mountain in the Segovias region to assemble his Army in Defence of the National Sovereignty of Nicaragua (EDSN), which by 1933 comprised 6,000 combatants. The US responded to his attacks with aerial bombardment after ground forces failed to dislodge him. Although labelled 'communist' by the US government, Sandino was in fact an anti-communist nationalist; though he did believe in agrarian reform and fostered peasant co-operatives in the area under his control. He never broke his ties with the Liberal Party.

US forces withdrew, having failed to defeat Sandino, on 1 January 1933, and in February he accepted a ceasefire and the disarming of all but 100 of his troops. His demands for control of an autonomous region in the north of country; the repeal of the Chamorro-Bryan treaty and an end to foreign involvement with the newly-created National Guard, were unacceptable to the government and to the US. After a negotiating session in February 1934, Sandino and a group of his generals were ambushed and killed by the National Guard, on the orders of future dictator Anastasio Somoza García. Within three years the last pockets of resistance by his followers were wiped out. Sandino's name was adopted by the Sandinista National Liberation Front (FSLN) guerrilla movement (f. 1961) which came to power in 1979.
See also **Somoza García; Sandinista National Liberation Front.**

Sandino Brigade: see **Caribbean Legion.**

Sandino Revolutionary Front (FRS): see **ARDE; Pastora Gómez.**

Sandoval Alarcón, Mario

b. 1923. Secretary general of the National Liberation Movement (MLN) of Guatemala from its foundation in 1960. A law graduate from a Spanish university, Sandoval participated in the 1944 'revolution' alongside Jacobo Arbenz and Juan José Arévalo, but sided with Francisco Javier Arana in the dispute between the latter and Arbenz which split the Popular Liberation Front. He moved sharply to the right after the death of Arana. Having plotted against the Arbenz government, he was in jail at the time of its overthrow by Castillo Armas. He subsequently served as private secretary to Castillo Armas and was a member of the constituent assembly which drafted the 1966 constitution, later becoming a congressional deputy and then president of congress during the presidency of Gen. Carlos Arana Osorio (1970–74). He was vice-president of the republic under President Kjell Laugerud (1974–8), but from 1975 onwards was at odds with Laugerud, whom he considered a 'leftist'. A leading member of the World Anti-Communist League, Sandoval was for decades the undisputed leader of the extreme right in Guatemala and headed a private army said at one time to number 3,000. He stood unsuccessfully for the presidency in 1982 and 1985, obtaining 12.5% of the vote on the latter occasion.

See also **National Liberation Movement** (Guatemala); **Castillo Armas; Arana Osorio; Arbenz Guzmán; Arévalo Bermejo.**

Sangster, Sir Donald: see **Jamaica Labour Party; Shearer.**

San José Agreement

An arrangement between Mexico and Venezuela, agreed in August 1980, whereby they would jointly supply up to 160,000 b/d of oil to the five Central American nations, plus Panama, Jamaica, Barbados and the Dominican Republic, on concessionary terms. Under these, 30% of bills would be converted into 5-year, 4% loans, which could be extended to 20-year, 2% loans if the savings were invested in energy and economic developments projects. Venezuela gained from the deal, since its 80,000 b/d share was less than it was already providing under an existing scheme (the Puerto Ordaz Agreement). It was hoped that the scheme would contribute to regional stability. Shipments to Haiti (briefly included as a tenth beneficiary) were halted after part of the first was diverted to South Africa. In September 1982, Venezuela suspended shipments to Nicaragua on grounds of non-payment, though political motives were suspected. Mexico stepped in until 1983, when it was forced to cut back San José agreement shipments to Nicaragua due to its own financial difficulties. In October 1984 both countries said they might suspend all such shipments because of payment arrears. In early 1985, Mexico cut off supplies to Nicaragua, and a plea by the latter to both countries for a resumption was turned down when the agreement was renewed in July 1987. By this time San José shipments stood at around 100,000 b/d. Belize became the tenth beneficiary in August 1988.

San José, Declaration of: see **Central American Democratic Community; Havana, First Declaration of.**

Saravia, Capt. Alvaro Rafael: see **Romero, Archbishop Oscar Arnulfo.**

Saunders, Adrian: see **United People's Movement** (St Vincent).

Saunders, Norman

b. 20 November 1943. Chief minister of the Turks and Caicos Islands 1980–85. A wealthy businessman, Saunders was first elected to parliament in 1967. He co-founded the Progressive National Organisation before the 1976 general election, which the party lost. He then launched the Progressive National Party, which won the 1980 election, after which he became chief minister. Saunders led the party to victory again in 1984 but he and two government members were arrested in Miami in 1985 by undercover FBI agents and accused of bribery and drug smuggling offences. He resigned and was sentenced to eight years in prison in the US. In 1987, after being freed from jail, he returned to the country.

See also **Progressive National Party.**

Schick, René: see Somoza Debayle, Gen. Anastasio.

Schlotter, René de León: see Christian Democrat Party (Guatemala).

School of the Americas (*Escuela de las Américas*)
A US military training school for Latin American officers which operated from 1946 to 1985 in the Panama Canal Zone. Under the terms of the 1977 Canal Treaties, ownership of Fort Gulick, which housed the school, passed to the Panamanian Defence Forces on 30 September 1984, and in 1985 the school was temporarily moved to Fort Benning, Georgia, while a new location was sought: Puerto Rico, Honduras and Belize have all been mentioned as possible hosts. By 1985 almost 45,000 Latin American officers had passed through the School of the Americas: the large number who were subsequently involved in military governments in their own countries earned the establishment its nickname of *Escuela de Golpes* ('School of Coups'). Two US military training schools for Latin Americans remained in Panama: the Navy's Small Craft Instruction and Technical Training Centre and the USAF's Interamerican Air Force Academy.
See also: **Panama Canal Treaties; Panama Canal Zone.**

Scoon, Sir Paul: see Grenada, US invasion (1983).

Seaga, Edward
b. 28 May 1930. Prime minister of Jamaica 1980–89. Born in the US of Lebanese-Jamaican parents, Edward Seaga graduated as a social scientist from Harvard. He was nominated to the legislative council in 1959 by the opposition Jamaica Labour Party (JLP), of which he became secretary in 1962. He was elected to parliament in 1962 and appointed minister of development and social welfare. From 1967 until the JLP lost power in 1972 he was minister of finance and planning. In 1974 he replaced Hugh Shearer as party leader.

After leading the JLP to defeat in the 1976 election, Seaga defeated Michael Manley and the People's National Party (PNP) in 1980, with strong backing from Washington, which saw him as a bulwark against the left in the region. In government he led other Anglo-Caribbean states in opposition to the left-wing regime in Grenada and enthusiastically backed the 1983 US invasion of the island by sending Jamaican troops. His attempt to cash in on the invasion backfired when the PNP boycotted the general election he called a few weeks later. In 1986 he led the formation of the US-sponsored Caribbean Democratic Union of conservative Anglo-Caribbean ruling parties. Seaga's laissez-faire economic policies produced no results for many years. He managed to satisfy international finance bodies, but conditions deteriorated badly for ordinary Jamaicans because of sharp health and social services cutbacks. Seaga and the JLP lost power to Manley and the PNP at a general election in 1989.
See also **Jamaica Labour Party; Manley, Michael; Grenada, US invasion (1983); Caribbean Democratic Union; Shearer.**

Second Republic (*Segunda República*)
The name chosen by José Figueres and his associates to refer to the political/governmental reorganisation in Costa Rica (including a new constitution) instigated by the victorious rebels after the 1948 civil war; much of which was based on ideas originally formulated by the Centre for the Study of National Problems. The Founding Junta of the Second Republic, headed by Figueres, ruled from May 1948 to November 1949, when the presidency was handed to Otilio Ulate, victor in the disputed election of 1948. It issued more than 800 decrees, including the nationalisation of the banks and of the electricity supply industry.
See also **Civil War** (Costa Rica 1948); **Figueres Ferrer; Generation of '48** (Costa Rica).

Second Vatican Council: see **liberation theology.**

Secord, Maj. Gen. Richard: see **Iran/contra affair.**

Secret Anti-communist Army (ESA): see **death squad.**

Section 936: see **Operation Bootstrap.**

Seraphin, Oliver: see **Dominica Labour Party; John, Patrick; Douglas, Rosie.**

Serrano Elías, Jorge: see **Democratic Party of National Co-operation.**

Sessán Pereira, Col. Rafael: see **Rebel Armed Forces.**

sexenio: see **Mexico.**

Shah, Raffique: see **Trinidad, 'black power' uprising (1970); Panday.**

Sharpe, (Sir) John: see **United Bermuda Party.**

Sharples, Sir Richard: see **Progressive Labour Party** (Bermuda).

Shearer, Hugh
b. 18 May 1923. Prime minister of Jamaica 1967–72. A protégé of Jamaica Labour Party (JLP) leader Alexander Bustamante, Shearer became number two man in the Bustamante Industrial Trade Union (BITU) in the early 1950s. He was nominated to the legislative council in 1951 and became minister without portfolio. In 1955 he was elected to parliament but he lost his seat at the 1959 elections. He was appointed a senator and on independence in 1962 was named Jamaica's deputy representative at the United Nations in New York.

In 1967, Shearer was elected to parliament again, became foreign minister and, a month after his election, succeeded to the premiership on the death of Donald Sangster. He was also unofficial head of the BITU. In 1968, his banning from the country of Guyanese 'black power' activist Walter Rodney set off serious rioting against Jamaica's white-dominated ruling class. The JLP lost the 1972 election and Shearer became opposition leader. But he was forced out in 1974 by Edward Seaga. When the JLP returned to power in 1980, Shearer became foreign

minister and Seaga's deputy prime minister until the party's defeat at the 1989 general election, when he held his seat by only seven votes.
See also **Jamaica Labour Party; Bustamante Industrial Trade Union; Seaga; Rodney riots (1968)**

Shoman, Assad: see People's United Party.

Shultz, George: see Ardito Barletta; Monroe doctrine.

SIECA: see Central American Common Market.

Silva Hérzog, Jesús: see Salinas de Gortari.

Simmonds, Kennedy
b. 12 April 1936. Premier, prime minister of St Kitts-Nevis 1980– .
After training in Jamaica as a doctor, Simmonds returned to St Kitts and in 1965 was a founder-member and first vice-president of the People's Action Movement (PAM). He worked as a doctor in the Bahamas 1966–8 and studied in the US 1968–9, when he returned to St Kitts. He took over from Billie Herbert as leader of PAM in 1976 and entered parliament at a by-election in 1979 caused by the death of premier Robert Bradshaw a year earlier. The government prevented him from taking his seat, won after a court battle, by dissolving parliament. After the general election in 1980, he formed a coalition with the Nevis Reformation Party to win a one-seat parliamentary majority and become premier and, after independence in 1983, prime minister. He won general elections in 1984 and 1989. He was the first regional head of government to have graduated from the University of the West Indies.
See also **People's Action Movement.**

Singh, Rickey
b. 1 February 1937. Guyanese-born Caribbean journalist. Singh was dismissed as chief reporter of the *Guyana Graphic* in 1973 after writing that the government had rigged its election victory that year. The paper's foreign owners, Thomson Newspapers, under government pressure, transferred him to one of their papers in England. He was appointed editor of the Caribbean Conference of Churches monthly organ, *Caribbean Contact*, in 1974 and it soon became the most widely-read regional paper. In 1978 he was forced to leave Trinidad, where the paper was edited, when the government refused to renew his work permit. He then ran the paper from Barbados. His strong Caribbean nationalist stance led him to condemn the Barbados-sponsored 1983 US invasion of Grenada. The paper was the only one in the region to do so. As a result he was forced out as editor by US and Barbadian government pressure, including withdrawal of his work permit. In 1986 he became first president of the Caribbean Association of Media Workers (CAMWORK). A new Barbadian government granted him immigrant status in 1987.
See also **Grenada, US invasion (1983); Caribbean Conference of Churches.**

Singlaub, Maj. Gen. John: see Iran/contra affair.

Sint Eustatius
The official name of the Dutch Caribbean island more often known as Statia (area 21 sq km; pop. 1900).
See **Netherlands Antilles.**

Sint Maarten
Capital: Philipsburg
Area: 34 sq km
Population (1989): 24,000
Pop. growth rate: 4.3%
Pop. density: 706/sq km
Main exports: tourism

Political system

One of the five constituent parts of the Netherlands Antilles. It is the smaller but more prosperous part of an island divided between the Netherlands and France. A Dutch-appointed lieutenant-governor presides over a partly-elected island council. The island elects three members to the central parliament in Curaçao.
Lieutenant-governor: Ralph Richardson (1987)
Island leader: Claude Wathey (1951)
Last elections: 1990

Political organisations

Parties represented in central parliament: Sint Maarten Democratic Party/DP-SM (Claude Wathey) (2), f. 1951; Sint Maarten Patriotic Alliance/SPA (Vance James) (1), f. 1989.
See also **Netherlands Antilles; Saint Martin; St Martin.**

Sint Maarten Patriotic Alliance/SPA: see **Wathey.**

Siqueiros, David Alfaro: see **Communist Party** (Mexico).

Sisniega, Leonel: see **National Liberation Movement** (Guatemala).

SITRATERCO: see **general strike** (Honduras/1954).

Skippings, Oswald
b. 19 February 1953. Chief minister of the Turks and Caicos Islands 1980, 1988– . An ex-schoolteacher, Skippings was co-founder of the pro-independence People's Democratic Movement (PDM) in 1975. He became chief minister in 1980 after the death of J. A. G. S. McCartney, but the PDM lost the general election later that year. Skippings was replaced as party leader in 1984 by Clement Howell, whose deputy he became, and was one of three politicians named as unfit to hold public office in the 1986 Blom-Cooper report on arson and corruption. He became party leader again in 1987 and after leading the PDM to victory at the 1988 general election, became chief minister once more.
See also **People's Democratic Movement.**

Soccer War: see **'Football (Soccer) War'.**

Social Christian Party (*Partido Social Cristiano*/PSC)
A conservative Christian Democrat party founded in Nicaragua in 1957, which joined the anti-Somoza UDEL coalition in 1974. It split in 1976, with the 'Edgar Macías' faction forming the Nicaraguan Social Christian Party (PSCN – later the Popular Social Christian Party/PPSC), while the 'José Esteban González' faction retained the original name. The PSC joined the Nicaraguan Democratic Co-ordinator (CDN) in 1984, although the CDN's decision to boycott that year's elections caused internal problems since the PSC – the only member with a significant following – was the party with the most to lose. It was banned by the government as a consequence of the boycott and its differences with other CDN parties increased. Its leaders disagreed with the decision to seek closer ties with the armed anti-Sandinista (contra) groups, and in February 1987 it joined the explicitly non-contra Civic Opposition.

By mid-1987 it had split in two over internal ballot-rigging accusations, with the faction led by party president Erick Ramírez securing the recognition of the international Christian Democrat movement (which provides most of the party's funds). The right-wing faction, headed by secretary general Agustín Jarquín and Eduardo Rivas Gasteazoro, seized the party HQ. This faction itself later split, with Jarquín heading the National Confidence Democratic Party (PDCN) and Rivas the National Action Party (PAN). In late 1987, Ramírez was appointed to the 8-member National Reconciliation Commission set up under the terms of the Arias peace plan. Another PSC leader, Azucena Ferrey, had already joined the leadership of the Nicaraguan Resistance, the contra umbrella body. In the 1990 elections the PSC joined the opposition UNO alliance, winning a single seat, through its ally the Yatama movement.
See also **Popular Social Christian Party**.

Social Christian Reformist Party (*Partido Reformista Social Cristiano*/PRSC): see **Balaguer**.

Social Christian Revolutionary Party (*Partido Revolucionario Social Cristiano*/PRSC): see **Balaguer**.

Social Christian Student Front (FESC): see **Cerezo Arévalo**.

Social Christian Unity Party (*Partido Unidad Social Cristiano*/PUSC)
More homogeneously right-wing than Costa Rica's other main political force, the National Liberation Party (PLN), the PUSC was founded in 1983 by the four member parties of the Unity (*Unidad*) coalition, the losers in the 1982 election. *Unidad* had held power under President Carazo since 1978, the year after its formation. Its four member parties were the Christian Democrat Party (PDC), the Democratic Renovation Party (PRD), the Calderonista Republican Party (PCR) and the Popular Union Party (PUP). The PDC was founded in 1967 by a group of young Catholic intellectuals formed in 1962. Despite the support of the Confederation of Christian Workers and Peasants, it performed poorly in the 1970 and 1974 elections. The weakest tendency within the PUSC, Christian Democracy none the less became its guiding principle.

The PRC, the biggest of the member parties, contributed half the members of the coalition and half the leadership. Founded in 1962 as the Republican Party (PR) by ex-president Rafael Angel Calderón Guardia, it became the PRC after his death in 1970. It formed part of the National Unification Coalition with the National Union Party (PUN) from 1965 to 1970. Calderón's son, lawyer Rafael Angel Calderón Fournier, was foreign minister to Carazo Odio, and a PRC deputy became president of the legislative assembly in 1979. Calderón Fournier became the PUSC presidential candidate in 1982, but lost to Luís Alberto Monge. In 1990, however, he became president after defeating Carlos Manuel Castillo of the PLN. The PRD was founded in 1971 by Rodrigo Carazo Odio, who had failed to win the presidential nomination of the PLN in 1970. As PRD candidate in 1974 he won about 10% of the vote, providing the base for the subsequent construction of the Opposition Unity coalition, whose successful presidential candidate he became in 1978. The PUP was founded around 1974 as a conservative, anti-PLN party/pressure group, by coffee barons led by Cristián Tattembach, but did not present candidates at national level. It backed the National Unification Coalition in 1974.

In 1985 a group led by Oscar Aguilar Bulgarelli, joint founder of the PRD, left to join the National Union Party (PUN), which Aguilar quickly took over as leader. He had alleged a lack of democracy in the PUSC and accused the Calderón leadership of 'converging' ideologically with the PLN, but after his PUN leadership was legally overturned he sought reconciliation with the PUSC. The PUSC lost the 1986 election, in which it again presented Calderón Fournier as presidential candidate, but increased its assembly seats from 17 to 25, as well as gaining control of 25% of local authorities (up from 2%). The PUSC platform in 1986 stressed the pruning of the state sector and opposition to agrarian reform. After the election the PUSC leadership said it would use its strong parliamentary position to press for tax reform, law and order and cheaper public transport. In 1987 the PUSC became a member of the Conservative International.

See also **Calderón Guardia; Carazo Odio; Calderón Fournier**.

Social Democratic Innovation and Unity Party (*Partido de Inovación e Unidad-Social Demócrata*/PINU-SD)

A small, centrist, Honduran party, founded in 1970 as the Innovation and Unity Party (PINU) though not legally recognised until 1978. Its support comes mainly from professionals and some labour groups. In the 1981 elections founder Miguel Andonie Fernández and two others, including Julín Méndez, the first ever peasant leader in the legislature, won seats in congress. Its three seats were reduced to two in the 1985 elections, one of them held by Luis Lagos, president of the peasant organisation Anach. The party formally declared itself social democrat in 1986, claiming the support of the West German SPD, and acquired its present name in 1988. Its current (1989) president is Jorge Illescas.

Social Democratic Party: see Nicaraguan Democratic Co-ordinator.

Social Democrat Party (PSD) (Costa Rica): see Generation of '48 (Costa Rica); National Liberation Party.

Social Democrat Party (PSD) (El Salvador): see Democratic Convergence; Democratic Revolutionary Front (El Salvador).

Socialist Democratic Coalition: see Batista y Zaldívar.

Socialist (Second) International

The world social democrat organisation, founded in 1864, which currently represents more than 80 political parties and organisations world-wide. The SI's origins are in late 19th- and early 20th-century European politics and its formal involvement with Latin America dates back to the 1976 Geneva Congress, at which it took the decision to broaden its scope beyond Europe. It has placed stress on arms control and disarmament, North-South dialogue, the democratisation of Latin America and mediation in regional conflicts. Member parties in Mexico, Central America and the Caribbean (* denotes consultative party) are: National Liberation Party (PLN/Costa Rica); National Revolutionary Movement (MNR/El Salvador); People's National Party (PNP/Jamaica); Dominican Revolutionary Party (PRD/Dominican Republic); Democratic Socialist Party (PSD/Guatemala); People's Electoral Movement (MEP/Aruba)(*); New Antilles Movement (MAN/Netherlands Antilles)(*); Puerto Rican Independence Party (PIP)(*); Progressive Labour Party (PLP/St Lucia)(*). The Sandinista National Liberation Front/FSLN (Nicaragua) has several times been granted observer status. The Democratic Revolutionary Party/PRD of Panama, which had consultative status, was expelled after the fraudulent May 1989 elections in that country. Jamaica's Michael Manley, the Dominican Republic's José Francisco Peña Gómez, Guillermo Ungo of El Salvador and Daniel Oduber of Costa Rica are SI vice-presidents.

SI mediation in the Central American conflict has been complicated by the widely differing views of member parties. The PLN of Costa Rica has taken a generally anti-Sandinista line, as have some other parties, both inside and outside the region. The fourth meeting of the SI Committee for Latin America and the Caribbean (SICLAC), due to be held in Caracas, Venezuela, in 1982 had to be cancelled after the host party (Democratic Action/AD) objected to the FSLN presence. The SI rejected the US economic embargo and military campaign against Nicaragua but supported the Costa Rican government. On El Salvador, support for the FDR/FMLN opposition coalition has been strengthened by the presence of the MNR (a member of FDR) and its president, Guillermo Ungo (both president of the FDR and a vice-president of the SI); but despite resolutions condemning the government for human rights violations there was increasing acceptance of the 'democratisation' of the country under President Duarte. The tendency towards more limited support of the Sandinistas and the FDR-FMLN was evident in the SI's first triennial congress to be held in Latin America (Lima, Peru, June 1986). The

International backed the Contadora peace process and the Arias (or Esquipulas) Plan.

At a meeting of the SI Commission for Latin America and the Caribbean held in Quito in January 1990 a resolution was passed condemning the December 1989 US invasion of Panama and calling for free elections there.

See also **National Liberation Party; People's National Party; Dominican Revolutionary Party; People's Electoral Movement; New Antilles Movement; Puerto Rican Independence Party; Progressive Labour Party** (St Lucia); **Democratic Revolutionary Party; Manley, Michael; Peña Gómez; Ungo; Oduber, Daniel; Contadora Group; Arias Plan**.

Socialist Workers' Party (PST): see **Mexican Workers' Party**.

Solidarity Action Movement (MAS): see **Democratic Party of National Co-operation; Union of the National Centre**.

Solís Palma, Manuel: see **Delvalle**.

Somoza Debayle, Gen. Anastasio
1925–1980. President of Nicaragua 1967–79. Son of the dictator Anastasio Somoza García and a graduate of West Point military academy, USA, 'Tachito' Somoza was given the rank of major and command of the 1st battalion of the National Guard (GN) on his return to Nicaragua. He was later appointed the first Nicaraguan director of the military academy. He became head (*jefe director*) of the GN on his father's death in 1956 and installed himself as president after fraudulent elections in 1967, succeeding René Schick (1963–7). Prior to the elections, the GN had killed some 600 demonstrators at an opposition rally.Under his rule the GN was modernised and its role as a private army consolidated. Somoza was re-elected in 1971 under a pact with the rump of the opposition Conservative Party (known as '*zancudos*'), led by Fernando Aguero, which gave the Conservatives 40% of the legislature.

A triumvirate (Aguero plus two Somoza nominees) held formal power from May 1972 to December 1974, but Somoza kept control of the GN and remained head of state. He exploited the aftermath of the December 1972 earthquake to his own advantage, appropriating reconstruction aid and speculating with land and property. By this stage he had expanded the family businesses into real estate, construction, finance and insurance. They also included: food processing, fisheries, retail outlets, recording firms, ports and cargo handling facilities, the state airline and merchant shipping line, hotel chains, newspapers, radio and TV stations, banks, plastics and chemical factories. One source cites 346 different registered companies. Family landholdings represented at least half of the nation's registered land and a quarter of its best arable farmland. The Somozas were also involved in drugs, gambling and prostitution. They evaded tax, used state power for personal profit and took bribes from local and foreign companies. Somoza Debayle's wealth was estimated at US$900m–1,000m by 1979.

Rival businessmen began to speak of 'unfair competition', and oppo-

sition, both armed (the Sandinistas) and unarmed, grew steadily during the 1970s. After the earthquake Somoza ruled by decree as president of the National Emergency Committee, though the triumvirate still formally existed. He gave up the title of *jefe director* of the GN in order to stand in the 1974 elections, but became Supreme Head of the Armed Forces. He easily defeated the token Conservative candidate and began a third term of office (only possible through a constitutional amendment). In December 1974 he declared a state of siege after a Sandinista (FSLN) action in Managua: emergency rule lasted until September 1977. In August 1977 he had a major heart attack and was temporarily hospitalised in Miami. The FSLN offensive which overthrew him was in three phases: September 1978, April 1979 and May-July 1979. On 8 July 1979 Somoza offered his resignation to the US ambassador, on condition that his Liberal Party (PLN) and the GN remained intact, but it was too late. He fled the country on 17 July for exile in Miami (and later in Paraguay, where he bought a 12,000 ha ranch). Congress named an interim president, Francisco Urcuyo, who promptly announced his intention of serving out Somoza's term. He too fled two days later. Somoza was assassinated in September 1980 in a bazooka attack in Asunción, Paraguay.
See also **Sandinista National Liberation Front; Somoza García; Somoza Debayle, Luis; National Guard** (Nicaragua).

Somoza Debayle, Luis

1922–67. President of Nicaragua 1956–63. Son of Anastasio Somoza García and brother of Anastasio Somoza Debayle. Luis Somoza led the negotiating team in talks with the US on military assistance after World War II. He became a congressman, then president of congress, inheriting the presidency from his father after the latter's assassination in 1956. He undertook the modernisation of the economy and boosted foreign investment before voluntarily handing over the presidency in 1963 to a faithful supporter, lawyer René Schick. However, the Somoza family retained real power through control of the Liberal Party by Luis and of the National Guard by his brother Anastasio. Luis died of a heart attack in 1967.
See also **Somoza Debayle, Gen. Anastasio; Somoza García**.

Somoza García, Gen. Anastasio ('Tacho')

1896–1956. President of Nicaragua 1936–56. Son of a Conservative senator and owner of a modest coffee plantation near San Marcos, Carazo, Somoza was educated in Granada and at the Pierce Business School in Philadelphia, USA. He married a member of the wealthy Debayle family, who belonged to the Liberal Party (PLN), became active in the PL and took up arms with party leaders against the Conservative regime of Adolfo Díaz in 1926, assuming the title of general. He became undersecretary for foreign affairs in the government of President José María Moncada. After working as a translator for the US intervention forces, Somoza was appointed commander (*jefe director*) of the newly-created National Guard (GN) by the US in 1933. He turned the GN into a power base and used it to force out of office the then president, Juan Bautista

Sacasa, in 1936. In 1934 he was responsible for the ambush and murder of guerrilla leader Augusto César Sandino, with whom he had been negotiating.

Somoza was elected president in 1936 against only token opposition. Three years later he had the presidential term extended from four to six years. In 1947, under pressure both from within Nicaragua and from the US not to stand for office again, he allowed his defeated 1936 opponent, Leonardo Arguello, to be 'elected' in his place, but had him declared 'incapacitated' and exiled less than a month after his inauguration when he showed signs of independence. Corrupt abuse of state power brought him a fortune of several million dollars in the first ten years of his rule, along with vast landholdings. A 5% levy was imposed on public employees' wages for the benefit of the PLN, which he had turned into a vehicle for his personal power. After initial resistance, the Conservative opposition signed pacts with Somoza in 1948 and 1950, under which they effectively renounced their ambitions to rule. He was shot in León on 21 September 1956 by the poet and nationalist Rigoberto López Pérez, as he prepared to be nominated by the PLN for a fifth term of office: he died a week later. Control of the National Guard passed to his son Anastasio ('Tachito') Somoza Debayle and the presidency to Tachito's brother Luis.

See also **Sandino; National Guard** (Nicaragua); **Somoza Debayle, Gen. Anastasio; Somoza Debayle, Luis**.

Somoza Portocarrero, Anastasio: see **National Guard** (Nicaragua).

Sotelo Borgen, Enrique: see **Democratic Conservative Party**.

Southern Opposition Bloc (*Bloque Opositor del Sur*/BOS)
A coalition of Nicaraguan contra groups. Founded in July 1985, BOS originally included the Pastora wing of the Democratic Revolutionary Alliance (ARDE); the National Rescue and Conciliation Movement (MRCN) under Alfredo César; and four other smaller groups. Members were mainly Costa Rica-based former Sandinistas opposed to union with the largest contra group, the FDN, because of its links with the former Somoza regime. BOS was formed after the creation of the United Nicaraguan Opposition (UNO) by the FDN, the Robelo wing of ARDE and the Nicaraguan Democratic Co-ordinator (CDN). It complained of discrimination by the contras' US backers and called for equal status with UNO members and an agreed political project as conditions for unification. Its 'triple dialogue' proposal, involving talks between the US and the USSR, Nicaragua and its neighbours, and the Sandinistas and the 'opposition', won support from Colombian President Belisario Betancur in August 1985. In May 1987, after Pastora had abandoned the war, BOS and UNO announced the formation of a new alliance, to be known as the Nicaraguan Resistance. However, BOS withdrew from the RN in July 1988 complaining of a shift to the right.

See also **ARDE; Nicaraguan Resistance; Pastora Gómez; Nicaraguan Democratic Force**.

Southwell, Paul: see Bradshaw; St Kitts-Nevis Labour Party.

Space Research Corporation: see Bird, Vere C.

Spadafora, Hugo: see Ardito Barletta; Noriega Morena.

Spanish Embassy siege (Guatemala): see Peasant Unity Committee.

Special Service Units (SSUs)
US-trained and equipped military units of some 50–80 men drawn from the police force and set up in each of four English-speaking Eastern Caribbean islands (St Kitts-Nevis, Dominica, St Lucia and Grenada). The units, part of the US-financed Regional Security System launched in 1982, are designed to prevent coups such as the 1979 leftist takeover in Grenada and other violence against elected or civilian governments. But they were denounced by many as a means to repress internal dissent. St Vincent prime minister James Mitchell disbanded the unit in St Vincent when he won power in 1984, charging that it was a waste of money and potentially subversive. Grenadian prime minister Herbert Blaize in 1987 was the first to call in SSUs from other islands to defend against expected unrest.
See also **Regional Security System; Mitchell, James; Blaize; Grenada, US invasion (1983); military bases (foreign) in the Caribbean.**

Spencer, Baldwin: see United National Democratic Party.

Springer, (Sir) Hugh: see Barbados Workers' Union.

Stable Centrist Republican Movement (MERECEN): see Christian Democrat Party (El Salvador).

Statia
The more common name for the Dutch Caribbean island of Sint Eustatius (area 21 sq km; pop. 1900).
See **Netherlands Antilles.**

Stimson-Moncada pact: see Sandino.

Stoutt, Lavity
b. 7 March 1929. Chief minister, British Virgin Islands 1967–71, 1979–83, 1986– . A building contractor, Stoutt was elected to the legislative council in 1957. He was put in charge of works and communications from 1960 until 1967, when the ministerial system was introduced and he became the colony's first chief minister. He and his Virgin Islands Party (VIP) were defeated in the 1971 elections and he became leader of the opposition. In 1975, after elections produced a draw, Stoutt took power with independent MP Willard Wheatley as chief minister and himself as health minister and later deputy chief minister. In the 1979 election the VIP won only four of the nine seats, but Stoutt formed a government with the help of independent MPs and became chief minister. In 1983, when the VIP and the United Party (UP) tied at the polls, the UP joined

up with independent MP Cyril Romney to force Stoutt into opposition. Stoutt became chief minister again in 1986 after the VIP won elections called by Romney, who was under pressure from a drugs scandal. See also **Virgin Islands Party; Wheatley; United Party; Romney.**

Strachan, Winifred: see **Grenada United Labour Party.**

Structure Party, The (*Partido La Estructura*/PLE): see **Dominican Revolutionary Party; Majluta.**

Suazo Córdova, Dr Roberto

b. 1927. President of Honduras, 1982–6. Suazo Córdova was a little-known member of the *rodista* wing of the Liberal Party (PL) prior to the July 1979 death of PL leader Modesto Rodas Alvarado. He succeeded Rodas shortly before the 1980 constituent assembly election, which heralded the end of an almost unbroken two decades of military rule. Suazo had been a student in Guatemala in the 1940s and became a country doctor by profession. In 1965 he was expelled temporarily from the PL for seeking a deal with the military government. The PL won the 1980 election by a narrow margin, and joined a military-civilian coalition government comprising two military officers and six each from the PL and the National Party (PN). Suazo increased his majority in the 1981 general elections and took office as president in January 1982 with a majority of 44–34 over PN. A secret deal with the armed forces, agreed by both parties beforehand, had left the military – soon under hard-line armed forces commander Gen. Gustavo Alvarez – holding an effective veto over many crucial areas of policy. The new constitution also entrenched the autonomy of the military in the fields of defence, internal security and its own appointments structure.

Under Suazo, Honduras was closely identified with US policy in the region and agreed to host contra rebels fighting the Nicaraguan government. Human rights groups, both local and international, alleged widespread abuses, including the disappearance of over 100 opponents of the regime whose arrest was denied by the security forces. The government also used its control of the supreme court and the National Electoral Tribunal to promote the takeover of opposition organisations (including the PN) by minority pro-government factions. A plot to kill Suazo, uncovered by the FBI in 1984, led to the jailing of seven people, including a Honduran general, José Bueso Rosa, and three Honduran businessmen. The conspiracy, which was to have been financed with drugs money, was apparently aimed at recovering assets seized by the government from businessmen accused of fraud. As the 1985 election (in which he was constitutionally forbidden to stand) approached, Suazo displeased the US embassy and many PL members by manoeuvring to have his term of office extended, although he took care never to be publicly associated with the proposal.

In the Easter 1985 constitutional crisis, sparked by dissent within the PL, he was forced to agree to a settlement allowing more than one candidate to stand for the presidency on each party ticket, thus giving

dissident *rodista* José Azcona the chance to challenge and defeat Suazo's chosen successor, Oscar Mejía Arellano. Suazo's supporters took only 18 out of 134 seats.
See also **Liberal Party** (Honduras); **Alvarez Martínez.**

Swan, Sir John
b. 3 July 1935. Premier of Bermuda 1982– . A black millionaire real estate operator, Swan was elected to the house of assembly as a member of the United Bermuda Party in 1972. He was named minister of marine and air services in 1976 and later of labour and immigration. He became premier in 1982 when David Gibbons stepped down. He moved away from the UBP's traditional conservative white wing but was obliged to bring them back into the government after the 1989 election, when many black UBP MPs were defeated.
See also **United Bermuda Party.**

Sylvestre, Louis: see **People's United Party.**

T

Taft, William Howard: see dollar diplomacy

Taitt, Branford
b. 15 May 1938. Barbadian politician. A business consultant and former diplomat, Taitt was named a senator in 1971 and was minister of trade and industry 1971–6. He was elected to parliament in 1976. In 1984 he was beaten by Errol Barrow in a Democratic Labour Party (DLP) leadership election. He was named tourism and industry minister when the DLP returned to power in 1986, but demoted to health in 1987 when Erskine Sandiford became prime minister on the death of Barrow.
See also **Barrow; Democratic Labour Party; Sandiford**

tanda
A group or shift in a working context; also a class of graduates from a military academy (especially in El Salvador). Traditionally, members of the *tanda* protect one another and assist each other's career advancement. They make alliances with other *tandas* to this end, though rarely with that immediately ahead of them in graduation or that immediately behind because of the system whereby new entrants are brutalised by those in their second year. The Salvadorean *tanda* system, under which promotion is based on seniority rather than merit, has hindered the introduction of any formal system of discipline or punishment for officers guilty of crimes against civilians, and made the military resistant to outside influences. The class known as the *Tandona* comprises 33 colonels from the class of 1966, who are committed to a hard-line counter-insurgency policy and to protecting colleagues against human rights prosecutions. Members include retired major Roberto D'Aubuisson and another leading member of the ARENA party, Col. Sigifredo Ochoa. By the late 1980s the Tandona dominated the military hierarchy, its most prominent member being Col. René Emilio Ponce, chief of the staff of the armed forces.
See also **D'Aubuisson Arrieta.**

Tandona: see *tanda.*

Tannis, Hudson: see St Vincent Labour Party; Beache.

Tapia House Group
Trinidad-Tobago political party. Founded in 1968 by university lecturer and economist Lloyd Best, Tapia (the word means the earthen wall of a

traditional hut) grew out of the radical New World Group and was the first major organisation of the 'new left' movement which emerged to challenge the Caribbean's post-colonial conservatism. It advocated greater popular control, nationalism and self-reliance. Tapia's ideas helped fuel the 1970 'black power' uprising in Trinidad.

The group founded a party, the Tapia House Movement, to contest the 1976 general election, but only won 3.8% of the vote. It then advocated a 'party of parties' to overcome ethnic voting and the three-party alliance it joined won 10 seats at the 1981 general election. In 1986, Tapia dissolved itself to join the four-party opposition National Alliance for Reconstruction (NAR) coalition which won the 1986 general election. Best and others refused to join the NAR, but three Tapia members entered the cabinet. In 1987, Best relaunched the original Tapia House Group.

See also **Best; National Alliance for Reconstruction; 'new left'; 'black power'; Trinidad, 'black power' uprising (1970); Williams.**

Tattembach, Cristián: see Social Christian Unity Party.

Tegucigalpa Group: see Contadora Group.

Terceristas: see Sandinista National Liberation Front.

Théodore, René
b. 23 June 1940. Secretary-general of the Unified Haitian Communist Party (PUCH). A mathematics and physics teacher, Théodore was in exile from 1963, mostly in France. In 1962 he became a central committee member of the Party of Popular Accord (PEP) (f. 1959) and a member of its politburo two years later. In 1969, he was a founder member of PUCH and several months later was one of the few top officials and the only member of the party's politburo not to have been murdered by the Duvalier dictatorship. In 1978 he became party leader under the assumed name of Jacques Dorsilien, and returned to Haiti after the Duvaliers fell in 1986. He ran for the presidency as an independent in aborted elections in 1987.

See also **Unified Haitian Communist Party.**

13 November Revolutionary Movement (MR–13): see Guatemalan Labour Party.

31 January Popular Front (FP–31): see Peasant Unity Committee.

Thompson, Curl: see Esquivel, Manuel.

TIAR: see Rio Treaty.

Ti Legliz: see Haiti, Roman Catholic Church.

Tirado López, Víctor: see Sandinista National Liberation Front.

Tlatelolco massacre
A violent attack by Mexican troops on a student protest rally in Mexico City's central Plaza de Tlatelolco on 2 October 1968, which led to the deaths of an estimated 200–300 people. The protest movement, partly

influenced by student unrest elsewhere such as the events of May 1968 in Paris, had been growing in the run-up to the inauguration of the Olympic Games in Mexico, scheduled for 12 October. Students opposed the authoritarian character of the Gustavo Díaz Ordaz administration and there had been clashes with police in June and July. Soldiers attacked high school students barricaded in Preparatoria No 1, firing a bazooka at the school door. In response there were demonstrations against repression, with strong middle-class support. An estimated 300,000 people marched on 13 August and a similar number on 13 September.

The army occupied both the National Autonomous University (UNAM) and the National Polytechnic Institute (IPN), after which secret negotiations began between the government and the student leaders and the mass mobilisations temporarily lost their momentum. There was therefore a smaller turnout for the rally at Tlatelolco on 2 October, but by 5.30 p.m. around 10,000 protesters, including children, were still in the square. Without warning, army helicopters began dropping flares and hundreds of soldiers who had been lying in wait opened fire with automatic weapons. The secret police also opened fire, moving in later to make arrests. The government admitted that 32 protesters had died, but independent estimates put the figure much higher. The bodies were quickly removed in army trucks. Although the president accepted responsibility, saying the action had been necessary to eliminate the 'focus of agitation', he rarely appeared again in public during the remaining two years of his presidency.

See also **Díaz Ordaz.**

Tlatelolco Treaty

The treaty establishing a nuclear-free zone in Latin America, more formally known as the Treaty for the Prohibition of Nuclear Weapons in Latin America, which was signed in the Tlatelolco district of Mexico City on 14 February 1967. The treaty invoked the need for world disarmament and noted that 'the existence of nuclear weapons in any country of Latin America would make it a target for possible nuclear attacks and would inevitably set off . . . a ruinous race in nuclear weapons . . .' It commits the signatories to developing nuclear energy for purely peaceful purposes. The treaty bans the 'testing, use, manufacture, production, or acquisition by any means whatsoever of any nuclear weapons'; there is also a ban on the deployment or storage of nuclear weapons in Latin America by the signatories or by third parties.

The treaty established a special agency for verifying its implementation, the Organisation for the Prohibition of Nuclear Weapons in Latin America (OPANAL). Despite the ban on nuclear weapons the treaty specifically permits what are described as 'explosions of nuclear devices for peaceful purposes'. Additional Protocol I of the treaty seeks to make its provisions binding on extra-regional powers who are responsible, *de facto* or *de jure*, for territories within Latin America. Additional Protocol II commits extra-regional signatories not to use or threaten to use nuclear weapons against Latin American countries.

Cuba was the only country within the region which refused to sign the Tlatelolco Treaty, in protest at the maintenance of US bases with nuclear weapons in Guantánamo, Puerto Rico and the American Virgin Islands. Argentina signed but did not ratify the treaty, arguing that some of its clauses were commercially discriminatory, allowing the preservation of an exclusive 'nuclear club' and imposing restrictions on developing countries' access to nuclear technology. Brazil expressed similar reservations when it ratified the treaty in January 1968. The US signed Additional Protocol II, but with important reservations: that it did not consider itself impeded by the treaty from transporting nuclear weapons by air or sea through the non-nuclear zone; and that, while it would not threaten to use nuclear weapons against Latin American countries, that guarantee would lapse should any Latin American state, with the help of another nuclear power, launch an armed attack on the United States.

Tobago
Part of the twin-island state of Trinidad-Tobago.
Chief town: Scarborough
Area: 187 sq km
Population: 44,000
Main exports: tourism, fish

Political system

A 12-member House of Assembly with limited powers is elected for a maximum four years. The island elects two members of the State House of Representatives.
House of Assembly chairman: Lennox Denoon (1989)
Last elections: 1988

Political organisations

Parties in House of Assembly (leader) (seats): Democratic Action Congress/DAC (Jeff Davidson) (11), f. 1970; People's National Movement/PNM (Patrick Manning) (1), f. 1956.

The island, which became part of Trinidad-Tobago in 1889, has been politically dominated since 1976 by A. N. R. Robinson, prime minister of Trinidad-Tobago since 1986. Tobago elected its first House of Assembly in 1980, with Robinson's Democratic Action Congress (DAC) beating the People's National Movement 8–4. At the 1984 local elections DAC increased its hold by winning 11–1, a result repeated in 1988. Robinson was chairman of the assembly from 1980 until 1986, when he was succeeded by Jeff Davidson. Lennox Denoon was elected to replace Davidson in 1989.

In January 1987, a few weeks after Robinson became prime minister, Tobago was granted internal self-government, with full control of revenue collection, economic planning and public services. Under Robinson's prime ministership, new hotels, a deep-water port, a racecourse and a modern airport are being built in Tobago. The island inspired Daniel Defoe to write his adventure story Robinson Crusoe.

See also **Robinson: Trinidad and Tobago.**

'To Hell With Paradise': see **Mitchell, James.**

Tontons Macoutes
A para-military force created by Haitian President François Duvalier in 1958 to defend his regime against an army coup and other opponents. Officially known as the National Security Volunteers (VSN), its members were nicknamed Tontons Macoutes (bogeymen). They were overwhelmingly drawn from the black rural and urban poor, wore blue denim uniforms and often dark glasses and were given licence to extort and kill to maintain order. To avoid any threat to the regime from them, there was no strong central command of the force, which was tens of thousands strong, but for many years their 'national supervisor' was the formidable Rosalie 'Madame Max' Adolphe.

During the slightly more relaxed presidency of Jean-Claude Duvalier, complaints against them grew and they were nominally placed under army control. But their power barely diminished. Many Macoutes became disillusioned with Duvalier after his marriage to the mulatto Michèle Bennett in 1980, seeing it as a betrayal of the *noirisme* preached by François Duvalier. Their lack of enthusiasm and the sacking in 1985 of their patron, interior minister Roger Lafontant, contributed to the regime's collapse in 1986. The force was dissolved the day after the Duvaliers fled and hundreds of Macoutes were beaten, lynched or roasted alive. But many remained in the wings, emerging to kill and burn for the Duvalierists trying to regain power. The word *macoute* has become a strong term of abuse among Haitians.

See also **Duvalier, François; Duvalier, Jean-Claude;** *déchoukage.*

Torres, Marta Gloria: see **Unitary Representation of the Guatemalan Opposition.**

Torrijista Party: see **Democratic Revolutionary Party.**

Torrijos Herrera, Brig. Gen. Omar
1929–81. Chief of government of Panama 1968–78. Born in Santiago (Veraguas), the sixth son of a Colombian immigrant teacher, Torrijos was educated at the Dominio de Canadá school, Santiago, and the Escuela Normal 'Juan Demóstenes Arosemena'. As a student teacher he won a scholarship to the military college in El Salvador, graduating with the rank of sub-lieutenant (infantry) and a *bachillerato* in science and letters. He joined the Panamanian National Guard in 1952 and was promoted to lieutenant (1955), captain (1956), major (1960), lieutenant colonel (1966), colonel (1968) and brigadier general (1969). His posts included: commander of the National Guard unit at Tocumán international airport; head of Atlantic Zone (Colón) and Chiriquí (David); executive secretary of the general command of the National Guard; chief of the general staff; and finally, commander-in-chief. When the National Guard deposed President Arnulfo Arias in 1968, the presidency was assumed by Col. José María Pinilla, who had taken over as Guard com-

mander from Vallarino (retired by Arias). Real power, however, was in the hands of Torrijos (now commander) and Boris Martínez (now chief of staff).

Torrijos assumed full control in March 1969 after Martínez had made a radical speech about agrarian reform. Martínez was exiled and Torrijos promoted himself to brigadier general. Pinilla and his deputy were replaced with civilians in December 1969 for failing to oppose an attempted coup against Torrijos (the day of the attempt became known as the 'Day of Revolutionary Loyalty'). By 1971, Torrijos was expressing admiration for the radicalism of the Peruvian and Bolivian military, and had formed a close relationship with Fidel Castro (re-establishing diplomatic ties with Cuba in 1974), although he never espoused Marxism and kept local marxist politicians at arm's length. (All political parties were in recess during his rule.) He gradually came to serve as a middle-man, through whom right and left in the region could talk to each other, and acted as mediator in various aspects of the Central American crisis. From 1972 to 1978 a National Assembly of Community Representatives (ANRC) governed by decree, while Demetrios Lakas held the title of president.

Torrijos is credited with 'taking the army out of the clutches of the oligarchy', but his most notable achievement (though he remained dissatisfied with it) was the negotiation of the so-called 'Carter-Torrijos' treaties of 1978 giving Panama sovereignty over the Canal by the year 2000. Having achieved this, he embarked on a controlled return to civilian rule, leaving the 'leadership' of the country in 1978 while remaining the behind-the-scenes strong man. Dr Aristides Royo was appointed president by a newly-elected assembly in 1978. Torrijos died in an aircraft accident on 31 July 1981, in circumstances which were never fully explained. (His family and supporters have alleged CIA involvement, while accusations have also been levelled at his successor, Gen. Noriega.)
See also **Panama Canal Treaties: Democratic Revolutionary Party; Noriega Morena.**

Tower, John: see **Iran/contra affair.**

Tower Commission: see **Iran/contra affair.**

Trade Union Co-ordination Committee of Latin American Workers: see **CPUSTAL.**

Trafficante, Santos: see **Bay of Pigs invasion.**

TRINIDAD AND TOBAGO, Republic of
   Capital: Port of Spain
   Independence (from Britain): 1962.
   Area: 5,128 sq km
   Population (1989e): 1.29m (52% urban)
   Pop. growth rate: 3%
   Pop. density: 252/sq km
   Infant mortality: 14 per thousand

Life expectancy at birth: 70
Literacy: 95%
GDP per capita (1988e): US$5,510
Foreign debt per capita (1990): US$1,610
Main exports: petroleum products, chemicals, sugar, tourism

Political system

Constitution: 1976. A figurehead president is chosen by parliament. A 36-member House of Representatives is elected for a maximum of five years. A 31-member Senate is nominated. Tobago has its own House of Assembly with limited powers and elects two members of parliament.
President: Noor Mohammed Hassanali (1987)
Prime minister: A. N. R. Robinson (1986)
Last elections: 1986

Political organisations

Parties in parliament (leader) (seats in House of Representatives): National Alliance for Reconstruction/NAR (A. N. R. Robinson) (27), f. 1985; People's National Movement/PNM (Patrick Manning) (3), f. 1956; United National Congress/UNC (Basdeo Panday) (6), f. 1989.
Parties outside parliament: Tapia House Group/THG (Lloyd Best), f. 1968; National Joint Action Committee/NJAC (Makandal Daaga), f. 1969; Movement for Social Transformation/Motion (David Abdulah), f. 1989.
Main trade unions: Trinidad and Tobago Labour Congress/TTLC (Carl Tull), f. 1966; Council of Progressive Trade Unions/CPTU (Cecil Paul), f. 1970; All-Trinidad Sugar Estates and General Workers Trade Union/ ATSEGWTU (Basdeo Panday), f. 1937; Oilfield Workers' Trade Union/OWTU (Errol McLeod), f. 1937; National Farmers' and Workers' Union/NFWU (Raffique Shah), f. 1970; Bank and General Workers' Union/BGWU (Wade Mark), f. 1974; Public Services Association/- PSA (Kenrick Rennie), f. 1938; Seamen and Waterfront Workers' Trade Union/SWWTU (Vernon Glean), f. 1937; Transport and Industrial Workers' Union/TIWU (Albert Aberdeen), f. 1962; National Union of Government and Federated Workers/NUGFW (Selwyn John), f. 1937; Amalgamated Workers' Union/AWU (Cyril Lopez), f. 1953; Communication Workers' Union/CWU (Lyle Townsend), f. 1953; Trinidad and Tobago Unified Teachers' Association/TTUTA (Anthony Garcia), f. 1979; Trinidad Island-wide Cane Farmers' Association/TICFA, f. 1957.
Employers' organisations: Trinidad and Tobago Manufacturers' Association/TTMA (Gary Voss); Trinidad and Tobago Employers' Consultative Association/TTECA (Ally Hilton-Clarke).
See also **Tobago.**

Trinidad, 'black power' uprising (1970)

Influenced by the US black consciousness movement and the regional 'new left' groups of the late 1960s, the radical National Joint Action

Committee (NJAC) of Geddes Granger led a demonstration in Port-of-Spain on 26 February 1970 against Canadian economic power in the region and in support of Caribbean students who were being tried for destroying computers at Sir George Williams University in Montreal. Spurred by unemployment and anti-trade union legislation, and rejecting Trinidad-Tobago prime minister Eric Williams's perceived 'Afro-Saxonism', protests and strikes spread. A. N. R. Robinson, deputy prime minister, resigned. When the government declared a state of emergency on 21 April, an army mutiny led by Lt Raffique Shah (b. 1940) and others broke out in sympathy with the demonstrations. With US and Venezuelan warships offshore, the revolt was put down and the crisis subsided, but it led to an opposition boycott of the 1971 general election and formation of the National Union of Freedom Fighters (NUFF) guerrilla group. Williams also speeded up 'localising' ownership of foreign firms.

See also **'black power'; National Joint Action Committee; Williams; 'new left'; Robinson; Canada and the Anglo-Caribbean.**

Trotter, Desmond: see dreads.

Trujillo, Generalissimo Rafael

1891–1961. Dictator of the Dominican Republic 1930–61. After joining the army during the 1916–24 US occupation, Trujillo, a former telegrapher and small-time thief, was rapidly promoted, becoming national police chief in 1925 and army commander in 1927. He seized power in 1930, arranged his own formal election, and stamped out all opposition. In 1936 he renamed the capital Ciudad Trujillo and Pico Duarte, the country's highest mountain, Pico Trujillo. He gave himself the title of 'The Benefactor' and his family eventually took control of most of the economy. In 1937 he ordered the massacre of some 20,000 Haitian migrants along the border with Haiti. In 1938 he appointed first Jacinto Peynado and then Manuel de Jesús Troncoso de la Concha as puppet president and did not resume the title until 1943. In 1952 he handed the nominal presidency to his brother Héctor and then in 1960 to Joaquín Balaguer.

A failed attempt that year by his agents to assassinate Venezuelan President Rómulo Betancourt drew international condemnation of his regime and the Organisation of American States urged member states to break ties with the Dominican Republic. Internal unrest also grew. Trujullo was murdered on 30 May 1961 by a group of soldiers and civilians with CIA backing. His eldest son, Ramfis, then held power for a few months before being forced into exile along with his relatives.

The family's fortune was estimated at some $500m. But despite the megalomania, excesses and savageries of his rule, during which thousands were murdered, Trujillo is regarded by most as father of the modern Dominican state, having set up many of its present institutions, a sound economy and good road network.

See also **Dominican Republic, Haitian border massacre (1937); Balaguer.**

Tucker, Sir Henry: see United Bermuda Party.

Tula River murders: see Durazo Moreno.

Turcios Lima, Luis Augusto: see Rebel Armed Forces.

TURKS AND CAICOS ISLANDS
Capital: Grand Turk
Area: 430 sq km
Population (1989e): 13,000
Pop. growth rate: 7%
Pop. density: 30/sq km
Infant mortality: 43 per thousand
Life expectancy at birth: 70
Literacy: 87%
GDP per capita (1988): US$5,215
Foreign debt per capita (1987): US$207
Main exports: offshore finance, tourism, lobster, conch

Political system

A British colony, with (since 1972) an appointed British governor responsible for external affairs, defence and internal security, representing the
titular head of state, Queen Elizabeth of Britain. The governor chairs a
13-member Executive Council. Constitution: 1976. After direct rule was
imposed in 1986 following a corruption scandal, constitutional amendments in 1987 gave greater powers to the governor and revised the
electoral system. A 19-member (13 elected, 3 nominated, 3 ex-officio)
parliament, the Legislative Council, serves for a maximum four years.
Governor: Michael Bradley (1987)
Chief minister: Oswald Skippings (1988)
Last elections: 1988

Political organisations

Parties in parliament (leader) (seats): People's Democratic Movement/-
PDM (Oswald Skippings) (11), f. 1975; Progressive National Party/PNP
(Robert Hall) (2), f. 1980.
Parties outside parliament: National Democratic Alliance/NDA (Ariel
Misick), f. 1987; Turks and Caicos United Party/TCUP (Glen Clarke),
f. 1985.

TV Martí: see Radio Martí.

20 December Movement (M–20): see Dignity Battalions.

'20 families' (Panama): see 'rabiblancos'.

28 February Popular Leagues (LP–28): see Democratic Revolutionary Front (El Salvador); People's Revolutionary Army (El Salvador).

26 July Movement (*Movimiento 26 de Julio*/M–26–7)
A political movement founded in 1955 by Fidel Castro and named after

the date of the attack on the Moncada barracks in 1953 (officially taken as the start of the Cuban revolution). Recruits were mostly from the reformist *Ortodoxo* party, based in the urban middle class. M–26–7 was the vehicle for the struggle against the Batista regime (1956–8). It merged into the Integrated Revolutionary Organisations (ORI/1961–3) and its successor, the United Party of the Socialist Revolution (PURS), and then into the new Cuban Communist Party (PCC) in 1965, along with the Popular Socialist Party (PSP) and the Revolutionary Student Directorate (DER).

See also **Communist Party** (Cuba); **Cuban Revolutionary War; Integrated Revolutionary Organisations; United Party of the Socialist Revolution.**

U

Ubico, Dr Arturo: see Ubico y Castañeda.

Ubico y Castañeda, Gen. Jorge

1878–1946. President of Guatemala 1931–44. The son of Dr Arturo Ubico, interior minister under President Justo Rufino Barrios and envoy to the US, Ubico served in the army as a lieutenant attached to the general staff during the 1906 frontier war with El Salvador, even though he had failed to graduate from the military academy. He was then appointed political and military commander of Alta Verapaz (1907–9) and Retalhuleu (1911–19) departments; and head of the National Sanitary Commission during the army's campaign to eradicate yellow fever. He became chief of staff in 1920. Ubico was one of the first Guatemalan officers to receive US training and later (post–1920) helped introduce US methods more widely into the army. In 1920 he took part in the coup which installed Gen. José M. Orellana as president, and he served as Orellana's minister of war 1921–3, but he then quarrelled with him and began to plot against him. In 1922 and 1926 he stood as a presidential candidate, without success, but after a coup in 1930 the US helped install him as president after perfunctory elections.

Despite a constitutional ban on consecutive terms of office, Ubico had his presidency extended to five terms by various fraudulent means. He was noted for the brutality of his rule, under which torture and summary execution were commonplace. He abolished municipal authorities; introduced a vagrancy law compelling Indians owning only small plots of land to work 150 days a year on plantations; centralised and greatly extended the political police system and banned all political parties except his own Liberal-Progressive Party (PLP). During World War II, Ubico supported the Axis powers until he was compelled by US pressure to expropriate German and Italian properties. He was eventually forced out of office in 1944 by mass demonstrations and strikes led by students, teachers, doctors and lawyers and finally joined by businessmen. He was briefly succeeded by Gen. Federico Ponce, before the outbreak of the military revolt which heralded the Guatemalan 'revolution'. He died in exile in New Orleans.

See also **Arévalo Bermejo**.

UDEL coalition: see Independent Liberal Party.

Ulate Blanco, Otilio: see Civil War (Costa Rica/1948); Second Republic (Costa Rica).

Unade (Democratic National Union): see National Liberation Coalition (COLINA).

Ungo, Dr Guillermo
b. 1931. President of the Democratic Revolutionary Front (FDR) of El Salvador. A law professor and businessman, Guillermo Ungo became leader of the National Revolutionary Movement (MNR) on its formation. He was vice-presidential running mate to José Napoleón Duarte in 1972 on the National Opposition Union (UNO) ticket, and joined the first junta formed after the 15 October 1979 coup. He resigned on 3 January 1980, along with most other members of the government, arguing that the armed forces were blocking reforms. Following the abduction and murder of Enrique Alvarez Córdova in November 1980, Ungo was elected to succeed him as president of the FDR, of which the MNR was a founder member. He is also a vice-president of the Socialist International. In 1988, Ungo returned from exile to help found the Democratic Convergence, an electoral alliance which backed his presidential candidacy in March 1989. However, the FDR's allies on the armed left disrupted the elections, lowering the turnout and contributing to Ungo's poor showing of less than 5%.
See also **Democratic Convergence; Democratic Revolutionary Front** (El Salvador).

Unidad: see Social Christian Unity Party.

Unified Haitian Communist Party (*Parti Unifié des Communistes Haitiens*/PUCH)
Founded abroad in 1969 as a merger of the pro-Moscow Party of Popular Accord (PEP) and the pro-Castro Union of Haitian Democrats Party (PUDA). Successor to the Haitian Communist Party founded in 1934 by Jacques Roumain. The party led a brief anti-government uprising in the village of Cazale in March 1969. The Duvalier dictatorship made communism a capital offence a month later and by July its agents had killed most of the party's top officials, including secretary-general Gérald Brisson, 16 of the 21-member central committee and four of the five-member politburo. Joseph Roney became secretary-general until 1972, after which the party was weakened by a quarrel over whether to adopt armed struggle.
René Théodore became secretary-general in 1978 under the name of Jacques Dorsilien. More than 1,000 PUCH supporters are estimated to have been killed by the dictatorship. Théodore returned to Haiti in 1986 after the Duvaliers fell and the party was allowed to function, and was an independent candidate in aborted presidential elections in 1987.
See also **Théodore; Duvalier, François; Duvalier, Jean-Claude.**

Unified Popular Action Front: see FAPU.

Unified Revolutionary Directorate (DRU): see Farabundo Martí National Liberation Front.

Union for Renewal (Martinique): see Lordinot.

Union Island revolt (1979)

About 30 young people, led by rastafarian Lennox 'Bumber' Charles, staged an uprising on the Grenadine island of Union (10 sq km, pop. 4,000) in December 1979 to seek autonomy from St Vincent and the government of Milton Cato two days after Cato had won a general election. Charles had complained about neglect of the island, over-fishing by foreigners, drug smuggling and foreign tourist exploitation. The ill-planned revolt was crushed by police from St Vincent and soldiers sent by Barbados in the first example of military aid by one independent Commonwealth Caribbean state to another. One civilian was killed. Cato declared a state of emergency which lasted six months. Charles escaped to neighbouring Carriacou and Grenada but was arrested and returned to St Vincent, where he was tried in 1980 and sentenced to eight years in jail with hard labour.

See also **Cato; Regional Security System; rastafarians; Grenadines.**

Union of the National Centre (*Unión del Centro Nacional*/UCN)

A Guatemalan party founded in 1983 as a vehicle for the presidential ambitions of newspaper publisher Jorge Carpio Nicolle, owner of the newspaper *El Gráfico*. The UCN lacked a firm political base, but in 1984, Carpio waged the first modern professional media campaign seen in Guatemala, winning 20 seats in the constituent assembly elections. He fought a run-off presidential round against Vinicio Cerezo of the Christian Democrats (DCG) in 1985, winning about one-third of the votes cast. It was widely alleged that he was (at least initially) the favoured candidate of the army and the US embassy, a theory to which his free-spending campaigns lent credence. The UCN's platform was right of centre, though its ideology was vague. It proposed no major reforms, concentrating on the need for more efficient agriculture and better tax collection. It formed alliances with two conservative parties, the Revolutionary Party (PR) and the Party of National Renovation (PNR), prior to the presidential elections, but these were short-lived.

In 1987 the UCN declined to sign the 'democratic commitment' (*compromiso democrático*) with other parties. Carpio described as 'farcical' this attempt by the DCG to form a common front against authoritarianism, even though the UCN had been involved in its preparation. Despite its openly anti-communist stance in 1984–5 and its decision to join the Liberal International, the UCN has at times sought to present itself as a party of the left, criticising the DCG for 'rightist' policies. In the run-up to the 1990 elections it held talks on a possible alliance with the Confederation of Guatemalan Trade Union Unity (CUSG), considered close to the US embassy.

Unitary Action Party (PAU): see Batista y Zaldívar.

Unitary Representation of the Guatemalan Opposition (*Representación Unitaria de la Oposición Guatemalteca*/RUOG)
A group of left-wing opposition figures who left the country in 1980–81 because of threats to their lives, and who now seek to represent the interests of some 200,000 Guatemalan exiles. Leading members of the group include labour lawyers Marta Gloria Torres and Frank Larue, campesino leader Rigoberta Menchú, and Rolando Castillo, former dean of the faculty of medicine at the University of San Carlos. The government has described them as guerrilla leaders who must seek amnesty in order to return. Despite this, a RUOG delegation visited Guatemala in April 1988 to assess the state of the 'political opening' there. In April 1989 they returned to participate in the National Dialogue established under the terms of the Arias peace plan. However, Larue, Torres and Castillo left the following month after receiving death threats.
See also **Arias Plan.**

United Bahamian Party (UBP)
Former ruling party in the Bahamas, founded in 1958 and representing the country's segregated white ruling class, known as the Bay Street Boys (after the merchants with premises on Nassau's main street), who dominated the country for 300 years. Amid charges of massive corruption involving foreign gambling and Mafia interests in the development of Grand Bahama, it was led to its electoral demise in 1967 by Premier Sir Roland Symonette. It was defeated by the black-dominated Progressive Liberal Party (PLP) of Lynden Pindling, which tied 18–18 with the UBP but took office with the support of independent MPs. The party won only seven seats at the 1968 general election. In 1970 the four remaining UBP MPs joined with defectors from the PLP to form the Free National Movement.
See also **Free National Movement; Progressive Liberal Party; Hawksbill Creek Agreement.**

United Bermuda Party (UBP)
Founded in 1964 by leading banker Sir Henry Tucker as the voice of Bermuda's ruling white business class (nicknamed the Forty Thieves) and in reaction to the formation of the black-based left-wing Progressive Labour Party (PLP) the year before. It immediately became the majority party in the house of assembly when most MPs, hitherto independents, joined it. It won elections 30–10 in 1968 on the granting of internal self-government and Tucker became government leader. Pre-election race riots spurred the party to push for an end to racial segregation and inequality, but racial disturbances erupted again in 1970.

Tucker handed over to the island's first black head of government, Sir Edward Richards, in 1971. The UBP won 30–10 once more at the 1972 election. Richards yielded the premiership in 1976 to his deputy, John Sharpe (b. 8 November 1921). The party lost ground in elections a few months later to the PLP but won 26–14. After a cabinet revolt, Sharpe resigned in 1977 and finance minister David Gibbons became premier. The UBP came within 150 votes of losing power to the PLP at the 1980

election when it beat the PLP 22–18. It appointed a black millionaire, John Swan, as leader and premier in 1982 in place of Gibbons and won general elections in 1983 (26–14) and 1985 (31–9). But in 1989 it only beat the opposition by 23–17. Seven of the eight seats it lost were held by blacks and Swan was obliged to appoint to the cabinet many conservative whites he had earlier opposed.
See also **Swan; Progressive Labour Party** (Bermuda); **'black power'.**

United Brands: see **López Arellano.**

United Democratic Party (UDP)

A Belizean political party, founded in 1973 out of a fusion of the Liberal Party, the National Independence Party (under Philip Goldson) and the People's Development Movement (under Dean Lindo), and formally constituted in April 1974. The UDP, whose ethnic base is in the black (creole) community, lost the 1974 general election, but won control of Belize City Council that year. In the 1970s, under the leadership of Dean Lindo, it argued that independence from Britain should be postponed for 10 years, pending settlement of the Guatemalan territorial claim. It fought the 1979 election on the accusation that the People's United Party government was communist, and won five seats. But Lindo was replaced as leader by Theodore Aranda. The party called without success for a referendum on independence. It boycotted both the parliamentary committee set up to study the issue and the September 1981 independence celebrations. A few months before independence some members organised the Belize Action Movement (BAM), which became involved in violent anti-government protests.

Aranda was forced out in 1982 and Manuel Esquivel became party leader. In 1984 the UDP took power for the first time, after a 21–7-seat victory in the general elections, which was quickly followed by sweeping gains in local government. The party is conservative and believes in development through foreign investment. It took Belize even further into the US sphere of influence than the PUP, despite a manifesto commitment to the preservation of sovereignty and a declaration that it would be 'non-aligned' though 'pro-western'. Factional fighting in 1988 suggested that the old rivalries among the UDP's constituent parties had not entirely been overcome. In 1989, Esquivel called an election in which he sought support for a continuation of his free market economic model, but he was defeated 15–13 by the PUP.
See also **Esquivel, Manuel; People's United Party.**

United Fruit Company: see **Castillo Armas; Carías Andino; banana strike** (Costa Rica/1934); **general strike** (Honduras/1954); **López Arellano; National Party; Villeda Morales.**

United Labour Front (ULF): see **Panday; National Alliance for Reconstruction.**

United National Congress (UNC): see **Panday; National Alliance for Reconstruction.**

United National Democratic Party (UNDP)

Antiguan political party. Founded in 1986 after a merger between surgeon Ivor Heath's National Democratic Party (f. 1985) and the United People's Movement (UPM) of ex-premier George Walter. Heath (b. 16 August 1926) was named leader, with the UPM's Baldwin Spencer (b. 8 October 1948) as his deputy. Spencer, also assistant general secretary of the Antigua Workers' Union, won the party's first seat in parliament at the 1989 general election, when the UPM received 31% of the vote.
See also **Walter**.

United National Front (UNF): see Irish.

United Nicaraguan Opposition (*Unidad Nicaragüense Opositora*/UNO)

A coalition of contra groups, founded in June 1985 in San Salvador by the leaders of the Nicaraguan Democratic Force (FDN) (Adolfo Calero), the Nicaraguan Democratic Movement (MDN) (Alfonso Robelo) and the Nicaraguan Democratic Co-ordinator (CDN) (Arturo Cruz). (Not to be confused with the National Opposition Union/UNO, which won the 1990 elections.) Funded by the US government, and allegedly supplied unlawfully between 1984 and 1986 by the US Central Intelligence Agency (CIA) and the National Security Council (NSC), UNO was the successor to the Nicaraguan Unity for Reconciliation group (UNIR, f. 1984). US government agencies were instrumental in its creation, which was intended not only to present a united anti-Sandinista front but to improve the public image of the contras. In January 1986, UNO leaders presented a Statement of Principles and Objectives, promising (*inter alia*) a pluralist political system, amnesty for political and related civil crimes and the creation of a National Army, largely composed of former contra combatants. Other proposals included: 'integral agrarian reform', with respect for private property; and the abolition of 'state centralism', returning to the private sector those areas of the economy which it could run 'more efficiently'. UNO promised to hold general elections within eight months of taking power.

From the beginning there were serious strains between Calero and the other two UNO leaders, and he was forced to resign in February 1987 over his opposition to internal reform. Pedro Joaquín Chamorro Jr took his place. UNO's small southern front (UNO-FARN) had already withdrawn from the alliance, alleging that its supplies had been blocked, and the Miskito Indian group Kisan had made similar complaints. Robelo and Cruz insisted on the integration of all contra forces, the expansion of the civilian directorate and clear-cut civilian control over military operations. In May 1987, UNO merged with the Southern Opposition Bloc (BOS) to form the Nicaraguan Resistance (RN).
See also **Nicaraguan Democratic Force; Nicaraguan Democratic Co-ordinator; Nicaraguan Resistance; Iran/contra affair; Calero Portocarrero; Cruz Porras; Robelo Callejas.**

352

United Party (UP)
Political party in the British Virgin Islands. The UP won the 1967 elections 4–3, but achieved only one seat in the 1971 election. It tied 3–3 with the Virgin Islands Party (VIP) at the 1975 poll, but the VIP took power in alliance with the lone independent MP, Willard Wheatley, as chief minister. After being dumped by the VIP following the 1979 election, Wheatley became leader of the UP, which had won no seats. In 1983 the party tied again (4–4) with the VIP and took power by making the single independent MP, Cyril Romney, chief minister. The party won only two seats in the 1986 poll, called after Romney had been tainted by a drug scandal. Former labour minister Conrad Maduro then became party leader. UP MP Ralph O'Neal (b. 15 December 1933), the parliamentary opposition leader, defected to the VIP in 1988 and became deputy chief minister, replacing Omar Hodge who had been sacked for alleged corruption. Hodge joined the UP but left it in 1989 to form the Independent People's Movement.
See also **Wheatley; Romney; Virgin Islands Party.**

United Party of the Socialist Revolution (*Partido Unido de la Revolución Socialista*/PURS)
A political party founded in 1963 by the Castro regime in Cuba as a replacement for the Integrated Revolutionary Organisations (ORI). The aim was to lay the foundations of a mass party of workers and peasants, subsequently founded in 1965 as the Cuban Communist Party (PCC). The secretary general of PURS was Fidel Castro.
See also **Communist Party** (Cuba)**; Integrated Revolutionary Organisations; Castro Ruz, Fidel Alejandro.**

United People (PU): see **Communist Party** (Costa Rica).

United People Party (PPU): see **Communist Party** (Costa Rica).

United People's Movement (UPM) (Antigua): see **Walter; United National Democratic Party.**

United People's Movement (MPU) (Nicaragua): see **Sandinista National Liberation Front.**

United People's Movement (UPM) (St Vincent)
Political party in St Vincent. Founded as a left-wing alliance just before the 1979 general election, the UPM comprised the Youlou Liberation Movement (Yulimo) (Ralph Gonsalves and Renwick Rose), Arwee (Oscar Allen) and the People's Democratic Movement (Kenneth John). It won no seats but its 14.4% of the vote marked the high point electorally of the region's 'new left', whose influence thereafter declined. The coalition broke up after the poll, but the UPM survived and first Rose then Allen became leader. Allen resigned in 1988 and Adrian Saunders (b. 1954) became UPM leader. The party took 3% of the vote at the 1984 general election and only 1% at the 1989 poll.
See also **Gonsalves; Movement for National Unity; 'new left'.**

United Resistance Front (FUR): see Rebel Armed Forces.

United Revolutionary Organisations Co-ordinating Group: see Omega 7.

United Workers' Party (UWP) (St Lucia)
Conservative party in St Lucia. Founded in 1964 by defectors from the St Lucia Labour Party (SLP), including John Compton, who joined up with the People's Progressive Party led by George Mallet to form the UWP. The party won the 1964 elections (6–4) and Compton became premier with Mallet as his deputy. It won again in 1969 (6–4) and 1974 (10–7) but was defeated (12–5) by a reinvigorated, left-leaning SLP in 1979. After three years of chaotic factional SLP rule ending in a brief all-party coalition government under Michael Pilgrim, the UWP and Compton returned to power after winning the 1982 elections (14–3). In two general elections in 1987 the UWP narrowly won (9–8 each time). It later increased its majority to 10–7 after an opposition defection.
See also **Compton; St Lucia Labour Party.**

Unity and Teamwork: see Bodden, Jim.

Unity of Labour and Popular Action (UAPS): see Peasant Unity Committee.

University and Allied Workers' Union (UAWU): see Workers' Party of Jamaica; Munroe.

University of the West Indies (UWI)
One of the few successful attempts at Anglo-Caribbean unity. Founded in 1949 as the University College of the West Indies, it took its present name in 1962. It has three campuses: Mona (Jamaica), St Augustine (Trinidad) and Cave Hill (Barbados). Vice-chancellor: Alister McIntyre (1988).
See also **Caribbean Community; Lewis, Sir Arthur; McIntyre.**

UNO-FARN: see United Nicaraguan Opposition.

UPT: see Popular Liberation Forces; Popular Revolutionary Bloc.

UR–19: see Popular Liberation Forces.

Urcuyo, Francisco: see Sandinista National Liberation Front; Somoza Debayle, Gen. Anastasio.

Urgent Fury: see Grenada, US invasion (1983).

Urrutia, Juan Pablo: see National Party.

Urrutia, Manuel: see Dorticós Torrado.

US Southern Command: see CONDECA; Panama Canal Zone.

US VIRGIN ISLANDS
Capital: Charlotte Amalie
Area: 355 sq km

Population (1988): 110,000
Pop. growth rate: 1.9%
Pop. density: 310/sq km
Infant mortality: 18 per thousand
Life expectancy at birth: 68
Literacy: 90%
GDP per capita (1986): US$12,264
Main exports: petroleum products, chemicals, tourism, rum, clocks and watches, meat, ethanol

Political system

A US possession since it was bought from Denmark in 1917 for $25m. A governor, elected (since 1970) every four years, represents head of state US President George Bush. A 15-member senate with limited powers is elected every two years. The islands have had a non-voting delegate in the US House of Representatives since 1972. Proposals for greater self-government have been rejected in referendums, mainly because this would mean higher taxation.

Governor: Alexander A. Farrelly (1987)
Lieutenant-governor (St Croix): Derek M. Hodge (1987)
Delegate to the US Congress: Ron de Lugo (1972)
Last elections: 1988

Political organisations

Parties in the Senate (leader) (seats): Democratic Party of the Virgin Islands/DPVI (Winston Hodge) (10); Republican Party of the Virgin Islands/RPVI (Charlotte Poole-Davis) (2); Independent Citizens' Movement/ICM (Virdin Brown) (1), f. 1968.
See also **St Croix.**

V

Valladares, Armando
b. 1937. Cuban ex-prisoner, appointed head of the US human rights delegation to the United Nations in 1988. Valladares is a former civil servant who was arrested in 1960 and, after a brief trial, sentenced to 30 years' imprisonment for illegal possession of firearms and explosives. A controversial figure, he is regarded by supporters, including the US government, as a writer who was unjustly imprisoned for expressing opposition to Marxism. The Cuban authorities say he was a policeman during the Batista dictatorship. He claims to have been subjected to brutal reprisals for his refusal to co-operate with the prison authorities and to have been paralysed for five years as a result of being denied food for 46 days in 1974. Adopted by Amnesty International as a prisoner of conscience, he was eventually released in 1982 at the request of President Mitterand of France. He became a US citizen in January 1987 and was chosen to head the human rights delegation, with the rank of ambassador, at a time when Washington was placing heavy emphasis on human rights in Cuba.
See also **Cuban Human Rights Party.**

Valverde, Carlos Luis: see Civil War (Costa Rica).

Vanguard Nationalist and Socialist Party (VNSP)
Bahamian political party. Founded mainly as a 'black power' group in 1971 by members of the Unicomm youth group who distanced themselves from other members who gave critical support to the ruling Progressive Liberal Party. Its first chairman was John McCartney, a Bahamian university lecturer in the US. The party then moved further left. McCartney was later succeeded by his deputy, Lionel Carey. The party won less than 1% of the vote at the 1982 general election.
See also **Progressive Liberal Party; 'black power'.**

Vargas, Azael: see Labour Party (Panama).

Vásquez Rojas, Genaro: see Nationalist Revolutionary Civic Association.

Vatican II: see Christian base community.

Vazquez-Sakio Treaty: see San Andrés dispute.

Velázquez, Fidel

Velázquez, Fidel

b. 1900. A long-serving Mexican labour leader whose support has been crucial to a succession of presidents. Velázquez was born into a poor family and started his working life as a milkman, soon becoming involved in the labour movement. He was one of the 'five little wolves', the group of officials which came to control the Mexican Workers' Congress (CTM) shortly after its foundation, and by 1941 had emerged as its undisputed leader. Strongly anti-communist in outlook, he forged close links with George Meany's American Federation of Labor (AFL) in the US, while domestically he developed the CTM into a formidable political machine which was used to support the ruling Institutional Revolutionary Party (PRI). The CTM leadership frequently imposed wage restraint at the government's behest and quelled outbreaks of rank-and-file radicalism. At the same time, however, Velázquez was careful to extract a *quid pro quo*.

In 1968 the CTM's opposition to the student protest movement prevented unrest from spreading throughout the country, and in return Velázquez secured President Díaz Ordaz's support for a new labour code. Relations between 'Don Fidel' and President Echeverría in the late 1970s were more tense, however, because of the latter's initial support for independent, left-leaning unions and his apparent desire to undermine the CTM leader's power base. But in the latter part of Echeverría's *sexenio*, when conflict between the government and the business sector sharpened, the president was forced to turn to Velázquez for help.

Under López Portillo, Velázquez accepted wage increases below the rate of inflation. In return the CTM was granted control of the state housing fund, a Workers' Bank was set up and the government persecuted the anti-Velázquez independent unions. In the more severe economic crisis after 1982, during the presidency of De la Madrid, the CTM again, rather than pressing wage demands, helped impose austerity on its members. Real wages fell drastically, by as much as 50% according to some calculations, without an outbreak of strikes or other protest action. There were, however, signs that Velázquez was impatient with the more technocratic government officials and their failure to recognise the need for sensitive political handling of the situation. In 1983, for example, the CTM leader threatened to call a general strike.

Velázquez angrily rejected suggestions that he retire, and in 1986, at the age of 86, he was re-elected for a ninth six-year term as CTM general secretary.

See also **Confederation of Mexican Workers; Institutional Revolutionary Party; Tlatelolco massacre; Díaz Ordaz; Echeverría Alvarez; López Portillo; De la Madrid Hurtado.**

Victory 82: see *fusiles y frijoles*.

Vieques

A 132 sq km island (pop. 8,000) 10 km east of Puerto Rico, of which it is part. Two-thirds of it is controlled by the US military, who use it for bombing practice and as a key centre of annual military manoeuvres

involving US, European and Caribbean troops. In 1981 it was used in an
'Ocean Venture' exercise by 120,000 troops as a rehearsal for the invasion
of Grenada two years later. For the exercise, Vieques was named 'Amber
and the Amberdines'. After five years of wrangling over the bad effects
of the military presence, the US navy signed an agreement with the
Puerto Rican government in 1983 to boost the island's economic development. In 1984 local fishermen and other Puerto Ricans protested against
the annual manoeuvres. In 1989, squatters occupied part of the military
area. The island was devastated by Hurricane Hugo in 1989.
  Mayor: Manuela Santiago Collazo (1987).
See also **Puerto Rico; Grenada, US invasion (1983); military bases
(foreign) in the Caribbean; Culebra.**

Villa, Francisco (Pancho): see Mexican Revolution.

Villalobos, Joaquín
b. 1951. Commander-in-chief of the People's Revolutionary Army (ERP)
of El Salvador and senior commander of the Farabundo Martí National
Liberation Front (FMLN). Born in San Salvador, the son of a printer,
Joaquín Villalobos studied economics and became a student leader, but
dropped out in the mid-1970s to join the guerrillas. He was among those
responsible for the 'execution' of poet and ERP dissident Roque Dalton,
killed in 1975. After the death of Popular Liberation Forces (FPL) leader
Salvador Cayetano Carpio, in 1983, Villalobos emerged as the dominant
guerrilla commander.
See also **People's Revolutionary Army** (El Salvador); **Farabundo Martí
National Liberation Front.**

Villeda Morales, Ramón
1908–71. President of Honduras 1957–63. Elected on the Liberal Party
(PL) ticket in the 1957 elections following the overthrow by the army in
October 1956 of the repressive *de facto* regime of Julio Lozano Díaz
(National Party/PN), Villeda was a moderate reformer and anti-communist. He won the support of the US in the Alliance for Progress years
after the Cuban revolution, introduced the first Honduran labour law
(1959) and took the country into the Central American Common Market.
He aroused the opposition of landowners and US fruit companies, however, by his 1962 agrarian reform programme, which sought to bring
idle land into production and ease the growing pressure from peasant
organisations. Amendments imposed by the United Fruit Co. effectively
prevented the expropriation of private land. The PN and the army were
alienated by Villeda's abolition of the (pro-PN) police force and his
creation of a Civil Guard, independent of the armed forces, as its replacement. When the PL seemed set to win the 1963 elections, the army
overthrew Villeda, killing many Guard members, and imposed Col.
Oswaldo López Arellano as president.
See also **Liberal Party** (Honduras).

Villeda Morales Movement: see Liberal Party (Honduras).

Virgin Islands: see British Virgin Islands; US Virgin Islands.

Virgin Islands Party (VIP)

Political party in the British Virgin Islands. Founded in 1970, the VIP won two of the seven elective seats at the 1971 election. In 1975 it and the United Party (UP) each won three seats and VIP leader Lavity Stoutt joined with independent MP Willard Wheatley to take power, with Wheatley as chief minister and Stoutt as his deputy. The VIP won only four of nine seats in 1979, but Stoutt was named chief minister with the backing of independents who held the other five. In 1983 the VIP and the UP tied 4–4 and the UP and the single independent MP put the VIP into opposition. The VIP won 5–4 in the 1986 elections and Stoutt again became chief minister. UP MP Ralph O'Neal, the parliamentary opposition leader, defected to the VIP in 1988 and became deputy chief minister, succeeding the sacked Omar Hodge, who in turn joined the UP.

See also **Stoutt; United Party; Wheatley.**

VSN (*Volontaires de la Sécurité Nationale*/VSN): see **Tontons Macoutes.**

Wade, Frederick: see **Progressive Labour Party** (Bermuda)

Walcott, Sir Frank
b. 16 September 1916. Barbadian trade union leader. Walcott became general secretary of the Barbados Workers' Union (BWU) in 1948. He was also a member of the island's Executive Council 1948–53 in charge of agriculture, communications and public works. He broke with Grantley Adams, who had jointly run the BWU as president-general, after Adams became premier in 1954, and in 1958 allied himself with the rebel Democratic Labour Party of Errol Barrow. He was a member of the House of Assembly 1945–51, 1956–66 and 1971–6, and was named to the senate from 1966–71 and again in 1976, later becoming its president.
See also **Barbados Workers' Union; Democratic Labour Party** (Barbados).

Wallace-Whitfield, Sir Cecil
1930–90. Opposition leader in the Bahamas 1971–2, 1976–81, 1987–90. A barrister, Wallace-Whitfield was works minister in the first government of Lynden Pindling, 1967–8, and then education minister from 1968 until 1970, when he and three other ministers resigned along with four more MPs of the ruling Progressive Liberal Party and formed the Free National Movement (FNM) in 1971. He succeeded Henry Bostwick, the party's first leader, and headed the party until 1972 when he lost his parliamentary seat and handed over to Kendal Isaacs. He took the post back from 1976 until 1981, when Isaacs returned again and Wallace-Whitfield became deputy leader. He resumed the leadership once more after the FNM lost the 1987 election.
See also **Free National Movement; Progressive Liberal Party; Isaacs**.

Walter, George
b. 8 September 1928. Premier of Antigua-Barbuda 1971–6. A trade union official, Walter became general secretary of the Antigua Trades and Labour Union but was expelled from it in 1967 after disputing the power of union president Vere C. Bird. Walter then formed the Antigua Workers' Union (AWU). He founded the Progressive Labour Movement (PLM) in 1968 and led it to victory in the 1971 elections to become premier. Laws curbing the press and political freedom led to the PLM's defeat at the 1976 election. Walter was jailed in 1979 for three years for

corruption in office and was replaced as party leader by Robert Hall. After a year in prison, he was acquitted on appeal a few days after a new PLM defeat in the 1980 election, from which he was legally barred. He was forced out of the party and in 1982 formed the United People's Movement (UPM) which, with the support of the AWU, won 22% of the vote at the 1984 election though no seats. After the UPM merged with the National Democratic Party in 1986 to form the United National Democratic Party he withdrew from politics.
See also **Progressive Labour Movement; United National Democratic Party; Bird, Vere C; Hudson-Phillips.**

Wathey, Claude
b. 24 July 1926. Leader of Sint Maarten 1951–   and architect of the island's conversion into a major Caribbean tourist resort. In 1951, Wathey co-founded the Sint Maarten Democratic Party (DP), which won all the island's seats in the central parliament in Curaçao that year and at every election until 1990, when it lost one seat to the Sint Maarten Patriotic Alliance and Wathey came only second on the DP list. Wathey was a member of the Netherlands Antilles central parliament in Curaçao from 1962 until 1977, when he did not seek re-election. He returned to the Curaçao parliament in 1982. His party won all the seats on the Sint Maarten council at the last elections in 1985. He resigned from the central government in 1987 and said in 1988 that he favoured complete independence for Sint Maarten.
See also **Sint Maarten; St Martin.**

Webster, Ronald
b. 2 March 1926. Council leader, chief minister of Anguilla 1971–7, 1980–84. A farmworker who inherited a substantial legacy from his Dutch employers in nearby Sint Maarten, the deeply religious Webster emerged in 1967 as leader of Anguilla's revolt against rule by St Kitts after the islanders rejected token autonomy. Webster demanded independence and when negotiations with Britain proved unsuccessful he unilaterally declared independence and a republic in February 1969. He accepted the British military invasion a few weeks later, and when in 1971 Britain agreed to resume formal control he was named island council leader. He founded the People's Progressive Party (PPP) in 1972 and won the general election that year (6–1) and in 1976 (6–1).

He was dismissed in 1977 after rebels led by Emile Gumbs, who were tired of his eccentricity and authoritarianism, voted no confidence in him. Gumbs replaced him but he won the 1980 elections 6–1 as head of the Anguilla United Party (AUP) and became chief minister again. A year later the AUP broke up and Webster founded the Anguilla People's Party (APP) which won new elections 5–2 the same year. He was defeated 2–5 by Gumbs in 1984, losing his seat, after which he resigned as APP leader. He then revived the AUP but narrowly failed to win a seat in the 1989 elections, when the party won two seats.
See also **Anguilla secession; Gumbs; Anguilla Democratic Party.**

Wessin y Wessin, Gen. Elías

b. 22 July 1924. Right-wing leader in the 1965 Dominican Republic civil war. Wessin y Wessin became politically powerful in 1962 when he foiled a coup as commander of the army's élite armoured corps. He became head of the armed forces training school and led the US-encouraged army overthrow of the leftist President Juan Bosch in 1963.

In 1965 he headed the US-supported rightist forces in the civil war. The political settlement of the conflict included his exile as consul-general in Miami. He formed the Quisqueyan Democratic Party (PQD) in 1968, was allowed to return to the country in 1969 and won 13% of the vote at the 1970 presidential elections. In 1971, President Joaquín Balaguer accused him of plotting to overthrow the government and he was again exiled, this time to Spain. He was named vice-presidential candidate *in absentia* in the 1974 elections in a coalition with the Dominican Revolutionary Party (the Santiago Accord) but the coalition withdrew from the poll at the last minute. He returned from exile in 1978 after Balaguer was defeated for re-election, and ran for president in 1982. Balaguer named him interior and police minister in 1986 and armed forces minister in 1988–90. The PQD is formally led by his son, Elías Wessin Chávez.

See also **Dominican Republic, US invasion (1965); Bosch, Juan; Balaguer; Dominican Revolutionary Party**.

West Indies

The colonial-era name for the Caribbean, especially the English-speaking islands. With independence in the 1960s and 1970s, the term began to be replaced by 'the Caribbean'. It survives in the names of various regional institutions, notably the University of the West Indies and the world-beating West Indies cricket team.

See also **Caribbean**.

West Indies Associated States (WISA)

The name given to six British eastern Caribbean colonies when they were granted internal self-government (except for defence and foreign affairs) in the late 1960s, without any further presence of white British administrators. Antigua, St Kitts-Nevis-Anguilla, Dominica, St Lucia and Grenada achieved associated statehood in 1967 but St Vincent, because of internal political complications, not until 1969. All became independent soon afterwards – Grenada in 1974, Dominica (1978), St Lucia (1979), St Vincent (1979), Antigua-Barbuda (1981) and St Kitts-Nevis (1983). The acronym WISA was used rather than WIAS because of the impolite meaning of the latter in West Indian slang.

See also **Caribbean Community; Organisation of Eastern Caribbean States; West Indies Federation**.

West Indies Federation (1958–62)

Britain and leaders of its Caribbean colonies formed a 10-state federation in 1958, believing that this would be the best way to move the small Caribbean states to independence. It was dominated by the larger islands – Jamaica, Trinidad and Barbados – and headquartered in Trinidad.

Other members were Antigua, Barbados, Dominica, Grenada, St Kitts, St Lucia and St Vincent. The Federal Labour Party, led by Jamaican premier Norman Manley, narrowly beat the Democratic Labour Party, headed by Jamaica's Sir Alexander Bustamante, in elections to a federal parliament in 1958. Manley's deputy, Sir Grantley Adams of Barbados, became federal prime minister.

The refusal of the leaders of the larger islands to leave their political bases, consequent reliance on politicians from the smaller islands, which were electorally over-represented, economic and political rivalry between Jamaica and Trinidad and weak leadership by Adams doomed the federation almost from the start. In 1959, Bustamante called for Jamaica to secede. By mid-1960, Trinidad and Jamaica were ignoring the small island leaders. After Manley lost a referendum in Jamaica in 1961 on a proposal to stay in the federation, he announced that Jamaica would move to separate independence. Trinidadian leader Eric Williams followed suit. Manley then lost power in Jamaica, and when both countries became independent in 1962 the federation died.

See also **Marryshow, T. A.; Barbados Labour Party; Jamaica Labour Party; People's National Party; Williams; Caribbean Community; West Indies Associated States; Organisation of Eastern Caribbean States**.

Wheatley, Willard

b. 16 July 1915. Chief minister, British Virgin Islands 1971–9. A schoolteacher and later a junior minister, Wheatley became chief minister in 1971, when after a general election, as the lone independent MP, he was picked by Democratic Party leader Q. W. Osborne to head a coalition. He retained the job after the 1975 election when the two main parties (the Democrats and the Virgin Islands Party/VIP) tied and he teamed up with the VIP. He lost power after elections in 1979 when his deputy, VIP leader Lavity Stoutt, assembled a majority and succeeded him. He then became leader of the United Party (UP). When the UP tied with the VIP in the 1983 election he became chief minister under independent MP Cyril Romney. He withdrew his support from Romney over a drug money scandal in 1986 but lost his seat at the elections Romney then called and was replaced as UP leader by Conrad Maduro.

See also **United Party; Stoutt; Romney; Virgin Islands Party**.

Wheelock, Jaime: see Sandinista National Liberation Front.

White Hand: see death squad.

White, Robert: see D'Aubuisson Arrieta.

Whiteman, Unison: see New Jewel Movement.

White Warriors Union (UGB): see death squad; D'Aubuisson Arrieta.

Williams, Dr Eric

1911–81. Chief minister, premier and prime minister of Trinidad-Tobago 1956–81. A historian and academic, Williams taught at Howard University in the US before working for the Anglo-American Caribbean Commission (1943–55). He founded the People's National Movement (PNM) in 1956, inspiring voters with lofty new anti-colonial ideas. The party won general elections later that year and Williams became chief minister. After the collapse of the West Indies Federation, Williams, by now premier, led the country to independence from Britain in 1962 and became prime minister.

By 1970 he had become preoccupied with supposed left-wing subversion and had taken repressive measures. Serious discontent, fed by 'black power' militancy originating in North America, erupted that year and a radical-led revolt and army mutiny broke out against his rule. He declared a state of emergency and the revolt failed. The opposition, part of which mocked him as an 'Afro-Saxon', boycotted the 1971 general election. He announced in 1973 that he would step down but then changed his mind. Thanks to the huge rise that year in the world price of oil, Trinidad's main resource, Williams was able to restore his political fortunes, and in 1976 he and the PNM won another general election. He died in office.

Reverence for William's intellectual talents and his reclusive nature also enhanced his power. His best-known book is *Capitalism and Slavery* (1944). Although Trinidad was an economic magnet for immigration from the smaller, poorer islands, Williams stood aloof from his neighbours, sometimes quarrelling with them, rarely attending regional summits and in the mid-1970s warning strongly against the danger of regional domination by Venezuela which, with its new oil wealth, had launched an aid programme for the Anglo-Caribbean states.

See also **People's National Movement** (Trinidad-Tobago); **West Indies Federation; 'black power'; Trinidad, 'black power' uprising (1970); James, C. L. R.**

Windward Islands

In the Anglo-Caribbean, the south-easterly islands of Dominica, St Lucia, St Vincent, Barbados and Grenada. In the Netherlands Antilles, the three northerly islands of Sint Maarten, Saba and Statia.

Worker-Peasant Movement (*Mouvement Ouvrier Paysan*/MOP): see **Fignolé; Duvalier, François.**

Workers' and Farmers' Party (WFP): see **James, C. L. R.; Panday.**

Workers' and Peasants' Bloc: see **Communist Party** (Costa Rica).

Workers' League: see **St Kitts-Nevis Labour Party; Bradshaw.**

Workers' Liberation Front-Social Independent Party (*Frente Obrero di Liberashon-Partido Social Independiente*/FOL-SI)

Political party in the Netherlands Antilles. Founded as the Workers' Liberation Front during the violent 'black power' demonstrations by Curaçao oil workers in May 1969 led by dockworkers' union leader Wilson Godett (b. 11 August 1932) and leftist schoolteacher Stanley Brown. Three months later the Curaçao-based party won three seats at a general election. Two of them were won by Godett and Brown, who were still in jail as a result of the disturbances. The FOL entered the

Democratic Party coalition government, but Brown left the party in 1970 after a dispute with Godett, who was appointed labour and social affairs minister by premier Juancho Evertsz in 1975. The FOL held its three seats at the 1973 and 1977 elections, but lost all of them at the 1979 poll. Brown returned to the party but left politics in 1986. With a tie-breaking one seat (gained at the 1985 election), it brought down the government of Don Martina in 1988 after objecting to mass economic layoffs of civil servants.

In early 1990, it merged with the Social Independent Party (SI) (f. 1986), a splinter group of the National People's Party, and the party assumed its present joint name. The SI leader, George Hueck (b. 1942), replaced Godett as party chief and the grouping won three seats at the 1990 general election.

See also **'black power'; Democratic Party** (Netherlands Antilles); **Martina; New Antilles Movement; National People's Party; Netherlands Antilles, oil refineries.**

Workers' Party of Jamaica (WPJ)

Founded in 1978 by marxist Trevor Munroe as successor to the Workers' Liberation League (f. 1974), the WPJ at first gave 'critical support' to the government of Michael Manley and then moved into an unofficial alliance with it. After its defeat at the 1980 election, Manley's People's National Party broke ties with the WPJ in 1981. The WPJ lost more support in 1983 because of Munroe's backing for the radicals who murdered Grenadian prime minister Maurice Bishop that year. In 1988 deputy leader Don Robotham and five other central committe members resigned, saying the party should drop its 'narrow and dictatorial' ideology. Munroe confessed to errors and over-rigidity and said the party should be more democratic and Jamaican. The WPJ's trade union arm, the University and Allied Workers' Union, in 1988 won bargaining rights at a sugar estate, the first time a small union had broken the monopoly of the two major unions in the sugar industry.

See also **Munroe; People's National Party.**

World Anti-Communist League: see **Iran/contra affair; Sandoval Alarcón.**

World Confederation of Labour (WCL): see **CLAT.**

World Federation of Trade Unions: see **CPUSTAL.**

Wright, Jim: see **Arias Plan.**

Y

Yatama

A Nicaraguan opposition group drawn from the Atlantic Coast communities. The biggest member group, Kisan, was founded in 1983 (as Misura) by Steadman Fagoth and Wycliffe Diego, taking its original name from the Atlantic Coast Indian tribes (Miskito, Sumo and Rama). The other main group, Misurasata, had previously split into a hard-line faction belonging to the ARDE alliance and a pro-negotiations group led by Brooklyn Rivera. Misura changed its name to Kisan ('Unity of the Peoples of the Coast') in 1985 after expelling Fagoth from the leadership, and joined the United Nicaraguan Opposition (UNO). Fagoth was replaced by Diego and Adán Artola, who accused him of corruption and of opposing unity moves. The Kisan leadership opposed negotiations with the Sandinistas, although a faction (Kisan-Zonal or Kisan-Pro-Peace) signed a peace agreement in 1985 under which its 480 combatants took on the defence of eight communities.

In 1987, under pressure from the US, Fagoth, Rivera and Diego formed Yatama ('Children of Mother Earth') and sought closer co-ordination with Nicaraguan Resistance (RN). But the following year eight Yatama leaders signed an agreement with the government under which their forces became the Indigenous Border Defence Militias (MAFE), while talks continued with Fagoth and Rivera. Diego was elected to the RN directorate in August 1988, a move repudiated by Fagoth and Rivera, but in 1989 all three agreed to abandon the armed struggle and take part in the 1990 elections. Lacking party status, the organisation first opted to support the campaign of the Social Christian (PSC) and Popular Social Christian (PPSC) parties, but just before the election it switched its support to the victorious coalition led by Violeta Chamorro. Rivera was given a cabinet post with responsibility for the Atlantic Coast and Yatama was disbanded in 1990.

See also **Atlantic Coast** (Nicaragua); **Nicaraguan Resistance; ARDE.**

Ydígoras Fuentes, Miguel: see Arévalo Bermejo.

Yon Sosa, Marco Antonio: see Rebel Armed Forces.

Youlou Liberation Movement (Yulimo): see Gonsalves; United People's Movement (St Vincent).

Z

Zacapa, Jackal of: see **Arana Osorio**.

zafra de los diez millones
In 1969–70, the 'Year of the Decisive Endeavour', the Cuban government mobilised maximum resources nation-wide in an attempt to achieve a ten-million-tonne *zafra* (sugar harvest). This marked the height of the process by which sugar came to occupy an even more important position in the Cuban economy than before the revolution, despite the early years (1960–62) in which its role was played down. The attempt, subsequently regarded as a serious error in that it paralysed the remainder of the economy, was acknowledged to have failed by May 1970. The final figure (which some observers believe was itself falsified) was under nine million tonnes. After this, more realistic targets were set and more effort put into economic diversification, but sugar continues to account for three-quarters of Cuba's foreign earnings.

Zamora, Mario: see **D'Aubuisson Arrieta**.

Zamora, Rubén: see **Democratic Convergence; Democratic Revolutionary Front** (El Salvador); **Christian Democrat Party** (El Salvador).

'*zancudos*': see **Somoza Debayle, Gen. Anastasio**.

Zapata, Emiliano: see **Mexican Revolution**.

Zapata, Mario: see *Matanza* (1932 massacre).

Zelaya, Lorenzo: see **Guerrilla movements** (Honduras).

Zeledón, Benjamín: see **Fonseca Amador**.

List of entries by country

Anguilla
Anguilla Democratic Party
Anguilla National Alliance
Anguilla secession (1967, 1969)
Dog Island
Gumbs, Emile
Webster, Ronald

Antigua–Barbuda
Antigua Caribbean Liberation
  Movement
Antigua Labour Party
Barbuda
Bird, Lester
Bird, Vere Jr.
Bird, Vere C.
Hector, Tim
Progressive Labour Movement
United National Democratic Party
Walter, George

Aruba
Croes, Betico
Eman, Henny
Netherlands Antilles, oil refineries
Oduber, Nelson
People's Electoral Movement

Bahamas
Abaco secession movement
  (1971–77)
Family Islands, The
Free National Movement
Hawksbill Creek Agreement
  (1955)
Isaacs, Kendal

Maynard, Clement
Pindling, Sir Lynden
Progressive Liberal Party
United Bahamian Party
Vanguard Nationalist and Socialist
  Party
Wallace-Whitfield, Sir Cecil

Barbados
Adams, Tom
Barbados Labour Party
Barbados Workers' Union
Barrow, Errol
Blackman, Don
Democratic Labour Party
Forde, Henry
Greaves, Philip
Haynes, Richie
Sandiford, Erskine
Taitt, Branford
Walcott, (Sir) Frank

Barbuda
Burton, Eric
Frank, Hilbourne

Belize
Belize dispute
Esquivel, Manuel
People's United Party
Price, George
United Democratic Party

Bermuda
Browne-Evans, Lois
National Liberal Party

Dominican Republic, Haitian
　canecutters
Dominican Republic, US invasion
　(1965)
Dominican Revolutionary Party
　(PRD)
Guzmán, Antonio
Imbert Barrera, Gen Antonio
Jorge Blanco, Salvador
Majluta, Jacobo
Morales Troncoso, Carlos
Peña Gómez, José Francisco
Reid Cabral, Donald
Trujillo, Generalissimo Rafael
Wessin y Wessin, Gen Elías

El Salvador
ARENA (Nationalist
　Revolutionary Alliance)
Christian Democrat Party (PDC)
Cristiani, Alfredo
D'Aubuisson Arrieta, Roberto
Democratic Convergence
Duarte, José Napoléon
EL SALVADOR, Republic of
FAPU
Farabundo Martí National
　Liberation Front (FMLN)
fourteen families
Martí, Augustín Farabundo
Martínez, Gen Maximiliano
　Hernández
Matanza (1932 massacre)
National Conciliation Party (PCN)
National Guard
Nationalist Democratic Union
　(UDN)
ORDEN
People's Revolutionary Army
　(ERP)
Popular Liberation Forces (FPL)
Popular Revolutionary Bloc
　(BPR)
Revolutionary Democratic Front
　(FDR)
Romero, Archbishop Oscar
　Arnulfo

Romero Mena, Gen Carlos
　Humberto
Salvadorean Communist Party
　(PCS)
tanda
Ungo, Guillermo
Villalobos, Joaquín

Grenada
Alexis, Francis
Bishop, Maurice
Blaize, Herbert
Brizan, George
Brathwaite, Nicholas
Carriacou
Coard, Bernard
Gairy, Sir Eric
Grenada United Labour Party
Grenada, US invasion (1983)
Grenadines
Louison, George
Marryshow, T. A.
Marryshow, Terry
Maurice Bishop Patriotic
　Movement
Mitchell, Keith
National Democratic Congress
New Jewel Movement
New National Party
People's Revolutionary
　Government
Radix, Kendrick
Revolutionary Military Council

Guadeloupe
Bangou, Henri
de Haenen, Rémy
Fleming, Albert
Guadeloupe, independence
　movements
Jalton, Frédéric
Larifla, Dominique
Michaux-Chevry, Lucette
Moutoussamy, Ernest
Reinette, Luc
Saint Barthélémy
Saint Martin
St Martin

Liberal Party
López Arellano, Gen. Oswaldo
National Party
Suazo Córdova, Roberto
Villeda Morales, Ramón

International
Alliance for Progress
American Institute for Free Labor
  Development (AIFLD)
Arias Plan
'black power'
'boat people'
border dispute (El
  Salvador/Honduras)
cacique
Canada and the Anglo-Caribbean
Caribbean
Caribbean Basin Initiative (CBI)
Caribbean Community and
  Common Market/Caricom
Caribbean Conference of
  Churches (CCC)
Caribbean Democratic Union
  (CDU)
Caribs
caudillo
Central American Common
  Market (CACM)
Central American Democratic
  Community (CADC)
Central American Parliament
Christian base community
CLAT
Commonwealth Caribbean
CONDECA
Contadora Group
continuismo
CPUSTAL
cuartelazo
death squad
Declaration of St George's (1979)
Demas, William
député-maire
dollar diplomacy
Economic Commission for Latin
  America and the Caribbean
  (ECLAC)

Family Islands
'Football (Soccer) war'
foquismo
Franco-Mexican declaration
Garvey, Marcus
good neighbour policy
Greater Antilles
Guyana
Hurricane Hugo (1989)
indigenismo
Inter-American Defence Board
  (IADB)
Inter-American Development
  Bank (IDB)
invasions and occupations by the
  United States
Iran/contra affair
junta
Kissinger Report
ladino
latifundio
Latin American Bishops'
  Conference (CELAM)
Latin American Economic System
  (SELA)
Latin American Energy
  Organisation (OLADE)
Latin American Integration
  Association (LAIA)
Leeward Islands
Lesser Antilles
Lewis, Sir Arthur
liberation theology
McIntyre, Alister
military bases (foreign) in the
  Caribbean
Monroe doctrine
Moyne Commission (1938)
'new left'
noirisme
Non-Aligned Movement
Organisation of American States
  (OAS)
Organisation of Eastern
  Caribbean States (OECS)
ORIT
personalismo
populism

premier
rastafarians
Regional Security System (RSS)
Rio group
Rio treaty
Rodney riots (1968)
San Andrés dispute
San José Agreement
School of the Americas
Singh, Rickey
Socialist (second) International
Special Service Units (SSUs)
Tlatelolco Treaty
University of the West Indies
  (UWI)
West Indies
West Indies Associated States
  (WISA)
West Indies Federation (1958–62)
Windward Islands

Jamaica

Bustamante Industrial Trade
  Union
Jamaica Labour Party
Manley, Michael
Munroe, Trevor
National Workers' Union of
  Jamaica
Patterson, P. J.
People's National Party
Rodney riots (1968)
Seaga, Edward
Shearer, Hugh
Workers' Party of Jamaica

Martinique

Césaire, Aimé
Crusol, Jean
Darsières, Camille
Lise, Claude
Lordinot, Guy
Louis-Joseph-Dogué, Maurice
Martinican Progressive Party
  (PPM)
Maurice, Emile

Mexico

Alemán Valdés, Miguel
Authentic Party of the Mexican
  Revolution (PARM)
Avila Camacho, Gen Manuel
braceros
Calles, Gen. Plutarco Elías
Cárdenas Cuauhtémoc
Cárdenas, Lázaro
Communist Party (PCM)
Confederation of Mexican
  Workers (CTM)
Cristeros
De la Madrid Hurtado, Miguel
Destape
Díaz Ordaz, Gustavo
Durazo Moreno, Gen. Arturo
Echeverría Alvarez, Luis
Institutional Revolutionary Party
  (PRI)
Lombardo Toledano, Vicente
López Mateos, Adolfo
López Portillo y Pacheco, José
Mexican Revolution
Mexican Socialist Party (PSM)
Mexican Workers' Party (PMT)
MEXICO (United Mexican
  States)
National Action Party (PAN)
National Democratic Front (FDN)
Nationalist Revolutionary Civic
  Association
Oil nationalisation
Party of the Democratic
  Revolution (PRD)
Party of the Poor
La Quina
Ruiz Cortines, Adolfo
Salinas de Gortari, Carlos
Tlatelolco massacre
Unified Socialist Party of Mexico
  (PSUM)
Velázquez, Fidel

Montserrat

Bramble, Austin
Fergus, Howard
Irish, J. A. George

Jaipail Mission (1975)
Osborne, Bertrand
Osborne, John

Netherlands Antilles
ABC islands
Antilles of the Five
Aruba
Democratic Party
Liberia-Peters, Maria
Martina, Don
National People's Party
Netherlands Antilles, oil refineries
New Antilles Movement
St Martin
Sint Eustatius
Sint Maarten
Statia
Wathey, Claude
Workers' Liberation Front

Nevis
Daniel, Simeon
Nevis Reformation Party

Nicaragua
ARDE
Atlantic Coast
Barrios de Chamorro, Violeta
Borge Martínez, Tomás
Calero Portocarrero, Adolfo
Chamorro Cardenal, Pedro
  Joaquín
contra
COSEP
Cruz Porras, Arturo
Democratic Conservative Party
  (PCD)
Fonseca Amador, Carlos
Independent Liberal Party (PLI)
National Guard
National Opposition Union
  (UNO)
NICARAGUA, Republic of
Nicaraguan Democratic Co-
  ordinator (CDN)
Nicaraguan Democratic Force
  (FDN)

Nicaraguan Resistance (RN)
Obando y Bravo, Cardinal Miguel
Ortega Saavedra, Daniel
Pastora Gómez, Edén
Popular Social Christian Party
La Prensa
Robelo Callejas, Alfonso
Sandino, Augusto César
Sandinista National Liberation
  Front (FSLN)
Social Christian Party (PSC)
Somoza Debayle, Anastasio
Somoza Debayle, Luis
Somoza García, Anastasio
Southern Opposition Bloc (BOS)
United Nicaraguan Opposition
  (UNO)
Yatama

Panama
Ardito Barletta, Nicolás
Arias Calderón, Ricardo
Arias Madrid, Arnulfo
Authentic Panameñista Party
  (PPA)
Christian Democrat Party
  (Panama) (PDC)
COLINA (National Liberation
  Coalition)
Delvalle, Eric Arturo
Democratic Alliance of Civic
  Opposition (ADOC)
Dignity Battalions
Endara Galimany, Guillermo
flag riots
Labour Party (PALA)
Liberal Party (PL)
Molirena
National Civic Crusade (CCN)
Noriega Morena, Gen. Manuel
  Antonio
PANAMA, Republic of
Panama Canal treaties
Panama Canal Zone
Panama, US invasion (1989)
People's Party of Panama (PPP)
rabiblancos
Republican Party (PR)

Maps

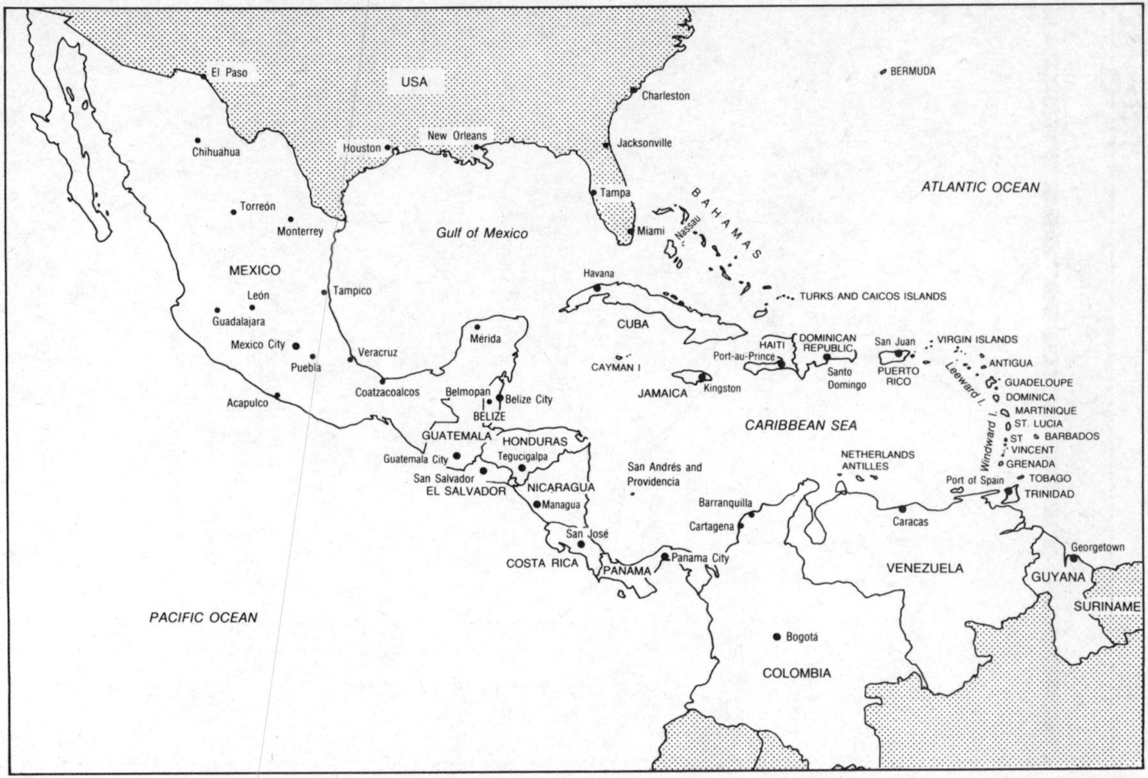

Map 1 Mexico, Central America and the Caribbean

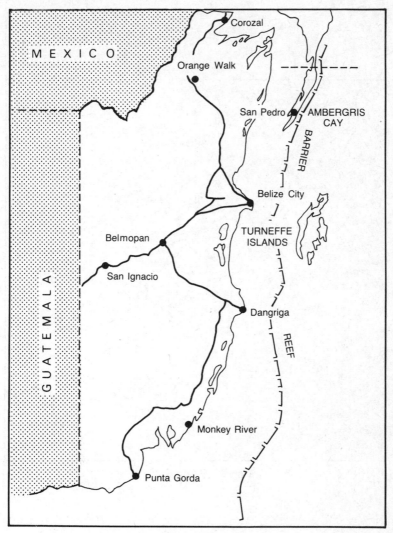

Map 2 Belize

Map 3 Costa Rica

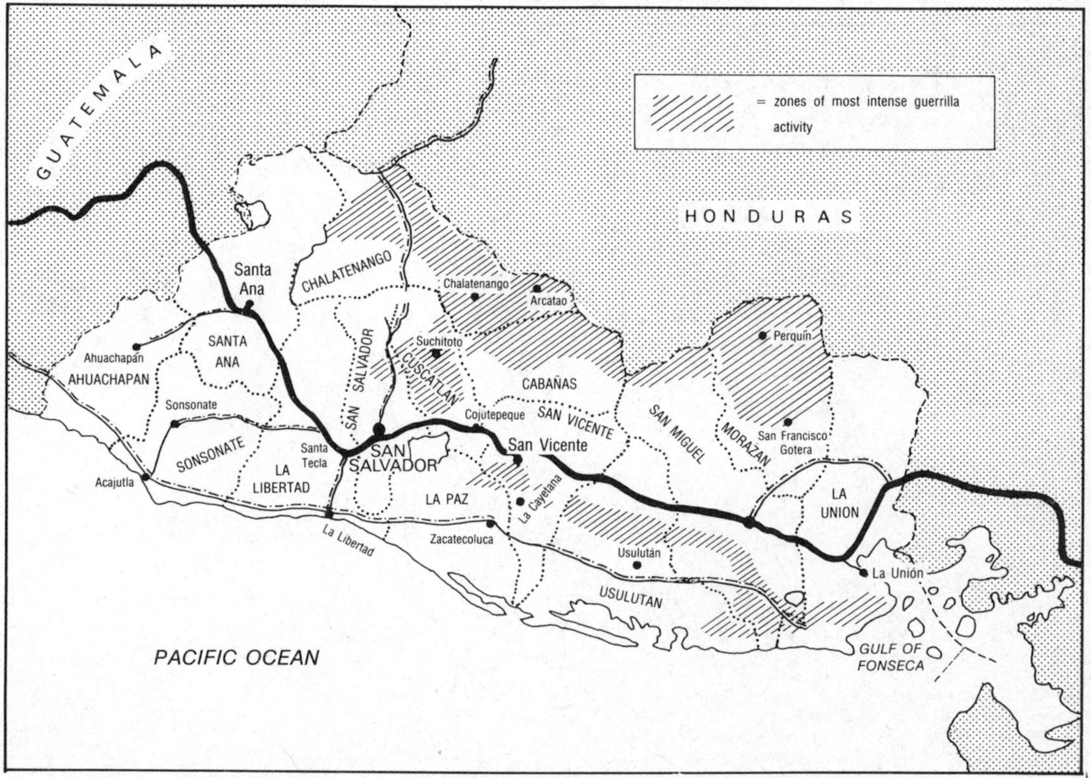

Map 4 El Salvador

Legend:
= zones of most intense guerrilla activity

HONDURAS

GUATEMALA

PACIFIC OCEAN

GULF OF FONSECA

LA UNION

MORAZAN

SAN MIGUEL

SAN VICENTE

CABAÑAS

CUSCATLAN

CHALATENANGO

SAN SALVADOR

LA PAZ

USULUTAN

LA LIBERTAD

SONSONATE

SANTA ANA

AHUACHAPAN

Perquín
San Francisco Gotera
La Unión
Usulután
Arcatao
Chalatenango
Suchitoto
Cojutepeque
La Cayetana
San Vicente
Zacatecoluca
La Libertad
Santa Tecla
Sonsonate
Acajutla
Ahuachapán
Santa Ana
San Salvador

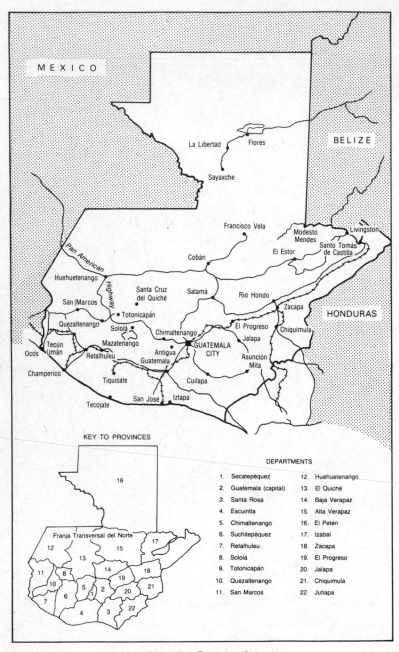

MEXICO

La Libertad   Flores

BELIZE

Sayaxche

Francisco Vela

Modesto
Mendes   Livingston

Pan American   Cobán   El Estor   Santo Tomás
de Castilla

Huehuetenango

Highway   Santa Cruz   Salamá   Rio Hondo
del Quiché

San |Marcos   Zacapa

Totonicapán   HONDURAS

Quezaltenango   Sololá   El Progreso   Chiquimula
Chimaltenango

Tecún   Mazatenango   Jalapa
Umán   Antigua   GUATEMALA
Ocós   Retalhuleu   Guatemala   CITY

Champerico   Asunción
Mita

Tiquisate   Cuilapa

Tecojate   San José   Iztapa

KEY TO PROVINCES

16

Franja Transversal del Norte   17

12   15

13

14   18

11   19

8

10   5   20   21

2

7   6

1

4   3   22

DEPARTMENTS

1. Secatepéquez	12. Huehuetenango
2. Guatemala (capital)	13. El Quiché
3. Santa Rosa	14. Baja Verapaz
4. Escuintla	15. Alta Verapaz
5. Chimaltenango	16. El Petén
6. Suchitepéquez	17. Izabal
7. Retalhuleu	18. Zacapa
8. Sololá	19. El Progreso
9. Totonicapán	20. Jalapa
10. Quezaltenango	21. Chiquimula
11. San Marcos	22. Jutiapa

Map 5   Guatemala

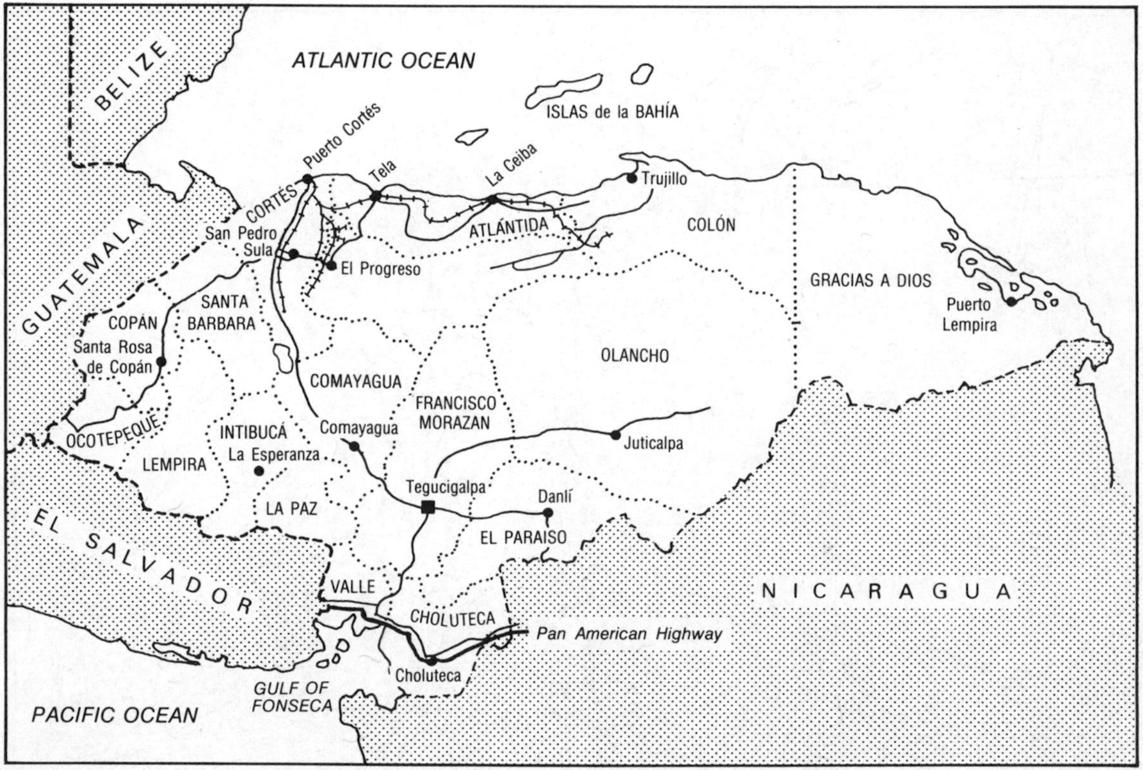

Map 6 Honduras

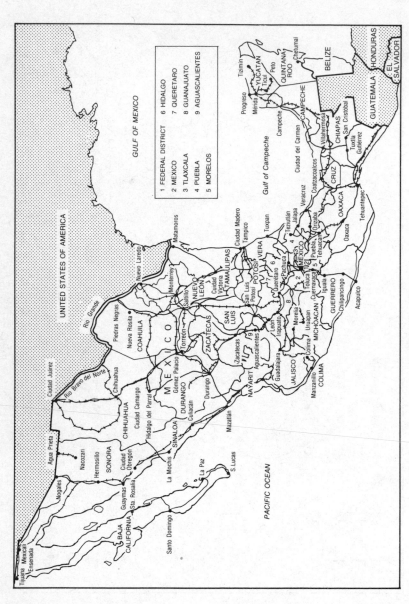

Map 7 Mexico

382

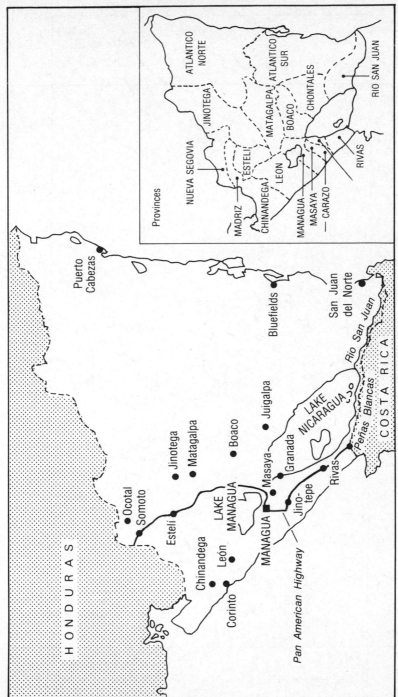

Map 8 Nicaragua

Provinces

ATLANTICO NORTE
ATLANTICO SUR
JINOTEGA
MATAGALPA
BOACO
CHONTALES
RIO SAN JUAN
NUEVA SEGOVIA
ESTELI
CHINANDEGA
LEON
MANAGUA
MASAYA
CARAZO
RIVAS
MADRIZ

Puerto Cabezas

HONDURAS

Bluefields

San Juan del Norte

Ocotal
Somoto
Jinotega
Matagalpa
Boaco
Juigalpa

Estelí

LAKE MANAGUA

Chinandega
León
Corinto

MANAGUA
Masaya
Granada
LAKE NICARAGUA

Jino-tepe
Rivas
Peñas Blancas
Rio San Juan

COSTA RICA

Pan American Highway

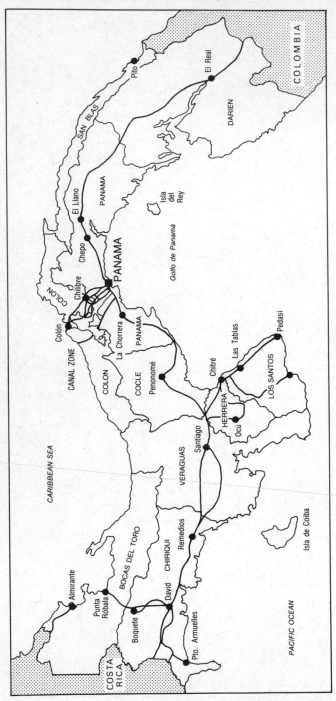

Map 9 Panama

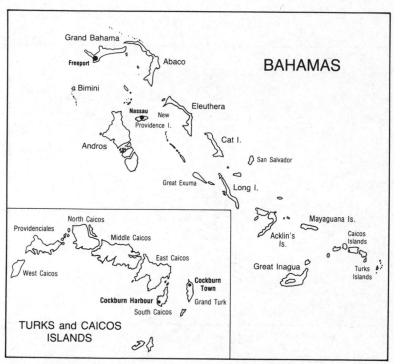

Map 10 The Bahamas and the Turks and Caicos Islands

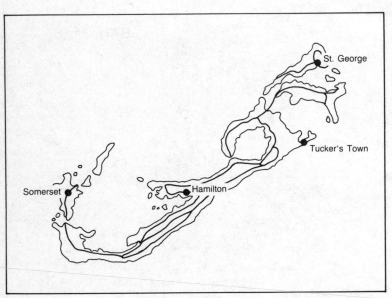

Map 11 Bermuda

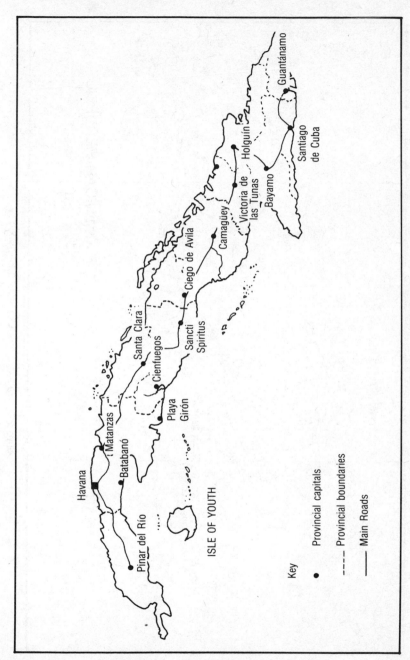

Guantánamo

Holguín

Santiago
de Cuba

Victoria de
las Tunas

Bayamo

Camagüey

Ciego de Avila

Sancti
Spíritus

Santa Clara

Cienfuegos

Playa
Girón

Matanzas

Batabanó

Havana

Pinar del Rio

ISLE OF YOUTH

Key

●   Provincial capitals

-----   Provincial boundaries

———   Main Roads

Map 12   Cuba

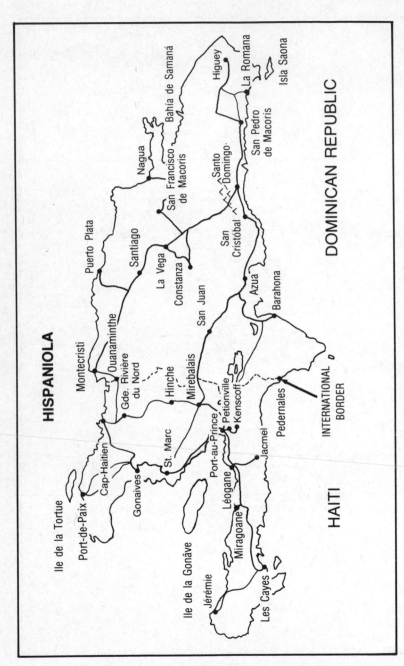

HISPANIOLA

Ile de la Tortue

Port-de-Paix

Cap-Haïtien

Montecristi

Ouanaminthe

Gde. Rivière
du Nord

Puerto Plata

Santiago

Nagua

Bahia de Samaná

Higuey

La Romana

Isla Saona

San Pedro
de Macoris

Santo
Domingo

San Francisco
de Macoris

La Vega

Constanza

San
Cristóbal

San Juan

Azua

Barahona

Hinche

Mirebalais

St. Marc

Gonaives

Ile de la Gonâve

Jérémie

Port-au-Prince

Pétionville

Kenscoff

Léogane

Miragoane

Jacmel

Les Cayes

Pedernales

INTERNATIONAL
BORDER

DOMINICAN REPUBLIC

HAITI

Map 13 Haiti and the Dominican Republic

388

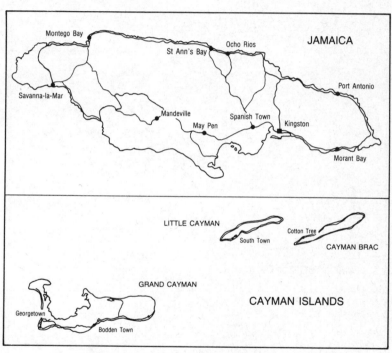

Map 14 Jamaica and the Cayman Islands

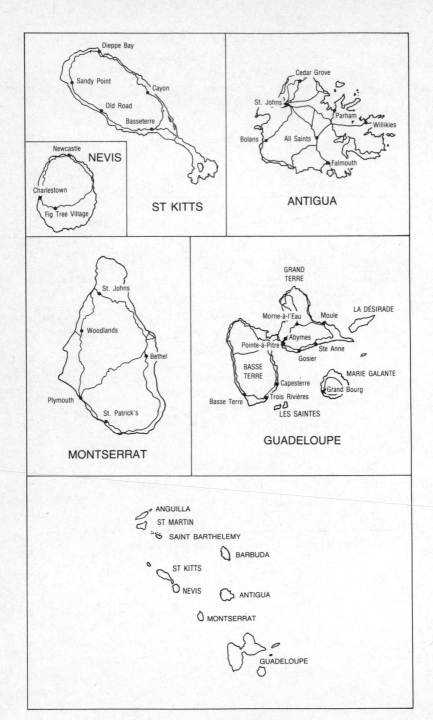

Map 15 The Leeward Islands

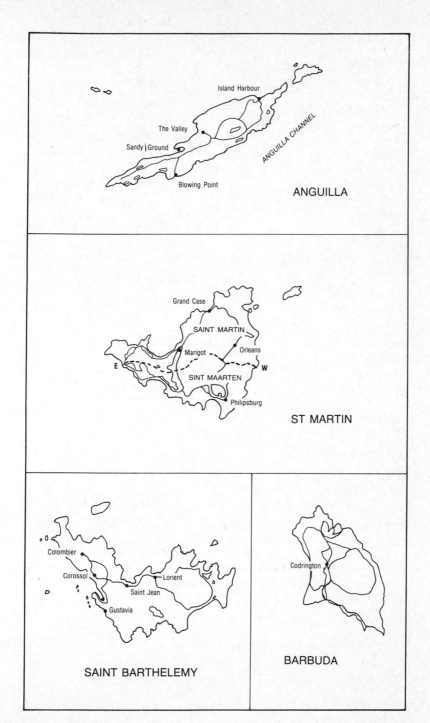

ANGUILLA

Island Harbour

The Valley

Sandy | Ground

Blowing Point

ANGUILLA CHANNEL

Grand Case

SAINT MARTIN

Marigot

Orleans

E

W

SINT MAARTEN

Philipsburg

ST MARTIN

Colombier

Corossol

Lorient

Saint Jean

Gustavia

SAINT BARTHELEMY

Codrington

BARBUDA

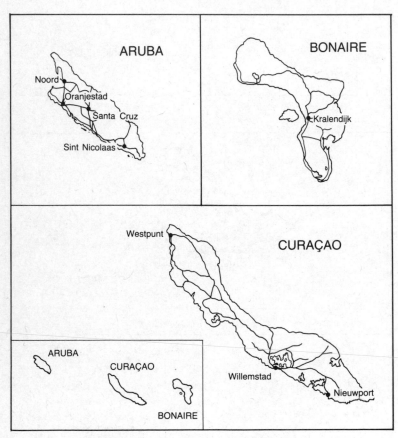

Map 16 The Netherlands Antilles

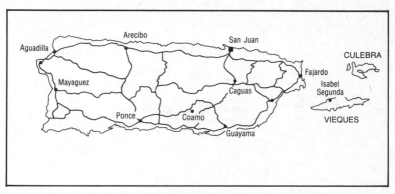

Map 17   Puerto Rico

Map 18 Trinidad and Tobago

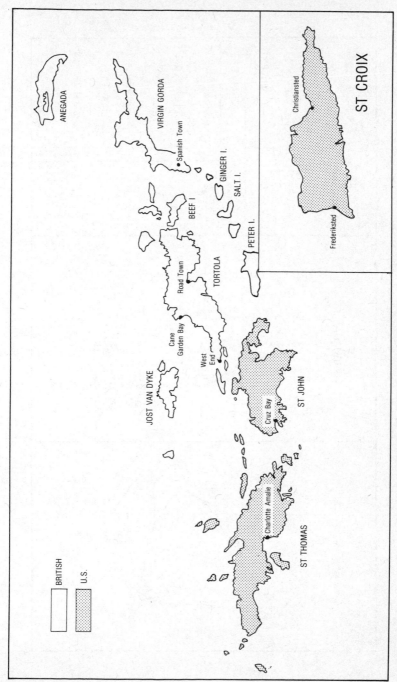

Map 19 The British and United States Virgin Islands and St Croix

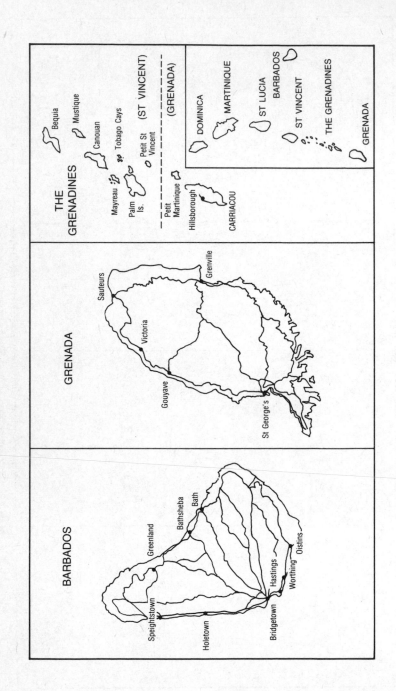

BARBADOS

Speightstown
Greenland
Bathsheba
Bath
Holetown
Bridgetown
Hastings
Worthing
Oistins

GRENADA

Sauteurs
Victoria
Gouyave
Grenville
St George's

THE
GRENADINES

Bequia
Mustique
Canouan
Tobago Cays
Mayreau
Palm
Is.
Petit St
Vincent
Petit
Martinique
Hillsborough
CARRIACOU

(ST VINCENT)

(GRENADA)

DOMINICA
MARTINIQUE
ST LUCIA
BARBADOS
ST VINCENT
THE GRENADINES
GRENADA

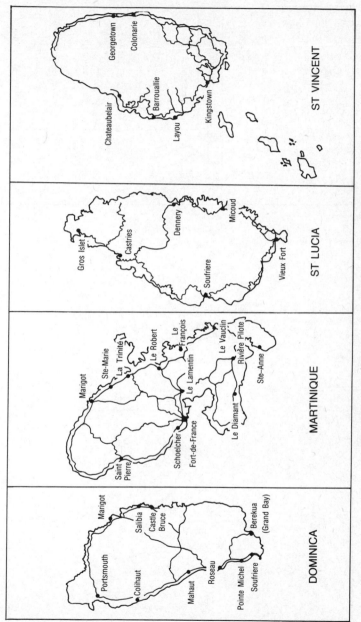

Map 20 The Windward Islands and Barbados